ISLAMIC MOVEMENTS
OF EUROPE

Islamic Movements of Europe

Public Religion and Islamophobia
in the Modern World

Edited by
Frank Peter and Rafael Ortega

I.B. TAURIS
LONDON · NEW YORK

Published in 2014 by I.B.Tauris & Co. Ltd
6 Salem Road, London W2 4BU
175 Fifth Avenue, New York NY 10010
www.ibtauris.com

Distributed in the United States and Canada Exclusively by Palgrave Macmillan
175 Fifth Avenue, New York NY 10010

Library of European Studies 21

ISBN: 978 1 84885 844 2 (HB)
       978 1 84885 845 9 (PB)
eISBN: 978 0 85773 673 4

A full CIP record for this book is available from the British Library
A full CIP record is available from the Library of Congress

Library of Congress catalog card: available

Printed and bound in Great Britain by T.J. International, Padstow, Cornwall.

CONTENTS

Part 1
ISLAMIC MOVEMENTS

Part 2
ISLAMIC MOVEMENTS IN EUROPE

ISLAMIC GUIDANCE AND PUBLIC DEBATES:
IMAMS, CHAPLAINS AND INTELLECTUALS

ISLAMIC KNOWLEDGE AND EDUCATION,
AND MUSLIMS AT UNIVERSITIES

Part 3
ISLAMIC MOVEMENTS IN EUROPE: ISLAMISM AND ISLAMOPHOBIA

LIST OF ILLUSTRATIONS

PREFACE

In controversies about Islam in Europe, fears about a variously named 'extremist Islam' – Islamism, political Islam, fundamentalism, revivalism – and about the radicalisation of European Muslims, constitute a seemingly unavoidable element of the political debate. This volume presents expert studies of the most visible groups and actors in Europe and of the institutional contexts – mosques, universities, Muslim representative bodies, prisons – in which public anxieties about radical Islam are particularly prominent. The studies are written by more than 50 scholars from Europe, North Africa and the United States who have worked extensively in their fields.

The premise of this volume is that the critical analysis of 'radical Islam' in Europe cannot be limited to the study of the groups or individuals who are labelled as radicals. We approach the question of 'radical Islam' as a three-dimensional one, as reflected in the structure of this volume. The first part of this volume contains a series of chapters dealing with Islamic groups in North Africa, the Middle East and Pakistan. These groups are variously related to Islamic groups in present-day Europe, which are the focus of the second and central part of this book. The volume ends with a study of Islamophobia in eight European countries. This three-tier structure is geared towards current debates on Islam in Europe. Two features of these debates pertaining to radical Islam are of particular interest to us. First, when discussing controversial Islamic groups in Europe, one notes that constant reference is made to their eponyms in the Muslim majority world, that is, the Middle East, North Africa and the Indian subcontinent. Descriptions and evaluations of the activities and aims of European Muslims thus tend to assume that the latter share a basic identity with movements in the Islamic world. Second, the debate about these so-called radical Muslim groups is abstracted from the broader societal contexts of the new Europe which today counts millions of Muslim citizens. The question of how the anxieties associated with radical Islam relate to the emergence of a Europe which is inclusive of Islam – and not merely to the features of radical Islamic groups – is rarely asked.

This volume addresses both these shortcomings. The first two parts offer studies about those Islamic groups and institutions which are in the centre of current European public debates. Contributors were asked to distinguish between the ideas and practices of these groups in Muslim majority countries and in Europe. Too often, European Muslim actors are read simply as offshoots of groups in Muslim countries. This runs contrary to the ample evidence demonstrating how the specific conditions under which European

Muslim groups function determine many aspects of their activities and, more generally, of the lifes Muslims live in Europe. Historical ties, forms of cooperation or shared religious references should not lead us to overlook or negate the differences between Muslim organisations in Europe and in the Islamic world. In important ways these Muslim organisations are 'European'. Sometimes the specific European context is explicitly reflected upon by these groups as a condition for their work; in many other instances it can be shown that Europe constitutes, broadly speaking, the social space which enables and makes meaningful many of their practices.

This claim that these Muslim organisations are European must nevertheless be qualified. The qualifier European is not based on the idea that there exists a clear boundary between European countries on the one hand and countries in the Islamic world on the other. The categories Europe and Islamic world are not mutually exclusive and there is no necessary contradiction between embeddedness in the nation states of Europe and various kinds of relations to the homeland of Muslim migrants or global Islam. Such relations are characteristic of many Muslim institutions in Europe, and by no means only those deemed 'radical'. Thus, the 'moderate' Islam favoured by some European governments is often promoted in partnership with various countries in North Africa or the Middle East. Indeed, it is striking to see how seemingly unavoidable it is to build relations outside of Europe when it comes to organising the practice of Islam. Concerning the debate about a specifically European Islam, one has to recognise that what is described by the adjective 'European' is fundamentally the result of the contingent and changing constitution of European peoples and their religious practices. This is not merely an empirical statement. Considering that European states are committed to freedom of religion, the ongoing process through which new meanings are given to what is European in terms of religiosity has a strong legal basis. This is all too often forgotten when calls are made for the construction of a new European Islam which fully conforms to the conditions of integration postulated by governments.

The last part of this volume responds in a different manner to current European debates on Islam. The chapters assembled in this part attempt to decentre the structure of the debate. Instead of engaging the question to which degree Islamic groups in Europe are problematic, they explore the ways in which current fears of Islam are related to general developments and structures of European nation states. In this way, they seek to redress one important flaw in public arguments about Islam in Europe, namely, the exclusive focus on Muslims and Islamic institutions. Notwithstanding regular reminders that integration is a two-way process, the assumption that the controversial debate about Islam is the result of problematic practices by Muslims continues to be widely held. It is this assumption which undergirds the constant scrutinising of European Muslims, their 'real' beliefs and aims, their practices and religious institutions. The chapters in Part 3 of this volume broaden and problematise this perspective. They examine the developments which have led to public interest in specific groups and issues, investigating how specific views of these issues become hegemonic, analysing the political functions of campaigns against certain Islamic groups and the factors which have enabled the emergence of powerful antagonism against Islam.

So far, the groups studied here have been understood only with reference to the way in which they are usually classified today, that is, as radical. Radical or extremist Islam designates a broad variety of groups and trends in Islam. The term is regularly criticised by academics (and rightly so) because of its vagueness. Indeed, it often seems that the main criterion for delimiting the field of radicalism is a constantly changing notion of normality which is rarely disclosed. Many other terms are used for designating these

Muslim groups. Ever since the academic and public interest in the more political aspects of Islam intensified in the aftermath of the Iranian Revolution of 1979, a great debate has erupted about how to name these groups. Islamism, political Islam, fundamentalism, militant Islam or revivalism have become key concepts. The studies presented in this volume do not rely upon any of these concepts in a strong sense. These terms certainly are useful, but their usage also inevitably leads to simplification. This is partly so because in debating these concepts and their respective merits, their features are defined in strongly contrasting terms. Thus, the concept of Islamic revival or resurgence is being used by those who wish to emphasise the factor of religion in the rise of these movements. In contrast, the term Islamism conceptualises them as primarily political groups engaged in struggles of power. This kind of rough distinction is important and probably unavoidable at first. Nevertheless, if we let our analysis become durably reduced to such frameworks, essential questions about how politics and religion are articulated, and how religion is defined in the first place, risk becoming obscured. Indeed, we should exercise restraint in using generalising categories. Considering the broad variety of contexts in which the groups presented here function in many countries – from Morocco to Indo-Pakistan – the heuristic benefit of classifying them is necessarily limited. Moreover, the time factor imposes further limits. The political processes in the Middle East and North Africa can change rapidly. The contributions to this volume were finished before the outbreak of the revolutions of 2010–11. At that time, the Tunisian movement Al-Nahdha had been prohibited for a long time and was credited only minor importance. Today it constitutes the most important political force in the country. A similar statement can be made with regard to the Egyptian Muslim Brotherhood, whose candidates have won the presidential and parliamentary elections in 2012.

There is another, less straightforward, reason for being cautious in the use of these concepts. This has to do with the status of exceptionality which these concepts ascribe to Islamic groups. In fact, these terms share a basic understanding of these Muslim groups as somehow exceptional and extraordinary. Structurally, this understanding implies the expectation that these groups are ultimately unstable and bound to disappear at some point in time. In many ways, the perception of these groups is determined strongly by the notion that their existence is due to unusual circumstances. There exists a variety of ways through which this exceptionality is inscribed into these groups. Perhaps the most important one is the constant emphasis which is placed on the experience of crises in narratives of these groups. Most accounts of political Islam thus go back to the nineteenth century and the history of Western imperial expansion through which Muslim countries have become colonised or part of informal hegemonical structures. This process of colonial modernisation brought rapid transformations of the entire social structure which destabilised social hierarchies, forms of authority and religious traditions, so it is argued. In brief, it brought about a period of crisis and it is in relation to this crisis-ridden environment that the first political–religious groups emerged. Sometimes such analyses emphasise the interests of specific groups as catalysts, sometimes it is the more general dislocations triggered by modernisation in Islamic societies which are referred to in explanations of these groups. Whatever the precise focus, many of the above terms, such as Islamism, fundamentalism, or militant Islam, convey the idea that these groups thrive because of unusual developments and circumstances. There are multiple ways in standard representations which function to name them and situate them at a distance to the supposedly normal functioning of society. Whether it is the anti-modernism of these groups, their anti-secularist stance or, on the social level, their reliance upon a disadvantaged clientele, they are defined through what they are not – or what they are against – and are seen as purely reactive forces thriving on extraordinary conditions which are bound to dissolve.

It is striking to note that these groups continue to be seen as exceptional in spite of the fact that they often exist for long periods of time. There is a real risk that the standard interpretation of Islamist groups in relation to the crises and failures the Islamic world experienced leads to a reductive perception of them as exceptional and ephemerous phenomena. Such a perception is indeed quite popular and widespread today. It comforts, in many instances, not only geopolitical interests in the West. It also makes it possible to maintain the belief that the processes of secularisation which are held typical for Europe have a universal value and define the basic route to follow for the rest of the world. Put differently, it obscures the fundamental question which radical Islam raises, namely, whether the ways in which these groups conjoin religion and politics is more than a deviation, more than an abnormality. Today there seems to be more reason than ever for discussing this question. Groups such as the Muslim Brotherhood have been existing for more than 80 years now. It has regularly been pronounced in decline and irrelevant. Today it constitutes the political leadership of Egypt and is directly involved in international politics. Whether this new situation will lead to changes in the Western evaluation of political Islam remains to be seen.

PART 1

ISLAMIC MOVEMENTS

INTRODUCTION

Frank Peter

This section offers case studies of major Islamic movements which have originated in Africa and Asia at different moments of history. The founder of the Wahhabiya, Muhammad Ibn ʿAbd al-Wahhab, was born in 1702 or 1703 in what is known today as Saudi Arabia; Tablighi Jamaʿat and Jamaʿat-i Islami originated in 1926 and 1941 respectively on the Indian subcontinent; and the originally Egyptian Society of the Muslim Brothers was created in 1928. All the other movements discussed here – in Palestine, Turkey and North Africa – were created in the decades following the end of World War II. As the following chapters will demonstrate, these groups are highly diverse with respect to their histories, their aims and the contexts in which they are embedded. Nevertheless, these groups do have in common that they are perceived in the West as being religious in ways which are both not normal and not acceptable. This perception is indeed the common element in the broad variety of names given to these groups: Islamists, Fundamentalists, political Islam, Islamic movements, radical or extremist Muslims, and so forth. What these names seek to capture and rationalise is the deviant nature of conjoining politics and religion.

The first question these chapters ask is how these movements seek to link Islam to the political order – and what counts for them as political. With the exception of the Tablighi Jamaʿat, which is usually considered apolitical, the most common characteristic ascribed to the groups studied here is their comprehensive articulation of Islam, which supposedly sees politics and religion as inseparable. While these groups certainly are inspired by the belief that politics and religion are intimately intertwined, a closer look at them quickly reveals that these two domains do not coincide in their objectives, strategies and activities. In the case of the Saudi Arabian Wahhabiya, the conjunction of religion and politics is founded on the alliance between the royal family, al-Saʿud, on the one hand, and the religious establishment headed by the scholarly family Al-Shaikh on the other. Far from being a relationship between equals, the religious establishment has been largely constrained in recent decades to serve the royal family's interests both in Saudi Arabia and abroad. Some of the decisions taken by the scholars, such as legitimising the presence of US troops in the kingdom, have seriously damaged Saudi Arabia's reputation as an Islamic state and contributed to the emergence, since the 1960s, of new Islamic – sometimes violent – movements which are, to various degrees, oppositional to the Saudi state.

Four of the other movements studied here – Jamaʿat-i Islami, Milli Görüş the Tunisian

Harakat al-Nahda and the Moroccan Justice and Development Party – have constituted themselves as political parties. While banned as a political party between 1948 and 2011, the Society of the Muslim Brothers repeatedly ran in elections through alliances with other Egyptian parties. In 2011, it created the Freedom and Justice Party and won the parliamentary elections. The Movement of Society for Peace in Algeria has participated in all elections since 1990 and in several governments. Refusing to see the relationship between God's sovereignty and that of the people as one of simple opposition, these groups endeavoured to participate in the democratic process, accepting all the restrictions accompanying it. In the course of the last decades, this option has often been denied them by authoritarian regimes. In the case of the Tunisian al-Nahda, this led to the radicalisation of part of the movement. In Algeria, the creation of the Islamic Salvation Front (FIS) and its success led the military and secular political forces to arrest its leadership and dissolve the group, which then took up armed struggle.

The engagement of these movements in the democratic process is regularly suspected to be merely a tactic in order to ultimately subvert the system. The intense debates inside these movements – sometimes leading to internal division – about whether and how to be politically active make it difficult to give credence to the thesis of an instrumentalist approach to democratic elections. Rather, the debates inside these groups demonstrate their awareness of what is objectively at stake when they enter the field of party politics, namely a commitment to participate in a process which exerts considerable constraints on their programme, activities and legitimacy. Some of the cases presented here point to the effects these constraints have generated over time.

A somewhat different case is presented by Hizb ut-Tahrir. Refraining from any social, educational or profession-based activism – so central to the activism of the Muslim Brotherhood – this group sees itself strictly as a political party. However, the conditions it places upon its entry into the political process are such that it has, by and large, abstained from participating in a democratic system which it ultimately rejects as un-Islamic. From a different perspective, the last movement studied here, Tablighi Jama'at, also rejects political activism within the existing frameworks. While the movement's founder was deeply concerned about the loss of political power by Muslims, direct involvement in politics was shunned in favour of reforming and strengthening the religious practice and identity of individual Muslims. In the view of Tablighi Jama'at (as well as other Islamic movements), personal piety and politics are thus fundamentally inseparable – there can be no Islamic state unless Muslims truly live as Muslims. Nevertheless, the separation between these two elements is a constituent feature of the movement's activities.

Secondly, these movements can be seen as social movements; that is, as movements – with an institutional basis in various voluntary associations, enterprises, or parties – which aim for social change, justice and political rights. Adopting a social movement perspective on these groups raises the question of how to explain their success. While this question has been addressed in many debates, one notes that little attention is paid to seeing their success in terms of the aspirations and needs of citizens and civil society. Numerous studies have attempted to explain the emergence and appeal of Islamist movements as the result of various social or cultural failures in the Islamic world. There has, however, been less research into how these groups meet social needs and expectations in civil society and how they succeed in mobilising citizens. Pursuing this line of analysis further, the question arises as to whether, and to what extent, characterising these movements as 'Islamic' is adequate or even helpful. Finally, in a broader perspective, the emergence of many of these groups is closely related to the creation of nation states. The anti-colonial struggle of the Muslim Brotherhood from the 1920s onwards, the crucial contribution of the Wahhabi movement to the creation of Saudi Arabia in the early twentieth century, and the emergence of the 'missionary' Tablighi Jama'at in the context of colonial India's communal politics are some examples of this. More generally, the nation is a crucially important space of action for these national-transnational groups. However, not all movements accept the national framework as final. Indeed one of them, Hizb ut-Tahrir, pursues the recreation of a supranational caliphate as one of its primary aims. However, while the acceptance by these movements of the nation state framework is often linked to simultaneous attempts to reshape and also transcend it, their embeddedness in specific national contexts, and their concern for national interests and the welfare of the population, nevertheless strongly condition their understanding of Islam and often render it highly specific to time and place.

The studies underscore how useful and necessary it is to speak of specific Islamic groups rather than of political or radical Islam in general. They demonstrate the very limited benefits of analysing the perceived 'threat of Islam' with reference to general observations on Islamic doctrine and practice. To an important degree these practices and interpretations are changing, and this is indeed something which some of these movements openly acknowledge. Arguably, the perspectives outlined so far will not put to rest all anxieties relating to these movements. Indeed, these worries do not merely result from the difficulty of seeking to rationalise these groups, nor can they be fully explained by geopolitical interests which might incite the opposition of Western countries. It is certainly possible, in many cases, to rationalise the emergence and the functioning of Islamist groups in their social contexts, and it is also possible to show that many of them fundamentally accept the rules of democracy. If these groups nevertheless provoke anxieties and fears in many quarters in the West, this has to do with the fact that they contest the paradigmatic value of the Western model. The idea that for a society to be modern its organisation needs to conform to the specific way in which Western societies have developed is one which these groups reject in often uncompromising terms. In contrast to the notion that central institutions of modernity, such as democracy or human rights, have been conclusively defined in Western contexts, these groups have engaged in formulating competing understandings of these institutions. It is this kind of challenge, aimed at the very vocabulary of Western self-understanding, which triggers many of the hostile reactions to these groups.

Having said this, another question needs to be raised when thinking about Islamic movements, and it relates to our understanding of what we mean by politics. In fact, much of the discussion in the following case studies centres on whether a specific movement can be qualified as political, and how precisely politics and religion relate to each other. This is indeed the major question being asked today in public debates about these groups, and the following studies seek to answer it in an informed and considered manner. However, while this is an important question to ask, it is also in part misleading and in itself insufficient for properly assessing these groups. When asking whether a specific group is political, we are presupposing, of course, that politics (as much as religion) constitutes an evident category. We are presupposing that specific practices have a definite meaning and are either political or not. On closer scrutiny, this assumption is difficult to maintain. In fact, one effect of the ongoing debates on Islam in Europe has been a growing awareness by European nations of their highly specific understanding of how they define religion, politics and the legal arrangement which separates them – namely, secularism. The ongoing debates in Europe about the Islamic headscarf, and its religious or political signification, are but one example of the fact that identifying what counts as a religious practice is highly contested. As an act of identification, it is inescapably already part of politics. The headscarf issue also demonstrates that the state-centred definition of politics is intuitively rejected by many citizens who are deeply convinced that very personal practices, such as dress code, do have a bearing on broader society and are, ultimately, politically relevant. It seems that this intuition needs to be made explicit if we want to make progress in the current debate on political Islam.

It is thus far from obvious that we can employ a ready-to-use concept of politics and religion which is universally valid and allows for an objective study of religions. Indeed, many have pointed out that the dominant understanding of the concept of religion today is in some ways inappropriate for a study of Islam. The last chapter in this part will take this as its point of departure. It will ask how we can study these movements differently if we abandon the assumption that the dominant notions of politics and religion are universally valid. It will offer a starting point for thinking about how politics and religion can be differentiated in ways other than those prevailing in Europe today, and it will ask how such a rethinking of Islamic movements affects the widespread belief that their joining of politics and religion is inherently dangerous to Europe.

THE MUSLIM BROTHERHOOD: CREATION, EVOLUTION, AND GOALS FOR THE FUTURE

Rafael Ortega Rodrigo

From its creation in 1928, by Hasan al-Banna (1906–49), as the first global Islamic and reformist organisation that aspired to implement comprehensive social change (religious, political, educational, social) and sought to represent the ideal society and a strategy for effecting that transformation, the Muslim Brotherhood (MB, Jama'at al-Ikhwan al-Muslimun) has become one of the fundamental political–social actors in many Arab and Muslim countries. Legalised or not, with or without representation in the state institutions, and with an undisputed social implantation, both the founding organisation – the Muslim Brotherhood of Egypt – and the organisations deriving from it in many other countries now represent a key political and social force. Various expansion strategies have converged in this process: social and educational strategies characteristic of an association or pressure group, and political strategies – such as alliances with various parties and in different contexts – characteristic of a traditional political party.

I. Rise and spread

The MB arose in reaction to the deep social, political, economic and cultural changes that have been taking place since the end of the nineteenth and early twentieth centuries in Egypt. These include substantial changes in Egyptian administration that affected justice (partial secularisation of legislation), education (religious education reforms), and other spheres, such as the economy, politics and morality, in a context characterised by contact with a Europe at once illustrious and colonialist, and by a duality in thought between a 'lay-liberal' tendency and a 'reformist-Salafi' tendency inherited from nineteenth-century Muslim reformers. The latter developed a reflection on the causes of the decline of Arab and Muslim societies, which they causally related to contact with Europe, and promoted a religious reform capable of adapting Islam to the needs of the era and a modernisation of government institutions. Jamal al-Din al-Afghani (1838–97) and his disciple Muhammad Abduh (1849–1906), the former with a revolutionary approach and the latter opting for a more gradual and 'rationalist' model of re-reading sources, were the most prominent protagonists of this trend. Their discourse was taken up by a disciple of Abduh, Muhammad Rashid Rida (1865–1935), who had witnessed how, in the name of state secularism, the caliphate had been abolished and the Ottoman Empire divided, and how British colonial presence in Egypt had caused profound changes in society. Like Afghani and Abduh, Rida had defended the return to the 'times of the pious forefathers' (*al-salaf al-salih*) as a mechanism for renewing the interpretation of religion and as a strategy to stir Arab and Islamic societies from what he considered was lethargy and regression. The MB embraced the ideas of Rida, and this had important consequences: while the reformism of the nineteenth and early twentieth centuries was basically intellectual and individual, Hasan al-Banna aspired to create a movement and strove to form a type of pressure group that would 'advise' government authorities on how to govern in an 'Islamic' way (*shura, shari'a,* Islamic economics) and not (as many might think) to hold power and establish an 'Islamic State'.

The MB organisation was founded in the Egyptian city of Isma'iliyya to fulfil the duties of a good Muslim: 'command that which is established and prohibit that which is reprehensible' (*al-amr bi-l-ma'ruf wa-l-nahi 'an al-munkar),* invite to Islam (*da'wa),* and erect mosques and schools that would broaden the possibilities for individuals, families and communities to live in conformity with the message of Islam. This was a reaction to what they considered a degradation of morals and social practices and the removal of Islam from the public sphere due to the influence of European presence. Al-Banna viewed European culture as degraded, even if it included certain elements that could be acceptably embraced by Islamic societies (e.g., labour management and science, mass media techniques, urban planning, social security, energy resources, etc.).

In 1932, after expanding to other cities in the Suez Canal zone, the organisation relocated its headquarters to Cairo and embarked upon a new phase of expansion. The group, strongly personified in the figure of its highest leader, the General Guide, to whom an oath of obedience is sworn, consolidated its position during the 1930s and World War II and deeply penetrated society. This was due to its activities and the numerous services it provided through the construction of private mosques, hospitals, modest commercial projects and the creation of educational foundations for religious teaching and the eradication of illiteracy; to its proselytism through the publication of books and magazines; and to its position on certain geopolitical issues, notably its support for the Palestinian uprising of 1936. This social, educational and propaganda activity has been an essential component of the MB movement from the beginning and throughout its history. Later, in the 1940s, the organisation's ideology began to spread among the urban middle class which had been excluded from political and economic power.

Together with the social and educational dimensions, even at the time of al-Banna, an internal debate was taking place on the benefit of creating a political party and working for the reform of social order from within. At the organisation's fifth congress, held in January 1939, the MB's ideology was revised, its programme and objectives outlined, and the group defined. The General Guide reasserted the strictly Islamic character of the MB's ideology, with a vision of a global Islam, reaffirming that any action taken by the organisation was, above all, Islamic:

we believe that the rules and the teachings of Islam constitute a whole that governs the worldly life and the eternal one [...] because Islam is doctrine and devotion, nation and nationality, religion and State, spirituality and action, Qur'an and sword.

Given this global character of Islam and the fact that the MB is an inherently Islamic organisation aiming for total reform, the Epistle of the Fifth Congress also defined the group in terms of its global character, namely: Salafi predication (Qur'an and Sunna), Sunni (purified Sunna), Sufi (purification of the soul), sports group (the strong believer is better than the weak one), scientific and cultural circle (the search for knowledge is a duty for every Muslim), economic enterprise (finance and goods managing) and social ideology (healing the evils of society). Among all the definitions of the group, al-Banna also described it as a political organisation (*haya siyasiyya*) that aims to achieve comprehensive reform of the form of government, with an ideology that addressed the most important issues of the time (Egyptian constitution, the caliphate, Arab unity, Islamic unity, and relations with Britain). Almost from the beginning, the organisation acted as just another political force and knew how to take advantage of the power struggle between the Egyptian monarchy and the main political party, al-Wafd, in order to increase its popularity. It also participated in the main public debates of the time, especially in matters relating to nationalism, a debate that the organisation placed within the broad scope of the caliphate.

At the end of the 1930s, the basis of its strategy was established: discussions and conferences at MB's headquarters and in the mosques; circulation of the internal statutes and the epistles of al-Banna on his vision of social change; publication of a weekly magazine (*al-Ikhwan al-Muslimin*); creation of groups in Cairo and in the provinces; formation of a body of 'scouts' (*al-Kashshafa*), and various sports activities aimed at young people; *da'wa* in schools and at the university; promotion of religious teaching; defence of the Islamic way; and the struggle against parties and governments that lacked Islamic legitimacy.

There are two elements in the history of the MB that are especially interesting when analysing the group's spread to other countries: on the one hand, its presence in schools and at Al-Azhar University, which is attended by many students from other Arab and Islamic countries (some joining the group and spreading its ideals upon returning to their country of origin), and on the other hand the movement's universal and global character which, according to its founder, supported its continued adherence to the institution of the caliphate as the symbol of unity and a link between all Islamic communities beyond any national ties. This notion of caliphate provided the theoretical basis of the activities carried out by members of the group in different countries such as Iraq, Syria, Lebanon, Palestine, Sudan, Yemen in the 1930s and 1940s, Jordan and Iraq in the 1950s, and Libya and Kuwait in the 1960s. Different mechanisms were used to disseminate these activities: the work of the Communication Office with the Islamic world, created in 1945; the exile of leaders due to the repressive Nasser regime; the presence in 'international associations' of students and in other sectors; and the official creation of the International Organisation of the Muslim Brotherhood in July 1982.

The analysis of the MB's expansion and the development of the branches created outside of Egypt, acting with greater or lesser independence from the founding organisation, suggests that the organisation, in spite of the theoretical principle of subordination to the Egyptian leadership and in spite of its call to overcome national barriers within the framework of *umma*, has adopted different models and strategies according to specific national contexts. Thus, the forms of political participation, the mechanisms to expand the movement, the use of violence in specific circumstances, the way in which the ideal society was imagined, and the strategies used to gain power, varied according to specific socio-historical contexts.

II. Objectives and strategies

The critique of society in the early publications of the MB was accompanied by a specific vision of an ideal society: an Islamic regime based on a number of general principles taken from the sources of Islam (Qur'an and Sunna) and the era of the Rightly Guided Caliphs, with a global concept of Islam that would regulate political, social and economic matters. The general framework of this order would be the caliphate, as the highest expression of the unity of the *umma*. The existing multi-party system and partisan attitudes were rejected as factors that divided the community (although this did not prevent the MB from entering into the political game of alliances with other groups).

A central concern of the movement in the early decades – apart from the creation of companies and economic institutions that either had the direct mission of spreading the group's ideology or involved investments in sensitive and strategic fields (such as the textile industry) – was legislation. The MB's activities in this field must be seen in relation to the changes in the legal system that occurred with the modernisation of the state and the introduction of positive law. The MB took advantage of the contradictions created by this process to emphasise the need for laws deriving from *shari'a* and Islamic jurisprudence *(fiqh)*, which would irredeemably lead to the Islamisation of society and stamp out displays of morality apart from Islam.

The strategy for achieving this transformation was based on preaching, education and Islamisation of the individual, family and society, so that once the process had been completed it would naturally lead to the creation of a truly Islamic state without resorting to violence or struggle; a concept, *jihad,* that the founder of the organisation continually postponed for future stages. Thus, the organisation sometimes resorted to violence, which was generally widespread in Egypt in the 1940s due partly to the degradation of parliamentary life through the Special Organisation *(al-Nidham al-Khass)*. Initially colonising forces were attacked and later, in 1945, the regime, which would lead to the organisation being declared illegal in 1948.

However, given that the resort to violence and the misdeeds of the Special Organisation had led to the illegalisation of the MB and to the assassination of its founder, the election of the second General Guide, Hasan al-Hudaybi (1951–73), justice advisor, would serve to reorient the activities of the organisation, return it to the political arena, corner the Special Organisation (the new General Guide publicly announced that there was no violence in Islam) and redefine relations with the other political forces.

The relationship of the Muslim Brotherhood of Egypt with the new regime inaugurated in 1952 was initially cordial, as the Free Officers movement was linked to the Islamic movement, and some participants in the coup or its preparation had even been active members of the group. However, at the end of 1950 Nasser began to reunite a group of comrades with different principles under the name of the Movement of Free Officers. This change in Nasser's approach coincided with a period of paralysis in the MB's activities that lasted from the assassination of al-Banna in 1949 up to the election of his successor, al-Hudaybi, at the end of 1951.

In spite of the presence of some members of the MB in the first Revolution Leadership Council, relations rapidly began to deteriorate once Nasser's power was strengthened and the MB declared illegal in January 1954. The assassination attempt on Nasser on 26 October 1954, of which the Islamic movement was accused, triggered a hard repression; the incarceration of around 4,000 members of the group, including Hasan al-Hudaybi, the sentencing to death of six leaders and the confiscation of the group's property.

The tension between the Islamic movement and the Egyptian regime reached a climax in 1965, when the regime accused the MB of conspiracy. This repression, which coincided with the defeat of 1967 and awareness of the failure of Nasserite nationalism, would have important consequences for the Egyptian and international Islamist movement. It fostered the emergence of the nucleus of the future International Organisation of the Muslim Brotherhood and triggered a radicalisation among some members, notably one of its greatest theorists, Sayyid Qutb. Executed in 1966, Qutb developed his thought in prison. Deeply hostile to Western culture, his thinking was based on the notion of God's sole sovereignty (*hakimiyyat Allah*). He accused the rulers of existing Muslim societies and their subjects – which were characterised as living in ignorance (*jahiliya*) – of unbelief (*takfir*) and insisted on the priority of action in order to provoke change. This line of thought exercised, and continues to exercise, a powerful influence on Islamic movements, which eventually opted for violence and direct confrontation with the regimes as a mechanism for transforming society. Qutb's position was contested by the MB in the work of al-Hudaybi, *Preachers, not judges.*[1]

After the repression of Nasser's regime, his successor Anwar al-Sadat changed strategy at the same time as he oriented the regime towards the West, and the members of the MB were released from jail, tolerated and used by the regime to counter the communist and Nasserist opposition that put its legitimacy in doubt. The association's third General Guide, Omar al-Tilmisani (1974–86) was responsible for returning the MB to social and political life and continuing its work of social Islamisation, as well as benefitting from the economic policy adopted by Sadat.

III. Transformations and future goals

During the 1980s, the organisation deployed a strategy of alliances with political parties in order to participate in the elections, first with the conservative al-Wafd and later with the Labour Party and Liberal Party, with a conservative social programme and a liberal economic policy. It was in this decade that the organisation launched the slogan 'Islam is the solution', corresponding to the MB's global vision of Islam and of the organisation itself, and that the internal debate began on the creation of a political party. According to the former First Deputy Guide of the organisation, Muhammad Habib, the *shura* Council of the MB adopted the decision to create a political party in 1989. However, pressure on the organisation from the Egyptian authorities forced it to shelve such aspirations. When Mustafa Mashhur was elected General Guide in 1996, the creation of a political party that would have official recognition was discussed. These deliberations led to the creation of Hizb al-Wasat (Centre Party), with the approval of the then member of the *shura* council, Muhammah Mahdi Akef, but without the support of the Orientation Office. Hizb al-Wasat was an attempt to create a separate political structure or platform from the MB. It resulted from the generational crisis within the group between a new generation of young Islamists, perhaps not fully committed to the organisation but feeling very represented by it, who endorse greater openness to democracy and more transparency in the MB's internal management, and the old guard, who defend most of the conservative positions. Thus, the former General Guide, Muhammad Mahdi Akef (2004–9), has shown, more than his predecessors in that position, a greater openness towards internal reforms and a clear tendency to reform the organisation into a political party, as shown with the presentation of the 'draft' political programme of the Muslim Brotherhood of Egypt in October 2007. The MB decided to announce the draft political party programme largely because the organisation obtained 88 parliamentary seats (approximately 20 per cent) in the 2005 elections. This confirms that it has become an important political actor over the years, and although the organisation lacks the status of a party it really acts like one: it competes in elections as much as possible, it has parliamentary representation, it has an internal structure similar to any traditional Egyptian party and participates in public debates.

Akef has defended internal democratisation and is the only General Guide to have submitted his nomination to the *shura* of the international organisation, scrupulously following the statutes that for decades were ignored, but his initiatives have fuelled a debate within the organisation that may lead to the modernisation of its structures and leadership.

The major challenge for the future is not the acceptance of the rules of democracy, since these were accepted by the group decades ago. In fact, for many years the MB has defended civil liberties, campaigned against the state of emergency and the military courts, and fought against corruption and for the limitation of the power of the president. It also believes in the people as the sole source of authority, the necessary election of a leader and power switching. Instead, the challenge is to recognise and accept differences, that is, to further the internal democratisation of the group. The MB also needs dialogue with other political forces, which the latter have been reluctant to do until now, which demonstrates two things: first, that the MB has become a political force on a par with other parties in Egypt with similar problems (renewal of leadership, splits, lack of dialogue), but with a larger social base, greater parliamentary presence and a greater capacity to mobilise women than the other political groups; and second, that, like the other political groups, it has so far failed to capitalise on or channel the social protest movement that has shaken Egyptian society for the last several years.

Nobody doubts that the MB is a powerful political and social force, least of all the Egyptian regime which, after the MB's success at the last parliamentary elections, has once again adopted a harder strategy of repression. The sentences handed down by the military courts in April 2008 against various MB leaders, businessmen, university professors and others accused of money laundering to finance an illegal organisation, are just one of the many indicators that reveal the regime's desire to marginalise the MB through political and economic pursuit of the organisation. However, this strategy seems to have the opposite effect, by increasing the organisation's popularity before what is seen as a corrupt and frightened regime.

Notes

1 Hasan al-Hudaybi (1977) *Du'at la qudat*. Cairo: Dar al-Tawzi' wa-l-Nashr al-Islamiyya.

References

al-Anani, Jalil (2007) *Al-Ikhwan al-Muslimun fi Misr. Shaykhukha tusari'u al-zaman?* Cairo: Maktabat al-Shuruq al-Dualiyya.
al-Banna, Hasan (1988) *Majmu'at rasail al-imam al-shahid Hasan al-Banna*. Alexandria: Dar al-Da'wa.
Carré, Olivier and Gérard Michaud (1983) *Les Frères musulmans. Egypte et Syrie (1928–1982)*. Paris: Gallimard.
Elshobaki, Amr (2009) *Les Frères musulmans des origines à nos jours*. Paris: Karthala.
al-Hudaybi, Hasan (1977) *Du'at la qudat*. Cairo: Dar al-Tawzi' wa-l-Nashr al-Islamiyya.
Martín Muñoz, Gema (1999) *El Estado árabe. Crisis de legitimidad y contestación islamista*. Barcelona: Bellaterra.
Mitchell, Richard P. (1969) *The Society of the Muslim Brothers*. Oxford: Oxford University Press.
Mustafa, Hala (1992) *Al-Islam al-siyasi fi Misr. Min harakat al-islah ila jama'at al-'unf*. Cairo: Markaz al-Dirasat al-Siyasiyya wa-l-Istratijija.

Ramadan, Tarek (1998) *Aux sources du renouveau musulman*. Paris: Bayard.
Tamam, Hossam (2005) *Tahawwulat al-Ikhwan al-Muslimun*. Cairo: Madbuli.
Ternisien, Xavier (2005) *Les Frères musulmans*. Paris: Fayard.
al-Tilmisani, Omar (n.d.) *Dhikrayyat la mudhakkirat*. Cairo: Dar al-I'tisam.

MILLI GÖRÜŞ

Jenny White

Milli Görüş, or National Vision, is Turkey's sole political Islamist movement. It emerged in the late 1960s, not as an underground revolutionary movement, but as a legitimate strain of political thought within a functioning democratic party system. The leader of the political Islamist movement was Necmettin Erbakan, who founded a series of political parties over the ensuing three decades. The term Milli Görüş derives from the party platform Erbakan wrote in 1975 that laid out his vision of a form of economic modernisation which was authentically Turkish and based on Muslim ethics. Islam was linked to nationalism and had a strong chauvinist and racialist component based on Turkishness, Turkish blood and history. The Ottoman Empire was posited as the locus of origin of the civilisation of Islam. In this way, Islam provided an authentic Turkish justification of modernisation that did not rely on the West. In other words, Milli Görüş used Turkey's Ottoman–Muslim heritage to construct a modern religio-ethnic Turkish national identity. The emphasis was on the national, rather than the Islamic, although this balance changed over time as Islam became a more overt justification for policy decisions.

The Milli Görüş view remained important in Turkish politics until the mid-1990s when the movement split and a new party the Justice and Development Party (AKP, Adalet ve Kalkınma Partisi), led by Recep Tayyip Erdoğan, eclipsed Erbakan's party (and his ideas) with a more moderate, liberal conception of the role of Islam in politics. The AKP viewed Muslimhood as a personal attribute of politicians, rather than Islam as an attribute of the party platform as Milli Görüş had done.[1] By 2008, Erbakan's political party was no longer represented in Parliament and the influence of his Milli Görüş movement had become more pronounced in Europe than Turkey.

History

From the founding of the Turkish Republic in 1924, the state extended its control over the public practice of Islam. All religious orders and educational institutions were closed and aspects of social practice, from the alphabet and calendar to clothing, were radically Westernised and cut off from Islamic references. The display of religious symbols in public places, such as schools, state buildings and hospitals, was banned. The public functions of Islam were co-opted by and subordinated to state institutions, such as the Directorate of Religious Affairs (Diyanet İşleri Başkanlığı). The Diyanet oversees mosques and Islamic education, distributes sermons, translates religious texts and interprets them.

Under the leadership of Turkey's charismatic founder, Mustafa Kemal Atatürk, religion in the new republic was to be severed from the political arena and relegated to citizens' private lives. This principle was referred to as laicism (*laiklik*), meaning state control over religion, rather than the more hands-off connotation of the term secularism, meaning separation of Church and State.

Several powerful Sunni religious brotherhoods (singular: *tarikat*) are found in Turkey, among them the Sufi orders of Nakşibendi, Süleymancı and Nurcu. Although religious brotherhoods and dervish orders were banned shortly after the founding of the republic and their lodges closed, they continued to operate clandestinely and to play an important role in Turkish society and politics.

Contemporary supporters of Mustafa Kemal Atatürk's laicist reforms are called Kemalists, as distinguished from Islamists. Both are self-ascriptive terms representing group boundaries based on shared beliefs about the proper role of religion in society and politics. Generally speaking, the Kemalist position combines a kind of authoritarian democracy with a Westernised secular lifestyle. Kemalists have tried to ensure a laic state and secular Turkish society through the government, judiciary, educational system and military.

Islamists are Muslims who, rather than accept an inherited Muslim tradition, have developed their own self-conscious vision of Islam and the ideal Islamic life, which they then bring to bear on social and political events. That is, rather than expressing their Muslim identity through prayer, veiling, almsgiving and other such ritual practices alone, these practices are singled out and critically examined for their meaning beyond the realm of religion, family and workplace. They are interpreted as potential frameworks for social betterment through political action. Islamism implies an activist understanding of being Muslim that goes beyond conversion of non-Muslims to the conversion of the entire social and political framework within which Muslims live, with the aim of producing one that better accommodates Muslim values. The delineation of what values are appropriate to this new order is elastic and a matter of continual negotiation between Islamists, their constituencies and the exigencies of the political environment. In Turkey, for instance, Islamists tend to see Muslim values derived from 'Turkish' Islam as better than those they associate with 'Arab' Islam, reflecting a racialist conception of nationalism.

Turkey's population today is almost entirely Muslim, with small minorities of Jews and Christians. About four-fifths of the Muslim population are orthodox Sunni Muslims; the rest are Alevis, a non-Sunni syncretistic Muslim minority. A 1999 survey showed a high level of religious practice in Turkey, with nine out of ten adults fasting during the holy month of Ramadan and almost half praying five times a day.[2] Between 40 and 60 per cent of all respondents rated themselves as religious and 40 per cent would define themselves as Muslim or Muslim Turk before Turkish citizen.[3] Muslim identity, however, is not a homogenous category in Turkey and also offers a code to express political ideas, social class position, or general life philosophy, in addition to specific religious beliefs or affiliation.[4]

Despite the erasure of Islam from public life, once Turkey introduced multi-party politics in 1945 the electorate demanded a broader role for religion in the public sphere. The Nakşibendi and Nurcu orders reappeared in political life when politicians realised the potential for religious leaders to deliver votes. Competition for votes prompted the government itself to add voluntary religious instruction to the elementary school curriculum in 1948, build more mosques, preacher-training schools and a school of theology. In turn, the Turkish military enacted changes in the constitution and advisory bodies, such as the National Security Council, that allowed it to assume the role of guardian of the laic nature of the Turkish state, with the right to intervene if the military deemed it under threat. This oppositional government/state framework, with the elected government representing a relatively devout population, and the state as guardian of laicism, continues to this day and is the root of much political turmoil.

Beginning with the 1950 election, Islam in politics mostly took the form of functional appeals to Islamic forms and practices to obtain votes, and an expansion of Islamic arenas by the state (more mosques and Islamic education) in an attempt to counter leftist ideologies prevalent at the time. It wasn't until the late 1960s that a political movement emerged with an ideology explicitly rooted in Islamic principles.

The Islamist Parties

The first overtly Islam-identified political party, the National Order Party (NOP, Milli Nizam Partisi), was founded in 1970 by Necmettin Erbakan, a professor of mechanical engineering with a degree from a technical university in Aachen, Germany. The party represented small independent businessmen, merchants and craftsmen who felt threatened by industrialisation.

The Nakşibendi Sufi brotherhood played an important role in founding what became known as the Milli Görüş movement. Erbakan belonged to the circle around the Nakşibendi Sheikh Mehmed Zahid Kotku (d. 1980) at the Iskenderpaşa mosque in Istanbul. In the 1970s, the influence of Pakistani, Egyptian, Indian and other Islamist writers made themselves felt with the translation of their works, particularly those by Mawdudi, Hasan al-Banna and Sayyid Qutb. Kotku was influenced by these writers who believed Westernisation had brought about the decline of their societies, that pan-Arab nationalism (and Turkish Kemalism) had been shown to be ineffectual, and advocated Islam as a political project. Kotku saw the need for a new model of Islam-derived modernity that emphasised economic development and moral probity. He inspired Erbakan's developing philosophy and mobilised networks of his followers to support his party.[5] Other Sufi orders and the Nurcu order also played active roles in founding the party.

The NOP was closed down in 1971, along with all other parties, as a consequence of Turkey's second military coup, a reaction to widespread violent right-left conflict. Erbakan fled to Switzerland, but returned to establish the National Salvation Party (NSP, Milli Selamet Partisi) in 1972. The NSP was a conservative party with a marginal following among provincial business people and followers of religious orders.

The party platform focused on expanding the role of small business within state-protected industrialisation, so its constituency was drawn mostly from small-town businessmen, who also tended to be conservative and pious. The NSP proposed that state-led industry be supported by large numbers of small capitalists, each owning no more than a 5 per cent share, thus giving small business a stake in industrialisation, rather than being threatened by it.[6] The NSP organised rallies that attacked the laicist system and even Atatürk himself, and called for the restoration of *sharia*, or Islamic, law. It did not do well in elections in the 1970s, suggesting that religion was an insufficient factor for mobilising political support. Nevertheless, as a result of political horse-trading, the NSP was part of three coalition governments in that decade.

In 1975 Erbakan wrote a platform for the NSP entitled Milli Görüş. It laid out his thoughts about industrialisation and economic development, emphasising Turkey's economic independence. Although the NSP's platform was officially secular, the Milli Görüş manifesto talked about the European Common Market as a European Catholic project that aimed to assimilate Turkey. Erbakan suggested that Turkey's economic and political partners should be in the Muslim world instead of Europe.

Milli Görüş was a middle way between the evils of Communism and monopolistic large capital, envisioned as multinational companies as well as state-sponsored large national enterprises. The party demanded that industrial enterprises be spread throughout the country rather than in big urban areas, that official assistance be given to promote industrialisation in Anatolia, and that interest rates be abolished. The Milli Görüş way was one of Islamic morality, justice and development within a totally national industry. Instead of unions, Milli Görüş encouraged an Islamic work ethic and Islam-inspired responsibility to one's workers. Relations with the Muslim world were envisioned as Turkey reoccupying the economic and political leadership role it had enjoyed in the region in Ottoman times.

Throughout the 1970s, Milli Görüş supporters tended to be small tradesmen, craftsmen and religious figures and their followers, especially in provincial areas. The NSP did well in elections in eastern and southeastern Anatolia, where the Nakşibendi Order and the Nur movement were particularly active. The party was closed along with other parties in the 1980 coup.

In 1983, Erbakan founded a new Islamic party, the Welfare Party (WP, Refah Partisi). While his earlier NSP had drawn its main support from towns in the underdeveloped eastern and central Anatolian provinces and did not do well in the cities, the WP's voter base included the urban poor living at the margins of cities, particularly small shop-keepers and urban migrants, many of whom had previously voted for the centre-left social democrats. Squatter areas were growing up around Turkey's major cities as a result of rural to urban migration, as farmers were driven from the land by mechanisation and other factors and drawn to jobs in large, state-run factories. Erbakan proposed a 'Just Economic Order' (*Adil Düzen*) to eliminate socio-economic inequality and corruption. He called for state withdrawal from economic activities and the promotion of individual small enterprise. Rather than seeing Milli Görüş as representing the conservative periphery, then, one could argue that it was driven by Turkey's increasing industrialisation and incorporation into global capitalism.[7] Milli Görüş wasn't against capitalism, except in its monopolistic form. Rather, its supporters wanted a share.

In the 1987 election, the WP failed to obtain the minimum 10 per cent of the vote and thus was not represented in Parliament. However, throughout the rest of the 1980s the WP added to its supporters, including members of an expanding Islamist business and professional community that did business explicitly within a framework of Islamic principles. They provided a stable economic underpinning for various aspects of an emerging Islamist movement – whether in the form of contributions to political parties, support for charitable organisations, scholarships, or the building of schools and gender-segregated dormitories – putting into practice both the economic and moral principles of the Milli Görüş movement.

In nationwide municipal elections held in 1994, the WP doubled its votes from the 1989 elections, winning 28 of 76 mayoral seats in provincial capitals, including six of Turkey's largest 15 cities. Istanbul and Ankara both elected Islamist mayors. The election results shocked Kemalists, who organised to counter what they perceived to be a fundamentalist threat that would culminate in a restrictive *sharia* -based state that they feared was the WP's ultimate aim.

In this period, the religious component of Milli Görüş eclipsed nationalism as the major framework for WP policy. Erbakan spoke against laicism and Westernisation and against Turkey's military cooperation agreement with Israel. He pledged to withdraw Turkey from NATO and the European Union Customs Union signed in 1996, in favour of political and economic alliances with other Muslim countries. He planned to pursue a brotherhood of Muslims around the world, replacing Turkey's ties with and reliance on the West. After the 1994 elections, several attacks were reported on women in Western dress in Istanbul, and attempts were made to separate women from men on public transport. Some WP mayors had statues of nudes removed from parks and tried to close or restrict restaurants and nightclubs that served alcohol. Party zealots proposed building an enormous mosque in Istanbul's Taksim Square, a direct affront to the institutional legacy of Kemalist secularism. While this plan did not succeed, other icons of Kemalism were transformed. When the WP won the 1994 municipal elections in Ankara, the new mayor changed the official city symbol from a Hittite sun to a symbol containing elements of a mosque. For the most part, however, WP mayors improved city services, which encouraged even secularist voters to favour the WP in 1995: two-fifths of those voting for the WP identified themselves as secularist.

In the 1995 national election, the WP emerged as the largest party with 21 per cent of the vote and 158 of 550 seats in Parliament. Called upon to form a government, the WP was unable to do so because the two leading centre-right parties refused to join it in a coalition government. Ultimately, in the summer of 1996, after some negotiation, Erbakan found himself Prime Minister in a coalition.

As prime minister, Erbakan tried to implement some of his Milli Görüş views about reorienting Turkey towards the Muslim world. However, he met with little success. Turkey's control of the water on the Tigris and Euphrates rivers through its massive South Anatolia Dam Project had already strained relations with downriver Iraq and Syria. On Erbakan's state visit to Libya, its leader, Muammar el-Qaddafi, criticised Turkey for its treatment of the Kurds.

The WP's turn towards Islam and its anti-system stance heightened public anxiety about the ultimate aim of the party. The WP tried to move hundreds of secular-minded judges to posts in rural districts and replace them with judges who might stretch the interpretation of Turkey's secular legal code, especially in the area of family law. This prompted a public outcry and the move was blocked by a government supervisory council. The press kept a watchful eye on the WP's actions, and public and civic organisations were quick to mobilise and demonstrate their displeasure. After winning municipal elections, the WP closed some community libraries and educational centres for women, sometimes replacing them with Qur'an courses.

The activities of the WP came under intense scrutiny by the military. The WP's radicalism eventually led to Erbakan's ouster and the party's demise. In June 1997 the military engineered what has become known as a 'soft coup', edging Erbakan out of power without actually taking over the government itself. In 1998 the Constitutional Court closed down the WP for allegedly threatening the secularist nature of the state, and banned Erbakan from political activity for five years.

The reasons for the WP's success in elections are multifold. In part, WP support was a protest against the corruption and incompetence of the other parties. The WP appealed to widespread religio-cultural values. The laic state's continued repression of religious expression led to public demonstrations and political activism, particularly by the conservative sector of the population aspiring to education and economic upward mobility. The ban on wearing the headscarf at universities in particular was seen as an attempt to keep conservative young women from getting an education and entering the professions. Issues of poverty and social class fuelled what appeared on the surface to be a purely religious issue.

What accounted for the WP's appeal to non-religious voters? WP election advertisements avoided religious language and presented the WP as a forward-looking party with a vision that encompassed all strata of society, regardless of their views about political Islam.[8] WP advertisements referred to issues such as pensions, affordable housing, health care and the environment. Religious themes and images were, for the most part, avoided. The WP mayor of Istanbul, Recep Tayyip Erdoğan, brought some order to municipal services and seemed, on the surface at least, to be less corrupt than previous administrations.

The WP also had a face-to-face, personalised political style that mobilised voters through a system of associations, foundations and informal organisations. The metaphor of family and its associated responsibility and obligation was carried over to the neighbourhood and work place, where it meshed with cultural and religious norms that gave neighbours, employees, and so on, rights to assistance and just treatment. In other words, human rights and citizens' rights were made personal obligations. People were asked, as their religious duty, to take personal responsibility for their neighbours. Unlike the other top-down, highly centralised parties that brought their projects to the voters for support, the WP built on local solidarities and wedded local projects and sensibilities to the party's project. The involvement of grassroots organisations lent flexibility and endurance to the Islamist political project, even in the face of the banning of the WP in January 1998 and the jailing of its politicians.[9]

The party also had the advantage of the strong Milli Görüş message that appealed across class, ethnic and gender divides. Islamists took over the role of champions of economic justice from the left that had been decimated in the 1980 coup, although the Islamist conception differed quite substantially from the class-based ideas of the left. Milli Görüş, with its Just Economic Order, appealed to the working class and to marginal people in the squatter areas, as well as to small businessmen and entrepreneurs. In the 1980s, Turkey opened its economy to the world market, creating new opportunities for small- and medium-sized businesses. At the same time, the government began to privatise industry, increasing unemployment, and to dismantle the already thin social safety net. The segment of the population left behind by the economic transformation also found a voice in the WP, which emphasised issues such as social justice, unemployment, poverty and social security, while respecting the more conservative lifestyle of the masses.

In sum, the political success of the WP reflected the increasing role of Islam in Turkish public life, as evidenced by the growth of Islamic schools and banks, Islamic businesses, and a politicised Islamist movement with its own organisations, dress and publications. State repression of religious expression galvanised Islamist activism. The WP's success also expressed voter dissatisfaction with government corruption and the performance of the centrist parties. Support for the WP came not only from the smaller towns in its traditional strongholds of central and eastern Anatolia, but also from major cities. The WP expanded its voter base from conservative rural people and small businessmen to include big business owners, young urban professionals, women, intellectuals, and crossovers from the left. In a pragmatic move, the party began to present itself not as a religious party, but as a modern party with a vision that encompassed issues of concern to all strata of society. Campaign advertisements depicted people such as pensioners, civil servants and unveiled women. The party's approach to organising took advantage of local grassroots organisations that brought it closer to the people. Despite this, the WP's activities continued to demonstrate the radical roots of Milli Görüş and the influence of Kotku and the Nakşibendi order. The WP was closed down by the Constitutional Court for violating the laic nature of the state, and Erbakan was banned once again from politics.

The WP was succeeded by the Virtue Party (VP, Fazilet Partisi), which Erbakan helped lead from behind the scenes. The WP's experience of persecution pushed the VP's platform and rhetoric in the direction of democracy and human rights, political freedom and pluralism. While the WP was a political party defined by its relation to Islam, its successor, the VP, represented itself as a Muslim party defined by its relation to politics. It claimed to be a moderate, modern meritocracy, populist, environmentalist and open to women and minorities in its organisation. Kemalists were cynical about the party's sudden discovery of democratic principles and saw it as self-serving, given the party's precarious legal state. It was also perceived to be yet another example of *takiyye*, of hiding one's true purpose in the interest of achieving one's ultimate goal, presumably to remake the Turkish state into an Islamic one.

Younger, populist, charismatic leaders such as Istanbul mayor Recep Tayyip Erdoğan began to dominate the party. Unlike the elder, more elitist Erbakan, Erdoğan appealed to the new Islamist constituencies – young, middle-class professionals, students and intellectuals. The younger Islamist generation was invested in current political issues, not loyalty to regional patrons and religious brotherhoods. Many were urban youth in their twenties and thirties, educated in secular institutions or theological schools, desiring upward mobility and economic security, but with few opportunities to participate in the global economy and booming service sector. They were open to new ideas and models of society that would incorporate these aspirations, while retaining an Islamic lifestyle and moral values. Erdoğan's rise to leadership of the Islamist movement, Turkey's globalising economy, and a new Islamic public made the Milli Görüş movement increasingly irrelevant. Although Erdoğan entertained Islamist ideas, he and Abdullah Gül, a 49 year old former economics professor from Kayseri, moved the VP further away from an 'Islam-referenced' party to what they called a 'new politics' based on democracy and freedom of belief. Nevertheless, in April 1999 the Constitutional Court opened a case against the VP on charges of anti-laic activities.

The VP was banned in June 2001, with the conservative faction, under Necmettin Erbakan, and the reformists, under Recep Tayyip Erdoğan, going their separate ways, each founding a new party. Erbakan's Felicity Party (FP, Saadet Partisi) continued to represent Milli Görüş views and did not do well in subsequent elections, unable to pass the 10 per cent vote threshold to take a seat in Parliament. Erdoğan founded the AKP and claimed to have abandoned Milli Görüş altogether, including both its ethno-nationalist and Islamist views, and to have become a conservative democratic party.[10] This has shown itself to be a winning formula, propelling the AKP into government leadership with an ever-increasing segment of the vote (47 per cent in the 2007 elections), with Erdoğan as prime minister and Gül president. The party's roots have shifted from Nakşibendi influence to the more globally oriented Nurcu, particularly the Fethullah Gülen movement that focuses on modernising Islam through education and popularising it through outreach.[11]

In Europe, Milli Görüş runs an extensive network of mosques. It has 54,000 members in Germany alone and branches in 11 countries. In the past, Milli Görüş raised money through its European mosques to support Erbakan's parties in Turkish elections but, starting in the 1990s, Milli Görüş began to distance itself from Turkish politics and reorient itself to its European constituency, focusing on obtaining official recognition for Islam and Muslim identity.[12]

Although the status of Milli Görüş in Europe is still being debated, it could be argued that political events in Turkey and the opportunities and exigencies of institutional survival in the European context, have transformed it from a movement that in Turkey used

Turkish-Muslim authenticity as a basis for rejecting the West, to a civic organisation that in Europe sees Turkish-Muslim identity as a basis for integration with the West. Both are broadly political projects, but differ substantially in their means and goals.

If this is so, it gives an important insight into the malleable nature, both structurally and ideologically, of what generally is lumped together under the unhelpfully broad rubric of Islamist movement. Rather, it points to the necessity of examining how such organisations are embedded within particular constituent cultures and nation state contexts. It begs the question of whether and how movements perceived to be radical and anti-systemic in one context may in another context or another time play a different and even contradictory role.

Notes

1   Jenny White (2005) 'The End of Islamism? Turkey's Muslimhood Model', in Robert Hefner (ed.), *Modern Muslim Politics*, Princeton: Princeton University Press, pp. 87–111.
2   Ali Çarkoğlu and Binnaz Toprak (2000) *Türkiye'de Din, Toplum ve Siyaset*, Istanbul: Türkiye Ekonomik ve Sosyal Etüdler Vakfı, p.45.
3   Ibid., p. 43 and p. 27.
4   Haldun Gülalp (2003) 'Whatever Happened To Secularism? The Multiple Islams of Turkey', *The South Atlantic Quarterly*, 102 (2/3), Spring/Summer.
5   Özlem Bayraktar (2007) *The National Outlook and Its Youth in the 1970s*, M.A. Thesis, Bosphorus University: Turkey.
6   Haldun Gülalp (1999) 'Political Islam in Turkey: The Rise and Fall of the Refah Party', *The Muslim World*, 89 (1), p. 27.
7   Bayraktar, *The National Outlook*.
8   Ayşe Öncü (1995) 'Packaging Islam: Cultural Politics on the Landscape of Turkish Commercial Television', *Public Culture*, 8 (1), Fall: pp. 60–2.
9   Jenny White (2002) *Islamist Mobilization in Turkey: A Study in Vernacular Politics*, Seattle: University of Washington Press.
10   Ahmet T. Kuru (2006) 'Reinterpretation of secularism in Turkey: the case of the Justice and Development Party', in M. Hakan Yavuz (ed.), *The Emergence of a New Turkey: Democracy and the AK Parti*, Salt Lake City: University of Utah Press, p. 8.
11   Berna Turam (2006) *Between Islam and the State: The Politics of Engagement*, Stanford: Stanford University Press.
12   Ahmet Yükleyen (2010) 'State Policies and Islam in Europe: Milli Görüş in Germany and the Netherlands', *Journal of Ethnic and Migration Studies*, 36 (3), pp. 445–63.

References

Bayraktar, Özlem (2007) *The National Outlook and Its Youth in the 1970s*, MA thesis, Bosphorus University: Turkey.
Çarkoğlu, Ali and Binnaz Toprak (2000) *Türkiye'de Din, Toplum ve Siyaset*, Istanbul: Türkiye Ekonomik ve Sosyal Etüdler Vakfı.
Gülalp, Haldun (2004) 'Whatever Happened To Secularism? The Multiple Islams of Turkey', *The South Atlantic Quarterly*, 102 (2/3), Spring/Summer: pp. 381–95.
——— (1999) 'Political Islam in Turkey: The Rise and Fall of the Refah Party', *The Muslim World*, 89 (1) January: pp. 22–41.

Kuru, Ahmet T. (2006) 'Reinterpretation of Secularism in Turkey: The Case of the Justice and Development Party', in M. Hakan Yavuz (ed.), *The Emergence of a New Turkey: Democracy and the AK Parti*, Salt Lake City: University of Utah Press, pp. 136–59.

Öncü, Ayşe (1995) 'Packaging Islam: Cultural Politics on the Landscape of Turkish Commercial Television', *Public Culture*, 8 (1) Fall: pp. 51–71.

Turam, Berna (2006) *Between Islam and the State: The Politics of Engagement*, Stanford: Stanford University Press.

White, Jenny (2005) 'The End of Islamism? Turkey's Muslimhood Model', in Robert Hefner (ed.), *Modern Muslim Politics*, Princeton: Princeton University Press, pp. 87–111.

—— (2002) Islamist Mobilization in Turkey: A Study in Vernacular Politics, Seattle: University of Washington Press.

Yükleyen, Ahmet (2010) 'State Policies and Islam in Europe: Milli Görüş in Germany and the Netherlands', *Journal of Ethnic and Migration Studies*, 36 (3), pp. 445–63.

THE JAMA'AT-I ISLAMI

Jan-Peter Hartung

The South Asian Jama'at-i Islami (JiI Islamic Society/Community) must be considered the second oldest Islamist movement after the Egyptian Muslim Brotherhood. Although founded by a gathering of 75 men in Lahore on 24 August 1941, its ideological foundation has to be set about a decade earlier, when Sayyid Abu l-A'la Mawdudi (d. 1979) began to develop the first self-contained modern theory of an Islamic state. Mawdudi must be considered the sole driving force behind the movement and his influence persists even today, even if not always readily visible in daily life.

Mawdudi was born in 1903 to a family that epitomised the struggle of Muslim intellectual elites between adaptation and emphatic attempts to maintain their cultural identity after the establishment of British rule in India post-1857. Trained in both secular and traditionalist religious institutions in approximately 1918, Mawdudi took to journalism and was editing a number of local newspapers and journals. This was during a period of major political developments: between 1919 and 1924 the young Indian independence movement had formed a massive campaign under the pretext of protecting the caliphate, held by the Ottoman sultan, from British interference after World War I. The disillusion of Mawdudi, when in 1924 he witnessed the abolition of the caliphate under Kemal Atatürk and the collapse of the Indian *Khilafat* movement, had a decisive influence on his religio-political ideas; ideas which began to take shape in his first major work in 1927 – *al-Jihad fi l-islam* (The Jihad in Islam).

The ideology which Mawdudi began to sketch out in the subsequent decade rested on the assumption that the Western political conceptions of secularism, nationalism, and democracy are incompatible with Islam. Being well aware of the requisites of his time, however, Mawdudi did not opt for a verbatim return to the practice of the original Muslim community. Instead, he thoroughly engaged with modern Western philosophical thought and used his thus gained knowledge as the prism through which he perceived the authoritative texts of Sunni Islam, that is, the Qur'an and the Sunna of the Prophet. The outcome was the first systematic outline of a modern Islamic state and a reinterpretation of Islam as an all-encompassing 'system of life' (*nizham-i zindagi*), a notion that came to have a tremendous influence on contemporary Islamist thought. An essential component of Mawdudi's elaboration of his system was his perception of Islamic history, which he understood as a constant struggle between 'Islam' and 'ignorance' (*jahiliyya*) that could only be solved by a reinterpretation of a traditional concept of cyclical renewal (*tajdid*). In his view, ignorance not only signified the pre-Islamic era, but every contemporary thought and practice that did not match his rigid criteria for Islam.

Mawdudi's systematic outline also rested on a handful of axiomatic terms which he had deduced by selective reading of the Qur'an, stating that the text of the revelation would be the only possible infallible source on which a stable and virtuous society could be built:

> Islam [...] is a well-arranged system, the basis of which had been determined as a fixed number of principles. From its corner stones to the least little detail everything is in a logical relation to its fundamental principles.[1]

It was this unmediated and selective approach to the authoritative sources that earned Mawdudi severe criticism from the formally trained Muslim religious scholars ('ulama), who accused him of neglecting an entire tradition of learned exegesis. His direct recourse to the Qur'an by means of foregoing the exegetical tradition was, however, not accidental but a logical consequence of Mawdudi's conception of history: It was the very 'ulama that, in his eyes, had contributed considerably to the decline of Islam, and this could only be overcome by an unmediated approach to the text.

The axiomatic terms assumed a legislative, as well as a receptive aspect of God's fundamental One-ness (tawhid), and determined similarly a receptive and a submissive relation of man to God: as master (rabb) God issues binding rules (shari'a) to man; as goddess (ilah) he receives obedience ('ibadat) from man. From this particular relationship between God and man Mawdudi deduced his next set of important key concepts that were to mark his career in Islamist political theory from this point on: 'God's absolute and unrestricted sovereignty' (hakimiyya-yi ilahi), and 'man's limited sovereignty as God's trustee on earth' (khilafat). With the latter concept, derived from his understanding of the Qur'anic verse 24:55, Mawdudi emphasised a non-historical notion of the caliphate, that is to say not the historical succession of the Prophet as leaders of the Muslim community, but as the earthly deputyship of the whole of mankind for God, provided that 'they believe and work righteous deeds', as the Qur'anic verse states.

The dichotomy of God's absolute and man's limited sovereignty allows nonetheless for a certain range of self-responsible action by man. This range is only limited by his understanding of the timeless edicts of the Qur'an and the Prophetic Sunna, and constitutes what Mawdudi would call the 'Islamic State' (islami hukumat). Each regulation for every single societal arena, be it economics, culture, morality or politics, had to meet Mawdudi's above-given definition of Islam as a self-contained System of Life. They were to be deduced by a Consultative Council (majlis-i shura) in a responsible manner. This council would, however, not be confined to a number of specially trained legal experts but to those 'who believe and work righteous deeds', that is, ideally, the entire Muslim community. This collective aspect of the decision-making process within the confines of the divine revelation was what Mawdudi labelled 'theo-democracy' (ilahi jumhuri hukumat).

The question that remained unanswered was how this theo-democracy would come about. In his endeavour to solve this issue, Mawdudi proposed an interesting semantic shift in his understanding of Islam by adding a dynamic aspect to it: in principle, Islam is the name of a movement that, on the concept of the sovereignty of the One God, strives to erect the entire building of human existence.[2]

It is from within this understanding of Islam that the JiI fits into Mawdudi's theoretical framework: it was conceptualised as a small avant-garde within the wider Muslim community (*umma*) that was to ensure the transition of the latter to an Islamic polity as imagined by Mawdudi. Herein lies the interesting semantic ambiguity of the carefully chosen term '*Jama'a*' as 'community' on the one hand, and 'society' on the other: In a process that Mawdudi described as a persistent and non-violent 'Islamic revolution' (*inqilab-i islami*), the avant-garde would eventually grow into the entire Muslim community. The JiI that was founded in August 1941 was thus understood as a motor of social and political change, as well as a small-scale model of the Islamic state. Of course, as an avant-garde who already 'believed and worked righteous deeds' it was they who aimed at leadership in the state-to-come: 'righteous leadership' would be granted to those who form the core of the newly established Islamic movement, those who consider themselves most able to bring about a revolution in leadership and who claim a monopoly of righteousness, with Mawdudi himself as the exemplary figure. It is understandable that, in order to ensure this monopoly to the avant-garde, its number had to be kept in manageable confines. For that reason, the JiI kept the number of its permanent members, the so-called 'pillars' (*arkan*), quite small for a long time and relied instead on increasing its number of loose supporters (*muttafiqan*), as Mawdudi himself had specified.

JiI in its valence as 'community' is similarly stratified. There seem to be different reasons for this: even within an avant-garde there has to be, according to Mawdudi, a structure of leadership that is instrumental in determining and reinforcing regulations deduced from the Qur'an and *hadith*. Here it was argued that men were deliberately created with different faculties in order to fit organically into a labour-divided society. The decision-making process within the JiI, which consists of a Consultative Council that is headed by a commander (*amir*) reflects this natural order without intending to impose a social hierarchy, even though this has proven hard to avoid in practice. The authority of the *amir* might even be seen as resembling God's authority, especially when considering the fact that the constitution of the JiI assigns him the right of veto on decisions of the Consultative Council.

On the other hand, leadership in the JiI has to acknowledge the Qur'anic assertion of man's equality before God, and therefore Mawdudi's own conception of an Islamic polity based on democratic principles. The *amir* of the JiI, elected by the General Assembly of permanent members for a term of five years (with the possibility of unlimited extensions), must thus be seen as just the first among equals, although he does possess a *de facto* absolute monopoly over definitions of what is commendable and what reprehensible, as stated in the Qur'anic verse 3:110. The founding congregation of the JiI in 1941 elected Mawdudi as its first *amir*, just as expected. It is interesting to note that the structure of the movement resembled that of a political party, even from the beginning. Regional cells were set up which were led by regional Consultative Councils, the heads of which were the members of the central consultative council. This way, Mawdudi was able to maintain utmost control from the uppermost to the lowermost and smallest units of the movement. In subsequent years, however, the JiI and its leader were confronted with drastic political developments in the subcontinent – the events leading to the independence of India from British colonial rule and the subsequent emergence of distinct nation states; these had a decisive influence on the numerous adjustments the JiI was compelled to make.

Mawdudi must be considered one of the most important ideologues of Islamism worldwide. His works have been translated into numerous languages and are constantly republished all over the world. Some of his core ideas have demonstrably had an impact in shaping the ideas of Sayyid Qutb (executed 1966) and his spiritual successors. Mawdudi's importance was even acknowledged by the Saudi religious and political establishment that co-opted him to the Board of Trustees of the International Islamic University in Medina, as well as the Constitutive Assembly of the Mecca-based Muslim World League (RAI, Rabitat al-'Alam al-Islami). With Mawdudi joining the RAI, it has been argued, the JiI became a basis for the RAI's intervention in South Asia.

Today branches of the JiI are found in almost all South Asian states with a Muslim population. To perceive the movement as a transnational one only, however, appears problematic, as all the national branches have developed different outlooks and doctrines due to their respective political circumstances. Thus one may consider the movement transnational only insofar as the general acceptance of Mawdudi's ideological framework is concerned, but one would have to clearly distinguish between the JiI's different national expressions. The roots for the development of distinct branches, however, were already laid before the partition of India in 1947.

From its inception, the inner circle of the movement was rocked by internal discord over the structure as well as the ideological principles of the JiI in view of the looming partition, which had been unanimously opposed by Mawdudi and his companions. Distinguished religious scholars ('*ulama*) resigned from their seats in the Consultative Council at a very early stage, arguing that the aim and methods proposed by Mawdudi were not appropriate in view of the recent developments. It is remarkable that these scholars became such a major influence in shaping the Indian branch of the JiI after 1947. Being aware of the fundamentally different political circumstances in India and Pakistan, Mawdudi gave his approval to the official foundation of the JiI Hind (JiI-H) in April 1948 in Allahabad. Its first *amir*, Abu l-Layth Islahi Nadwi (d. 1992), had to navigate the movement through the formative period of the Republic of India, which was characterised by a strong emphasis on secularism and socialist tendencies. Although clearly opposed to the idea of a secular state and upholding the idea of Islam as a natural and perfect system of life, it clearly appears from the resolution of the Central Consultative Council in 1961 that the leadership of the JiI-H had fully acknowledged the minority situation of Muslims in India, and that the main goal would be a contribution to a polity safeguarding minority rights. Although the text of the constitution of the JiI-H corresponds to that of its Pakistani counterpart, it nonetheless remained a mass movement that, besides numerous charity activities, had aligned itself with various non-governmental Muslim pressure groups in order to advocate its cause.

In Pakistan, the JiI was, from the beginning, confronted with the problem of a Pakistani state that, while founded explicitly on religious grounds, did not correspond with the JiI Pakistan's (JiI-P) idea of an Islamic state. Thus this branch, until 1972 headed by Mawdudi himself, became vigorously engaged in the constitutional debate between 1948 and 1956 – epitomised in their slogan 'Our Demand: An Islamic Constitution!' – and later objected to the politics of almost every prime minister or president, with the exception of the pro-Islamic rule of General Diya al-Haqq between 1977 and 1988 (the time of the latter's mysterious death). In 1953 as well as 1977 the JiI-P and later also its student wing, the Islami Jama'iyyat-i Tulaba (IJT, Islamic Student Society), took a leading role in the partially violent anti-Ahmadiyya Movement of the Finality of Prophethood (Tahrik-i Khatm-i Nubuwwat), that eventually led to the imprisonment of Mawdudi and his death sentence in 1953 that was cancelled shortly after. This, however, could not prevent an internal schism in 1957, following a vote of no confidence in Mawdudi's leadership, after which the JiI-P transformed more and more into a political party. This move did not stay undisputed within the movement itself because the adaptation to the existing political system and participation in a parliamentary form of government considerably rocked the fundamentals of the JiI ideology, over and above the widespread reluctance to accept any polity other than the Islamic state as conceptualised by Mawdudi in the 1930s.

Martial law resulted in a ban of the JiI-P only a year later, preventing the party from partaking in the parliamentary process until 1965. This, in turn, led to an increase in militant tendencies, especially among the IJT, which directed its often-violent protest against the government's secularist course and the rise of leftist groups. After the ban on the JiI-P was lifted, the party took part in the elections of 1970 and gained four seats in the National Assembly, and four more in provincial assemblies, both of whose numbers have increased ever since. However, immediately after the schism the JiI-P lost its intellectual momentum and the active role of Mawdudi gradually declined. Although his person and works are still respected, the JiI-P turned increasingly away from the initial idea of the movement and today is an established Islamist party that has been able to maintain its considerable influence, especially over the urban Pakistani middle class. This latter fact still requires some explanation, as it has recently been argued that it was the open-endedness, in particular, of the original JiI ideology in opposition to politics of nationalism that was attractive to the urban middle class: similar to many left- and right-wing ideologies in the first half of the twentieth century, it had served as an instrument to overcome the constraints of societal politics that proved inefficient as a tool of self-expressionism. This is important because it helps to explain why the JiI-P had pursued a policy that alternated between being a political party that served the aspirations for power of its leadership, and its identity as an NGO, an ideal community-cum-society that served the aspirations of the urban middle class.

This hybrid nature of the JiI-P explains why, on the one hand, its agenda has repeatedly been subjected to amendments, the most dramatic one being perhaps the abandonment of the understanding of revolution as a top-down process while, on the other hand, the JiI-P still appears as a major opposition movement to the respective current rule. The latter is perhaps best illustrated by the fact that the JiI-P has, over time, entered into a variety of different alliances, the most recent one being the Muttahida Majlis-i 'Amal (United Council of Action), a coalition of five Islamist parties founded in the wake of the national elections in 2002, and headed today by the present *amir* of the JiI-P, Qadi Husayn Ahmad (b. 1938).

In addition, in today's Bangladesh the JiI constitutes one of the largest Islamic political parties. Its origins are rooted in the East Pakistan wing of the movement that was then led by Ghulam A'zham (b. 1922). During East Pakistan's struggle for independence, and a major military operation to curb the Bengali nationalist movement in 1971, the JiI actively rejected the country's aspiration for independence and was therefore banned from political activities by the rather secularist and pro-Indian first government of Bangladesh. Ghulam A'zham was divested of citizenship and lived in Pakistani and British exile until 1994, when he was officially granted Bangladeshi citizenship. During the years in exile he was actively travelling in the Middle East, attempting to gain support for a military coup against the Dhaka government.

A rather positive attitude to militancy clearly distinguishes the JiI Bangladesh (JiI-B) from its West Pakistani and Indian counterparts. It is rooted in the party's activities during the War of Independence, when offshoots such as the *al-Badr* militia under Mati al-Rahman Nizhami (b. 1943), the current *amir* of the JiI-B since 2001, waged guerrilla attacks on secularist forces as well as on Hindus. The years of illegality may have added to this attitude; after all, Bangladesh was predominantly Muslim and should, in the eyes of JiI activists, be ruled according to Islamic standards. Even though a military coup in 1975 and a referendum in 1978 brought the country back to more religious lines, lifted the ban on the JiI-B and opened a path of democratic participation, allegations that the latter's perspective on militancy never entirely vanished still persist. Although in 1991 and 2001 they managed to successfully enter the national Parliament, and its *amir* even served as Minister of Industries, the JiI-B was, to a large extent, blamed for not having discouraged the politically motivated violence that flared up in Bangladesh around 2004–5, driven by religious extremism that aimed at the establishment of an Islamic order and the suppression of any secularist tendency.

A special case that has to be mentioned is the JiI Jammu and Kashmir (JiI-J&K), because it constitutes to some extent a mixture of the JiI-P and JiI-H. It owes its special status to the disputed political status, as well as cultural particularities, of Kashmir. The questions of belonging of Kashmir after 1947 made the strategic region a major bone of contention between India and Pakistan that has repeatedly led to war and to an ongoing military presence of Indian troops in the Kashmir valley. The so-called Delhi Agreement of 1952, however, granted Kashmir a de facto independent political status until a plebiscite was held to decide over its political future. This, in turn, led the JiI-H to suggest the formation of a separate organisation in Kashmir. The JiI-J&K, officially established in 1954 and headed by Sa'd al-Din Tarabali (1912–99), can be seen as a major advocate for an understanding of Islam that does not meet the widespread popularity of Sufism in the valley. Even though the JiI-J&K upheld the position that the political status of Kashmir is a disputed one, it nonetheless decided to actively participate in the state elections from the 1970s onwards, thus actually acknowledging Jammu and Kashmir as a state of the Indian Union. However, the outbreak of armed resistance in the valley in 1989 marked the end of the JiI-J&K's parliamentary engagement, and its current *amir* Sayyid 'Ali Shah Gilani (b. 1929) openly advocated militant means, the result of which was that the party was officially banned by the Indian authorities.

Notes

1   Abū l-A'lā Mawdūdī (1996) *Islam ka nazhariyya-yi siyasi*, Delhi: (n.d.), p. 5.
2   Abū l-A'lā Mawdūdī (1993) *Islami hukumat kis tarah qa'im hoti hai?*, Delhi: (n.d.), p. 26.

References

Ahmad, Khurshid and Zafar Ishaq Ansari (eds) (1979) *Islamic Perspectives: Studies in Honour of Mawlana Sayyid Abul A'la Mawdudi*, Leicester: Islamic Foundation.

Ahsan, Abdullah (ed.) (2003) 'A Special Issue on 'Allama Mawdudi and Contemporary Pakistan', *The Muslim World*, 93: pp. 3–4.

Hartung, Jan-Peter (1999) 'A Contribution of Islamic Revivalists to Modernity: The Ğamā 'at-i islāmī as a Practical Approach for the Realization of an Islamic Concept of History', *Folia Orientali*, 35: pp. 41–54.

—— (2001) 'Reinterpretation von Tradition und der Paradigmenwechsel der Moderne. Abū l-A'lā Mawdūdī (1903–79) und die Jamā'at-i Islāmī', in Dietrich Reetz (ed.), *Sendungsbewußtsein oder Eigennutz: Zu Motivation und Selbstverständnis islamischer Mobilisierung*, Berlin: Das Arabische Buch, pp. 107–26.

—— (2004) *Viele Wege und ein Ziel: Leben und Werk von Sayyid Abū l-Ḥasan 'Alī al-Ḥasanī Nadwī (1914–99)*, Würzburg: Ergon.

—— (2013) *A System of Life: Mawdūdī and the Ideologisation of Islam*, London / New York: Hurst / Oxford University Press.

Jackson, Roy (2008) *Mawlana Mawdūdī and Political Islam: Authority and the Islamic State*, London: Routledge.

Mawdūdī, Abū l-Aʿlā (1993) *Islami hukumat kis tarah qaʿim hoti hai?*, Delhi: (n.d.), p. 26.

Mawdūdī, Abū l-Aʿlā (1996) *Islam ka nazhariyya-yi siyasi*, Delhi: (n.d.), p. 5.

Nasr, Seyyed Vali Reza (1994) *The Vanguard of the Islamic Revolution. The Jama'at-i Islamic of Pakistan*, Berkeley / Los Angeles: University of California Press.

—— (1995) 'Mawlāna [sic] Mawdūdī's Autobiography', *The Muslim World*, 85 (1/2): pp. 49–62.

—— (1996) *Mawdudi and the Making of Islamic Revivalism*, New York / Oxford: Oxford University Press.

Schulze, Reinhard (1990) *Islamischer Internationalismus im 20. Jahrhundert. Untersuchungen zur Geschichte der Islamischen Weltliga*, Leiden: Brill.

Schwerin, Ulrich von (2005) 'Die Muttahida Majlis-e Amal - Ursachen des Wahlerfolges der Islamisten bei den pakistanischen Wahlen im Oktober 2002', *Asien*, 97: pp. 76–83.

Sikand, Yoginder (2002) 'The Emergence and Development of the Jama'at-i-Islami of Jammu and Kashmir (1940s–1990)', *Modern Asian Studies*, 36 (3): pp. 705–51.

Rashiduzzaman, Mohammad (1994) 'The Liberals and the Religious Right in Bangladesh', *Asian Survey*, 34 (11): pp. 974–90.

—— (2002) 'Bangladesh in 2001: The Election and a New Political Reality?', *Asian Survey*, 42 (1): pp. 183–91.

TABLIGHI JAMA'AT

Dietrich Reetz

The Tablighi Jama'at (TJ) is a global missionary movement of Sunnite Islam. By various accounts it is the largest transnational Islamic grassroots movement in the world. Estimates of the number of its followers range widely between 12 and 80 million people. It originated in South Asia where it was founded in 1927 by Maulana Muhammad Ilyas (1885–1944), an Islamic scholar following the tradition of the Sunnite purist school of Deoband in north India. Its global headquarters is in Delhi (Nizhamuddin). Its European regional headquarters is located in the UK, in Dewsbury, Yorkshire. In a growing number of Muslim countries it has transcended communities of South Asian migrants and established a solid presence. There it has become a major force of orthodox Islam, strengthening conservative and pietist attitudes. It refuses to take a programmatic stand on social or political issues, although it strongly impacts them in various ways.

Religious mode of operation

The TJ operates as a lay preaching movement, which aims at strengthening the faith of nominal believers by instructing them in the rituals and practice of correct religious worship and behaviour. It invites common Muslims to join missionary walks (*gash/jawla*), which they conduct in their neighbourhood, but also by travelling to other cities and countries. For this purpose they form missionary groups (*jama'at*) of five to ten people headed by a leader (*amir*). They visit a local mosque where they reside and also sleep. From there, they invite Muslims from the neighbourhood for prayer and inspirational talks (*bayan*), during which they call for volunteers for further missionary travels following the same pattern. There is a fixed roster of missionary tours for followers which are cumulative and undertaken in ascending order: three days, 40 days (*chilla*), four months (*grand chilla*), seven or 12 months. After exploring the neighbourhood, other cities and countries are targeted for a missionary sortie (*khuruj*). Those who complete the grand *chilla* are considered part of a spiritual elite. In many countries, special congregations are held for them. After returning from their travels they are supposed to give a report (*karguzari*) on the local conditions and results of their missionary efforts.

The Tablighi preachers are easily recognisable by their flowing white gowns, beards and traditional headgear, which many of their preachers wear in accordance with the customs of local Muslims, mainly from South Asia, but also North Africa and other regions.

Regular congregations represent another form of participation in Tablighi activism. They are part of a regular roster of meetings in every region and locality where the TJ is represented. The Jama'at's annual congregations (*ijtima'*) in South Asia and other regions attract up to one million followers, making them the largest gatherings of Muslims after the *hajj*. However, as a measure of the Tablighis' impact on Muslim society, its weekly Thursday night gathering (*shab-e jum'a*) is much more important, as it is conducted at every centre (*markaz*) of the movement across the world, although the day may sometimes vary.

The Tablighi message and its format are very fixed; critics at times call it rigid. The Tablighi understanding of Islam is put forward in six points. They demand to focus attention on (1) the re-confirmation of faith (*shahada*), (2) the correct performance of prayer (*salat*), (3) religious knowledge and the ritual remembrance of God (*'ilm-o-dhikr*), (4) respect for fellow Muslims (*ikram-i muslim*), (5) the purification of intentions (*niyyat*), and (6) spending time preaching as a servant of God (*nafr*). Their leaders and followers regard these as essentials, but their critics believe these points are reductionist, if not uneducated. Other recommendations have been grouped in sets of four points for the purposes of providing guidance to new members. They include the four things to do more (preaching, worship, education and service), to do less (eating, sleeping, spending time out of the mosque and talking idly), not to do (question, desire, spend and take from others without express permission) and to avoid (rejection of others, criticism, competition and pride).

Religious education (*ta'lim*) is considered another pillar of Tablighi activism. Tablighi workers are required to read essays written by Maulana Muhammad Zakariya (1898–1982). He was a nephew of Ilyas, a co-founder of the movement and a scholar of prophetic traditions (*hadith*) at the Saharanpur *madrasa*. These essays were compiled in a single edition, first as *Tablighi Curriculum* (*Tablighi nisab*), later known as *Virtues of Good Deeds* (*Fada'il-i A'mal*). The different chapters of the collection discuss life stories of the companions of the Prophet, the spiritual virtues of prayer (*salat*), of the ritual remembrance of God (*dhikr*), of charity, pilgrimage (*hajj*), ritual salutation to the Prophet, and the Qur'an. Written in plain Urdu and based mostly on inspirational traditions and anecdotes, some of which may not be historically sound, these essays also constitute, with little alteration, the basic source material for the formulaic speeches delivered by the Tablighi missionaries throughout the world. There are other Islamic classics which are in use throughout the global network of the Tablighi Jama'at. In Europe, the *hadith* collection by Nawawi (1233–77), *Gardens of the Righteous* (*Riyad al-Salihin*), enjoys strong popularity at Tabligh congregations. Another classic *hadith* collection by Tirmidhi (d. 892), *Shama'il-e Tirmidhi*, translated by Zakariya himself, helps members of the movement to emulate the behaviour of the Prophet in all aspects of daily life. For the Sufi-inclined followers, the collection of supplication prayers (*du'a*) al-husn al-hasin by Ibn al-Jazari (1350–1429) is often taken up for reading, although more in Asia and Africa than in Europe, apparently. In addition, every Muslim is encouraged to learn how to read the Qur'an in Arabic, with correct pronunciation.

Coming from the highly sectarian background of South Asian Islam, the Tablighi Jama'at seeks to unite Sunni Muslims on the basis of the reformist and purist tradition of the Deoband seminary founded in 1866. However, the TJ is heavily criticised by activists of the rival Barelwi tradition for its defence of Deobandi concepts. Deobandis are known for their strict interpretation of Islam. In particular, they criticise the worship of shrines and other Sufi-related rituals practiced by followers of the Barelwi tradition, although the Deobandis do not oppose Sufism in general. The Tablighis take the middle ground. While they teach their followers to avoid certain practices and rituals, they also retain some Sufi influence. To combat the Tablighi influence, in 1980 the Barelwis created a rival group, Da'wat-i Islami, that also operates globally. Salafi preachers, on the other hand, believe the TJ is not strict or knowledgeable enough. They often regard the TJ as simplistic, although they admire its mobilising potential. While the TJ claims to welcome all Muslims, it keeps out those seen as deviant or heterodox such as Shi'as and Ahmadis. Yet globally, the TJ is evolving into a source of normative Sunni Islam that is increasingly regarded as non-sectarian.

The Jama'at's reliance on lay preachers rather than on religious scholars has helped it reach and attract common Muslims in suburban communities and small towns. Their dissemination efforts have mainly been conducted by word of mouth. However, over the years a growing body of informal religious literature has emerged, mainly in Urdu, with some in Arabic as well. Most of the important literature has also been translated into Western languages, such as English, French and Spanish. This literature has served to induct new followers into the movement and satisfy the demands of religious students close to the Jama'at.

Younger followers have also delved into new media, especially in Europe. Tablighi leaders are reconciled with their speeches being widely distributed on cassettes and CDs. Enthusiasts discuss moral issues and organisational matters in internet forums, and provide related reading material at sympathetic Internet sites. They also confront critical interventions at social networking sites such as YouTube and My Space. The Pakistani cleric and Tablighi elder, Tariq Jamil, running a *madrasa* in Faisalabad, is an example of this growing marriage of popular media and spiritual guidance. His speeches have achieved cult status on the internet and in CD format; there is even a fan website in his name.[1]

Tablighi leaders present their movement as entirely grassroots, devoid of any central organisation and solely resting on the activism and motivation of rank members. However, the movement has gone through a process of growing formalisation and institutionalisation. It has established a network of regional and national centres (*marakiz*), usually attached to mosques and religious schools (*madaris*) of the Deobandi tradition. The movement has developed an extensive internal bureaucracy with elaborate procedures. In most places it is run by councils (*shura*); as a matter of principle decisions are taken in council (*mashwara*), with elders and elected or nominated leaders (*amir/umara*) having clear precedence. In what used to be a highly egalitarian movement, the administration, although largely obscured from ordinary followers, has become more elaborate, bureaucratic and hierarchical. The administrative centre of the global movement is still in Delhi, although some of the burden is shared by the Pakistan centre at Raiwind.

The format and history of the movement suggest a strong bond between the religion of Islam and the culture of the South Asian subcontinent. This relates as much to the unquestioned centrality of their Indian headquarters as to the prominence of the language of Urdu, spoken by South Asian Muslims, and the specifics of their relations with Islamic sects and other religions hailing from South Asia. The movement came into being in response to reclamation efforts of Hindu missionary groups trying to re-convert nominal Muslims back into the fold of Hinduism to which their ancestors had belonged. The Tablighi centres of the movement in India, Pakistan and Bangladesh are popular destinations for preaching tours of Western followers. They are seen as shrine-like places of worship where young Western adherents can be best initiated into the ranks and concepts of the movement. Transnational South Asian trading castes, mainly from Gujarat, are behind much of the expansion of Tablighi networks across the world.

Yet despite its culturally coded, simple message and pre-set approach, the TJ has been able to expand its influence steadily across cultural, linguistic and political boundaries. While the core of its followers hails from India, Pakistan, Bangladesh and South Asian migrant communities around the world, the TJ has been able to transcend these ethnic limitations in regions such as North Africa, South East Asia, Central Asia and Western Europe.

Social concerns and rewards

Throughout its history the Tablighi Jama'at has been remarkable for its adaptation to different social contexts. It started out as a movement among tribal groups in the Mewat region around Delhi, India, where it aimed at reconfirming them in the faith of Islam. These tribes were considered 'neo-Muslims' and faced efforts by Hindu activists to reclaim them for the Hinduism of their ancestors. It later spread to include mobile Muslim strata from the rural areas and the urban lower-middle classes.

Tablighi activism is seen as a way for members not only to reform themselves but also society at large, applying its lessons to their own social environments, without directly implicating the Tablighi Jama'at. This (rather secular) separation of religious observance and worldly affairs is a way to reconcile other professional, commercial, educational or ideological identities with participation in Tablighi activities. It was a tremendous help to the TJ in penetrating different strata of society, regardless of their non-religious profiles and interests.

In reality, the TJ has evolved into a public organisation, confidently joining the mainstream of Muslim activism, even though its religious activism and its social and political impact remain rather distinct. In South Asia the movement often cooperates with the State to conduct its activities, notably in the case of the large congregations attended by millions of believers, where army, police, water, fire and health services cooperate to secure the events. For many years the movement had been encouraged in its activism by various governments, which saw them as an ideal antidote to political and militant Islam. Bureaucrats, politicians and officers from the army and security agencies attended their congregations in the hope of benefitting from the popularity, legitimacy and authority of the movement.

Sections of the middle and upper middle classes started joining the movement more recently. Their functionaries are often businessmen, traders, university or college teachers and other professional classes. Colleges and universities have become a main recruiting and operating area for the TJ in South Asia.

Through growing mass participation the TJ has evolved from a fringe phenomenon to part of the Muslim mainstream. The movement provides a growing system of communication which serves the varying requirements of its participants, representing the concerns of mainstream society. Students use it for networking and cheap travel; traders and businessmen for commercial contacts; and political parties and militant groups as contact areas and recruiting grounds. The leadership is clearly aware of these tendencies and has sought to discourage them, feeling they might distract the movement from its missionary goals.

The Tablighi movement has also left its mark on the social attitudes of Muslims; regular followers tend to move away from movies, television, Western dress, mixing with the opposite sex and lavish weddings. Tablighi congregations began celebrating mass marriages (*nikah*), free of the excessive expenditure that generally characterises wedding ceremonies in many parts of Asia and Africa. In some countries, separate girls' *madrasas* have opened at the initiative of Tablighi elders (Winkelmann 2005). Women have come to play an increasingly important role in the movement. They have developed their own format of preaching, and do so accompanied by a male guardian (*mahram*). Tablighi women also meet for Islamic education, largely conducted on the basis of the Zakariyya volume *Fada'il-i A'mal*. Thus, the impact of the movement on women has been equivocal. While the movement has contributed to the increased segregation of Muslim women, it has also provided them with a social agency to expand their public and private roles.

Ideology and politics by design and default

Since the Tablighis' main activity is to propagate their missionary message, secular critics and their competitors often see them as highly ideological. Many non-Muslim observers in the West confuse them with political activists of the Salafi or Muslim Brotherhood variety. Unlike the latter, however, they exert their political influence by proxy. Their ideological message is primarily confined to their programme of missionary walks, tours and congregations, and to their education and reading sessions of Islamic literature. Their organisation, in the form of local associations of mosques and religious centres, has led them to gradual intervention in society. Thus the TJ has been active in taking over the control of mosques and in setting up mosques and Islamic centres where they don't exist. Their activists and elders initiate Islamic training camps and retreats for Muslim youth and set up confessional schools which teach a secular curriculum.

While the Jama'at's leaders have refused to take public positions on political issues, they have allowed politics to seep into the movement. Leading politicians started attending their congregations looking for religious sanction and legitimacy. Stalwart supporters of the movement have been elected to local bodies. Sectarian and radical Islamists occasionally seek refuge in their preaching tours.

Tablighi elders tacitly accept encouragement from governments in countries such as Pakistan, India, Indonesia and Malaysia, and promote the Jama'at as an antidote to militant Islam. But Tablighi leaders have repeatedly rebuffed attempts by political Islamists to get the movement involved in political controversies and militant mobilisation. At the same time, it is assumed that Tablighi activism has indirectly helped to consolidate the vote banks of religious-political parties and groups in South, South East and West Asia in particular. By default the movement has therefore turned much more public and its impact more political than before.

Global player of Islam

The Tablighis have created global structures and concepts which not only aim at religious revival but also intervene in societies around the world, with far-reaching consequences that are cultural, social and political. They largely rely on the descendants of former migrant communities. While their South Asian origins still play an important role, in many countries they are shaped by their association with local Muslim traditions. Moreover, they have contributed to a more general process of de-linking local Muslim religious activism from cultural roots in order to revive normative religious observance.

The Tablighis have become a visible socio-religious force with a strong local impact in places where they have organised their centres (*markaz*). They have increasingly been accepted by other Muslim players as a legitimate and useful source of knowledge and piety in relation to Islam, even though many regard them as limited in outlook and practice, and some even consider them as heretical.

They have gone through a process of differentiation and social adaptation which has created distinct national, provincial and local profiles in their branches – despite their transnational and global networking. Their political impact is not uniform and relates to the maturity of their activism in each country. Where they are newcomers or without large local support networks they are held responsible for destabilising and polarising local Muslim communities. They are associated with supporting and serving (illegal) migration (as in Spain) and the radicalisation of individuals (as in Germany). In countries with an extensive and longstanding local presence, with developed institutions (as in Britain and France), they could be seen as a stabilising conservative religious force providing value education and the re-validation of the religious identity of European Muslims with immigrant backgrounds.

In the 'Islamic field' in Europe they provide the conservative colour of choice for Muslims reconciled with and desirous of Western modernity and civic engagement, who want to live there in consonance with, and in full observance of, their religious dictates. The tendency of their evolution in Western Europe is of a growing adjustment to the legal and political reality of the West. This process has been rocked and disturbed by the post-9/11 political polarisation. Political and media-based attacks in particular saw their representatives partly retreating to a more claustrophobic and anxious mode of operation. In the face of such adversities they have fallen back on resilience, frugality and sufferance as they are confident that they cannot be defeated.

Notes

1 http://www.tariqjamil.org/. (link last accessed 19 June 2014)

References

Masud, Muhammad Khalid (2000) *Travellers in Faith: Studies of the Tablīghī Jamā'at as a Transnational Islamic Movement for Faith Renewal*, Leiden: Brill.

Mayaram, Shail (1997) *Resisting Regimes: Myth, Memory, and the Shaping of a Muslim Identity*, Delhi: Oxford University Press.

Nadwi S. Abul Hasan Ali (1964) *Hazrat maulana muhammad ilyas aur un ki dini da'wat* (*Revered Maulana Muhammad Ilyas and His Call to the Religious Renewal*), Lucknow: Tanwir Press.

Qadiri, Arshadul (1969) *Tablīghī Jamā'at: haqā'iq wa ma'lumāt* (*Tablighi Jama'at: facts and information*), Lahore: Maktaba Nabwiya.

Reetz, Dietrich (2006a) 'Sufi spirituality fires reformist zeal: The Tablighi Jama'at in today's India and Pakistan', *Archives de Sciences Sociales des Religions*, 51(135): pp. 33–51.

—— (2006b) *Islam in the public sphere: religious groups in India, 1900–1947*, New Delhi: Oxford University Press.

—— (2008) 'The "Faith Bureaucracy" of the *Tablīghī Jamā'at*: An Insight into their System of Self-Organisation (*intizām*)', in Gwilym Beckerlegge (ed.), *Colonialism, Modernity, and Religious Identities: Religious Reform Movements in South Asia*, Oxford / Delhi: Oxford University Press, pp. 98–124.

Sikand, Yogindar (2002) *The Origins and Development of the Tablīghī Jamā'āt, 1920–2000: A Cross Country Comparative Study*, New Delhi: Orient Longman.

Winkelmann, Mareike Jule (2005) '*From Behind the Curtain: A Study of Girls' Madrasa in India*', Ph.D. dissertation, International Institute for the Study of Islam in the Modern

World. Amsterdam: Amsterdam University Press.
Zakarīyā, Muhammad (1940) *Tablīghī Niṣāb* (Tablīghī Curriculum), Delhi: numerous editions, later *Faḍā 'il-i A'māl* (The Virtues of [Correct] Religious Practices).
——, Ihtishamul Hasan Kandhlawi and Ashiq Ilahi (1994) *Faza'il-E-A maal*, New Delhi: Idara Ishaat-e-Diniyat.

THE WAHHABIYA, SAUDI ARABIA AND THE SALAFIST MOVEMENT

Guido Steinberg

I. The Wahhabiya

The Wahhabiya is a purist reform movement of the eighteenth century. Its opponents named it after its eponymous founder, Muhammad b. 'Abdalwahhab (1703/4–92), thereby suggesting that the Wahhabis in fact follow Ibn 'Abdalwahhab rather than God and his prophet, as they themselves claim to do. Wahhabis call themselves *muwahhidun* (professors of the unity of God), *ahl al-tawhid* (people of monotheism), and – more recently – Salafis.

The Wahhabiya is a radically purist movement which invests considerable efforts in differentiating between Wahhabi believers and all other unbelievers. This isolationist tendency has decreased considerably since the 1930s due to practical constraints. However, this trend has not yet led to a rethinking of Wahhabi doctrine, and the distinction between believers and unbelievers has remained an important factor in Wahhabi lore and Saudi society.[1] A non-Wahhabi Muslim is not considered to be a believer unless he fully accepts the Wahhabiya's theological interpretations and its strict code of social and individual conduct. Wahhabis believe that the Qur'an and the Sunna have presented to them an authentic and detailed account of early Muslim life in the times of the pious forefathers (*al-salaf as-salih*), that is, the early Muslims in Mecca and Medina during the seventh century. They claim to follow this ideal by putting into practice God's commandments as they derive them from scripture. This includes the five daily prayers in the congregation and the prohibition of music, tobacco and silken garments, as well as the banishment of women from public life.

Their opponents accuse them of wrongfully declaring non-Wahhabi Muslims to be unbelievers (*takfir*) and thereby excommunicating them. Indeed, the *takfir* has always been an important element of Wahhabi ideology, although many Wahhabi religious scholars (*'ulama'*) have taken a much less militant stance in this regard than their opponents would claim. Nevertheless, the Wahhabiya have provided all Saudi states with a religious-ideological foundation for perpetuated military expansion against its Muslim neighbours, propagating the duty of fighting a Holy War (*jihad*) against anyone they consider a non-Wahhabi unbeliever. Wahhabi radicalism has been moderated only through the Saudi rulers' desire to build a strong and lasting central state, which – as they discovered in the nineteenth century – could not survive unless the Wahhabi radicals were subjected to tight governmental control.

II. Actors and Institutions in Saudi Religious Policy

The Saudi state emerged as the result of a mutually beneficial alliance between the Saudi ruling family and the Wahhabi religious scholars. The Saudi rulers were able to gain legitimacy by portraying themselves as defendants of the true faith, and they established three consecutive states, the first one between 1744 and 1818, and the second from 1824 until 1891. The third, which was founded in 1902, still exists today. The Wahhabi scholars, for their part, profited greatly from their alliance with an emerging state that gave them the opportunity to spread their vision of an Islamic society through the use of the State's coercive mechanisms. The alliance proved so essential for the political survival of the two partners on the Arabian scene – especially after the destruction of the first two Saudi states in 1818 and 1891 – that they preserve it until this day. Mainly, it endows the ruling family with a religious legitimacy for which it has not yet found an adequate substitute. Consequently, the 'ulama' have established themselves as the second most important social group in Saudi Arabia. However, their position has been considerably weakened by governmental modernisation policies since the early 1930s. While in the early decades of the twentieth century the leading Wahhabi scholars managed to influence even strategic political decisions, they have by and large been reduced to junior partners of a royal family that has built its power increasingly on the country's oil revenues. While the Wahhabi 'ulama' nowadays have no influence on political matters, they remain firmly entrenched in Saudi society. Even today, they dominate the administration of justice and play an important role in the educational system. Furthermore, they are accepted by most inhabitants of Najd (central Arabia) – where the ruling family and the Wahhabi movement have their origins and power base – as the interpreters of divine law in a deeply religious society.

While the survival of the Saudi state has depended on the legitimacy derived from the support of the Wahhabi 'ulama' they have also had a tendency to obstruct the State's modernisation and centralisation policies. Particularly after the advent of oil production in commercial quantities after 1945, the State had to cope with the Wahhabi 'ulama' resistance to the opening of the country to foreign influences. In essential matters pertaining to the very survival of the Saudi state, such as the alliance with the United States and the presence of Americans on Saudi soil, the government has not tolerated dissenting voices. On less important issues, however, the Saudi family has tended to negotiate various solutions with the scholars. For example, when public girls' schools were opened for the first time in 1960, King Faisal overcame the scholars' resistance by granting them control of the General Directorate of Girls' Education. Until 2003, when the Directorate was dissolved and the responsibility for girls' education transferred to the Ministry of Education, Wahhabi scholars held the presidency of this institution. In an even more telling example, the Wahhabi scholars were allowed to maintain control over the central institutions of Saudi religious policy.

Traditionally, the ministries responsible for religious policy are headed by Wahhabi or other 'ulama' in many cases descendants of Muhammad b. 'Abdalwahhab, members of the so-called 'family of the Shaikh' (Al al-Shaikh). These ministries are the Ministry of Islamic Affairs, the Ministry of Justice and the Pilgrimage Ministry. Out of these, the Ministry of Islamic Affairs, Endowments, Da'wa and Guidance is clearly the most important, dealing with all religious affairs except the pilgrimage.[2] Furthermore, the Wahhabi scholars control the two central institutions of religious policy outside of government, the Council of Senior Scholars (Hay'at Kibar al-'Ulama') and the Fatwa Council (Dar al-Ifta wa-l-Ishraf 'ala al-Shu'un al-Diniya).

The Council of Senior Scholars was founded in 1971 and is the most important institutional partner for the government in religious affairs and matters of religious policy. Its members are drawn exclusively from the Wahhabi establishment, hailing mostly from central Arabia. Sunni scholars from provinces conquered by the Saudi state in the west, south-west, and east of the country are only very rarely represented in this institution, and only if they started their careers from their early youth in Wahhabi educational institutions. Non-Wahhabi Muslims are not represented at all. The members of the Council form the very top of the Wahhabi hierarchy and pronounce – individually and collectively as an institution – legal rulings (fatwa, pl. fatawa) on all issues of public and private life. In times of crisis, the Council of Senior Scholars legitimises controversial decisions taken by the government such as, for instance, the deployment of American troops on Saudi soil in the run-up to the 1990 Kuwait war.

The Fatwa Council, or Dar al-Ifta, was founded earlier in 1953 in order to centralise and control the issuance of religious legal opinions. The head of this institution is the grand mufti who, in theory, is considered the leading legal counsellor in Saudi Arabia and, in practice, is the leading scholarly figure in domestic religious policy. He also serves as head of the Council of Senior Scholars, making a clear-cut differentiation between the two institutions difficult. Although he still holds a powerful office, the grand mufti has become a state functionary in recent decades, effectively surrendering his scholarly independence. By institutionalising his position and the issuance of legal rulings, the State subordinated the Wahhabi *'ulama'* to governmental control. In this process, which started with the emergence of the first institutions of Saudi religious policy in the early 1950s, the government compensated the Wahhabi scholars for their loss of domestic influence by supporting their proselytisation efforts abroad. The main result of these efforts was the emergence of a new, Wahhabi-inspired but nevertheless independent movement called Salafism, or 'traditional Islamism'.

III. Religious Foreign Policy and the Emergence of the Salafist Movement

The twentieth century brought the Wahhabiya into closer contact with the surrounding world. It had never been an insular movement, but had hitherto limited its contacts to similar-minded scholars in the neighbouring countries and India. With the conquest of the Holy Sites of Mecca and Medina in 1924, the Wahhabis suddenly encountered non-Wahhabi Muslims and were forced to relinquish their radically isolationist attitudes. Since the 1930s, they increasingly developed their own relations to non-Wahhabi scholars who came to Saudi Arabia for the pilgrimage. The Wahhabi *'ulama'* realised that in a modern state they would have to forge their own international contacts if they wanted to retain their relevance for the Saudi rulers. As a consequence, they chose to ally themselves to Salafists and Islamists from other Muslim countries.

This trend was given a boost by the influx of Islamists from the Arab world. Egyptian Muslim Brothers had arrived in larger numbers in Saudi Arabia after a government crackdown in their home country in 1954 forced them to flee. Many Syrian Muslim Brothers followed suit in the 1960s. Members of the Muslim Brotherhood were employed in large numbers in Saudi educational institutions and, since the 1960s, in the Muslim World League and its affiliated organisations.

The foundation of the Muslim World League (Rabitat al-'Alam al-Islami) in Mecca in 1962 was a first result of this cooperation between the Wahhabi and non-Saudi Islamists. The Muslim World League was founded as an organisation of Muslim scholars and intellectuals and, although it is often described as a Wahhabi institution, it is rather the institutional embodiment of a rapprochement of the Saudi Arabian religious establishment, the Islamist Muslim Brotherhood and Salafist scholars worldwide. In the following decades, the League built a dense international web combining educational and cultural efforts with charity and health projects. The League commands a wide and diffuse infrastructure of more than 30 offices abroad, cultural centres – among them five big Islamic centres in Europe – and numerous educational institutions. However, through a wide array of subordinate and affiliated organisations, mosques, institutions and individuals, the Muslim World League controls a much larger network. It spearheaded the export of the new amalgam of Wahhabi and Islamist thinking which a growing number of specialists today call Salafism. In fact, Salafism might be defined as 'all the hybridisations that have taken place since the 1960s between the teachings of Muhammad bin 'Abd al-Wahhab and other Islamic schools of thought.'[3]

IV. The Salafist Movement

The close and at times complicated interaction between Wahhabis and Salafis – and the Wahhabis' self-identification as Salafis – makes a clear-cut distinction between the two movements difficult. On the one hand, Salafism has developed as an outgrowth of the Wahhabi tradition in Saudi Arabia and might be considered a result of its interaction with non-Saudi Islamist organisations and individuals since the 1920s. This becomes especially clear when leading Wahhabi scholars such as the late 'Abdelaziz Ben Baz (1912–99) and Muhammad b. 'Uthaymin (1929–2001) are quoted as important references for Salafis worldwide. On the other hand, the Islamist influences from Egypt and Syria and the development of Salafi thinking (and Salafi thinkers) outside of Saudi Arabia clearly changed the Wahhabi movement. In fact, from the 1970s different Salafi–Wahhabi schools developed which distanced themselves from the original movement that was led by the establishment scholars. Three main trends are usually differentiated, the purists (or quietists), the political or mainstream Salafists, and the jihadists.[4]

1. Purists and Quietists

The purists are those Salafists who focus primarily on the reform of individuals and societies, while shunning politics or keeping their distance from the political sphere. While it is somewhat difficult to clearly differentiate between the strands of Salafism, the adherents of the purist school are easily discernible by their choice of religious references – often scholars of the generation born in the early twentieth century who have died in the meantime and most of whom had focused on the study of *hadith* as a means to establish the way the pious forefathers lived.

Perhaps the most important reference for this group of Salafists is the Albanian–Syrian scholar Nasir al-Din al-Albani (1914–99).[5] Albani's family had left his native Albania for Syria in 1923, where he soon became a well-known scholar. When confronted with an ever more hostile government, his friend Ben Baz invited Albani to Saudi Arabia in 1961 to teach at the Islamic University in Medina. However, his teachings soon became subject to controversy. While agreeing on all important aspects of the Wahhabi lore, his focus on *hadith* studies and rejection of the Muslim schools of law brought him into conflict with parts of the religious establishment. The Wahhabis had always argued that the jurisprudent should base his judgements primarily on Qur'an and Sunna, thereby reducing the influence of the schools of law on the administration of justice and legal counselling. In practice, however, the Hanbali school of law – which predominated in central Arabia for centuries – had become the official school of law in Saudi Arabia.

This was mainly due to the Wahhabi alliance with the Saudi rulers, who insisted on a reliable and stable basis for the justice system in the country. By criticising the Wahhabi position and pointing out that the Wahhabis in fact ignored Muhammad b. 'Abdalwahhab's hostility towards the schools of law, Albani provoked resistance which finally forced him to leave the country in 1963. He returned to Syria, which he again left in 1979 for Jordan.

'Abdelaziz Ben Baz (1912–99) is another important figure for the more purist-minded Salafists worldwide. His positions on the role of the schools of law and the importance of *hadith* were similar to those of Albani, and his reputation for piety and scholarly erudition was so impeccable that his central involvement in the religious hierarchy in Saudi Arabia did not taint his public image as much as in other cases. Even among mainstream Salafists and some jihadist circles, he has remained a much-revered scholar. This is partly due to his resistance to the Saudi government in instances where he deemed certain measures contrary to the Muslim creed. Ben Baz rose to prominence in the 1950s. He had by then already developed his reputation as a steadfast supporter of the original tenets of the Wahhabiya. In the following decades, he rose to the highest echelons of the Wahhabi religious establishment and was appointed Grand Mufti of Saudi Arabia in 1993. However, his loyalty to the Saudi ruling family was severely tested on several occasions. Most importantly, in 1990, Ben Baz and the Council of Senior Scholars, which he headed at the time, supported the government's decision to call American forces into the kingdom. After the occupation of Kuwait by Iraqi troops, the ruling family feared an Iraqi invasion. At first, the *'ulama* are said to have categorically refused to issue a fatwa endorsing the government decision, but were later convinced of the imminent danger.[6] These and other decisions led many Salafists to rethink their admiration of Ben Baz and his Wahhabi colleagues. Within and outside the kingdom, those scholars who kept more of a distance from the authorities gained increasing credibility and influence in Salafist circles.

2. The Political Salafists or the Salafist Mainstream

The political Salafists or the Salafist mainstream have been labelled the Islamic awakening (*al-sahwa al-islamiya*) in the Saudi context. The group had its intellectual origins in the growing influence of the Muslim Brotherhood in the Saudi educational system since the 1950s and 1960s. Its adherents combined the more politically oriented Islamism of the Muslim Brotherhood with the Wahhabi focus on the ideal society of the pious forefathers and the Wahhabiya's purism and conservatism in social affairs. The result was an interpretation of Wahhabism which was much more oriented towards contemporary political matters, with its adherents taking a greater interest in regional and world affairs than the traditional Wahhabis did.

The representatives of the *Sahwa* – most notably Safar al-Hawali (born 1950) and Salman al-'Awda (born 1955) – rose to prominence in Saudi Arabia in the latter half of the 1980s, when they protested against what they perceived as the growing influence of 'liberals' in Saudi society: a debate dominating the Saudi political scene in those years. However, they only started targeting the Saudi ruling family after the occupation of Kuwait by Iraqi forces. Hawali and 'Awda, together with lesser-known figures such as 'A'id al-Qarni and Nasir al-'Umar, campaigned against the government's decision to allow American forces to deploy in the Kingdom. Apart from foreign policies, the preachers attacked the Saudi rulers for their alleged neglect of Islamic rules and values and widespread corruption. Furthermore, they criticised the religious establishment for legitimising the Saudi rulers' decision.

Hawali and 'Awda gained importance in a growing Islamist protest movement, which sent petitions to the king demanding a thorough Islamisation of the country's foreign policies and domestic affairs. The regime hesitated, but in 1993 and 1994 it cracked down on the increasingly organised Islamist opposition. Many popular preachers were imprisoned, among them Hawali and 'Awda. In Salafist circles in Saudi Arabia and abroad, the prison terms only added to their popularity. After their release in 1999, both adopted a more circumspect strategy, combining cooperation with a marked distance towards the regime. They avoided criticising the ruling family and toned down their demands for political reform. On the other hand, they became important critics of the jihadist movement once the attacks of al-Qaeda in Saudi Arabia began in 2003. Hence, they served as an important legitimising factor at a time when – after the death of Ben Baz – the religious establishment had lost its remaining credibility in more radical circles.[7]

Outside of the kingdom, 'Awda and Hawali became important references for all those Salafists who adopted a more politicised Salafism which distanced itself from the brutal violence of the jihadists. 'Awda became particularly popular in the Arab world and in Europe.[8]

3. The Jihadi Salafists

The jihadists are the smallest of the three trends, but the most visible. The jihadist movement has its roots in several Arab states, among them Egypt, Saudi Arabia and Algeria. In Saudi Arabia, the seizure of the Grand Mosque of Mecca in November 1979 heralded the emergence of a revolutionary trend within the Wahhabi movement. Between 500 and 1000 rebels seized the mosque, took several hundred pilgrims as their hostages and held out for about two weeks against Saudi forces.[9] The leaders of the group demanded a return to the Islamic society of their pious forefathers and harshly criticised the Sa'ud family for their corruption, the oppression of the population and their alliance with infidel powers, especially the USA.

However, while the events of 1979 bore a clear Saudi hallmark, it was the Afghanistan experience in the 1980s which led to the emergence of a more transnational trend. Its leader was 'Abdallah 'Azzam, a Palestinian Muslim Brother with good relations to the Saudi religious establishment. Today, the most important religious references of this trend are Palestinians; Abu Qutada al-Filastini (born 1960) – a Jordanian citizen currently imprisoned in the UK – and Abu Muhammad al-Maqdisi, also a Jordanian citizen imprisoned in his home country. The jihadi Salafists might be subcategorised as follows:

The nationalists: These are jihadi groups fighting primarily their home regimes, that is, the 'near enemy'. These groups had their heyday in the 1980s and 1990s. It took, for instance, long and arduous debates before the Egyptian jihad group would adopt a more internationalist stance, joining al-Qaeda in the second half of the 1990s. The Libyan Islamic Fighting Group (LIFG) and the Algerian Salafist Group for Preaching and Combat (GSPC) were two other notable examples. After 2001, several of these organisations broadened their strategies to include the fight against the 'far enemy', that is, the USA and the West.

The classical internationalists: The classical internationalists stand in the tradition of the Afghan jihad and 'Abdallah 'Azzam's teachings. According to these, Muslim territory occupied by a non-Muslim invader has to be liberated by all Muslims. After Afghanistan, the classical internationalists fought in countries such as Bosnia, the Philippines and Chechnya. Since 2001, the fight against coalition troops in Afghanistan and – from 2003 – in Iraq gained prominence. Iraq in particular became a popular destination for fighters from all over the Arab world and Europe.

The anti-Western internationalists: The anti-Western internationalists are the youngest of the three groups and have risen to prominence in the jihadist movement under the leadership of Osama Bin Laden and Aiman al-Zawahiri from the mid-1990s. They fight both the 'far' and the 'near enemy' with a focus on the United States. With the American 'War on Terror' and the subsequent American-led wars in Afghanistan and Iraq, they have broadened their appeal worldwide – particularly in Europe – and benefited from a trend towards internationalisation in jihadist circles.

Notes

1   Guido Steinberg (2002) Religion und Staat in Saudi-Arabien. Die wahhabitischen Gelehrten (1902–1953), Würzburg: Ergon, pp. 92–102.
2   See http://www.moia.gov.sa/. Accessed 7 April 2008.
3   Stéphane Lacroix (2008) 'Al-Albani's Revolutionary Approach to Hadith', *ISIM Review* 21, Spring: 6–7.
4   This differentiation mainly follows Quintan Wiktorowicz (2006) 'Anatomy of the Salafi Movement', *Studies in Conflict and Terrorism*, 29 (3): pp. 207–39. Wiktorowicz uses the term 'political Salafists' instead of the Salafist mainstream.
5   On his life and works see his website http://www.alalbany.net/. (accessed 19 June 2014)
6   Nawaf E. Obaid (1999) 'The Power of Saudi Arabia's Islamic Leaders', *Middle East Forum*. See http://www.meforum.org/meq/sept99/saudipower.shtml (accessed 19 June 2014)
7   International Crisis Group (2004) 'Saudi Arabia Backgrounder: Who are the Islamists?', *ICG Middle East Report*, 31, p. 10.
8   See Awda's popular website in Arabic, English, and French: http://www.islamtoday.net. (accessed 19 June 2014)
9   James Buchan (1981) 'The return of the Ikhwan, 1979', in David Holden and Richard Jones, (eds), *The House of Saud. The Rise and Rule of the Most Powerful Dynasty in the Arab World*, New York: Holt, Rinehart and Winston, pp. 511–26.r

References

Buchan, James (1981) 'The return of the Ikhwan, 1979', in David Holden and Richard Jones, (eds), *The House of Saud. The Rise and Rule of the Most Powerful Dynasty in the Arab World*, New York: Holt, Rinehart and Winston, pp. 511–26.
International Crisis Group (2004) 'Saudi Arabia Backgrounder: Who are the Islamists?', *ICG Middle East Report*, 31, p. 10.
Lacroix, Stéphane (2008) 'Al-Albani's Revolutionary Approach to Hadith', *ISIM Review* 21, Spring, pp. 6–7.
Meijer, Roel (ed.) (2009) *Global Salafism: Islam's New Religious Movement*, London / New York: Hurst / Columbia.
Obaid, Nawaf E. (1999) 'The Power of Saudi Arabia's Islamic Leaders', *Middle East Forum*. See http://www.meforum.org/meq/sept99/saudipower.shtml
Schulze, Reinhard (1990) *Islamischer Internationalismus im 20. Jahrhundert: Untersuchungen zur Geschichte der Islamischen Weltliga*, Leiden: Brill.
Steinberg, Guido (2007) 'Saudi-arabische religionspolitik nach 2001: Instrument zur fortsetzung eines zweckbündnisses', in Sigrid Faath (ed.), *Staatliche Religionspolitik in Nordafrika / Nahost: Ein Instrument für modernisierende Reformen?*, Hamburg: GIGA-Institut für Nahoststudien, pp. 175–96.
Wiktorowicz, Quintan (2006) 'Anatomy of the Salafi Movement', *Studies in Conflict and Terrorism*, 29 (3), pp. 207–39.

HIZB UT-TAHRIR

Suha Taji-Farouki

Emergence and history

Hizb ut-Tahrir was established in Jerusalem in 1953 by Taqi al-Din al-Nabhani (1909–77), an Al-Azhar graduate, high school teacher and *qadi* (religious judge) from Ijzim in northern Palestine, and colleagues who had left the Muslim Brotherhood (MB). It declared itself a political party with Islam as its ideology and the revival of the Islamic community of faith (*umma*) – purged of the vestiges of colonialism and restored to an Islamic way of life – as its goal. It would achieve this goal by creating a single pan-Islamic state on the ruins of existing regimes, which would implement Islam completely and immediately, convey it worldwide and restore Palestine to the Islamic fold. Although it never obtained official sanction there, the movement enjoyed modest successes in Jordan and the West Bank, until opposition to the pro-Western monarchy was suppressed and martial law imposed in response to the political crisis of 1957. It indoctrinated recruits, disseminated its ideas through leaflets, lectures, and sermons, and contested parliamentary elections. Branches appeared in Syria, Lebanon, Kuwait and Iraq as early as 1953 and 1954. The ascendancy of Nasserism hindered its effort to gain popular support during the 1960s, yet the movement's growing confidence culminated in two coup attempts in Amman in 1968 and 1969, coordinated with simultaneous arrangements in Damascus and Baghdad.

Similar plots emerged in Baghdad (1972), Cairo (1974) and Damascus (1976). Under 'Abd al-Qadim Zallum, a founding member who, in 1977, succeeded al-Nabhani as leader, the movement expanded across the Arab world, but it still failed to gain a high profile. The activities of Hamas and Islamic Jihad, and the electoral success of the MB's Islamic Action Front from the late 1980s, underscored Hizb ut-Tahrir's marginal status in Palestine and Jordan, its original strongholds.

More recently, there is evidence of renewed vitality in Palestine (especially the West Bank, where it has benefited from the conflict between Hamas and Fatah), Jordan and Syria, and of continuing activity in the Arab Gulf countries, North African countries, Sudan and Iraq. This is in spite of the movement's proscription, based on a perception that it seeks the violent overthrow of their regimes, in all Arab countries except Yemen, the United Arab Emirates (UAE) and, since 2006, Lebanon. If mainstream political Islam has presented serious competition in Arab countries, the movement has found fertile ground elsewhere in the Muslim world. Its activities have spread to South Asia (Pakistan – where it operates openly despite a 2003 ban by presidential ordinance – and Bangladesh), South East Asia (Indonesia – where its 2007 annual global conference was held in a 100,000 capacity Jakarta stadium, but where it nonetheless has relatively minor influence – and

Malaysia) and, visible since the mid- to late-1990s, Central Asia (Uzbekistan, Tajikistan and, most recently, Kazakhstan – where in each case it has met with severe repression – and Kyrgyzstan, where the State response has been more moderate; Russia banned it in 2003). The movement has spread to Turkey, where it was classified a non-terrorist organisation in 2004, and has reached East Africa, with widespread activities in Tanzania (Zanzibar, 2006). It has been active among Muslim communities in Australia, the United States (where it remains off the terrorist organisations list) and Western Europe.

The movement's expanding geographical reach has been matched since the late 1990s by increasingly effective use of the internet and other new media to create a more integrated and accessible global perspective; the adoption of English as a major language of dissemination; and the granting of greater tactical and administrative autonomy to regional branches. These developments reflect an acknowledgement of the realities of globalisation and the presence of significant membership cadres outside the Arab Muslim world by Zallum and, in particular, his successor as leader since 2003, the media-savvy Palestinian 'Ata' Abu al-Rushta (b. 1943), an engineer and former Jordanian branch spokesman. Recent international media attention has centred on the movement's surging activities in Central Asia, where it has responded effectively to the ideological vacuum created by the collapse of Communism and problems of socio-economic deterioration: total regional membership is estimated at 18,000. This has led some to argue that the region is the focus of its global strategy and that the movement represents a threat to American strategic interests there; other analyses suggest that its impact is limited. The movement's growing adaptability and pragmatism are showcased by its high profile in London; although important to its international media campaign, it does not see the city as its global headquarters as some have claimed.

Ideas and worldview

Hizb ut-Tahrir has a distinctive and coherent system of thought, reflecting al-Nabhani's original attempt to construe Islam as an ideology superior to capitalism and Socialism. The Islamic ideology comprises a rational doctrine that shapes thought and conduct, and a system for ordering all aspects of life. Al-Nabhani's views concerning the foundations of this doctrine are controversial and rejected by Islamic thinkers and movements, from traditionalists to Salafis. Issuing from the doctrine, the Islamic system is the *shari'a*, elaborated through *ijtihad*. Al-Nabhani developed a distinctive articulation of the sources of the *shari'a*, displaying some affinity with trends in Islamic jurisprudence that reduce the role of reason and suspend mechanisms that serve the community's interests and accommodate change. He considered re-establishment of the sovereignty of the *shari'a*, now absent worldwide, as the lynchpin in restoring an Islamic way of life: this can only be achieved by an Islamic state. He posited the model of the caliphate as detailed by classical Islamic jurists, synthesised with modern political processes, as the divinely prescribed form of Islamic government. His uniquely comprehensive draft constitution (1953) details Islamic legal rules for the State's political, economic and social systems, and its foreign policy. According to this, executive and legislative powers are vested in an elected caliph, in whom most state functions are centralised. Citizens call the State to account through specific institutions and a political opposition expressed through Islamic political parties. Political participation forms a 'collective religious duty' (*fard kifaya*), but 'consultation' (*shura*) is not considered a pillar of Islamic government. Al-Nabhani's call to restore the caliphate was originally counter-posed to secular pan-Arabism in the struggle to reverse the fragmentation caused by the implantation of nation states

and the creation of Israel. Today, it is revitalised as a vision of a utopian order that promises justice and inclusion, challenges the exploitative global hegemony of Western capitalism, checks its neo-colonial exploits, and restores to Islam its worldly status. Al-Nabhani
described a world divided between Islam and 'unbelief' (*kufr*)– which seeks to destroy
Islam and finds its most virulent expression in capitalism, itself organically connected
to secularism, democracy and colonialism – and headed by America and Britain. Like
democracy, nationalism is a construct of unbelief, used to divide Muslims, while international organisations are vehicles of unbelieving states.

The movement has construed the Islamic resurgence of the last few decades as evidence
that its ideas have taken root. Its optimism has grown since the first Gulf crisis, the 'War
on Terror', and the Afghanistan and Iraq wars which, in its view, have exposed Western
designs on the Muslim world, the treachery of 'puppet' Muslim regimes, and the failure
of other political movements.

Organisation, membership and strategy

Using an Islamic discourse, al-Nabhani legitimised adopting modes of political organisation and mobilisation characteristic of the modern nationalist parties that emerged in
the Arab East from the 1930s (significantly, he had himself been closely involved in
proto-Ba'ath and early Ba'ath party circles during the 1940s). He developed a centralised,
hierarchical and disciplined framework for the movement, where executive power is
vested in one individual at each level of organisation. There is a central leadership
committee (located in the Arab world), committees in administrative regions (an administrative region or *wilaya* typically corresponds to an individual country), and local committees that oversee individual urban centres and clusters of small indoctrination cells there.
Decision-making authority is vested at the top of this pyramidal structure, with instructions flowing downwards. To maintain ideological homogeneity the central leadership
'adopts' material as 'party canon' (*thaqafa hizbiyya*), which becomes binding on members;
membership follows a period of intensive indoctrination and is marked by a pledge of
loyalty to the movement's views and obedience to its decisions and orders. The movement has maintained a remarkable degree of ideological and operational cohesion across
its career, and there have been few and relatively insignificant internal divisions and splits
(in Jordan, Britain and Uzbekistan). Membership has drawn heavily on secondary school
and university students and recent graduates, but profiles vary within and across regions,
from middle-class professionals to the uneducated and poor. Female members are visibly
active in some countries, but the movement operates strict internal segregation. Evidence
concerning the movement's finances points overwhelmingly to internal sources (including
member donations) and private donations from sympathisers.

Al-Nabhani elaborated a coherent political programmefor the movement modelled
on the Prophet's precedent in establishing the Medinan city state and comprising three
consecutive stages, designed for implementation in Muslim societies, beginning with the
Arab countries. First, to build its cadres through indoctrination of individuals with its
ideology, and second, to interact with society in order to supplant erroneous concepts
– spawned by decline and the colonialist legacy – with the movement's ideology, such
that the movement assumes intellectual leadership of society and creates within it a public
base of support for the revolutionary state. The establishment of this state forms the
third stage, namely, seizing government through a *coup d'état* executed by various power
groups – including the armed forces – that have been won over to the movement's cause.
In stage two the movement politicises Muslims, exposing conspiracies hatched by Islam's

enemies and Muslim rulers' collusion in these; this has produced sustained analysis of international politics. The movement confines its role to the political-intellectual struggle exclusively; it does not participate in charitable, social or educational projects. Meanwhile, its rejection of other Islamist groups' tactics makes cooperation with them difficult; relations with the MB have been particularly problematic, having been marked from the outset by mutual animosity, rivalry and a fundamental incompatibility of ethos and approach.

In recent years Hizb ut-Tahrir's increased visibility and extensive geographical reach have generated conflicting perceptions of its actual and potential impact, bringing to the fore significant challenges in the attempt to understand Islamic movements and key questions in associated public debates. The following themes illustrate these challenges and questions.

Squaring the circle: radicalism and non-violence

Hizb ut-Tahrir upholds an uncompromising ideology and a revolutionary vision that rejects all gradualist approaches to the establishment of an Islamic state and the implementation of Islam in society. However, while it openly campaigns for the overthrow of Muslim governments and deliberately fuels Muslim resentment at American and Israeli hegemony, it explicitly repudiates violence as a method of political change. In the post-9/11 climate a determination to link it to the radicalisation of young Muslims and to acts of violence have driven some analysts to advance the so-called 'conveyor belt' thesis. This argues that individuals primed by Hizb ut-Tahrir's worldview and who become frustrated by its slow progress might embrace violent means. The evidence linking the movement with individual acts of violence is tenuous and tangential rather than demonstrably causative: attendance of the movement's events at some point in their career by individuals subsequently convicted of terrorist activity in Western Europe; the emergence of two small violent splinter groups in Central Asia; and glorification of terrorist acts and channelling of individuals to *jihad* training camps by al-Muhajiroun, which was created in 1996 by Omar Bakri Muhammad, Hizb ut-Tahrir's 'aberrant' former leader in the UK. Set against the movement's 55 year career and substantial membership body, this list is remarkable for its brevity. Nonetheless, the assumptions underlying the conveyor belt thesis have become widespread, including among intelligence and policy communities.

In spite of its explicit repudiation of any role for *jihad* and acts of violence in the work to reinstate Islam, the consistent evidence of this furnished by its lengthy career, and its own condemnation of terrorist tactics as forbidden by Islam, some analysts have lumped Hizb ut-Tahrir together with various jihadi movements – including al-Qaeda – based on superficial rhetorical similarities that reflect a common repertoire of symbolic motifs. However, their public rhetoric cannot be used to explain how Islamic movements operate in the political arena, or the methods they adopt in their bid to change political realities. Al-Nabhani's nuanced treatment of *jihad* is at times obscured in Hizb ut-Tahrir's own public rhetoric, adding to the confused perception of some observers. A significant feature of this treatment – and a central plank of the movement's ideology – is the conviction that the *jihad* to liberate Muslim lands from occupying unbelievers before the restitution of the caliphate would merely divert resources from this pivotal duty, which aims ultimately to end all such occupations. This stance has become justification for the indefinite postponement of *jihad*, even in the clear-cut case of Palestine. In a climate increasingly dominated by the radical Islamist 'competition' with its emphasis on immediate 'defensive' *jihad*, however, the movement has been constrained to underline its own acknowledgement of this as a universal Islamic duty in its public rhetoric. This serves to establish its Islamic credentials and to defend its stance against its Islamist critics, but it does not amount to a repudiation of its non-violent strategy, as some analysts have suggested. Practical preparation or training for *jihad* remains alien to its culture, and members' energies are relentlessly focused away from *jihad* and onto the goal of establishing the caliphate through avenues of ideological and political struggle.

Politics and religion in an Islamic political party

Hizb ut-Tahrir was one of the first Islamic movements to fashion itself as a modern political party. This is its self-defining characteristic: it projects itself as a political party exclusively, sharing neither the concerns nor the methods of any other Islamic associations, be they religious, moral-social, charitable or educational. Participation in the institutionalised politics of the State through elections is, of course, organic to the methods of political parties in the democratic milieu, but Hizb ut-Tahrir refuses to participate in parliamentary elections in Muslim countries unless certain (unrealistic) conditions can be met: the upshot is that such participation has remained overwhelmingly hypothetical across its career. Nonetheless, the movement sees politics as integral to its purpose and mission. Defined simply as 'managing people's affairs according to particular ideas', al-Nabhani attempted to rehabilitate it as a field of activity in Muslim life; by projecting involvement in politics as a religious duty, he also sought to instate it as an obligatory part of this. Its clear theoretical self-understanding makes Hizb ut-Tahrir an illuminating case within which to explore the categories of politics and religion, and their interrelation, in Islamic movements more broadly. Although it endeavours to distinguish between them, members experience a subtle conflation of political and religious spheres within the movement. Thus they must accept Hizb ut-Tahrir and its adopted canon and strategy as the divinely prescribed vehicle and method for an Islamic restoration. They become subject to internal sanctions not only if they fail to carry out instructions or are remiss in the specific responsibilities of membership in the movement, but also if they fail to adhere to the prescriptions of the *shariʻa* (by committing a prohibited act or refraining from an obligatory one, for example). And if a member puts a question to the central leadership concerning some personal matter (relations between the sexes, for example), the Islamic jurisprudential opinion issued in response can become incorporated into the adopted canon, thereby extending the movement's authoritative reach beyond the purely political. Yet Hizb ut-Tahrir on principle does not adopt jurisprudential opinions concerning acts of worship, leaving these to individual members to deduce or adopt for themselves. This is a corollary of its self-consciously exclusive concern with the political duty of establishing an Islamic state, rather than with Islam as a religion.

Transnationalism, centralisation and regional-national differentiation

Although recent geographical expansion, a growing multi-lingual internet presence and effective use of live communication technologies have fuelled threatening spectres of a 'global' Islamic state, the movement's goal remains to establish the caliphate in a Muslim majority (Arab) country, under which Muslim countries will in theory become unified. It is important to emphasise the peripheral status of Western settings in Hizb ut-Tahrir's overall strategy, arising out of the fact that, like all other non-Muslim countries, these are not considered a potential locus for the caliphate.

The British branch is illustrative in this regard: when activists fleeing Arab countries arrived there during the early 1980s they initially targeted temporary Muslim residents, preparing them for the 'real' work back home: this changed only during the 1990s.

Active in some 40 countries, Hizb ut-Tahrir illustrates the operational sophistication and pragmatic adaptability of transnational Islamic movements more broadly. Hizb ut-Tahrir posits the worldwide Islamic community of faith as every Muslim's exclusive focus of allegiance and source of identity – an emphasis that has undoubtedly facilitated its transformation from Arab-centric to genuinely international movement – and has proved especially attractive to some second- and third-generation European Muslims. It vehemently rejects nationalism but is, of course, compelled to work within nation state frameworks, which shape its modes of operation. Given the prevailing security situation in Uzbekistan, for example, the movement's branch there remains clandestine; in Britain, in contrast, it makes full use of the liberal climate to disseminate its propaganda internationally. Recent moves towards de-centralisation appear to have produced only a modest degree of regional-national autonomy; for example, committees in administrative regions have been authorised to issue leaflets in their own name (signed, for example, 'Hizb ut-Tahrir, *wilaya* of Pakistan'), but only those issued by the central leadership carry the movement's official signature. This modest degree of autonomy allows for a more rapid response to specific events and more sustained analysis of relevant issues in terms of the movement's worldview than the central leadership might accomplish, with senior cadres across the sphere of operation now shaping campaigns based on intimate contextual knowledge. While strictly adhering to the adopted canon, the movement's propaganda can thus be framed to resonate with its immediate audience.

For example, leaflets issued in Central Asia might focus on specific local realities relating to economic insecurity, social ills and unjust authority, contrasting these with the just and secure society that will be formed under the future Islamic state.

Meanwhile, the British branch (which has increasingly tried to present a 'respectable' public profile) has implicitly compared the caliphate to the Western liberal system, styling it as a contractual, representative, accountable and welfare-oriented government that protects minorities. In all environments, Hizb ut-Tahrir operates as a social movement that does not offer immediate, concrete solutions but a single, utopian response to all problems, whether political, economic or social: the creation of an ethical order that will stand up to the twin evils of global capitalism and American hegemony.

References

Baran, Zeyno (2004) *Hizb ut-Tahrir. Islam's Political Insurgency*, Washington DC: The Nixon Center.

Karagiannis, Emmanuel (2006) 'The Challenge of Radical Islam in Tajikistan: Hizb ut-Tahrir al-Islami', *Nationalities Papers*, 34 (1): pp. 1–20.

Mayer, Jean-François (2004) 'Hizb ut-Tahrir. The Next Al-Qaeda, Really?', *Program for the Study of International Organization*, Occasional Paper, 4.

International Crisis Group (2003) 'Radical Islam in Central Asia: Responding to Hizb ut-Tahrir', *ICC Report*, 58.

Taji-Farouki, Suha (1996) *A Fundamental Quest: Hizb ut-Tahrir and the Search for the Islamic Caliphate*, London: Grey Seal.

—— (2000) 'Islamists and the Threat of Jihad: Hizb ut-Tahrir and al-Muhajiroun on Israel and the Jews', *Middle Eastern Studies*, 36 (4): pp. 21–46.

—— (2008) 'Hizb ut-Tahrir al-Islami', in John L Esposito (ed.) *The Oxford Encyclopedia of the Islamic World*.

HARAKAT AN-NAHDA AND ISLAMIC MOVEMENTS IN TUNISIA

By Lutz Rogler

What is known today as the Tunisian Renaissance Movement (Harakat an-Nahda) can be traced back to the beginning of the 1970s when some young men, at that time in their twenties and early thirties, engaged together in collective 'Islamic action' ('amal islami), mainly inspired by *tablighi* methods of preaching and supported by some older scholars of the marginalised *Zaytuna* milieu. Their main activities consisted of giving religious lessons in mosques and schools, and their slowly growing audience was composed of other young people, namely pupils and students. In 1972, this nucleus formed a clandestine organisation that was called al-Jama'a al-islamiya (the Islamic Group). During its formative period of the following years, this new Islamic movement became more and more influenced, both in regard to its ideology and its organisational structures, by the (Egyptian and Syrian) Muslim Brotherhood (MB), but remained far from playing an explicitly political role. Until the second half of the 1970s, the movement's endeavours concentrated on religious and moral 'education' and on spreading a message of re-Islamisation in a society perceived as increasingly Westernised and alienated from its Arab-Islamic identity. Although the leaders of the movement were certainly aware of the political dimension of the contradiction between their own ideological orientation and the 'modernist' ideology – and, in their view, secularising and Westernising policy – of President Bourguiba's regime, they articulated their critique of the situation at this stage in rather general cultural and religious terms. This propensity in turn had an ideological basis, at least in part, in the writings of the late Sayyid Qutb, which had exercised a strong influence on the members of al-Jama'a al-Islamiya in the 1970s: his call for a departure and an 'emotional' isolation from the ambient non-Islamic (*jahili*) society by the community (*jama'a*) of true believers, which should work for the transformation of society by its own expansion, led the Tunisian movement to adopt and practice a certain degree of political and social isolationism. It was only at the end of the decade that the movement changed this course and started to undergo a process of politicisation as a result of the conjunction of several factors and circumstances. Against the background of a deep social crisis in the country, under the impression of the increasing ideological interaction between Islamist students and leftist groups at the university, and due to the political and ideological impact of the Islamic Revolution in Iran, the movement's discourse and practices turned rapidly to political and social issues of the moment: from 1977 onwards, students at the university began to publish official statements and leaflets signed in the name of 'the Islamic trend' (*al-Ittijah al-Islami*), and it was in fact the student wing that pushed the movement's leadership to get more and more involved in politics.

For the movement as a whole, this shift in 'Islamic action' implied a major reorientation in its ideological foundations, as it had to abandon an approach based more or less explicitly on the rejection of 'non-Islamic' Tunisian reality and build a 'realistic' position regarding the concrete political and social problems of the country. This reorientation was achieved only gradually, at least as far as the members-at-large were concerned, and it was accompanied by a certain degree of critical revision of the movement's former ideological concepts. In the course of the internal debates taking place at this moment, a small group of intellectuals and students developed a particularly severe criticism of the movement's religious ideology, challenging namely the dominant MB influence, especially in its Qutbian version. These internal critics came to the conclusion that the Islamic movement needed a complete *aggiornamento* of its intellectual foundations and therefore, while approving the necessity of a 'realistic' turn to the current Tunisian situation, they refused a rapid and direct involvement in political affairs. In their view, neither the movement's actual theoretical background, nor the contents of the 'education' given to its adherents, were providing a sufficiently clear, concrete and coherent vision for political action.

Indeed, some other leaders of the movement might have shared some or even most of these self-critical concerns, especially with regard to the necessity of adapting its vision – largely inspired by previous ideological elaborations in the Middle East – to the specific national context of Tunisia. At this stage, however, the movement witnessed an important quantitative expansion mainly among secondary schools pupils and teachers, as well as students at the institutions of higher education, who were highly motivated by the success of the Islamic Revolution in Iran. In August 1979, the mainstream leaders held the first official – but still clandestine – conference of the movement, in order to prepare it ideologically and organisationally for the coming developments. In the movement's history, this meeting is regarded as the 'founding conference (*al-mu'tamar at-ta'sisi*) of al-Jama'a al-Islamiya in Tunisia'. It proclaimed that the movement belonged to the international organisation of the MB, and the participants also agreed on giving a more elaborate hierarchical structure to the movement, including 'cells' as the basic units, a territorial division, a functional division with separate organisational entities for the university and the secondary schools, an elected consultative council (Majlis ash-shura) and an elected executive bureau headed by a leader (*amir*). Rashid al-Ghannushi (b.1941), a teacher of philosophy at a secondary school in Tunis, and one of the movement's founding fathers at the beginning of the 1970s, was elected as *amir*. Despite the growing public visibility of its activities, not least in the media, and the authorities becoming increasingly aware of its political role, the conference decided that the organisational structures should be kept secret.

In contrast, H'mida an-Naifar (b.1942), also one of the founding members, and some other intellectuals and students of the 'self-critical' group decided to leave the *Jama'a* and, in 1980, they formed a new informal group under the name of the Progressive Islamists (al-Islamiyun al-Taqaddumiyyun). This group devoted itself to a critical rethinking of Islamist ideology and practice in terms of a departure from historically constituted 'Islamic' concepts and models and, consequently, of an elaboration of a 'progressive' vision that could provide the mental framework for a positive interaction with modern institutions and developments. Hence, in their view, the Islamic movement still had to undergo a deep ideological transformation and should give priority in its Islamic action to cultural and social dimensions instead of concentrating on political contention.

The whole decade of the 1980s confirmed, nevertheless, the highly disputed nature of the political activism of the mainstream Islamic movement in Tunisia, with regard to both its internal debates and the interaction with the Tunisian regime. In December 1980, the police arrested two of the Executive Bureau's members. Although they were released a few days later, the incident supplied the authorities with documents and information about the secret structures of al-Jama'a al-islamiya. In order to save the organisation from a government crackdown on it, the central structures of the movement were dissolved, and al-Ghannushi then proposed to publicly announce the creation of a political formation, thus pre-empting any action by the government. Once again, this option of a step towards full and open 'politicisation' met some opposition from inside the movement, but this time it came from students and leaders, who saw in the will to integrate with the official political scene a kind of recognition and legitimisation of the existing regime. These tensions between the advocates of a realistic and moderate position, and the partisans of a more revolutionary and radical course, found a temporary end during an 'extraordinary conference', held in April 1981, where a majority approved the political party option.

In a press conference on 6 June 1981, Rashid al-Ghannushi announced the creation of Harakat al-Ittijah al-Islami (Islamic Tendency Movement) and presented himself as its president and four others as members of its Political Bureau. In its Founding Manifesto, the new political formation refused violence 'as a means of change' and expressed its intention to participate in a coming pluralistic political system and democratic elections.

What should and could have been the beginning of a new phase in the movement's evolution quickly turned out to be its probable end. Some weeks later, about 150 members of the Islamic Tendency Movement were arrested, and between August and October more than a hundred were given prison sentences ranging from six months to 11 years. Al-Ghannushi was sent to prison for a period of ten years. This wave of state repression inaugurated a period of about ten years, during which short phases of truce, even dialogue, alternated with phases of partial or total confrontation between the mainstream Islamic movement and the authoritarian regimes of Bourguiba and, later on, Ben Ali. During this period, the movement never succeeded in gaining its formal legalisation. In 1984 when, after the release of its leaders, Harakat al-Ittijah al-Islami entered a period of truce with the authorities, a national conference of the movement once again confirmed the priority given to a political role in general and to the problem of an official recognition as a political formation in particular. While this insistence on the political dimension once again met some resistance from a group of intellectuals inside the movement (some of whom formed a group called The Independent Islamists and published in 1985 – together with former or current members of the movement – a collective self-critical document about the 'Islamic action' in Tunisia), the mainstream witnessed an ongoing rise in popularity as the – from then on – main force of political opposition in the country. Notably, the movement extended its visible presence and influence, not only among pupils and students, but also in the trade union and middle class milieus as well as – via communiqués and interviews – in the independent press.

In the face of the growing political activities of the Islamist movement, in particular at the universities and, increasingly, by means of street demonstrations, the Bourguiba regime reacted with a new wave of repression at the beginning of 1987, leading not only to the imprisonment of hundreds of the movement's members but, in August and September 1987, to the trial of dozens of its leaders by the state security court. The verdicts included seven death sentences; al-Ghannushi was sentenced to life imprisonment with hard labour. Meanwhile, amidst the atmosphere of sympathy for the movement in the country, some leaders working in secret or in exile prepared a military coup against Bourguiba. What was later called 'the security group', which included members of the movement inside the army and the security services, was charged with the execution of the plan on 8 November 1987. However, the Islamists were anticipated by Bourguiba's prime minister, Ben Ali, who deposed the president on 7 November by a so-called constitutional *coup d'état*.

The new regime of Ben Ali brought about a sort of détente. The Islamists welcomed the removal of Bourguiba and, for some time, forms of dialogue and cooperation were set up between them and the regime. In May 1988, al-Ghannushi was released and, later on, all prisoners belonging to the movement were amnestied. In addition to some symbolic measures taken by the new regime in order to reconcile the country with its Islamic identity, the authorities adopted what seemed to be a more conciliatory attitude towards the Islamic movement. The Islamist Student Organisation, already founded in 1985, received an official recognition in September 1988. A prominent member of the Islamic Tendency Movement participated in a committee that had been charged with drawing up a national pact between the political forces of the country, and his signing of the document, in November 1988, was regarded as expressing the movement's acceptance of the general principles for a new political consensus. The movement's demands for legalisation as a political party, however, continued to remain without success. In December 1988, the movement decided to change its name to Harakat an-Nahda (Renaissance Movement), since the Parties Law banned explicitly religious parties. Although still lacking official recognition as a political party, an-Nahda took part in the first pluralistic elections by presenting its candidates on 'independent' lists. According to the official results, the Islamist candidates gained an average of 17 per cent of the vote, realising about 30 per cent in the capital and 24–28 per cent in some other urban districts. However, they didn't win any seats in the parliament because of the majority vote system.

In retrospect, the parliamentary elections held in April 1989 seem to be the turning point in the interaction between the Islamic movement and the new regime. While the Islamic movement emerged through the election results as the second-largest political force, the electoral campaign had revealed the fundamental bipolarisation of the political landscape in the country. As far as the leadership of an-Nahda was concerned, the elections strengthened its will to make the legalisation issue a priority of the movement's political action. The movement's popularity seemed to be at an unprecedented peak, in particular among large sectors of the urban youth and the lower-middle class. Moreover, its members and supporters felt encouraged by the ascension of FIS and other Islamist forces in Algeria in 1990–1. However, the developments in its neighbouring country had the opposite effect, not only on Tunisia's ruling political circles, but also on a wider intellectual elite and parts of the secular political opposition forces. Against this background the bipolarisation was not only on the political level, between the regime and its ruling party on the one hand and an-Nahda and its sympathisers on the other, but there was an ever-sharper ideological confrontation in the country, between those who defended the right of the Islamic movement to have its own recognised party in a pluralistic political system, and those who feared an overwhelming wave of fundamentalism or obscurantism in the region generally and in Tunisia itself. Among the latter were large parts of the leftist milieus and the 'modernist' elites of the country.

The confrontation escalated in the context of the Second Gulf War and the political and emotional agitation that came with it. Once again it was mainly the student wing of the movement which contributed – by means of street demonstrations, strikes, gatherings, leaflets, etc. – to a deepening antagonism between the regime and the Islamists. The escalation of tension also resulted in some acts of violence. The movement's leadership condemned these acts but, by the end of 1990, state repression had started again by arresting members, suspending the movement's journal *al-Fajr* and banning the Islamist Students Union (March 1991). After the government had accused an-Nahda of plots aiming at overthrowing the regime by force, in May and in September 1991, thousands of leaders and members were arrested during a wave of repression between October 1991 and May 1992. Most of them were put on trial and sentenced to imprisonment. With those not arrested going underground or leaving the country, an-Nahda found itself completely paralysed in Tunisia.

From 1992 onwards, the total wiping out of the Islamic movement soon proved to be the beginning of the marginalisation, or neutralisation, of all kinds of independent opposition. While the repression of the Islamists was, especially in the first half of the 1990s, ideologically backed by large fragments of the secularised, secularist and leftist elite, by and by civil social organisations like the Tunisian League for the Defence of Human Rights and other political opposition forces fell victim to the increasingly authoritarian character of Ben Ali's regime.

The foregoing remarks on the historical evolution of Harakat an-Nahda, and its political and societal context, make it clear that the mainstream Islamist movement in Tunisia can hardly be considered as having been a clearly defined collective force, either sociologically or ideologically. During its history it underwent significant ideological shifts and changes due to the changing political and social context in which it evolved, and depending on how its leaders, and also its members-at-large, perceived this context. Growing from about a dozen to several hundred members in the 1970s, to several thousand members, and even more sympathisers, in the second half of the 1980s, it moved from a small, relatively isolated 'avant-garde of believers' (in the Qutbian sense of the term), to a political and social mass movement, in which players of different social situations and sensibilities – radical students, religious conservatives, organisational hardliners, moderate intellectuals, middle-class professionals, civil servants etc. – were active, sometimes in ways that contradicted the orientations suggested by the decisions and declarations of the movement's leaders. The long periods of repression and, hence, the pressure on ensuring cohesion and unity, more than once prevented internal contradictions from fully breaking out and compromising the 'collective' identity of an-Nahda. The most important split in the movement's history – that of the group later known as the Progressive Islamists in the late 1970s – left its mark not on internal tensions alone. All in all, the Progressive Islamists remained, indeed, a small group of intellectuals. However, mainly through their journal *15–21* (referring to the Islamic calendar and the 'global' calendar'), which they were permitted to publish between 1982 and 1991, they critically accompanied the political and ideological evolution of the mainstream movement, thus helping to sustain a mentality of self-reflexivity and sometimes of self-criticism and openness, at least among some leaders, intellectuals and student circles, which clearly affected the political discourse and practice of the Islamic Tendency Movement (an-Nahda) in the 1980s and 1990s. Several times, namely in 1985, 1991 and 1998, leading members of the mainstream movement challenged the focus on political activism and called for a more cultural and civilisational orientation of Islamic action.

Since the mid-1990s, indeed, exiled leaders of the Renaissance Movement made some self-critical attempts to evaluate the experience of their movement, including its escalation tactics in the period following the elections in 1989. This appeared in official declarations published by the organisation and in statements made by former and current leaders. Among them is Rashid al-Ghannushi, who left Tunisia after the elections in 1989 and who enjoys high standing as one of the movement's historical founding figures and intellectuals, without being a 'charismatic' leader and theoretician. Though often contested, he has played, and still plays, since the mid-1990s too, certainly the most prominent role inside the movement for his tactical choices, as 'president' of an-Nahda (in exile in Great Britain since 1991), in view of the movement's long-lasting political dilemma. From his exile in London, Rashid al-Ghannushi became, mainly through his numerous writings and interviews in the European, Arab or Arab-speaking media, not only the most widely known personality of an-Nahda, but he also gained the reputation of being one of the most outstanding and influential intellectuals in the contemporary Islamist mainstream in the Arab world and beyond.

After its complete paralysis in Tunisia at the beginning of the 1990s, the leadership of an-Nahda in exile developed close and regular contacts – and forms of coordination and cooperation – with other Tunisian opposition forces, and national, as well as international, human rights organisations. These were denouncing the general political status quo in the country and calling for a pluralistic 'democratic front' of all opposition forces. At the same time, on both organisational and ideological levels, members of an-Nahda have played (and partly still play) a notable and visible role in Muslim contexts in Europe, mainly in France, Belgium, Great Britain and Germany. Since the first wave of repression in the early 1980s, some leading figures exiled in France have participated prominently in the creation of associational networks of Muslims in France and Europe (namely the Union of Islamic Organisations of France (UOIF) and the Federation of Islamic Organisations in Europe (FIOE)); others have been actively involved in running educational structures affiliated with such associations.

Undoubtedly, after two decades of repression, which for thousands of members and supporters meant either imprisonment and torture or hiding and exile, the events of 2011 seem to mark a decisive turning point for an-Nahda in Tunisia. In fact, after the overthrow of Ben Ali's regime by the revolutionary mass movement of January 2011, a completely new historical era began for the country's most important Islamist movement. For the first time since its foundation in the early 1970s, an-Nahda could legally develop organisational structures and become socially active without any interference by state bureaucrats. On 1 March 2011 it received official permission to form a political party, almost 30 years after the unsuccessful attempt in June 1981 to gain formal recognition as the Islamic Tendency Movement.

Moreover, in the elections for a constituent assembly on 23 October 2011, an-Nahda gained 89 of 210 seats (around 41 per cent), far outstripping the other political groupings. Thus, during the envisaged transitional period of one year, during which the National Constituent Assembly is charged with drawing up a new constitution and functioning as the legislature, the Islamist movement has been able to achieve an importance that hardly anyone had reckoned with. Also, in mid-December 2011, Tunisia's transitional president, Munsif al-Marzuqi, charged an-Nahda's secretary general, Hamadi al-Jabali, with forming a government. In the coalition government established soon after that (with two other secular parties alongside an-Nahda) the Islamists provided the foreign, interior and justice ministers, as well as filling other posts.

The question – much-discussed during the pre-electoral period – of whether Harakat an-Nahda would play a decisive part in the post-revolutionary Tunisian political landscape thus received a clear-cut answer. It is in fact rather surprising that, after 20 years of absence from the country's political life and unprecedented state persecution of its members, the movement was capable within just a few months of both redeveloping its organisational structures and mobilising such a wide range of voters – including young people who could hardly have known the movement from their own previous experience. Remarkable too is the reintegration, obviously without any major problems, of hundreds of members after years of being exiled abroad.

On the other hand, the movement's basic policies since the revolution have scarcely been surprising, with its orientation towards change through rapid creation of democratic (and above all democratically legitimated) institutions, and its striving for consensus with other political forces in the country, including – indeed, especially – secular parties. Taking into account what the movement declared as early as 1996, in a programme setting out objectives for the period following Ben Ali's dictatorship, the present coalition government really does seem to be an implementation of that concept of a joint 'front' of the most important opposition forces against the regime which fell in January 2011. Furthermore, just as in 1981, when the movement had first attempted to embrace the pluralistic political order then seemingly coming into existence, in 2011 it similarly refrained from urging the establishment of an 'Islamic state' or calling for the 'application of *shari'a*'.

Indeed, in its programme published a few weeks before the October 2011 elections, the movement summarised its political objectives as entailing freedom, democracy and 'Power to the People'. The details of this programme for a new political order in Tunisia make clear an-Nahda's commitment to a broad-based social system: freedom, justice and development are stated to be the central values of state and society. Human rights and individual and collective freedoms are to be guaranteed – especially freedom of belief and thought, and the rights of religious minorities. Torture is to be banned. In addition, an-Nahda proclaims its support of independence for civic society, the principle of pluralism and peaceful transfers of power, separation of powers and an independent legal system. The functions of legislation and control are to be exerted by a parliament consisting of a single chamber, which is also responsible for possible changes in the constitution and election of the president of the republic.

In the fundamental orientation demonstrated in its election programme, and in many public statements since the revolution, the movement's positions clearly accord with recent theoretical reflections by Rashid al-Ghannushi and other an-Nahda intellectuals. These include the central idea that the State has no right to prescribe to citizens specific religious convictions and norms laid down by law. In the election programme there was no mention of *shari'a*. Similarly, the an-Nahda leadership has also urged that the old constitution's formulation that 'Tunisia is a free and independent state, with Islam as its religion and Arabic its language' should remain unchanged in the new constitution. When, in July 2012, Harakat an-Nahda held its first party convention after the revolution in Tunis, the movement's orientation towards democratic change and the principle of achieving consensus with other political and ideological forces regarding the essential steps in the country's ongoing transition were clearly reiterated. On the same occasion, Rashid al-Ghannushi, who also seems to have played an important mediating role between different ideological sensibilities within the movement, was re-elected as the movement's president with 72.5 per cent of the votes.

Yet, the coalition government led by an-Nahda had – right from its start - not only to face, in a persisting difficult economic situation, growing social unrest in the country, but also the challenges of distrust and misrepresentations in a much-polarised political and ideological environment. A number of Tunisian politicians are thus repeatedly fuelling doubts about the credibility of an-Nahda's democratic discourse, and are presenting the movement as demonstrating provisional pragmatism in order to retain power, or even as explicitly resorting to deceitfulness. It is claimed that the movement's real objective consists of using its new position of power within the State to reverse the achievements of 'modernity', particularly women's rights and freedom of opinion and belief. Nonetheless, current presumptions and fears, especially on the part of intellectuals, activists for women's rights, and left-wing parties, are not only shaped by decades of state rhetoric in the struggle against 'religious extremism'. In the months after the fall of Ben Ali's regime they have been nourished by a series of public declarations and actions by religious groupings belonging to the Salafist trend that had already emerged, mainly among younger Tunisians, throughout the 2000s. While still mostly disapproving explicitly any involvement in formal political engagement, these Salafist groupings are utilising the country's new political context to draw attention to themselves and to mobilise youth at a grassroots level, in particular in marginalised areas and milieus. At the same time, several events in the 2000s already revealed the emergence of more radical and violent milieus on the margins of this trend, which are more or less connected to, or inspired by, al-Qaeda networks and forms of action. To some extent, this Salafist trend might constitute a challenge for future prospects of an-Nahda in Tunisia, as far as the country's political stability and the ideological polarisation of the political landscape is concerned. In addition to Salafist groupings, the Islamic Liberation Party, which gained its official recognition in July 2012 and which calls explicitly for 'application of *sharia*' and re-establishment of an Islamic caliphate, seems to challenge Harakat an-Nahda by rather 'radical' ideological viewpoints in the Islamist spectrum.

All in all, with its supporting of the principle of a democratic civic state, Harakat an-Nahda adopts a position similar to that of the MB in Egypt or Morocco's Justice and Development Party. In fact, an-Nahda's current positions appear to be the result of political experiences gained and processed during decades of authoritarian rule in Tunisia – and also the outcome of debates and conflicts between different tendencies within the movement, reflecting self-critical assessments of the movement's own ideology and praxis. These theoretical reflections have crucially shaped an-Nahda's self-image today, with its guiding impulse of symbiosis between Islam and modernity making the movement even closer to the Turkish Justice And Development Party (AKP) than to the MB.

References

Ayari, Michael Bechir (2007) 'Rester le même tout en devenant un autre: les islamistes" tunisiens exilés en France', *Maghreb-Machrek*, 194 Winter, pp. 55–69.

Burgat, François (1988) *L'islamisme au Maghreb: la voix du Sud*, Paris: Karthala.

Camau, Michel and Vincent Geisser (2003) *Le syndrome autoritaire: politique en Tunisie de Bourguiba à Ben Ali*, Paris: Presses de Sciences Po.

Hamdi, Mohamed Elhachmi (1997) *The Politicisation of Islam: a case study of Tunisia*, Boulder: Westview Press.

Hermassi, Abdelbaki (1995) 'The rise and fall of the Islamist movement in Tunisia', in Laura Guazzone (ed.), *The Islamist dilemma: the political role of Islamist movements in the contemporary Arab world*, Reading: Ithaca Press, pp. 105–27.

Krichen, Zyed (1997) 'Le mouvement fondamentaliste islamique en Tunisie, 1970–90: histoire et langage', in Mahmoud Ben Romdhane (ed.), *Tunisie: mouvements sociaux et modernité*, Dakar: CODESRIA, pp. 193–268.

Rogler, Lutz (2001) 'Zu Erfahrung, Kritik und Selbstkritik im politischen Selbstverständnis tunesischer Islamisten', in Dietrich Reetz (ed.), *Sendungsbewußtsein oder Eigennutz:*

Zu Motivation und Selbstverständnis islamischer Mobilisierung, Berlin: Das Arabische Buch, pp. 199–223.

Tamimi, Azzam S. (2001) *Rachid Ghannouchi: a democrat within Islamism*, Oxford: Oxford University Press.

THE MOROCCAN ISLAMIST MOVEMENT, FROM SECESSIONISM TO PARTICIPATION

Mohamed Darif

Ever since the appearance of the first visible expressions of organised political Islam in Morocco in 1969, represented by the Islamic Youth Movement, the varied actors within Moroccan Islamism have maintained a continuous interaction among themselves on the one hand, and the political field on the other. In a political system where the monarchy is a key actor, and where the king exerts his monopoly over religious interpretations by virtue of his role as commander of the faithful (*amir al-mu'minin*), the Moroccan Islamist movement is significantly affected by the monarchy's strategy when it comes to managing the religious field. In order to preserve religious stability, the monarchy has continuously played on the contradictions that plague different religious actors. Following the Islamic Revolution in Iran in 1979, it used the Wahhabi-inspired Salafist trend against the Islamist currents, while relatively ostracising the Sufis. However, after the 9/11 attacks on the United States in 2001, the monarchy initially used the Sufi groups trend to confront the jihadi Salafists trend, after which it partially 'neutralised' the Islamist trend by using the traditionalist forces.

The evolution of Moroccan Islamism reflects a continuous chain of transformations and reevaluation processes that eventually led to its distancing from the subversive option, initially embodied by the Islamic Youth Movement. Eventually the movement was forced to undergo a process of self-criticism in order to reconcile itself with the political system. The movement can also claim to have created some sort of 'integrated Islamism' by way of the different fractions that split from it. Among them, we shall cite the most important one, the Jemaa Islamiya (al-Jama'a al-islamiyya) – later on renamed as Unification and Reform Movement (Harakat al-Tawhid wa-l-Islah) – and the Justice and Charity collective (Jama'at al-'Adl wa-l-Ihsan), which represents a brand of restorative Islamism that has ceaselessly reevaluated its position. Justice and Charity aims at implementing a series of reforms not from the outside, but within the State's institutions. Even though Moroccan Islamism in its integrationist as well as in its subversive trends may have achieved its goals, both the 9/11 attacks in 2001 and the 16 May attacks in Casablanca in 2003 abruptly limited religious extremism in Salafist circles.

I. The retreat of subversive Islamism: the Islamic Youth Association and its splinter groups

Abdelkrim Mouti founded the Islamic Youth Association (IYA, Harakat al-Shabiba al-

Islamiyya) in 1969, in an effort to counter the leftist tide in Morocco. The founding of the IYA converged with the goals of the political authorities who needed ideological help when it came to containing leftist ideas. However, this ideological meeting of minds turned sour and was soon followed by a breakup following the assassination of one of the leaders of the left-wing opposition, Oman Ben Jelloun, on 18 December 1975. Ben Jelloun's assassination was attributed to the Islamic Youth Movement. From that point onwards, the movement's leaders were arrested and harassed. In turn, this affected the movement's organisational structure. Omar Ben Jelloun's assassination marked the beginning of the fragmentation of the Islamic Youth Movement, which would lead to subsequent 'revisions' of its ideological and political line on two different levels: 1) the reevaluation of the breakup at the organisational level within the Islamic Youth Movement, and 2) a second level of reevaluation pertaining to the organisation itself.

In September 1980, Abdelkrim Mouti was sentenced, *in absentia*, to life imprisonment for Omar Ben Jelloun's assassination. The ruling incited him to openly declare his hostility against the Moroccan regime on the pages of the magazine *al-Mujahid* (*The Militant*), issued in March 1981. A swift reaction from some of the movement's leaders ensued and, in April 1981, Abdelkrim Mouti was suspended. At the same time, some of the movement's leaders opted for 'freezing his activity' until a clearer vision of the situation emerged. In this context, we may speak of two revisionist stances that led to the organisational breakup within the Islamic Youth Movement.

1. The 1981 reevaluation process and the founding of the Jemaa Islamiyah
After adopting the decision to split from the Islamic Youth Movement following the publication of the magazine *al-Mujahid* in March 1981, secessionist groups were forced to opt between two different paths in the 1981–4 period: a path of secrecy and a path of openness. This period witnessed several detentions of members that belonged to the splinter groups. It was in 1983 that the Rabat-based group led by Abdelillah Benkiran submitted a petition to the authorities, with the purpose of establishing the Islamic Collective or Jemaa Islamiyah (al-Jama'a al-islamiyya). Right at the start of 1985, the political vision of the secessionist organisations that had split from the IYA became quite clear: they decided to follow the lead of the Rabat Group. In addition, the Casablanca Group, led by Saad Eddine Othmani, followed Abdelillah Benkiran's lead and submitted its own petition to the authorities, leading to the establishment of a branch of the Jemaa Islamiyah in October 1986.

The initiative of setting up the Jemaa Islamiyah as an organisation separate from the IYA unveiled a series of ideological revisions in search of legitimacy, while rejecting violence. The search for legitimacy and the opposition to the use of violence led the leadership of the Movement for Reform and Renewal (Harakat al-Islah wa-l-Tajdid) to establish a political party in 1992: the Party for National Renewal (Hizb al-Tajdid al-Watani), which did not achieve legal status. In this context there seemed to be no use in insisting on political action through an Islamic party. Instead, a dialogue ensued on the legitimacy of working through 'a political party with Islamic leanings'. From the beginning, the option was the Popular Constitutional Democratic Party, headed by Dr Abdelkrim Khatib. The roots of the party went back to 1967. The party held an extraordinary convention in the summer of 1996, after which several of the leaders belonging to the Movement for Reform and Renewal (a.k.a. the Movement for Reunification and Reform) became members of the party's General Secretariat. The party took part in the legislative elections on 14 November 1997 and endorsed the government – despite not participating in it – although maintaining a critical stance. In December 1998, the party changed its name to the Justice and Development Party (JDP, Hizb al-'Adala wa-l-Tanmiyya) and took part in the elections of 27 September 2002, coming third in the number of seats in the House of Representatives.

The JDP, which has become an example of the integration of Islamists in the political game, still faces a significant challenge related to the nature of its relationship with the Movement for Unification and Reform. Moroccan authorities reject any exploitation of religion for political purposes on the part of political parties, and the normalisation process with the JDP was based on this premise, in order to avoid any overlap between politics and religious preaching. The JDP accepted the rules of the game, and it started to talk of a functional differentiation between the Movement for Reunification and Reform as a religious missionary movement, and the party itself as a political organisation. However, these debates and analyses did not make it any easier to differentiate between the political and the religious levels in the actions of the JDP. Before the events of 16 May 2003, the party thought of itself as an Islamist party. It currently considers itself to be a political party with Islamic leanings.

2. The 1995 reevaluation process and the establishment of the Civilisational Alternative (al-Badil al-Hadari).

The Movement for a Civilisational Alternative or 'Alternative Civilisation' (Harakat al-Badil al-Hadari) emerged out of the core of the Islamic Youth Movement. It categorically rejected the use of violence and clandestine action, and tried to achieve legal status. Nevertheless, the movement's vision differed from that held by the Movement for Unification and Reform. Its views largely coincided with those held by the democratic forces with which it was in dialogue. In contrast to the Movement for Unification and Reform, which demanded a 'governing monarchy', the Movement for a Civilisational Alternative demanded a 'parliamentary monarchy', which it considers to be the closest model to the spirit of Islam. Three years into this, the remaining members in favour of the Islamic choice established the Umma Movement (al-Haraka min Ajl al-Umma) in 1998, under the leadership of Muhammad al-Marwani.

Following Abdelkrim Mouti's sentencing to life imprisonment *in absentia* in September 1980, he explicitly declared his hostility to the Moroccan regime. Mouti's organisation suffered several splits, both in its missionary and military wings, the latter headed by Abdel Aziz al-Numani who, in 1984, established his own movement: the Organisation of Moroccan Mujahidin (Munadhdhamat al-Mujahidin al-Maghariba). Abdelkrim Mouti set out to establish without delay a new military wing by the name of the Jihad Cell (Fasil al-Jihad), in charge of carrying out armed operations inside Morocco. The authorities detained two groups associated with it: the first, during the summer of 1983, was the so-called Group 71. The second, in the summer of 1985, was Group 26. Abdelkrim Mouti was sentenced to two consecutive life sentences following the arrest of these two cells.

It appears as if Mouti's failure in carrying out armed operations inside Morocco, and the emergence of new Islamic organisations rallied around the IYA in particular (Justice and Charity), prompted him to reconsider his political and intellectual philosophy. This reconsideration, which was clearly expressed after the death of King Hassan II on 23 July 1999, took form in a call for reconciliation with the existing political system, and also triggered an exercise of self-criticism. Immediately following Hassan II's death, the IYA moved to announce its rebirth with the goal of searching for a place in the map that was being drawn in this 'new era'. The movement's leadership issued a series of statements in the summer of 1999, through which it confirmed its firm rejection of subversive ideology and any implicit violence and takfirisation. The movement also announced the need to strengthen its peaceful stance in the new era, in order to preserve Moroccan unity amidst the secessionist military conflict in the Moroccan Sahara. It welcomed the opening of a dialogue with the pertinent authorities (more specifically, with the Interior Ministry) leading to the re-establishment of trust inaugurated by the granting of the royal pardon to all prisoners and exiles, without exception.

In 2000, Abdelkrim Mouti, the spiritual leader of the Islamic Youth Association, published a book entitled *Fiqh al-Ahkam al-sultaniyya: Muhawalat Naqdiyya li-l-Ta'sil wa-l-Tatwir (Jurisprudence of the principles of government: A critical view of its origins and its evolution)*. The book strongly criticised the trajectory of the Islamist movement in the Arab and Islamic world in general, as well as the Moroccan IYA. The book highlights the deep transformation in the thought and choices of Abdelkrim Mouti. He does not present himself as an activist working to forcefully change the political system in place, but as an Islamic 'intellectual' with a new vision that could push the work of the Islamic movement in a different direction. The ideas expressed in the book make us wonder: are we witnessing the unannounced ending of the Islamic Youth movement, or its rebirth? In the summer of 2004, Abdelkrim Mouti changed the organisation's name to Moroccan Islamic Movement and took on the role of spiritual leader.

II. The reevaluation process of subversive Islamism: Justice and Charity

The revision processes undergone by subversive Islamism are best represented in the trajectory of the Justice and Charity collective (Jama'at al-'Adl wa-l-Ihsan), both during its founding stage and its later development.

Abdesslam Yassine established the Justice and Charity movement following an in-depth reexamination of the concepts used by the IYA, with the goal of achieving a better grasp of the Moroccan situation. In this process, he criticised the concepts used by the 'subversive trend', the ideas formulated by both Abu al-A'la al-Mawdudi and Sayyid Qutb, and Abdelkrim Mouti's attempt to adapt such concepts to the Moroccan reality on the ground. Abdesslam Yassine rejects the idea that society is spiritually ignorant, proposing an alternative instead: the idea of 'civil strife', or *fitna*. In his book *Islam Tomorrow*, Abdesslam Yassine writes: 'We are not spiritually ignorant, but rather confused. If there are apostates among us, the humbled *umma* remains, and that is the *umma* of our Prophet Muhammad, sound in its faith.' The rejection of the concept of spiritual ignorance is thus justified as follows:

> When we judge our society to be ignorant, that is, out of God's path, then we've just judged ourselves as ignorant individuals. It is God's law that we may only be hostile to the oppressors (*al-dhalimin*), and the Prophet's judgement that we ought to be kind and non-violent, particularly in an era of civil strife (*fitna*) and confusion. Contemporary Islamic societies are not spiritually ignorant, but rather live through times of confusion and civil strife, in which the Truth gets mixed with falseness.

From its inception, the Justice and Charity movement reaffirmed its rejection of violence. In his book *The Prophetic Path*, Abdesslam Yassine writes: 'We shall never call for violence', asserting that the future Islamic renaissance will not shed blood and will not persecute anyone.

The Justice and Charity movement was established in the context of a wide re-evaluation of the concepts that had served as a basis for the subversive Islamist trend within the Islamist milieu. Out of it emerged an absolute rejection of secrecy and the decision to carry out its actions both publicly and legally. The movement's evolution is characterised by continuous revisions in terms of strategies and concepts. 1994 marked the beginning of an important political re-evaluation process in the movement, which now emphasised its wish to participate in the political process and its willingness to put forward new proposals. The reevaluation of Yassine's ideas was motivated by the wave of violence that swept Algeria, starting with the 'White Revolution' – a *coup d'etat* against President Chadli Bendjedid in January 1992 – and a series of reforms initiated by King Hassan II starting with the issuing of the 1992 Constitution. These reforms were combined with the attempt to get political parties then represented in the opposition to participate in the government, through the 14 October 1993 initiatives. In the period after 1994, the organisation replaced the discourse on uprising (that is, revolution) with a discourse based on the idea of reform, that is, the need to introduce a series of reforms in the political system. Following the attacks of 16 May 2003 which targeted Casablanca, Justice and Charity reaffirmed its stance against violence. The authorities were cognisant of the key role that the movement had played in delaying violent outbursts, keeping many young Moroccans away from the arms of the Wahhabi-Salafi trend supported by the State. The Justice and Charity movement viewed the 16 May 2003 attacks in Casablanca as an opportunity to demand a new religious policy from the authorities, leading to the reconciliation between the State and the religious milieu. Their goal was to bring religious fanaticism under control. The movement also drew a line separating spiritual training (which became the purview of the Council's Assembly) and political education, which came under the Political Department, created in July 1988. In order to send a clear message to the authorities, proving the movement's intention to participate in the political process, the closing statement of the Political Council, issued at the end of November 2005, contained several recommendations regarding the need to draw up a political programme and put forward basic proposals demanding the revision of the existing Constitution. At the same time, the Justice and Charity movement organised several meetings throughout 2006 during which it made public the organisational makeup of its political structure.

Starting in May 2006, the authorities began to restrict the group's activities. These actions were not designed to damage the government's relationship with the movement, but rather to exert pressure on the movement to make it further relinquish some of its stances in order to establish a 'political settlement' of sorts between the authorities and the movement in the post-Yassine era.

III. The critical situation of Salafism: the limits between the 'traditional' and the 'jihadist' trends

When Morocco achieved its independence in 1956, Salafism's most prominent figure was Sheikh Taqy Eddin al-Hilali, who died in Casablanca in 1987. After al-Hilali's death, Sheikh Muhammad Ben Abd al-Rahman al-Maghraoui became the movement's foremost representative. Al-Meghraoui was the founder of the collective for the Propagation of the Qur'an and Sunna (*Jama'iyyat al-Da'wa li-l-Qur'an wa-l-Sunna*), which still represents the spirit of Moroccan Salafism. Out of the movement emerged many Salafists, including the founders of the al-Hafidh ibn 'Abd al-Barr Collective (Jama'iyyat al-Hafidh ibn 'Abd al-Barr) in 1993, or those who would be known as 'jihadi Salafists', like Muhammad al-Fizazi.

Given the Salafists' ability to safeguard the political needs of the regime (and not only the religious ones), the Moroccan state maintained both a positive and negative attitude towards Salafism. After the establishment of the Islamic Republic in Iran, Moroccan Islamists reacted by trying to emulate the experience in Iran. It is worth noting that the establishment of the Justice and Charity project was directly related to the success of the Iranian Revolution. Despite the fact that King Hassan II understood that most Moroccan Islamist groups could not be attracted to Shi'ism to the same extent that they could be attracted by Khomeinist ideology (particularly in terms of political strategy), he nevertheless believed the Iranian Revolution represented a Shi'ite threat to Moroccan Sunnism. In this context, the crown bet on Moroccan Salafism as a way to oppose both the 'Shi'isation' of the country and fundamentalism. The Movement for the Preaching of Qur'an and Sunna, founded in 1975 by Muhammad ibn Abd al-Rahman al-Maghraoui, played a key role in opposing Shi'ite doctrine through its Qur'an schools. At the same time, it confronted Islamism by criticising the reformist preaching propagated by Islamist circles. In one of his essays, entitled *Our need for the Sunna*, al-Maghraoui writes:

> What reformation will come from those [i.e. Islamists] when they are not well versed in our Prophet's Sunna? What reformation will come to the *umma*, unless we reform their dogmas, purifying them and freeing them from superstition, heretical innovations, their interpretations, the falseness spread by the ignoramus and the deception of windbags?

Joining the strategy of the State and pledging obedience to it did not prevent Salafists from simultaneously pledging allegiance to al-Maghraoui and Taqy al-Din al-Hilali. Even Salafists who seceded from Meghraoui's school of thought, such as Muhammad al-Fizazi and Umar Haddushi, became integrated into the State's strategy, particularly when it came to confronting the Justice and Charity movement.

The Salafists' relationship with the State can be divided into two different stages: a first stage (1979–2001) during which the religious strategy was based upon the idea of employing the Salafists and using their services in the State's confrontation with the Islamists, to the exclusion of Sufism; and a second stage, beginning in 2001 and continuing until the present, during which the Sufis were used to confront the Salafists, to the exclusion of the Islamist trend. Following the 9/11 attacks, the Moroccan government changed its position on Salafism. In the official discourse, Salafism became synonymous with religious extremism. Starting in 2002, the State began to differentiate between several trends among Moroccan Salafism: a moderate trend represented by al-Maghraoui and al-Hilali and his followers, and a second trend that the media came to define as jihadi Salafism. Hence, numerous Salafists who were also considered to be jihadis were arrested. More than 1,200 of them were brought to trial, among them several jihadi Salafist *sheikhs* such as Muhammad al-Fizazi, Abd al-Karim al-Shadhili, Umar Haddushi, Hasan al-Kattani and Abu Hafs.

Whenever the State disapproved of those accused of extremism within the Moroccan Salafist movement, the accused made public their loyalty to the State during the trials. Umar al-Haddushi said: 'We're preachers, not revolutionaries. It is not our job to judge others, which is a prerogative of the Sultan and his delegates'. As to the reasons for the State's changing stance towards the moderate strand of Moroccan Salafism, represented by Muhammad al-Maghraoui, two factors might explain this transformation. Decision-makers believed that moderate traditional Salafism is a bridge leading to jihadi Salafism. Several incidents supported this belief, such as Yusuf al-Suli's case; a traditional Salafist who turned to jihadi Salafism and eventually blew himself up in Iraq. The second factor has to do with the nature of some of Muhammad al-Maghraoui's statements. In an interview with a Moroccan weekly on January 2003, al-Maghraoui said that under Hassan II's government nobody had been deprived of their freedom, except for those who had abused it and were unable to make proper use of it. It was understood that Sheykh al-Maghraoui had meant that Muhammad VI's reign had further restricted the preachers' activities, and that freedoms had dwindled.

Muhammad al-Maghraoui was aware of the fact that after the Casablanca attacks on 16 May 2003, Salafists were in the eye of the storm. Thus, the day after the attacks he issued a statement disapproving of the attacks and criticising them. In spite of maintaining such a clear stance, Moroccan authorities had already decided to disavow traditional Salafism (albeit gradually), while simultaneously putting an end to the projects of the al-Hafidh ibn 'Abd al-Barr Collective and closing down the Qur'an and Sunna Propagation Collective in 2008, including its Qur'anic schools.

References

Darif, Muhammad (1999) *Al-Islamiyun al-maghariba*, Casablanca: Matba'at al-najah al-jadida.
Zeghal, Malika (2008) *Islamism in Morocco*, Princeton: Markus Wiener Publications.

THE ISLAMIC MOVEMENT IN ALGERIA: THREE TRENDS, THREE PATHS

Mohamed Darif

Algerian Islamism emerged from the confluence between different groups in the religious realm. With the exception of the Ikhwani trend represented by the Movement of Society for Peace (Harakat Mujtama' al-Silm) and the Renaissance Movement (Harakat al-Nahda), the populist trend represented by the Islamic Salvation Front (FIS, al-Jabha al-islamiyya li-l-Inqadh) was born out of the union of a set of principles previously unable to coexist. The FIS's establishment was the result of a rapprochement between Abassi Madani's political Islam and Ali Belhadj's *salafi* Islam. This combination resulted in the birth of a populist kind of Islamism, whose victim became the FIS itself. The result was the Islamic Armed Group (GIA, al-Jama'a al-islamiyya al-Musallaha) emerging from the union of a large number of different religious associations.

Algerian Islamism, which coalesced in the early 1990s, distinguished itself by the inability of its different components to coexist. The FIS opposed the representatives of the Ikhwani trend (both the Movement of Society for Peace and the al-Nahda movement). Meanwhile, the GIA defied all other Islamist trends, including the FIS itself. Perhaps it was these contradictions, which permeated Algerian Islamism, that helped the Algerian authorities manage the confrontation with armed movements. This began in 1992, at times through the inclusion of the Islamist representatives of the Ikhwanist trend in government coalitions (from 1996 until 2009), and at other times by playing on the internal contradictions within the Islamic Salvation Front, following the decision to dissolve the party in 1992.

Abdul Aziz Bouteflika's arrival at the presidency of the republic in 1999, together with the launching of the Charter for Peace and National Reconciliation, clarified the map of Algerian Islamism, which may be divided into three main trends:

- The populist trend, represented by the Islamic Salvation Front (FIS), currently undergoing a slow death.
- The Ikhwani trend, embodied in the Movement of Society for Peace, which has become part of the political game.
- The jihadi Salafist trend represented by the Salafist Group for Preaching and Combat (al-Jama'a al-Salafiyya li-l-Da'wa wa-l-Qital), now witnessing a slight recovery.

I. The slow death of the populist trend: the Islamic Salvation Front

The establishment of the FIS was announced on 10 March 1989 and the party achieved legal status in September that same year. From the onset, the FIS was aware that its strength derived from the streets and the organisation established the mechanisms that would allow it to benefit from street mobilisation. In a country devastated by a crisis at all levels, the FIS attracted members and supporters from among the shabby urban proletariat and soon reached a membership of three million. With such a vast membership and ample support it was able to contest the first regional elections on 12 June 1990, which gave the party a notable victory.

The organisational structure of the FIS has three distinctive features. First, it distinguishes itself by the open nature of its aims. It speaks of itself not as a political party, but as an organiser of the Algerian people. Second, the movement is not a unifying project, but a collective one. It brings together not a series of harmonious currents with a unified vision, but rather a conglomerate of different trends, each with their own ideas about the State and the regime. The third characteristic is embodied in the FIS's 'compromising' nature at the leadership level, where decisions are reached through a consensus. On occasion, this can hinder the organisation and fragment it. That is what actually happened on May 1991, when the FIS decided to call for a general strike. Despite the fact that the decision was supported by a majority inside the National Consultative Council (Majlis al-Shura al-Watani), which set the strike to commence on the twenty-fifth of that same month, a minority against the principle of a general strike issued an opposing statement three days later. The statement, dated 28 May 1991, carried the signature of the FIS's National Consultative Council.

The FIS bet on the streets, which it tried to control through its organisational structure, while pursuing street mobilisation through the movement's political programme. The organisation's goal was to reach power and establish an Islamic state through the ballot box for the first time in history. The FIS was aware of the fact that the authorities would not allow it to claim an election victory either at the legislative or at the presidential level without exerting a modicum of pressure, particularly after the resounding victory obtained at the municipal and provincial elections of 12 June 1990. In effect, the authorities took an arbitrary stance on the electoral strength of the FIS by adopting new electoral law, enacted by the National Council in 1991. The FIS reacted by demanding new presidential elections parallel to the legislative elections. As proof of the seriousness of its demands, the FIS hinted at the possibility of resorting to tactics of civil disobedience through a general strike. In response to delaying tactics on the part of the authorities, the FIS decided to call for a general strike starting 25 May 1991. The situation came to an end with the president of the republic's decision to impose martial law on 5 June, the announcement of the postponement of the legislative election, and the resignation of the prime minister, Mouloud Hamrouch. The following day, 6 June, Abassi Madani and Ali Belhadj issued their famous statement, trying to guarantee the continuity of civil disobedience and illustrating the different levels on which it operated. Nevertheless, the authorities resorted to violence. Due to the lack of balance in strength, the FIS decided to put an end to the general strike on 8 June, just a few days after the issuing of the Madani–Belhadj declaration. On 30 June the authorities arrested Abassi Madani and Ali Belhadj.

The decision to arrest the FIS's dual leadership not only had the goal of putting an end to the civil disobedience tactics, but also of weakening its electoral strength. In the absence of Abassi Madani and Ali Belhadj, legislative elections took place on 26 December. The FIS obtained a resounding victory in the first round and was very close to reaching power through democratic means. However, secular-oriented political forces allied them-selves with the military establishment to put an end to this experiment. Following Chadli Bendjedid's dismissal, the army returned to power disguised under a constitutional 'heresy': the State Supreme Council. Among the Council's most important actions were the disso-lution of the FIS in March 1992, and bringing its leaders to justice on 27 June that same year. Abassi Madani and Ali Belhadj were both sentenced to 12 years in prison.

The failure of the civil disobedience tactic, and the army's subsequent return disguised behind the figures of Mohamed Boudiaf and Ali Kafi, prompted Ali Belhadj to issue his 'Blood fatwa' on February 1993, calling for *jihad*. The violent option required the FIS to have an armed wing, which it lacked. Other organisations unrelated to the FIS carried out armed operations, although there were coordinated actions through Qarm al-Din Karbani and Said Makhloufi. These factors led to the establishment of the Islamic Salvation Army (al-Jaysh al-Islami li-l-Inqadh).

The dissolution of the FIS following the arrest of its leaders represented a sudden turn of events that had, and continues to have, negative consequences for the move-ment's evolution. The FIS's leadership was represented on four different fronts: (1) the imprisoned sheikhs; (2) the sheikhs that had been released from prison; (3) the secret leadership inside the country; and (4) the executive leadership abroad. The visible lack of coordination among these four sectors put both the FIS's existence and credibility at risk. When the sector represented by Abd al-Razzaq Rajjam signed the decision to dissolve the FIS and incorporate it into the GIA other sectors within the organisation rejected the decision. Differences in opinion affected the FIS's membership abroad: the execu-tive branch abroad was split when Anwar Haddam favoured the FIS's integration into the GIA. The remaining members of the organisation rejected this idea and hurried to separate him from the organisation. President Liamine Zeroual's initiatives against the FIS contributed to further deepen differences.

These differences not only affected FIS members inside the country, but also those living abroad. Rabih Kebir, who lived in Germany, became Abassi Madani's right arm, whereas Washington-based Anouar Haddam became Ali Belhadj's representative. Differences reached an extreme after Rabih Kebir acknowledged the legitimacy of Liamin Zeroual's election for the presidency in 1995. Anouar Haddam interpreted this acknowl-edgement as treacherous to the Islamist cause. Abdelaziz Bouteflika's arrival to power and the launching of the National Reconciliation Initiative changed many things. The Islamic Salvation Army, headed by Madani Merzak, accepted Bouteflika's proposal to join the initiative. Ali Belhaj felt under siege following his release from prison and Abassi Madani opted for moving to Qatar, whereas Germany-based Rabah Kebir returned to Algeria in 2006. Once there, he hinted at establishing a new political party, indicative of a clear distancing between him and the FIS. As the dispersal of the FIS's former members continued, the Algerian authorities insisted on opposing its return to the political arena.

II. The integration of the Ikhwani trend: The Movement for Peace Society

The Movement for an Islamic Society (Harakat al-Mujtama' al-Islami) is, by far, the most important representative of the Ikhwani trend in Algeria. The movement changed its name to Movement of Society for Peace (HAMAS, Harakat Mujtama' al-Silm) following the issuing of the 1996 decrees that banned the involvement of the State in the political action of political parties. It is not possible to understand the Movement for an Islamic Society without reflecting on the life and experience of Mahfouz Nahnah, a preacher who synthesised the movement. Nahnah established the Society for Reform and Guidance

(Jama'iyyat al-Irshad wa-l-Islah) on 12 February 1989. Through this organisation, Nahnah tried to articulate the transformation that Algeria was undergoing. The first of these changes was the issuing of a new constitution on 23 February 1989. In a declaration dated 22 February 1989 Nahnah wrote, regarding the constitution:

> Algeria is the home of Islam and *jihad*, as proved by our many uprisings. After independence, the pillars of this *umma* were abandoned. Now, a constitutional reform project that hides among its articles a myriad of negative aspects is being put forward to the Algerian people. Consequently, the Islamist movement proposes the following:
>
> 1. The Qur'an is the only source of the Constitution.
> 2. To be established, fundamental freedoms must be in accordance with the constituent principles of the *umma*.
> 3. The family and the educational system derive their inspiration from Islamic education and its goals.
> 4. The functions of the Islamic Supreme Council ought to be established by the Presidency.

The February 1989 Constitution contained positive aspects, including the recognition of the plurality of political parties. In this context, Nahnah announced the founding of his own party on 9 November 1990: the Movement for an Islamic Society. The party held its inaugural convention on 29 May 1991. As soon as the institutional convention had taken place, the movement started to recruit followers among workers. It established the Islamic Trade Union Association (al-Ittihad al-Islami li-l-Niqabat): more than 5,000 workers were present at its first meeting in July 1991. The Movement for an Islamic Society relied on a well-trodden path of absorption, based on gradual progress and cooperation with different social forces and the authorities. This path was based, first, on the belief in dialogue and the need for flexibility. During the party's founding convention, Nahnah said in this regard:

> We reject neither democracy nor consultation (*shura*). Whoever accepts democracy, we shall accept them, saying: 'We are democratic'. Whoever rejects democracy but believes in consultation, we shall open our arms to them, saying: 'We're in favour of consultation'. Democracy is not a monster or a dinosaur, but a lamb. Thus I tell you that not all secularists are of the same stock: there are among them some you can dialogue with and whom you can convince, and there are those who will not be convinced today, but they

The second factor, as reflected in the recommendations of the founding convention, was the belief in the progressive nature of the movement's missionary work, since the building of an Islamic state requires invoking all necessary means to achieve victory and what comes with it. It is by limiting itself to the progressive, thematically focused and realistic nature of its work that the movement can achieve its goals in the realms of knowledge, work, justice and goodness for all. On the basis of this belief in the progressive nature of its missionary action, the movement rejected the FIS's invitation to participate in the organisation of the May 1991 general strike. When the crisis between the State and the Islamic Front flared up, Nahnah favoured the option of a military intervention, which he justified in the following terms:

The Algerian people were about to be torn to pieces. Had the situation kept deteriorating, there existed the possibility of a foreign power intervening, which is why I said (and still hold this opinion) that the army's intervention was a wise move, notwithstanding some excesses. Today, we believe in the rule of law and the Algerian constitution. We must all respect this, including the opposition, the army and the Algerian authorities.

Generally speaking, the recommendations issued during the course of the inaugural convention of the Movement for an Islamic Society fully embody the movement's character and are represented in this comprehensive path. Among these, we shall cite the following:

- The support for using democratic means and the upholding of political pluralism.
- Working towards the establishment of an Islamic state through legal means, according to both the Qur'an and Sunna.
- Freeing public institutions from the tutelage of political parties.
- Practicing moderation and dialogue among all citizens of the *umma*, including the government, political parties, associations and individual members of society.
- Renouncing violence and radicalism in all its forms.
- The participation of women in the decision-making process, granting them the opportunity to freely collaborate in the political, economic, social and cultural realm, as prescribed by the *shari'a*.

Since its inception, the Movement for an Islamic Society tried to portray political Islam in a different light from that of the FIS or the Armed Islamic Group. The movement participated in all election processes starting 12 June 1990, and expressed its wish to be represented in the State's institutions. The party had adopted the strategic decision to participate – a decision it upheld in spite of its president being banned from running in the elections – following Liamine Zeroual's resignation as president of the republic. Following Mahfouz Nahnah's death on 19 June 2003, the movement held its Third Institutional Convention on 8 August 2003, choosing Bouguerra Sultani as its new president. Sultani reasserted his unequivocal will to follow in the path of Mahfouz Nahnah, a stand that was later affirmed with the movement's participation in the coalition leading to the re-election of Abdel Aziz Bouteflika in April 2004, in conjunction with the National Liberation Front (Jabhat al-Tahrir al-Watani) and the National Democratic Assembly (al-Tajammu' al-Watani al-Dimuqrati).

The challenge currently facing the Movement for Peace Society is the ability to maintain its unity, particularly following the Fourth National Convention in 2008, which witnessed the emergence of two trends: one supporting Bouguerra Sultani, and a second trend in support of Abdelmajid Mnasra. Even though the conference ended with Sultani's re-election for the presidency, there were clear signs of fragmentation inside the movement which led to the establishment of a new organisation: the Movement for Preaching and Change (Harakat al-Da'wa wa-l-Taghyir).

III. The restoration of the jihadi trend: the Salafist Group for Preaching and Combat

The Algerian situation shows how the overturning of the election victory claimed by the FIS in the early 1990s paved the way for the violent outbreak that eventually drowned the country in a tide of blood. The Islamic Armed Group (GIA) was born in 1992 with the goal of putting into practice a violent ideology on the ground, against the Algerian system. From the ranks of the GIA a new organisation emerged in 1999: the Salafist Group for Preaching and Combat (al-Jama'a al-Salafiyya li-l-Da'wa wa-l-Qital), an organisation that made excessive use of violence before being consumed by the contradictions that plagued it following the deposition of its leader, Hassan al-Khattab, and his replacement with Abdel Malek Drudkal, a.k.a. 'Abu Musab Abd al-Wadud'. Abu Musaab had close ties with al-Qaeda and allied himself with this organisation, adopting its strategy and eventually changing the group's name to Al-Qaeda Organisation in the Islamic Maghreb (Tandhim Qa'idat al-Jihad fi Bilad al-Maghrib al-Islami).

Even though Salafist ideology has maintained a strong presence in the Arab Maghreb region since the late 1990s, its organisational structure differs from one country to the next. In Algeria, it is represented by the Salafist Group for Preaching and Combat, a group that was not initially related to al-Qaeda. However, other countries in the Maghreb region witnessed the formation of organisations that were part of al-Qaeda, such as the Moroccan Combat Group (al-Jama'a al-Maghribiyya al-Muqatila), the Libyan Combat Group (al-Jama'a al-Libiyya al-Muqatila), or the Tunisian Combat Group (al-Jama'a al-Tunisiyya al-Muqatila). Al-Qaeda seized this ideology as an opportunity to put together the different fragments of jihadi Salafism in the Maghreb and create a centralised organisation under the meaningful name of Al-Qaeda Organisation in the Islamic Maghreb. The circumstances behind the establishment of the group are related to the transformations and changes that have taken place in the Maghreb region. Some have to do with the jihadi Salafist organisations in the region; others are related to al-Qaeda's 'motherly' strategy. To begin with, following the 9/11 attacks, Salafist organisations in the Maghreb were dealt numerous blows that resulted in a loss of effectiveness following the arrests of the organisation's leaders in Libya, Morocco and Algeria. Such blows forced many jihadi Salafists in the Maghreb region to look for hiding places outside their own countries, particularly in the countries of the Sahel region, south of the Sahara. Moving was not a choice, but an obligation.

The pressure exerted on the Salafist Group for Preaching and Combat demanded a revision of the movement's priorities and the nature of the alliances it had established. The leadership of the Salafist Group was split into two: one trend defended the need to maintain a 'regional' character, in terms of organisation, that would later focus on the Algerian interior. This position was defended by Hassan al-Khattab. A second trend favoured the idea of widening its organisational scope to other jihadi Salafists in the Maghreb region, and widening the confrontation arena throughout the Maghreb. At the end of the day, this second trend finally prevailed, not because of its strength within the organisation, but because the objective reality on the ground did not allow for a different choice. This fact limited the nature of the coalitions and determined the organisation's future. Before the Salafist Group for Preaching and Combat's leader, Abu Musaab Abd al-Wadud, made public his allegiance to al-Qaeda on 9/11, and before the declaration of the birth of al-Qaeda in the Islamic Maghreb in January 2007, Salafist groups had already widened the confrontation arena with the attacks on the 'Muguiti' military barracks in Mauritania, in June 2005.

The changes that affected jihadi Salafist organisations in the Maghreb (and in particular the Salafist Group for Preaching and Combat) coincided with al-Qaeda's adoption of a brand new strategy at the end of 2003, following the American invasion of Iraq. The military invasion meant the 'rebirth' of Osama Bin Laden and Aiman Zawahiri's organisation. The new strategy was based upon the founding of an Islamic state in the Arab world, preconditioned by the need of first establishing an Islamic state in Iraq. Thus, achieving victory in the Iraq war became the movement's utmost priority. To achieve this goal, al-Qaeda put in practice a recruitment effort looking for 'combatants'. The Arab Maghreb became a strategic objective and a reservoir of men to fuel the Iraq war. The interaction between the changes undergone by the Salafist Group for Preaching and Combat, and its desire to rebuild its sanctuaries in the Maghreb following the blows it had been dealt, together with the transformation of al-Qaeda's strategy after the occupation of Iraq and the wish to create a 'Maghrebi' framework that allowed for the recruitment of combatants, were all contributing factors to the establishment of the Al-Qaeda Organisation in the Islamic Maghreb.

Al-Qaeda's organisational priorities in the Islamic Maghreb do not currently differ from the circumstances that gave birth to the movement. First, the organisation aims at reaffirming its presence in the region and thus responding to those who questioned the new organisation's ability to carry out its threats and thought of it exclusively as a media phenomenon. Abu Musaab Abd al-Wadud's followers carried out several violent armed operations, which they themselves considered as propagandist actions starting 11 April, followed up by other actions on 11 July and 11 December 2007. The second priority relates to the organisation's wish to emphasise the conferring of legitimacy on the regional' dimension, to which the new name of the organisation referred. Abu Musab Abd al-Wadud rejects the idea that his organisation means nothing but a change in name of the Salafist Group for Preaching and Combat. Instead, he believes it to be a new movement that aims at uniting all jihadi Salafists in the Maghreb region. Meanwhile, and in order to further legitimise the regional dimension of the movement, he admitted two new non-Algerian members from other Maghreb countries into the council, and widened the scope of the movement's activities to other countries in the region, particularly Mauritania. The third priority is to directly incorporate al-Qaeda's new strategy into the organisation, as evidenced in the recruitment of combatants from the Maghreb who are later sent to Iraq.

References

Burgat, Francois (2003) *Face to face with political Islam*, London: I.B.Tauris.
Darif, Muhammad (1994) *Al-Islam al-siyasi fi l-jaza'ir*, Casablanca: Al-Majalla al-maghribiya li-'ilm al-ijtima' al-siyasi.

POLITICS OF ISLAMISM

Salman Sayyid

In June 2009 the recently elected president of the United States, Barack Hussein Obama, made what was touted as a landmark speech, in which he would reset the relations between the USA and the Muslim *umma* after the excesses of a neo-conservative crusade on terror. The idea was that a more emollient approach to Muslims would do much to improve the image of the USA globally, especially among Muslims, and thus help restore its much-frayed legitimacy and hegemonic position in the world. In this speech Obama's biography, with its diverse heritage, drew attention to global multiculturalism, including his association with Islam. There was a tremendous desire among many in the world, both Muslim and non-Muslim, that this speech would mark a radical break with the Bush regime and its policies of the past eight years.

Perhaps the expectations of such a diverse audience could never be satisfied, and it may have been unrealistic to hope that one speech on its own could dismantle the administrative and disciplinary assemblage which had coordinated and consolidated the logic of the War on Terror (I refer not only to the use of torture by the USA and its allies, or the continuation of Guantanamo, nor the various security measures, but also to the new financial controls and the intensification of surveillance, and the carefully calibrated curtailment of liberal rights). It is possible to see Obama's speech as signalling the continuation of the War on Terror by other means. For at the heart of this campaign was nothing short of an attempt to restore Western hegemony and thus eradicate Islamism as a meaningful political horizon. This multi-dimensional struggle against Islamism raises the question about its nature. This is more problematic than it seems since, from its inception, Islamism has been seen as a strange sort of fad that will imminently vanish, and one cannot help but notice how, at regular intervals, one encounters commentaries declaring that Islamism and its cognates have come to an end. These arguments for the decline of political Islam are quickly cast aside when the next instance of 'Islamic fundamentalism' hits the headlines. As such, prior to the attacks on New York, Washington, Bali, London and Madrid, there were a number of commentators pointing to the end of Islamism. The inability to treat Islamism as something more than a set of pathological reactions to developments in the world means that Islamism as an object of analysis remains obscure, being represented as either a form of fascism, or fundamentalism or libidinal displacement.

Seldom are Islamist projects presented as distinct political movements, with all the ambiguities and contradictions that are entailed. This is partly a function of the way in which the end of the Cold War has led to a general depoliticisation. With the unravelling of the communist project of transnational radical transformation, politics has been reduced to liberalism which, it can be argued, is not a politics at all, but rather the expansion of an economic logic from the market to the State. The effect has been to produce a definition of politics in which political activity becomes a branch of economic calculation. At the same time, politics is viewed as what Western plutocracies do. Therefore, by definition, Islamism, with its projects of re-founding an Islamic order within Muslim communities, is seen to be engaging in anti-politics, a politics that is not about the art of the possible, but of trying to make the impossible possible. The political ambition of Islamism to institute a new society, and to abandon the status quo, is represented as its proclivity for violence and fanaticism, thus denoting Islamism as the negation of politics. Furthermore it is argued that the Islamist project is unable to provide answers to what may be called the bread-and-butter issues and, as such, the majority of Muslims are unable to accept that it has much to say about improving their ordinary lives. These sets of arguments are based on the characterisation of the Islamist agenda as being dominated by the impossibility of adhering to Islam outside the borders of an Islamic state; the necessity of taking part in *jihad* against infidels and corrupt Muslims; the equation of modern Muslim societies with *jahiliyya*, and the description of most Muslim leaders as *kafir* (that is, unbelievers). Therefore, what Islamists want to establish is not a prosperous society, but an Islamic moral order.

It is also argued that Islamism does not offer a clear and consistent pattern of government. This conclusion is often reached either by comparing Maududi, Qutb and Khomeini and finding not only that they do not agree with each other, but that they also contradict each other, or by pointing out the differences between political parties such as Hizbullah or the Muslim Brotherhood. Islamists are often dismissed as peculiarly prone to disagreements, for having vague public policies, and for focusing on trivial issues.[1] These inconsistencies are considered to weaken the appeal of Islamism, and can also be found in the policies of Islamist regimes, for example the Iranian alliance with Ba'athist Syria during its war with Iraq, in spite of Syria's anti-Islamist and pro-secularist polices,[2] or sectarian conflict in occupied Iraq between Shi'a and Sunni Islamists.

Olivier Roy makes an interesting distinction between revolutionary and salvationary aspects of the assertion of Muslim subjectivity.[3] For him the former is characterised by attempt to capture state power, while the latter is characterised by attempt at individual reforms. Islamism for Roy is only political if it is able to capture the State. The failure, since the Iranian Revolution, of any Islamist project to capture state power for any sustained period of time demonstrates, according to Roy, the political failings of Islamism and its replacement by a 'neo-fundamentalist' focus on personal piety. This judgement on Islamism's failure has been fairly influential. Roy's conceptualisation of the political, however, is state-centric and seems to see social transformation in terms of a single founding act (the revolution) which concentrates power and allows for the re-organisation of society. Such a narrow conception of the political, and of the process of politically motivated social transformations, does not do justice to the complex way in which social transformations occur. It fails to recognise the ontological character of the political by reducing it to the product of a specific institutional ensemble.

To see the political in terms of the following four sets of interrelated concepts is more useful. One, the political is the moment of making a decision (not a choice). Two, the political is the institution of the social. Behind all social relations we have the political or the struggle to bring the new into the world. Three, the political is about the process of identification, of creating subjectivities and maintaining those subjectivities. And four, the political exists whenever it is possible to make a distinction between friend and enemy, and this distinction is a public one.[4] That is to say, any sphere of social life can become politicised. Social transformation produces antagonisms: a distinction is drawn between the enemies and friends of change. Projects of social transformation seek to institute a new set of relations; the act of institution takes place in terrain in which the distinction between friend and enemy is at its sharpest, since at the moment of institution the mechanisms for transforming friends and enemies into opponents is not established. Roy, by seeming to suggest that the political is to be 'housed' in the State, would seem to discount the political nature of, for example, the feminist movement, which transformed gender relations throughout the world without ever directly seizing state power.

As Gramsci argues, there are a number of different pathways to bringing about social transformation, not all of which begin with the capture of the State. The State is not the only 'container' of power; rather, the capture of the State is the culmination of a long process of 'intellectual-moral' reform and struggle, which delegitimises the exercise of state authority and articulates an alternative vision of the organisation of state and society.[5] By discarding the possibility of a process of social transformation that operates through 'intellectual and moral reform' without holding state power, Roy privileges the idea of revolution as the moment of the foundation of a new order. There are many examples in which social transformation has culminated in the formation or capture of the State. For example, the history of early Islam is precisely one in which initial transformation is accomplished by the dissemination of the Prophetic message and expansion of the Prophet's following in the absence of state power (a model of transformation that resonates with many Islamists).

A more complex schema than the one provided by Roy is needed to take into account the way in which the assertion of a Muslim subjectivity has been transformed by its inclusion into a set of social relations that stitch together the Muslim *umma*. The first step in such an endeavour is to understand Islamism as a discourse rather than just an ideology. A discourse has many points of enunciation – it is not articulated from one particular centre – this accords with the case of Islamism which is articulated from a plurality of sites. A discourse consists of a diverse number of statements. Similarly, Islamism is not reducible to the statements from purely political parties; it is constituted by a variety of interventions. These statements have a non-random and systematic relationship with each other.[6] Islamism's specificity arises when its constitutive elements are organised in terms of a frontier, which excludes elements that are considered to have an antagonistic relationship with elements internal to Islamism. In other words, Islamism seeks to differentiate itself from the discourse of Kemalism via the establishment of such a frontier. For these reasons, Islamism cannot be seen simply as an ideology. Its discursive character includes both linguistic and extra-linguistic elements. Islamism as discourse cannot be simply contained within the institutional ensemble of the State. In most of Muslimistan the State has proved impermeable to direct Islamist advances.[7] This failure to capture the State does not, however, imply a failure of political Islam, as Roy and others would suggest. The failure or success of Islamism depends, however, on the criteria that we deploy to make such judgements, and this, of course, depends on what exactly we consider Islamism to be. There is no doubt that Islamists face four main challenges in their capacity to acquire state power.

First, in most Muslim societies a large section of the population remains committed to Westernisation and, for various reasons, Islamists have not been successful in winning over this group. This section of the population believes itself to be secularist, liberal and democratic, and it certainly presents itself in these terms to Western audiences. Despite their much-proclaimed love of liberalism and democracy, however, many of these people have been willing to support the most illiberal and anti-democratic measures taken by state machinery against Islamists.

Second, the current divisions of the Muslim world are sanctioned and manipulated by an international order and enforced by the new concert of mainly European powers based around the leadership of the United States (G8), constituting what Martin Shaw has described as a 'conglomerate global state'.[8] It is this conglomerate global state that is the main defender of the current world order, which includes the current distribution of Muslimistan into rival and often contending nation state blocs. As such, most Islamist groups are forced into making accommodations to the nation state, with the consequence that nationalism begins to penetrate their discourse (for example, the parties in Kuwait, who claim to be Islamist, are unwilling to allow non-Kuwaiti Muslims to become members). This nationalisation of Islamism means that Islamist groups are prone to being isolated, and are often forced into political positions that undermine their Islamist objectives (for example, the way they have to pander to policies of ethnic and cultural homogenisation even when dealing with Muslim minority ethnic groups).

Third, the current global order is dominated by the discourse of capitalism, which privileges the subjectivity of a sovereign consumer. In this way, all values and convictions become matters for individual choice and consumption. Islamists, despite the energy spent on devising 'Islamic economics', have largely failed to counter the discourse of global capital. Their attacks have been based on questions of moral regulation and rectitude rather than transcending the terms of global capitalism.

In this environment Islamism, as an attempt to articulate a political order centred on Islam, has so far been successful only in Iran; other Islamist regimes have only been able to hold on to power for relatively short periods of time, for example in Sudan and Afghanistan. In general, they have found (as many before them) that the power of the modern post-colonial state is formidable and unrelenting. The international discourse of terrorism, articulated by the United States and subsequently used by authoritarian regimes, has become hegemonic to the extent that the category of 'freedom-fighter' has almost disappeared. Moreover, challenge to state authority is considered to be terrorism – this has the effect of de-legitimating any resistance to repressive regimes. Unrepresentative regimes have been very successful in articulating Islamist opposition as terrorism, thus creating the excuse for 'dirty wars' against Islamists. Even Islamists who have tried the electoral route have been forced on the defensive by being branded 'terrorists', thus allowing the ruling elites of Muslimistan to declare them a national security threat – a threat that justifies the State using extra-constitutional means, including violence, to combat it. Currently, the electoral as well as the revolutionary route to an Islamic state seems to have been diverted or blocked by the Westoxicated elites' use of death squads and torture centres.

Given the current strategic difficulties faced by Islamists, it is interesting to note that in many ways most Muslim communities are becoming increasingly 'Islamic'. More and more Muslims are beginning to adhere with greater conviction and regularity to Islamic norms and values. In many ways, this can be seen as the conceptual analogue to the sovereign consumer of free-market fundamentalism, the idea being that once we have a society full of good Muslims then we shall have an Islamic order. Such an approach is locked into a methodological and epistemological position in which the individual is the basic building block of social order. The sovereignty of the individual hollows out the idea of society. The logical conclusion to such a strategy would be Muslims without the *umma*. In other words, this is a world of individual pious Muslims enclosed in their private spheres, where public spaces remain Islam-free zones. In Muslimistan this Islamisation is encouraged as a vaccine against Islamism. The Islamisation from below, however, has heightened the difference between the Westoxicated elite and the Islamised section of society – in this way, even this gradual Islamisation risks eroding the legitimacy of the existing regimes.

The problems that beset Muslimistan are not likely to be solved by a slavish imitation of the Western template. At the same time, there is no reason to assume that the qualities that most people would want in their ideal society cannot be generated from within Islamic cultural formations. Values with universal significance are not the monopoly of the West. The greatest trick the West has played has been to convince the world that only Western culture knows what is good and what is evil, and only by following the lead of the West can other societies partake of universal values. It is time to recognise this trick for what it is. Muslims can have a good life, a good society and good governance without trying to force their history, their traditions and their culture into a pale imitation of the Western historical development. The events that shaped the West (the Renaissance, the Reformation, the Counter-Reformation, the Enlightenment, Modernity) are part of a contingent and political sequence; they are not a necessary or logical development that has to be imposed upon Muslim societies with very different starting points and very different locations within the current world order.

The very condition of the possibility of Islamism is the decentring of the West. Islamism is only possible if the gap between what is universal and what is Western is opened up. Thus it is possible for Muslims to imagine a project of transformation without having to route that project through the western cultural heritage. Islamists believe it possible to think of a better way of life by drawing on the Islamicate resources to articulate a project for the future reconstruction of social relations. This puts into question the notion that only Western cultural resources are useful for building a future for all societies.[9]

The argument that Islamists have been checked in their drive for state power depends on treating the Islamists as narrowly conceived political movements reacting to the conditions found in specific parts of Muslimistan. Such arguments do not take into account that Islamists operate in a global context and their emergence is not simply related to local situations (though it would be foolish to deny that local factors have their part to play in the variety of forms that Islamism has taken). Islamism challenges not just the various Kemalist regimes that hold sway in Muslimistan, it threatens to overturn the current world order, by undermining the principles that legitimise the status quo.

The growth of nineteenth-century nationalism in Europe was a hesitant, complicated and ambiguous process. Nonetheless, the tide of nationalism proved that only those statesman who were willing to accommodate and channel it were able to ensure the survival of their regimes. If Islamism is a similar force, it is unlikely to be checked for long by the use of coercion – even on a global scale – or ill-conceived persuasive measures that remain in denial about its nature. Islamism denotes not any particular organisation or movement but rather it is an expression of Muslim political agency.

Notes

1   Abdulwahab Saleh Babeair (1990) 'Contemporary Islamic Revivalism: A Movement or a Moment?', *Journal of Arab Affairs*, 9 (2) p. 133.

2   Anwar-ul-Haq Ahady (1992) 'The Decline of Islamic Fundamentalism', *Journal of Asian and African Studies*, 27 (3/4) p. 240.
3   Olivier Roy (2006) *Globalized Islam: The Search for a New Ummah* (CERI Series in Comparative Politics and International Studies), New York: Columbia University Press.
4   Carl Schmitt (1996) *The Concept of the Political*, Chicago: University of Chicago Press, and Jacques Derrida (1999) *The Politics of Friendship*, London: Verso.
5   Gramsci's conceptions of social transformation were coloured by the Orientalist division between the West and non-West, and while he was willing to accept the need for 'intellectual-moral' leadership in 'advanced capitalist societies', he did not think such an effort was necessary in the case of 'Asiatic' societies. See Antonio Gramsci (1971) *Selections from Prison Notebooks*, Quinton Hoare and Geoffrey Nowell Smith, (ed. and trans.) London: Lawrence and Wishart. The idea that non-Western societies lacked civil society is, of course, a staple of Orientalist scholarship. Recent historical research does not support the idea that civil society was absent outside the West. See Christopher Alan Bayly (2004) *The Birth of the Modern World, 1780–1914*, Oxford: Blackwell; and Amira El-Azhary Sonbol (2000) *The New Mamluks: Egyptian Society and Modern Feudalism*, Syracuse: Syracuse University Press.
6   This distinction between ideology and discourse is based on Stuart Hall (1992) 'The West and the non-West: discourse and power' in Stuart Hall and Bram Gieben (eds), *The Formation of Modernity*, Cambridge: Polity Press, pp. 291–2.
7   Muslimistan refers to countries in which Muslims predominate demographically and socially.
8   Martin Shaw (2001) *Theory of a Global State*, Cambridge: Cambridge University Press.
9   Islamicate is a term introduced by Marshall Hodgson to refer to social relations that cannot be reduced to Islam but are informed by its venture.

References

Ahady, Anwar-ul-Haq (1992) 'The Decline of Islamic Fundamentalism', *Journal of Asian and African Studies*, 27 (3/4) p. 240.
Babeair, Abdulwahab Saleh (1990) 'Contemporary Islamic Revivalism: A Movement or a Moment?', *Journal of Arab Affairs*, 9 (2) p. 133.
Bayly, Christopher Alan (2004) *The Birth of the Modern World, 1780–1914*, Oxford: Blackwell.
Derrida, Jacques (1999) *The Politics of Friendship*, London: Verso.
Gramsci, Antonio, Quinton Hoare and Geoffrey Nowell Smith (ed. and trans.) (1971) *Selections from Prison Notebooks*, London: Lawrence and Wishart.
Hall, Stuart (1992) 'The West and the non-West: discourse and power' in Stuart Hall and Bram Gieben (eds), *The Formation of Modernity*, Cambridge: Polity Press, pp. 291–2.
Roy, Olivier (2006) *Globalized Islam: The Search for a New Ummah* (CERI Series in Comparative Politics and International Studies), New York: Columbia University Press.
Sayyid, Salman (2003) *A Fundamental Fear*, London: Zed Press.
Schmitt, Carl (1996) *The Concept of the Political*, Chicago: University of Chicago Press.
Shaw, Martin (2001) *Theory of a Global State*, Cambridge: Cambridge University Press.

Sonbol, Amira El-Azhary (2000) *The New Mamluks: Egyptian Society and Modern Feudalism*, Syracuse: Syracuse University Press.

Volpi, Frédéric (2010) *Political Islam observed. Disciplinary Perspectives*, London / New York: Hurst / Columbia University Press.

PART 2

ISLAMIC MOVEMENTS IN EUROPE

INTRODUCTION

Frank Peter

It is a peculiar feature of debates about Islam in Europe – and this certainly applies to debates about 'radical' Islam – that they conastantly refer to a reality which is not immediately perceptible. In other words, these debates are largely are about what Muslims 'really' mean when, for example, they affirm their commitment to European societies. They are about what Muslims do not say publicly but firmly believe. Debates are triggered by threats to national security which have not yet materialised, but whose symptoms can supposedly be identified. And these debates set out to establish how those Muslims who do not have a public voice – the so-called silent majority – go about living their lives. It is this wish to go beyond 'mere appearances' and to identify who Muslims truly are that fuels current attempts to map Europe's Muslim communities, to construct social profiles of Muslims, to measure their religious practice and to classify their modes of religiosity.

A central part of this mapping consists of identifying groups inside Europe's Muslim communities and establishing links between European Muslim actors on the one hand and Islamic movements in Africa and Asia on the other. In some cases, these links are evident and uncontroversial. Sections of Hizb ut-Tahrir in Europe consider themselves part of a global movement whose message is intended to transcend any geographical divisions and create a global caliphate. In the case of other groups, however, it is far more difficult to ascertain what exactly connects them to Islamic movements in Asia and Africa and in what ways they converge or diverge. European Muslims grouped here under the category 'Salafis', for example, are regularly identified with Saudi Arabia and the Wahhabiya. The following studies demonstrate not only the internal diversity of these groups, but also how – notwithstanding close ties to Saudi Arabia – they are deeply embedded in Europe. Other Muslim groups emphasise that their historical links and current contacts with Islamic movements outside Europe do not indicate any kind of institutional affiliation and that they are independent in their activities. Such claims – regularly made, for example, by those European Muslim organisations usually seen as belonging to the Muslim Brotherhood (MB) – are heavily contested by various state security services, think-tanks, journalists and writers. Indeed, the latter have undertaken many attempts to establish the 'real' identity of European Muslim actors.

These attempts are flawed, partly because it is not clear what exactly follows from the claim that a European Muslim group 'belongs' to a given Islamic movement. As the preceding chapters showed, these groups have espoused different programmes and ideas, depending on when and where they are active, and it is not always possible to ascribe a uniform outlook to their members. Consequently, the benefit that might be derived from thinking in terms of categories such as 'Muslim Brotherhood', 'Milli Görüş', and so forth is not as evident as is usually presumed. There are different ways of being a 'Muslim Brother' in the Middle East, and this fact should be taken into account when debating whether there are 'Muslim Brothers' in Europe. Likewise, the fact that a given European Muslim group counts among its references writers or scholars from certain Islamic movements can indicate different things to the observer about the beliefs of these European Muslims. It does not offer an analytical shortcut for identifying what they are really up to. How these references are used by Muslims in Europe needs to be investigated, rather than taken as a sign of identical views between European Muslims and Islamic movements elsewhere.

The following studies are inscribed into a different perspective. Instead of asking whether a given European Muslim group conforms to reified notions of Islamism, they start out by recognising that the groups examined here function within specific European contexts. Their aims and activities necessarily differ to some degree from related groups in Islamic countries. The task is to find out how they differ, and hence how we can conceptualise these national contexts in Europe and what distinguishes them from Muslim countries. These questions are answered in different ways below. Some authors examine the activities and development of these Muslim groups primarily in relation to the changing social makeup of Muslim communities and the religious needs of Muslims. In this respect, as many studies have previously pointed out, intergenerational change – that is, the rise of European-born Muslim generations beginning in the 1980s – is of great importance. Most notably, it has initiated various processes of reforming and restoring the authentic Islamic message. The coming-of-age of European-born Muslims is a central factor underlying the spread of Salafi groups, whose distinctive trait is their claim to follow the message in complete conformity with the practice of the first three Muslim generations. In partial opposition to this trend, intergenerational change has also initiated processes of reform, which link a return to the foundational scriptures to the idea of 'contextualising' Islam and engaging with society. These European discourses about the contextualisation of Islam often draw heavily on notions concerning the adaptability of Islam, re-elaborated since the nineteenth century by Muslim reformist thinkers in the Middle East, and by later writers associated with Islamic movements. In the current European context, these ideas partly serve a new purpose. Whereas in earlier times adaptability related to efforts to ensure the relevance of Islamic traditions in the present-day world by returning to the authentic revelation, the adaptation European Muslims have in mind is framed primarily in geographical terms, that is, by a distinct European space. The partial reconfiguration of Islamist thought thus triggered should encourage us to think carefully about citational practices by European Muslims and the conclusions we can draw from them.

In contrast to this perspective, which emphasises the relevance of doctrinal orientations and divisions between Muslim groups to understanding why they are more or less successful in assembling believers, other studies highlight the relative fluidity of these boundaries. How and why the 'common believer' relates to supposedly radical Muslim associations whose services he uses in one way or the other is a real question. For one thing, believers may simply ignore or willfully transcend doctrinal lines of separation. In fact, talking about doctrinal lines of separation presupposes a relatively high degree of structuration in European Islam. Some of the studies assembled here suggest that it is well worth questioning the extent of that structuration. More importantly, perhaps, when thinking about doctrinal orientations, it should be borne in mind that the activities of the groups studied here are, to a large degree, geared to satisfying very basic demands that Muslims have. Public debates about the construction of a small number of mosques with minarets, and anxieties about wealthy Islamic foundations financing European Muslim groups, easily make us forget that building Muslim community structures in Europe is a slow process. Muslim groups in Europe are mostly occupied with the provision of places for prayer, basic religious instruction and activities for young people and women. With this in mind, we need to ask how their work is shaped by an environment in which Islam is still very weakly institutionalised, rather than simply examining these groups in light of historical links to Islamic movements. Is it more pertinent to regard them as Islamist or as minority groups functioning in a (post-)migration context?

The studies also demonstrate what a huge impact the legal frameworks of European nation states exert on the functioning of these Muslim actors. The work of religious associations is conditioned by numerous legal provisions which determine the form Muslim organisations can take, the fields of activity open to religious actors (and those from which they are excluded), and also the kind of direct or indirect public funding they can tap for some of their activities. In particular, the studies on imams, chaplains and Islamic educational actors underline the significant effects produced by multiple interrelations, between Muslim institutions on the one hand, and the legal frameworks and political processes of the nation state on the other. Most of the organisations studied here consider that the legal provisions concerning religion are sufficient for Muslim needs and perfectly applicable to Islam. However, they have often criticised, together with other civil society actors, their discriminatory application to Islam. Especially since the new counter-terrorism measures were devised after 2001, a broad range of activities by Muslims has been targeted by various types of surveillance and state policies. These policies are not simply exclusionist. Looking back at the 1990s, European nations actually seem, at least in some respects, more willing to accept Islam as a durable part of Europe than before. However, this partial transformation has been accompanied by an increased willingness to adopt interventionist policies in the management of Islam and to shape the kind of Islam which is being institutionalised. The most visible example of this trend is, perhaps, the attempt by several European states to create Muslim councils which are both 'representative' and staffed by 'moderate' Muslims. These acts of discrimination, some of which are analysed more closely in the following section of this book, are a crucial factor propelling Muslim organisations in the public sphere and resetting their agenda. Many of the groups discussed here devote a considerable amount of their resources to the struggle for recognition of their equal rights as adherents of one religion among others. Whether it be in the field of educational policies, the labour market, the construction of mosques or the representation of Islam, the need to fight for equality and for rights, which these groups see as essential, has largely determined what kind of activities they undertake in public. This simple observation has important consequences for how we approach these Muslim organisations. Instead of trying to identify the 'real' aims of these groups with reference to the Islamic organisations they branched off from, it seems more profitable in light of this observation to examine how their agenda is shaped by the need to confront the very tangible problems of discrimination in Europe.

What is at stake here, as elsewhere in debates about European Islam, is how we understand the structures of power within which these groups function. Claims that 'radical' Islam poses a threat in Europe dismiss the fact that Muslims are largely marginalised. It is frequently assumed that Muslim organisations can choose what they say at will, independently of what they do. The basic assumption here is that saying and doing or, for that matter, saying and being, are two unrelated things, and that one can decide at will which discourse to articulate. The studies assembled here offer evidence to the contrary. They show how the discourses of these organisations constrain them in their activities and how the pledges they make do indeed shape their work and are put into practice. Indeed, it is difficult to ignore the important interconnections between discourses, practices and identities inside these groups. The related argument made by those who make such claims about the Islamic threat consists in maintaining that these groups systematically practice 'double talk'. The claim is that, while they purport to accept the secular frameworks of European nation states, their activities are partially at odds with these orders and indeed sometimes designed to subvert them. This frequent argument obviously has a highly negative impact on the ability of Muslims to enter into public debates and make themselves heard. This argument and the impact it produces depend upon a problematic presupposition. The anxiety which the thesis of double talk by Muslims provokes is based on the assumption that they have (or can muster) the resources which would allow them to pursue such a strategy of subversion or infiltration of state structures, and with reasonable chances of success. As the following studies show, there is no evidence for these assumptions. Their plausibility does not reside in evidence. Rather, to understand them we must refer back to those who hold these views. This topic will be examined in the final section of the book.

(1) THE EUROPEAN LINEAGE OF THE MUSLIM BROTHERS

THE INTERNATIONAL ORGANISATION OF THE MUSLIM BROTHERHOOD

Hossam Tamam

The Muslim Brotherhood (MB) has been undergoing very important changes since its creation in the 1920s. Probably one of the most important of these has been the establishment of what can be called the International Organization of the Muslim Brotherhood (IOMB, al-Tandhim al-Duwali li-l-Ikhwan al-Muslimun). The mother organisation, which was born in Egypt in 1928, witnessed a growth which covered the majority of Arab and Islamic countries. It even spread to Europe where several branches of the MB were established. So the IOMB in this sense was an international manifestation of a movement of coordination and reconciliation, the objective of which had been the union of all the branch organisations of the MB at the beginning of the 1980s. The goal of this union was to become a type of international group whose members shared the common objective of the creation of an Islamic state. However, an examination of historical developments shows how the International Movement would end up falling apart.

Historical Context of Its Birth

The creation of the IOMB was officially announced on 29 July 1982. However, the historical context shows us that the ideology behind the movement was born with the rise of the movement itself in 1928. Despite the fact the founder of the movement, Hasan al-Banna (1906–49), had registered the group as a charity association in 1928 (Muslim Brothers Charity Association), he saw in it the seed with which the Islamic Caliphate, the symbol of political unity of the Islamic *umma* that had fallen just four years before in 1924, could be recovered.

Sheykh al-Banna would maintain contact with important Islamic celebrities throughout the world such as Abdulkarim al-Khattabi and Allal al-Fasi in Morocco; Emir Idris later to become King of Libya; Kuhy al-Din al-Qulaybi in Tunisia; Prince Shakib Arslan in Syria; and Navab Sarafi, founder of the Fada'iyan-e Islam movement, and the al-Nadawi family in India. He would also direct the mobilising efforts of the movement towards Arab and Muslim students who were studying at the Azhar University. Some of these very same students would later become the seed of the branch organisations of the MB in their home countries such as Syria, Sudan, Iraq, Kuwait, Yemen and Afghanistan. To implement this strategy the group would set up a communications division with the Islamic world which in itself should be considered an initial phase in the march towards the construction of the IOMB.

The biggest strike against the MB during its struggle with the revolutionary regime of July 1952 was the decisive turn which would quickly take it away from the path towards international expansion and the establishment of regional organisations. This would come after many of the group leaders such as Kamal al-Sharif and Sa'id Ramadan left the country in order to escape arrest. They fled to the Gulf countries where the branch organisations were receiving support and there they created a strong network of relations and communications which expanded even more thanks to the group's activities. By the same token, they founded many associations and companies, as well as social, cultural and religious institutions, which would constitute a foundation upon which the International Organization would later be established.

The Islamic Center of Geneva, Switzerland, founded by Sa'id Ramadan[1] was the most important base for the MB in Europe. It was from here that a whole network of centres and other MB institutions would be erected, such as the Islamic Centre of London and the Islamic Center of Munich, Germany, which was witness to the final phases of the official birth of the International Organization in 1982. The birth of the IOMB can be considered a natural development within the general growth of the MB as well as its expansion in and outside the Islamic world.

The Dynamics of the Protagonists

The role of Mustafa Mashhur, known for his excellent organisational abilities, was essential in the establishment of the International Movement. He became active when he left prison in 1973, with the collaboration of a number of the most important leaders of the Special Regime[2], through the unification of the MB organisations worldwide, especially in the Arab countries. Mashhur's liberation from arrest in Egypt at the end of Anwar Sadat's rule in 1981 contributed to his dedication to achieving the necessary conditions for the official announcement of the establishment of the IOMB. This announcement took place while he was in Germany, on 29 July 1982, which was the date when the statute of 'The General Regime of the Muslim Brotherhood' was passed. In this statute, the conditions of membership in the IOMB were specified. It also administered relations between the different regional organisations throughout the Arab world and Europe, and the mother group in Egypt, which was responsible for the coordination of all the groups.

Mustafa Mashhur was the real founder of the IOMB and one of the hardliners who had a dominating position deep within the organisation, as well as in its ideological tendencies, before becoming head of the MB officially in 1996. While the ideological guide number three, 'Umar al-Tilmisani, who died in 1986, and the ideological guide number four, Muhammad Hamid Abu al-Nasr, who died in 1996, were more worried about Egypt and its versatile and volatile political issues, Mashhur dedicated his efforts to the construction of the IOMB inside and outside of the country. Hence, he was the most outstanding figure in its foundation and administration, with continuing Egyptian support which underpinned a period of ripeness and expansion of the organization. In 1983 the Union of Islamic Organizations in France was established, later changing its name, in 1989, to the Union of Islamic Organizations of France. The founder of the union and its first president was the Egyptian Ahmad Nasha who was continuing his higher studies in architecture at French universities. He was also the son-in-law of Mashhur.

When Mustafa Mashhur, who died in 2002, became General Guide of the group in 1996, the circumstances occasionally changed his tendency towards the continuation of the building of the international organisation, governed by a central administration, the headquarters of which was to be located in Egypt. As a result, the historical leadership of the group in Egypt quickly became concerned with what was happening on a national and local level. This concern was materialised through a wide and growing participation in local and legislative elections, as well as paying close attention to internal issues along with demands for the establishment of a political party, which would sometimes turn into a call for the transformation of the organisation into a political party.

By the same token, there was a rise in the influence of the second man in charge of the group, Ma'mun al-Hudaybi which, practically speaking, converted the organisation into a national political party in its discourse and practice. Ma'mun al-Hudaybi was most influential during his term as vice-president, under Mashhur, and as official spokesman of the group. He began to marginalise members of the MB outside of Egypt, reserving the right of leadership for Egyptians only and rejecting any non-Egyptian role in determining its path and tendencies. When al-Hudaybi passed away in 2004, having served as leader of the group from 2002, the IOMB had been following the path he had designed for it. With his passing the path would change direction, with the IOMB becoming a coordinating umbrella of the other national organisations. These national organisations were more like national groups and parties, gradually diminishing the international character of the group and becoming more independent from the central administration, while relying ever more on local initiatives.

This transformation came about during the term of the sixth guide, Mahdi 'Akif, who had completely immersed himself in local Egyptian affairs, becoming more of a leader of a political party than the guide of an international organisation. This despite the fact that he had been one of the most important historical leaders involved in its foundation. He was leading the administration of the IOMB in Munich when its statute was announced at the beginning of the 1980s. 'Akif acknowledged these transformations, which reduced the centralised leadership of the IOMB in exchange for greater reliance on regional leaders – who were individually prepared for their roles, as members of the IOMB – in Egypt. This process confirmed the independence of each regional organisation of the MB and authorised them to make their own decisions.

Internal and External Debate

The combination of regional and international circumstances, along with internal factors in the MB's regional organisations, and ideological and political developments within the mother organisation in Egypt, have clearly indicated the waning influence of the IOMB. These indicators also suggest the growing possibility that it may cease to exist, or remain in stasis at best.

The discourse of the MB, which calls for the establishment of the Islamic state, enjoyed a presence, and effective influence, in the Arab and Islamic world during the 1980s. The regional offices of the MB in more than one country were successful in many areas. Their participation under the banner of the establishment of the Islamic state, in itself a path towards the recovery of the 'lost' Islamic Caliphate, represented the unifying framework and motor behind the construction and strengthening of the IOMB which, at the same time, united all the regional divisions. This situation began to undergo a fundamental change at the beginning of the 1990s, due to regional and international factors which affected the MB both ideologically and administratively.

The Iraqi invasion of Kuwait and the ensuing war of liberation conducted by the international coalition, under the leadership of the United States, led to the first and most important schism in the IOMB. MB organisations in the Gulf countries manifested their solidarity with the Muslim Brotherhood of Kuwait, who had withdrawn in protest at what they considered to be a pro-Iraq bias after the leadership of the Muslim Brotherhood in Egypt, as well as other countries, rejected the presence of foreign forces. The Gulf War would hit the ideological roots of the IOMB, and priority would be given to the nation at the expense of the *umma*. The movement withdrew into regional organisations of the MB as opposed to the vision of a united Islamic world or *umma*, which had previously been the foundation upon which the group and IOMB were erected.

With the attacks of 9/11, the dynamic transforming the MB from an internationally styled organisation to a number of national ones was hastened. The MB organisations have remained withdrawn within the borders of the countries they work in, paying little attention to maintaining international ties. This is due to their desire to avoid burdens and costs, both on a political as well as a security level, especially after the expansion of the international War on Terror led by the United States. This position has been reinforced after the MB's Bank of Taqwa was included on the list of institutions which support terrorism, and the subsequent legal persecutions carried out against its founder, Yusuf Nada.

Confrontations between governing regimes and the MB have been on the rise in a number of countries, especially Egypt, Saudi Arabia and Yemen. The IOMB was infiltrated in other countries, such as Oman, after intelligence services there discovered members of a 'secret' organisation of the MB right after the arrival of its representatives at an IOMB meeting, some of whom were arrested. There has also been a reduction of the central organisation's binding authority over the regional ones. This is illustrated by the candidature of Mahfoud Nahnah in the presidential elections of the organisation in Algeria, despite the disapproval of the IOMB. Another example was when the Iraqi Islamic Party participated in the transitory governing council, under the supervision of American occupation in 2004, despite the rejection of the majority of the other MB organisations, particularly the Muslim Brotherhood of Jordan. Finally, the Muslim Brotherhood of Syria joined an opposition coalition supported by the United States to remove the governing Ba'athist regime.

The changes which have befallen the mother group in Egypt are considered to have affected most of all the Egyptian ideology of the IOMB, upon which basis the latter was founded and supported by the Egyptian leadership. From the beginning of the 1990s the authority of the Egyptian sector, and consequently its influence, began to diminish, both in the local Egyptian political equation and internationally. Since then, the group has plunged into a confrontation with the governing regime, which has led to its political encirclement, along with its diminishing popularity; especially after the campaign of arrests and military tribunals, which reached into the governing elite of the group. This has included the end of its presence in the labour unions, as well as the siege of its social and economic associations and institutions. Add to this the continuous growth of the regional organisations of the MB, which have been successful politically and electorally in Jordan, Yemen and Kuwait. The strength of the MB in the Gulf countries generally has increased thanks to the peculiar economic circumstances of the region. Freedoms in the 1990s have helped strengthen the presence and influence of the MB of Europe and America with regard to the organisation as a whole, elevating ideological and legal figures of non-Egyptian background, such as the Tunisian Rashid al-Ghannushi; the Sudanese Hasan al-Turabi; and the Lebanese Fathi Yakan. This has been to the detriment of previous ideological authorities like Sayyid Qutb, who was considered a reference for jihadist ideologies. This has diminished Egyptian influence on the MB internationally, depriving the mother group of the legitimacy of its leaders, whether it be in the field or from a legal-historical perspective. The legal and historical dimension was diminished by the passing on of the historical leadership, such as Ahmed al-Malat, Nafis Hamdi, Abbas al-Sisi and others, who were contemporaries of the founder of the group and played such an important role in the construction of the IOMB.

Egyptian influence in the IOMB had shrunk to the point where the leadership, which had historically been Egyptian, became the object of debate and even the target of objections by some of the regional organisations. In 1996, the MB outside Egypt protested against Ma'mun al-Hudaybi, because of the way Mustafa Mashhur was chosen during the burial of his predecessor Abu al-Nasr (the swearing of allegiance in the cemetery). It was here that the control of the IOMB by the Egyptians was evident. This protest was successful in imposing the election of the Syrian, Hasan Huweidi, resident in Jordan, as the second vice-president to the Guide (along with the first vice-president, al-Hudaybi). And just before the attacks of 9/11, there was a secret conversation between some of the leaders outside of Egypt concerning the possibility of presenting a non-Egyptian candidate to the position of Guide. One of the names which was discussed was the Lebanese, Faisal Mawlawi.

Developments from within the regional organisations of the MB indicate that the movement has switched from being an international organisation to completely submerging itself into national affairs. It has become governed by regional realities and condemned to pay its dues. The movement is aware of this transformation, even though it has not directly acknowledged it. The clearest indication of this transformation, and its strength, is not what happened to the MB in Egypt, nor the founders of the IOMB, or even those who transformed it into a completely national organisation, whose international role is limited to the general discourse of the need for Muslim unity, emphasising, however, the priority of internal reform and independence of the regional organisations.

The MB's ideology, with respect to the political unity of Islam through the recovery of the Islamic Caliphate, theoretically has not changed. No formal statement of disavowal of the IOMB's ideology has been issued, nor do we expect it to be. Reality stipulates, however, that the IOMB has lost its purpose and is no longer effective in the creation of policies for the smaller regional ones. It is not even capable of defining its major options or tendencies.

The format suggested by the Egyptian leader Abdulmunem Abu al-Fattuh seems to be the most appropriate and pragmatic for the future of the organisation, as it poses the idea of transforming the organisation into an intellectual or political forum far away from its organisational and secretive nature. He is following the pattern of groups such as the Arab National Conference, which has annexed national movements and parties, or the International Socialist Forum, which has united left-wing organisations and parties.

Notes

1 Sa'id Ramadan was able to build a strong relationship with the governing regime in Saudi Arabia where he participated in the establishment of the Organization of the Islamic Conference of the 1960s. After leaving for Switzerland and becoming a Swiss national he founded the Islamic Center of Geneva, from which the Muslim Brothers' ideology was spread throughout Europe. It is worth observing that Sa'id Ramadan is the son-in-law of Sheykh Hasan al-Banna, founder of the group, as well as father of the well known intellectual Tariq Ramadan who was born in Switzerland.

2 The Special Regime was a secret organisation, quasi-military in nature, which had conducted many assassination operations against the British occupation. It was later

involved in the internal political struggles, the most important of which was the assassination of the Egyptian Prime Minister, Fahmi al-Nagrashi. It would later be dissolved after the revolution.

References

Tamam, Hossam (2008) *The Egyptian Regime and the Brotherhood: Policies of Total Confrontation.* (in Arabic) March. http://www.islamonline.net/servlet/Satellite?c= ArticleA_C&cid=1203758450961&pagename=Zone-Arabic-News/NWALayout (link no longer accessible)

THE MUSLIM BROTHERHOOD IN SPAIN

Elena Arigita and Rafael Ortega

The Muslim Brotherhood's (MB) presence in Spain is determined by the internal dynamics of this transnational organisation, the experience it brings from its countries of origin, particularly Syria, and by the specific national context of Spain. In the beginning, its capacity to act was highly irregular and the organisation had become practically invisible by the 1990s. However, the dominant image of the MB in the media and in scientific literature in Spain is as an organisation associated with radicalisation and terrorism, as the source of and breeding ground for violent extremism and various terrorist acts. Not only is the MB in no way responsible for these acts, but also the organisation's integration into democratic politics in the Arab countries is ignored.

The presence in Spain of active members and supporters of the MB dates back to the late 1960s. At that time, Spain's cultural policy towards the Arab world offered young people from different Middle Eastern countries the opportunity to study at Spanish universities. Moreover, the escalation of repression and violence in Syria forced many militants and supporters of the local branch of the MB into exile, seeking shelter as refugees in different European countries, including Spain. The MB was established in Spain during the period spanning the end of the Franco regime, characterised by the awakening of civil rights activism and its subsequent political transition to democracy. These circumstances, which fostered the consolidation of religious freedom, also influenced an incipient Muslim community which, albeit irrelevant statistically speaking and in terms of social visibility, had the symbolic force to challenge the monolithic image that National Catholicism had imposed on Spanish identity under the Franco regime. Therefore, Muslim associationism during that period must be examined within this context of Spanish society, largely marked by the struggle for the acquisition of civil rights.

The Law of Associations of 24 December 1964 and the Law on Religious Freedom of 28 June 1967 paved the way for the creation of the first Muslim associations, among them the Centro Islámico de Granada (Islamic Centre of Granada), set up in 1966 in Granada by students, mainly Syrians, Jordanians and Palestinians.

During that early period, discussions of the Syrian situation caused a conflict, and divisions similar to those that took place in the Syrian movement in the 1970s between, on the one hand, followers of the branch of 'Isam al- 'Attar (General Supervisor of the MB of Syria between 1961 and 1980), who had gone into exile in 1964, settling in Germany in 1968 and who supported political participation, and on the other the more radical Abdelfattah Abu Gudda. Thus, in 1971, al- 'Attar's followers in Spain founded the Islamic Association of Spain in Madrid, breaking off from the Islamic Centre of Granada. This association revised its statutes in 1974 in order to be able to create centres and mosques. The first mosque to be built was the Abu Bakr mosque in Madrid. Work on the mosque was financed with donations from its members as well as external aid, mainly from Saudi Arabia, but it was not completed until 1988. The association gradually consolidated its position and spread to different cities. Both the Islamic Centre of Granada and the Islamic Association of Spain operated as meeting places for young militants and sympathisers more or less committed to the MB, where they used to discuss the future of the group, the documents published by the group in other countries, and their own situation in Spain.

The events and divisions within the organisation in Syria (al-'Attar abandoned the leadership at the Amman congress in 1980), the uprising of the armed group al-Tala'i' al-Muqatila (Fighting Vanguards) – which raised tension with the Syrian regime in a spiral of violence, culminating in the Hama massacre in 1982 – leadership struggles, and the ambiguous discourse of leaders on the acceptance or rejection of al-Tala'i' al-Nuqatila's strategy, prompted the dispersion of its members in the 1990s and a gradual break away from Syria, with the formation of a specifically Spanish project. Of course, this process of 'nationalisation' in Spain was not free of tension. One example of these internal disputes was the attempt to end the authority enjoyed by the Abu Bakr mosque since the 1970s, by young members of the MB of Syria who arrived in the 1980s, and who did not recognise this authority and possessed a more radical discourse. This new generation also included young radical and violent representatives, notably Mustafa Setmariam Nasar (Abu Musab al-Suri). Setmariam was initially a member of the MB in Syria until 1983 and later became an activist in Tala'i' al-Nuqatila. He spent a long period travelling, including an attempt to settle in Spain (1985–7 and 1991–4). He established links with the Armed Islamic Group of Algeria (as Editor in London of the bi-monthly magazine *al-Ansar*), joined the administration of the Taliban regime in Afghanistan, and was an iconic figure of the global *jihad* until his arrest in 2005 in the Pakistani city of Quetta.

The leader of that first stage of establishment and organisation of the MB of Spain was the Syrian Nizar Ahmad al-Sabbagh. A native of Homs, al-Sabbagh came to Spain in the late 1960s as a student, and began to develop his activism among both the Arab population and the young population of Spanish converts to Islam. The latter considered him the perfect mediator for obtaining financial aid that the Muslim World League and the World Assembly of Muslim Youth were seeking to make available to, in particular, Spanish converts to Islam, at a time when the MB was the only organisation capable of managing these resources. Consequently, al-Sabbagh is still an important reference among the eldest generation of Muslim leadership in Spain.

As acknowledged by Abdallah al-'Aqil, former Deputy Secretary General of the Muslim World League,[1] al-Sabbagh was considered a charismatic leader around whom an organisation could be built similar to those in other countries such as Germany, Switzerland or the United Kingdom. At the same time, and largely due to the work of al-Sabbagh, during the 1970s Spain became a good place for the MB to hold meetings, under the umbrella of the Islamic Centre of Granada and the Islamic Association of Spain in Madrid, with the participation of distinguished preachers and converts who presented their ideas, and discussed ways in which Islamic activism should develop in the West, and specifically in Spain where this activism was still in its early stage. Emphasis was placed on considering the particularity of the Western context when thinking about mechanisms required for the proper development of activism (e.g., sermons appropriate to the specific social contexts, new ways of inviting individuals to Islam, proper Islamic conduct, etc.) and the dissemination of translations into Spanish of reference works on Islam. Al-Sabbagh worked tirelessly, organising meetings, promoting Islamic culture in numerous articles and books published in Spain (on polygamy, prayer, pilgrimage, *hadith*, marriage, divorce, etc.) and other classical works on Islamism (such as *The Political Theory of Islam* by Abu l-A'la Mawdudi) through the publishing company La Casa Islámica, based in Granada.

A network of MB associations thus developed, but before it could fully form it was already in decline by the end of the 1980s. One particular event and one trend determined the MB's evolution in Spain and undermined its relevance when compared with the position of equivalent organisations in other European countries. The event in question was the assassination, on 21 November 1981 in Barcelona, of Nizar al-Sabbagh through circumstances that remain unknown. That incident arguably halted the consolidation of the leadership and associationism of the MB in Spain and was followed by another period of fragmentation within the structure of the associations linked to the MB.

The trend, which is important for understanding the MB's failure to consolidate its presence in Spain, was due to the actual evolution of Muslim associational life. The dialogue initiated with the Islamic Community of Spain by the Spanish government to reach a Cooperation Agreement, which was eventually signed in 1992 and which provided the Muslim community with rights and institutional representation, led many associations to focus on this new institutional visibility, which guaranteed stability, rights and an associative structure. They also began to integrate greater ethnic and ideological diversity in response to the growing presence of Muslim immigrants, especially from North African countries. Institutional developments and the immigration-fuelled sociological evolution of the Muslim community are the main reasons for this, together with the fact that the organisation was left leaderless, which had prompted the associations initially linked to the MB to gradually, and relatively effortlessly, distance themselves from its directives.

Attention attracted by the activities of certain individuals such as Setmariam, internal divisions and differences regarding the direction and leadership of the MB in Spain after al-Sabbagh's death, coupled with the propaganda of the Arab regimes demonising the MB, are elements that have prompted the organisation to be linked to, or suspected of, all types of violent incidents.

However, since the 1990s the MB's presence has been very limited, even though it continues to be an intellectual and moral reference that inspires many. Since its beginnings as an incipient association in the 1970s, it has now become a discreet, highly individualised entity, with little or no importance at an institutional level. The old members and supporters of the MB have gone separate ways and gradually distanced themselves from the MB's structure. This is the result of the evolution of both individual members and the organisation's associative structure over almost four decades, as well as its adaptation to the national context of Spain. The process that culminated in the 1992 agreement prompted the transformation of the Islamic Association into a purely Spanish structure, reconverted into an umbrella federation called the Union of Islamic Communities of Spain – now completely separate from the MB. This federation focused all its energy on the new task of managing resources, acting as an intermediary with the government and attracting new Muslim immigrants to vindicate its position as an official representative body of Muslims in Spain. Although its leaders maintain contacts with organisations that have evolved in a similar way in other European countries, the MB's influence is now essentially intellectual and very different from that exerted by the organisation during its first stage of direct involvement in the Syrian structure.

Notes

1   See Abdallah al-'Aqil (2000) *Min a'lam al-haraka al-islamiyya*, Cairo: Dar al-Tawzi' wa-l-Nashr al-Islamiyya, pp.27–8.

References

Al-'Aqil, Abdallah (2000) *Min a'lam al-haraka al-islamiyya*, Cairo: Dar al-Tawzi' wa-l-Nashr al-Islamiyya.

Darif, Muhammad (1999) *Al-Islamiyyun al-Maghariba*, Casablanca: Al-Majalla al-Maghribiyya li-'Ilm al-Ijtima' i al-Siyasi.

Lia, Brynjar (2008) *Architect of Global Jihad: the life of Al-Qaeda Strategist Abu Mus'ab al-Suri*, London / New York: Hurst / Columbia University Press.

Marechal, Brigitte (2008) *The Muslim Brothers in Europe: Roots and Discourse*, Leiden / Boston: Brill.

Maududi, Abul Ala (1969) *The Political Theory of Islam*, Kazi Publications Inc.

Meijer, Roel and Bakker, Edwin (eds) (2012) *The Muslim Brotherhood in Europe*, London / New York: Hurst / Columbia University Press.

GERMANY: ISLAMISCHE GEMEINSCHAFT IN DEUTSCHLAND AND ISLAMISCHE ZENTREN

Melanie Kamp and Jörn Thielmann

The Islamische Gemeinschaft in Deutschland (IGD, Islamic Community in Germany) is an organisation of Muslims of mainly Arab origin. Its establishment is closely connected with the foundation of the Islamisches Zentrum München (IZM). Some observers, including security agencies, journalists and researchers regard the IGD, together with the Islamic centres in Munich (IZM) and Aachen (IZA) and a number of related associations, as part of the international network of the Muslim Brotherhood (MB), which is classified as an Islamist organisation with anti-constitutional aims and ideology. This perception is based primarily on the fact that prominent representatives of the Egyptian and Syrian branches of the MB had been involved in the creation of these associations in the late 1950s and early 1960s. In addition, the IGD is a founding member of the Federation of Islamic Organisations in Europe (FIOE), of which, among others, the European Council for Fatwa and Research (ECFR) is a specialised institution. In all of them, some alleged members of the MB are involved. A further argument for the security agencies' observation of the IGD and the Islamic centres is that their activities to strengthen the Muslim identity of their adherents may contribute to the establishment of parallel societies and may initiate radicalisation processes. Due to the security reports, Islamic associations that are affiliated to or cooperate with the IGD and the Islamic centres occasionally get excluded from publicly funded social integration projects and encounter difficulties in realising their projects. Besides, the reports and public pressure make an open debate about their actual relation to the MB, their understanding of Islam and their position to the non-Muslim majority society difficult.

The IGD developed from a local mosque-building initiative in Munich and extended its influence gradually throughout Germany. The IZM was built in the late 1960s and inaugurated in 1973. The mosque, with an adjacent student hostel, was the sixth purpose-built mosque in Germany at the time. Initiated by the organisation of former Muslim members of the German army during World War II (mainly from the Balkans, the Caucasus and Central Asia), the Geistliche Verwaltung der Muslimflüchtlinge in der Bundesrepublik Deutschland – Musulman Mültecilerin Dini İdaresi – e.V. (founded 1958 in Munich and supported since 1971 by the Federal Government) the initiative was soon joined by Arab students in Munich. On 9 March 1960, a Moscheebau-Kommission e.V. (Mosque Construction Committee) was established to build a mosque, an Islamic cultural centre, a student hostel and a children's home. The Arab students brought into the committee, as president, Dr Saʿid Ramadan (d. 1995), the son-in-law of Hasan al-Banna, founder of the Egyptian Muslim Brotherhood and father of Tariq Ramadan. At that time living in Geneva, Ramadan acted as the secretary general of the Islamic General Congress of Jerusalem and was co-founder of the Muslim World League. Vice-president of the committee was Nurredin Nakibhodscha Namangani, an Uzbek imam, former imam of an SS division in World War II and president of the Geistliche Verwaltung. The Muslim refugees soon clashed with the Arab students on alleged political plans and connections with the MB, as well as with Sa'id Ramadan, and left the committee altogether in March 1962. In February 1962, the committee had been renamed as Islamische Gemeinschaft in Süddeutschland e.V. (Islamic Community in South Germany) and Said Ramadan remained its president until 1968. In 1982 the organisation's name was changed to Islamische Gemeinschaft in Deutschland e.V (Islamic Community in Germany). Until 2003 the IGD bought property, founded 12 Islamic centres in different German cities and established close cooperation with more than 50 other mosque communities. When, in 1999, the IGD lost its status as a charitable organisation due to fiscal irregularities, former branches of the IGD formally split from the IGD in order to apply for charitable status as independent Islamic centres. This way the IGD appears now to be more like a loose network of Islamic associations than a strict hierarchical organisation. When Ibrahim El-Zayat was appointed as president of the IGD in 2002, the headquarters of the IGD moved from the IZM to Cologne. Since 2008 the IZM has been formally independent from the IGD.

From the 1970s to 1990s the IZM became one of the most important centres of Islam in Europe, with numerous activities. Education was and is important: the IZM has initiated several student and youth associations. It also established a Muslim kindergarten (in 1974) and a German–Islamic Primary School (in 1981). Both were closed by the German administration in September 2005, on the basis of the assumption that the association running the school since 2003, the Deutsch-Islamisches Bildungswerk e.V. (DIBW, German–Islamic Educational Service), was a disguise for the IGD, which had been running the school before losing its charitable status in 1999. This fact was hidden from the school authorities until 2003 for fear of losing public refinancing and, therefore, closure. The IZM has also been a recognised organisation for Civil Service since 1986 as the first Muslim organisation. This recognition, however, was revoked some years ago by the Federal Office for Civil Service. It used to run a bookshop (now transferred to Cologne), published the quarterly *Al-Islam* between 1978 and 2005 (founded in 1958; it reappeared for a short time online), and still publishes the *Schriftenreihe des Islamischen Zentrums München*, a series covering various aspects of Muslim life. Discussion circles for men and women, also German-speaking ones, meet on a regular basis. Arabic lessons take place, as well as seminars on religious issues. The IZM was a forerunner of 'open mosque' activities, starting in May 1986, serving from the outset as a meeting and conference centre for European Muslims, and was visited by important personalities from the Muslim world. However, due to the emergence of a differentiated Islamic field throughout Germany as well as in Munich, the 'Arabisation' of the IZM in recent years and the continuing harassments by security agencies, the activities seem to be a somewhat in decline.

Due to the fact that the first president of the IZM was Dr Sa'id Ramadan, a figure-head of the Egyptian Muslim Brotherhood (MB), and that Muhammad Mahdi 'Akif, the former *al-murshid al-'amm* (General Guide, 2004–9) of the MB in Egypt, served from 1984 to 1987 as the director of the IZM, it is assumed by the German security agencies as well as by academics that the IZM is at least the German, if not the European, head-quarters of the MB. Its third president (1973–2002), Ali Ghalib Himmat, who came to Munich in the 1960s as a student but lived for a long time in Switzerland, resigned following US-led accusations of being a financier for terrorist activities, as he was one of the principals of Bank al-Taqwa, supposedly the financial arm of the MB. Suspicions were also nurtured by the trial *in absentia* of Ibrahim El-Zayat, along with 39 other Muslim Brothers (from in and outside Egypt, including Ali Ghalib Himmat), before an Egyptian military court, which eventually led to his sentencing to ten years in prison in April 2008. The documents published by the MB have been purged of any mention of el-Zayat's name after he made public refutations of his membership of the MB. For a long time, both the IZM and the IGD have been watched by the various security agencies and regularly raided by the police for various reasons, mostly connected to illegal business activities, money laundering and support of terrorist organisations abroad; so far, however, without leading to arraignment before a tribunal.

Parallel to the establishment of the IZM and the IGD, another Islamic centre was established in Aachen. In 1958, students of mainly Arab origin, as in Munich, took the initiative to set up a mosque. Nine years later, in 1967, the Bilal mosque, today registered as Islamic Centre Aachen (IZA), was opened. The first president of the IZA was 'Issam al-'Attar who had been the elected leader of the Syrian MB since 1961. Shortly after his election he had to leave Syria for political reasons and from 1968 he lived in exile in Aachen, forming Muslim community life there. When the conflict between the Syrian regime and the MB escalated at the end of the 1970s and the beginning of the 1980s, al-'Attar distanced himself from the Syrian MB because he objected to the use of violence in its struggle against the Syrian regime. However, he continued to be involved with the Islamic movement, giving it a new direction under the notion of Islamic avant-garde (*al-Tala'i' al-Islamiyya*). This step also created some distance between the IZA and the IGD, who had closely cooperated together in the past.

Like the IZM, the IZA offers a variety of activities and several smaller associations are attached to it: the IZA arranges lectures and religious instruction for adults; children are instructed at the Bilal-Schule, a weekend school that provides religious education in German; and student and youth groups regularly meet there. Closely connected with the IZA is the Islamischer Informationsdienst e.V. (Islamic Information Service), a small publisher of Islamic books. It also publishes the periodical *ar-Ra'id* (the Pioneer) that is well known beyond German Muslim circles. The IGD, the IZM and the IZA are founding members of the Zentralrat der Muslime in Deutschland (ZMD, Central Council of Muslims in Germany) and in this way indirectly represented in the Koordinierungsrat der Muslime (KRM, Coordination Council of Muslims).

The stated aims of the Islamic centres and the IGD are threefold: first, they wish to offer Muslims in Germany a suitable framework to practice their religion. Above this they wish to strengthen their Muslim identity and at the same time foster the social integration of Muslims in Germany. Programme headings of conferences and meetings that the IGD and the Islamic centres organise annually express these aims, with titles such as 'The Islamic culture and the western culture. Interaction and completion' (IZA, 2007), '...and thus We made you a community of the middle' referring to the Qur'an (IGD, 2007)[1] and 'Participating – being part of [the society]' (IGD, 2008). It is also apparent in their early efforts to lecture and publish in German. At a very early stage they also started bilingual Friday sermons or offered translations of Arabic sermons into German. Compared to other Islamic organisations in Germany, mainly established by Turkish working migrants, the IGD and the Islamic centres were pioneers in this field.

In its self-portrayal, and especially in statements, the IGD stresses that Islam is the religion of the middle way, referring explicitly to the concept of *wasatiyya* that was popularised by the Muslim scholar Yusuf al-Qaradawi. He and the ECFR play an important role for the IGD and the mosque congregations linked to it. The relatively young Council of Imams and *Da'is* in Germany, designed to connect imams with each other and to form a religiously authoritative body, is also part of the IGD network but not yet so very well known.

The IGD, its centres as well as associations that cooperate with them, are held in suspicion and mistrust by German security agencies. The case of the Berlin-based association Inssan illustrates this quite well. Inssan had planned to establish an Islamic cultural centre, including a mosque and further educational and cultural functions. When it was divulged that the president of the IGD, Ibrahim El-Zayat, had concluded the sales contract for the building site – he was acting in his function as representative of the European Trust – the authorities withdrew the provisional planning permission. The European Trust, now called Europe Trust, also belongs to the FIOE's network and is designed to financially support Islamic communities and projects in Europe. In spite of the support of some politicians and church representatives, and the association's diverse projects in the realm of interfaith dialogue and social integration, a second attempt to buy a building site in another part of Berlin also failed and Inssan was several times excluded from state-funded social integration projects.

Although the IGD is one of the oldest Islamic organisations and its name claims influence throughout Germany, it was unable to establish itself as the leading Islamic organisation. Its influence is restricted to some 60 to 70 mosque congregations and some specialised associations. The number of members is supposed to be less than 2000 people.

However, the actual influence among Muslims with an Arab background, or among certain converts, seems to be much higher than this because a much higher number attend religious and other services provided by the mosques and participate in their activities, without officially being members of the mosque association.

Notes

1   Qur'an, Sura al-Baqara, verse 143.

References

Denffer, Ahmed von (1995) *Moscheeführer Islamisches Zentrum München*, Munich: Islamisches Zentrum München.

Federal Ministry of the Interior (2008) *2008 Annual Report on the Protection of the Constitution*. http://www.bmi.bund.de/cae/servlet/contentblob/754736/publicationFile/42104/vsb_2008_en.pdf;jsessionid=8B47BCBD162F92E4F932DACD7630D61A. Accessed 30 November 2009 (link no longer working).

Lemmen, Thomas (2001) *Muslime in Deutschland. Eine Herausforderung für Kirche und Gesellschaft*, Baden-Baden: Nomos.

Schulze, Reinhard (1990) *Islamischer Internationalismus im 20. Jahrhundert. Untersuchungen zur Geschichte der Islamischen Weltliga*, Leiden: Brill.

Weismann, Itzchak (1993) 'Sa'id Hawwa: the making of a radical Muslim thinker in modern Syria', *Middle Eastern Studies*, 29 (4): pp. 601–23.

http://euro-muslim.net/. (Accessed 11 December 2009 link no longer working).
    http://www.europetrust.eu.com/. (Accessed 15 November 2009).

http://www.igd-online.de. (Accessed 8 September 2009).

http://www.islamisches-zentrum-muenchen.de/. (Accessed 11 September 2009).

http://www.inssan-ev.de/. (Accessed 15 November 2009).

http://www.izaachen.de/. (Accessed 15 November 2009).
http://rigd.de/index.html. (Accessed 15 November 2009).
http://web.archive.org. for some stored old websites of the IGD: www.i-g-d.com and
   www.i-g-d.de (link no longer working).

BEING AND BECOMING A GERMAN MUSLIM YOUTH: MUSLIMISCHE JUGEND IN DEUTSCHLAND

Synnøve Bendixsen

The religious youth organisation Muslimische Jugend in Deutschland e.V. (MJD, Young Muslims in Germany) was established under the aegis of Haus der Islam by eight young Muslims between the ages of 17 and 20 years old in 1994. Starting modestly with the idea of creating a religious association for youths born in Germany, the association was later made independent from Haus der Islam and registered in a small village in Baden-Württemberg. Comprising approximately 50 branches Germany wide, the organisation is today considered the second-largest Muslim youth organisation in Germany, after Milli Görüş. A weekly meeting in Berlin gathers sometimes a mere ten young women, while the annual national meetings have to set a participation limit of approximately 1200 youths.[1] Similar Muslim youth organisations exist in Austria, Italy, France, Sweden and Norway, and MJD is represented at the European level by FEMYSO (Forum European Muslim Youth and Student Organisation), established in Leicester, UK, in 1996. The German organisation is funded by annual membership fees, events, donations (from former members, parents and friends), and income from the religious bookstore Green Palace which, in 2000–1, was owned by MJD. Since 2003 the organisation has faced negative media attention. In 2005 the Verfassungsschutz (Federal Office for the Protection of the Constitution) in Baden-Württemberg and, since 2006 in Hessen (where the annual national MJD meeting takes place), stated that the MJD was on their list of Islamist organisations under surveillance.

Aims of MJD

'Youth' is the main focus of MJD, the stated goal being 'to integrate Muslim youths by providing an opportunity to develop their creativity and talents as young German Muslims in the German language.'[2] One of the main reasons why MJD was established, according to one of the founders, was that youths felt uncomfortable in the mosques established by their parents. These organisations were (and continue to be) ethnically oriented with Arabic or Turkish as the language of communication and instruction, and organised with a hierarchical structure. In contrast, the MJD is organised inter-ethnically – the members have, among others, Turkish, Egyptian, Sudanese, Palestinian and German (converted) backgrounds; it is organised by and for the youths (15–30 years old), and the weekly local meetings are prepared by a leader elected by the participants. The local factions have gender-segregated weekly meetings, where the youths pray together and discuss various religious themes, such as interaction with parents, the life of the Prophet (*Sira*), friendship and time management. At the head of the MJD network is a ten-member *shura* (consultation council), currently evenly split between males and females, which is elected every two years by the general member-assembly. The *shura*, representing the MJD nationwide, meets in different German places every four to six weeks and bears the ultimate responsibility for planning and coordinating all MJD activities. This includes dealing with general questions from other organisations or the local group, planning future events and deciding on its religious message. Different working groups execute the assignments.

MJD activities are informed by a specific pedagogy, three aspects of which should be stressed. First, the seminars seek to convey the difference between a 'pure' Islam versus that of a 'traditional' Islam. This distinction is made by emphasising Qur'an and Sunna as the exclusive basis for Muslim life. For example, especially tearful prayers during Ramadan will be criticised as mere 'performance' and it will be stressed that such a behaviour pertains to tradition and is not 'correct religious behaviour'. Second, workshops and discussions regularly focus on how internal motivation should relate to external motions. The participants are encouraged to work on themselves in order to achieve harmony between 'correct' external bodily practise and 'correct' internal focus. Third, discussions are concerned with how to be a 'good' Muslim living in German society. Seminar discussions are often about various religious dilemmas young Muslims face, such as their desire to 'be like the others', the danger of fashion trends and how to deal with experiences of discrimination. The leaders and elder participants promote the idea of being 'Muslim and proud of it'. The youths are encouraged to focus on what is more important: either this worldly life or the hereafter. Furthermore, certain values, such as punctuality, honesty and being hard-working, are posited as both German and Muslim, with an effort of bridging these two frames of identifications.

Profile of the members

The official national membership numbers of 600 (in 2007), of which two-thirds are female, is not representative of actual participants in the meetings. The relevance of the group in the German sphere is larger than its numbers, because during annual meetings only around 30 per cent of the participants are official members; some youth groups are unofficially attached to the MJD, and the organisation is publicly active in the media and the German public. Most of the MJD participants belong to an upwardly mobile part of the migrant population either because of their parents' education, or because of their own educational level. The organisational structure can partly explain the popularity among highly educated youth; all are encouraged to actively present religious topics and to partake in the administration of activities and (public) events.

At the national level, the MJD sends out nationwide emails on Friday, and arranges regional monthly seminars, *Tarbiyya* (education in values in Islam) and annual regional and national camps. Implementation of new MJD branches is either directly organised or coordinated from the national level.

The organisation is not promoting fixed, already-designed religious instruction, but draws on authorities which they believe follow an 'Islam of the middle way', including Tariq Ramadan, Yusuf al-Qaradawi and the Egyptian television preacher Amr Khaled. The messages of these authorities are not followed entirely; whereas some positions promoted by al-Qaradawi, such as 'women are allowed to travel alone' will be adopted, some of his positions regarding, for example, the Palestinian resistance[3] are rejected.

Furthermore, whereas some members respect Khaled's profile, other members will find him objectionable. The MJD, like any other organisation, has developed a particular internal culture which finds expression in its idelogical programme, its structure and modes of communication. A given *shura* might carry on that of the previous *shura*, but also modify it. Alteration of acceptable conduct (such as whether or not hip-hop is suitable at religious meetings) may reflect that the organisers are becoming more experienced, that they are growing up and thus less afraid of doing something 'incorrect'.

Facing Public Distrust

MJD received little public attention until it ventured out of the margins, receiving public recognition through state funding for the project *Ta'ruf/Kennenlernen!* [Getting to know Each Other!]. This project aimed to counter prejudice and racism, and received funding from a German state agency in 2002 until MJD was accused in the media of recruiting 'Islamist offspring'. During the witch-hunt that followed, the MJD suddenly received public attention, and journalists found a 'Friday talk' (*nasiha*) on MJD's home page with anti-Semitic overtones. The MJD, publicly regretting the text, wrote a press statement defending itself against the media's accusations. Nevertheless, the public funding was withdrawn and the project stopped.

During this process, MJD's connections to other Islamic organisations and the profile of individual members of the organisation were questioned. The Verfassungsschutz suddenly considered MJD Islamist and a part of the international MB – an assertion rejected by the MJD. The link to the MB was primarily made by pointing to the fact that one of the *shura* members in 2004 was the brother of Ibrahim El-Zayat, the president of IGD, and considered as representing the MB in Germany by the Verfassungschutz. It was also regularly mentioned that its Islamic bookshop, Green Palace, was selling books of questionable content, such al-Qaradawi's *The Allowed and the Forbidden in Islam*. Furthermore, Fereschta Ludin had been a long-time member of the organisation. The Afghan-born Ludin had fought the longest case in Baden-Württemberg for her right to veil as a teacher.[4] A circular argumentation followed where Fereschta Ludin is considered as a fundamentalist because she was a member of MJD, and MJD is considered as fundamentalist because Fereschta Ludin used to be a member of the organisation. The 'logic of rumours'[5] in this media campaign is reinforced by the practise of 'infection': any group who has contact with people distrusted by the German Verfassungsschutz will be infected with the 'virus' of Islamism.

Conclusion

The allegations brought against MJD remain based on generalisations about MJD's ideological orientation and the public national activities of the youth organisation, disregarding what takes place at the local weekly meetings with the youths – the main work of MJD. The local meetings have been not been unduly influenced by the media's negative attention, although public projects have become more difficult to pursue, including borrowing public spaces for events such as Islam Connecting People. While it might be true that it is harder to attract new members, there was an increase in membership at the beginning of 2007, from 350 to 600. Nevertheless, the negative press and the surveillance by German security agencies not only make it unlikely that public funding for new projects will be available, but also ensure that MJD will not be integrated into public debates. One unfortunate outcome of the public accusations is that this organisation, and others, may in the future decide against active participation in German public life, choosing instead to remain on the outskirts of the public sphere.

Notes

1 Synnøve Bendixsen (2013) *Young Female Muslims Crafting a Religious Self in Berlin*, Brill: Leiden.
2 See www.mjd-net.de. (accessed 19 June 2014)
3 See European Council of Fatwa and Research Website. http://www.e-cfr.org/en/ (link no longer working).
4 Heide Oestreich (2004) *Der Kopftuchstreit. Das Abendland und ein Quadratmeter Islam*, Frankfurt am Main: Brandes & Apsel.
5 Werner Schiffauer (2006) 'Der unheimliche Muslim. Staatsbürgerschaft und zivilge-sellschaftliche Ängste', in Levent Tezcan and Monika Wohlrab-Sahr (eds), *Konfliktfeld Islam in Europa*. Munich: Nomos, pp. 111–33.

References

Bendixsen, Synnøve (2013) *Young Female Muslims Crafting a Religious Self in Berlin*, Brill: Leiden.
Oestreich, Heide (2004) *Der Kopftuchstreit. Das Abendland und ein Quadratmeter Islam*, Frankfurt am Main: Brandes & Apsel.
Roy, Olivier (2004) *Globalized Islam*, New York: Columbia University Press.
Schiffauer, Werner (2006) 'Der unheimliche Muslim. Staatsbürgerschaft und zivilge-sellschaftliche Ängste', in Levent Tezcan and Monika Wohlrab-Sahr (eds), *Konfliktfeld Islam in Europa*, Munich: Nomos, pp. 111–33.

THE UNION OF ISLAMIC ORGANISATIONS OF FRANCE

Frank Peter

The Union of Islamic Organisations of France (UOIF) was created in 1983. Today it is the most well-structured of France's three major Muslim federations. Apart from 65 mosques which are federated in the UOIF, the network also comprises associations for students (Muslim Students of France, created in 1989), women and youths (French League of Muslim Women and Young Muslims of France, both created in 1993). In 1990, the UOIF set up a charity for Palestine; it was the driving force behind the European Institutes for Human Sciences (Institut Européen des Sciences Humaines, created in 1991), located in France and Wales, and it also runs a media outlet, Edition Gedis. Importantly, the kind of formal relations which link these associations and institutions to the UOIF vary considerably. In the last couple of years, the UOIF has set up private schools in Lille, Lyon and Marseille. The UOIF is also a central component of the Conseil Français du Culte Musulman, the State-created representative body of French mosque associations.

Due to its various links to people and institutions associated with the Muslim Brotherhood movement, the UOIF is usually considered to be the main Islamist group in France. Although after 9/11 public interest in the UOIF has been somewhat eclipsed by concerns about Salafism, the UOIF continues to face severe criticism and accusations from various sides. The central element of these accusations is the claim that the UOIF's activities in France are surreptitiously aimed at goals that threaten the secular republican order.[1] Put differently, it is claimed that statements from the activists of the UOIF are often mere double talk. Effectively, what is being questioned are statements with important implications, such as those asserting that the secular framework is fully adapted to the needs and expectations of French Muslims and that the UOIF seeks to promote French citizenship among Muslims.

Examining grand claims such as this one is not a task easily accomplished. One general objection to the above view can be made, however, in order to offer a starting point for a different kind of analysis of the UOIF. In fact the claim reported above, that the UOIF engages in double talk, is based on the problematic assumption that one can decide at will which discourse one articulates, that is, that saying and being are basically two unrelated things.

Contrary to this view, it needs to be asked how speech acts constrain the speaker and how they durably transform subjectivities, intersubjective relations and social environments. Also, the question of how the ability to successfully communicate a message relates to one's subjectivity and social position needs to be raised. Both questions are frustratingly left unaddressed by the critics of the UOIF.

A brief look at the history of the UOIF makes it immediately clear that the thesis of double talk is not of much help in analysing this group. It is difficult to ignore the important interconnections between discourses, practices and identities. The history of the UOIF in the past two decades demonstrates the tight correlation between reorientations in its discourse, changes in the social profile of its members and audiences, and new directions taken in the process of institution building and cooperation with the State. Discourses are taken seriously inside the group; they are the objects of numerous discussions among members and they are acted upon, often in environments where the members of the UOIF face important opposition from public authorities and various other institutions and actors. Likewise, the discourse of the UOIF has been crucial to its ability to reach out to new audiences in France. At the same time, the partial inclusion of these audiences has contributed to the internal transformation of the group.

In 1983, the UOIF (at that time named The Union of Islamic Organisations *in* France) started out as a group which was solidly rooted in the milieu of foreign Muslim students in France. While limited discussions about the legal status of non-Islamic countries (and the presence of Muslims in these countries) were already underway during the 1980s in this group, its geographic orientation was nevertheless primarily towards various parts of the Islamic world outside Europe. In the context of the 'Islamic awakening' or the 're-Islamisation' of French youth in the 1980s and 1990s, the federation soon became more strongly embedded in French society. Through the work of its youth groups, its preachers and activists, the UOIF has made great contributions to the process of spreading the message of Islam among French youth, and at the same time its own identity has partly changed. On the one hand, this process led to the creation of a kind of Muslim spirituality, whose notion of self-development was specifically attuned to the realities of French youth. On the other hand, this process changed the kind of questions and problems to which Muslim discourses responded and it modified the goals of the work of Muslim associations. The question of the modalities of Islam belonging to France, the defence of the compatibility between a public and visible Islam on the one hand and the French secular order on the other, and the problem of how to deal with anti-Muslim discrimination emerged as major issues at that time. The mere fact that these questions were now debated increasingly by French-born Muslims who made strong claims to their rights as citizens and articulated a natural feeling of belonging to France gave a new kind of public legitimacy to the UOIF as a French-Muslim group. It also raised the UOIF's potential to irritate the numerous individuals in France who were unwilling to recognise Muslims as equals. The creation, since the late 1980s, of associations and various media products specifically addressing youth, primarily in French, provided the space in which these issues were debated, and new discourses and arguments in favour of the compatibility of Islam and French secularism were forged. In these discourses, the trope of the adaptability of Islam to different time and space contexts plays a central role. Over the years, many of these arguments have been popularised and have found their way into the wider public sphere and are today no longer specific to the UOIF.

It is important to point out that inside the federation relatively diverse opinions coexist. There are a number of consensual positions with respect to fundamental issues, such as that of the legitimacy of Muslims living in France, even though here as well the modes of argumentation may vary considerably. Opinions differ when it comes to other no less important issues concerning, for example, the question of how to put into practice the principle of an intrinsic relation between belief and practice, which is constitutive of the

UOIF's self-presentation as a distinct actor in French Islam. Questions concerning what strategy to pursue in dealing with Islamophobia or the position to take in the Palestine conflict are also hotly debated. More generally, it has to be noted that diverse opinions can be articulated inside the federation, even if it is discouraged from speaking openly about differences of opinion. This diversity of opinion has not left the structure of the federation unaffected. For instance, one of the groups originally founded by the UOIF, Muslim Students of France, has recently cut its formal ties with its mother organisation and now acts in total independence. This event needs to be considered in light of the internal debate about whether Muslim activism can be made relevant and beneficial to the wider society. As to the Muslim Students of France, its aim is to not restrict itself and not be perceived as the exclusive representative of Muslims. This aim has triggered an ongoing process of reconstituting internal structures and modes of operation, which includes cutting ties with its explicitly religious mother organisation.

Another major field in which the UOIF's proclaimed aim to reconcile Islam with French citizenship has been put into practice is the Conseil Français du Culte Musulman. Since its inception in 2003, the UOIF has been a member of the council. The UOIF's leaders had placed great hopes in their participation in the council as a means to unify Muslims and give them a voice in French society. These hopes have been largely disappointed due to ongoing internal power struggles in the council which have severely limited its overall effectiveness. Nevertheless, the participation in the council has had a significant impact on the UOIF. Most importantly, its participation entailed for the UOIF a kind of self-censorship of its public discourse. Its reluctance to join the protests against the prohibition of headscarves in public schools in 2004 and its tendency to limit its interventions into the debate on the Palestine conflict to humanitarian appeals are two significant examples of this development, for which the organisation is regularly criticised by some of its members. However, in other respects the UOIF does not shy away from taking controversial positions which potentially endanger its self-presentation as a moderate Muslim organisation when this is seen as necessary for the defence of Muslim interests. During the Cartoon Crisis, it thus stood firmly with its decision to seek legal redress against the publication of selected cartoons by a French journal, in spite of the broad alliance of actors who had criticised this decision as an attempt to limit freedom of expression.

Over the years, the various components of the UOIF have thus become deeply enmeshed in French society. Nevertheless, the organisation maintains important links to scholars and institutions outside France, notably in the Arab-Islamic world. These relations to actors who often closely identify with the tradition of the Muslim Brotherhood, notably Yusuf al-Qaradawi, are a central and enduring source of the accusations directed against the UOIF in France. In the current context, the contacts and cooperation between the UOIF and these foreign actors are regularly presented as implying an approbation of all positions taken by the latter. This representation runs counter to the way in which the members of the UOIF conceive of these relationships. One reason for this is that the possibility and sometimes even necessity to interpret Islamic sources differently in function of time and space is a crucial element of the UOIF's methodology. Not everything these scholars say can thus necessarily be relevant to the lives of French Muslims, from the point of view of the UOIF. The UOIF's understanding of France (and more generally of Europe) as a space which is relatively distinct yet remains part of the universal Islamic community of believers is a complex one. This complexity contributes to the UOIF's difficulties in its sometimes quite limited attempts to make explicit the basis and implications of its transnational cooperations. Given the current tendency to imagine

Europe and the Islamic world as two radically distinct entities, the issue of the UOIF's transnational network will, in all likelihood, continue to tarnish its reputation.

Notes

1   Fiammetta Venner (2005) *OPA sur l'islam de France. Les ambitions de l'UOIF*, Paris: Calman Lévy.

References

Amghar, Samir (ed.) (2006) *Islamismes d'Occident, état des lieux et perspectives*, Paris: Lignes de repères.

Marechal, Brigitte (2008) *The Muslim Brothers in Europe: Roots and Discourse*, Leiden / Boston: Brill.

Peter, Frank (2011) 'Die Union des Organisations Islamiques de France und die Tradition der Muslimbrüder im Zeitalter der Integrationspolitik', in Dietrich Reetz (ed.), *Islam in Europa – Religiöses Leben heute*, Münster: Waxmann, pp. 145–70.

Venner, Fiammetta (2005) *OPA sur l'islam de France. Les ambitions de l'UOIF*, Paris: Calman Lévy.

MUSLIM ASSOCIATION OF BRITAIN

Sadek Hamid

The Muslim Association of Britain (MAB) is a Muslim Brotherhood (MB) inspired Islamist movement officially formed in November 1997. While marketing itself as an indigenised European Islamic organisation, it does not conceal the fact that many of its personnel were members of the MB originating from different parts of the Arab world. The organisation's publicity materials present the MAB as a vehicle for Islamic evangelism and the promotion of social integration, but its achievements have mainly been in the areas of raising awareness of the Palestinian cause and anti-war political mobilisation. Its founding members include Kemal al-Helbawy, Azzam Tamimi and Anas Tikriti. A prominent MB figure, Helbawy settled in the UK in the mid-1990s, where he was briefly 'MB spokesman to the West' and the organisation's first president. Tamimi is another well-known figure who has written extensively on Islamism and is acknowledged to be sympathetic to Hamas. Tikriti is also a previous organisation president and leading Muslim anti-war activist; his father Osama Al Tikriti was the leader of the MB in Iraq.

The MAB has around 12 branches across Britain in areas with significant Muslim populations – London, Leeds and Manchester are probably the most active. Its services range from running Islamic educational projects for scouts, youths and students, to a dedicated media and public relations department producing booklets and publications, such as *Inspire* magazine. Its early mission statements suggest that the MAB was created to fill the gaps left by other UK Islamic movement groups and to complement their work. However, according to activists from other movement organisations, the inception of the MAB was resented among many of its peers, notably the Islamic Society of Britain (ISB), whose leadership was unhappy that the MAB had poached a number of its executive members from its youth organisation, Young Muslim UK (YM). There was also a wider grievance that the creation of the MAB signalled a failure of attempts to create a unified Islamic movement for the UK. The MAB is said to have been formed because of what it perceived as the failure of South Asian reformist organisations such as the UK Islamic Mission, YM and the ISB to provide Islamist leadership to Muslim communities in Britain. Its critics argue that the MAB's arrival represented a return to more ethnically based loyalties among Islamist organisations – an 'Arab take-over' as some pejoratively describe it – further fragmenting the less than harmonious relationships between British Islamists.

The organisation is among the few Islamist groups to penetrate mainstream public consciousness as a result of its involvement in the British anti-war movement between 2002 and 2003. Working exposure to the political left led to their alliance with the Stop the War Coalition and the Socialist Workers Party. The MAB's participation in the commemoration of the anniversary of the second Palestinian uprising, and subsequent role in the huge anti-war demonstration in March 2003, created a strong media profile. This was followed by cooperation with the ex-Labour MP, George Galloway's new Respect Party. The newfound friendship with non-Muslim groups encouraged former president Anas Altikriti to run as a Respect candidate during the European elections in Yorkshire and Humberside in June 2004. The MAB leadership also built good relationships with then Labour mayor of London Ken Livingstone, who controversially helped them host influential Sheikh Yusuf al-Qaradawi for a 'Pro-*Hijab*' conference in July 2004. This was used by the MAB to promote Qaradawi's European Council of Fatwa, and to demonstrate how it could benefit wider community cohesion. The MAB's political pragmatism did not go unchallenged, as some elements of the left were unhappy with the cooperation of secular leftists with what they deemed a socially conservative religious movement. In addition, MP Louise Ellman, a member of Labour Friends of Israel, has accused the MAB of anti-Semitism and terrorist connections, singling out Azzam Tamimi for his links with Hamas. The MAB returned to the media spotlight in 2005, when they took over the management of Finsbury Park mosque in North London, after wresting control from notorious extremist preacher Abu Hamza and his followers.

The MAB's relationships with other Islamic organisations is limited, due to either insufficient ideological affinity – with the majority of British Muslim religious trends such as the South Asian Barelwi and Deobandi theological communities – or competition with rival tendencies such as the various conservative Salafi groups. The MAB seems to be only interested in working with other non-Islamist groups when their interests converge – for example, in their large-scale *Islam Expo* exhibition events in 2006 and 2008 – or when conducting Muslim rights based campaigning. The MAB's strength lies in its consolidation of its own network of MB influenced institutions; it has created subsidiaries such as the British Muslim Initiative, The Cordoba Foundation and the Centre for the Study of Terrorism, where Tikriti and al-Helbawy play leading roles. It also works with older organisations such as the Palestine Return Centre and The European Trust, and is a vocal affiliate within the umbrella body, the Muslim Council of Britain.

Like other diasporic MB organisations, the MAB remains independent but broadly sympathetic to MB aspirations in the West, working for pan-Islamic consciousness raising, gaining political influence in its adopted countries and sympathy for Islamist projects in the Middle East. For the MAB, religious proselytisation, the issue of Palestine and liberation of Iraq remain principal priorities which they have pursed more assertively than most other similar organisations. It views its role as being at the forefront of defending Muslim political rights, such as the championing of women's right to wear the *hijab*, challenging Islamophobia and critiquing government policies intepreted as discriminatory against Muslims. The MAB's appeal to the majority of Muslim communities is limited due to the predominantly South Asian Muslim demography of Britain's Muslims and its accompanying sectarian and ethnic diversity. It also remains beleaguered, due to continued targeting by the pro-Israeli lobby in the UK and the current government's hostile perception of political Islamist groups.

References

Maréchal, Brigitte (2008) *The Muslim Brotherhood in Europe: Roots and Discourse*, Leiden: Brill.
Whine, Michael (2005) 'The Advance of the Muslim Brotherhood in the UK', *Current Trends in Islamist Ideology*, 2: pp. 30–40.
http://mabonline.net/ (accessed 19 June 2014)

THE UNION OF ISLAMIC COMMUNITIES AND ORGANISATIONS AND RELATED GROUPS IN ITALY

Annalisa Frisina

The Union of Islamic Communities and Organisations in Italy[1] (UCOII) was created officially in 1990 in Ancona, central Italy, as a federation of mosque associations. Since its creation, its president has been Dachan Mohamed Nour, a doctor of Syrian origin who has lived in Italy for 40 years. Its leadership is mainly composed of citizens of Syrian origin. A significant number are Muslim Brothers who escaped from repression by the Asad regime in the early 1980s, but Palestinians, Jordanians, Egyptians and Italian converts are present too. The members of UCOII are recruited primarily from the Maghreb, in particular Morocco, but there are also Muslims from the Middle East, Sub-Saharan Africa and the Balkans. In 2005, the number of mosque associations represented by UCOII was estimated at 133, of which more than half were situated in northern Italy. At the European level, UCOII is a member of the Federation of Islamic Organisations in Europe (FIOE).

Since the creation of the UCOII its major aim has been the representation of Muslims to the Italian state and the extension of state accommodation of religion to religious practices of Muslims. To this end, the UCOII has repeatedly presented a draft agreement (*Intesa*) to be concluded between Muslims and the Italian State, in compliance with Article 8 of the Italian Constitution. Here it is stated that:

> All religious confessions are equally free before the law. Religious confessions other than the Catholic faith have the right to organise themselves according to their statutes in so far as they are not in conflict with the Italian laws. Their relationship with the Italian State is regulated by agreements (*Intese*) drawn up between the Italian State and organisations which represent that faith.

The conclusion of an *Intesa* would encode and guarantee certain rights whose exercise by Muslims is today largely dependent on discretionary decisions at the local level. The requests from the UCOII include notably: access to *otto per mille* (eight per thousand: public funding for religious organisations whose amount is calculated based on the religious affiliation indicated on individuals' tax declarations); the facilitation of new mosque construction; the employment of Muslim chaplains in hospitals and jails; the possibility of wearing the *hijab* in official document photos; the recognition of civil effects of marriages celebrated according to Islamic rites; the opening of Islamic cemeteries; the recognition of Islamic celebrations; the introduction of Islamic religious education in public schools; the provision of *halal* food in public schools and the facilitation of Islamic ritual slaughter;

and the possibility of Friday collective prayer by Muslim workers.

The political dispute on the *Intesa* with Muslim organisation is still ongoing, for several different reasons. On the one hand, the Muslim organisations which are seeking official recognition from the Italian state do not recognise each other. In fact, they sometimes accuse each other of not following the 'real' Islam, lacking representative legitimacy and, as concerns the UCOII, being a 'societal danger'. On the other hand, there is strong resistance by the dominant majority to fully recognising Islam as part of Italian society (see Part 3).

Until now the State has not responded to most UCOII demands. The cooperation between the UCOII and state authorities is problematic, mainly because the UCOII is branded as anti-Semitic and its support for the Palestinian cause is often constructed as support for terrorism. Cooperation is further rendered problematic by the fact that the UCOII, in contrast to the dominant opinion in Italy, does not only want Islam to change in function in the European context, but also seeks a change in Italian policies concerning immigration and citizenship. This fact decisively influenced the results of the Consulta per l'Islam Italiano (Advisory Board for Italian Islam) in which the UCOII takes part. The Consulta per l'Islam Italiano was established in 2005 by Home Officer Pisanu, who nominated 15 Islamic 'experts'. The framework inside which discussion took place was that of security, and the State's main aim was to promote a 'moderate Islam'. The UCOII presence became controversial on two occasions in particular. First, the UCOII refused to sign the *Manifesto dell'islam in Italia* (Manifesto of Islam in Italy), because the president of the UCOII considered it to be too insistent on rejecting terrorism and failed to state the necessity of changing the Italian immigration and citizenship laws. Second, during the conflict between Israel and Lebanon in 2006, the UCOII published advertisements in various Italian newspapers titled 'Yesterday Nazi massacres, today Israeli massacres' where the number of civilian victims from Palestine and Lebanon were counted, from 1937 to 2006. The intention of the UCOII leaders was to provide some kind of 'counter-information' to the representations of other media. However, the reactions were overwhelmingly negative and ranged from 'an unacceptable provocation' to accusations of racism, anti-Semitism and terrorism.

The organisations which make up the UCOII are heterogeneous and they relate in very different ways to the heritage of the Muslim Brotherhood (MB). As a matter of fact, there are social players linked to the UCOII which seem to follow a strategy of 'functional separation' between Muslims and the rest of the Italian population. These organisations seek to gain social visibility and to mark the symbolic borders between Islam and others. This border is marked both externally (by stating their own superiority over a 'decadent society') and internally, in order to work against the 'privatisation of belief' and the 'reduction of Islam to a cultural heritage'. The concern is that an increasing number of Muslims are affected by a reduction of Islam to mere folklore.

Women and youth are two groupd within the UCOII that have been the most active and have led to several transformations within the organisation. For example, one member group of the UCOII is the Associazione Donne Musulmane d' Italia (ADMI, Association of Muslim Women in Italy), founded as a female section of the UCOII and subsequently separating from it institutionally in 2001. While the majority of members in the ADMI (and generally in the Italian society) are from North Africa and are in low positions in the social hierarchy, the past leaders of the ADMI were from the Middle East (often housewives married to professionals). It seems that this discrepancy was a major reason for the separation of the ADMI from the UCOII. Today the president is Fatima Abdel Hakim, a businesswoman of Algerian origin who has lived in Italy for 30 years.

During the meetings of the ADMI, it was common to observe the defensive attitude towards Italian society which was seen as discriminating against Muslims. The relationship with non-Muslim Italian women was marked by mutual stereotyping: on one side 'the half-naked woman and her body as commodity', on the other side 'the veiled women and their submission to men'. More recently, those views have become more complex and there is an attempt to increase exchange and cooperation on both sides, for instance concerning the education of children and the relationship with schools. The role of 'daughters' – young Muslim women of the so-called second generation – is important to effect this change, since they continue trying to help their mothers to interact more with Italian society and to challenge gender stereotypes.

Another example of conflicting transformations related to the UCOII, concerns the activities of the Giovani Musulmani d'Italia (GMI, Association of Young Muslims of Italy),[2] which is no longer a member of the UCOII, from which it separated in 2001. The association is composed of about 350 members between 16 and 30 years old. The majority of members are women but the first four presidents were all male; the most active sections are in Emilia Romagna, Lombardy (the headquarters is in Milan) and Piemonte. Members were born or raised in Italy, while their working-class parents are mainly from the Maghreb (but there is a significant section from the Middle East among the leaders). The majority of members of GMI attend high schools, while the leaders study at university. What characterises these youths is their attempt to try to 'break the defensive logic' of the previous generation and enter the public sphere by declaring themselves 'Italian citizens of Islamic faith'. In this way, they challenge the collective representation of Italy as a Catholic country and contribute to showing the limits of Italian secularism. They contest the apologetic and normative version of Islam described as 'out of history' and reduced to a matter of distinguishing between *halal/haram*. Rather, they search for a 'critical brotherhood', based on pluralism and active participation.

The Islamic Alliance of Italy (before 2005 its name was Association of Islamic Culture and Education in Italy, led by Boubakeur Gheddouda, of Algerian origin) is also a member of the UCOII and acts more as a movement (i.e., there is no formal membership, participation is voluntary) and its work focuses on the Islamic education of youths and the training of activists.

Inside the Alliance, the heritage of the MB is openly assumed (for instance, in the centrality of 'making *da'wa*', also involving themselves in the public sphere), but it is strongly emphasised that there is no link from an organisational point of view and that they do not share the politics of the MB in Arab countries. The emphasis, therefore, is on the building of a European Islam, partly through cooperation with the Federation of Islamic Organisations in Europe (FIOE) of which the Alliance (as well as the UCOII) is a member. Thus, the European Council for Fatwa and Research (ECFR) and the Institut Européen des Sciences Humaines (France) sent their experts to the recently held courses for imams, which the Alliance started in order to further their inculcation of imams to the Italian context. However, young Muslims did not show much interest in these courses. According to some of them, the problem was the teaching method: the teaching was still in Arabic even if it was then translated into Italian, and above all the style was considered old-fashioned, in that it was too directive. According to others, the more general problem was the specific cultural references of the first generation. These references, it was said, helped to lead the older generation to adopt a defensive attitude towards changes in Islamic practices, and ultimately nurtured a certain kind of traditionalisation of Islam in Italy.

Notes

1   See http://www.islam-ucoii.it. (link no longer functional)
2   See www.giovanimusulmani.it. (link accessed 19 June 2014)

References

Allievi, Stefano (1999) *I nuovi musulmani. I convertiti all'islam*, Rome: Edizioni Lavoro.

Campanini, Massimo and Karim Mezran (2007) *Arcipelago Islam. Tradizione, riforma e militanza in età contemporanea*, Rome / Bari: Laterza.

Frisina, Annalisa (2005) 'Famiglie musulmane e scuola: la parola alle donne', in Antonio Marazzi (ed.), *Voci di famiglie immigrate*, Milan: Franco Angeli, pp. 119–28.

—— (2007) *Giovani Musulmani d'Italia*, Rome: Carocci.

Furstenberg, Nina (2007) *Chi ha paura di Tariq Ramadan?*, Venice: Marsilio.

—— (1999) 'Attori sociali e processi di rappresentanza nell'islam italiano', in Chantal Saint-Blancat (ed.), *L'islam in Italia. Una presenza plurale*, Rome: Edizioni Lavoro, pp. 67–90.

Guolo, Renzo (2005) 'Il campo religioso musulmano in Italia', *Rassegna Italiana di Sociologia*, 4, October–December: pp. 631–58.

Pace, Enzo and Fabio Perocco (2000) 'L'islam plurale degli immigrati in Italia', *Studi Emigrazione*, 137: pp. 2–20.

THE EUROPEAN COUNCIL FOR FATWA AND RESEARCH AND YUSUF AL-QARADAWI

Alexandre Caeiro and Bettina Gräf

The European Council for Fatwa and Research

The European Council for Fatwa and Research (ECFR) was founded in London in 1997 upon the initiative of the Federation of Islamic Organizations in Europe (FIOE). While most of its members are Muslim scholars living in Europe, the Council includes a number of 'ulama' based in the Muslim world, including Yusuf al-Qaradawi (see below) and Faysal Mawlawi, respectively chairman and vice-chairman of the ECFR. Based in Dublin, the ECFR meets once or twice a year to produce religious opinions, or fatwas, on issues relevant to Muslims living in the West. These fatwas, disseminated via the mass media, are accompanied by a more specialised reflection on what is called a Muslim jurisprudence of minorities (*fiqh al-aqalliyyat* or minority *fiqh*): an attempt to think of Islamic norms in contexts where Islam is disconnected from the State and the majority society.

Advocates of *fiqh al-aqalliyyat* share both a commitment to the Islamic legal tradition (*fiqh* or *shari'a*) and a perception of minority status as a particular kind of problem for this tradition. However, the understandings of what the status of minority entails, and whether it is adequate at all when applied to citizens of liberal democracies, are issues which have been highly debated internally. Likewise, although *fiqh* remains the terrain in which solutions to the problems of Muslims in the West are sought, what this normative tradition precisely amounts to is sometimes unclear, given the simultaneous emphases placed on 'reform' and 'contextualisation'. In the case of the ECFR, given the complex nature of the collective deliberations within the fatwa body, one can speak of minority *fiqh* only as an evolving project, diversely understood and variously implemented, by the heterogeneous members of the European Fatwa Council.

The fatwas issued by the ECFR purport to make Muslims in Europe pious and law-abiding citizens. The emphasis is on 'integration' without 'assimilation'. Integration in the fatwas of the ECFR is mainly understood in legal terms: Muslims are repeatedly enjoined to obey the laws of the countries in which they live; when European laws forbid certain practices which are allowed in Islamic law, these practices usually become Islamically prohibited. In the more difficult cases when European laws contradict perceived Islamic obligations, such as the headscarf ban from public schools in France, Muslims are urged to protest and to keep their protest within legitimate legal channels. Although local customs are recognised as a source of Islamic normativity, and participation in non-Muslim cultural practices may be allowed, cultural assimilation is by and large rejected.

Generally speaking, the fatwas of the ECFR oscillate between an emphasis on the powerlessness of Muslims (which justifies exceptions to the Islamic norm) and a defence of the contemporary relevance of the Islamic tradition (which stresses the individual responsibility of believers and minimises the importance of the context).

Gender issues have been a matter of particular concern for the ECFR. The vision of gender relations articulated by the all-male fatwa body is one of 'complementarity' of gender roles rather than equality of rights. The fact that many questions sent to the ECFR continue to come from female Muslims suggests that such opinions are not out of tune with the aspirations of at least some Muslim women in Europe.

The ritualistic and detailed nature of many of the questions appear unintelligible to secular subjects, who often dismiss them as fundamentalist rhetorics. For the petitioners who ask the questions, as well as for the scholars who answer them, such detailed issues are nevertheless often considered important because they constitute pathways for creating or maintaining a link to the divine and to the Islamic tradition. One should be careful when attempting to draw any inferences regarding this kind of religiosity and wider political attitudes.

The enterprise of minority *fiqh* has sometimes been perceived as posing a legal challenge to European secular orders. Critics point in particular to the demands made by the ECFR for state recognition of Muslim family law in Europe. While this demand is highly problematic in certain contexts (France), it is clearly feasible in others (UK). For many of the members of the ECFR, the ability to self-regulate family matters is a basic dimension of freedom of religion; one which these scholars staunchly defend in the case of Muslim minorities in the West, as they do in the case of Christians and Jews in Muslim lands. Given the legal recognition granted in some Western countries to the decisions issued by rabbinic authorities regarding matters of Jewish family law, members of the ECFR perceive the refusal to extend this recognition to *shari'a* councils in Europe as a form of discrimination. Although this complex issue cannot be fully dealt with here, the challenge seems to be political rather than strictly legal: in many cases, the main argument for preventing *shari'a* councils from becoming legally binding procedures of alternative dispute resolution hinges on a simplistic view of Muslim women as 'oppressed'. The evidence provided to substantiate this view is often problematic.

The transnationalism of the ECFR – and in particular its links to the agenda of the Islamist movements in the Muslim world – has also been a recurrent point of contention in public debates. The FIOE itself is often directly linked to the Muslim Brotherhood (MB) in Egypt. Many of the members of the ECFR are affiliated with Islamist movements; some even hold important political positions in the Muslim world. While these movements all seek to promote an Islamic alternative to current regimes in the Arab world, their political objectives are often local. The members share a rejection of terrorism, which they distinguish from 'legitimate defence' in those lands which are perceived to be under attack (Palestine, Kashmir, Chechnya, etc.). Although the leadership of the Council supports the actions of Hamas in the Palestinian–Israeli conflict, for example, the ECFR itself has been careful not to issue a detailed fatwa on the topic: contrary to what is often claimed in the media, the ECFR never claimed that suicide bombings are martyrdom operations, but simply distinguished 'terrorism' from 'resistance from occupation'.

Yusuf al-Qaradawi

Yusuf al-Qaradawi, born in Egypt in 1926 and based in Qatar since 1961, is a scholar trained in Al-Azhar who chairs the ECFR and the International Union of Muslim Scholars. Although he is often presented as the leader of the Muslim Brotherhood (MB), al-Qaradawi was a member of this only until 1956. While he continues to be regarded as a major authority within the movement, his commitment lies not in the MB itself but in constructing a viable Islamic alternative to the secular authoritarian regimes of the Arab world, and to Western hegemony more largely. Mass media and the institutional-isation of fatwa bodies have been the tools through which al-Qaradawi has tried render Islam relevant in the contemporary world, while guarding the boundaries of legitimate religious authority against the fragmentation that has allowed – in his eyes – both the consolidation of the Arab secularist regimes and the rise of radical Islamist terrorist networks.

Al-Qaradawi's views of Islam as a 'rational', 'comprehensive' and 'easy' way of life appeal to large sections of Muslims worldwide. A champion of *ijtihad*, al-Qaradawi is committed to a religious reform that builds on the modes of reasoning of the classical Islamic tradition and takes into consideration the contemporary reality and interests of Muslims in a globalised and pluralist world. He has come under attack from more conser-vative scholars for his willingness to contextualise traditional Islamic norms, and from modernists for reaching conclusions that often fall short of liberal standards. Al-Qaradawi has, in turn, depicted his conservative interlocutors as extremist (in their literalist under-standing of the texts) and his modernist challengers as neglectful (of mankind's duties to God), claiming for himself the position of moderation (*wasatiyya*).

When viewed in terms of the conservative-versus-liberal or traditionalist-versus-modernist categories, al-Qaradawi appears as a highly ambiguous personality. These ambiguities stem in part from al-Qaradawi's eagerness to unite Muslims, an eagerness which requires him to address multiple audiences and to respond to their varying expec-tations. The ambiguities are also related to the difficulties involved in the attempt to bring about change in the Muslim world, while trying to provide an alternative to Western political, social and economic models. Al-Qaradawi and his peers are acutely aware that they operate in a politicised setting where the project of Islamic reform is linked in complex ways to secularist agendas and imperial projects which they are opposed to.

In the West, al-Qaradawi is most (in)famous for his support for Hamas, which has led to bans from entering the United States and Britain. Although al-Qaradawi's condem-nation of terrorism in other settings has made him a valuable ally of Western govern-ments in the so-called War on Terror, his support of kamizake operations in Israel, on grounds that the Jewish state is a militarised society where civilians are always real or potential soldiers, has proved embarrassing for the pragmatic Western governments which have sought to engage him after 9/11.

References

Caeiro, Alexandre (2010) 'The Power of European Fatwas: The Minority Fiqh Project and the Making of an Islamic Counterpublic', *International Journal of Middle East Studies*, 42 (3): pp. 435–49.

European Council for Fatwa and Research (1999) *First and Second Collection of Fatwas (Qararat wa fatawa li-l majlis al-'urubbi li-l-ifta' wa-l-buhuth)*, Anas Osama Altikriti and Shaikh Nasif Al-Ubaydi (trans). Cairo: Islamic INC/Al-Falah Foundation.

Gräf, Bettina and Skovgaard-Petersen, Jakob (eds) (2009) *The Global Mufti: The Phenomenon of Yusuf al-Qaradawi*, London: Hurst.

GROUPS AND FEDERATIONS
(2) MILLI GÖRÜŞ

THE MILLI GÖRÜŞ COMMUNITY IN GERMANY: ISLAMISCHE GEMEINSCHAFT MILLI GÖRÜŞ

Werner Schiffauer

The story of the Milli Görüş community in Germany unfolds in four clear-cut phases: (1) The foundational phase (1973–83); (2) crisis and reconstruction (1983–97); (3) reorientation (1997–2002); and (4) the post-Islamist phase.

I. The foundational phase (1973–83)

In the early 1970s hundreds of backyard and storefront mosques were established by self-organised mosque communities of Turkish migrants in almost all major cities of Germany. As a result, there was a structural need for setting up an umbrella organisation in order to organise practical problems associated with running the mosques (such as organising preachers or solving legal questions). Affiliation to the newly founded Salvation Party (MSP, Milli Selamet Partisi) of Necmettin Erbakan seemed to be a particularly promising way for getting an umbrella organisation established. It connected the ideas of industrialisation and modernisation with Islamisation, implying the promise of return to Turkey. Allying an umbrella organisation with that particular party would provide it with a specific profile and give it access to resources in Turkey. This would allow it to compete with other umbrella organisations, in particular with the one that had already been set up by the Süleymancı movement. After initial contacts were made in 1974 the Turkish Union of Europe was founded, with active support from the MSP in Turkey in 1976. In these early years the network between Turkey and Europe, and also between the Milli Görüş communities in Europe, was quite loose. The local communities were independent and organised most of their affairs themselves. The overall Milli Görüş network was a hybrid of a movement in Turkey and mosque communities in Europe.

During the state of emergency in Turkey from 1980 to 1983 many members of the MSP went into exile in Germany in order to avoid persecution. The Milli Görüş communities in Europe radicalised considerably during these years. The disillusionment with the situation in Turkey went hand in hand with pan-Islamic enthusiasm triggered by the Iranian Revolution (1979) and the Muslim resistance in Afghanistan after the Soviet invasion. The communities in Germany were characterised by long-distance radicalism aiming for an Iranian-style Islamic revolution in Turkey.

II. Crisis and reconstruction

When Erbakan decided to establish the Welfare Party (WP) to succeed the MSP in Turkey, in order to participate in the elections of 1983, two-thirds of the German Milli Görüş communities, headed by Cemaleddin Kaplan, split off. Kaplan argued that the *coup d'état* had proven that regime change brought about by Parliament was impossible. Instead, one should go for the Iranian model of an Islamic revolution. The adherents of Erbakan found themselves in a minority position. This seemed to be the end of the Milli Görüş communities in Europe.

Milli Görüş Europe was reconstructed with considerable help from the newly founded WP, who sent the charismatic preacher, Şevki Yilmaz, and the theologian, Osman Yumakoğulları, to Germany. The rather loose network of Milli Görüş communities was transformed into a hierarchical organisation with its centre in Turkey and its sub-centre in Cologne. The local mosques transferred their property rights to Milli Görüş and thus tied themselves firmly to the umbrella organisation. The leadership positions had to be affirmed by the centre, while cohesion was achieved by establishing a highly competitive structure. Communities, regions and local mosque communities competed with each other with regard to recruitment of new members, fundraising or providing services (*hizmet*). The combination of growing complexity, functional differentiation and professionalisation changed the ad hoc style of the organisation's early years. The organisational set-up started to resemble more and more that of an established religious organisation.

During these years a specific organisational culture emerged. It centred around the idea of empowering Muslim immigrants. This was spelled out to mean combating poverty and (religious) ignorance, and promoting Islamic ethics. A particular clientele to be addressed was the second generation. A very effective and disciplined youth organisation was built up. It was supposed to counter the negative impact of Western society on the second generation (such as sex and drugs and rock 'n' roll). This aim was pursued by developing a diversified programme ranging from religious education to sports activities. More important yet was setting up a career system. One in three members in the youth association became a functionary. A career system was installed. Promising young men were offered positions on the regional and even the national level. Thus a regime of recognition was created. Another feature of the organisational culture was the charisma attributed to Erbakan, particularly among members of the first generation. They felt stranded in Europe. He was increasingly seen as a saviour who would bring his people home and put an end to the bitter years in exile. The topic of exile was taken up by Milli Görüş by paralleling the situation in Germany with the situation of *hijra*, Muhammed's forced exile in Medina, which was ended by the glorious return to Mecca in 632.

In the years between 1989 and 1996 the transnational cooperation between the WP in Turkey and the German Community Milli Görüş was extremely intensive. The religious communities in Germany profited from the enthusiasm which resulted from the successes of the WP in regional and national elections in Turkey. The creation of an Islamised state which would allow for a glorious return to Turkey seemed to be imminent. This connected with individual dreams about political careers in the home country. All this motivated Milli Görüş members in Germany to donate heavily to the campaigning of the WP, thus contributing to its electoral successes. Euphoria was also related to the boom years of the 1990s, which saw the growth of 'green capital'. Islamic holdings were thought to be steps towards an Islamic economy.

III. Reorientation

Erbakan won 21.4 per cent of the votes in the national elections in 1996 and became prime minister. The short life of his government led to disappointment among many followers, as it became evident that the leeway for Islamic policies tolerated by the military was extremely narrow. The dream finally collapsed when Erbakan had to step back after the postmodern *coup d'état* of 28 February 1997. Just as important as the failure of the political dream was the collapse of the economic dream. The Islamic Holdings went bankrupt only two years later. The collapse had a strong impact on the communities in Europe, as the establishment of the Islamische Gemeinschaft Milli Görüş (IGMG) had allowed the holdings to advertise in the mosques in support of the investment. Many members who had lost their savings blamed the leadership.

The delegitimisation of the leadership allowed a second generation in the community to take over. This generation differed considerably from the first. They had gone through the European school system and had developed strong ties to the country of immigration without giving up their ties to Turkey. Whereas the first generation had felt they were in exile, the second felt they were in diaspora. The second generation had been much less affected by the developments in the 1990s than the first generation. It was Mehmet Sabri Erbakan, who had been general secretary of Milli Görüş from 1995 to 1999 and its president from 1999 to 2003, who developed a vision with which this second generation could identify. He propounded that Muslims should consider Germany to be their home and thus the dichotomies of Islam and West should be overcome. The existence in Germany, far from being deficient, would allow them to work in an efficient way for the Islamic cause. He called on Muslims to apply for citizenship. They should make their way into European society and in order to do so send their children (girls as well as boys) to European schools. They should fight for their right for difference within the framework of secular society. 9/11 was seen as a chance by Erbakan and his close associates to push through this agenda within the community: the necessity of opening up the mosques and of entering into dialogue with German society and with the churches had become clear to everyone.

Looking back, Mehmet Sabri Erbakan seems to have been predestined for this role. He came from a Turkish-German background and was culturally competent in both cultures. Intellectually brilliant, he was able to design a position for a diasporic Islam which would develop strong ties to the country of immigration while keeping up the links to home country. Being the nephew of Necmettin Erbakan he enjoyed the trust of the latter and shared his charisma. It seems unlikely that anybody else could have dared to formulate a vision so far from the original message.

When the split between the Justice And Development Party (AKP) and Saadet Partisi occurred in 2002 the German community tried to stay out of the conflict, although many of the second generation felt politically closer to Erdoğan. They did not want, however, to alienate the Erbakan loyalists of the first generation. In the diaspora a heightened feeling of complementarity and mutual dependence, as well as gratitude, was characteristic of the intergenerational relationship. The first generation needed the second, because the latter was able to represent the community to the outside. The second generation in turn needed the first, which had founded the mosques and is still today the financial and spiritual backbone of the community.

IV. The post-Islamist period

Mehmet Sabri Erbakan resigned in 2002 after information about an extramarital affair came to be known. After his resignation, the troika of Karahan, Oğuz Üçüncü and Mustafa Yeneroğlu began to take over. Whereas Karahan represented the IGMG in Turkey, Yeneroğlu and Üçüncü represented it in Germany. The troika drew practical consequences from Mehmet Erbakan's visions and institutionalised them. They can be summarised in three points:

A first decision was to refrain from direct action (such as demonstrations or mass rallies), which had characterised much of the Milli Görüş activities in the 1990s, and rather to engage in procedural strategies (such as cooperation in consultative bodies or legal claim-making).

This engagement was institutionalised by building up a remarkable legal department within the general secretary's office. Promising (and critical) young academics were recruited by Yeneroğlu to work with him in this department. He brought together not only students of law, but also students of political and social science and Islamic studies. Over the years a centre of competence emerged which is unique for Muslim organisations in Germany. A culture of rational discussion became characteristic for this centre, and charismatic preachers such as Şevki Yılmaz, who had set the tone at many Milli Görüş rallies in the 1990s, became more and more marginalised.

A second decision was to establish a *fiqh* for Europe. The necessity of *ictihad* is again and again repeated. This stands in strong contrast to the theology advocated by the Milli Görüş movement in the 1980s which critisised any attempt in this direction as *bid'a*. In the 1990s the IGMG supported the European Council for Fatwas and Research (ECFR). Today, however, the leadership of the IGMG feels that the ECFR is not going far enough. The Islamic authorities on the council, who in their majority stem from the Arab-Islamic world, tend not to have firsthand knowledge of Europe. This, however, is required in order to develop legal verdicts that do justice to the situation. Nevertheless, the leadership of Milli Görüş does manage to push this process forward as they challenge the *ulema* in the community with hypotheses they develop about key questions, and call upon them for answers (thus, even though they are not entirely qualified, the theologians are taking the initiative in the legal quest). A firm decision to stay within the Islamic law is thus combined with a legal search.

The third characteristic is a reformulation of secularism. In fact, this generation draws the theoretical consequence from the experience that secularism provides space for minority religions like Islam in Germany. This is a remarkable difference from the experience of the first generation which tends to equate secularism with anti-Islam, repression and even totalitarianism. This rethinking of secularism is particularly important as it coincides with a growing scepticism about the possibilities of an Islamic state. The Islamic Republic of Iran seems especially to highlight that the mingling of religion and politics is corrupting and leads to widespread alienation from religion. In this context, models of secularism that allow for the expression of religion in the public sphere (like the German or the British model) seem to be attractive also for Muslim countries.

This led to an attempt to rethink the relationship between religion and politics. The fight for a 'Just order' (*Adil Düzen*), which had been the programme of the Milli Görüş movement in the 1980s, is replaced by a generalised fight for more justice. According to the leadership of the IGMG, Islam does not provide readymade recipes for curing social ills, but it points out injustices and intolerable circumstances and demands that the believer fight them. Islam does not provide answers, but rather stimulates a search for a better society.

All these developments led to an increasing tension with the Saadet Partisi in Turkey which had responded to the electoral defeats with radicalisation. Positions which had already been given up or at least ameliorated during the late 1990s were again re-emphasised: a vision of a just order was again propagated, an antagonism between Islam and the West constructed, and conspiracy theories formulated. Erdoğan himself was declared to have fallen from faith and to have become an agent of Zionism. All these positions caused problems for the German communities as they were taken as proof by the Verfassungsschutz that the positions developed in Germany were nothing but a facade set up in order to deceive the German public. There was an increasing feeling in the German community that the course steered by Erbakan would be detrimental for their attempts to get recognition as a religious organisation. The criticism by the German community again made Erbakan fear that the European communities would break away.

The conflict broke out in 2005 when Erbakan summoned the regional and European leaders of IGMG to Ankara. Erbakan tried to abolish the European centre in Cologne, which he charged with ideological aberration (Erbakan spoke of 'protestantism') and lack of loyalty. He was planning to tie the regional leadership directly to Ankara. It reflects the balance of power that this attempt was unsuccessful. Relations improved in 2008 when Numan Kurtulmuş was elected to head the Saadet Partisi, after yet another catastrophic defeat in local and regional elections. In many aspects he represents a similar position to those held in Cologne.

References

Schiffauer, Werner (2010) *Nach dem Islamismus. Eine Ethnographie der Islamischen Gemeinschaft Milli Görüş*, Frankfurt am Main: Suhrkamp Verlag.

THE CALIPHATE STATE

Werner Schiffauer

The community of Cemalettin Kaplan was formed in Germany in the early 1980s as a breakaway from the National View – the European branch of the National Salvation Party (NSP, later the Refah (Welfare) Party), the party of the later prime minister of Turkey Necmettin Erbakan. In 1983–4 the leadership of the former NSP split on the issue of whether the party should be re-established after the 'state of exception' (1980–3). All parties had been outlawed, but now new national elections were scheduled. When Erbakan and the party establishment opted to found a successor party to the NSP (the Refah (Welfare) Party), a revolutionary wing headed by Kaplan, the former Müftü of Adana, separated. For them the history of the *coup d'état* had demonstrated the impossibility of a parliamentary route to Islamic rule. Instead, he propagated an extra institutional grassroots movement that would position the Qur'an as the sole foundation for overcoming a perceived split among European Muslims, try to establish a mass movement and seize power in Turkey in an attempt to finally reinstate the caliphate. This model was clearly inspired by Khomeini's triumphant return to Iran. The movement got off to a good start, and great majority of Milli Görüş followers left their communities or transferred their mosques to the Kaplan movement.

Kaplan initially did not just want to found a new community which would join other already existing groups, but rather a community which encompassed all others. It was the vision of an open movement under his leadership. The power of such a charismatic movement rests in its promise to transcend all kinds of borders. Everybody is invited. Institutional ties and social background lose their relevance. The more people follow this invitation the more the aim of a new world seems to be within reach. In a way, the enthusiasm which prevailed in the beginning allowed the community to experience the future state of salvation. It was a 'spontaneous communitas'.[1] The feeling prevailed that all problems can be solved if the community just manages to keep the spirit alive. It is this boundary-transgressing character which carries the promise of salvation, and which distinguishes open charismatic movements from all other parties and organisations. All other organisations, the mystical brotherhoods as well as the parties reaffirming boundaries and working for their individual good, would be overcome by Kaplan. He stood for the promise of a community of passion.

Very early on, however, disenchantment and disillusionment made itself apparent. Hopes that the message would be interpreted as an oriflamme were not realised. Neither had the other communities in Germany joined forces with Kaplan; nor had he been able to mobilise the *hocas* in Turkey. The revolution in Iran had lost much of its initial appeal to the believers during the dirty war with Iraq. Disillusionment of this kind is particularly problematic for a charismatic and boundary-transcending movement. Just as easily as new members had been able to join the movement, they now left. The movement first stagnated and then began to crumble visibly. The number of followers attending the Hegira festival (the central festivity of the community) dropped over the years from 10,000 in 1987 to 2,500 visitors in 1990. In 1987 Ahmet Polat, a co-founder of the movement, left. Conversely, the Milli Görüş movement recovered from the blow it had received and soon began to outnumber the Kaplan community.

In this situation Kaplan had to either accept defeat or find an organisational response to the challenge. He chose the latter and transformed the open movement into a sect. In a series of interrelated measures he kept the community together by drawing symbolic boundaries and by increasing hierarchisation and centralisation. In a way his answer to dissolution was fortress building. In a programmatic sermon, held on 15 August 1988, he sketched his vision of transforming an open movement into an elitist brotherhood of Islamic warriors:

> The movement has hit the road, commencing with the principle: 'The source is the Qur'an, the example is the Prophet.' On this way there are three phases of maturation. They are tied to three locations: The *medrese*, the *tekke* and the barracks. In the *medrese* our adherents will get to know the *seriat*, in the *tekke* they will learn about the mystical way and in the barracks they will learn to shoot.[2]

It is the vision of a mystically inspired covenant of *mücahits* which is expressed here. His son Metin would explain further:

> All believers are soldiers and the apartments, mosques and so on are barracks. The preparation consists in registering the names of families, the registration of video players and TV sets; guaranteeing the availability of teaching material (videos) and the organisation of support. Each month the families are called into the mosques where they are controlled by teachers...Thus a good education will be effectuated and the movement will be able to work effectively.[3]

In 1988 the members of the organisation were registered. For the first time it was formally established who was a member of the organisation and who was not. The same year Kaplan began asking others to take an oath of allegiance to him. An open movement had been turned into a sworn-in community. Furthermore, to separate from the movement not only meant to renounce loyalty towards Kaplan, but also to commit a sin. This far-reaching restructuring of the community led to conflicts and further loss of members. In 1988–9 a number of students who were obviously close disciples of Kaplan revolted against the increasing authoritarian control in the community and left. This event was re-interpreted by Kaplan in his own terms. Those who left the brotherhood of warriors were either afraid of fighting or too much interested in inner-worldly goods and pleasures. They were interpreted as half-hearted, and what was lost in quantity was understood as gained in quality. Those who remained in the movement could proudly consider themselves the avant-garde of a revolution. In this process a highly integrated collective of equal-minded followers emerges. They share a wide-reaching consensus. The discussions in the in-group become more and more important, whereas discussions with outsiders (which so far had formed an important counterweight) become exceedingly rare. This insularity leads to the adoption of ideas, discourses and practices that are increasingly distant from and out-of-touch with those in the broader society. In closed circles, hermetical lines of thinking and arguing develop, which face increasing difficulties in making themselves understood to outsiders. The greater the distance to others, the more closed and narrow the worldview, the greater again the tendencies to centralisation, hierarchisation, cleansing and elite formation. A circular process develops which consists of the following steps: boundary drawing; centralisation; hierarchisation; purification and elite formation; in-group formation; and nonconformism. The Kaplan community is an example of a movement which deals with potential failure by becoming increasingly nonconformist. This laid the grounds for the second step of radicalisation. On 18 April 1992, Kaplan proclaimed the Islamic Federation of Anatolia and was declared *locum tenens* of the caliph by his excited followers. This was declared to be the first step towards the restoration of the caliphate. Kaplan would hold the position until a *şura* of Islamic states would appoint the caliph himself. For the time being, however, Kaplan claimed the right to speak in the name of the *umma*. In that name he demanded that the territory of Anatolia should be returned to the Muslims by the Kemalist occupiers. Kaplan sought to be legitimised in this way for two reasons. A placeholder for the future caliph could only come from Turkey since the last caliph had been an Ottoman. Among Turkish pretenders he again was legitimised as the head of the purest community. There was, however, another problem, because the small number of followers posed a problem of its own. The majority of Islamic scholars hold the position that the most powerful Islamic ruler should become caliph because only he can guarantee the unity and power of Islam. In the backdrop of this thoroughly realistic concept it seems absurd for anybody to claim the title of a caliph 'who can be arrested and put to jail by two policemen'. (Kaplan used to answer this position by stating that he did not claim the caliphate itself, but acted only as *locum tenens*, his intention being only to mark a necessarily symbolic policy. Anybody claiming something else would be guilty of defamation).

The emergence of a close-knit group of followers was a necessary condition for such a presumptuous step. The step effectively put Kaplan outside the consensus of the communities in Germany. It was considered to be an act of sheer insanity and Kaplan was considered to have lost touch with reality. With that step Kaplan entered into the sectarian circle for the second time. First, the boundaries to the other communities were emphasised. Kaplan started to condemn the leaders of other communities as polytheists (*müsrik*). He thus made use of a weapon which is heavily disputed in the Islamic community, namely the branding of a fellow-Muslim as apostate before he himself had declared leaving Islam. All other communities were declared to be illegitimate. 'We say: "There is only one true organisation or community; all other communities and organisation are either unjust or they conflate the just and the unjust." The community also started to distinguish itself visually from the other communities. The members of the movement were asked to wear Islamic garb – wide pants, the turban, a cloak – and to separate themselves thus from the other believers. Even more importantly, Kaplan forbade marriages outside the community. With that step he placed loyalty towards the community over loyalty to kin. Second, hierarchy and centralisation were again emphasised. The quest for loyalty became more absolute. While in the early phases of the movement he had stated that those who do not fight for the caliphate would die the death of ignorance; the death of ignorance was now predicted for those who did not take the oath of allegiance to Kaplan.

The declaration of the government in exile led to the exodus of almost all members of the first generations, who had combined revolutionary zeal with the realism of a generation born and raised in Anatolian villages. The step Kaplan took now was in sharp contrast to what they felt to be adequate. The presumption which lies in the act of declaring oneself the head of the government was immodest by all their standards. In short, the whole act of declaring the government in exile was in contradiction to what they felt to be Islamic. They were replaced by students of the second generation who admired in Kaplan his uncompromising attitude, and who were quite happy to accept the role of a revolutionary avant-garde. In a way the movement became more intellectual, which was very much in line with Kaplan's own dreams and his mild contempt for the unsophisticated followers of the first generation. All this increased the cohesion of the in-group. Thus the foundation was laid for the last step in the radicalisation process: on 8 March 1994 Kaplan declared himself caliph proper. Again there was the hope for setting a precedent. In order to legitimise this step Kaplan introduced a new philosophy of history. According to this theory one is at the turning point of history. Islam has reached the state of total decline where only 1,200 dedicated believers are left. They constitute an elite and are determined that they are able to swing the tide around. From now on the work of reconstruction begins. Those who still have doubts should ask how many soldiers Muhammed had at hand in the battle of Badr (300) or in the battle of Uhud (1,000).

This further radicalisation again had interesting consequences with regard to boundary drawing. A qualitative change is observable. Originally one was supposed to distance oneself most radically from those whose positions were fundamentally different (as the positions of the Diyanet or the Süleymancı). Now the biggest enemy seems to be the one whose position is the closest. 'The other parties are more distant from Islam. In Erbakan's party Islam is an issue. Exactly because of that reason it is the worst. The more they seem to take up Islamic issues the more intriguing they are. So Kaplan's party is worse than others.'[4] The dynamic of in-group formation, boundary drawing and increasing nonconformity raises the costs of exit. The more this process is advanced the more difficult it becomes to separate from this group. An exit does not only mean a break with almost all social ties, but also a break with a reality which one has taken for granted. It seems to be related to this fact that Kaplan managed to stabilise finally the number of adherents to around 1,200 followers.

In 1995 Cemaleddin Kaplan died. He appointed his son Metin as successor in the caliphate but Metin, however, possessed neither his charisma nor his knowledge. In 1996 a split occurred when Ibrahim Sofu, a medical doctor in Berlin, was appointed counter-caliph by a yet smaller group of followers. Metin responded with fatwas declaring the appointment of a counter-caliph during the time of an acting caliph as an unlawful act deserving the death penalty. On 5 May 1997 Ibrahim Sofu was killed in his apartment by a professional hit squad. The murderer remained undetected, but suspicion fell on adherents of Metin Kaplan. There were pertinent rumours in the Turkish community (not only from within the Kaplan movement) which blamed the Turkish secret service. In November 1998 the Istanbul police reported that it had prevented a suicide attack on the Atatürk memorial which was supposed to take place during the ceremonies marking the seventy-fifth anniversary of the Turkish Revolution. Again inconsistencies in the police report brought forth rumours that this was also a set-up by the Turkish secret service. In 1999 Metin Kaplan was arrested by the German police and charged with having set up a terrorist organisation. The organisation was outlawed in 2001.

Notes

1   Victor Turner (1969) *The Ritual Process. Structure and anti-Structure*, New York: Ithaca.
2   Werner Schiffauer (2000) *Die Gottesmänner – Türkische Islamisten in Deutschland*, Frankfurt am Main: Suhrkamp.
3   Ibid.
4   Ibid.

References

Schiffauer, Werner (2000) *Die Gottesmänner – Türkische Islamisten in Deutschland*, Frankfurt am Main: Suhrkamp.
Turner, Victor (1969) *The Ritual Process. Structure and anti-Structure*, New York: Ithaca.

THE ISLAMIC FEDERATION OF BELGIUM: THE BELGIAN BRANCH OF THE MILLI GÖRÜŞ MOVEMENT

Ural Manço

The Islamic Federation of Belgium (FIB)[1] is Belgium's second Turkish organisation after Diyanet (the Turkish–Islamic Union – Turkey's official religious body in Belgium). Contrary to Diyanet, the FIB does not enjoy official recognition and, like all the Milli Görüş movement's national federations, relies on its own finances. Thirty Turkish mosques in Belgium are controlled by the FIB, while the Diyanet mosques number 62. At present, the FIB's audience is composed of around 15,000 people. The FIB holds that the number is more than 40,000.[2] In comparison, the current audience of Diyanet approaches 100,000 people (according to Diyanet)[3]. The figures put forward by the organisations seem exaggerated, given that in 2005 Belgium's total population of Turkish origin was estimated at 142,000.

In 1982, a segment of the Turkish population of Brussels split from the rest of the community to organise their own Qur'an classes. This minority group allied itself with the Islamic-populist political movement led in Turkey by Necmettin Erbakan since 1969. It criticised the intervention of Turkish diplomats in Islamic spaces in Belgium. Since 1983 its followers have merged under the name of the Belgian Islamic Federation (Belçika Islam Federasyonu), the Belgian branch of the Milli Görüş movement. The FIB was established as a non-profit organisation on 24 September 1986.[4] Its cadres describe it as a social assistance organisation for immigrants, yet religious services are by far its most important activity and an FIB-affiliated local association is first and foremost a mosque. The 1990s was the golden age of this body that, parallel to the development of Milli Görüş throughout Europe, was able to continually expand its activities and number of sympathisers. In 2002 the FIB was affected by a schism from which it is only beginning to recover today. Better trained cadres from the FIB left it to regroup in the European Turkish Democratic Union (UETD, Union européenne des Turcs démocrates). This new association, which has distinct branches in Germany and the Netherlands, appeared in Europe at the time when the current prime minister, Recep Tayyip Erdoğan, and his followers broke with the Islamist party of the historic leader Necmettin Erbakan. Presenting itself as a conservative but non-religious political organisation, the UETD effectively backs Prime Minister Erdoğan's Justice and Development Party (AKP).

The classic formulation of the historic leader Erbakan's thought willingly conflates the 'confessional view' and 'national(ist) view' (the two possible translations of Milli Görüş). This discourse, wherein the pan-Islamic utopia of a unified Muslim world under the Turkish flag is palpable, ultimately turns out to be populism lined with clever electioneering, that castigates the entrenched Kemalist establishment. From Belgium, the federation's members adhere to the values of Turkish–Islamic traditions and the idealised view of the Ottoman Empire as a conquering force that made the Christian West tremble. Yet they do not reject the technical and economic progress generated by that selfsame West so disparaged for its moral decay. Each profane venture of Milli Görüş or the FIB necessarily finds an Islamic justification. The federation member is a believer subject to *shari'a*, that is, to all the cultural, moral and social obligations of a holistic concept of Islam, which is his or her daily guide. Socio-political activism is likewise included among obligations. Members are required to dedicate one day a week to proselytising or to benevolent participation in the organisation's social and charity activities. Since the second half of the 1990s, integration, which primarily means economic success in European society, has not represented the antithesis of Muslim existence for the FIB. According to the federation's discourse, the community should prosper under Islamic guidance in order to gain respect. The subject of individual assimilation, which instilled so much fear among members in past decades, is no longer tackled in this century. For the FIB the community, which in Belgium is able to perpetuate its religious and national traditions, should respect the law and remain on good terms with the native populations and authorities.

Yet reasons for joining the FIB are not only ideological or religious. The quality of services rendered and the warmth of human relations also seem to be influential factors. Family tradition and region of origin may also play a role. Especially in Brussels and Ghent, cities where most Turkish immigrants come from one single district (Emirdag), it has been noted that families who belong to the FIB are not usually from that area, nor are the majority of FIB leaders. It is as if the Muslims who are not from Emirdag prefer not to join the Diyanet mosques, which are inevitably managed and attended by people from Emirdag. The public who attend FIB mosques are noticeably evenly split between first-generation (the elderly) and second-generation immigrants, that is, the adults and young people resulting from immigration. For this public a mosque is a place for socialising or organising other activities besides prayer: Qur'an courses; moral and religious counselling; insurance for repatriating the deceased and funeral arrangements; organisation of the pilgrimage; payment of the *zakat* and sacrifice; and the possibility of buying *halal* meat, books or other cultural items. As of the 2000s the FIB has offered travel options (Paris, London, Andalusia) and activities in non-mixed groups: visits to amusement parks or museums, conferences and sporting activities.

Women are notably visible and active in the Milli Görüş movement. The women's branches of the FIB appeared in the early 1990s, and adult women are regularly urged to make donations during women-only meetings called *süvari*. Such donations can be very fruitful. Given the low education level of most FIB women, there is ample interest in the social work undertaken by the female sections. It focuses on areas such as consumer topics, hygiene, child education, sexuality and contraception. In 1991 the FIB opened, near Mons (in the south of the country), the Avicenna (*Ibn-î Sina*) Institute of Islamic Sciences for young women. Every year this institution hosts several dozen adolescents during the summer vacation period who are given religious instruction in Turkish. The training is complemented by learning to recite the Qur'an in Arabic and by a French language course. Participants come from all around Europe. Wearing the headscarf is mandatory for the students. During the academic year the institute becomes a boarding school for girls. Boarders come from French-speaking Belgium and France. They continue their ordinary secondary education at Belgian schools in the region, and in the evening there are also courses on Islamic religion given in Turkish. The institute is currently run by a pair of theologians trained in Turkey.

The imams and other officials of the organisation are often 'imported' from Turkey via marriage with a daughter of immigrants, and live in symbiosis with the FIB's followers. Their missionary zeal comprises the federation's force. These cadres often have a Turkish university degree (in theology or other fields), but are also educated in Turkish official secondary schools for those who conduct religious worship. Their aim is to sustain the political movement and to channel the gathered funds to Turkey. Some hope the FIB stage will open up a future in the international leadership of Milli Görüş, in the political party or in companies pertaining to leading community members. Since the 1990s, four people have shared the job of running the federation, of whom only one has a degree in theology. Differences between the national Milli Görüş branches are due to the quality of cadres and leaders from the standpoint of educational background, profession and mastery of the host country's language. For example, Turks from the Netherlands benefit from a more organised Milli Görüş branch, which presents a better public image than the FIB. The appearance in Belgium of some young second-generation organisers who have higher education degrees has not yet changed this situation.

Recognition by the Belgian authorities, press and public has been a constant goal in the FIB's activities. Since 1997 the federation has actively taken part in interreligious dialogues in much of Belgium. In 2000, the federation offered a ton of meat to the *Restos du Cœur*[5] to mark the festival of sacrifice. The FIB published a communiqué condemning the 9/11 terrorist attacks and, since 2002, the FIB has offered Qur'an courses in French and Dutch, as well as sermons in those languages. Open-door workshops in mosques and meals to break the fast during Ramadan month are often organised. One novel activity is the holding in Brussels of informative gatherings in the form of bazaars and similar events before local council or regional elections (11 March 2004 and 14–15 March 2009). These activities enable the FIB to promote itself and earn income through the sale of books, multimedia material and food. Politicians of Turkish origin in the traditional parties (Socialist, Liberal, Christian-Democratic) are invited, along with Turkish diplomatic representatives. The federation usually avoids participation in political demonstrations, but two recent exceptions must nevertheless be noted. In October 2007 the FIB condemned the Kurdish guerrilla group PKK for massacring 12 Turkish soldiers in south east Turkey, as well as the violence committed by Turkish youths from Brussels after their protest in response. The FIB's participation in the demonstration against Israel's attack on Gaza (11 January 2009) was notable for its discipline and order. The FIB's collaboration with other Turkish religious organisations (especially Diyanet) is non-existent, in contrast to what has been observed in the case of Milli Görüş in Cologne and Strasbourg. The FIB has otherwise worked, since very recently, with non-religious Turkish organisations to arrange recreational and cultural activities such as a Turkish poetry festival and a Turkish book fair.

In Europe, the Milli Görüş constellation is the biggest social and religious organisation of Turkish emigrants, created as fully independent of Turkey and without official recognition from European governments. This success is its members' pride and joy. The FIB must nevertheless deal with chronic problems, both internally and externally. Internally, there are indications of corruption during the 1990s (dues money may have gone missing on various occasions). The FIB's management seems somewhat chaotic and dues collection is difficult. The problem of training qualified cadres also seems prevalent. For these reasons, the FIB may have lost any chance to compete against the official Diyanet Islam controlled by the secularist Turkish state. These external difficulties characterise the Belgian authorities' suspicious view of the FIB. The FIB has been continually associated with Islamism, political Islam and fundamentalism. In 1989, for example, the FIB's local mosque was taken to court by the Schaerbeek local authorities over non-regulation reno-vation work. The local Diyanet mosque was in the same situation but was left unboth-ered. In 1991–3, when the FIB founded the Avicenna Institute of Islamic Sciences, the Belgian press insisted on labelling it a 'fundamentalist' initiative. In 2007–8, the Belgian regional governments recognised and accepted the financing of 56 mosques, a majority of them Turkish, yet none associated with the federation.

Notes

1 http://www.fibif.be/tr/ (link no longer functional)
2 M. El Battiui and M. Kanmaz (2004) *Mosquées, imams et professeurs de religion islamique en Belgique*, Brussels: Fondation Roi Baudouin, p. 19 http://www.kbs-frb.be/uploadedFiles/KBSFRB/Files.
3 http://www.belcikadiyanet.be/du/ (accessed 19 June 2014)
4 Date of publication in the *Moniteur belge*, identification number: 26481/86.
5 Translation – Restaurants of the Heart. A charity organisation which provides meals to those in need.

References

Battiui, Mohamed El and Meryem Kanmaz (2004) *Mosquées, imams et professeurs de religion islamique en Belgique*, Brussels: Fondation Roi Baudouin, p. 19. http://www.kbs-frb.be/uploadedFiles/KBS-FRB/Files/FR/PUB_1448_Mosquees_imams_prof_islam.pdf (link no longer working).
Manço, Ural (1997) 'Des organisations socio-politiques comme solidarités islamiques dans l'immigration turque en Europe', *Les Annales de l'Autre Islam*, 4: pp. 97–133.
———(2000) 'La présence musulmane en Belgique: dimensions historique, démographique et économique', in Manço, Ural (ed.), *Voix et Voies Musulmanes de Belgique*, Brussels: Publications des Facultés Universitaires Saint-Louis, pp. 17–39.

MILLI GÖRÜŞ IN FRANCE

Samim Akgönül

In France, the networks of Turkish religious associations are shared by different types of structures, which conform to the socio-religious configuration in Turkey. All Turkish associations in France belong to a network, and 'independent' prayer groups do not exist. Regarding those originating in Turkey, two networks dominate the Turco-French landscape. First, about 45 per cent of the associations receive imams sent and paid for by the Turkish government. These associations (approximately 120 in France) may be considered within the Diyanet İşleri Türk İslam Birliği (DITIB, Turkish–Islamic Union for Religious Affairs) network, an emanation of the Turkish Presidency of Religious Affairs (Diyanet), itself reporting directly to the prime minister.[1] Second, approximately 25 per cent of the associations (around 50)[2] are part of the Milli Görüş network. The distinction between belonging to the DITIB versus the Milli Görüş network must be made clear from the outset.

Since the DITIB was founded in 1983, partly to counter the Milli Görüş network (active in Cologne from 1975), hundreds of associations have either joined or been founded within the former. However, importantly, the fact that an association is within this network does not necessarily imply an ideological orientation or attachment to official Islam, given that ties with the DITIB are accompanied by many advantages that can hardly be deemed insignificant. Not only does such affiliation mean good relations with the consulates, it also allows an imam (and perhaps a religious teacher) to be obtained at Turkish government expense. So belonging to the DITIB network has much less to do with ideological considerations than is the case with Milli Görüş or the Süleymancı. That said, the faithful who attend Milli Görüş mosques are not necessarily all as politicised as the functionaries. Attendance may be solely for religious practice or social reasons. Consequently, one must always bear in mind that Milli Görüş is not a brotherhood, nor a sect, nor even a distinct religious allegiance.

Milli Görüş in France: structure and hierarchy

In France Milli Görüş has, since 1981, been organised within the framework of the National Islamic Union Movement of France (TNUIF, Tendance Nationale Union Islamique de France), whose French centre is found on the Rue de Faubourg Saint-Denis in Paris. It is headed by Mustafa Doğan, one of the old guard very much involved in Turkish internal politics. The network is affiliated with the National Federation of French Muslims

(FNPF, Fédération Nationale des Musulmans de France) and boasts 1,500 members.[3] Since 1998 the network's associations have met within the framework of the Milli Görüş Islamic Community of France (CIMG, İslam Toplumu Milli Görüş Fransa). At its head is a member of the young generation, Ahmet Bakcan, although the old guard is still very influential.

The CIMG's role is not solely confined to religious practice. Analysis of the association's multiple activities shows that religious practice is marginal compared to other socio-religious and educational activities. Among the most significant are the following: arrangements for the pilgrimage to Mecca (*Hajj* during the pilgrimage period, *'Umra* at other times); of ritual slaughter; sacrifices during the festival of *'Id al-Adha*; funeral services (burials in France or transport to Turkey – the CIMG has a death insurance fund); organisation and distribution of the religious tax (*Fitr* and *Zakat*); and above all religious courses and other activities meant for children, such as holiday classes. Also, the magazine *Perspektive*, issued by the Islamische Gemeinschaft Milli Görüş (IGMG, the Cologne centre), is distributed in France and the radio station imgm.fm has a large internet audience. The associations with prayer rooms are spread over six regions headed by Paris on the one hand, but also by Cologne at the European level, and evidently by Turkey as well.

Discourse and position in the French landscape

As in Germany or the Benelux countries, Milli Görüş France is an ideological and political organisation as much as a religious one. The network's top concern has consequently

DIE ISLAMISCHE GEMEINSCHAFT - COLOGNE COMMUNAUTE ISLAMIQUE *MILLI GÖRÜŞ* FRANCE					
ALPES Albertville	OUEST Blois	ÎLE DE FRANCE Beauvais	EST Belfort	SUD-OUEST Bordeaux	RÉGION LYONNAISE Ambérieu
Annecy	Châteaudun	Creil	Colmar		Annonay
Annemasse	Vendôme	Fontenay	Strasbourg		Avignon
Bellegarde		Mantes-La-Jolie	Haguenau		Bourgoin
Chambéry		Montfermeil	Metz		Clermont-Ferrand
Grenoble		Poissy	Morhange		Feurs
Nantua		Ris Orangis	Mulhouse		Le Creusot
Oyonnax		Sarcelles	Neufchâteau		Firminy
Sallanches		Sevran	Niederhaslach		Le Creusot
Ugine			Saint-Avold		Péage de Roussillon
			Saverne		Saint-Chamond
					Saint-Etienne
					Salon de Provence
					Vaise
					Vénissieux
					Vienne
					Villefranche

always been Turkey, at least its political life and the religious values of Turkish society. The discourse by the network's officials in France has therefore always addressed that country. Only recently have we noted a change in both discourse and effect. Indeed, since the late 1990s it has been possible to make out a different orientation in the network's activities, now more concerned with local community problems. The Milli Görüş's arrival in power in Turkey, first through government coalitions and then after 2002 with the Justice And Development Party (AKP) government issued from its ranks, has certainly played a role in this. But the shift does not mean the umbilical cord with Turkey or the mother movement there has been cut – far from it. That said, regarding hot topics in European public opinion such as the Islamic headscarf or interreligious dialogue, the Milli Görüş's discourse has been considerably toned down. It has become increasingly 'moderate' and altogether more consensual than that of the Süleymancı brotherhood, for example. After enactment of the 2004 law against conspicuous symbols in public schools, specifically targeting headscarves, Milli Görüş remained notably silent while the Süleymancı organised both media and legal resistance. Another sign of changed orientation is seen in the process of enhancing Islam's representation in France through the French Council of the Muslim Faith (CFCM, Conseil Français du Culte Musulman) and the Regional Councils of the Muslim Faith (CRCM, Conseils Régionaux du Culte Musulman). Milli Görüş remained entirely disinterested throughout this process and its numerous ups and downs,[4] maintaining that it was an issue between the Maghrebis and the French authorities. Moreover, during the 1999 consultation, *Istishara*, Milli Görüş was rejected by the French government in favour of the DITIB. However, once the structure was put in place Milli Görüş also joined the path towards representation.

The Milli Görüş is facing three important tasks. The first is acquiring legitimacy with respect to French officialdom. Lest we forget, for a decade (approximately 1985–95) Turkey pressured its European partners, and particularly Germany, to label Milli Görüş a dangerous if not 'terrorist' organisation, and to limit its activities. Through its determined participation in the CFCM and CRCM context Milli Görüş has, little by little, gained respectability. Second, like the other Muslim federative organisations in France, Milli Görüş wants to show its capacity to represent the body of Islam in France, and this despite the historic and numerical minority of Turks in that country. Lastly, what is really at stake is the aim to show the Turkish community that the representative ground is not solely occupied by the DITIB, and that Milli Görüş's influence matters in France's relations with Turkey, at least concerning religion. Such market strategies are well known by the rival networks and should certainly not be minimised. Yet neither Milli Görüş nor the DITIB are competing for the faithful. The rivalry is over representation and not supporters or dogma. The DITIB did not counterattack when Milli Görüş tried (unsuccessfully) in the 1990s to place France's newly arrived Balkan Muslim refugees under its aegis.[5] Like the other networks, Milli Görüş has also played alliance and rivalry games during the three successive elections, even though its leaders have basically been sceptical about the usefulness and function of the CFCM. During the first elections, Milli Görüş made common cause with the Union of Islamic Organisations of France (UOIF). During the second elections it tried to go it alone, without much success. But this lack of alliance harmed the UOIF, which lost the Alsace CRCM presidency. The June 2008 elections saw an alliance with the UOIF at national level and local alliances of opportunity, such as in Alsace, where the Strasbourg Grand Mosque obtained its backing.

Conclusion

It is now legitimate to ask whether the 'radical' label is appropriate for Milli Görüş France, as the organisation has been integrated into both the French system and the Turkish one. Admittedly the Milli Görüş members, current supporters or those who just use the mosques to pray, form a conservative population that aspires to more religion and more Islam in both public and private lives. In that sense they can be therefore called 'Islamists'. But there are other networks and other tendencies, Muslim or not, which have the same sort of aspirations. It is true that during the period when official Turkish Islam and Milli Görüş were very much at odds the risks of radicalised discourse existed. But Milli Görüş has never been a violent organisation – this is evidenced by the fact that the Turkish radical Islamic movement, *Kaplancı*, broke with Milli Görüş in the 1980s, deeming it too moderate. In the first decade of this century even the discourse has been toned down and the network seems to be refocusing on the Turkish political landscape, albeit also on European Islam. That said, a number of positions remain very low profile, such as the subject of Judaism or Zionism already noted by Bilici.[6] However, from now on it will be totally out of place to state that Milli Görüş advocates the establishment of *shari'a* in Turkey by way of France.[7]

Notes

1   Samim Akgönül (2005) *Religions de Turquie, religions des Turcs : nouveaux acteurs dans l'Europe élargie*. Paris: L'Harmattan, p. 129.
2   According to Ternissien, Milli Görüş controls 70 associations in France. See Xavier Ternissien (2002) *La France des mosquées*, Paris: Albin Michel, p. 183; I was able to count 62 in 2004; Samim Akgönül (2006) 'Millî Görüş : institution religieuse minoritaire et mouvement politique transnational', in Samir Amghar, (ed.), *Recompositions contemporaines de l'islamisme en situation de diaspora*, Paris: Lignes de Repères, pp. 63–86. The CIMG official website lists 52. http://milligoruş.cimgfrance.fr/. (accessed 19 June 2014)
3   Jean-Pierre Touzanne (2001) *L'islamisme turc*, Paris: L'Harmattan, p. 129.
4   See to that end Franck Frégosi (2008) *Penser l'islam dans la laïcité*, Paris: Fayard, pp. 278–94.
5   Xavier Bougarel (2005) 'Islam balkanique et intégration européenne' in Rémy Leveau and Khadija Mohsen-Finan (eds), *Musulmans de France et d'Europe*, Paris: CNRS éditions, p. 39.
6   Faruk Bilici (1997) 'Le parti islamiste turc et sa dimension international', *Les annales de l'Autre islam*, 4, p. 45.
7   Birol Caymaz (2002) *Les mouvements islamiques turcs à Paris*, Paris: L'Harmattan, p. 212.

References

Akgönül, Samim (2005) *Religions de Turquie, religions des Turcs : nouveaux acteurs dans l'Europe élargie*, Paris: L'Harmattan.
—— (2006) 'Millî Görüş : 'Institution religieuse minoritaire et mouvement politique transnational', in Samir Amghar (ed.), *Recompositions contemporaines de l'islamisme en situation de diaspora*, Paris: Lignes de Repères, pp. 63–86.

Bilici, Faruk (1997) 'Le parti islamiste turc et sa dimension international', *Les annales de l'Autre islam*, 4: pp. 44–58.

Bougarel, Xavier (2005) 'Islam balkanique et intégration européenne' in Rémy Leveau and Khadija Mohsen-Finan (eds), *Musulmans de France et d'Europe*, Paris: CNRS éditions, pp. 21–48.

Caymaz, Birol (2002) *Les mouvements islamiques turcs à Paris*, Paris: L'Harmattan.

Frégosi, Franck (2008) *Penser l'islam dans la laïcité*, Paris: Fayard.

Ternissien, Xavier (2002) *La France des mosquées*, Paris: Albin Michel.

Touzanne, Jean-Pierre (2001) *L'islamisme turc*, Paris: L'Harmattan.

MILLI GÖRÜŞ IN THE NETHERLANDS

Thijl Sunier

In the Netherlands, Milli Görüş consists of two separate branches with an independent administration. One operates mainly in the southern part of the country under the name of Nederlands Islamitische Federatie (NIF, Dutch Islamic Federation). The other is based in Amsterdam and operates in the middle and northern parts of the country and calls itself Milli Görüş Noord Nederland (Milli Görüş Northern Netherlands), or simply Milli Görüş. The NIF coordinates the activities of 17 local mosques and another 50 associations for women, youth, students, etc. Milli Görüş Noord Nederland coordinates 22 mosques and a variety of other associations. In terms of numbers, Milli Görüş is mid-range. Officially their mosques are owned by a European foundation under the supervision of Avrupa Milli Görüş Teşkilatları (Organisation of the Milli Görüş in Europe) in Germany. As in the case of all Turkish-Muslim organisations, the rank-and-file of Milli Görüş in the Netherlands consists of ordinary Turkish labour migrants and their offshoots, and imams are recruited from among Turkish residents in the Netherlands. Due to the strict immigration laws in the Netherlands it is very difficult to recruit religious personnel from Turkey, except through the Turkish state's Diyanet İşleri Başkanlığı (Presidency of Religious Affairs). Within the Milli Görüş organisations there is a strict separation between religious duties and activities that concern the local community and Dutch society. The latter activities are the responsibility of the board of the association. All theological issues are the responsibility of the imam. The NIF generally concentrates more on core activities such as running the mosques, religious teaching and organising meetings for the members, whereas the northern branch has been very active in their efforts to develop the local associations with a clear rooting in the neighbourhood.

The first coordinated activities of Milli Görüş in the Netherlands date back to the early 1980s. After the military coup in Turkey in 1980, Milli Görüş shifted its attention more to Europe in general. It intensified the development of a religious infrastructure in the Netherlands specifically because of the growing influence of the Diyanet İşleri Başkanlığı among Turkish migrants. In the late 1970s the competition between several Islamic movements among Turkish migrants was very fierce. Until the early 1990s the Dutch branch of Milli Görüş was firmly under the influence of the German headquarters. The attempts of some young leaders to achieve greater autonomy from Cologne resulted in a severe conflict with the German headquarters in 1990. Since then, the maintenance of an independent agenda has remained a sensitive issue in Dutch Milli Görüş circles.

In 1997, Dutch Milli Görüş split into southern and northern branches. The origin of the separation between the two branches is still a topic of conjecture. The relations with the Turkish and German sister organisations may have played a crucial role. Some have argued, however, that the separation had to do with the scission of the the Welfare Party in Turkey, between the younger generation that in 2001 would found the Justice and Development Party and Erbakan's supporters that organised themselves in the Felicity Party. Milli Görüş Noord Nederland would side with the former, whereas the southern branch would consist of supporters of the latter.

Among the Dutch public Milli Görüş is probably the most well-known Islamic organisation in the Netherlands, both in a positive and in a negative sense. Under its former spokesman Haci Karacaer, who presided over the northern branch of Milli Görüş from 1999 until early 2006, the association developed from a low profile organisation of Turkish migrants into a high-profile movement that very actively initiated and participated in public debate, and which reaches the press on a regular basis. Under his leadership, the Aya Sofya mosque in Amsterdam turned the yearly *iftar* gathering, when local officials, politicians and companions were invited, into a happening where national politicians, the mayor of Amsterdam, academics, journalists and opinion leaders took part in a public debate. It was also under the leadership of Karacaer that the planning of the so-called 'Wester mosque' took shape, a huge complex consisting of a mosque, apartments, a shopping centre and a service centre. Milli Görüş had bought a plot of land in an old quarter of Amsterdam with the intention of building a new mosque there. Since the movement had a reputation of being Islamist, there was massive resistance to the plans. Articles appeared in the newspapers in which the whole project was depicted as a means to increase the influence of Turkish Islamism among Turkish migrants in the neighbourhood. It was mainly through the careful strategy of Karacaer and his companions that the mosque project turned from a presumed threat into an example of interethnic and interreligious cooperation. The mosque would be built in the architectural style of the famous 'Amsterdam School'. According to officials of the municipality, the project was a sublime act of cooperation between several collective actors in the neighbourhood and a model for future projects. The Dutch Secretary of Justice even laid the first stone for the building.

This dream was abruptly put to an end in April 2006 when the German branch of Milli Görüş ousted the board of the mosque and replaced it with people who would listen more carefully to the directives of the German headquarters. Since Germany had labelled Milli Görüş as fundamentalist, the shift was immediately depicted by the local Dutch authorities as a *coup d'état* that put an end to the 'liberal' experiment. In addition there were rumours about fraud. Since the image of the 'new' Milli Görüş was still fragile, and the German branch was depicted as radical, most of the Dutch partners in the project were immediately ready to take up this version of events and withdraw from it entirely. It is uncertain whether the Wester mosque will ever be built.

This incident nicely captures the position in which Milli Görüş still finds itself. In spite of the important transformations it is undergoing and its loosening ties to Turkey, Milli Görüş continues to be depicted in a simplistic way as the outpost of the Turkish anti-secularisation movement with a hidden political agenda for immigrant populations in Europe. In the current context, this perception of Milli Görüş (by the State and the dominant majority) generates increasingly negative effects. The fears of a globalised threat of Islam, and the related attempt by the Dutch government to encourage the development of a so-called liberal Islam by curtailing any international influence on Dutch Islam, have altered the threshold of acceptance for movements such as Milli Görüş. It is for this reason that initiatives such as the Wester mosque continue to be monitored very closely by Dutch authorities.

References

Landman, Nico (1992) *Van mat tot minaret*, Amsterdam: VU Uitgeverij.

Sunier, Thijl (1996) *Islam in Beweging. Turkse Jongeren en islamitische Organisaties*, Amsterdam: Het Spinhuis.

—— (2006) 'The Western Mosque: Space in Physical Place', *ISIM Review*, 18: pp. 22–4.

MILLI GÖRÜŞ IN DENMARK

Jørgen Bæk Simonsen

Milli Görüş has been present in Denmark since the mid-1970s. At this time, when Turkish migrant workers began to unify their families, a number of social, cultural and religious issues surfaced among the parents and many felt a dire need for advice and assistance. Some parents approached the Turkish embassy, but requests for assistance were declined, ostensibly due to the official Turkish principle of secularism. From the early 1970s on, a growing number of Turkish migrants became involved with Islamic Turkish circles active in the major cities of Germany. These circles housed large numbers of Turkish migrant workers in a strategic effort to mobilise them for the political struggle inside Turkey. It eventually became clear in these circles that many Turkish parents living in Denmark needed guidance in bringing up their children. Accordingly, a number of *hoças* (imams) with affiliations to Milli Görüş began to visit Denmark for short periods, offering the parents the Islamic guidance they requested. When this was realised by the Turkish embassy, the embassy decided to change its policy. As the needs of Turkish parents living in Denmark were recognised, it was decided, by way of Diyanet İşleri Türk-Islam Birligi, linked to the office of the prime minister, that the Turkish embassy in Copenhagen would in the future try to assist Turkish migrant groups in Denmark in obtaining educated imams. The Diyanet initiative was successful. Within a few years local Turkish mosques were established in a number of cities where the Turkish migrants were living. Turkish migrants with links to Milli Görüş were generally outmaneouvred by Diyanet but were able to succeed in establishing local mosques and associations in the greater Copenhagen area, as well as in Aarhus (the second-largest town in Denmark) and in a number of mid-sized cities throughout Denmark.

Milli Görüş in Denmark was formally organised in 1985 in an organisation called Danimarka Milli Görüş Teşkilati, with a strong commitment to sustaining the role of Islam in the country of origin (Turkey), as well as among Turks who were settled in the world at large as a result of migration. The name was changed in 1986 to Danimarka Müsülman Göcmenler Teşkilati (DMGT). Islam became accordingly part and parcel of the formal network established in Denmark, and the importance of Islam was exposed in the official name of the union, Sammenslutningen af Muslimske Indvandrerforeninger (Federation of Muslim Immigrant Associations).

DMGT was formally part of Avrupa Milli Görüş Teşkilaleri, set up in Germany in order to disseminate the ideology of Milli Görüş. The reason for establishing DMGT was based on a principal recognition of the new realities for Turkish migrants and their families, who were to stay and remain outside of Turkey. Milli Görüş defines Islam as a comprehensive way of life and, as such, it must be activated as a point of reference in both the collective and the individual lives of Muslims. The local associations of DMGT organise a number of initiatives in the local mosques, including courses in the Qur'an and courses on classical Islam for children and young people, and lectures and discussions for adults. The DMGT is also involved in organising *hajj* for Turks, and Muslims in general, living in Denmark, and has established well-functioning links to the Saudi authorities to fulfil this goal.

For decades the split between Milli Görüş and Diyanet kept the Turks from cooperating with other Muslim groups and organisations in Denmark. As the political scene in Turkey slowly changed, relations between Milli Görüş and the Turkish embassy and Diyanet improved, especially after the inauguration in 2002 of the first Justice And Development Party (AKP) government. In line with this, from 2003 onwards Milli Görüş became involved in an effort to establish a Muslim graveyard in the greater Copenhagen area with a number of other local Muslim groups and organisations. The initiative materialised in 2007, and a Muslim graveyard was officially established in Brøndbyerne, a greater Copenhagen suburb. Inspired by this Milli Görüş, in cooperation with other Muslim groups, tried to organise a nationwide umbrella organisation to represent Islam and Muslims in Denmark, by formulating a declaration of principles. Even though their efforts did not gain wider support due to intra-Muslim disagreements, in March 2006 Milli Görüş, in cooperation with others, established Danmarks Muslimske Union (DUM), and other groups in 2007 were able to establish Muslimernes Fællesråd.

In 1994 parents associated with Milli Görüş applied to the Ministry of Education for permission to establish a private Muslim school. Permission was granted and the school was opened. In the early years most of the children came from families supporting Milli Görüş, but during recent years the school has been approached by many other Muslim families, presumably due to the very high results it has gained in various external evaluations conducted by private think-tanks and the Ministry of Education.

The present chairman of DMGT, who was elected in the autumn of 2006, indicates that the present number of members is approximately 2,500.

References

Bæk Simonsen, Jørgen (1991) *Islam i Danmark. Muslimske institutioner i Danmark 1970–1989*, Aarhus: Aarhus Universitetsforlag.

Petersen, Lars (1999) *Newer Islamic Movements in Western Europe*, Aldershot: Ashgate.

Schmidt, Garbi (2007) *Muslim i Danmark – muslim i verden*, Uppsala: Universitetstryk-keriet.

(3) SALAFIST GROUPS

SALAFI POLITICS IN THE NETHERLANDS

Martijn de Koning

In the Netherlands, Salafi movements have become the focus of attention and are regularly linked to intolerance, promoting violence against 'infidels' and inciting hatred against politicians and other opinion leaders. In particular, 9/11 and the murder of Theo Van Gogh by Mohammed Bouyeri in November 2004, serve as the exemplary events in the public debate that are used to explain what is wrong with Islam or, conversely, what is wrong with the host countries of Muslim migrants. Based upon their own claims to follow a *Salafi Manhaj* (Salafi method of learning and training Islamic knowledge), six main Salafi groups can be identified, distinguished by the different Islamic authorities they base their teachings on.

In the 1990s, two new groups of migrants to Europe appear: militant representatives who asked Muslims in Europe for financial support on the one hand, and people who were victims of political Islam and victims of the prosecution of political Islam in their home country on the other. Among the latter were representatives of Salafi groups in the Middle East. During the 1990s, and with increasing speed after 9/11, the different branches of Salafism in the Netherlands developed into social movements by building up their own mosques, websites and informal networks used for resource mobilisation and dissemination. Nowadays we can distinguish between six main groups, each with its own internal divisions. First there are the Selefies (Salafi as it can be pronounced in Dutch, Selefie is the label they give themselves), a quietist group that follows Sheikh Rabi' al-Madkhali (a Saudi Arabian scholar of Islam who is a very active antagonist of the politicised Salafi movements in Saudi Arabia). The main preachers within this group are Abdelillah Boushta (born in Morocco, 1958) and several native Dutch Muslims who have studied in Saudi Arabia. The second group consists of mosques in Amsterdam (its imam is Shershaby, born in Egypt, 1957), The Hague (its imam is Fawaz Jneid, born in Lebanon, 1964, of Syrian nationality, who worked as imam in Saudi Arabia and the United Arab Emirates (UAE) and came to the Netherlands in 1992 after having problems in the UAE because of his anti-American stance) and Tilburg (its imam is Ahmad Salam, born in Syria, 1949, who arrived in the Netherlands from Yemen in 1989 and started working with the Al Waqf Foundation in Eindhoven, his son Suhayb being one of the main preachers of the Dutch Salafi groups). In 2001 they established the Stichting Islamitisch Comité voor Ahl as-Sunna in Nederland (Foundation Islamic Committee for Ahl as-Sunna in the Netherlands). The Stichting Islamitisch Comité voor Ahl as-Sunna in Nederland is part of the Committee for Ahl as-Sunna in Europe, with members in

Spain, France, Germany, Belgium and England and Adnane Al-Aroor, also from Syria, as president. In the past there have been connections between leaders of this movement and Salafi leaders such as Muhammad Suroor, who was the teacher of several Salafi leaders within the Saudi *Sahwa* (awakening) movement. The fourth group is closely tied to the Ahl as-Sunna committee but not a member of it: the Fourqaan mosque in the south of the Netherlands. The fifth group is led by a Dutch Salafi who broke away from the Fourqaan mosque, Dutch convert Abdul-Jabbar van de Ven (born in the Netherlands, 1977, who converted to Islam in 1992 and studied for one year in Saudi Arabia at a language course). He was a follower of some of the *Sahwa* sheikhs in Saudi Arabia and has established a (loose) network that can be seen as the fifth group. In the past, he was accused of being part of the sixth strand of the Salafi movements in the Netherlands – the *jihadi/takfiri* branch of Salafism in the Netherlands – although he seems to keep some distance now. While most of the Dutch Salafi groups refrain from using and/or endorsing violence, the *jihadi/takfiri* branch of Salafism in the Netherlands is characterised by a strong commitment to violent action, in response to injustice against Muslims worldwide and in the Netherlands, as well as to a very narrow idea of what a Muslim should or should not do, resulting in the practice of excommunicating (*takfir*) all those Muslims who do not conform to their definition. In almost all instances this branch is directly or indirectly connected to the core of the old Hofstad network (of which the assassin of Van Gogh, Mohammed Bouyeri, and his friend Samir Azzouz are the most well-known members).

Radical politics

The politics of the Salafi movements are often labelled by politicians and security services as 'radical', meaning at odds with democratic values and even anti-democratic. In contrast to this view, 'radicalisation' among Moroccan-Dutch Muslim youth could be seen as a means of engaging with society. The Salafi movements provide these young people with means and a religious and political framework to engage with society in a critical way by taking on three different types of politics: politics of resistance, politics of distinction and lifestyle politics. Instead of focusing on a typology that characterises the Salafi movements by one of these types, we should describe and analyse how all the different movements make use of all of these types of politics in particular circumstances.[1] Politics in this sense does not mean party politics or dealings with the State only but involves the negotiations and competition over particular symbols and institutions in society.[2]

Lifestyle politics

This form of politics is based upon a primarily cultural orientation in which questions of identity and identity politics are primary, for example with regard to clothing, the position of women in Islam, and expressing one's identity as a Muslim in a secular environment. In political debates this is often seen as a sign of 'Islamising' the public sphere or on the contrary as apolitical or cultural (i.e., without any impact on institutional power as is emphasised by some of the Salafi groups). It can nevertheless be analysed as a particular kind of politics, not necessarily aimed at 'Islamising' society but in relation to identity formation. Identity construction always involves negotiations over the interpretation of particular symbols. In particular with regard to female attire such as the headscarf or *niqab*, which are frequently discussed in public and political debates, and given the fact that Islam is highly politicised in Dutch society, personal lifestyle has by definition political dimensions. Although for individual Muslims lifestyle issues are very personal issues in the search for their own identity and means of being and becoming a good Muslim, the politicisation of Islam leads to a situation wherein Muslim lifestyles (for example wearing a headscarf) are considered to be political statements whether the individual Muslim wants it to be so or not.[3] All of the major currents of the Salafi movements in the Netherlands engage in some sort of lifestyle politics. Examples can be found on the internet and in meetings where books are sold explaining the correct Islamic lifestyle, in electronic gadgets such as mobile phones that signal the times for prayer, in lectures and books concerning the Islamic aspects of the relationship between men and women and the correct dress for Muslim men and women.[4] It is in particular the lifestyle politics that attract many young Moroccan-Dutch Muslims. It enables them to re-write their own life stories and to construct their sense of self as strong and self-confident people who find their purpose of life in Islam by connecting their own individual experiences with the larger narratives of Islam and the *umma*.[5]

Politics of distinction
Politics of distinction entail rejecting an undiscerning mainstream culture by claiming the right for one's own identity.[6] Also all of the Salafi currents engage in politics of distinction but they do this in different ways. The Madkhali Selefies for example state more often than not that they do not intervene in Dutch politics; however, they do have established institutions for Islamic home care and youth work, thereby aiming at building up alternatives to Dutch institutions that, according to these movements, do not take into account Islamic norms and values. The Salafis of the Ahl as-Sunna committee are also trying to establish such an infrastructure but use petitions, open letters to politicians and to newspapers as a means of contention. They have, for example, criticised Dutch politicians for trying to ban the *burqa* from the public sphere, written an open letter to the Dutch parliament after Geert Wilders announced his release for the film *Fitna* and used their sermons to harshly condemn the practices of people such as Wilders, Hirsi Ali and in the past, Theo van Gogh. In particular, in the case of the *burqa* they are responding to the threat of a ban by tailoring their language to fit within the secular public sphere. In most slogans and in their petition references they used concepts such as emancipation, a right to (religious) identity, dignity, tolerance and so on. In sum, the politics of distinction is meant to secure the minority position of Muslims in society, protecting their rights to freedom of religion and practicing Islam (according to the Salafi interpretation). At the same time it aims to enhance the awareness of Muslims of their minority status in the Netherlands and mobilise them to defend it.

Politics of resistance
The politics of resistance means rejecting a powerless structural position and aiming to transform the structure of society.[7] With regards to the Netherlands we cannot see that the Salafi movements engage in a politics of resistance. Although in the past the Amsterdam Tawheed mosque has expressed a desire to strive for making the Netherlands an Islamic society, most of the activists are aiming at being pious Muslims in Dutch society, emphasising the right for a religious identity (politics of distinction) and performing *da'wah* among other Muslims. An exception is the core of the so-called Hofstad network with Mohammed Bouyeri and Samir Azzouz, both of whom saw the Netherlands as part of the battleground for the struggle between 'good and evil', 'truth and falseness' and 'light and darkness', and Van Gogh's murder as part of 'defending Islam'.[8] The jihadi Salafis and in particular the Hofstad network have been heavily criticised by both the Madkhali

Selefies and the Salafis of the Ahl as-Sunnah committee. With regard to politics in the Middle East in particular the jihadi Salafis and the Ahl as-Sunnah committee are much more critical than the Madkhali Salafis and they have more or less made political struggle part of their doctrine and reduced the evaluation of political and religious leader to a question of belief or disbelief.[9] While some of the jihadi Salafis accuse religious and political leaders of being 'infidels', the Ahl as-Sunnah committee are much more reluctant with regard to the practice of *takfir*. The Madkhali Salafis abstain from a politics of resistance. According to the Madkhali Salafis it is not allowed to criticise leaders let alone violently attack them and they believe it is better to have a 'bad Muslim leader than no Muslim leader'.

The Dutch Salafi movements

The Salafi movements have been labelled as 'radical' in many of the official government publications where radicalisation is conceptualised as a process in which groups develop and actively engage with anti-democratic values. However, for the Moroccan-Dutch Muslim youth the Salafi movements offer a kind of repertoire that make the complex and sometimes contradictory realities of modern society understandable. The Salafi movements allow young people to engage with society in different ways by framing the correct Islamic lifestyle (lifestyle politics), by defending the rights of Muslims in the Netherlands (politics of distinction) and by engaging with international politics – in particular the Middle East (politics of resistance).

Notes

1 See Steven M. Buechler (1995) 'New Social Movement Theories', *The Sociological Quarterly*, 36 (3): pp. 441–64.
2 See Dale F. Eickelman and James Piscatori (1996) *Muslim Politics*, Princeton: Princeton University Press.
3 See Anthony Giddens (1991) *Modernity and Self Identity. Self and society in the late modern age*, Cambridge: Polity Press, and Buechler, 'New Social Movement Theories'.
4 Martijn de Koning (2008c) *Identity in transition. Connecting online and offline internet practices of Moroccan–Dutch Muslim youth*, London: London Metropolitan University – Institute for the Study of European Transformations.
5 See Martijn de Koning (2008b). *Zoeken naar een 'zuivere' islam. Geloofsbeleving en identiteitsvorming van jonge Marokkaans–Nederlandse moslims*, Amsterdam: Bert Bakker, and Martijn de Koning (2009a) 'Changing worldviews and friendship. An exploration of the life stories of two female Salafists in the Netherlands', in Roel Meijer (ed.), *Global Salafism. Islam's New Religious Movement*, London: Hurst, pp. 372–92.
6 Mary Bucholtz (2002) 'Youth and cultural practice', *Annual Review of Anthropology*, 31: p. 541.
7 Ibid.
8 Martijn de Koning (2008a). '"You follow the path of the Shaitan: we try to follow the righteous path." Negotiating evil in the identity construction of young Moroccan–Dutch Muslims', in Lourens Minnema and Nelly van Doorn-Harder (eds), *Coping with Evil in Religion and Culture: Case Studies*, Amsterdam / New York: Rodopi, pp. 137–48.

9   Jonathan Birt (2005) 'Wahhabism in the United Kingdom. Manifestations and reactions', in Madawi Al-Rasheed, (ed.), *Transnational connections and the Arab Gulf*, London / New York: Routledge, p. 177.

References

Al-Rasheed, Madawi (2007) *Contesting the Saudi State. Islamic Voices from a New Generation*, Cambridge: Cambridge University Press.

Birt, Jonathan (2005) 'Wahhabism in the United Kingdom. Manifestations and reactions', in Madawi Al-Rasheed, (ed.), *Transnational connections and the Arab Gulf*. London / New York: Routledge, pp. 168–84.

Bucholtz, Mary (2002) 'Youth and cultural practice', *Annual Review of Anthropology*, 31: pp. 525–52.

Buechler, Steven M. (1995) 'New Social Movement Theories', *The Sociological Quarterly*, 36 (3): pp. 441–64.

Buijs, Frank J., Froukje Demant and Atef Hamdy (2006) *Strijders van eigen bodem. Radicale en democratische moslims in Nederland*, Amsterdam: Amsterdam University Press.

Eickelman, Dale F. and James Piscatori (1996) *Muslim Politics*, Princeton: Princeton University Press.

Giddens, Anthony (1991) *Modernity and Self Identity. Self and society in the late modern age*, Cambridge: Polity Press.

Koning, Martijn de (2008a) '"You follow the path of the Shaitan: we try to follow the righteous path." Negotiating evil in the identity construction of young Moroccan–Dutch Muslims', in Lourens Minnema and Nelly van Doorn-Harder (eds), *Coping with Evil in Religion and Culture: Case Studies*, Amsterdam / New York: Rodopi, pp. 137–48.

—— (2008b) *Zoeken naar een 'zuivere' islam. Geloofsbeleving en identiteitsvorming van jonge Marokkaans–Nederlandse moslims*, Amsterdam: Bert Bakker.

—— (2008c) *Identity in transition. Connecting online and offline internet practices of Moroccan–Dutch Muslim youth*. London: London Metropolitan University – Institute for the Study of European Transformations.

—— (2009) 'Changing worldviews and friendship. An exploration of the life stories of two female Salafists in the Netherlands', in Roel Meijer (ed.), *Global Salafism. Islam's New Religious Movement*, London: Hurst, pp. 372–92.

Waardenburg, J.D.J. (2001) *Institutionele vormgevingen van de Islam in Nederland gezien in Europees perspectief*, The Hague: Scientific Council for Government Policy.

Wiktorowicz, Quintan (2006) 'Anatomy of the Salafi Movement', *Studies in Conflict & Terrorism*, 29: pp. 207–39.

THE SALAFIST GROUPS IN FRANCE: A PLURAL AND ANTAGONISTIC MOVEMENT

Samir Amghar

Among all European countries, France is doubtless where the Salafist phenomenon is most expressive. Far from being a homogenous and organised movement, Salafism is built around three competing and antagonistic poles. While the first two forms of Salafism are ultra-minorities in the Salafist panorama on mainland France, the third is ultra-majority by comparison.

The first is the so-called revolutionary Salafism, also known as jihadi. This tendency was associated early on with the political doctrine of the Muslim Brotherhood (MB). It has only kept one idea from Islamic ideology: that political and social actions should necessarily be seen from an Islamic perspective – one joined to a literal reading of Qur'anic texts with political connotations on how power is wielded, the caliphate and authority, with the whole tending towards revolutionary action. Discourse is radical and against any sort of compromise or collaboration with Muslim or Western societies. The idea is to oppose the powers, even in the West, and to fight for the establishment of an Islamic state and eventually the caliphate. They are partly inspired by the religious opinions of the thirteenth-century Damascene theologian Ibn Taymiyya, who justified the recourse to *jihad* against the Mongols as he doubted their membership in the *umma*. This tendency advocates direct action to establish the Kingdom of God on earth. Hostile to religious action that is limited to preaching (*da'wa*), the revolutionary Salafists place *jihad* at the centre of Islamic belief.

While revolutionary Salafism urges *jihad*, the second tendency focuses by comparison more on politics and protest. They favour lawful political action and believe Muslims in France must be defended through actions such as demonstrations and petitions. That is why its supporters were out demonstrating during the 2006 affair involving caricatures of the Prophet and during rallies against the draft law on conspicuous religious symbols in 2004 and 2005. Besides defending Muslims living in France, they believe in the urgent need to establish an Islamic state in the Muslim countries. They are therefore very critical of the Arab regimes and rail against the political and social situation in their countries of origin.

This attitude, neither structured nor organised, is mainly manifested through charismatic figures, although it also borrows from the political Islam of the Front Islamique du Salut (FIS). Developed by followers close to the ideas of the Algerian Islamist Ali Belhadj, this tendency has now largely disappeared in France. Mosques on the Rue Myrrha and Rue Polonceau in the eighteenth arrondissement of Paris served as poles for spreading this Salafism. This pro-FIS tendency was also found in a southern French mosque in Valence, where partisans of Ali Belhadj tried to attract followers in the first years of this century. Among the most active were Farid Aouidi, Miloud Bourzig and Mourad Zemour. The latter lived in Medina in 1995 and 1996 in the company of Farid Zemmour; both waged a subversive anti-French and anti-Algerian campaign among young Maghrebi pilgrims. More recent is the charismatic leader Ali Benyetou, a young Franco-Algerian 20-odd years old, who arranged for a number of youths to go to fight American troops in Iraq; he also defended a political view of Salafism. A follower of Ali Belhadj's theses, he learned the FIS's Salafist ideology through the preaching of his brother-in-law, himself a member of the Algerian Islamist party. During this decade he has remained in Algeria to complete religious training in contact with old FIS members. He was arrested in January 2005 for terrorist activities. Yet despite the existence of this tendency in mainland France, such political Salafism increasingly tends to approach the quietist Salafism, and therefore to disappear.

While political Salafism gives priority to political activism as a means to instill the imperative need for an Islamic state and society among the Muslim masses, the third tendency stresses Islamic education and training. Indeed, this form of Salafism is opposed to all political engagement in the name of Islam. It has no intention of becoming involved in European societies and no political plan besides messianic expectation (bereft of any immediate application): it defends an apolitical and non-violent view of Islam grounded on the willingness to organise its entire existence around the religious opinions of the Saudi scholars. This marks a difference between Salafism and the Islam of the MB. Indeed, while the Salafist theologians think the Muslim faith has been tarnished by dross inherited from Maraboutism, ideology associated with the MB holds that the religious fibre of Muslims is sound, hence preaching should be used at political level to convince the faithful of the urgent need to establish an Islamic state (*dawla islamiyya*).

Salafism is afraid of *fitna* (division) and defends the idea of not contesting political authority for fear of anarchy, even when power is in the hands of non-Muslims. Far from the heightened revolutionary ardour encouraged by the FIS's Salafism, this Salafism has capitalised on the disappointment of Islamic militants upset over the failure of the political Islam model. Its preachers, such as Sheikh Ibn Baz (died 1999), assert that the only solution to the Muslims' problems is not to be found in Islamisation of the state, but in what they call '*al-tasfiyatu wa-l-tarbiyya* (purification and education): on the one hand, to cleanse the Muslim religion of all 'innovations' which have marred its precepts and dogmas, to go back to the original religion as it was transmitted by the Prophet, and on the other hand to educate Muslims so that they conform to this purified religion and leave off their bad habits.[1]

It is quite obvious that this unobtrusive Salafism's approach to public affairs is not based on a strictly religious view of Islam. Its discourse also has a significant political content in many aspects. In the Arab world, Salafism's apparent neutrality regarding political life implies support for the existing regimes.[2] In Morocco, the Salafist theologian Muhammad al-Maghraoui asked his religious counterparts to refrain from violent and political action in the name of Islam and considered that country's monarchy to be the ideal framework for guaranteeing national unity. In Tunisia, the Ben Ali regime has allowed numerous Salafists to preach, although any Islamic activism is usually forbidden. In Algeria, President Bouteflika has encouraged the development of Salafism to counter Salafism with a jihadi bent. He has institutionalised and made functionaries many followers of this tendency. Algeria has consequently witnessed an exponential development of this sort of Salafism. From Algiers to Constantine via Béjaïa, Salafism has become its number one re-Islamisation movement, well ahead of the MB or the Sufi groups. Even though the Saudi theologians defend a quietist view of Islam, they openly back the monarchy which they deem the best way to uphold the country's national cohesion and Islamic values. These pro-government positions are a major bargaining chip for the Salafist religious figures who exchange their backing for social control over society.

Whereas Salafism develops a form of loyalism and weaves non-conflicting relations with the Arab regimes, in mainland France it is a powerful basis for criticising Western political systems. The Salafist preachers installed in France, and also the Arab world, regularly rail against the political, moral and social values of the West. This notwithstanding, neither their verbal outrage against France, nor their orthodox view of Islam, should be considered a prelude to engagement in *jihad* (even if such was the case in the 1990s). On the contrary, the militants' religious radicalism and anti-Western imprecations act as a 'safety valve' that discourages followers from taking direct action. Consequently, violence is no longer necessary. Furthermore, the Salafists living in France often insist that they respect the current laws in their host country. They say they are not calling for violence, and protest every time their movement is labelled terrorist.

This doctrine's expansion was mainly due to the proselytising of former European students at Saudi Islamic universities (and training centres in Yemen), especially the one in Medina. In France, the Netherlands, Belgium and even Great Britain, it resulted from the preaching of the first European graduates who had studied religious sciences in Saudi Arabia, and through whom Saudi Salafism gained a foothold in the old continent. Such is the case of Abdelkader Bouziane, at the movement's origin in the Lyon region. Before becoming an imam of numerous mosques in the Rhône-Alpes region in the 1990s, he spent two years in Medina studying Islam with the Salafist theologians. Pressed by certain European students, Saudi religious scholars, Egyptians or even Jordanian Salafist followers, he travelled to mainland France to give conferences. Sheikh Abdel Salam al-Bourjis, a disciple of the old mufti of Saudi Arabia, regularly visited France (and also Great Britain and the United States) to give conferences. Sheikh Muhammed Bazmoul, an Egyptian national and teacher at the University of Mecca, came to France several times.

Up to 2001 this quietist strain of Salafism evolved and achieved significant success, notably with the arrival of the Saudi scholars. Mosques were created or won over and there was even a push to create Salafist pole in France. In mainland France nearly 20 centres of worship were Salafist (including Marseille, Paris, Lyon, Roubaix, Valence, Romans-sur-Isère, Aix-en-Provence and Stains) and numerous demonstrations were organised. Every year from 1998 a major Salafist congress was held in the Paris suburbs on the initiative of Yacoub Leenen, a Dutchman in his forties now resident in Saudi Arabia, head of the Anas publishing house specialising in religious works in French. In 2001 this gathering drew nearly one thousand people from all over France and also Germany.

As the movement was beginning to consolidate its institutional and organisational structure, the French police authorities decided to cut short its development the day after the 9/11 attacks. The public powers accused this kind of Salafism of being behind terrorist attacks in the West; the Salafist sheikhs were forbidden to stay in France. A Salafist congress scheduled for June 2001 in Paris was suspended and the Saudi theologians, meant to give the conferences, were all arrested at Charles de Gaulle airport and deported to their country. Many imams were also expelled or placed under house arrest. The imam Abdelkader Bouziane, responsible for introducing Salafism in the Lyon region, was likewise sent back to Algeria due to his misogynous outbursts. The imam of the Argenteuil mosque, Ali Yashar, of Iraqi origin, was removed from his post and has since lived under house arrest in southern France.

Contrary to other movements seeking to inject new life into French Islam, such as the MB, which are essentially backed by the re-Islamised middle classes, Salafism recruits in the manner of the Tabligh movement in the impoverished areas of big cities. Workers, welfare recipients, the jobless and employed form the social clientele of this tendency. Salafism is hence an Islam of exclusion: a 'blue collar' Islam. The overrepresentation of young working-class people is explained by the congruence of numerous elements; a homology effect occurs between the Salafist project outlined in its discourse and excluded youths in search of Islam. Salafist Islam is an easy-to-understand Islam, much easier for a population with little education *a priori* to grasp and comprehend. It provides a mental framework for exclusion and social and economic domination, endowing them with religious meaning. This Islam appeals to people because it emphasises its ability to deal with the economic and social malaises linked to exclusion by proposing a simple solution: a return to Islam.

Within Salafism the emergence of a business-oriented petit bourgeoisie has nevertheless been noted; a class of entrepreneurs and independents. Increasing numbers of young people have thus opened businesses and the suburbs have witnessed the appearance of Islamic bookstores, sandwich shops or even public call offices run by Salafists. Material success has become a sign of divine election: 'because Allah helps people who follow his path' and also 'if my business is successful I owe it to God who has compensated me for my actions', a Salafist tells us. For the most part, they say that 'lots of luck comes from doing commerce'. With a new way of worshipping Allah, these young people reinvent a new relationship with religion, no longer inclined only towards devoted fulfilment of the different pillars of Islam, but henceforth expressed by a mundane willingness to succeed in business. Businesses are opened for religious, albeit pragmatic, reasons. Indeed, religious discrimination and problems finding jobs lead these youths to set up independent activities.

The desire to escape from the oversight of a superior hierarchy seems to be a recurring argument for the business motives of the Salafists. This success often takes on a protesting and vengeful attitude towards French society. A new religious configuration emerges, wherein a new spirit of capitalism is arranged according to performance and competitiveness; a theology of prosperity is outlined which is not only particular to Salafism in France but also defended by other Islamic movements (for example the MB and Ahbash) and by preachers such as the Egyptian Amr Khaled. Islamic products such as the Bilal Wear or Salam apparel lines were created by young suburban Salafists. The founder of the Salam brand is a former Moroccan rapper.

Notes

1   Olivier Roy (2005) *L'islam face à la laïcité*, Paris: Seuil.
2   The Algerian Salafist preachers have always backed the Algerian regime and especially Abdelaziz Bouteflika, who had encouraged the movement's development. Even the Saudi Sheikh 'Uthaymin, before his death in 2001, praised the Algerian president for his policy of national reconciliation via civil concord.

References

Samir Amghar (2008) 'Le salafisme en France: de la révolution islamique à la révolution conservatrice', *Critique internationale*, 3 (40) : pp. 95–113.

—— (2011) *Le salafisme d'aujourd'hui. Mouvements sectaires en Occident*, Paris: Michalon.

Roy, Olivier (2005) *L'islam face à la laïcité*, Paris: Seuil.

THE DEVELOPMENT OF SALAFI DOCTRINE IN SPAIN

Jordi Moreras and Sol Tarrés

The establishment of Salafiyya in Spain

Salafiyya first appeared in Spain in the early 1990s, and much more discretely than Wahhabism, which is identified with the cultural centres financed by Saudi Arabia (Madrid, Marbella, Fuengirola and Malaga).

In Spain, Salafi doctrine is most strongly established in local communities in Catalonia. In 1992, a group of *sheikhs* from Saudi Arabia were invited to give a series of conferences throughout Catalonia. The first Salafi-inspired prayer rooms were opened in various towns in the province of Tarragona. In 1998, the Pastoral Islamic Community of Tarragona was created in El Vendrell, federating different Salafi places of worship from the region. In May 2004 it was estimated that there were around 15 Salafi places of worship in all Catalonia, mostly in the province of Tarragona. This number has increased substantially and it is estimated that there are now between 25 and 30 in Catalonia. The towns where the first Salafi oratories were established also hosted the first Salafi meetings and gatherings, fostering the spread of this doctrine, first in Catalonia and then throughout the rest of Spain. At these meetings, interpersonal contacts facilitated the establishment of social relations and information networks that fuelled the development of the Salafiyya movement in Spain. For example, at these meetings the members of communities without permanent or resident imams could request that a member of the movement visit their place of worship to cater to the spiritual needs of their communities. This practice is being observed elsewhere in Spain, for example in Andalusia.

Although the informal organisation of the Salafiyya movement in Spain was based on a structure of extremely complex personal relations and contacts, important differences still existed between self-proclaimed Salafi communities, ranging from the formation of new Salafi communities or the penetration of the doctrine in established communities to communities with greater or lesser visibility, as well as differences in their composition and structure (communities of national origin or formed by various nationalities, communities with or without the presence of women, etc.), or because they follow different *sheikhs*. Important channels for the establishment of the Salafiyya movement among Muslim women are women's networks on the internet. Forums, chat rooms or blogs are important spaces, especially for converted or neo-Muslim women, where they can share feelings, daily events, concerns or mutual support. Sometimes these virtual contacts become interpersonal meetings in which participants read the

Qur'an and the texts of the most noteworthy *sheikhs*, learn to perform rituals correctly and exchange *halal* recipes or life experiences. All this helps build a solid, active and discrete identity.

The structure of the Salafiyya movement in Spain

The Salafiyya movement is not a structured and hierarchical Islamic movement such as, for example, the Muslim Brotherhood (MB), but rather a doctrine that fosters the creation of a 'network of shared meanings' (according to the concept proposed by Alberto Melucci) based on an 'epistemological promise', which professes that the needs and obligations of Muslims today must be solely deduced from the original textual sources of the Qur'an and the Sunnah. To this end, it proposes a simple reference framework in which concepts such as *tawhid* (unicity of God), *bid'a* (innovation) or the rejection of legal schools are of great importance. Its main characteristics are extreme literality, the centrality of religious observations and the genealogical purification of any innovation in the doctrine. Followers are therefore committed to this reference framework and not to a formally structured movement, with more emphasis on convictions than on affiliations.

The organisation of the Salafiyya movement is based on the complementarity between three types of social actors. First, there are the main promoters, who act as 'private promoters of religious matters' and who aim to keep the doctrinal reference active by controlling places of worship and organising meetings. These actors are normally entrepreneurs or traders, with a higher-than-average status to local Muslims, thus legitimising their community leadership. Second, there are the heads of local communities with very close links to the main promoters (for example work, professional or other links) who enjoy the latter's trust and promote or lead the establishment of new places of worship, or 'reorient' existing members in accordance with Salafi doctrine. This second level is crucial for obtaining the support of local communities for Salafi doctrine and their participation in meetings. Third, there are sympathisers of the Salafiyya movement and those who participate actively in the activities organised by the aforementioned actors. In short, these are the people who socially legitimise these initiatives.

Due to the lack of a formal organisation and the contingency and volatility of relations among different members, the movement has to find ways to strengthen personal links. Regular educational meetings are held (since 1993 in southern Catalonia, normally coinciding with the Christmas and Holy Week or Easter holidays, thus guaranteeing the attendance of Muslim families) to build camaraderie among members; this is one dimension of the commitment to the Salafi community. These kinds of activities generate social capital that enhances the quality of interpersonal relations and helps spread the doctrine. These meetings, which are the most important Salafi gatherings in southern Europe, take the form of training seminars (similar to the Islamic congresses organised by the different Islamic federations and communities in Spain). They are structured around conferences given by *sheikhs* from different Muslim (Syria, Egypt, Saudi Arabia) and European (France, Belgium, the Netherlands) countries. Given their different origins, these speakers refer to subjects and debates taking place in their societies of origin, thus strengthening the transnational nature of these meetings. In their master classes they tend to address issues relating to the main Salafi doctrinal arguments, linking these with the daily lives of Muslims, particularly those living in Europe, in a non-Muslim context. The *sheikhs* normally use arguments that emphasise the individual responsibility of Muslims to actively practice their faith and express their belonging to Islam, even if this means contradicting the society in which they live.

The formulation of a dual rupture

Faithfully adhering to the original message of the Revelation implies an initial exercise of doctrinal cleansing of all innovations, cultural influences and political interpretations considered alien to Salafi doctrine. However, it also entails a commitment on two levels: individual and community. Literal readings, and the desire to reconfigure doctrinal reference in the form of a code regulating daily conduct, constitute the individual commitment of Muslims, faithful to their own faith and religious identity. This is combined with community endogamy that responds to a context which tends to favour precisely the opposite, that is, social exogamy. This distancing, expressed not only with respect to the society in which they live but also with respect to the collective to which they belong, prompts attention to emotions expressed before the possible rupture (or cooling) of links with the collective and, more importantly, with the family. The emotional component should not be ignored in the analysis since it reveals the types of relationships that are woven within these collectives. In addition, the incorporation of discourses proclaiming a firmer commitment to Islam may give rise to situations and arguments of differentiation.

This argument may be used to consider one of the fundamental principles in the Salafi reading of the community development of Muslim collectives, which they believe consists of the establishment of effective limits and boundaries with respect to non-Muslim society. Since populational proximity is clearly an important factor, these limits may not always be physical and must sometimes be symbolised. Manuel Castells referred to 'identities of resistance' as generators and legitimators in the construction of differentiated communities, including, as Castells mentions, those conceptualised as religious fundamentalists. Alternatively, Emmanuel Sivan refers to the notion of 'enclave culture' as an argument used by fundamentalist-inspired groups as a way to define the group's internal and external relations. Within this framework, the exclusive community spaces demanded by this collective and even their clothing and general appearance will establish these symbolic limits in contexts of proximity.

If this rupture has a significant impact on the Muslim collective, it is significant because it affects more complex aspects of the collective's internal organisation. By making a strong distinction between Muslims who earnestly follow the principles of Salafi doctrine and those who maintain a banal or superficial relationship with the same, a series of criteria and arguments are introduced that reinforce the practices of social control and supervision of social behaviour. By generating new social ethics they intervene in relations between equals, generations, sexes, and in relations with non-Muslims, substantially altering previous parameters. The patrimonialisation of the principle of religious authority inscribed in Salafi doctrine has an effective impact on the cultural disconnection (the 'deculturalisation' described by Olivier Roy) of religious practices, thus fuelling a conflict of visions between religiosity expressed by adults and parents in relation to their children, who may be more inclined to endorse this non-cultural reading of their belonging to Islam. Moreover, the introduction of these principles clearly influences alterations in the parameters of their relationship with Spanish society as a consequence of the imposition of a new public community morality brimming with endogamic characteristics. The rupture within the heart of Muslim communities is much deeper and more significant, but it is also less visible and perceptible from outside the collective. This aspect is especially significant in the context of Muslim communities living in Spain. However, although certain changes can be observed in relations with Spanish society, these are interpreted in a banal and superficial manner (for example clothing habits) as simply another argument supporting the thesis of the difficult integration of Muslim collectives into Spain.

References

Meijer, Roel (ed.) (2009) *Global Salafism: Islam's New Religious Movement*, London / New York: Hurst / Columbia University Press.

Rougier, Bernard (ed.) (2008) *Qu'est-ce que le salafisme?*, Paris: Presses Universitaires de France.

SALAFISM IN GERMANY

Jörn Thielmann

Since the mid-1990s, a grid of Salafi mosques has emerged across Germany (with some concentration in the Rhineland, the wider area around Cologne), loosely linked together without formally belonging to an organisation but united through a strict adherence to the Qur'an and the Sunna, the tradition of the Prophet (as collected in the *hadith*). The common denominator for all Salafi groups is an essentialisation of Islam in their lifestyle by imitating the model given by Prophet Muhammad and lived by the first three Muslim generations, the *al-salaf al-salih* (the pious ancestors). Most of the Salafi mosques were set up by Muslims of Arab origin, but are visited by a supranational attendance, united by a shared understanding of Islam and Islamic practice, among them a particularly high number of German converts. In the scene, people know each other through seminars, conferences and meetings and are, furthermore, connected by travelling preachers and activists, such as Pierre Vogel, Abu Anas (or Ebu Enes, AKA Muhamed Ciftci, the head of the *Islamschule* in Braunschweig), Ibrahim Abou-Nagie, Abu Dujana, Hassan Dabbagh (Abul Hussain, the imam of Al-Rahman mosque in Leipzig), Abdul Adhim Kamouss (preacher in the Al-Nur mosque in Berlin) and others, and through the internet and other modes of modern communication.

Although Saudi Arabia has sponsored Salafi movements all over the world and helped spread its worldviews and theology, and continues do so, an animosity exists inside the Salafiyya movement towards Muslims identified with Saudi Arabian Wahhabism. This animosity is also visible in German mosques and on German Muslim websites and includes mutual *takfir* (charge of unbelief). In some Salafi mosques visitors considered to be Wahhabis are frequently asked not to return or are even directly denied access.

The theology as presented in the videos and podcasts is focused on dualistic, Manichaean terms: hell for unbelievers (that is, every non-Muslim) versus paradise for true Muslims, and punishment versus reward. Fear of God and of his judgement – all Salafis speak of hell and eternal punishment in vivid terms – and the hope of entering paradise through practising 'true Islam' play an important role. The background illustration of the new website of Pierre Vogel and his circle, named *Einladung zum Paradies* (call to paradise), is a picture of a white beach with palm trees, thereby visualising the possible gains for prospective followers. Muslims who do not follow the *Salafi manhaj* (method or manner) are often considered to be *kuffar* (unbelievers). So, for example, Salafis condemn *Sufis* (mystics) as *kuffar* on the basis that they practise the intercession by a sheikh in possession of secret knowledge and specific *barakat* (divine blessing) – this being in contradiction to the revelation – and on the fact that no Sufism and Sufi practices existed in the times of the Prophet Muhammad and the *al-salaf al-salih*. Muslims who insist on adherence to an Islamic school of law (*madhhab*) are sometimes considered as *kuffar*, however a Salafi preacher like Pierre Vogel recommends learning a *madhhab* to become acquainted with Islamic rules and practices, but not to follow it blindly in every case and to instead always choose the practice with the best and strongest proof.

The Salafiyya has a scriptural approach to Islam, based exclusively on the literal interpretation of the Qur'an and the Sunna. Important is the moral and social formation of Muslims through (self) education, thus the stress on teaching on all websites and in all mosques. All these groups are inspired by a relatively small number of sheikhs – often Saudi – among them Muhammad ibn Salih al-'Uthayunin, 'Abd al-'Aziz Ibn Baz, and Muhammad Nasir al-Din Al-Albani.

In addition, for all sides, the Islamic principle of 'commanding right, forbidding wrong' (*al-amr bil-ma'ruf wan-nahy 'an al-munkar*, Qur'an 3:104) is crucial, due to the fact that its realisation is considered a litmus test for Islamicness and distinction as a Muslim community. Another guiding principle for Salafis, *al-wala' wa-l-bara'* (friendship with fellow Muslims and enmity towards and separation from non-Muslims), is found among every Salafi group in Germany, and brotherliness is reclaimed. Nevertheless, according to their specific understanding of Islam and of who is in and who is not, Salafi groups gain shape and identity through drawing sharp lines between themselves and others. So it comes as no surprise that various Salafi groups are intensively fighting against each other. Via videos on YouTube or their own websites, they denounce views and practices of others in the Salafi scene, and even ridicule each other, for example, by mocking the Arabic pronunciation of other Salafis.

Quite often, the acceptance of the German legal order is stressed on the websites, in documents or in sermons. However, it is also openly said that an authentic depiction of true Islam and of certain practices of an Islamic state with an Islamic legislation are in contradiction with the German legal order, however the authors underline that they do not want to change the German system, but to simply present an authentic Islamic view. They also consistently condemn violence and terror. Nevertheless, German security agencies consider all these groups, mosques and preachers to be extremely dangerous, because in their opinion they pave the way to radicalisation and jihadi forms of the Salafiyya due to their clear-cut Manichaean view of Islam and its place in a multi-religious and multi-cultural society, and of true Muslim behaviour. Thus, a great part of presumed Salafi mosques are under supervision, as well as certain preachers accused of being *Haßprediger* (preachers of hate).

The internet is important in Germany, as elsewhere, for *da'wa* (preaching, missionary activity) and for maintaining and enlarging the Salafi networks. Here, numerous websites are aimed at informing and educating Muslims in the Salafi way, presented as the only true Islam, and at proselytising among non-Muslims. These websites and the related networks of preachers and active supporters consist of native Muslims of Arab as well as Turkish origin and German converts. Modern media and communication (e.g., Paltalk, SMS, Weblogs, Chat, Podcasts, etc.) serve as linkages between the virtual and the real; that is, mosques, associations and local groups.[1] Lectures and seminars all over Germany are filmed and presented on the internet, now increasingly as live streams. The majority of the audiences consist of young people. Saudi scholars and their books, especially al-'Uthayunin and Ibn Baz, often serve as references. So the *Islamschule* in Braunschweig, run by Muhamed Ciftci, is proud to offer the Islamic instruction of the Islamic University of Medina as long-distance learning to interested people in Germany.[2]

The use of Arabic and of Islamic phrases and eulogies is quite noteworthy among all groups. Many lectures are introduced by lengthy formulaic introductions in Arabic – the same used by different speakers – and the speeches are blotched with formula such as *al-hamdu li-Llah* (praise be to God), *baraka Llahu fikum* (the blessing of God be with you) and so on. In the case of converts like Pierre Vogel, this might confer authority in certain settings, but can also provoke harsh reactions by other groups who mock pronunciation and mistakes.

One of the most famous Salafi preachers in Germany is the German convert Pierre Vogel, known also as Abu Hamza. Born in 1978 near Cologne, he grew up as a Protestant Christian and was educated at a private Catholic school. From 1994 to 1999, he attended an elite sport school in Berlin where he took his *Abitur* (A-Levels). During his time as a professional boxer, he worked with a Turkish-Muslim colleague and had an American convert, Khalid Jones, as a sparring partner. When, one day in 2001, Vogel accompanied Khalid to the Friday prayer, he converted to Islam and stopped fighting as a boxer two fights later. From 2004 until 2006 he studied at Umm Al-Qura University in Mecca, like the majority of Salafi preachers in Germany who studied in Saudi Arabia. Back in Germany he started preaching, earning his living with part-time jobs.[3] In early 2009 he set up a new website with other people around Muhamed Ciftci.[4] Since the end of 2009 he has been in an intense feud with Ibrahim Abou-Nagie and www.diewahrereligion.de. Basically, they differ on collecting donations for the *da'wa* (practised by Pierre Vogel), on life insurances (accepted by Pierre Vogel) and on other issues that have not been mentioned – and both sides denounce the denunciatory style of the other. Due to his biography, his outlook, his personal charisma and style – he always speaks with a heavy Cologne accent and makes jokes – Pierre Vogel soon became famous and successful, especially among young people, being perhaps the preacher who 'attracts' the most converts. Converts are overrepresented among Salafis, counting for perhaps up to one-quarter (against their share of perhaps one per cent of the total Muslim population of 3.8–4.3 million.) This also brought him to the attention of German security and media. However, he counterattacks the accusations that his teaching and preaching prepares the ground for radicalisation and subsequent terrorism by addressing the negative media reports, or the fact of being supervised by security agencies, in his lectures. Pierre Vogel qualifies them as unjustified by pointing at his lectures, especially those on *jihad* and terrorism. For him, these accusations are part of a bigger campaign against Islam and practising Muslims residing in Germany.

Notes

1   Most websites are related to particular mosques, for example, www.diewahrereligion.de to the Omar-Ibn-El-Khattab mosque in Moers; www.einladungzumparadies.de (link no longer working), to the As-Sunnah mosque in Mönchengladbach; www.islamschule.de to the *Islamschule* in Braunschweig; and www.islamvoice.de and http://tauhid.org to the Al-Nur mosque in Berlin. (links accessed 19 June 2014)

2   Muhamed Ciftci is also responsible for the website www.einladungzumparadies.de. (link no longer functional)

3   He also had support from www.diewahrereligion.de. (accessed 19 June 2014)

4   www.einladungzumparadies.de. (link no longer functional)

References

Becker, Carmen (2009) '"Gaining Knowledge": Salafi Activism in German and Dutch Online Forums', *Masaryk University Journal of Law and Technology*, 3(1), pp. 79–98. Available at: http://www.digitalislam.eu/article.do?articleId=2348. (Accessed 18 December 2009).

Die wahre Religion (2009) n.p./n.d.

http://www.einladungzumparadies.de/videos/referenten/pierre-vogel/mein-weg-zum-islam-22-03-2009-63.html#63 (Pierre Vogel on his way to Islam. (Accessed 23 January 2010 link no longer functional).

http://www.einladungzumparadies.de/videos/referenten/pierre-vogel/sufismus-395.html#395. Pierre Vogel on Sufism. (Accessed 23 January 2010).

http://www.einladungzumparadies.de/videos/referenten/pierre-vogel/die-antwort-auf-diejenigen-die-die-muslime-wahhabieten-nennen-102.html#102. Pierre Vogel on accusations of being *Wahhabi*. (Accessed 23 January 2010. Link no longer working).

http://www.salaf.de or http://www.al-islaam.de. (Accessed 18 December 2009).

(4) JIHADI SALAFIST GROUPS

JIHADI MOVEMENTS IN THE UNITED KINGDOM

Yahya Birt and Sadek Hamid

A number of young British Muslim men fought in Afghanistan in the 1980s against the Soviet occupation, a resistance that was backed by the Americans and the Gulf States at the time. This participation was described as life changing, as standing up for Muslim people in their struggle for self-determination. Participation in this *jihad* by these young men was seen at the time as fulfilling a religious obligation and emulating the way of the earliest Muslims rather than as a political act. It is clear that a series of conflicts in the Muslim world had a major effect upon the jihadi movement in Britain. The Bosnia conflict (1992–5) played the central role in galvanising the *jihad* movement in Britain and considerably strengthening it because of proximity and access.

The key trigger to split the movement was its division over what constituted true Salafism (ideology evolved by those who claim to follow the first generation of Muslims), *jihad* and *takfir* (religious excommunication). These issues arose in the context of the Saudi support for the American recapture of Kuwait from Saddam Hussain in 1990. The romantic sheen around 'standing up for the oppressed Muslims' began to fade for some, because some British Muslims involved in the Bosnian *jihad* were targeted by *takfiri* elements for recruitment, and they began to cause problems upon returning home. The second divisive issue was that the major Saudi Salafi scholars of the day, Ibn Bin Baz and al-'Uthaymin, both condemned the post-1992 situation in Afghanistan after the communist Najibullah government fell in Kabul. It was no longer a *jihad*, in their view, as the former Muslim factions were now killing each other.

The ideational patterns of *takfiri* ideology can be represented as being parts of a seven-piece jigsaw. These pieces not only form the basic components out of which a religious outlook justifying violence is created, but they also determined the bases upon which sectarian splinters among violent *and* non-violent radical groups were defined in Britain. In brief they are:

1. *Takfir* of Muslim leaders for failing to rule by the entirety of the *shari'a* and, in some cases, of the generality of Muslims for their complicity in this misrule or for failing to practise or believe in a form of Islam acceptable to violent radicals.
2. *Jihadism.* Rather than an ethically circumscribed concept of moral struggle and just war, this conception of *jihad* has three elements. Jihadism is (1) a permanent and (2) individual obligation that may be (3) called for by non-state actors.

3. *The World as Dar al-Harb (the Abode of War)* This means that states in both the Muslim world and the non-Muslim world are presumed to be hostile enemies at war with Islam and Muslims until the rule of *shari'a* is established in the Muslim world.

4. *Attacking the Far Enemy.* Involves a strategic switch from targeting the 'near enemy', or apostate Muslim governments, to attacking America and its Western allies directly. Both the 'near' and 'far' enemies fit within the paradigm of the World as the Abode of War. The strategy is tactically justified in order to create the Islam–West polarisation necessary to draw support to the cause.

5. *The Principle of Indiscrimination between Civilian and Military Targets.* This is tactically necessary in asymmetric warfare as no terrorist organisation can by definition directly confront the military forces of the state conventionally. This is justified either through an argument of culpability – civilians support or serve in the military, civilians are military reservists (used in the case of Israel) or civilians pay taxes to or vote for governments that oppress the Muslim world – or by a version of the 'collateral damage' argument.

6. *Suicide Bombing.* This tactic comes out of the principle of indiscrimination and is similarly justified as a necessary tactic of asymmetric warfare, due to the poverty of alternative and more powerful means of force.

7. *Killing Muslims.* This is justified on the grounds that either (1) they are complicit, through either voting for, or by paying taxes to, Western governments or apostate Muslim governments, or (2) they oppose the establishment of an Islamic state, or (3) they are collateral damage but may be considered paradoxically as martyrs to the cause. This issue has proved controversial within al-Qaeda and Takfiri jihadi circles because attacking the near enemy, or fellow Muslims, has quickly lost it support.

Jordanian cleric Abu Qatada al-Filistini and Syrian scholar Abu Basir al-Tartusi were crucial transnational interlocutors in providing religious endorsements for elements of this model. The key figures in Britain were those able to bring the arguments of the Arab Takfiri jihadi discourse to the attention of multi-ethnic Muslim communities, particularly South Asians, though it was Omar Bakri Mohammed, Abu Hamza al-Masri and Jamaican convert Abdullah el-Faisal who were able to connect young South Asian Muslims with these issues and had a national impact in Britain. Abdullah el-Faisal was also appointed as a teacher at Brixton mosque in South London in 1991, but was ousted two years later when he made his extremist views more apparent and attempted unsuccessfully to take over the mosque. Abu Hamza and Abu Qatada both started their work in Britain in 1993. Abu Hamza's Supporters of Shari'a (SOS) was set up in 1994. The groups at the forefront of promoting jihadi ideas were Abu Hamza's SOS, and Omar Bakri's al-Muhajirun movement until it disbanded in 2004 and was replaced by successor organisations *al-Ghuraba'* (The Strangers) and The Saviour Sect, both of which were proscribed by the British government in 2006. Omar Bakri Mohammed probably had the greatest propagandist influence, both as leader of Hizb ut-Tahrir Britain in the early 1990s and even more so as leader of al-Muhajirun, as his group was larger and better organised nationally. This assessment is based on the fact that many of the terrorist cells involving British-born or -raised recruits had some past connections with al-Muhajirun. Moderate Islamist movements, like most of the Muslim communities, while disagreeing with the religious arguments of the jihadi trends, had some sympathy with their political critique of repressive Muslim governments and the call for resistance to Western hegemony.

Through the late 1990s and onwards, Omar Bakri Mohammed and Abu Hamza were in competition to gain access and influence in similar circles. Omar Bakri described himself as the spokesman for Osama Bin Laden's International Islamic Front for Jihad Against Jews and Crusaders. If Abu Hamza described the 9/11 attacks as 'a towering day in history', Omar Bakri Mohammed praised the perpetrators as 'the magnificent 19', much to the consternation of British Muslims. Both claimed to be sending volunteers to Afghanistan, both before and after 9/11.

For the most part, in public rhetoric Takfiri jihadi preachers in Britain invoked the argument about the covenant of security throughout the 1990s and the early 2000s by which they were left relatively free to propagate their ideas, raise funds and send recruits abroad for training so long as they did not attack the home country directly. In response to the tightening controls after 9/11, in January 2005, Omar Bakri was found to be declaring privately to his core followers that the covenant of security had been rendered null and void. However, it is clear that moving into the 2000s many of the British-based cells were able to receive terrorist training abroad, prior to striking the United Kingdom (as seen with the 7/7 and fertiliser bomb cells for instance) whatever public rhetoric there was about the persistence of a covenant of security remaining in place between the Takfiri jihadis and the British state. The military invasions of Iraq and Afghanistan by American and Allied troops have weakened the distinction between the near and far enemy.

Since 2001, Britain has driven much of the open propaganda for Takfiri jihadism underground. Abu Hamza was arrested in 2004 and convicted in 2006 of inciting race hate and murder, and on one terrorist charge. Al-Muhajirun was disbanded and proscribed and Omar Bakri was exiled to the Lebanon in 2005. Abdullah Faisal was jailed for soliciting murder and inciting racial hatred in 2003, and was deported back to Jamaica in 2007. Abu Qatada, detained without charge at Belmarsh Prison between 2002 and 2005, was released under a control order and was then put back into custody. He has since then fought legal battles to resist his deportation back to Jordan. Their disciples who have taken up that propaganda role have headed a number of the British-based terror cells.

The materials of such propagandists are still in circulation and may be used to culture seekers or recruits to a quite a high level of theological sophistication and political reorientation. At the same time, there is now the propaganda of the deed; iconic attacks such as 9/11 or 7/7, or the use of simple slogans to send out powerful public messages – such as Mohammed Sidique Khan's 'I am a solider and we are at war' – that have their own rationale of exploiting the narrative that the Muslim world and the West are bound to be in conflict. This narrative has become more plausible since the military response to 9/11 commenced.

References

Abbas, Tahir (ed.) (2007) *Islamic Political Radicalism. A European Perspective*, Edinburgh: Edinburgh University Press.
——(2011) *Islamic Radicalism and Multicultural Politics. The British Experience*, Ashgate: Routledge.
The Change Institute (2008) *Studies into violent radicalisation; Lot 2 The beliefs ideologies and narratives*. Available at http://ec.europa.eu/home-affairs/doc_centre/terrorism/docs/ec_radicalisation_study_on_ideology_and_narrative_en.pdf (link accessed 19 June 2014)

ABU HAMZA AL-MASRI AND SUPPORTERS OF SHARI'A

Dominique Thomas

Supporters of Shari'a was founded in 1994 – although it became active on the British Islamist scene only in 1996 – by the preacher of Egyptian origin Mustapha Kemal, otherwise known as Abu Hamza al-Masri. Born in 1958 into a family of small traders in Alexandria, he decided in 1979 to emigrate to Brighton in Great Britain to continue his studies in architecture. In order to finance his studies, he worked as a porter in various pubs and discos and, by his own assessment, led a life without any religious commitments. Having obtained British citizenship by marriage to an English Catholic woman of Spanish descent, he began to pray regularly and read the Qur'an after the birth of their first son, Mohammad, in 1981. He became increasingly interested in the Islamic sciences and began studying the basics of the *shari'a* on his own.

Persuaded by the call from preachers from Saudi Arabia, who at that time enjoyed full liberty to preach in British mosques, he went to help the wounded Afghanis being treated in British hospitals. These visits nurtured in him the belief that he had to emigrate and settle in Afghanistan with his family. His encounter with Sheikh 'Abdallah 'Azzam, whom he met at a conference in 1987, convinced him to put his knowledge of civil and military architecture at the service of the *mujahidin*. He joined up at Peshawar in late 1989 and then emigrated with his family in 1990, staying there until 1993. He participated in the building of camps for Afghan refugees on the road between Kabul and Jalalabad and, in 1993, decided to help the *mujahidin* in the Kashmir region. He was wounded during an operation involving explosives and lost sight in one eye and both his forearms.

Abu Hamza returned to the United Kingdom in 1994 and became involved in support efforts for Bosnia where he often travelled as part of humanitarian missions. These missions stopped after the signing of the Dayton agreements on 21 November 1995, which he considered to be a Western usurpation of the victory of his Muslim brothers in Bosnia. He then returned to settle permanently in London and became an imam. He started to preach in one of the big mosques in North London at Finsbury Park with another former fighter from Afghanistan, Abu Qatada al-Filastini. In their messages they called upon British Muslims to be in solidarity with Muslim fighters and reproached them for their lack of political commitment.

In 1996, he decided to launch his own organisation called the Supporters of Shari'a and, by playing off alliances, he managed to take control of the Finsbury Park mosque. This episode is important in the structuring of the movement because it marks his territorial anchorage in the heart of the British capital. From Finsbury Park, the eloquent Abu Hamza, building on his reputation as *mujahid*, extended his influence through preaching and attending conferences in Britain. He based his discourses on the principle of *al-Wala' wa-l-Bara'* to advocate a total separation of Muslims from impious people and environments, and he rejected the democratic system and integration into Western society. Furthermore, he stressed the obligation to contribute to the defence of Muslims wherever they live in the event of occupation. Praising the virtues of armed *jihad* in places such as Yemen, Pakistan, North Africa and Afghanistan, he supported the Taliban regime and the al-Qaeda movement. His sermons proved relatively successful and attracted British Muslims of African and West Indian descent as much as immigrants from North Africa, the Balkans and the Caucasus.

From its inception, Supporters of Shari'a gave material support to assorted *jihad* causes. It managed to raise funds and bring media attention to bear on two new fronts: the Chechen Muslims' separatist campaign against Russia, and support for the armed Islamic movements in Algeria. Supporters of Shari'a provided support through its publications, financial aid and logistics to the Groupes Islamiques Armés (Armed Islamic Groups). Abu Hamza was one of the rare preachers in Europe to support this group until 1998. Subsequently he rallied to the Groupe Salafiste pour la Prédication et le Combat (Salafist Group for Preaching and Combat) founded the same year by Algerian fighters with direct links to the radical Islamist scene in London. His support for these groups soon triggered reprisals from various states. The first protests came from Yemen, after five members of his organisation, including his own son, were arrested at Sana'a in December 1998, on suspicion of having links with an Islamic opposition movement, Jaysh 'Aden Abyan (Adan Abyan Army). After 2001, the United States of America accused Abu Hamza of inspiring various failed terrorist plots planned by individuals who had, for periods of varying length, attended his mosque. These included an American convert, James Jumaa, a resident of Seattle accused of attempting to finance training camps in the state of Oregon; the French–Moroccan Zacarias Moussaoui, arrested on American soil prior to 9/11 and subsequently convicted for membership of the al-Qaeda network; and the Briton, Richard Reid, who attempted to blow up the Paris–Miami flight in December 2001.

Abu Hamza was forbidden to preach within the confines of the mosque in November 2002. New arrests of militants from the Algerian network triggered police operations in January 2003 that led to the closure of the Finsbury Park mosque. For more than a year, Abu Hamza continued to preach in front of the closed mosque. Maintaining his position on armed struggle, his sermons were becoming increasingly violent towards the British system, which he had previously spared; Britain's intervention in Iraq alongside the United States in 2003 shattered this fragile balance forever. The authorities, fearing the influence of this preacher on young militants, finally arrested him in May 2004. His trial, which began during the summer of 2005, found him, along with another preacher of Jamaican origin, Abdullah el-Faisal, guilty of charges of soliciting murder and intending to stir up racial hatred. Soon after, the Supporters of Shari'a found itself again in the sights of the British authorities when it became apparent that the perpetrators of the failed attacks on 21 July 2005 had regularly attended Finsbury Park mosque.

After the attacks on 7/7, and the subsequent expulsion of more militants, the Supporters of Shari'a continued its preaching, this time in small groups. The organisation has since been declared illegal and banned from British soil. After the arrest of Abu Hamza, a 43-year-old Briton of Cypriot origin, Aziz Ahmet – otherwise known as Abu Abdallah – has since become the new unofficial leader. Born in London, he became a fervent practitioner in 1992, while he was pursuing a career in education. In 1998, he studied with Abdullah el-Faisal, the imam of the Brixton mosque. Next, he rejoined the mosque in Finsbury Park and became a member of Supporters of Shari'a. He took over preaching duties after the arrest of Abu Hamza, along with the preacher's son, Mohammad Kemal.

The discourse of Supporters of Shari'a is today fully in line with Abu Hamza, fiercely and simultaneously condemning British politics, its impious society and Muslim organisations maintaining links with the authorities. The representatives of the Muslim Council of Britain (MCB) thus embodied a new target for the movement. In fact, after the reopening of the Finsbury Park mosque in February 2005, the group entered into conflict with the new leadership of the mosque, who had come under the influence of the MCB, the most important Muslim federation in Britain. It openly accused the MCB of collaborating with the British authorities in the latter's attempts to discredit Supporters of Shari'a and like-minded groups. More generally, it condemned the MCB for its proximity to groups supposedly promoting unlawful innovations, such as the Muslim Brotherhood and certain Sufi brotherhoods.

The followers of Supporters of Shari'a left the Finsbury Park mosque for good to join the Whitechapel mosque, where they again came into conflict with its leaders, still influenced by the MCB. Aziz Ahmet was also arrested in September 2006, under the remit of the Terrorism Act and the Public Order Act. He was accused of having organised recruitment and training camps in the British countryside. His trial took place in October 2007 and he was sentenced to eight years' imprisonment. After its prohibition, and in the absence of any real leadership, the Supporters of Shari'a would seem to be very weak in terms of its ability to mobilise militants. Today it constitutes a very small, fragmented group of clandestine individuals, making it difficult to mobilise around any sort of unified platform.

References

Thomas, Dominique (2003) *Le Londonistan. La voix du Jihad*, Paris: Michalon.

AL-MUHAJIRUN AND AL-GHURABA'

Dominique Thomas

The al-Muhajirun (the emigrants) was founded in 1996 by the Syrian preacher Omar Bakri Mohammad. Born in 1959 into the Sunni bourgeoisie of Damascus, he associated for many years with the oppositional circles of the Syrian Muslim Brotherhood and later with the Hizb ut-Tahrir in Lebanon. He then moved to Saudi Arabia where he worked as a businessman, and claims to have set up a local branch of Hizb ut-Tahrir in Mecca. However, his militant activities in the 1980s embarrassed the Saudi authorities and he was forced into exile in the West where he took refuge in the United Kingdom in 1986. Right from the start, he continued with his militant action in the ranks of the British branch of Hizb ut-Tahrir. However, towards the middle of the 1990s, Omar Bakri distanced himself from this movement.

The creation of al-Muhajirun was a result of this split from Hizb ut-Tahrir and had its roots not only in a conflict of power among its leaders, but also in ideological differences. Omar Bakri did not reject violent operations as a method of action and held the opinion that *shari'a* must be installed in whichever land its partisans find themselves, in this case Great Britain. In contrast, this latter option was not seriously considered by Hizb ut-Tahrir which conceived of non-Muslim countries such as Great Britain only as support bases for militancy in countries with a more sizeable Muslim population. According to Bakri, armed *jihad* was also part of a method of action when the defence of Muslim territories requires it, as for example in Palestine, Iraq or Afghanistan. In order to achieve its objectives in the field, al-Muhajirun equipped itself with an efficient and exclusively anglophone communications network, in contrast to Hizb ut-Tahrir's reliance on Arabic media; al-Muhajirun also used all available means of communication: magazines, bulletins, publications, information networks through text messages and internet sites.

The activities of al-Muhajirun revolved around Islamic education and, above all, targeted young people by means of touring activities, university societies and summer camps, organised in the countryside in the south of England. Al-Muhajirun appeared to be the most structured movement on the British radical Islamic scene. It was also the most often mentioned in the British press, as a result of the fact that it admitted into its ranks Muslims of Pakistani origin, by far the most numerous component of the British Muslim population. Moreover, the group did not limit itself to developing its political activities around the London area, but was also present in other large cities such as Manchester, Birmingham and Leeds. Since its foundation, many activists who have been members in the past have been arrested in Britain and abroad (Pakistan, United States, Morocco and Israel). The group was banned under the Terrorism Act in 2004 for inciting violence and racial hatred. It was disbanded on 13 October 2004 and the movement then reconstituted itself in several splinters; this was also due to its spiritual leader Omar Bakri's exile to Lebanon in August, 2005.

A first group made its appearance right after the disbanding under the impetus of a 36-year-old convert, Simon Sulayman Keeler, previously a sergeant in the British army, who came under the influence of Omar Bakri during lectures in his home town of Crawley in West Sussex. The group took the name of Saviour Sect in reference to the one group of Muslims who, because they do not deviate from the Qur'an and the Prophetic tradition, will be saved according to a saying of the Prophet. This group brought the Islamic identity of its militants to the fore by advising them not to follow the dominant way of life in British society. Two other British people of Pakistani origin, engineering graduates in their thirties, have also played an important role in the ranks of this movement: Sajid Sharif and Abdul Rahman Saleem. The latter was arrested under the Public Order Act and found guilty in July 2007 for incitement to violence, after having called for violent actions in response to the publication of cartoons of the Prophet. The group was again dismantled on 17 July 2006 and its members joined the ranks of another called Ahl al-Sunna wa-l-Jama'a.

The second movement to appear is considered the ideological heritage of the preacher Omar Bakri. It was created in November 2004 and was initially placed under the authority of Bakri until his exile. The group takes the name of al-Ghuraba' (the Foreigners). The spokesperson was a close relative of Omar Bakri, Trevor Omar Brooks, a 31-year-old Jamaican who converted to Islam in 1994. He had joined the ranks of al-Muhajirun in 1996, and he too was arrested in February 2007 and placed under judicial monitoring, pending trial, for having made violent utterances and inciting hatred towards the country's authorities. Al-Ghuraba' extolled a discourse founded on the principle of total adherence to Islamic values and the rejection of all secular, British or Western influence present in society, a principle known by radical Islamists under the name al-Wala' wa-l Bara' (loyalty or alliance and disavowal). This association also disbanded voluntarily after the July 2005 attacks, as it was blamed for radicalising British youth and was put on the list of banned organisations.

In November 2005 a new group appeared on the London Islamic scene. It took the name of Ahl al-Sunna wa-l Jama'a and followed the preceding groups. After the exile of Omar Bakri, the people in charge today are the preacher's old-guard 'spiritual sons'. The movement was launched at the initiative of Sulayman Keeler and Anjem Choudary. The latter is considered a first-class militant at the heart of al-Muhajirun and was the right-hand man of Omar Bakri. This British Muslim aged 39, of Pakistani origin, is a lawyer by training, a graduate of Southampton University. One of the other leaders is a British citizen of Bangladeshi origin aged 25, Abdul Muheed Eslam, who was also arrested and tried in July 2007 following demonstrations against the cartoons of the Prophet.

The discourse extolled has not varied much since the al-Muhajirun years. It continues to focus on the re-Islamisation of young people by giving them a new education based on separation from the British Western model. Thus, enrolling in the army or the police force is considered an act of apostasy. Voting and encouraging others to vote are equally acts to be condemned, and so is giving allegiance to a British political party. Asking for a British passport as an expression of desire to form part of the British nation also forms part of this category of nonconforming acts, as too is the registration of a marriage in the civil court. Militants 'legalise' their unions and occasionally divorces through the intermediary of the imam or in unofficial Islamic courts, such as those created by Omar

Bakri in the 1990s and taken over by Anjem Choudary and Omar Brooks after 2005. On the social level, Muslims are also asked to avoid contact with non-Muslim friends, visiting mixed venues, cinemas or even listening to music. The other important axis of this discourse concerns working or collaborating with representative organisations of British Muslims, such as the Muslim Council of Britain, which also constitutes a reprehensible act. The doctrine initiated by Omar Bakri in fact rejects the policies of British Muslim associations considered to be at the service of the State. Their militants therefore find themselves in a Catch-22 situation: on the one hand rejecting Western society, and on the other hand criticising all forms of Islam that refer to any of the four legal schools of Sunni Islam or Sufi lineages. The followers of Ahl al-Sunna define themselves as Salafi, just following the Qur'an and the Sunna without precise reference to the four legal schools.

The organisation today claims to have roughly 1,000 members, although a figure of several hundred militants seems more realistic. Most of these are between 18 and 25 years of age and are essentially of Pakistani or Bangladeshi origin. They come from densely populated areas with high immigration; from London, Birmingham, Leeds or sometimes smaller cities such as Leicester, Stoke, Oldham or Derby. The Ahl al-Sunna wa-l-Jama'a organises conferences on themes around the role of Muslim youth and the British state. Just like the previous organisations, the group has a modern information network using internet sites, discussion forums, blogs and text alerts. The organisation also has dynamic branches in Birmingham and Stoke-on-Trent in Staffordshire and has expanded its activities throughout East London where its implantation is strongest due to the presence of a considerable Muslim population. With unwavering commitment to the defence of Islam, it was at the forefront of the demonstrations staged against the Danish cartoons, the controversial statements of Pope Benedict XVI in Regensburg and, more recently, during gatherings in support of the Muslims in Iraq or Palestine.

References

Thomas, Dominique (2003) *Le Londonistan. La voix du Jihad*, Paris: Michalon.

VIRTUAL JIHADIST MEDIA

Akil N. Awan

The ideological conflict that underlies the global War on Terror is increasingly conducted on the internet's battlefield. Virtual forums are recognised as one of the most important fronts, with an exponential growth in jihadist websites from 14 to over 5,000 between 2000 and 2005 alone.

The constituency of the transnational audiences of this virtual corpus of jihadist media is extremely difficult to ascertain, unless users willingly disclose this information themselves. Audience demographics are, however, dictated to a large degree by extraneous factors pertaining to accessibility of the medium itself such as age, gender, location, socioeconomic status etc. In addition, the audience profile is further limited by the content available, in particular its linguistic demands. The overwhelming majority of virtual jihadist forums are published in Arabic alone and so are inaccessible to a large proportion of non-Arabic-speaking audiences (for example, British Muslim audiences are predominantly (around 74 per cent) of South Asian extraction). Nevertheless, despite the Arabic monopoly on these forums for close to a decade, other languages such as English, French, German, Turkish and Urdu are increasing in importance, both through multilingual sites and translation facilities, and through foums catering to specific parochial audiences. Moreover, much of the audio-visual content of these forums inherently transcend linguistic constraints.

Jihadist forums are very diverse in nature, however they generally serve four key inter-related functions:

1. News: many jihadist forums consider their news coverage to be an important part of their *raison d'être*, particularly as existing coverage of Muslim conflicts is deemed to be unrepresentative and skewed towards their opponents' viewpoints.
2. Propaganda: perhaps the most important role of virtual forums is the uncensored publication and dissemination of the ideology and culture of jihadism. This ranges from the ideological treatises and theological evidences underpinning the culture of jihad, and official statements and communiqués from jihadist groups and leaders, to the circulation of 'acts of jihad' such as graphic beheading videos or IED attacks on coalition targets in Iraq.
3. Training: aside from propagating ideology, virtual forums also provide the means through which those with the inclination may actualise their jihadist aspirations. A plethora of technical and military manuals cover topics as diverse as hostage

kidnapping, weaponry manufacture and deployment, guerrilla warfare, training and tactics and bomb-making.

4. Expression: the relationship between some users of jihadist forums and the pursuit of violence is incontrovertible in some cases. However, for other, less hardline audiences, jihadist forums may serve an important function in subsuming diverse strains of political activism, unrest and dissent, and so provide a conduit and framework for its non-violent expression. Consequently they can serve a cathartic function, allowing audiences to vent their anger and frustration without resorting to violent means, similar to the role played by Al-Jazeera with Middle Eastern audiences. It can indeed be argued that while Al-Jazeera has increased awareness of certain issues, it has also inadvertently engendered some paralysis, particularly as it has led to the withdrawal of people who feel content with being discontent viewers.[1]

Despite the patent fact that much of the material produced by virtual jihadi media constitutes propaganda and aims at indoctrination, its actual efficacy in radicalisation is extremely difficult to ascertain. Some jihadist groups and their media arms such as the Global Islamic Media Front (GIMF) are well aware of the internet's potential radicalising efficacy and appear to be explicitly focusing their energies upon virtual radicalisation and recruitment.[2] Although this recruitment drive is clearly proving fruitful in some cases (the 2004 Madrid train bombings, the 21 July 2005 London abortive bomb plot and the 2006 Canadian bomb plot are all prime examples), it is difficult to ascertain the degree to which virtual jihadist forums influence wider audiences and users. For all we know, they may be proverbially 'preaching to the converted'. For example, Omar Bakri Mohammed's internet relay chat sessions on the Paltalk network in January 2006, where he publicly exhorted to violence and jihad, were solely targeted at the small coterie of his followers, with little attempt to reach a wider audience. Similarly, the vast majority of messages posted on the jihadist forum Mujahedon.net originated within a very small core group of active users: 99 per cent were passive or casual users.[3]

Jihadist media often fulfil some of the same functions as particularistic ethnic media. If one ignores the extreme and sometimes violent tone and content of jihadist sources, they are often concerned with the same issues and topics as are deemed important by mainstream and moderate Muslim news media. In diasporic Muslim communities in Britain and elsewhere, the consumption of alternative news media can be based upon mistrust and cynicism towards 'Western news', and thus motivations for production as well as content can converge in both cases.

Jihadist websites may also converge with non-Muslim sources, although in more limited ways. A number of mainstream websites (such as welfarestate.com, truthseeker.co.uk and loosechange911.com) support conspiracy theories, a staple of some jihadist media. Another shared aspect is extreme audio-visual content, such as the images and videos of beheadings, civilian casualties and other graphic violence, also a staple of 'gore sites' such as Ogrish.com and Rotten.com. The video beheading of Nick Berg was downloaded from Ogrish a staggering 15 million times, granting the material a far higher profile than could possibly have been envisaged by the perpetrators and immediate disseminators of the act.

Content-sharing platforms can also contribute to the wider availability of jihadist media. The popular jihadist-inspired rap video, *Dirty Kuffar*, by the UK group 'Sheikh Terra and the Soul Salah Crew', has been hosted on a very small number of jihadist forums including Tajdeed.org.uk. The video has not gained widespread acclaim or notoriety through the jihadist community, who most likely consider it to be amateurish and perhaps even offensive in using Western-style rap music. Instead, it has relied upon more mainstream platforms such as Putfile, Google Video, and YouTube to gain a fairly high profile.

However, perhaps the most important aspect in which jihadist media converge with non-jihadist sources is in their presentation of alternate narratives and paradigms to those of the mainstream media, and particularly those originating with coalition forces or the US administration. Many websites and blogs are intensely critical of mainstream media 'collusion' with the coalition, which they see exemplified by the statement of CBS news anchor Dan Rather in 2003: 'When my country is at war, I want my country to win ... there is an inherent bias in the coverage of the American press'. jihadist media reports bear some resemblance in their news reportage to sites which claim to present the fuller picture by utilising a greater diversity of non-mainstream sources.[4] Stories originating with jihadi sources can quickly gain currency in the context of a growing mistrust of news and propaganda originating with the US administration and coalition forces and disseminated by what are viewed as its proxies, the mainstream news agencies. This mistrust has many roots. In addition to suspicions over the true motives for the invasion of Iraq, and damning indictments of the United States and coalition partners in the light of the lurid excesses witnessed at Guantanamo Bay, Abu Ghraib and elsewhere, evidence of falsification, concealment or infiltration of untrue 'news' into the mainstream media has undermined trust. Examples include the Pentagon's fictitious account of the 'heroic rescue' of Private Jessica Lynch from al-Nasiriyah, the claim that white phosphorous was only used for illumination purposes in the assault on Falluja (and subsequent admission that it was used indiscriminately as an incendiary weapon)[5] or the denial that napalm was used in Iraq (and subsequent admission of the use of MK77 bombs, the more deadly successor to napalm).[6] Similarly, perceptions of hypocrisy and double standards have also been detrimental both to the coalition's claim to the moral high ground, and to the credibility of mainstream news media. Images of Abu Musab al-Zarqawi's bloodied corpse are paraded in mission briefings and relayed in the mainstream media, while images of dead coalition soldiers on Al-Jazeera spark moral outrage. The US administration extols the virtues of freedom of press and speech while apparently unable to tolerate alternative viewpoints, as epitomised by its sustained 'war' on Al-Jazeera. Beside such attempts to deter reporting from the other side, government-made television news segments have been found to constitute improper covert propaganda by both the Government Accountability Office and the Federal Communications Commission in 2005. All such actions exacerbate distrust and grant alternative paradigms and narratives far greater legitimacy. Overall, the use or adoption of jihadist stories by non-jihadist and non-Muslim media has had a considerable effect in countering the marginalisation of jihadist voices.

The exponential growth of jihadist websites, forums and blogs with increasingly high-end production values, sophisticated critiques of prevailing narratives and ostensive attempts at impartiality has not occurred in a vacuum. To a great extent they are reactive, their *raison d'être* being supplied by the mainstream media's perceived collusion with governmental misinformation or at least uncritical acceptance of it. jihadist media are far from alone in these critiques, and there has been a growing convergence of interests with other non-mainstream media outlets. The general proliferation of sources of news, information and commentary, coupled with increasingly media-savvy audiences, who are far less likely to accept the veracity of any one narrative and more likely to evince dissatisfaction with conventional modes of mediation, is challenging 'media imperialism'. Web 2.0 applications, with their blurring of the boundaries between traditional categories of producer and consumer on the internet are increasingly playing a major role in allowing the jihadist message to gain wider circulation and, significantly, outside of its traditional ambit too.

Notes

1   Mohamed Zayani (2006) 'Arabic public opinion in the age of satellite television: the case of al-Jazeera', in Elizabeth Poole and John E. Richardson (eds), *Muslims and the News Media*, London: I.B.Tauris.
2   Akil N. Awan (2007) 'Virtual jihadist media: Function, legitimacy, and radicalising efficacy', *European Journal of Cultural Studies*, 10 (3): pp. 389–408.
3   Ibid.
4   See whatreallyhappened.com; thetruthseeker.co.uk; iraqbodycount.net; and informationclearinghouse.com. (first two links accessed 19 June 2014, last two links no longer accessible)
5   BBC News (2005) *US used white phosphorus in Iraq*. November. Available at http://news.bbc.co.uk/2/hi/middle_east/4440664.stm (link accessed 19 June 2014)
6   Colin Brown (2005) 'US Lied to Britain Over Use of Napalm in Iraq War', The *Independent*, November.

References

Awan, Akil N. (2007) 'Virtual jihadist media: Function, legitimacy, and radicalising efficacy', *European Journal of Cultural Studies*, 10 (3): pp. 389–408.
BBC News (2005) *US used white phosphorus in Iraq*. November. Available at http://news.bbc.co.uk/2/hi/middle_east/4440664.stm (link accessed 19 June 2014)
Brown, Colin (2005) 'US Lied to Britain Over Use of Napalm in Iraq War', The *Independent*, November. (link accessed 19 June 2014)
Zayani, Mohamed (2006) 'Arabic public opinion in the age of satellite television: the case of al-Jazeera', in Elizabeth Poole and John E. Richardson (eds), *Muslims and the News Media*. London: I.B.Tauris.

(5) TABLIGHI JAMA'AT

TABLIGHI JAMA'AT IN THE UK

Imran Mogra

Through alleys into huts and via boulevards into skyscrapers

Tablighi Jama'at (TJ) attains a transnational character through a theological basis, as it considers itself and others as being designated representatives to pass on the eternal message of the final messenger – Muhammad. Since the line of prophethood has been terminated and new messengers will not be sent to the world to invite humanity to God, the mantle of this responsibility, TJ maintains, lies on the entire Muslim nation. This responsibility is being fulfilled in part by TJ, they argue. Hence they aim to take the message of Islam to every household on earth by adopting a global character. According to them, the evidence for embracing this duty is categorically declared in the Qur'an and *hadith* (saying of the Prophet). To encapsulate the essence of this belief, some TJ's are often heard positing: 'we have not brought a message from India. This is not a message of an Indian rather we have brought the message of Madinah'.[1]

The inspiration to become a global movement is also attained from the fact that the *Sahaba* (companions of the Prophet) dispersed from the holy lands to many countries – and were buried there – for spreading the message. Knowing that the *Sahaba* left their home and died in foreign lands motivates some TJ's to supplicate for such engagement. Some aspire to die while in *jama'at* (outreach) and would consider it to be a commendable death.

TJ is international because the message of Muhammad is international. By this, TJ understands that every Muslim should have a concern for every human being to be led to heaven and saved from hell. In order to achieve this, TJ in the UK, like their global counterparts elsewhere, maintain that Muhammad gave this responsibility to the *Sahaba* who dispersed to the four corners of the world leaving the blessed cities. Justification for the multicultural nature of TJ is also derived from the hagiographies of companions such as Salman, Suhaib and Bilal, who were from Persia, Rome and Abyssinia respectively, and who were engaged in the service of Islam. TJ asserts that the *Sahaba* were 'multi-coloured' and therefore they cannot be otherwise.

In understanding the movement's work, it is significant to note that their *che bāten* (six points) are used as key tools for re-orientating Muslims and are not innovations or articles of belief specific to TJ. Rather, they are common characteristics identified by TJ's founder Maulana Ilyas (1885–1944), popularly known as Hadhrat Ji (respect sir), which were found among all the *Sahaba* and which, he felt, if adopted by Muslims would bring about change in thought and action.

In the UK, based on questionnaires and interviews, it appears that TJ has, to a great extent, shed its image of being attractive to the older generation and lower classes.² In fact some respondents, when discussing the particular characteristic of UK, opined that there were more young people active in the UK. The claim of exclusiveness based on socio-economic grounds is rejected by appealing to everyone to join TJ on the basis that in the early days of Islam, all sections of the Maccan community began the invitation: Abu Bakr was rich, 'Ammar was destitute and Sumayya, a female, was brutally murdered. Hence TJ claims to be open for everyone. Indeed, observations at various TJ gatherings show that their participants come from a very wide spectrum of society and include doctors, teachers, surgeons and dentists; some are self-employed and others are unemployed, both young and aged. TJ also takes pride and showcases celebrities and sport stars to recruit new members, convince sceptics about the 'legitimacy' of their movement and bolster their enthusiasts.

The key aim of TJ also contributes to its transnational character. TJ endeavours to be wholly engaged with the reformation of the self. The reformation of the self involves talking to others about Islam and ostensibly TJ's six points. This process has a dual purpose as it makes the conviction of the person delivering the message spiritually renewed and may also become the means of guidance for the invitee. In so doing, TJ facilitates counselling and it reminds Muslims of their duty in a systematic way by starting with the self, the family, neighbours, the locality, the country and the world.

The practice of *hijra* (travelling) and *nusra* (assisting) as exemplified during the life of Muhammad are strong mechanisms used by TJ to create identity around particular TJ characteristics and communities of *sāthis* (acquaintances) living in modern urban spaces and beyond. Their weekly activities remain within local areas of individual mosques, but their monthly or annual activities take them out of town and to other countries. Geographically, such networks can be mapped across the world. In fact, the details of their initial activities, and their analysis of the state of Muslims in England and in remote villages of Africa during the Fifties and Sixties, were available for the elders at the *markaz* in Nizamuddin, India.³

Tablighi Jama'at in the UK

One of the great achievements of Maulana Yusuf, son of Maulana Ilyas was that during his leadership the *da'wa* and *tabligh* had been extended to foreign countries rapidly and vigorously: 20 January 1946 marks the day when the first *ghasht* (rounds) was conducted in England.⁴ Muslims in the then-Indian quarter of London responded earnestly to their call and since then TJ has been growing.

However, it was not until 1982 that a *markaz* was established in Dewsbury, Yorkshire, to operate as a European *markaz*. Having such a centre provided several advantages: in the *diyar ghair* (foreign lands) a permanent abode was created, the *akabir* (elders) could replicate the activities of the subcontinent; as commitment to various needs of TJ deepened and progress was made, the layers of organisation and efforts could be passed on incrementally within the country; and the responsibility for UK and Europe was laid more on their own people.

In recent years, the expansion of their participants can also be gauged by considering the pattern of their *jhor* (gathering), conducted for reinvigorating those who have given 40 days itinerant. At one time, such members from all over the country were assembled in Dewsbury for a weekend, but currently the *markaz* is no longer able to coordinate and accommodate them effectively. As a result, such members are called from particular regions across the country over different weekends. This suggests not only a huge increase in the number of members who have spent 40 days, but also indicates their continued commitment. Every quarter, prominent 'elders' from all European centres have a consultation meeting where European issues are discussed. Dewsbury host these meetings too. The rate of increase in Europe appears to be faster whereas in the UK it has stabilised, according to a respondent.

Consequently, from the single *markaz* of the early 1980s, the next step was the creation of a *markaz* within various regions of the UK and these were established within major cities in these regions. In other words, the status of *markaz* was devolved to local areas which continued to have strong links with the national *markaz,* where national consultations are usually held on a monthly basis. In 2009, this formation has meant that 'elders' from abroad were able to reach more members when they toured the UK by attending more than one of these *marakiz*, sometimes in a single day, rather than Dewsbury organising a huge gathering. For the more active members, such an arrangement is convenient and less time intensive. In other words, from the industrial towns of the 1970s, TJ is no longer a Yorkshire or Midlands phenomenon, instead, smaller leafy suburbs and affluent areas are not only visited by TJ but they have their presence. In part this is sometimes facilitated by those who give their time in what is termed as *pedal jamaʻat* (mobile group), by those who have relocated out of the inner city periphery, professionals whose jobs have been transferred, or students.

This devolvement, in part, played a significant role in the establishment of a network of mosque infrastructures in the UK, since a *markaz* is inevitably encapsulated within a mosque. TJ also assists in the establishment of mosques beyond the dominant sectarian lines of the Deoband/Barelwi traditions. The former tend to provide them with fertile grounds to conduct their programmes mostly unhindered, and also because its origins lie with it. Some mosques have been established by leading members of TJ in some local areas. The running of these mosques would predominantly be conducted by members of TJ and former TJ members would, in some cases, have a role on the committee. This is not to suggest that the establishment of mosques consists of definitive rules. While this may be the case in a group or two, support for the establishment of mosques in the UK often crosses sectarian lines. The concept of *biraderi* (tribal networks) also has a role in gaining support for creating mosques beyond sectarian divides, just as theological and eschatological motives do. Active participants of the TJ have also established independent schools, *dar al-ʻulum* and *makatib* in some cities of the UK.

In some cities TJ have had their programme in mosques managed by followers of the Barelwi tradition who are content with TJ conducting some of their activities but have reservations for letting them sleep therein. During the 1980s, the central Ahl-e-Hadith mosque provided them with access to conduct their programmes. Some mosques established by Muslims originating outside the subcontinent communities also tend to be sympathetic towards TJ especially for bringing change among some wayward youths.

Some members of TJ in the UK claim that, in principle, there is nothing specific about being a Tablìghi in the UK. However, there is a perception among some of them that more youngsters are involved in this effort, as stated earlier. Perhaps this is facilitated by the vacation system, both in education and employment, which makes it easier to participate. Holding a British passport affords its own privileges, as receiving visas to travel abroad becomes relatively easy for them, unlike their *sāthis* visiting the UK.

For some Muslims in the UK, TJ appeals due to its simple and basic, yet true and effective message that relates to all members of the Muslim society. In addition eschatological beliefs and promises of virtues for treading in 'the path of God' have a strong appeal. The freedom for religious expression also provides confidence to many individuals, as participating in TJ brings out positive qualities of a person, and one is drawn to practice the religion and live in a country which freely allows this.

Conclusion

From humble beginnings, Maulana Ilyas initiated a programme of reminding Muslims of their true status and duty. Today TJ boasts of being a global movement. In the UK there are signs of its continued growth among many sections of the Muslim community, although the response to them is not uniform from other Muslim groups. The youth, in particular, seem to be attracted by the changes that TJ is able to bring about within individuals, and give a positive sense of purpose and responsibility. Nevertheless, a challenge remains: how to ensure that the intermittent participants become regular and dedicated ones.

Notes

1   *Fieldnote* 5 October 2009.
2   Yoginder Sikand (1998) 'The origins and growth of the Tablighi Jamāt in Britain', *Islam and Christian–Muslim Relations*, 9 (2): pp. 171–92.
3   Sani Hasani (1982) *Sawaneh-i-Hazrat Maulānā Yusuf Kandhlawi*, Lucknow: Maktabah Darul Uloom Nadwat-ul-Ulama.
4   Ibid.

References

Hasani, Sani (1982) *Sawaneh-i-Hazrat Maulānā Yusuf Kandhlawi*, Lucknow: Maktabah Darul Uloom Nadwat-ul-Ulama.
Mogra, Imran (2006) 'Intervention for Transformation. Activities among Young Muslims of Britain', *Youth & Policy*, 92: pp. 133–49.
Sikand, Yoginder (1998) 'The origins and growth of the Tablighi Jamāt in Britain', *Islam and Christian-Muslim Relations*, 9 (2): pp. 171–92.

THE TABLIGHI JAMAʻAT IN SPAIN

Sol Tarrés

Brief historical overview of the Tablighi Jamaʻat in Spain

The first reliable information on the presence of Tablighi communities in Spain dates back to the mid-1980s in Catalonia, and always in relation to immigrant Maghreb and, to a lesser extent, Pakistani groups.

The Tablighi movement entered Spain by three main routes: Catalonia and nearby communities in the North; Morocco via Ceuta, Melilla and Gibraltar in the South; and Portugal in the West. *Daʻis* (preachers) from Great Britain and Northern Europe also came to Spain at that time and regularly travel around the Iberian Peninsula. Today, there are Tablighi communities in almost all Spanish autonomous communities, although their precise number is unknown due to the lack of a general census of Muslim communities.

The establishment of the Tablighi community in Spain can be divided into three phases. The first phase, from the mid-1980s to the mid-1990s, was characterised by the first visits by *daʻis* to Spain, preaching *daʻwa* on closed mosque circuits. These *daʻis* contacted potential groups and people related with these collectives who later created the first communities linked to the Tablighi movement in Catalonia, on the Mediterranean coast and in the autonomous cities of Ceuta and Melilla.

The second phase, from the mid-1990s to the beginning of the twenty-first century, was characterised by community construction and the start of the institutionalisation process. Most citizens see the Tablighi communities that have established themselves in Spain as closed and largely self-sufficient groups because they have developed based on the *siffat* or Tablighi principles. This process involves both the creation of strong networks, characterised by their solidarity and mutual support among their members, and the strengthening of a solid Islamic identity based on a strict religious praxis and constant Islamic education.

The third stage, which began with the 11 March attacks in Madrid, has been characterised by the spread of these communities throughout almost the whole of Spain (particularly in regions recently affected by immigration), as well as attempts to open the community to the rest of society. Most Tablighi communities are legally recognised religious organisations federated with the Union of Islamic Communities of Spain (UCIDE). Moreover, since they comply with Spanish legislation, they enjoy all the rights recognised in the 1992 Cooperation Agreement,[1] including access to financing for their social and cultural activities (Spanish courses, Arabic courses, festive events, etc.), such as financial aid offered by the Fundación Pluralismo y Convivencia (Pluralism and Coexistence Foundation).[2] The oldest Tablighi communities in Spain belong to autonomous community Islamic institutions (for example Islamic Councils).

The profile of Tablighi communities in Spain

Tablighi communities in Spain are very similar to other Islamic communities in the country. They are multicultural but are mainly formed by Maghrebi immigrants. The presence of immigrants from the Indian subcontinent (Pakistanis and Bangladeshis) is only significant in certain parts of Catalonia and Madrid. Since the intensification of international migratory flows to Spain and the strong growth of Muslim communities took place in the second half of the 1990s, the members of most of these communities are first-generation immigrants; hence, generational renewal has yet to take place. The pre-eminence of immigrants in Tablighi communities, especially in those created in the last decade, has led to the construction of communities with strong structures characterised by group solidarity, the intensification of Islamic sociability, social control, strict compliance with religious praxis and the temporary self-segregation of the majority society in order to strengthen both the community and Islamic identity and minimise acculturation. Additionally, mosques with close ties to the Tablighi are often a reference for Muslims in each region, due to both their congregation capacity and their social work.

Spanish converts to the Tablighi movement are in effect invisible, proportionally speaking, in these communities (although there are many Spanish women who have joined the group after marrying Tablighi members). This is because the proselytising work of the Tablighi is aimed at other Muslims and because Spanish converts see them as closed communities with few common cultural codes. Exceptions are the communities in Ceuta and Melilla, where there are more Spaniards due to the unique historical and geographical characteristics of the Muslim communities in these autonomous cities.

Lastly, the communities display different levels of adherence to the Tablighi Jama'at movement, ranging from communities that are fully integrated to those that sympathise with the movement and those that are only stopovers for the *da'is* on their missionary voyages.

The debate on the Tablighi Jama'at

Until 2001–4, the Tablighis went completely unnoticed in Spanish society due to both the discretion of their actions ('we prefer working to talking' claimed one of their leaders) and to the prevailing ignorance of the different Islamic groups and trends in Spain. Since their arrival, the Tablighi have carried out intense social work from the Islamic perspective, that is, through *da'wa* and supporting Muslims and their families in the area of influence of their communities, especially in the case of people engaging in clearly illicit behaviour or marginalised individuals (dysfunctional conduct; for example alcoholism, drug addiction, inmates in prison, young people and petty criminals, etc.). Although this work is largely ignored by most citizens, the same is not true of institutions because the Tablighi have always been careful about their image and the attention they have received from national law enforcement agencies: they officially announce the opening of mosques/oratorios, invite them to Friday prayer and inform them when a *mashura* is going to be celebrated at their mosques.

The Tablighi Jama'at suddenly attracted media attention after 9/11, when the movement was mentioned as a possible source of jihadist recruits for Abu Dahdah's network. The Madrid attacks on 11 March and the arrests of alleged terrorists in subsequent years continued to cast suspicion over the Tablighi as those arrested had been in contact with the Tablighi movement at some point in their lives. Furthermore, the media included the Tablighi in the same group as other very different Islamic groups, political parties and trends. The same media organisations fail to mention (or ignore) the difference between different Islamic trends, and present an essentialist and determinist vision that identifies strict religious practice with political radicalism. This situation is exacerbated by information originating from North African countries, warning of the possible radicalisation of the discourse of pro-Tablighi imams, essentially concealing the failure of institutions in those countries to exercise sufficient religious, ideological and institutional control of their communities.

The Tablighi Jama'at is a strongly apolitical and pacifist movement. The community's leaders are very careful to prevent any type of publicity or political propaganda in mosques/oratorios and expel people who do so from such places. Active commitment to the Tablighi movement is incompatible with aggressive militancy: according to one of its leaders, 'if a person joins the radicals, they automatically cease to be a Tablighi'. Political concerns or opinions are kept out of daily community life and are therefore not used to respond to the ideological needs or socio-political opinions and social justice concerns of certain members, especially the younger members. As a result, the latter participate in other Muslim groups where politics are welcomed. Leaving the Tablighi movement is relatively simple and common, as membership of the movement is an individual decision and permanent membership is not obligatory.

In the debate on integration, there is a common belief that Tablighi communities oppose the integration of its members in Spanish society. As mentioned previously, the explanation given for this is the construction of Tablighi communities. However, the Tablighi support social peace, peaceful coexistence and participation in Spanish society in the Islamic way, based on the belief that being a good Muslim means being a good citizen. Through their communities, they support respect and compliance with the laws of their country of residence, provided that these laws do not contradict Islamic rules (something which does not happen in Spain). They also ensure that the community's religious leaders have knowledge of the society in which they live in order to adequately resolve problems and contradictions that arise in daily life, as well as promoting better coexistence. This indirectly makes it easier for their communities to open up to the society in which they live.

Reflections

The Tablighi Jama'at movement is part of a society that now includes second- and third-generation Muslims with different concerns and needs to first-generation Muslims. This society is characterised by increasing, complex, plural and competitive religious Islamic pluralism, in which different institutions and/or different religious groups compete for the loyalty of real and/or potential believers, as well as for their survival. In short, a highly dynamic social reality.

Notes

1   The 1980 Organic Law on Religious Freedom gave minority confessions with the recognised condition of *notorio arraigo* (clear and deep-rooted influence) the ability

to sign a series of legally binding cooperation agreements recognising these rights. In 1992, the Spanish government signed these agreements with representatives of the three religious confessions that, at that time, were considered to comply with the condition of *notorio arraigo*: Jews, Protestants and Muslims.

2   The Fundación Pluralismo y Convivencia (Pluralism and Coexistence Foundation) was founded in 2003 as a state foundation. It aims to support the cultural, educational and social integration programmes of minority religious confessions that have signed a cooperation agreement with the State, or that comply with the condition of *notorio arraigo* (clear and deep-rooted influence) in Spain, as well as the promotion of the full enjoyment of religious freedom.

References

Beltrán, Joaquín and Sáiz, Amelia (2002) 'Comunidades asiáticas en España', *Documentos CIDOB, relaciones España-Asia*. No. 3. Barcelona: Fundació CIDOB.

Metcalf, Barbara D. (2002) '"Traditionalist" Islamic activism: Deoband, Tablighis, and Talibs', *ISIM Papers*, Leiden: ISIM.

Moreras, Jordi (2005) 'Ravalistán? Islam y configuración comunitaria entre los paquistaníes en Barcelona', *Revista CIDOB d'afers internacional*, 68, pp. 119–132.

Sikand, Yoginder (2006) 'The Tablighi Jama'at and Politics: A Critical Re-Appraisal', *The Muslim World*, 96 (1), pp. 175–95.

LAÏCITÉ AND PIETY – THE TABLIGHI JAMA'AT IN FRANCE

Dietrich Reetz

For the Tablighi Jama'at (TJ), France hosts its most important, numerous and influential European national branch. Inside France, the Tablighi Jama'at managed to become one of the most influential Sunni Islamic forces. According to a 2001 study by French security agencies, out of 1,534 places of worship the TJ was reported to control 163 mosques, occupying second place behind the Union of French Islamic Organisations (UOIF).[1]

The successful expansion of the Tablighi in France thus presents a number of paradoxes: It reconciles demonstrable piety with a combative secularist environment. The TJ, being much shaped by the culture of Indian Islam, has been able to win over Muslims from a different cultural background, Maghebian, and is even dominated by them in France. The TJ ethos and practical ritual runs against French predilections for intellectual debate and extensive discourse. The key to its influence is the social status of many Muslims. TJ identity politics have helped it to acquire cultural capital and social status. In this sense, it is the social marginalisation of French Muslims and many of its Muslim immigrants, and offensive public attitudes towards Islam and its rituals, which have encouraged young French Muslims to seek mental and spiritual refuge in the Tablighi Jama'at.

The TJ presence in France developed in proto-typical ways that carry significance for its expansion to the West in general.[2] Its expansion proceeded in stages which could be roughly distinguished as that of: the travelling preacher, the religious migrant, the religious citizen, the pious citizen, and the defiant believer.

While those stages overlap they mark the major direction of activism during that period.

(1) Preaching groups of the TJ began coming to France regularly in the 1960s. In the early phase they were invited by pious followers who happened to live in Europe, mostly students or businessmen. They would come as visitors, not thinking of staying in Europe, but the compulsions of the Tablighi mode of operation soon forced them to make arrangements for the travelling preachers.

(2) After a period of makeshift arrangements for prayers and meetings, they were looking for proper places of worship and religious centres where they could receive the arriving groups. As facilities were small and often provisional, it was the authorities that pushed them to go for more formal arrangements due to

concerns over hygiene, fire or construction safety. Sometimes state regulations would be more stringently enforced on their prayer rooms as the Tablighis were newcomers and migrant representatives. Thanks to the needs of the travelling groups they formed in the 1970s and early 1980s, low-key associations and established religious centres where they could receive arriving preachers and conduct the weekly congregation on a Thursday night. The Tablighis first registered in France as an association in 1972 (l'Association Foi et Pratique). During this phase they would feel that the settled migrants needed and wanted to be more knowledgeable about their religion. The Tablighis were seeking to provide them with spiritual and religious guidance representing the rightly guided pious and religious migrant.

(3) During the late 1980s and early 1990s Tablighi institutions were growing in number and influence. In France the number of units belonging to the Association Foi et Pratique rapidly increased. The associations and their local centres started seeking interaction with local authorities in order to settle issues or disputes over the mosques, these centres or the travelling groups. As state supervision in France was, and is, very close and also perceived as intrusive, the need for local mediation often arose. Functionaries of the Tablighi Jama'at started self-consciously consulting with local authorities to get mosques and prayer centres established. A good example of that is the Tablighi unit in Marseille. Under the moderate leadership of Sheikh Yassine, in daily life a self-employed interpreter of Moroccan descent, it managed to build its own mosque, the first new-built mosque in Marseille, which opened to a wider Muslim public in 2005.[3] Thus, this phase was marked by a period of normalisation and integration where Tablighi leaders sought to make a home in Europe. They probably reflected on their own personal situation in countries where they had succeeded in striking family roots in local society. Within the Islamic field they established a conservative option that found its niche without being seen as hostile. Thus they became involved in the

Institutionalisation of the Tablighi Jama'at

1962	Arrival of first Tablighi group		Sanaullah Khan – later Professor of Statistics in Aligarh University, India
1968	Arrival of second Tablighi group		Sanaullah Khan
1972	*Association Foi et Pratique*	79 Rue Jean-Pierre Timbaud, 75011 Paris	Mohammed Hammami
1973	*Mosquée Abou Bakir*	39 Boulevard Belleville, 75011 Paris	
1979	*Mosquée Omar Ibn Al-Khattab*	79 Rue Jean-Pierre Timbaud, 75011 Paris	
1986	*Association Culturelle de Tabligh et Daawa ila-LLAH,* together with *Ar- Rahma Mosquée*	52, Av Paul Vaillant Couturier 93200 Saint-Denis	Younès Ben Mohamed Tlili *alias* Mohamed Younès
1995–2005	First purpose-built Tablighi mosque in Marseille, Mosquée Khalid Ibn Walid	24, rue Malaval, 13002 Marseilles	Mohamed Yassine

Sources: Kepel (2000); Khedimellah (2005); author's research (2008).

production of a 'religious citizen'. This was in marked contrast to their pattern of operation in South Asia where they avoided all forms of public civic involvement.

(4) The 1990s saw a period of pious mass activism, where the institutions rapidly expanded numerically among believers and citizens of migrant descent. In France, this phase was embodied in the split of the Tablighi Association and the establishment of the rival Tabligh-o-Dawah group. The latter, more conservative and demonstrably more pietist than the former, soon gained the upper hand under the charismatic but highly ideological Sheikh Younès and currently enjoys majority support among French Tablighis.

During this period the expression of public pietism in the name of Islam was still seen as politically correct in Western Europe. Conservative Sunni Islam at the time was a close political ally of NATO in Afghanistan, against Iraq and Iran.

(5) With the events of 9/11 the political perspective on Islamic pietism changed. It was soon regarded as a threat laying the foundation for political and radical or militant Islam.[4] Tabligh activists in France were subjected to close and primarily hostile scrutiny by the mass media. Tablighi centres and their leaders turned defiant and dug in for the long haul. They had established a secure legal and institutional presence and felt wronged by public attitudes. Groups and centres were now the object of intrusive coverage by the media. They were officially put under surveillance in France, who now saw them as harbingers of terrorism.[5]

The TJ has thus grown into the daily fabric of Muslim life in France. Nevertheless, it has not become a major player in the Islamic field in terms of political consequences and decision-making and is not likely to become one. It shuns public attention and activism beyond its rituals of piety. Perhaps this helped the TJ to become a positive test case for reconciling French laïcité with public religiosity. The French political and administrative system appeared flexible enough for the Tablighis to create and develop its institutional presence of demonstrable piety. It takes protection from the same legalism and secularism, in terms of separation of State and religion, that form the core of the laicist French political ethos.

Notes

1   Christophe Deloire and Christophe Dubois (2004) *Les islamistes sont déjà là. Enquête sur une guerre secrète*, Paris: Albin Michel, p. 43.
2   Ben Halima Abderraouf (2004) *Tabligh: Etape IV*, Paris: Le Figuier.
3   See http://www.20minutes.fr/article/152337/France-Nouveau-retard-pour-le-projet-de-grande-mosquee-a-Marseille.php. Accessed 16 April 2008.
4   Marc Gaborieau (2006) 'What Is Left of Sufism in Tablighi Jama'at?', *Archives de Sciences Sociales des Religions*, 135: pp. 53–72.
5   Christoper Deliso (2007) *The Coming Balkan Caliphate: the Threat of Radical Islam to Europe and the West*, Westport: Praeger Security International, p. 90.

References

Abderraouf, Ben Halima (2004) *Tabligh: Etape IV*, Paris: Le Figuier.
Deliso, Christoper (2007) *The Coming Balkan Caliphate : the Threat of Radical Islam to Europe and the West*, Westport: Praeger Security International.

Deloire, Christophe and Christophe Dubois (2004) *Les islamistes sont déjà là. Enquête sur une guerre secrete*, Paris: Albin Michel, p. 43.

Gaborieau, Marc (2006) 'What Is Left of Sufism in Tablighi Jama'at?', *Archives de Sciences Sociales des Religions*, 135: pp. 53–72.

Kepel, Gilles (2000) 'Foi et pratique: Tablīghī Jama'at in France', in Khalid Masud (ed.), *Travellers in Faith: Studies of the Tablīghī Jama'āt As a Transnational Islamic Movement for Faith Renewal*. Leiden: Brill, pp. 188–205.

Khedimellah, Moussa (2000) ' Le mouvement Tablīgh en Lorraine', in Richard Lioger (ed.), *Une anthropologie religieuse en Lorraine*, Metz: Editions Serpenoise, pp. 149–62.

—— (2001) 'Les jeunes prédicateurs : la dignité identitaire retrouvée par le puritanisme religieux?', *Revue Socio-Anthropologie*, 10. Available at http://socio-anthropologie.revues. org/index155.html (link accessed 19 June 2014)

—— (2005) 'La mosquée Al Rahma, le centre français du Tablīgh a Saint-Denis'. July. Available at www.bladi.net/forum/51933-mosquee-al-rahma-centre-francais-Tablīgh/ #post1014329 (link accessed 19 June 2014)

Masud, Muhammad Khalid (2000) *Travellers in Faith: Studies of the Tablīghī Jama'āt As a Transnational Islamic Movement for Faith Renewal*, Leiden: Brill.

Reetz, Dietrich (forthcoming) 'Public Piety among European Diversity: The Tablīghī Jama'at between Traditionalism and Transformation', in Dietrich Reetz (ed.), *Living Islam in Europe: Muslim Traditions in European Contexts*, Leiden: Brill.

(6) HIZB UT-TAHRIR

HIZB UT-TAHRIR IN THE UNITED KINGDOM

Sadek Hamid

The feature that distinguishes Hizb ut-Tahrir (HT) from rival Islamic movements is its conversion of Islam into a revolutionary self-sufficient, rational ideology or its totalising politicisation of religion. Islam for party members is understood as an Islamised *weltan-schaung* enclosed within series of integrated systems which cover political, economic, legal and social affairs. HT's *raison d'être* is the reunification of all the Muslim lands, or the reconstructing of a modern caliphate, which is believed by them to be the only viable method of restoring Muslim sovereignty and religio-cultural authenticity.

HT in the UK has arguably emerged through three phases since its establishment in the 1980s. The party first began to gain media attention in the early 1990s after Syrian exile and party member Omar Bakri Mohammed was asked to become its leader. His controversial public pronouncing on British domestic issues and international relations, such as calling for the assassination of the British prime minister at the time, began to cause tension with the international leadership who were unhappy that he, and not the party's ideas, had become the focus of public interest. Under the period of his leader- ship Bakri, with the active assistance of his loyal deputy Farid Kassim, was able to recruit hundreds of members across the UK, most of which were college and university students from South Asian backgrounds. Differences with the central leadership came to a head in 1996 after which Bakri resigned, claiming that HT had violated Islamic law, in his view, by constricting the demands of the *shari'a* in areas such as: where to re-estabilish the caliphate; separating law from belief; and not accepting that *jihad* is an indvidual duty, as opposed to one defined by legitimate authority. This resulted in him reactivating his HT front group Al-Muhajirun, created in Saudi Arabia in 1983, and taking a signif- icant number of members with him.

The period between 1996 and 2002 marked a period where HT seemed to struggle to reorganise after Bakri's departure, preferring instead to quietly rebuild its base of support. From 2002, to the present, HT has attempted to rebrand itself as a moderate Islamist movement. Since the 7/7 attacks in London, they have made major efforts to tone down their anti-Western rhetoric and distance themselves from allegations connecting them with violent extremism. London has provided HT with the ideal hub for coordi- nating its international communications, administrative and publishing operations and also, importantly, freedom to function in a way not possible in other Western or Muslim states. The main preoccupations of HT in Britain are to mobilise Muslim public opinion and educate non-Muslim political and intellectual elites, so that they become favourable to their interpretation of Islam. It has also allowed Western educated cadres opportunities for spreading the party's ideas; in this regard British trained members have helped to establish HT branches in Bangladesh and Pakistan.

To be able to disseminate its core message HT is continuously in the process of finding new recruits. Its actual total membership is difficult to ascertain due to its highly secretive nature and therefore could number anywhere from hundreds of *Shabb* (youth) to a few thousand supporters and sympathisers. It succeeds in recruitment by disseminating its particular theo-political analysis of events affecting British Muslim communities and Muslim societies through various media and community platforms. In practice this is achieved by distributing flyers outside colleges, universities and mosques, and by organising study circles, conferences, demonstrations and vigils. Young British Muslims searching for satisfying religious identities are drawn to HT ideology for a number of reasons. For some, it is the first Islamic group that provides them with a convincing explanation for their marginalised condition in society; in terms of religion, it offers a deculturalised Islam that is free from the folkloric, patriarchal religion of their parents' generation; for some it becomes a shelter against racism and Islamophobia; while for others it provides the conceptual vocabulary to resist the perception of a Western war against Islam.

The core of HT Britain's religious and political activism revolves around raising awareness; what they would term as 'disseminating Islamic intellectual and political thoughts' to 'remove misconceptions about Islam and the Muslim community'. To trigger interest in their message, any Muslim social concern or issue is invariably rationalised, by way of a linear cause-effect process, to prove the need for the restoration of the *Khilafa* (caliphate). A lynchpin of HT in Britain's strategy is to create a socio-psychological dissonance between the idea of being both a British citizen and Muslim; this culminated in the organising of its conference in 2003, which disputed the idea that such a valid hybrid identity could exist. The conference, entitled 'Are you British or Muslim?', aimed to challenge the discourse of mainstream British Muslim organisations and to assert an Islamic supranationality, in other words asking people to put their faith before nationality.

The other issue, which animates the concerns of British members of HT, is the refusal to recognise the legitimacy of current Muslim governments. This position forms the majority of HT content on its English websites such as HT in Britain, khilafah.com and 1924.org. The websites carry news and analysis on events in the Muslim world, updates of HT activities in other countries, articles uploaded from external news agencies and critiques of the ruling governments in Muslim countries. In addition, they periodically produce documents challenging Western foreign policy, such as its strategy document on Iraq, the treatment of party members by the Uzbek government and a policy paper on the future of Pakistan. Furthermore, it devotes a portion of efforts to providing responses to political issues that affect Muslims domestically, for example it has produced reports on radicalisation, a response to the UK government's anti-terrorism legislation and a statement to the British government on its consultation on diversity and community cohesion. Since the London bombings of July 2005, HT have faced the threat of government proscription and have since been keen to prove their non-violent credentials, repeatedly rebutting any link between their party's ideas and terrorism. The allegation that HT is a 'conveyor belt for terrorism' continues to be maintained by a number of analysts who have yet to substantiate their claims beyond a very weak evidence base suggesting guilt by association. In Britain, HT has so far survived proscription after the Association of Chief Police Officers and the intelligence services opposed the ban on the grounds that there was insufficient evidence and that it did not directly advocate violence.

In the 1990s, HT was also notorious for its provocative behaviour towards other Muslim organisations. Attempting to assume the leadership of Muslim communities, they were known for frequently ridiculing the work of other Muslim activist movements such as the Young Muslims UK. The aftermath of the London bombings produced a major change in their attitude to those with whom they differed. It was no longer deemed wise to antagonise people who could provide support, so they began sharing platforms with other Muslim groups and engaging non-Muslim organisations and individuals on issues that concerned them. Examples of this pragmatism include softening of their language and animosity to rival Islamist movements and broadening the sphere of their concerns to include the importance of youth and community development work. In the May 2006 local elections, instead of condemning Muslim participation in the election as religiously unlawful, they asked Muslims to 'consider Muslim issues when voting'. They also worked with their campus nemesis, the Federation of Student Islamic Societies (FOSIS), against a ban in university student societies.

HT in Britain, like its counterparts in the Muslim world, appears to be going through a transition. As Whine has observed, this is either due to the force of historical events or local conditions which have necessitated a change of emphasis to avoid problems with the police and to appear less threatening to the media and potential recruits. The threat of proscription seems to have had the effect of moderating it, although it continues to suffer from an image problem. In late 2006, there were allegations that a street gang in South London were members of HT who robbed rival gangs in order to prove their loyalty. Perhaps the most problematic development has been the sustained campaign by three of its ex-members – Shiraz Maher, Ed Hussain and Majid Nawaz – to discredit the party's ideas. The fact that the people have left and continue to do so illustrates a problem with retention and its ability to remain relevant to young Muslims in a competitive activist scene – people either 'grow up and out' after entering into adult life and responsibilities or become ideologically disillusioned. For example, some disgruntled ex-members have set up support groups, such as The Union of Former Hizb ut-Tahrir Members and Students, and corresponding websites.

According to other insiders, there appears to an ideological diversity with the movement – hardliners and pragmatists with the HT leadership transmitting different vibes – and so it is difficult to identify what its future plans are and how they coordinate with the international leadership. What is clear is that HT, at least on the surface, has developed a much more sophisticated image, and media-savvy spokespeople, representing a break from its confrontational approach of the past, which ensures that HT continues to attract attention and remains a force within British Muslim communities.

References

Birt, Yahya (2007) 'Dangerous Minds', *New Statesman*, May.
Connor, Kylie (2005) '"Islamism" in the West? The Life Span of the Al-Muhajiroun in the United Kingdom', *Journal of Muslim Minority Affairs*, 25 (1): pp. 117–33.
Hizb-ut-Tahrir website. www.hizbuttahrir.org (link last accessed 19 June 2014)
Hamid, Sadek (2007) 'Islamic political radicalism in Britain: the case of Hizb-ut-Tahrir', in Tahir Abbas (ed.), *Islamic Political Radicalism, A European Perspective*, Edinburgh: Edinburgh University Press, pp. 145–59.
The Union and Former Hizbut-Tahir members and students.

Whine, Michael (2006) 'Is Hizb ut-Tahrir Changing Strategy or Tactics?', *Center for Eurasian Policy Occasional Research Paper*, 1 (1). Available at http://64.233.183.104/search?q= cache:tQRnbszTJAEJ:www.thecst.org.uk/docs/EurasianPaper_Aug42006.pdf+hizbut+t ahrir&hl=en&ct=clnk&cd=57&gl=uk (link no longer functional)

HIZB UT-TAHRIR IN DENMARK

Jørgen Bæk Simonsen

Hizb ut-Tahrir (HT) surfaced in Denmark in the early 1990s as a result of the arrival of a number of refugees of Palestinian and Lebanese origin who had obtained political asylum in the late 1980s. They organised the party in Denmark and directed their campaign towards Danish Muslims in an effort to attract potential members to the party. In December 1994 the party published the first issue of their journal *Khilafah Magasinet* (in Danish) introducing the party and its goals to the Muslim public and underlining its commitment to incite Muslims all over the world to take part in the work needed to re-establish the caliphate – the *raison d' être* of the party since its establishment in Jerusalem in 1953. According to the first issue, the magazine was edited by a group of Muslim students. The magazine stated its wish to guide Muslims in Denmark and invited fellow Muslims to write articles. The party's anti-Western attitude was highlighted in the first issue, which emphasised the need to combat ideas and values considered to be dangerous for the Muslim *umma.*

The internal organisation of HT in Denmark has always been a secret to the general public. All communication between the party and the general public is conducted by the party's spokesman. A few years after its establishment the party began to organise courses introducing the party's ideology to the public and, from the late 1990s, it also began to organise public meetings which frequently focused on issues of general interest for Muslims living in Denmark (headscarves, the Palestinian issue, the political conflicts in the former Yugoslavia and in the former USSR where Muslims were involved, and the like). The exact number of enrolled members is not known, but most observers estimate the number to be a few hundred. A former member of the party in an interview with the Danish paper *Jyllands-Posten* in April 2008 stated that the party had 100 full members.

During the early years HT directed its efforts towards other Muslims living in Denmark and avoided participation in general public debate. In line with the ideology of the party, members were always present at public meetings organised by other Muslim groups or organisations. HT also presented its points of view in articles published in its magazine, or by way of small books or translations into Danish or English of important contributions by the founder of the party Taqi al-Din al-Nabhani (1909–77) or other publicly known leaders from the party.

The terror attacks on New York and Washington in September 2001 changed this situation. HT's magazine had, from its first issue, been characterised by articles with strong anti-American and anti-Israeli rhetoric. When the international War on Terror was launched in October 2001, the party strongly opposed the initiative at a public meeting it organised. In March 2002 the party published a leaflet on its home page and a printed version was distributed, strongly criticising events on the West Bank. The party was accused of racism and, in October 2002, the spokesman was convicted by the City Court of violating the Criminal Code § 266b. The judgement was confirmed by the High Court in March 2003.

In March 2003, the Danish government supported the US-led invasion of Iraq, and Danish media continued to focus on the party and its strong critique of government policy in this matter. A number of politicians demanded an investigation of the party. Subsequently, the public prosecutor stated that HT had broken no laws in its political work. The minister of Justice, in line with the investigation, announced that the government had no intention of trying to have the party declared unconstitutional, and HT itself announced its commitment to continue its work in Denmark.

HT has been the focus of widespread public interest since 9/11, and all initiatives taken by it are given ample media attention, to the annoyance of other Muslim groups who have difficulty garnering such headlines. The party has proven its ability to benefit from this interest and thus its activities and its points of view are often found in the public sphere. Nevertheless, HT still considers Muslims living in Denmark to be its prime target. Judging by the presence of its supporters, the party recently seems to have been able to attract young Danes who are converting to Islam.

References

Grøndahl, Malene, Torben Rugberg Rasmussen and Kirstine Sinclair (2003) *Hizb ut-Tahrir i Danmark. Farlig fundamentalisme eller uskyldigt ungdomsoprør?*, Aarhus: Aarhus Universitetsforlag.

Schmidt, Garbi (2007) *Muslim I Danmark – muslim I verden. En analyse af muslimske ungdomsforeninger og muslimsk identitet i årene op til Muhammad-krisen*, Uppsala: Universitetstrykkeriet.

(7) OTHER GROUPS AND MUSLIM REPRESENTATIVE BODIES

AL-'ADL WA-L-IHSAN IN SPAIN: AN EMERGING ACTOR IN THE MUSLIM FIELD

Elena Arigita

The presence of members of al-'Adl wa-l-Ihsan in Spain dates back to 1986. Yet it was not until the end of the 1990s that a certain structure began to be set up, at first sight following the typical dynamic of the Moroccan Jama'a adapted to the associative fabric in Spain: there is no system of *usar* (families) but rather of associations (such as women's groups, in favour of human rights or mosques) with a representative. Above these, there are regional organisations and a national structure, run by a *muraqib*, which changes every three or four years and is elected by secret ballot. Therefore, there is a national structure that reproduces or adapts the form of *tanzim* (organisation) of the Moroccan *Jama'a* as far as possible. Nonetheless, both in the continued ties to the movement and in the details of that Spanish structure, repeated in other European countries, the kind of activity shown cannot be defined solely and exclusively as part of the project of the Moroccan movement, not at least in its political dimension.

The members of al-'Adl wa-l-Ihsan in Spain, or those holding positions of emerging leadership, albeit not necessarily acknowledged in the form of an appointment, have categorically rejected any organic link to, or dependence on, the Moroccan *Jama'a*. Despite the close ties maintained with the movement in Morocco, they qualify or lessen their identification as members or leaders of al-'Adl wa-l-Ihsan in Spain. Whenever members of the *Jama'a* emigrate, they formally cease to be members. This is an essential point to understand how they participate as Muslims in Europe, what ties bind them to the Moroccan movement and also their interaction with other Islamic movements in Europe, as the example of the Muslim Brothers is recurrent when they explain their presence in Europe.

All of the members of al-'Adl wa-l-Ihsan share the *suhba* with Sheikh Yassine and a strict ritual that consists of fasting twice weekly, on Mondays and Thursdays, and the *qiyyam al-layl* (night prayer) in small groups, that is, sessions of *dhikr* (remembrance of God) and study of the Qur'an and the *hadith*; a Sufi discipline that keeps them tied to Sheikh Yassine in his most spiritual dimension.

The *suhba* is a core concept in Sufism and takes on vital importance for the *murshid* (guide) of *al-'Adl wa-l-Ihsan*. A *murid* (disciple) cannot follow the path of God without the *Sahib* (master) and the *suhba* is the tie that bonds the *murid* with his *sahib*. He has to follow the same route in order to attract others to this path. But unlike the traditional *tariqas*, Sheikh Yassine, in his *al-Minhaj al-Nabawi* (the Prophetic Method), places *al-suhba wa-l-jama'a* as the first pillar. In other words, the spiritual path and the political commitment are on the same level. Thus, the *suhba* is an integral part of the *jama'a*, and it is part of the *tarbiyya* (spiritual education), also understood as the driving force for social change.

If the *suhba* with the Sheikh is a core belief for the movement's followers, what can be said of the commitment with *al-jama'a* for those living abroad? The answer is complex and has a lot to do with the experience of migration among the members of the movement and their *da'wa* outside Morocco. Although political activism is central to the movement on the Moroccan scenario, the debate on the need to separate spirituality and political commitment in Morocco has been ongoing since the 1990s. This is where the dynamics for building a European Islam take on central importance.

The key to a young emerging leadership in Spain involves education and demands for civil rights. Its participation strategy is seen only marginally in the field of institutional representation as a religious minority and focuses on the social and cultural field in many diverse ways: as associations in favour of human rights, as women's associations, as a socio-cultural association at national or local level, although also as mosque or religious association.

The associative movement of a social and cultural bent, as opposed to the institutional structure of religious bodies grouping Muslim associations together, is seen by them as a strategy to avoid state control in the religious sphere. In that sense they are, like many other leaders of religious associations, highly critical of the manner of institutional representation and demand greater plurality for the Islamic Commission of Spain. Without waiving its presence in state-wide bodies, its forms of participation are not as an organisation but on an individual basis.

The modes of participation in the associative level, the configuration of an emerging leadership and their networks of contacts with Morocco and other groups in Spain and in Europe show that the Moroccan Islamic movement al-'Adl wa-l-Ihsan has a structured presence around the idea of *suhba* with its Moroccan guide and a close contact with the Moroccan structure. However, the reflections of the emerging leadership in Spain on how to organise and participate in the Spanish 'Muslim field' denotes an effort that goes beyond Morocco or the transnational Moroccan–Spanish space, as they show a commitment to the development of new formulae for participating in and contributing to Spain. Not without difficulty. As a result of the pressure they feel (and express) for their political activism and opposition to the regime in Morocco, this emerging leadership being groomed in Spain establishes ways of participating that they themselves describe as 'discreet', and insist on separating all forms of organisational ties with Morocco's *jama'a*. It must not be overlooked that many of those leaders who are participating in the creation of an associative movement have emigrated on political grounds. However, over and above a strategy for the survival of the movement outside Morocco, its forms of participating at both the local and national levels have structured a kind of participation as Muslim citizens in Spain, at the same time as they participate in European networks with the same goals.

Although contact with the movement in Morocco continues, militancy from Europe is undergoing a process of reformulation and that process includes the expression of the need to distance themselves from the political project in order to create a European project. Significantly, the project of that emerging leadership in Spain has not been defined by its Moroccan reference, or at least not exclusively, but as a function of different levels: basically through its competition with other formulae (mainly other Islamic movements and pro-Moroccan groups) located within the scope of religion and the Spanish associative movement and by the institutional framework and associative fabric in which they take part, both at the Spanish level and in the wider framework of Islam in Europe. Seen the other way around, their reconceptualisation of the notions of *suhba* and *jama'a* allows these activists in Spain to set a new frame in which they are reconfiguring the transnational space of Morocco and Spain, and position themselves in different planes of participation.

References

Arigita, Elena (2010) 'Al-'Adl wa-l-Ihsan en España: un proyecto nacional para un movimiento islámico transnacional?', *Revista de Dialectología y Tradiciones Populares*, 65 (1), pp. 113–36.

Darif, Mohammed (1985) *Jama'at al-'Adl wa-l-Ihsan*, Casablanca: al-Mayalla al-Maghribiya li-'ilm al-litima' al-siyasi.

Macías Amoretti, Juan Antonio (2008) *Entre la fe y la razón: Los caminos del pensamiento político en Marruecos*, Alcalá la Real: Alcalá.

Mohatar Marzok, Mokhtar (ed.) (2009) *Marroquíes en Andalucía: Dinámicas migratorias y con-diciones de vida*, Seville: Fundación Centro de Estudios Andaluces.

Tozy, Mohamed (1997) *Monarchie et islam politique au Maroc*, Paris: Presses de Sciences Po.

Zeghal, Malika (2008) *Islamism in Morocco: religion, authoritarianism, and electoral politics*, Princeton: Markus Wiener.

THE ISLAMIC FOUNDATION IN THE UNITED KINGDOM

Seán McLoughlin

Since 7/7 especially, previously hidden diasporic and transnational Muslim public spheres in Britain have become subject to new levels of visibility, scrutiny and regulation unknown even in the years immediately after 9/11. Despite a track record of engagement with New Labour and civil society, media and think-tank reports across the political left and right have sought to challenge certain prominent Muslim organisations' claims to moderation.[1] Revealing the origins of organisations such as the Islamic Foundation (IF) in Jama'at-i Islami (JiI), a political movement founded in India by Abul Ala Mawdudi (d. 1979) in 1941, critics highlight the incongruity of liberal-democratic values and what is identified as an extremist Islamist heritage.[2] Certainly in the writings of Mawdudi, who propagated the idea of an Islamic state in Pakistan after Partition, Western society emerges as the dystopia to his projected Islamic utopia. However, such an analysis does not make enough allowance for the reformist, gradualist and pragmatic character of JiI. Moreover, a significant transformation of the JiI tradition in the UK diaspora has been underway since the 1990s especially. Not only has the movement travelled from a Muslim majority to a non-Muslim state context, but the social capital of a British-born, university-educated, newly professionalised middle class with a good deal invested personally and professionally in the mainstream, has also begun to impact organically on the life of these organisations.

The IF is just one of several JiI-related organisations in Britain, all established since the 1960s and 1970s. Compared to other first-generation migrants from South Asia, the majority of whom were illiterate and of rural peasant farming origin, JiI activists tended to be well-organised and highly motivated students and young professionals. Indeed, the IF was founded in 1973 by Khurshid Ahmad (b.1932) who began life in JiI as a student activist in Pakistan before making his name in the field of Islamic economics. He returned to Pakistan from England to become an (ultimately short-lived and critical) member of the Islamising military government of General Zia (ruled 1977–88). However, the fact that Ahmad was a generation younger than Mawdudi made him more aware of the interdependence of a globalised social and economic order.[3] Indeed, while remaining critical of the Western tendency to dichotomise the secular and the sacred, Ahmad emphasised the need for relations and dialogue with the West rather than rejecting it outright. His ideas were reflected at the IF during the 1970s, where he oversaw the establishing of an Interfaith unit (1977) – alongside the Islamic Economics unit (1976) – intended to engage in interfaith dialogue but also, significantly, to monitor post-colonial Christian missionary activity worldwide. During the 1970s, the interfaith arena represented one of the few public spaces in which Muslims as a religious minority could engage with the mainstream in secular Britain.

Although the IF has no official links to JiI, something in keeping with the movement's tendency to develop quite independently in the diverse nation states of modern South Asia, key IF staff during the 1970s and 1980s often had overlapping membership of JiI and/or JiI-related organisations. The IF was also fairly unique among Islamic institutions in the UK in not being entirely dominated by South Asian heritage Muslims, a mark of its openness to movement Islam *per se*. Nevertheless, one of the main activities since its beginning – publishing – was generally concerned with the writings of JiI's ideologues, especially Mawdudi himself, Khurshid Ahmad and Khurram Murad (d.1996) an engineer, Ahmad's successor at the helm of the IF in 1978 and another past vice-president of JiI Pakistan. In keeping with JiI's Sunni revivalist credentials, IF publications in the 1970s and 1980s routinely presented Islam within a selective (and arguably sectarian) framework hostile to Sufism and Shi'ism. Notably, the availability of World Muslim League funding during this period identified the institution with a Saudi Arabian axis network of pan-Islamic organisations, linkages which persist to this day, although such financial support has never simply bought ideological conformity. A centre for the Islamisation of knowledge and *da'wa* (mission) in Britain – a New Muslims project – was established in 1993; the IF proved to be of little relevance, however, for the vast majority of first-generation of South Asian heritage Muslims in Britain.

Some questioning of Mawdudi's legacy among the youth of JiI-related organisations in Britain was evident during the late 1970s and early 1980s. The writings of Khurram Murad, for example, reveal a reluctance to discuss Islamist politics, with the rhetoric of the Islamic state being abandoned for the idea of creating a 'counter culture' to revive Islamic lifestyles among Muslims in Britain. Global crises such as the protests against Salman Rushdie's *The Satanic Verses* (1988) – during which the IF and its networks played a key coordinating role – raised consciousness of such questions of identity among a new and demographically significant 'bulge' of young British Muslims born in the diaspora. The upwardly mobile segment of this constituency especially, one destined for college and professional life, became exposed to revivalist thinking in ways their parents and grandparents could never have been, with the IF and other JiI-related organisations meeting much of the demand for Islamic materials available in English at that time. The Rushdie affair also widened the IF's opportunities for faith-based public engagement with wider society. Precipitating a crisis in the race and ethnicity paradigm of minority affairs in Britain, into the 1990s the state and public services gradually sought to take Muslims as 'Muslims' more seriously. This meant that interfaith and multifaith markets for the IF's unique packaging of Islam for English-speaking audiences began to consolidate, this at a time when streams of Saudi funding were running dry.

Like other Muslim organisations with an increasingly mainstream national profile in Britain, the IF also began to imitate more secular institutions, being more 'professional' and circumspect about publicly announcing its ideological inspirations. In the last decade especially, the IF has deliberately de-emphasised its original concern for *da'wa* and countercultural Islamisation, especially in the neutralised marketing of some key initiatives and subsidiaries. The Markfield Institute of Higher Education (MIHE), established in 2000 and directed by Dr Ataullah Siddiqui – interfaith scholar and author of the government report *Islam at Universities in England*[4]– offers postgraduate qualifications in Islamic Studies, Muslim Community Studies and Islamic Banking Finance and Management. Cultural awareness training programmes on Muslims in Britain, described as 'warts and all'[5], are delivered to non-Muslim government officers and professionals including the Foreign and Commonwealth Office. For over a decade the IF has also worked in partnership with The Citizen Organising Foundation which trains activists in the art of politics, emphasising broad-based alliances not least among faith-based organisations in London.

Despite these developments, however, the IF is still often seen by its critics as having profited from naive multiculturalism's failure to interrogate an opportunistic and largely successful presentation of Islamism as representative of Islam *per se*, thus marginalising the voices of more mainstream and progressive Muslims. However, citing Siddiqui and Hussain as examples, Mandaville argues that, given the religious and political freedoms of the diaspora, and intensified encounters with Muslim 'others', Islamist intellectuals and activists in the West are actually evolving innovative, cosmopolitan and self-critical re-formulations of their traditions. He overstates the widespread acceptance of such a trend in Britain, as any transformations at the IF or among JiI-related organisations are still very much in transition. Nevertheless, a critical mass hospitable to such perspectives has undoubtedly emerged at the institution since the 1990s, a period of important re-intellectualisation and engagement with democratising forces among reformist Islamists worldwide.

So, while the IF was initially inspired by the tradition of Mawdudi and JiI – 'first-generation' Islamism – it also reflects the values and experiences of a 'second generation' more aware of the global interdependency of 'Islam' and 'the West'; that is, Khurshid Ahmad. The contention here is that it is now necessary to speak of a 'third generation' of (diasporic) intellectual-activists who are, moreover, far more reflexive concerning their Islamic lineage than many commentators, including Western journalists and politicians, would seem to allow. Within the academic and policy-oriented research units of the IF especially, those of South Asian heritage are joined by Muslims of other ethnicities, including converts to Islam, with whom they share similar cultural capital, lived experiences and investments. Together they confidently embrace and successfully negotiate relationships, education, activism and careers in the in-between spaces that constitute 'British Muslim' identity.

Some remain well-networked in terms of JiI-related organisations such as the Islamic Society of Britain (ISB) and seek to practice the good citizenship preached in Tariq Ramadan's *To be a European Muslim* which was published by the IF as part of a bid to broaden its portfolio. However, given the largely undocumented 'fragmentation and breaks' within the JiI-related tradition during the 1990s, some members of such organisations can be very much out on a limb, with concepts key in the 1970s and 1980s all now 'up for grabs'. Indeed, other individual members of staff are more determinedly non-affiliated, perhaps reflecting something of a post-Islamist trend. Even individuals who identify with a 'neo-traditionalist' heritage, a lineage attached to the authority of the *'ulama'* and Sufis that Islamists generally reject, have found in the IF unusual opportunities to work ecumenically on concerns common to all British Muslims.

The argument here, then, is not that third-generation or post-Islamism has entirely displaced its forbears at the IF, but rather that the two now cohabit in the same space. Unlike many of his younger colleagues, Director General Khurshid Ahmad, for whom the IF is now mainly a summer retreat for writing and research, is still committed to 'Islamisation from below'.[7] He does not exclude the non-Muslim state from such transformation, although, 'the route to the State is through the individual, community and civil society... there is loyalty to the society but we also to try to improve it'. Nevertheless, he welcomes the fact that 'it is no longer necessary to import staff' to work at the institution and that a growing 'British Muslim ethos' is finally 'detaching the institution from Pakistani culture'.

This process of transition and transformation has been further and forcefully accelerated by the impact of the London bombings of 7/7. As suggested by way of introduction, the IF – like the Muslim Council of Britain and the East London mosque – has been the subject of several exposés all concerning its Islamist heritage. Former activists such as the Quilliam Foundation's Ed Husain, now making a career in the preventing violent extremism industry, are also repeating such accusations.[8] With its back against the wall and increasingly 'seeing themselves as others see them', staff of different generations and orientations at the IF have been forced into difficult 'do or die' conversations about such accusations.[9] The old guard may remain in post but their options are now becoming increasingly limited. While a public break with the past is unlikely, it is no longer a case of them giving their blessing to reforms. The world has changed.

Notes

1   See, for example, *The Observer*, 14 August 2005 and *The Telegraph*, 14 April 2008.
2   *The Times*, 29 July 2004.
3   John Esposito and John Voll (2001) *Makers of Contemporary Islam*, Oxford: Oxford University Press.
4   Ataullah Siddiqui , *Islam at universities in England : meeting the needs and investing in the future*. Report submitted to Bill Rammell MP (Minister of State for Lifelong Learning, Further and Higher Education) on 10th April 2007.
5   Dilwar Hussain, 3 February 2003, in author interview.
6   Peter Mandaville (2001) *Transnational Muslim Politics*, London: Routledge, pp. 132–6.
7   Khurshid Ahmad, 17 October 2003, in author interview.
8   The *Guardian*, 8 September 2009.
9   Dilwar Hussain, 2 April 2008, in author interview.

References

Esposito, John and John Voll (2001) *Makers of Contemporary Islam*, Oxford: Oxford University Press.
Mandaville, Peter (2001) *Transnational Muslim Politics*, London: Routledge.
McLoughlin, Seán (2005) 'The State, new Muslim leaderships and Islam as a resource for engagement in Britain', in Jocelyne Cesari and Seán McLoughlin (eds), *European Muslims and the Secular State*, Abingdon: Ashgate, pp. 55–69.
Ramadan, Tariq (1999) *To be a European Muslim. A study of the Islamic sources in the European context*, Leicester: The Islamic Foundation.
Rushdie, Salman (1989) *The Satanic Verses*, London: Viking.
Siddiqui, Ataullah (2007) *Islam at universities in England : meeting the needs and investing in the future*, Report submitted to Bill Rammell MP (Minister of State for Lifelong Learning, Further and Higher Education).

SHEIKH ABDALQADIR AL-MURABIT AND THE ISLAMIC COMMUNITY IN SPAIN

F. Javier Rosón Lorente

To speak about the Islamic Community in Spain (CIE) is to speak about Sheikh Abdalqadir al-Murabit 'as-Sufi' ad-Darqawy, about the Murabitun Worldwide Movement (MWM), about Sufism and about processes of conversion to Islam. However, above all it entails recreating the historical roots of al-Andalus, of Andalusian nationalism and the emergence of contemporary Islam in Granada, in the Andalusia region and in Spain.[1]

The origins of this community must primarily be sought in the incipient conversion process which began during the 1960s and 1970s. The conversion of Spaniards to Islam had roots in a climate of socio-political dissatisfaction, mainly among left-wing academics and intellectuals aged between 20 and 30, some of them from Christian communities.[2] It started life in Córdoba and later (1980) moved its headquarters to Seville. In the specific case of Granada (the current headquarters of the CIE), the measures taken to prepare it as a European city of culture and the attempt to establish a Euro-Arabic University offered the CIE a gateway to the city, given that 'selling' the cosmopolitanism and Orientalism of Granada called for the recovery of this social actor, no longer within the religious sphere but rather the socio-cultural one.

In order to understand this process, the position of Granada and consolidation of the first communities of converted Muslims in the city and in Spain, we have to consider several points. First, the 1970s saw the first significant conversions of Spaniards, initially linked to the Jama'a Islámica Al-Andalus-Liga Morisca (Islamic Community of Al-Andalus). In parallel fashion, a group of young people from different ideological and geographical backgrounds (Ciudad Real, Guadalajara, Pontevedra, etc.) converted to Islam and became the first Spanish disciples of the Murabitun community in England. Second, the existing Murabituns, led by a charismatic but widely criticised leader, Sheikh Abdalqadir, were established in Granada in the mid-1980s and granted legal status by the Ministry of Justice under the name of Sociedad para el Retorno al Islam en España (Society for the Return to Islam in Spain) (1978).[3] Third, alongside the configuration of Spanish neo-Muslim communities, a series of hippie communes formed in the Alpujarra region of Granada, which broadly accepted the rhetoric of the Sheikh and eventually joined in. In fourth place, the structure of the current CIE is defined by the union of these two communities with the addition of other sporadic groups. The initial idea was to extend Islam to every city in Spain populated by 'Muslims from Granada', with the final aim of restoring the worldwide caliphate as this is, according to Abdalqadir, an obligation that concerns all Muslims.[4] In fifth and final place, the new community began to organise an infrastructure, established in the Albayzín district of Granada, although it has representation in cities such as Majorca, Tarragona, San Sebastián, Orense and Madrid, among others.

The Sheikh was 'proclaimed' successor to the *Tariqa Darqawiyya* of Morocco in 1968, after receiving spiritual authority from Sheikh Muhammad ibn al-Habib. He leads a wide community of converted Muslims who embrace Sufism and follow its guidance as the best way to conclude the process of establishing Islam in Granada and contemporary Spain. However, the hostile environment they encountered and the latent rejection they were to meet in Granada, Spain and the rest of the world in connection with the MWM and the terrorist attacks of 9/11, 11 March and 7/7 conditioned subsequent stages towards achieving community visibility.

The development of the neo-Muslim community has gone through three stages: an initial stage of appearance and isolation, when the CIE was established within the symbolic Muslim quarter of the Albayzín district; a second stage when community structures were consolidated, with the creation of Qur'an schools (*madrasa*), mosques and a series of infrastructures to facilitate local development (bookshops, craft shops, etc.); and a third stage of presence or local visibility, with public engagements and the creation of identity procedures (speakers in public squares, demonstrations, etc.), both within the community itself and towards the outside population of Granada.

These stages closed the 'cycle' of identity creation for the CIE and the early neo-Muslims, but in turn they generated a new cycle (internal evolution with regard to Islam) involving several of its most prominent members, which led to Mansur Escudero and Abdelkarim Carrasco (among others) leaving the community and shortly thereafter becoming the national representatives of Islam through the Spanish Federation of Islamic Religious Entities (FEERI) and the Junta Islámica (Islamic Council). This led to an internal struggle which challenged the CIE's 'monopolistic representation', its vision of Islam and its limited or zero relationship with the immigrant Islam that had recently gained a foothold in the city. While (immigrant) Islam in Spain is increasingly visible – at federal and municipal level through the Union of Islamic Communities in Spain (UCIDE), FEERI and the Islamic Commission of Spain – internal regression now set in, marked by the political, economic and social problems (neighbourhood protests, political pressure from conservative sectors of the city, lack of funding, etc.) which accompanied the undertaking of one of its greatest objectives: the construction, 500 years after the expulsion of the Moors, of the first Great Mosque in Granada.

After endless conflicts following the purchase of land by the CIE (1981), the Great Mosque in Granada opened on 10 July 2003. The last period of construction was funded by the government of Sharjah (United Arab Emirates), thanks to an agreement between the various representatives of the Muslim communities of Granada, which enabled decision-making by the CIE to be 'diversified and decentralised' by creating the Patronage of the Fundación Mezquita de Granada (2003), made up of Spanish Muslims and a representative from the Sharjah Emirate. New structures (foundations) began to be generated around the mosque: Fundación Educativa Al-Andalus and the European Muslim Union (2005) (CIE, the Society of Islam in England and the Weimarer Institut für Geistliche und Zeitgeschichtliche Fragen).

At that time, the new mosque and the foundations, which had already been widely criticised from different Muslimophobic angles, far from being a space for knowledge and dissemination of the *Din* of Islam, a gathering place, became more like a 'new' place not to meet for the rest of the population, and even for (immigrant) Muslims who were trying to detach themselves from the criticism heaped upon the CIE. Shortly afterwards, both groups were confronted with the essentialist stigmatisation of the Muslim world that followed the Madrid bombings of 11 March (11M), when ordinary local residents were identified as terrorists while the mosque and its environs were identified as a focal point that attracted 'the poor, the illiterate, troublemakers, chauvinists, fanatical and intransigent Muslims.'[5]

This led to an (even greater) polarisation of the CIE's stance on the immigrant population and vice versa. 'Immigrant Islam' and neo-Muslims who had split from the community openly criticised its hierarchical (pyramidal) structure, the reverence for the Sheikh that at times exceeded or obscured reverence for the Prophet, the fierce control over social bases (used as tokens to obtain external funding), the isolation and secrecy of the community (with the construction of the Grand Mosque, the education of children outside the public school system, the sources of funding, arranged marriages, etc.), and the use of a separate currency (gold and silver dinars and dirhams).

The CIE is now undergoing another period of internal regression following criticism from local residents (about the construction of a mosque in Seville, and an attempt to build a large Arabic studies centre with a sports complex in the village of Jun, Granada) but, above all, attacks in the national press and international publications, which classify it as an 'Islamic fundamentalist sect'. This prompted several active members of the community to sell their businesses and shift their habitual residence and that of their families to South Africa where, in 2006, the Sheikh opened the Jumu'a mosque of Cape Town and a centre for the education of Muslim leaders, away from the essentialist scrutiny of sections of the Spanish population.

However, a lot of Muslims in Granada, many of whom have openly criticised the 'sectarian' (or better, exclusivist) posture of the CIE, now express a degree of acceptance and admiration for the infrastructure it has achieved, its clear and purposeful organisation (despite the external attacks that sought to undermine), its fight for Islam, and its efforts to introduce more plurality in its discourse (bringing it closer to other Muslims), thanks to the current Moroccan Imam of the Grand Mosque.

Notes

1   F. Javier Rosón Lorente (2005) 'Tariq's return? Muslimophobia, Muslimophilia and the formation of ethnicized religious communities in southern Spain', *Migration: European Journal of International Migration and Ethnic Relations*, 43–5: pp. 87–95.
2   Sol Tarrés Chamorro (1999) 'Religiosidad musulmana en Sevilla', in Salvador Rodríguez Becerra (ed.), *Religión y cultura*, Seville: Fundación Machado, pp. 199–207.
3   See Tomás Navarro (1998) *La mezquita de Babel. El nazismo sufista desde el Reino Unido a la Comunidad Autónoma de Andalucía*, Granada: Galería Virtual; Javier Valenzuela (2002) *España en el punto de mira. La amenaza del integrismo islámico*, Madrid: Temas de hoy; José Luis Sánchez Nogales (2004) *El islam entre nosotros: cristianismo e islam en España*, Madrid: Biblioteca de Autores Cristianos; and Rosa María Rodríguez Magda (2006) *La España convertida al islam*, Barcelona: Altera.
4   Abdalqadir As-Sufi (1998) *El retorno del califato*, Palma de Mallorca: Kutubia.
5   Gema Martín Muñoz (2004) 'Emigración e Islam', in Gemma Aubarell and Ricard Zapata-Barrero (eds), *Inmigración y procesos de cambio: Europa y el Mediterráneo en el contexto global*, Barcelona: Icaria, pp. 366ff.

References

As-Sufi, Abdalqadir (1998) *El retorno del califato*, Palma de Mallorca: Kutubia.

Martín Muñoz, Gema (2004) 'Emigración e Islam', in Gemma Aubarell and Ricard Zapata-Barrero, (eds), *Inmigración y procesos de cambio: Europa y el Mediterráneo en el contexto global*, Barcelona: Icaria, pp. 351–74.

Navarro, Tomás (1998) *La mezquita de Babel. El nazismo sufista desde el Reino Unido a la Comunidad Autónoma de Andalucía*, Granada: Galería Virtual.

Rodríguez Magda, Rosa María (2006) *La España convertida al islam*, Barcelona: Altera.

Rosón Lorente, F. Javier (2005) 'Tariq's return? Muslimophobia, Muslimophilia and the formation of ethnicized religious communities in southern Spain', *Migration: European Journal of International Migration and Ethnic Relations*, 43–5: pp. 87–95.

—— (2008) *El retorno de Tariq? Comunidades etnorreligiosas en el Albayzín granadino.* Ph.D Thesis, University of Granada: Spain.

Sánchez Nogales, José Luis (2004) *El islam entre nosotros: cristianismo e islam en España*, Madrid: Biblioteca de Autores Cristianos

Tarrés Chamorro, Sol (1999) 'Religiosidad musulmana en Sevilla', in Salvador Rodríguez Becerra (ed.), *Religión y cultura*, Seville: Fundación Machado, pp. 199–207.

Valenzuela, Javier (2002) *España en el punto de mira. La amenaza del integrismo islámico*, Madrid: Temas de hoy.

SÜLEYMANLIS IN GERMANY

Gerdien Jonker

Süleymanlıs is the name of a Turkish religious lay movement whose mission is the spread of knowledge of the Qur'an among Muslims. Its founder is preacher Süleyman Hilmi Tunahan. The movement's origin is intimately entwined with the birth of the Turkish republic in the 1920s. Originally the Süleymanlıs opposed the republic's laws, which severely restricted Islamic practices – notably Sufi practices – and brutally severed Turkey's ties to its religious past. Migration to Europe finally offered the movement a chance to stabilise and grow. The European organisation builds on this history and turns it into a tale of religious renewal.

In 1959, when Süleyman Hilmi Tunahan died in Istanbul, he left behind approximately one hundred students. They were rural peasants, the majority illiterate, whom Tunahan had taught to read and recite the Qur'an in order to perform simple religious services such as the weekly prayer, marriage services and prayers for the dead. Because religion was heavily controlled by the state in the Turkish republic of the 1940s and 1950s, acquiring religious knowledge and fulfilling religious services on one's own initiative was already an act of resistance for which many ended up in prison. In his lifetime, the preacher was not able to find all that many people willing to become his students. Those who were willing belonged to groups that had lost out in Turkish modernisation; war fugitives, second sons of poor peasants, coalers, miners, and others whom the republic had robbed of their social moorings and for whom religious community life remained an option.

Tunahan studied the religious sciences before the Kemalist revolution. Just as he finished his studies, Kemal Atatürk implemented forced modernisation upon Turkey, declaring religion a major obstacle to progress and issuing laws that discontinued the wealth of religious traditions. His republic did away with Arabic script and Sufi organisations, forbade Ottoman headgear and traditional gendered roles and razed mosques to the ground. It also ended Tunahan's religious career. From the preacher's point of view, he made the best of it. Saying farewell to his elite prospects he turned to the poorest classes where he found a willing ear. He taught them during long bus rides, while doing farm work together or working as a coaler, gaining him the nickname 'the coaling *hoca*'. Next to the Arabic alphabet and the ability to read simple passages from the Qur'an, he also taught his students the silently uttered *Dhikr* prayers, which belong to the Sufi tradition, groping for a way to let them not only learn the basics by heart but also understand 'the inside of the letter'. In addition to the five daily prayers, they help participants to reach a trance-like state, which is experienced as union with God. This form of practice having been forbidden, the silent *Dhikr* became a tool for silent protest.

After his death, his son-in-law Kemal Kacar, himself a dedicated student of Tunahan, proceeded to reorganise the preacher's heritage. He created the worldwide administration that today we know by the name of the Islamic Cultural Centres (ICC). In Turkish pejorative speech, members were more commonly known as Süleymancı, 'those of Süleyman'. The aim of the organisation was the spreading of the Qur'an ('A Qur'an in every hotel room!'). Engaging in politics was explicitly forbidden. Some members took an oath to dedicate their lives to teaching the Qur'an and to performing the *Dhikr* for the rest of their lives. Furthering the mission became intimately entwined with a search for religious essence.

Some 15 years after Tunahan's death, migration to Europe, and especially to Germany, was well under way. In the 1960s, his students managed to establish 150 prayer halls in Germany. In 1973 these were united under the label of the ICC, with headquarters in Cologne. As in Turkey, the congregations attracted poor workers with very little learning and very few resources. For many adults, the Arabic alphabet was the very first one they learned to master. Prayer circles were the glue that held the community together, functioning as solidarity groups and extended families and exercising severe social control. Members dedicated their lives to the proselytising activities that have gained the organisation another pejorative designation: *Koranschulen* (Qur'an schools). The schools offered Arabic grammar, the ability to read the Qur'an and recite parts by heart, public Qur'an recitation and personal conduct derived from religious law. It was a very traditional offer, but Turkish parents who found themselves confronted with the difficulties involved in raising children in European societies embraced it. The schools attracted children from conservative religious and republican laic households in equal numbers.

In 1979, the ICC went to court to demand the right to be recognised as a corporation of public law; a Muslim community with the same rights as the majority churches in Germany. Secular Turks and representatives of the Turkish state in Germany vigorously objected to this plan and revived old accusations from Turkey to incriminate the ICC. Some remembered that Tunahan's students had refused to wear a Western hat and only read the Qur'an. Others insinuated that Tunahan was a Nazi sympathiser. The ICC's devotional life, and the impenetrable social closure it erected around itself, added to the general miscomprehension. In the end, the demand was rejected on the three grounds that defined a German 'church': membership, durability and a religious credo which distinguishes it from the next.

In the years that followed, the organisation retired from whatever public life it had engaged in and stopped communicating with the outside world. Instead, it steadily enlarged the network of local associations, the number of which rose to 300. The suspicion that surrounded the ICC also rose at the same pace.

Fifteen years later, in 1995, the newly appointed head of the German organisation, Dr Nurettin Akman, himself a former colonel of the Turkish army, realised that, for the local communities, achieving acceptance in German society was as important as spreading knowledge of the Qur'an. His slogan was 'normalisation instead of isolation'; his ideal the building of a genuine Islamic elite. Being a man of action, he simply relegated the elder generation of local leaders to doormen and shop sellers and installed young people born and raised in Germany in their stead. Communication with the outside world was now the word of the day. Everywhere in Germany, young ICC members rapidly organised dialogue circles, invited policy makers to discuss religious and secular values and tried to break down the community's borders. In Cologne they established the first Islamic

Academy, where domestic violence and Islamic gender relations, subjects that within this community were considered impossible to discuss, were offered for public discussion. The response of German society was overwhelmingly positive. Akman treasured his growing elite and swept aside protesting voices from inside the community warning him that 'he is going too fast'. 'Their parents still sat knee-deep in the weeds', he told them, 'but in ten years time we will have one thousand intellectuals'.

In 2000, in the middle of all this innovation, Kemal Kacar died in Istanbul. At that point the German ICC counted 20,000 registered, paying members. But as each member also represented an entire family, the number of people active in the German organisation might actually have numbered about 80,000. Kacar's heir, Ahmed Arif Denizoğlun, himself a grandson of Tunahan, immediately terminated the path on which the German ICC had embarked. The aim of the organisation, he declared, was the rescuing of the souls of Turkish children, not communication with European society. Once again, the ICC took an authoritarian turn and disappeared behind the walls of social closure. To underline this new direction, Denizoğlun expelled the young men and women from their positions. Those who dared to protest were threatened with expulsion. A few months later, the old leaders returned to their former posts. The new watchword was 'boarding schools', which were considered to offer Turkish children a safe haven in the midst of what was generally considered a godless society.

Ever since, local communities have focused on the erection of boarding schools. In the eyes of the organisers, they were the logical continuation of the Qur'an schools, the majority of which had already installed dormitories for weekend pupils. Turkish parents, who were sympathetic to the offer to imbue their children with a conservative religious outlook, also accepted the prospect of placing them in a controlled environment, safeguarding them from the dangers modern society held in store.

But the requests for planning permissions to enlarge the schools have run into major political difficulties in every instance. Municipalities object to building measures, which from their point of view heighten self-isolation, hamper transparency and impede the integration of this organisation into German society. In neighbourhood initiatives that object to the erection of such schools in their vicinity, fear is repeatedly expressed that the ICC in general, and the boarding schools in particular, nurture anti-Western, anti-modern, Islamist sentiments.

Beginning in 2008, when the Cologne police released to the press a quotation from a (secret) document apparently proving this organisation's political involvement in right-wing circles and anti-Jewish resentments, it rekindled old suspicions against the ICC. The media created a spectacle; the ICC leaders reacted helplessly. Building boarding schools simply has not proven to be a successful course of action.

References

Jonker, Gerdien (2002) *Eine Wellenlänge zu Gott. Der Verband der islamischen Kulturzentren in Europa*, Bielefeld: Transcript.

—— (2004) 'Muslim lay communities between Turkey and Germany', in Jamal Malik, (ed.), *Muslims in Europe. From the Margin to the Centre*, Berlin: LIT, pp. 61–75.

—— (2005) 'Sufi piety in Europe. The transformation of a Sufi order into lay communities' in Jocelyne Césari and Seán MacLoughin (eds), *European Muslims and the Secular State*, London: Ashgate, pp. 24–49.

THE SÜLEYMANLI MOVEMENT IN THE NETHERLANDS

Thijl Sunier

In terms of size, the Dutch branch of the Süleymanlı movement today is a mid-range. The Süleymanlıs refer to themselves as *talebe*, followers or pupils of the Turkish Sunni teacher of Islam, Süleyman Hilmi Tunahan (1888–1959). The reason for extending their activities to Europe in the early 1970s was the tightening grip of the State on Islamic learning. They have over 40 local mosque organisations in the Netherlands and this number has been more or less stable over the past decade. Most of the attendants of the Sülemanli mosques are ordinary Turkish migrants. The main task of these organisations is to run the local mosque and to develop activities such as Qur'an classes, homework classes, running the mosque shop, establishing contacts with other local institutions, politicians and officials and to represent the local Muslim community and defend their interests. In general, local Süleymanlı branches are typical neighbourhood associations. In addition to the mosque associations, there are another 40 or so organisations which are loosely associated with the Süleymanlıs. The activities of all these local organisations are coordinated by the Stichting Islamitisch Centrum Nederland (SICN, the Islamic Centre Foundation in the Netherlands), founded in 1972 as the Stichting Islamitisch Centrum and based in the city of Utrecht. The local organisations are formally independent foundations, each of them registered separately, but there is a clear top-down structure with respect to decisions taken at a local level. The centre in Utrecht appoints local board members and decides about new initiatives. Due to the rejuvenation of the board and the stepping down of the rather authoritarian head of the Dutch branch of the movement, Ibrahim Nalbantoğlu, in the early 1990s, a gradual decentralisation started and local associations are now more than before able to adopt their own policy based on local circumstances.

Until the mid-1990s the organisation concentrated largely on its two main goals; establishing and running local mosques and organising Qur'anic teaching. Imams are recruited and trained in the Netherlands. They work full time and are supposed to do more than just conduct services. They should guide the local community and take part in local neighbourhood activities outside the mosque. For that reason the organisation emphasises that imams should speak Dutch more than sufficiently and should have lived in the Netherlands long enough to know the country and to understand specific needs of the local community. Süleymanlı mosques attract people by offering well-organised religious services, mainly educational in nature, and their reputation as organisers of solid Qur'an education stretches way beyond their own direct circles. Many Turkish

Muslims prefer Süleymanlı courses over those offered by the Diyanet. In some Dutch cities the organisation has opened boarding houses where children can stay for a while and be taught in Qur'an. In the press they were accused of adopting a very rigid teaching regime, and this contributed to their bad image in the 1980s and early 1990s.

The Süleymanlıs had a reputation of being inward-looking without any interest in cooperation with other institutions. During the 1990s, however, the SICN developed into one of the most active umbrella organisations in all kinds of local and national initiatives concerning Islam, integration and anti-discrimination. The most important reason for this change was the increasing number of younger, relatively well-educated people on the boards. The SICN participates in the Contactorgaan Moslims en Overheid (CMO, Dutch National Council of Muslims) and they are members of the board of the Inspraakorgaan Turken in Nederland (Advisory Board Turks in the Netherlands). In most cities where they founded mosque organisations they take part in local councils and cross-cultural initiatives.

Unlike other Islamic movements in Europe, the Dutch Süleymanlıs consider their relations with sister organisations in Turkey not very important when it concerns their local activities. Whereas in other Islamic movements this relation still constitutes one of the main controversies among the rank-and-file, in Süleymanlı circles in the Netherlands this has never been a big issue. Most adherents do of course have personal relations with Turkey, but these are not very instrumental in daily activities. The relation to sister branches in other parts of Europe are not institutionalised and are only activated on specific occasions, such as the movement's conferences or celebrations.

The Süleymanlıs were the first Turkish–Islamic movement in the Netherlands to organise and coordinate mosque activities. In 1972 a Dutch convert, Abdulvahid van Bommel, founded the SICN in Utrecht. The aim of the foundation was to help local Süleymanlıs in their effort to organise room for prayer, to assist them with teaching, to find imams, and in general to stimulate the development of religious accommodation. Under his successor, Ibrahim Nalbantoğlu, the SICN tightened its grip on the local associations.

In 1978 the SICN was reorganised and centralised. From then on the headquarters in Utrecht appointed local board members and set out the local political agenda. Until the end of the 1970s, the Süleymanlıs could operate relatively freely because they were the only set up with this aim. They exerted a disproportionate influence among Turkish Muslims. Between 1978 and 1983 the SICN founded 23 local associations. All of these local organisations were now an integral part of the Süleymanlı movement. Already in 1977, however, there were developments that would gradually undermine the monopoly position of the SICN as the sole provider of religious accommodation for Turkish Muslims. In the city of Rotterdam, a city with a relatively large Turkish community, a local church had put their building at the disposal of the Muslim community on the occasion of Ramadan. Because on such special occasions a professional imam is required, it was decided to bring somebody from Turkey. Two delegations travelled to Turkey to find the right person. They came back with two imams, one from Süleymanlı circles and one trained and employed by the Turkish state's Diyanet İşleri Başkanlığı (Presidency of Religious Affairs). Because the community could not decide which of the two imams would minister the service, there was a vote. The vast majority of the more than 1,000 Muslims present voted for the Diyanet imam. For the Süleymanlıs this was a disaster. The Diyanet now argued that they were the main representative of the Turkish Muslims in Rotterdam. The local *cemaat* (congregation), it was argued, had turned down the 'extremist' Süleymanlıs. In other Dutch cities conflicts such as this one also became manifest, and this constituted the beginning of a fierce ideological competition between Turkish–Islamic movements for the rank-and-file. In addition, Süleymanlıs were accused of backing the fascist Grey Wolves who were, at that time, very active in recruiting rank-and-file among Turkish migrants in the Netherlands and elsewhere in Europe. This was in a period when the Dutch government was looking for allies among the Muslim population to support their integration policy. The Diyanet organisations successfully occupied that position.

Today the situation has fundamentally changed. The Süleymanlıs are generally considered as moderate-profile mainstream Muslims who contribute to the continuous rooting of Islam in Dutch society. The fierce competition that characterised the 1970s, 1980s and much of the 1990s has almost died out and been put off the agenda in the wake of contemporary concerns about the radicalisation of young Muslims born in the Netherlands.

References

Landman, Nico (1992) *Van mat tot minaret*, Amsterdam: VU Uitgeverij.

Sunier, Thijl (1996) *Islam in Beweging. Turkse Jongeren en islamitische Organisaties*, Amsterdam: Het Spinhuis.

THE MUSLIM COUNCIL OF BRITAIN: FROM PIOUS LAY PREACHING TO POLITICAL LOBBYING

Mohammad Siddique Seddon

The emergence of minority Muslims in Britain onto the wider political forum is a rela-. tively recent phenomenon triggered by an increasingly 'Islamised' identity as a result of developments both internal and external to the British Muslim community. For the last decade, the Muslim Council of Britain (MCB) has been at the forefront of dialogue and representation between British Muslims and government, but the transformation from apparently disparate groups of Muslim pious lay preachers to a unified political lobbyist organisation has not been an easy one.

The MCB was established in 1997 with the primary objective of promoting 'cooperation, consensus and unity on Muslim affairs in the UK'.[1] It sought to achieve its aims by developing and positioning itself as a powerful lobby group that would become the primary interlocutors between the British Muslim community and the government. The MCB was preceded by a number of organisations; the Union of Muslim Organisations (UMO) (1970), the UK Action Committee on Islamic Affairs (UKACIA) (1991), and the National Interim Committee for Muslim Unity (NICMU) (1996) which eventually proved to be the precursor of the MCB. The creation of Muslim organisations historically traces developing engagement with wider British society. For example, the UMO concerned itself with issues relating to provision for Muslims in state education and discrimination against Muslims in the realms of employment, health care and immigration. These particular issues directly reflected the primary anxieties of first-generation migrant Muslims whereas the UKACIA, established two decades later, was a direct result of unifying Muslim sentiment, protests and responses, firstly to the publication of *The Satanic Verses* by Salman Rushdie in the late 1980s and then later to the first Gulf War, 1990–1.

Although the MCB has consistently claimed that it has a clear mandate to represent the wider and complexly diverse British Muslim community by virtue of the sheer number of affiliates, which currently number around 350, its members' list displays only a small number of affiliates from the largest ethno-theological sub-group from the British Muslim community – Kashmiri Sufis.[2] Kashmiris of Pakistani origin represent the single largest Muslim group in the UK. They are overwhelmingly charismatic Sufis, with a distinct, syncretic geo-cultural form of Sufism, a theological expression that does not find favour with most political Islamist movements because of the emphasis on, and allegiance to, charismatic sheikhs or pirs, which is interpreted by more literalistic Islamic expressions as a form of *shirk* (polytheism).

By the time the MCB was established in the late 1990s, most of the issues and concerns relating to Muslim provision in education, employment and civil society were largely resolved. Although aspects of racial and religious discrimination still remained, they were legally addressed with the introduction of the Employment Equality Regulation Act in 2003 and the Racial and Religious Hatred Act of 2006. However, the problem of Muslim mobilisation on key issues affecting the whole community, beyond narrow ethnic and theological divisions, was primarily one of political leadership and representation. In fact, despite alarming increases in Islamophobia, particularly in the wake of the 9/11 terrorist attacks in the US, the key issues facing the Muslim community were not just confined to equal opportunities and discrimination in wider British society. There was also the perennial problem of 'who speaks for British Muslims?' Inevitably, whenever Islamic-related issues were publicly discussed, Muslim responses were all too often both confusing and contradictory. In the process of engaging with the UK government, media and general populace on Muslim-related issues, at both national and local levels, it became clear those most able to converse with wider society were the political Islamists. This is perhaps because they were able to speak in relative and cognate political terms to politicians, journalists and civil service mandarins. As a result, the various political Islamist groups in the UK represented in the unifying umbrella organisations preceding the MCB sought to fill the power vacuum that existed in community–government dialogue. After the relatively successful mobilisation of Muslims by the UKACIA against the publication of The Satanic Verses, in 1992 the pro-Iranian, former Saudi-backed Muslim Institute, led by its director, the late Kalim Siddiqui, astutely established the Council for British Muslims which became dubbed the 'Muslim Parliament'. In the ensuing battle of words over the publication of The Satanic Verses, Sir Iqbal Sacranie, first Secretary General and later to be knighted in 2005, said in response to the Khomeini 'death fatwa' on Salman Rushdie that, 'death, perhaps is a bit too easy for him'. Sacranie's rather glib comment in relation to the death fatwa placed on Rushdie has been frequently referred to in the British popular press as an example of the MCB's 'hardline' Islamist ideology. However, in the aftermath of The Satanic Verses furore, the government desperately needed to interface with a Muslim body, similar to the Board of Deputies for British Jews, in order to defuse tensions. Both the MCB and the Muslim Parliament vied to become the democratic national representatives of Britain's Muslims. What developed in the process was a discernable shift from the transnational politics of the diaspora Muslim communities with which various Islamist groups were associated, for example, the UK Islamic Mission with Pakistan, Daw'atul Islam with Bangladesh, etc. The evolving politicisation of British Muslim community issues, from The Satanic Verses affair and beyond, presented an opportunity to both further politicise and 'Islamise' a seemingly socially detached and supposed secularised British Muslim populace. The formation of the MCB also coincided with two significant and specific developments within the British Muslim community.

The first development was a distinct political identity shift from ethnicity to religiosity in the constructions of evolving British 'Muslimness'. While it may have been more appropriate for first-generation migrant Muslims in Britain to identify within a broader ethnic identity, for example, as 'Asians', thereby allowing a grouping together of smaller minorities of multi-ethnic, cultural and religious groups to formulate a larger and more significant political voice, the newly emerging identities of Muslimness among second- and third-generation British-born offspring produced a distinct, hybrid British–Islamic identity in which ethno-cultural manifestations are becoming increasingly redundant. The second important development within the British Muslim community is the generational distillation from diverse theological expressions of distinction and difference into a wider definition and acceptance of what represents Islamic orthodoxy, or

Muslimness. That is to say, where previous first-generation identity politics tended to divide Muslims by both ethnicity and theological expression, a practical engagement and pragmatic experience of Muslim pluralism, set within a new geo-social context of liberal democracy, diversity and plurality, allowed for a greater synergy and tolerance between conflicting Islamic theological expressions for British-born progeny. In addition, where legal protection was implemented by government legislation via anti-racism and discrimination laws, which protected specific ethno-religious minorities such as British Jews and Sikhs, Muslims as a distinct religious group not only remained largely unprotected but actually became specific targets of increasing Islamophobia. It is clear that both these major developmental shifts in British Muslim identity politics were directly shaped by particular significant events – The Satanic Verses affair (1989), the Gulf War (1991) and the Bosnian situation (1990s).[3]

For the MCB, The Satanic Verses affair proved extremely important in their bid to represent the British Muslim community as they later managed to find the ear of the newly elected Labour government in 1997. However, relations between the MCB and central government have not always been harmonious. In the beginning New Labour and the MCB entered into a political marriage of convenience with neither harbouring much genuine love of the other but both sharing a common goal of political power. Perhaps the first real embarrassment for the government was the very public condemnation of the British forces' bombing of Afghanistan, made outside 10 Downing Street immediately after an all-faiths meeting with the then prime minister, Tony Blair. Further, when British Muslims rallied together with the 'Stop the War' campaigners in a demonstration by around two million people through the streets of London against the invasion of Iraq, relations between the MCB and the government were fraught. More uncomfortable moments followed later when it was uncovered that civil servant Mockbul Ali, working from the Engaging with the Islamic World Group (EIWG) at the Foreign Office, had written speeches for both Sacranie and former Secretary of State, Jack Straw when they shared a public platform after the 7/7 London suicide bombings in 2005. While the government had continuously presented the MCB as the authentic representatives of the British Muslim community, opinion polls have found that less than 4 per cent British Muslims believe the organisation represents them, with many Muslims revealing they had never heard of them. These facts lend themselves to the continued claim that the MCB does not in fact represent the overwhelming majority of British Muslims. There are also rumours regarding government funding received by the MCB which allude to hand-outs in the region of £500,000 although the MCB claim they were never direct recipients but, rather, that the grants were paid instead to their affiliates. However, in January 2008 they did submit a funding bid for £500,000 entitled 'British Muslims: From Alienation to Engagement', in which the MCB clumsily claims that Muslim alienation equals radicalisation. The bid was submitted to the Community and Faith Unit (CFU) at the Communities and Local Government Department (CLG). The MCB's rather abrasive response to governmental policy on preventing extremism and counter-terrorism has forced the government to look for, and fund, more willing Muslim partners and organisations, such as the Progressive Muslims, the Sufi Muslim Council and the Quilliam Foundation, to rubber-stamp its security policies relating to British Muslims. Another problem that has caused much annoyance to the government is the MCB's consistent boycott of the Holocaust Memorial Day; reasons for refusing to attend range from the Bosnian genocide to Israeli attacks on Gaza. But the latest row came on the eve of the launch of the government's revamped initiative on tackling extremism within the Muslim community; the inappropriately named CONTEST 2. The government insisted that the MCB remove Dr Duad Abdullah, deputy Secretary General, with former minister Hazel Blears issuing a letter demanding Abdullah's resignation. It is claimed that Abdullah signed a document allegedly to advocate attacks on both Jewish communities and British military forces. In response, Abdullah published an open letter in which he stated that 'entirely untrue' allegations had been made after he signed a pro-Hamas declaration against Israeli violations of international laws during the recent invasion of Gaza. Abdullah then issued legal proceedings against Blears for libel. The current situation remains one of stalemate, officially termed as 'disengagement' between the government and the MCB, although there have been a number of discussions between the two to try to heal the rift.

Notes

1   http://www.mcb.org.uk/aboutmcb.php. Accessed 26 October 2009.
2   Sufis are devotes of Sufism, an esoteric form of Islamic spiritualism usually taught through enlightened teachers or guides known as *sheikh*, *murshids* and *pirs*.
3   See Muhammad Anwar (2003) 'British Muslims: socio-economic position', in Mohammad Siddique Seddon et al. (eds), *British Muslims: Loyalty and Belonging*, Leicester: The Islamic Foundation, pp. 60–1.

References

Anwar, Muhammad (2003) 'British Muslims: socio-economic position', in Mohammad Siddique Seddon et al. (eds), *British Muslims: Loyalty and Belonging*, Leicester: The Islamic Foundation, pp.60–1.
Birt, Yahya (2005) 'Lobbying and marching: British Muslims and the State', in Yahya Birt (ed.), *Muslim Britain: Communities Under Pressure*, London: Zed Books, pp. 92–106.
Pędziwiatr, Konrad (2007) 'Creating New Discursive Arenas and Influencing the Policies of the State: The Case of the Muslim Council of Britain', *Social Compass*, (54), pp. 267–80.
Rushdie, Salman (1989) *The Satanic Verses*, London: Viking.

GERMAN MUSLIM FEDERATIONS: ZENTRALRAT DER MUSLIME IN DEUTSCHLAND AND KOORDINIERUNGSRAT DER MUSLIME

Schirin Amir-Moazami

The Zentralrat der Muslime in Deutschland (ZMD) has been largely criticised and sometimes openly accused by German political authorities, by the media and also by some competing Islamic organisations of hosting contested groups and movements such as the Shi'ite oriented Islamisches Zentrum Hamburg (IZH), connected to the Iranian regime, or the Islamische Gemeinde in Deutschland (IGD), observed by the secret service, and because of its ties to the Muslim Brotherhood (MB). Another more diffuse accusation concerns its alleged lack of loyalty to the German constitutional order. Umbrella organisations such as the ZMD and also the Koordinierungsrat der Muslime (KRM) therefore merit closer scrutiny.

Both should be contextualised within the dynamics of legal arrangements of church and state institutions in Germany and a long-lasting struggle by organised Muslims to gain public recognition within these existing patterns. The German constitution defines, on the one hand, a church–state separation by confining itself to religious and ideological neutrality. On the other hand, it guarantees a relatively close cooperation of state and church agents. One of the most important aspects is the 'status of corporation of public law' (*Körperschaft des Öffentlichen Rechts*), which Christian churches and a number of other religious communities inhabit. This ensures privileges such as the collection of church taxes or the right to teach confessionally bound religious classes in state schools. Muslim organisations have attempted to gain this status since their inception back in the late 1970s. The most recurrent objection has been their 'lack of representativity', and the 'guarantee of duration', which other religious communities with a more centralised structure and established character could prove more easily. By this request Muslim associations were encouraged to reunite into larger federations, first into the Islamrat der Bundesrepublik (1986) and then ZMD (1994). Yet all efforts to gain the corporation status remained unfulfilled so far. The formation of the ZMD thus results from a longer struggle for political and legal recognition of Muslim groups in Germany.

Constituted as a follow on from the Islamischer Arbeitskreis, the ZMD contains at present 19 associations representing around 20,000 Muslims from Maghrebi countries, the Middle East, the Balkans and a growing number of converts. Its current chair is the convert Ayyub Axel Köhler. In 2002 the ZMD published the Islamic Charta,[1] signed by all member associations and later on also by the concurring federation Islamischer Rat für die Bundesrepublik Deutschland (IRD). Driven by the post-9/11 climate of suspicion *vis-à-vis* Muslim organisations, the main aim was to provide a declaration about the commitment of Muslims organised in Germany to Islam and to German constitutional norms. The Charta thus explicitly takes up some of the main accusations against Muslims in Germany and elsewhere in Europe.[2] It can also be interpreted as an initiative of interfaith dialogue, as it addresses normative standards of how Muslims should ideally interact within a Christian-based society and vice versa.[3] Inspired by similar efforts in other European countries, the 21 paragraphs of the Charta contain issues ranging from theological basics through reflections on the conditions of Muslims within the German legal order to a list of requirements towards political authorities to further the institutionalisation of Islam in Germany.

The Islamic Charta triggered a wide scope of reactions among politicians, church representatives, the media and other Muslim organisations and individuals alike.[4] On a general level, the effort was welcomed as a necessary step to officially document the compatibility between Islamic doctrines and national and supranational norms. However, a number of commentators objected that the Charta did not go far enough in confessing Muslims' loyalty to German society.[5] A recurrent objection concerned the terminology employed in the Charta, for example the fact that it states to recognise the constitution merely 'in principle' (*grundsätzlich*), which can be interpreted as hiding reservations. Others were troubled by the Charta's 'conservatism' with regard to normative issues. Passages such as 'Islamic law demands equal treatment of what is identical and permits unequal treatment of what is not identical'[6] were, for example, interpreted as reflecting and confirming a general inequality between men and women 'in Islam'.[7] On the other hand, a commonly welcomed gesture also emphasised by critics, was the Charta's confession to the 'right to change one's religion, to have a different one or none at all'.[8]

A matter of contestation with which the ZMD has frequently been confronted was the personal backgrounds of representatives involved, in particular the personality of the former head, Nadeem Elyas, a doctor born in Saudi Arabia. Some of his statements in interviews were interpreted as an indicator of the ZMD's goal to support the establishment of *shari'a* in Germany and as undermining Muslims' loyalty to the German constitution. Looking at the ways in which representatives of the ZMD relate to *shari'a*, it becomes obvious, however, that such assessments are rather based on a stereotypical and generalising understanding of *shari'a* itself and the possibilities of its adaptation within a liberal–democratic context. Reasoning about the role and place of *shari'a* law in Germany, representatives of the ZMD tend to contextualise this institution in the first place as a moral instrument to regulate the right conduct of Muslims. Both Elyas and Köhler emphasised repeatedly that a *shari'a*-based legislation had no validity in a liberal–democratic context like Germany.[9]

The ZMD has become an important force which, in particular through a rich and dynamic website,[10] actively engages in public debates surrounding the Muslim presence in Germany. What it has not managed, in turn, is to form a representative body successful in achieving the status of corporation of public law, but this is definitely where the KRM is heading.

Similar to the ZMD, the KRM, formed in April 2007, is an umbrella organisation constituted by various religiously, ethnically and ideologically diverse larger Muslim federations such as the ZMD, IRD, Türkisch-Islamische Union der Anstalt für Religion (DITIB) and Verband der Islamischen Kulturzentren (VIKZ). The KRM's spokesmen are elected rotationally every six months. The foundation of the KRM has to be analysed both in light of the above-mentioned efforts of organised Muslims to reunite in order to gain legal recognition and also in view of changed political strategies, in particular of the German state and its security organs to ensure the 'integration' of Muslims into German society. Paralleled by enhanced processes of securitisation after 9/11, the German state has recently initiated measures exclusively targeting Muslims in order to ensure their integration through dialogue and discipline. These measures range from integration courses and citizenship tests to dialogue initiatives with the organised Muslim field. The most important example of this kind is the Deutsche Islam Konferenz (DIK), formed in September 2006 by the Minister of the Interior, Wolfgang Schäuble. It serves as a forum of dialogue between the German state, Muslim organisations and individual Muslims (intellectuals, scholars and outspoken 'secular/liberal' Muslims), in order to 'ameliorate the situation of Muslims in Germany' and to ensure their 'integration'.[11] The DIK combines broader security aims with efforts to recognise Islam as 'a part of German society' on the basis of the 'liberal–democratic order'.[12]

It is divided into four working groups that meet regularly, in which issues ranging from 'German community values' to security threats by 'Islamic fundamentalism' are the subjects of discussion. Driven by the joint goals of integration and security, one reason to also include contested groups such as the Islamische Gemeinschaft Milli Görüş is the requirement from Muslim organisations and movements of their 'internal democratisation' and public 'transparency'. The DIK can therefore be interpreted as an attempt to empower organised Muslim groups in Germany via their regulation and control.

The formation of the KRM can be interpreted as an unintended effect of this initiative. Encouraged by the DIK, the KRM reunited hitherto competing Muslim federations into one umbrella, serving as the representative dialogue partner of the State. The common basis is one shared interest that is, again, to gain official recognition as a representative Muslim body similar to Christian churches in order to organise practical matters such as the institutionalisation of Islamic classes in state schools, or church taxes.

The outspoken basis of KRM is similarly the confession to Germany's 'liberal–democratic order' and the Qur'an and the Sunna. So far the KRM has not specified what this 'both-and-logic' in practice consists of, nor has it made explicit the binding elements and concerns between the various organisations, directions and movements involved in the KRM. One reason for this is that the KRM has only been formed very recently. Another explanation is probably the effort to avoid falling into similar traps as the ZMD with its Islamic Charta.

Although the four federations of the KRM represent around 80 per cent the 2,500 mosque associations in Germany, the KRM is confronted with difficulties to be recognised as a legitimate partner and representative of Muslims in Germany. Scepticism is articulated by politicians, academics and non-religious migrant organisations. The most recurrent objection is that the KRM only represents a small proportion of Muslims living in Germany because only around 15 per cent of 3.5 million were organised at all. In a more general vein, associations of Secular Muslims or the Türkischer Bund object to the artificial 'churchification' of Islam in Germany as generally illegitimate for Islam itself. The more substantial reason for the dismissive stance towards the KRM is yet again the suspicions towards the politico-religious directions of some of the member federations and their alleged connections to Islamist movements in Turkey or the Middle East (especially of the IGMG, IGD and IZH). What is worth noting is a common and repetitive scheme with regard to the aims of organised Muslims to gain a representative voice and their recurrent confrontation with limitations to this, based on a 'hermeneutics of suspicion'. Their repetitive confession to the German constitutional order and confinement to German society as the centre of their belief and belonging will probably also continue to stir up the suspicion of various parts of the German non-Muslim majority society as characterising a 'double talk', divided into an 'external' discourse, tactically pleasing German society, and an 'internal' one which is still mired in Islamist currents in Muslim majority contexts. However, in the long run the postponement to attribute Muslim federations the status of a corporation of public law will be challenged on the basis of the principles of religious freedom and equality themselves, which are so intensively defended once it comes to the German self-understanding *vis-à-vis* Islam.

Notes

1   See http://zentralrat.de/3035.php (link accessed 19 June 2014)
2   *Islamic Charta*, art. 12: 'We do not seek to establish a clerical theocracy'.
3   Friedemann Eissler (2008) 'Christian–Muslim encounter – recent issues and perspectives', in Ala Al-Hamarneh and Jörn Thielmann (eds), *Islam and Muslims in Germany*, Leiden / Boston: Brill, pp. 161–181.
4   Ibid.
5   See Ludwig Amman (2004) *Kola und Koran. Das Wagnis einer islamischen Renaissance*, Freiburg: Herder, and Ursula Spuler-Stegemann (2002) *Muslime in Deutschland*, Freiburg: Herder.
6   *Islamic Charta*, art. 13.
7   See, for example, Spuler-Stegemann. *Muslime in Deutschland*, p. 162; Amman, *Kola und Koran*, p. 87; and Johannes Kandel (2002) 'Die Islamische Charta. Fragen und Anmerkungen', p.7.
8   *Islamic Charta*, art. 18.
9   See, for example, Elyas in *FAZ*, 1 February 2005 and Köhler in *Die Welt*, 4 March 2006.
10 http://www.islam.de. (link accessed 19 June 2014)
11 DIK Website. http://www.deutsche-islamkonferenz.de. (link accessed 19 June 2014)
12 Ibid.

References

Amman, Ludwig (2004) *Kola und Koran. Das Wagnis einer islamischen Renaissance*, Freiburg: Herder.
Eissler, Friedemann (2008) 'Christian-Muslim encounter – recent issues and perspectives', in Ala Al-Hamarneh and Jörn Thielmann (eds), *Islam and Muslims in Germany*, Leiden / Boston: Brill, pp. 161–81.
Kandel, Johannes (2002) 'Die Islamische Charta. Fragen und Anmerkungen'. Available at http://www.fes-online-akademie.de/download.php?d=KANDEL_ISLAM CHARTA.PDF. Accessed 30 September 2009.
Spuler-Stegemann, Ursula (2002) *Muslime in Deutschland*, Freiburg: Herder.

(II) ISLAMIC GUIDANCE AND PUBLIC DEBATES: IMAMS, CHAPLAINS AND INTELLECTUALS

IMAMS IN BRITAIN: AGENTS OF DE-RADICALISATION?

Philip Lewis

Until 9/11 the world of the imams in Britain, their influence, training and institutions was largely a matter of indifference to the government. Subsequently, that world has become the focus of intense scrutiny by both the government and the media. Unsurprisingly, this interest has intensified exponentially since 7/7. Initially, after 9/11, the intelligence services began to identify, monitor and prosecute a few notorious individuals – often self-styled 'sheikhs' such as Abu Hamza al-Masri, Abdullah El-Faisal and Abu Qatada – who had been pumping out virulent anti-Western diatribes against the *kuffar* (unbelievers) as well as romanticising and recruiting for jihadi activities from a few mosques in London. The temptation to see the imams through the prism of these individuals began to give way to a more nuanced understanding of violent extremism and its carriers, whether takfiri Salafis or violent Islamists. Indeed, the government has sought to mobilise and equip imams as part of a coordinated attempt to de-radicalise young British Muslims vulnerable to the siren calls of violent extremism. The government has begun to create and valorise the good imam as a counterpoint to the likes of Abu Hamza and Omar Bakri Muhammad. One who is outward looking and able to engage confidently with British Muslim youth, local schools and public and civic bodies, as well as being hospitable to members of other religions. It is hoped he will embody – as mainstream Christian clergy do – 'bridging' social capital, that is, enable trust and reciprocity across different communities.

Before rehearsing some of the measures the government has introduced to encourage such developments, we need to consider the provenance, status, training and social roles of imams in Britain. Almost three-quarters of Britain's 1.6 million Muslims (2001 census) have roots in South Asia. The majority of mosques have been created to serve these communities. The most comprehensive mapping of Britain's mosques with regard to location, ethnicity and 'school of thought' to which they belong, suggests that 600 are Deobandi, 550 Barelwi, 60 Islamists, 75 Salafi and 65 are Shi'ite, along with a number of ethnic-specific mosques serving Turks, Somalis, Arabs and so on.[1] In short, most reflect the different traditional, 'Sunni schools of thought' active in South Asia – especially Deobandi and Barewli. While British Deobandis with roots in India tend to belong to a pious and apolitical tradition, some with roots in Pakistan are the same ethnic group which has generated the Taliban. Barewlis have suffered from the 'Talibanisation' of Pakistan and, unsurprisingly, are bitterly hostile to them.

In Britain, most of the mosque committees are dominated by the elders, whose experiences in rural and small-town Pakistan continue to shape a limited set of expectations about the imam's status and role. Most are reimbursed well below the minimum wage and lack contractual security. Their roles are generally confined to the mosque where they are to lead the five daily prayers, teach children after state school, give the Friday address, preside over the 'rites of passage' and offer advice, when sought, within their competence on the application of Islamic teaching and law. Traditionalist Muslims occasionally seek amulets from them, for example, to ward off the evil eye.

In the last quarter of a century, side by side with mosque building, a new phase of institution building has begun with the proliferation of Dar al-'Ulum (Islamic seminaries). There are at least 24 registered seminaries in Britain: 16 Deobandi, five Barelwi, one Shi'ite, one of the Muslim Brotherhood and one founded by the late sheikh Dr Zaki Badawi (d. 2006), who trained at Al-Azhar in Cairo. These probably have a capacity to train about 250 'ulama' (religious scholars) each year. This means there is already a surfeit of Deobandi but a shortage of Barelwi scholars. One reason is that in the Barelwi tradition the key figure is the Sufi sheikh – a spiritual guide – who appoints the imam, often considered a low-level functionary.

The training and ethos of most of these seminaries indicate that only minor concessions have been made to their new location in Britain. The syllabus is a thinned-down version of that taught in South Asia. In the case of the Deobandi school of thought, the focus is on mastering Arabic to understand the Qur'an and canonical collections of hadith. There is minimal study of Qur'anic commentaries and Islamic law, no Islamic history beyond the first couple of generations after Muhammad's death and no Islamic philosophy. The medium of instruction often remains Urdu. Further, even if students study the few 'A' levels taught in such institutions – Arabic, Urdu, ICT, law and accountancy – their knowledge of British society and its history, culture and institutions will remain minimal.

The ethos of South Asian seminaries can still be characterised as rejectionist of modernity and of discourses developed outside its circumscribed world. In a recent survey of Pakistani students studying at Urdu and (elite) English-medium schools and universities, both public and private[2] (Rahman, 2008), between 65 and 90 per cent across the different institutions favoured equal rights for women – this is in marked contrast with 'seminarians', for whom the figure was 17 per cent. Significant differences were also evident with regard to treating non-Muslims equally and a willingness to make peace with India. A cursory look at traditional websites of seminaries and those of many traditional scholars in the UK evince similar attitudes, certainly with regard to gender, and often negative attitudes to non-Muslims. One other worrying import into Britain from South Asia has been a ratcheting up of intra-sectarian bigotry, exacerbated by both Pakistani governments and Saudi petrol dollars. However, there have been a few welcome changes from within the world of British seminaries. Since 9/11 and 7/7 some have begun to open up in a limited way to wider society, its civic and religious dignitaries, as well as to the police. Some of their scholars go on to study in a limited number of British universities or further afield. The best are beginning to find jobs as religious education teachers, chaplains in prisons, hospitals and further education where they are developing new intellectual and social skills. One or two are even barristers.

Unfortunately, many mosque committees still seem reluctant to employ such British trained imams – perhaps because they press for realistic salaries, contracts and pension rights. In the ten years after 1997 some 420 imams from Pakistan have been granted visas to come to Britain to discharge their duties. A survey of 300 mosques in 2008[3] indicated that 92 per cent of the imams were foreign born and trained, with only 6 per cent speaking English as their first language. This creates a significant disconnect between many mosques and the 52 per cent of British Muslims under 25 years old, most of whom were born and educated in the UK.

It is this disconnect which is seen as a major factor in a process of radicalisation: British Muslims unable to get answers to their questions often look outside the mosque altogether. Recourse is had to 'Sheikh Google'! There is an emerging consensus that radical anti-Western ideas do not translate into violent extremism without the presence of three combustible factors: a Manichean world view (Muslim versus the *kuffar*); Islam understood as a supremacist political ideology; and a commitment to violence to achieve goals. Research into violent extremists in Britain suggests an additional nuancing of these variables: a sense of moral outrage at crimes committed against Muslims globally and locally; such grievances interpreted as part of a larger war of the West against Islam; and a perspective which resonates with personal experience of discrimination, whether real or imagined. A few individuals are then mobilised through extremist networks, whether face-to-face or online. Insofar as imams embody a rejectionist, anti-Western stance, they can be seen as part of the problem.

To address these issues, the government has adopted a twin-track policy. It excluded some 79 'preachers of hate' between 2005 and 2008 while seeking to enhance the capacity of imams to build more resilient cross-community links and to de-legitimise the extremist narrative. It has raised the bar for imams to get into Britain – they now have to speak the same level of English as would be expected of a foreign student applying for a post-graduate course of study – and supported the creation in June 2006 of the Mosques and Imams National Advisory Board (MINAB), inclusive of most sectarian traditions, to improve the governance of mosques and the training of imams.

Most significantly, it has funded a flagship project, the Radical Middle Way,[4] which organises visits by prominent Muslim scholars from across the world to preach against extremism and to urge engagement with mainstream society. Further, the Foreign and Commonwealth Office's Projecting British Islam has been designed to undercut the narrative of Islam versus the West by showcasing British Muslims as an integral part of the UK. Between 2005 and 2009, over 30 trips have been organised to Muslim countries, in which younger imams and religious leaders participate. The government has also funded an innovative Islam and Citizenship Education (ICE) project which has an advisory board of Islamic specialists drawn from most of the 'schools of thought'. This is being piloted in a range of mosques across the country.

These welcome initiatives, along with some imams moving out of their comfort zones to become chaplains and teachers, may, in the long term, equip a new generation to engage with wider society. However, the Radical Middle Way unwittingly exposed the paucity of front-rank British Muslim scholars at ease with wider society. There was only one British Pakistani scholar and he did not belong to either Barelwi or Deobandi tradition. As a result the Deobandis responded with their own roadshow.

Notes

1   See www.muslimsinbritain.org. (link accessed 19 June 2014)
2   Tariq Rahman (2008) 'Madrasas: the potential for violence in Pakistan?', in Jamal Malik (ed.), *Madrasas in South Asia: teaching terror?*, Abingdon: Routledge, pp. 61–84.
3   Ron Geaves (2008) 'Drawing on the Past to Transform the Present: Contemporary

Challenges for Training and Preparing British Imams', *Journal of Muslim Minority Affairs*, 28 (1), April: pp. 99–112.

4   www.radicalmiddleway.co.uk. (link accessed 19 June 2014)

References

Birt, Jonathan and Philip Lewis (2013) 'The pattern of Islamic reform in Britain: the Deobandis between intra-Muslim sectarianism and engagement with wider society', in Martin van Bruinessen and Stefano Allievi (eds), *In Producing Islamic Knowledge: transmission and dissemination in Western Europe*, Abingdon: Routledge, 91–120.

Geaves, Ron (2008) 'Drawing on the Past to Transform the Present: Contemporary Challenges for Training and Preparing British Imams', *Journal of Muslim Minority Affairs*, 28(1), April: pp. 99–112.

Lewis, Philip (2007) *Young, British and Muslim*, London: Continuum.

Rahman, Tariq (2008) 'Madrasas: the potential for violence in Pakistan?', in Jamal Malik (ed.), *Madrasas in South Asia: teaching terror?*, Abingdon: Routledge, pp. 61–84.

IMAMS IN FRANCE

Frank Peter

In France, public anxiety about imams and their contribution to the spread of Muslim religiosities considered to be in conflict with the nation's legal and cultural norms has been widespread since the late 1980s. In 1989, when the French government formulated its first policies aiming to integrate Muslim institutions into the French state, the first projects to set up French institutes for training imams also took shape. During *The Satanic Verses* affair, the mobilisation of French Muslims in response to the Fatwa by Ayatollah Khomeini in February 1989, however small, was perceived by the French state and public as an indicator of the capability of French and foreign Muslim religious authorities to mobilise French Muslims against the interests of the State. Set against the backdrop of the rapid growth and fragmentation of Muslim institutions in France since the early 1980s, this incident (and subsequent events such as the Gulf War of 1990–1, the Algerian crisis and civil war and the various headscarf affairs) put the twin issue of the representation of French Muslims and their religious authorities durably on the agenda of the French state. The term imam has quickly become the most recurrent symbol of the issue of religious authorities in French Islam. Over the past two decades, representations of the well-integrated imam and of his anti-republican counterpart have changed to some degree. However, the two-tier state policy of promoting (largely unsuccessfully) the creation of new kinds of training facilities for French imams while at the same time surveilling mosques and deporting imams accused of endangering the public order has continued.

Concerns about imams are founded upon the widespread notion that imams occupy a central position in Muslim communities comparable to that of priests, ministers or rabbis. This notion is in part dependent upon the confusion surrounding the term imam. In principle, the term imam when it is employed in the context of mosques simply designates the person leading the prayer. While this function can be professionalised this is often not the case in French mosques, contrary to what is assumed in public debates. According to figures from the French intelligence agency Direction Centrale des Renseignements Généraux from 2004, only 60 per cent of mosques have a full-time imam at their disposal. The group of people leading the prayer, including Friday prayer which comprises a sermon, fluctuates. Also, the assumption that French imams are figures of authority for Muslims has to be considered in light of the often precarious and dependent status of full-time employed imams. About two-thirds of French imams are working on a voluntary basis or are remunerated through donations. Those imams who receive a salary by their mosque are usually only paid the minimum wage, a fact which also reflects their weak position *vis-à-vis* the mosque committee. The residence status of imams – only 20 per cent of whom have French nationality – can also contribute to creating insecure working conditions for them. Finally, the position of imams inside French mosques has to be considered with regard to the diversity of languages spoken therein. While many mosque associations are dominated by people from specific countries this does not necessarily equate with linguistic homogeneity. The usage of French by imams is increasing, but communication is not always without problems in a multi-ethnic community which continues to receive sizeable numbers of new immigrants.

Concerns about the limited knowledge of French by imams are indeed widespread and a major reason for the mostly vague anxieties by the French public about imams. According to the above-mentioned survey, one-third of imams have 'difficulties of articulation' in French and another third only an 'average mastery of French'. The concern with this aspect of the imam's qualifications springs forth from the idea that weak knowledge of French prevents a proper embeddedness in French culture and society (which is mostly imagined in a uniform manner) and paves the way for processes of radicalisation. While the French public is, since the appearance of the first 'home-grown terrorists' in the 1990s, well aware of the existence of French-born radical Muslims, their conversion to this kind of Islam is regularly explained with reference to the influence of 'foreign imams' on young Muslims suffering from social exclusion.

The second related source of anxiety about imams lies in their reputed spread of extremist ideas. Compared to other European countries, there have been few cases of prominent imams accused of preaching an extremist Islam. In part, this has to do with the simple fact that very few imams are known to the broader public. This is in spite of the increasing number of imams who claim for themselves a position of religious authority as Islamic scholars and is also in direct contrast to the perception of imams as Muslim leaders held by the French public. Today the public representatives of French Islam are, by and large, people with limited knowledge in Islamic sciences who do not exercise the function of an imam. More generally, it has to be noted that the accusations levelled against imams often remain unspecified. The most important exception to this is Abdelkader Bouziane from Vénissieux. Bouziane had become notorious for giving an interview in 2004 in which he notably claimed that the Qur'an legitimates beating one's wife 'under certain conditions'. Bouziane also expressed his desire to see France become Islamic while rejecting violence and declaring that he 'always asked Muslims listening to me to respect the law of the land in which they live'.[1] This interview had the effect of accelerating a procedure of expulsion that had been started earlier and Bouziane was deported to Algeria in April 2004. Although Bouziane succeeded in returning to France after the law courts temporarily suspended the decree, he was deported for a second time shortly afterwards.

The fact that the incriminated statements of Bouziane are available contrasts with the usual scarcity of public information about the discourse of imams considered to be radical. This scarcity is also related to the fact that state action taken against radical imams consists mainly of expelling them through administrative decrees rather than initiating a juridical procedure whose outcome would be quite uncertain due to French and European laws on free speech and the general regulations concerning legal evidence in court procedures. While long-time foreign residents in France benefit under certain conditions from protection against expulsion, this latter measure is authorised when there is an 'imperious necessity for the security of the State or public safety'.[2] Expulsions are also legal in case of acts that threaten the 'fundamental interests of the State', are linked to 'activities of terrorist nature' or 'constitute acts of explicit and deliberate incitement to discrimination, hatred or violence against a specific person or group of persons'.[3]

Both articles are used to expel imams and other Muslim activists from France. The evidence marshalled by the State in order to initiate this kind of procedure often consists only of short anonymous reports produced by the intelligence agency. The fact that the authors and sources of these reports are unknown has often been criticised, but their usage continues in spite of pledges made to abolish them by previous ministers of the interior – Sarkozy and de Villepin. Not surprisingly the reported content of incriminated speeches is regularly contested by the imams as are the interpretation of these speeches and their illegal character. It is noteworthy that the deportation of many imams has been criticised by a variety of Muslim representatives from divergent orientations. The fact that foreign residents are, in these cases, treated differently from French citizens and the systematic avoidance of legal mechanisms by the State contribute to sustaining this criticism. Notwithstanding this opposition, a significant number of imams have been deported. No comprehensive numbers are available for the 1990s. However, according to government figures, there were 15 people identified as 'imams' among the 71 'Islamic fundamentalists' expelled from French territory between September 2001 and September 2006.[4] Furthermore, there are a significant number of cases where the decrees of expulsion are not executed for fear of public reaction and imams are instead put under surveillance. In 2007, 17 imams were placed in such a situation.[5]

Over the past two decades the French state has undertaken numerous attempts to restructure the training of imams in France and to reform the chaplaincy system in prisons and the armed forces. With regard to Muslim chaplains, the government is, indeed, slowly augmenting their number and started creating chaplaincies in the armed forces in 2006. The Institute al-Ghazali of the Algerian Grand Mosque of Paris, the preferred Islamic partner of the government, has been offering, since 2003, two-year courses specifically aimed at chaplains, and it has also been charged by the government with the training of military personnel who will take up the task of chaplain.

In 2008, a six-month complementary study programme – 'Religions, laïcité, interculturality' – held at the Catholic Institute of Paris and organised initially in cooperation with the Grand Mosque of Paris, was inaugurated. While the graduation of the first group of students was widely covered by French media, this was indeed the first time that any students have been awarded diplomas by the Institute al-Ghazali, which has been in existence, with interruptions, since 1994. The convention concluded between the Grand Mosque of Paris and the Catholic Institute is noteworthy, since it is the only concrete attempt by the French government in almost 20 years to create new study programmes for imams. However, it proved impossible to find a public university willing to cooperate with the Grand Mosque of Paris. The fact that the new programme is conducted at the Catholic Institute was criticised by many Muslims. On a regional level, some training in continuation programmes for imams, primarily French language classes, have been set up by public authorities. So far, in spite of regular debates, the government has not been willing to make use of the possibility to create a state-funded faculty for Islamic theology complementing those for Catholic and Protestant theology in Strasbourg.

The extensive political debates on the need to create new and state-approved training programmes for imams thus contrast with the meagre results of state policies. While the number of institutes of Islamic sciences is rapidly expanding all over France, very few of these institutes offer full-time training or aim to train imams, the main exception being the Institut Européen en Sciences Humaines (IESH).

Notes

1   *Lyon Mag*, April 2004.
2   Code de l'entrée et du séjour des étrangers et du droit d'asile, art. L 521–2.
3   Ibid., art. L 521–3. This last article was in fact modified in 2004 in reaction to the Bouziane case and the previous reference to discrimination based on the 'origin' or the 'religion' of persons replaced by the broader category 'specific person or group of persons'.
4   Human Rights Watch (2007) *Au nom de la prévention. Des garanties insuffisantes concernant les éloignements pour des raisons de sécurité nationale*, Vol. 19(3): p. 55. Available at http://hrw.org/french/reports/2007/france0607/france0607frwebw cover.pdf. Accessed 6 June 2007.
5   *Le Figaro*, 2 November 2007.

References

Human Rights Watch (2007) *Au nom de la prévention. Des garanties insuffisantes concernant les éloignements pour des raisons de sécurité nationale*, Vol. 19(3): p. 55. Available at http://hrw.org/french/reports/2007/france0607/france0607frwebwcover.pdf. Accessed 6 June 2007.
Mondot, Jean-François (2009) *Imams de France*, Paris: Editions Stock.

AGENTS OF RADICALISATION OR AGENTS OF MODERATION AND INTEGRATION? THE GERMAN DEBATE ABOUT IMAMS

Melanie Kamp

In Germany, public attention began to focus on imams after 9/11. Before the attacks, a debate had already existed among experts on different issues concerning Islamic instruction at public schools and the standards of religious education at German mosques, but the wider public had not been interested in mosques or their personnel. Moreover, the fact that some of the perpetrators of the attacks had lived in Germany raised questions about the ideology transmitted in German mosques and the danger of political and religious radicalisation occurring there. At the same time, the integration of Muslims and Islam, socially as well as legally, became a major topic on the political agenda. In this context the background, education and functions of imams became widely discussed. The public image of imams oscillates between two extremes. They are either regarded as agents of radicalisation or as agents of moderation and integration. How are these images justified?

Security agencies state that only 39 out of approximately 2,500 German mosques can be identified as places of radical teachings. There are also several cases of imams suspected of hate speech being expelled in the past. The most prominent example is the so-called 'Caliph of Cologne'. Additional cases from Berlin, Bremen and Bavaria have been reported in the media, but the exact number of deported imams remains unclear because these cases are not centrally registered.

Despite this relatively small number of incidents, the mosques in Germany arouse suspicion not only because of their close ties with either the Turkish state or transnational Islamic networks such as the Islamische Gemeinschaft Milli Görüş (IGMG), but also because of their all-encompassing social services. Mosques have become community and neighbourhood centres that care for the many needs of their believers. Sports activities, small businesses and educational services such as language training, computer classes and homework-tutoring for children, as well as special programmes for women such as sewing instruction and religious education, are often housed under the same roof. This multifunctional mosque is perceived as the home and infrastructure of a 'parallel society' that separates Muslims from the majority society and is therefore seen as an obstacle to the social integration of Muslim migrants. The use of foreign languages such as Turkish or Arabic in sermons as well as in ordinary communication adds to this image.

As the majority of imams still come from abroad, the debate focuses on their lack of language skills and their ignorance of the German context and the needs of believers, as well as their dissemination of religious ideas and values contrary to European standards. This criticism is partly shared by the Muslim communities because they are directly confronted with the communication problems between Muslim youth, German converts and the imams of foreign origin. The exact role and function of an imam depends very much on his status, his educational background and the congregation he is working for. His main responsibility is leading the communal prayer. This is a ritual function that every adult male Muslim who is familiar with the ritual prayer can perform. Therefore two types of imams are prevalent. Larger mosques employ religious scholars as full-time imams; in smaller mosques respected people from the congregation, knowledgeable lay men or men with a basic religious education lead the prayer on a voluntary basis. The majority of employed imams in Germany are employees of the Turkish Office of Religious Affairs and work for Diyanet İşleri Türk İslam Birliği (DITIB, Turkish–Islamic Union for Religious Affairs), the largest Islamic organisation, with roughly 900 mosques. Statistical data about the status of the imams from the remaining approximately 1,600 mosques are not available.

Generally speaking, the scope of the activities of imams is larger in Germany than, for example, in Turkey and corresponds with the multifunctional character of the mosques. In addition to their genuine religious tasks such as leading the communal prayer, preaching on Fridays, lecturing and teaching religion to children and adults, imams are also expected to perform representative functions because outsiders usually perceive the imam as the head of the congregation. Similar to Christian chaplains, imams are supposed to engage in interreligious dialogue activities, to represent the mosque in public and to cooperate with the municipal administration. Believers also seek their advice in religious matters as well as in more routine daily affairs. Imams give oral fatwas, act as mediators in family disputes and take up pastoral duties. Obviously their education, their language skills and their familiarity with German society largely determines if they are able to meet all these expectations. In larger mosques, additional personnel often manage responsibilities such as public relations, interreligious dialogue or neighbourhood activities.

The complementary stereotypes of imams as preachers of hate or agents of integration are derived from the idea that they are respected authorities within the Muslim communities who influence the religious concepts and the social behaviour of individual believers. This perception correlates with the self-image of the imams who see it as their main responsibility to impart the correct understanding of Islam to believers. According to them, their authority is based on their education, their religious knowledge and on their positive social relationship with the visitors of the mosque. Therefore, they regard their influence as limited to the people they personally know.[1] However, the authority of imams gets challenged in many ways. As mentioned above, they are usually dependent employees of the mosques. In case of conflict with the mosque administration or the congregation they risk losing their positions. This is not a mere theoretical issue but happens quite often and occasionally causes an imam or preacher to establish his own congregation. Reasons for conflict may be, for example, the salary, differences in the religious orientation of the imam and the congregation and all kinds of power struggles within the community. Furthermore, imams are forced to compete with new types of lay preachers and new media that are very popular, especially among young Muslims who inform themselves about religion on the internet or watch religious programmes on satellite television, listen to taped sermons and lectures or read the cheap booklets that are available at the mosques bookshops. The imams are critical about these forms of self-study, insisting that it is necessary to study with a learned man who can immediately correct any false interpretations of the religion.

Understandably, the German debate about imams focuses on the issue of imam training. The idea is to establish a suitable infrastructure for Islamic learning in order to put an end to the recruitment of imams from Turkey, the Middle East, North Africa and South Asia. Politicians hope that imams raised, educated and trained in Germany will have the necessary attitude, knowledge and social skills to perform an integrative role. Recently, chairs for the study of Islam, Islamic theology and Islamic religious pedagogy have been established at the universities of Münster, Osnabrück, Erlangen and Frankfurt am Main. For the time being, these institutions focus on teacher training for Islamic instruction at public schools, but imam training is part of future plans. Islamic organisations also wish to establish institutions for Islamic learning because they have a genuine interest in German-speaking imams who are familiar with the lifeworlds of the believers. Moreover, for most communities, except for those who are affiliated to the DITIB, the recruitment of imams from abroad is a difficult process. For them, the possibility of recruiting imams who hold German citizenship and who have been trained in Germany will be a real advantage. However, they criticise how the State authorities privilege teachers and curricula that the mosque communities do not approve of, such as was reflected by the hiring of Professor Muhammad Kalisch from the University of Münster, whose questioning of the historical existence of the Prophet goes far beyond traditional scholarship and the traditional understanding of most Islamic communities in Germany.

Respected imams have an influential position in their congregation and might contribute to the integration of their adherents. However, any reflection on the role of imams in processes of radicalisation or integration has to consider the delicate relationship among imam, mosque administration and community. At the same time, it has to take into account the competing authorities and the growing self-empowerment of Muslims who have become more and more self-determined in their quest for religious knowledge and guidance. For the success of any kind of university-based imam training it is crucial to find a balance between the expectations of the majority society and the expectations of Muslim communities, because they are the ones who will decide in the end if they employ these imams or not.

Notes

1   Melanie Kamp (2008) 'Prayer leader, counselor, teacher, social worker, and public relations officer – on the roles and functions of imams in Germany', in Ala al-Hamarneh and Jörn Thielmann (eds), *Islam and Muslims in Germany*, Leiden: Brill, pp. 133–60.

References

Kamp, Melanie (2008) 'Prayer leader, counselor, teacher, social worker, and public relations officer – on the roles and functions of imams in Germany', in Ala al-Hamarneh and Jörn Thielmann (eds), *Islam and Muslims in Germany*, Leiden: Brill, pp. 133–60.

Malik, Jamal (2005) 'Ausbildung und rolle der Imame in der moschee', in *Ausbildung von Imamen und Seelsorgern in Deutschland für die Herausforderungen von morgen. Tagung der Georges-Anawati-Stiftung*, 27: pp. 11–199.

Schiffauer, Werner (2000) *Die Gottesmänner. Türkische Islamisten in Deutschland*, Frankfurt am Main: Suhrkamp.

Schmid, Hansjörg (2007) 'Auf dem Weg zum Integrationslotsen? Das Rollenverständnis der Imame in Deutschland ändert sich', *Herder Korrespondenz*, 61(1): pp. 25–30.

IMAMS IN BELGIUM: INTEGRATION FACTOR OR RADICALISATION INSTRUMENT?

Mohamed El Battiui

A mosque designates a public place where God is collectively worshipped. Other terms designating a mosque are often used by Belgium's Muslim population: *jama'a* in Moroccan dialect, *msala* in Algerian dialect, *tamzida* in Berber and *camii* in Turkish.[1] In local usage these terms generally refer to a place where the faithful gather for the practice of Islam in the Belgian context. The term mosque has been increasingly replaced by the term 'centre' – *markaz* (in Arabic) or *merkez* (in Turkish) – depending on the respective activities. If most people go there to pray, then it remains a mosque. If most come for other activities, it is normally called a centre. This terminology is a recent phenomenon. More than just a simple change of name, it reflects a real desire for change.[2] These places have a specific area for prayer, but often for Qur'anic studies, Arabic or Turkish language learning as well. In addition, there is sometimes a cafeteria around which cultural and community life centres. Thus, they are multipurpose spaces.

The first mosques were founded in 1975 in the form of non-profit associations. Some were set up by movements associated with various Muslim traditions, although most resulted 'from the action of family heads on the basis of nationality, vicinity, village or small town of residence, and quite often on ethno-family ties'. Moreover, 'sometimes a place of worship is created by splitting off from a pre-existing mosque, for religious or more often political (notably in the case of Turkish mosques) or ethno-family reasons'.[3]

According to our sources and counts, there are 328 mosques in Belgium. Most are situated in Flanders, with 162 mosques; there are also 89 in Wallonia and 77 in Brussels.[4] Of the 77 mosques in Brussels, 36 are Arab and 22 Turkish. Most of the Arab mosques are financed and run by Berber populations from northern Morocco. Regarding the Turkish mosques, 60 per cent pertain to the Diyanet (Turkish state), 30 per cent to the Milli Görüş movement and the remaining 10 per cent to different minority groups such as the Alevis, Süleymanlı and different Sufi brotherhoods. Of the 89 mosques in Wallonia, 45 are Turkish and 44 Moroccan; of the 162 mosques in Flanders, 82 are Arab and 67 Turkish.

Imams in Belgium – diversified role against radicalisation

Since its election, the Exécutif des Musulmans de Belgique (Muslim Executive of Belgium) has sought to clarify current terminology with a view to establishing a hierarchy among imams, as follows:

Grand Imam of Belgium (Mufti) – able to issue fatwas (legal opinions).

Imam-khatib (first ranking imam) – concentrates on preaching, delivers the Friday sermon and opines on theological questions.

Imam-ratib (second ranking imam) – leads the five daily prayers and all other prayers.

Third ranking imam – a more technical function. Has charge of material required for worship and conditions at the place of worship. Also replaces the second ranking imam should the latter be absent.

Assistant imam – an auxiliary function, particularly for teaching religion and Arabic language to both adults and children.

Mujawwid – main duty is to recite portions of the Qur'an, especially during religious festivals.

Mu'adhdhin (muezzin in Turkish) – in charge of summoning the faithful to prayer.

The Diyanet imams account for the vast majority of Turkish imams. All hold a theology diploma and have at least four years of professional training. They are recruited and paid by the Turkish state. However, to benefit from the services of these imams (who are sent abroad for three-year periods), the faithful must pay a 60-euro fee. Other Turkish imams from the likes of Milli Görüş, Süleymanlı and Alevis are mostly trained at private institutions, some in Europe, having arrived as part of family migrations. These imams are paid through a system of fees and donations from the faithful.

For the imams of Moroccan mosques the situation is different. Most Muslims from Morocco are of rural origin and most of their mosques were founded along ethnic or family lines often based on 'clan solidarity'. That explains why so many of their imams are village imams. They are either classically trained by religious institutions or just traditionally trained in the village, limited to learning by heart the indispensable Qur'anic texts that suffice for prayers. Many Turkish and Moroccan imams either do not speak, or speak only a little of, the country's languages (French, Dutch and German). Furthermore, these imams are remunerated through fees paid by heads of families that benefit from the mosque's services, and sometimes by anonymous donations.

Mosques well guarded – but imams defenceless against radicalism

Belgian mosques are, in effect and above all, spaces transplanted, and are organised along ethnic or national lines. Most are 'traditional' mosques in the hands of first-generation immigrants who concentrate on the mosque's role as a prayer space and locale for socialising and Muslim education. This is a general scenario and these mosques do not meddle in politics in the broad sense of the word, which ensures they remain closed to any attempts at radicalisation. In the Moroccan mosques there is, nevertheless, a notable tendency among new generations of the faithful towards independence vis-à-vis the founding fathers. The diversification and schisms within this community have also been driven by events and developments in the Middle East (the second Palestinian Intifada, Iraq's occupation by the American army, the 2006 Lebanon war, etc). This divergence of views between the parents' and children's generations causes the latter to abandon the mosques in search of other spaces and preachers. Some of these youths are courted by Jama'at al-Tabligh in their neighbourhoods and in public parks, metro station exits and cafés, or by al-'Adl wa-l-Ihsan on university campuses. Others who are vulnerable and frustrated are recruited by neo-fundamentalists before being indoctrinated among the jihadi Salafists. Regarding the latter, imams are defenceless. These imams, who speak no Belgian national language and have no knowledge of the Belgian and European context, are no match for the radical militants.

The current situation of the mosques and imams in Belgium therefore gives cause for concern. Not all mosques typically have enough means to engage an imam. Vacant posts in mosques are often much-coveted by radical groups (neo-fundamentalists and jihadi Salafists) seeking contact with the faithful. This obliges us to state that it is more imperative than ever to speed up the process of recognising mosques, training imams in a Belgian and European context and having them paid by Belgium. To that end, a slowgoing though potentially fruitful process is coming to light with the birth of the Unions of Mosques and League of Imams. The main purpose of such 'unions' is to represent the imams' interests in matters of remuneration, residence and other vocation-related claims. They recently put forward the idea of organising a type of training that would encompass theology, general information and language learning. It is a promising start in the fight against radicalism.

Notes

1   Mohamed El Battiui and Meryem Kanmaz (2004) *Mosquées, imams et professeurs de religion islamique en Belgique. Etats de la question et enjeux*, Brussels: Fondation Roi Baudouin.
2   Ibid.
3   Felice Dassetto and Albert Bastenier (1984) *L'islam transplanté: vie et organisation des minorités musulmanes de Belgique*, Antwerp : EPO.
4   El Battiui and Kanmaz, *Mosquées, imams et professeurs de religion islamique* Brussels: Fondation Roi Baudouin..

References

Dassetto, Felice and Albert Bastenier (1984) *L'islam transplanté : vie et organisation des minorités musulmanes de Belgique*, Antwerp: EPO.
El Battiui, Mohamed and Meryem Kanmaz (2004) *Mosquées, imams et professeurs de religion islamique en Belgique. Etats de la question et enjeux*, Brussels: Fondation Roi Baudouin.
────── (2007) 'Islam et sécularisation', *La Pensée et les Hommes*, 65: pp. 55–65. Brussells: Université de Bruxelles.
Maréchal, Brigitte (2008) 'Courants fondamentalistes en Belgique', *Journal d'étude des relations internationales au Moyen-Orient*, 3(1), March : pp. 65–78.

IMAMS AND RADICALISATION IN THE NETHERLANDS

Firdaous Oueslati

In 2007, 475 mosques existed in the Netherlands, of which 50 per cent were Turkish, 40 per cent Moroccan and 10 per cent Surinamese. These three groups constitute the oldest, most established groups of Muslims in the Netherlands. Research carried out recently shows that of the approximately one million people who define themselves as Muslims – which is around 6 per cent of the Dutch population– only 210,000 pay a weekly visit to a mosque.[1]

Mosques are mostly frequented by people characterised by one or interrelated ethnicities. Most ethnic communities are served by imams of their own origin, although there is an occasional Syrian or Egyptian imam leading a Moroccan congregation. Friday sermons are delivered in the language of the countries of origin in the majority of the mosques; Turkish is used in Turkish mosques and Arabic in Moroccan mosques. However, for the majority of the Moroccans in the Netherlands Arabic is not the first language, but rather Tarifit – the Berber language spoken in the Rif area of northern Morocco. There are still very few initiatives – apart from in the Surinamese mosques – for delivering sermons in Dutch.

Being an imam in the Netherlands is not an easy task. In addition to miserable working conditions – a very low salary and insecure terms of employment – most imams that are employed have not received their education in the Netherlands. This means that there is often a language barrier besides the problem of lacking knowledge of, and expertise in, dealing with Dutch society. This problem is widely acknowledged among Muslim communities who want to employ an imam rooted in Dutch society, and it is expected that over time more and more imams will be home-grown, or at least Dutch speaking.

In Dutch public opinion the office of an imam is often equated with that of a Christian minister, priest or Jewish rabbi. This is one of the reasons why – as public debate has evolved – the imam has been assigned more and more tasks. In historical contexts – or in the countries of origin – the office of an imam would entail one or more of the following tasks: leading the congregation during the five daily prayers; delivering the Friday sermon; and giving advice on practical religious issues. Nowadays, however, public opinion along with politicians and policy makers expect the imam to take on several social tasks that originally were not at all part of the office. The imam is expected to play a positive role in the process of integration of the Muslim communities in Dutch society by being a role model to his community, organising events that bring together Muslims and non-Muslims and by acting as a youth worker solving problems involving

Muslim youngsters. Apart from this, his own community expects him to act as an inter-mediary in cases of marital discord, and to provide advice and counselling in all kinds of other situations.

Radicalisation

In the second half of the 1990s, processes of radicalisation among small segments of the Muslim communities became more and more the focus of public debate, although the topic had long before provoked the interest of Dutch intelligence services. Particularly from the beginning of the new millennium onwards, small groups of youngsters – mostly of Moroccan descent – clustered in groups with a Salafi orientation in which they intensely professed their faith and developed strong opinions on Dutch society: it was regarded as a society of infidels. Some of these groups were closely linked to mosques, but other yet smaller groups broke away from the mosque they were previously attached to, and continued their activities in the private spheres of their homes.

Whenever the issue of 'radical imams' is related to mosques, it is related to Moroccan mosques, as Turkish or Surinamese mosques are rarely touched by this phenomenon. Another noteworthy point is that, in most cases, those designated as radical imams and preachers are not from a Moroccan background. There are some exceptions to this, but the radical imams that are known to the Dutch public sphere are of a Syrian, Egyptian and Dutch (convert) origin. One of the interesting questions to be asked is why the constituency designated as radical imams or preachers in the Netherlands mostly consists of Moroccan youngsters and of freshly converted people from Dutch or other origins. Why are Turkish youngsters significantly less susceptible to radical ideologies and/or charismatic leaders? One explanation could be that – contrary to the Moroccan commu-nity – the Turkish community is already well-organised, and these organisations and associations provide the young with sufficient support in their processes of identity construction. In other words, they do not need to search for a group that gives them a sense of belonging and that articulates their relation to wider society.

There has been considerable attention to radical preachers or imams in the Dutch media during the last decade. Three different types of what Dutch public opinion considers to be radical preachers or imams may be distinguished: first, there are a small number of imams that champion Salafi thought as it was developed in the twentieth century on the Arabian peninsula by scholars such as Nasir ad-Din al-Albani, Ibn Baz and Ibn 'Uthaymin. These imams have been leading four established mosques, one in each of the following Dutch cities: Amsterdam, The Hague, Tilburg and Eindhoven. These imams are considered to be adherents of a radical ideology. Second, there has been a recent phenomenon of radical preachers who preach at peoples' homes – so-called *huiskamer-bijeenkomsten* (gatherings at home) – since they do not recognise the legitimacy of the existing mosques and their constituencies. The third instance in which imams are labelled radical is when they publicly declare views or opinions that go against a perceived consensus on certain values and standards in Dutch society, even though they are usually not counted among those who advocate a radical ideology. An example of this category is imam El Moumni, whose case will be discussed below.

Several incidents involving imams ignited public debate on the supposed detrimental effect radical imams have on Muslims and wider society. Among other incidents featuring imams, the following three were the main triggers in the discussion on imams, radical-isation and the question of compatibility of Dutch and Islamic values and the opportu-nities for coexistence.

First, there is the case of a Moroccan imam, Mr El Moumni, who was interviewed for a current affairs programme (NOVA, 3 May, 2001) on Dutch TV on the topic of homosexuality. He explained his point of view in Islamic terms, stating that same-sex relationships were reprehensible and warning Dutch society about this 'disease' which would disrupt the natural order of things and threaten its existence. Second, there is the case in which the same current affairs programme (NOVA, three broadcasts in June 2002) secretly recorded some sermons from so-called radical imams who, in addition to some political anti-American and anti-Israel statements, advocated a view of Dutch society in which Muslims were supposed to interfere as little as possible with non-Muslims, and Muslim women for their part should not interfere with public life. Finally there is the case of imam Salam – also one of those imams whose sermon was secretly recorded and broadcasted – who refused to shake hands with the Minister of Immigration and Integration Affairs when she attended a conference for imams organised with the aim of discussing the topic of 'freedom of speech' and issues related to the tense atmosphere resulting from the murder of Dutch filmmaker Theo van Gogh in November 2004.

In debates on these three instances, what becomes evident time and again – in addition to disproportionate media attention for 'radical imams'– is the underlying assumption that the main task of an imam is the reconciliation of Islamic teachings with the values of secular Dutch society.

Imams are held responsible for the smooth integration of Muslim communities into Dutch society, even though they are ill-equipped for this task, and one might wonder whether there are more obvious choices to be charged with this. Apart from the fact that it is undesirable to hold a small group of people accountable for the behaviour of larger groups, one might wonder to what extent the voice of an imam is authoritative and of overriding importance to a large part of the various Muslim communities. It is, of course, possible – and within their range – to play an auxiliary role in the process of integration, but it would be highly unrealistic to expect the imam to be one of the key figures.

Can imams prevent the radicalisation of elements of Muslim youth? In most cases it is very hard for imams to connect to youngsters who are isolating themselves from the rest of society. In this process they slowly withdraw from the view of the imam, who will not be able to reach out to them anymore. Moreover, they regard the imam to be part of the system they are dissociating from which, in their eyes, strips from him all legitimacy. Radicalisation of elements of Muslim youth, as it were, will take place outside the view and range of influence of the imam.

Notes

1 *Nederland Deugt* (2007) pp. 53, 57.

References

Boender, Welmoet (2007) *Imam in Nederland, Opvattingen over zijn religieuze rol in de samenleving*, Amsterdam: Bert Bakker.

Oudenhoven, Jan Pieter van, A. Blank, F. Leemhuis, M. Plomp and A. F. Sluis (2008) *Nederland Deugt*, Rijksuniversiteit Groningen: Instituut voor integratie en sociale weerbaarheid.

IMAMS AND PROCESSES OF RADICALISATION IN DENMARK

Inge Liengaard

Mosques in Denmark are, to a large extent, organised along ethnic lines. The ethnic communities who have been most successful in organising prayer rooms and mosques are the ones who have spent the longest time in Denmark: the Turks and the Pakistanis who arrived in the early 1970s, and the Arabs who arrived from the mid-1980s. While both the Turkish and Pakistani religious environments are dominated by transnational organisations (e.g. Diyanet, Milli Görüş and Minhaj ul-Qur'an), the Arab mosque communities are much more local and fragmented. While Arab imams or mosques may have ties to Salafi and/or Wahhabi networks or to the Muslim Brotherhood (MB), they are rarely formal members of international organisations. Only a small number are affiliated with Hizb ut-Tahrir, Jama'at al-Tabligh and the Ahbash.

The terms 'mosque' and 'imam' have within recent years become a part of the Danish vocabulary but, as most non-Muslim Danes are unfamiliar with the Islamic tradition, an imam is often understood as the Islamic version of an average Danish Protestant minister, who has received his education at a public university. This analogy between a Christian pastor and an imam is, however, often misleading for several reasons.

Only about half of the approximately 114 prayer rooms and mosques in Denmark have an imam who is formally trained in Islamic sciences. For the remaining half, the person who performs the basic duty of the imam – that is, leading the prayer – is a man from the mosque community who has taken on this responsibility. Such people do not consider themselves as holders of a religious office and normally do not take on other religious responsibilities other than leading the prayer. This is contrary to the mosques that have religiously educated staff.

Most of the imams who have religious qualifications, have arrived in Denmark in one of two ways: either they are employed by a transnational religious organisation, in which case they are in Denmark on a time limited 'preachers' visa' of two to four years, or they have obtained refugee status. It follows from the aforementioned organisational pattern that the educated Turkish and Pakistani imams are often in Denmark on a preachers' visa, while the Arab imams have arrived in Denmark as refugees.

The majority of the formally educated imams have acquired their religious qualifications in a Muslim country, but the types of qualifications vary considerably, from summer courses at Indian Deobandi universities or mosque classes to many years of study at Al-Azhar, Medina University, *hawzas* in Qom or Turkish *ilahiyats*. Having religious qualifications, though, seems to be an important prerequisite in being accepted as an imam with religious authority, since all the influential imams in Denmark make reference to such qualifications when explaining their own position within the religious community. With the recognition as a religious authority several duties follow: not only do these imams lead the prayer and give the Friday sermon, they also give Islamic classes in the mosque and give religious advice to those who seek it.

Public interest has been concerned especially with the influence of mosque organisations or imams if they hold points of view that are considered to be contrary to Danish values. Danish values are, in this context, understood to secure gender equality and, depending on the position of the discussant, to be either secular or Protestant Christian.

The public interest in the positions and influence of the imams grew during the Cartoon Crisis in 2006, when four Danish imams of Arab origin travelled to the Middle East in order to make politicians, religious scholars and the general public aware of the cartoons that had been published in a Danish newspaper. This prompted questions in Denmark regarding the loyalty of these Danish Muslims. The fact that they were imams, holding positions from where they could influence the opinion of ordinary Muslims, was seen as especially dissatisfying.

However, although imams undoubtedly occupy an influential position in the Islamic field in Denmark, it is important to remember that their impact is limited to those Muslims who recognise them as an authority. There are no reliable numbers as to how many of the approximately 200,000 Muslim migrants and their descendants actually visit a mosque, but in a research project conducted in 2006 it was estimated that approximately 5–7 per cent of people who originate from a Muslim country participate in the Friday prayer on a given Friday.[1] Another report from 2007 concluded that 46 per cent of people originating in a Muslim country seldom or never visit a mosque, nor frequent an imam for personal advice.[2]

The differences in patterns of institutionalisation have affected public views concerning radicalism and radicalisation in the mosques. As regards the Turkish and the Pakistani communities, the criticism has been directed against the organisations rather than the people themselves, while it is specific imams who have been criticised within the Arab environment.

The criticism directed against organisations and imams who are believed to be radical are articulated by others who have different agendas. In some cases, such as the Hizb ut-Tahrir who have been very active in Denmark, the criticism has been unanimously launched by media, politicians and public commentators. In other instances, for example Milli Görüş, the criticism has been less widespread. The explanation behind this is probably that, although Milli Görüş expresses a religio-political agenda with reference to Turkey, the organisation does not promote these views with reference to a Danish context. Accusations of Islamic fundamentalism and radicalisation against Milli Görüş are thus not based on their deeds in a Danish context but on their transnational ties to Turkey. Often their critics are concerned with what they see and understand as a growing Islamisation of Western European societies.

It is imams and religious ideology from the Sunni Arab communities who have attracted most public attention when discussing Islamic radicalisation in Denmark. The explanation behind this is complex. One reason is related to the processes of institutionalisation in Denmark. While most organisations have a rather stable position and seem to think that they do not gain from attracting public interest: their imams tend to keep a low profile in public debates. By contrast, the Sunni Arab mosque communities are often local institutions, organised around a religious leader. This has caused less stability and increased competition among the Sunni Arab imams. As a consequence they are more prone to display controversial religious viewpoints publicly.

Another explanation behind the public interest in Sunni Arab imams is the fact that several of the prominent imams have been identified as sympathisers of the Muslim Brotherhood (MB) or Salafis. Some have been affiliated with the MB while they lived in their country of origin, one imam was educated at the Institut Européen des Sciences Humaines in Château Chinon, France, while another is a former member of The European Council for Fatwa and Research (ECFR). Both institutions are often seen as working in the tradition of the MB.

Several of the imams related to the MB have attracted public attention: Abu Bashar, who was one of only two paid prison imams in Denmark, took part in the 'imam delegation' that travelled to the Middle East when the Cartoon Crisis was escalating. Muhammad Fuad al-Barazi has given a fatwa condemning female circumcision, while the late imam Abu Laban suggested that paying 'blood money' could be part of a juridical solution if a murder case involved Muslims. This suggestion caused an intense public debate in which professors in criminal law were acting as both proponents and opponents.

While these imams share the conviction that Islam would constitute a better societal framework than liberal values do, they also stress the societal responsibility of Muslims wherever they live. They often mention the Islamic duty of keeping a contract, arguing that Muslims in Denmark, by taking on residence or citizenship in this country, have concluded a contract with the Danish state which they are obliged to keep according to the respective Qur'anic injunction. Their stance on violent actions as a legitimate means of promoting the Islamic cause is complex and seems to be a matter of geographical context. While they define the use of violence in the Palestinian conflict as a legitimate means of self defence, their criticism of Denmark or other Western countries does not entail legitimation of violence.

The Salafi ideology is a newer ideological trend among Danish Muslims. Its actual circulation and influence in mosques is not easy to estimate, although observers agree that it has gained momentum in recent years. In 2006 two influential mosques, the *Lighed-og Broderskabsforeningen* in Århus and *Det islamiske Trossamfund på Fyn* in Odense, had imams who openly subscribed to Salafi ideas, while three other large mosques had imams who have expressed ideas close to that of Salafism. Furthermore, a couple of small mosques with no educated imam propagated Salafi ideas.

Like the imams associated with the MB, the Salafi imams voice their criticism against Western societies, but their arguments tend to focus on gender issues and morality rather than politics. These imams do not publicly encourage Muslims to engage in violent acts in Denmark (although some do encourage Muslims to leave Denmark and resettle in a Muslim country), but several people who are currently on trial, accused of having planned violent actions, either in Denmark or in other European countries, have frequented mosques where Salafi imams preached.

In the end it remains unclear what role imams and mosques play in the Islamic radicalisation that undoubtedly takes places within certain Muslim segments in Denmark. Accusations of radicalisation may be made fairly easy, since what is meant by 'radicalisation' remains vague. In public debates, the view that a society based on Islamic principles is an ideal worth hoping for is quite often labelled 'radical' or 'fundamentalist'. With such a definition most of the Pakistani and Arab imams, as well as some Turkish, could be characterised as radicals.

If radical Islam is understood as a worldview that sees Islam as a complete and authentic way of life, both on an individual and a societal level, and whose adherents seek to implement this with whatever means they find necessary, one finds fewer than a handful of prominent imams in Denmark who would agree with such an understanding. Whether Muslims are introduced to radical ideas in a mosque, or to what extent such ideas are nurtured, is still difficult to say.

Notes

1   Lene Kühle (2006) *Moskeer i Danmark. Islam og muslimske bedesteder*, Højbjerg: Univers.
2   Tænketanken om udfordringer for integrationsindsatsen i Danmark (Think tank on the challenges for integration in Denmark), 2007.

References

Kühle, Lene (2006) *Moskeer i Danmark. Islam og muslimske bedesteder*, Højbjerg: Univers.
Tænketanken om udfordringer for integrationsindsatsen i Danmark (2007) *Værdier og normer blandt udlændinge og danskere*, Copenhagen: Ministeriet for flygtninge, indvandrere og integration.
www.nyidanmark.dk/bibliotek/publikationer/rapporter/2007/taenketanken_vaerdier_og_normer.pdf. (link no longer functional)

IMAMS AND RADICALISATION IN SPAIN

Jordi Moreras

When, in May 2004, the Spanish Minister of the Interior issued a call to 'control imams in small mosques, which are the cradle of Islamic fundamentalism',[1] he was legitimising the theory that linked imams with the radicalisation of Muslim groups in Spain. As one of the collateral effects of 11 March, the relationship inferred by José Antonio Alonso gave credibility to the permanent suspicion of imams and also further intensified (police and media) pressure on them. Spanish society as a whole still remembered very clearly the news of the sentence imposed on the Imam of Fuengirola, Mohamed Kamal Mustafa, for his work *La mujer en el Islam* (Women in Islam), which was interpreted by the judge as a declaration in favour of gender violence. This was the first time a legal sentence had been imposed on an imam in Western Europe, and served as a paradigmatic reference that revealed the direct relationship between imams and the radicalisation of Muslim communities.

This chapter re-examines this relationship, based on the assumption that there are consistent arguments for questioning the theory that there is a direct link between these religious figures of authority and radicalisation processes. For this purpose, first a brief definition is proposed of what is understood as 'radicalisation', as a contextual process involving different agents and circumstances. This is followed by a description of the conditions in which an Islamic religious authority is exercised in Spanish society, emphasising its precariousness and fragmentation. Finally, the circumstances concurring in the development of this imam–radicalisation relationship are examined. These circumstances are based on a series of preconceptions that must be examined, since these inspire public administration action aimed at Muslim communities.

Radicalisation is a social process that entails a change in the doctrinal and referential paradigm of a specific community in its relationship with its social context. This process causes such communities to become gradually distanced from their social environment and also leads to the development of a different and reactive identity. This process does not in itself prompt a shift towards the use of violence, as suggested by security advocates. The way in which Islam has been constructed in Spain in recent decades has given rise to a scenario in which these ruptures and radicalisation processes arise and develop. The circumstances and the agents driving these processes are different. The prominent doctrinal leadership role adopted by imams in these community contexts may be involved in these processes. However, a series of circumstances must coincide for this to occur, with the participation of other actors and institutions within and outside the community.

Spanish society considers that imams, due to their influence, interrupt the process of integration embarked upon previously by collectives of Muslim immigrants. The 'arrival of the imam' is interpreted as evidence that this process has been inverted. The increasing visibility of elements associated with the religiousness of these groups (especially clothing habits or demands in public establishments) is seen as evidence of the imams' influence, but this ignores the fact that this visibility – together with other factors such as the hiring of imams for local oratories – evidences the development of a community construction process.

Imams' influence on their collectives of reference is used as an argument to infer that they may condition or guide their communities towards specific doctrinal interpretations. The problem is this alleged religious authority of imams has an extremely contextual dimension, which entails accepting that they may not have such a direct or conditioning influence. The way in which this religious authority has been constructed in Muslim communities in Spain reveals its fragile and fragmented nature. The difficulties inherent in the development of a specific field of religion and its adaptation to Spanish society have strongly conditioned the forms of this authority, to the extent of revealing the appropriateness of questioning that supposed influence and impact on the group. The weakness of the mosque as a social institution undermines the figure of the imam as a religious authority. Furthermore, the imam's traditional basic education, which is inappropriate for performing their function in non-Muslim societies, their scarce knowledge of the social environment (with poor knowledge of the Spanish language) and their job insecurity (very few are hired as imams by their communities), show that the aforementioned leadership is taken for granted.[2]

Nevertheless, evidence of this institutional fragility is not normally recognised openly. In the survey of 2,000 Muslim immigrants carried out in October 2008 by the Spanish Ministry of the Interior, the following question was included: 'To what extent do you follow the advice and/or guidance of the imams at your mosque?' 59 per cent of the interviewees claimed that they followed their teachings strictly, while the rest said that they followed them only a little or not at all. It is important to bear in mind that the denial of the imam's authority would constitute openly questioning their traditional consideration as figures of reference, hence these results must be put into the context of relations of authority that develop between Muslim collectives and these traditional and other emerging figures.

The use of this traditional authority is a sufficiently valuable resource not to be claimed by existing doctrinal interpretations in Islam in Spain. An example of this would be the *salafiya*,[3] in which imams are fundamental for 'doctrinally redirecting' the group and preventing it from straying from strict adherence to the revealed message. Their role in education and preaching is claimed over and above simply acting as guides during collective worship; hence, the importance of the *khutba* (sermons) and conferences, and the role of an authority based on knowledge of doctrine.

The theories linking imams to radicalisation tend to highlight cases in Spain in which people acting as imams in local mosques have been arrested in anti-terrorist operations. According to this theory, such cases evidence the active link of imams with violent radicalisation activities. Such theories often fail to consider that the vast majority of these people are released without any charges shortly after their arrest.[4] Considering the violent radicalisation of Muslim communities in Spain as a collective process fuelled by the actions of imams would be to deny evidence of how such processes develop. Four conditions concur in these processes: they are developed discretely, on a small scale, very specifically and through the intervention of agents who lack the public condition of imams in mosques. Other figures with prior experience of radicalisation and continuing with a firm activist commitment seem to be better candidates than imams for carrying out this co-optation process.

The existing confusion between pastoral influence and indoctrination means that the notion of imams' alleged involvement in such activities cannot be ruled out categorically. Their actions and declarations are still monitored closely and their surveillance by different intelligence or information services continues to cast a shadow of suspicion over imams, making the situation very uncomfortable and uneasy for them.

In recent years Spanish public administrations have launched initiatives to prevent radical ideas penetrating Muslim collectives, by supervising the religious activities carried out at prisons after discovering that these were places where Islamist political proselytism was having a stronger influence. The voluntary nature of these religious activities – in which the Tablighi movement was particularly involved – was seen by prison authorities as a weak point for the penetration of these ideas; hence, these monitoring activities were organised with the representative Islamic entities in Spain, in order to establish a prior ideological filter.[5] Security pressures have re-defined the imam's role in prisons, attributing greater importance to cult matters (leading prayer) or personal guidance (catering for the demands of prisoners), than to proselytism (sermons, conferences or dissemination of doctrinal documentation). The imams responsible for this task are also entrusted with the task of actively containing such radical ideas, which at the same time allows them to demonstrate their 'moderate' doctrinal profile.

Second, another initiative to prevent the potential radicalisation of imams has been to offer them specific education activities. The first initiatives, geared to overcoming these imams' shortcomings in terms of language and knowledge of Spanish society, are being complemented by other initiatives that include more fundamental material on legislation, human rights and democratic procedures. This is based on the clearly naive assumption that theoretical education or training on the functioning of a democratic society can serve as an antidote to counteract the spread of doctrinal radicalisation. If this were the sole objective of that education or training it would hardly improve conditions for the professional exercise of Islamic worship in Spain, something that Muslim communities strongly desire.

Notes

1 *El País*, 2 May 2004.
2 Jordi Moreras (2009) *Garantes de la tradición. Viejos y nuevos roles en el ejercicio de la autoridad religiosa islámica en contexto migratorio. El caso de Cataluña*, Ph.D thesis, Universitat Rovira i Virgili: Spain
3 Ibid.
4 The study by Jordan (2007) includes a table listing the 16 imams arrested in anti-terrorist operations in Spain between 2004 and 2007. Eleven of them were later released without charge, while the remainder are awaiting trial.
5 Antonio Baquero and Jesus Albalat (2007) 'El Islam irrumpe en prisión', *El Periódico de Cataluña*, December.

References

Baquero, Antonio and Jesus Albalat (2007) 'El Islam irrumpe en prisión', *El Periódico de Cataluña*, December.

Jordan, Javier (2007) 'Las redes yihadistas en España: evolución desde el 11-M', *Athena Intelligence Journal*, 2(3): pp. 77–102.

Moreras, Jordi (2009) *Garantes de la tradición. Viejos y nuevos roles en el ejercicio de la autoridad religiosa islámica en contexto migratorio. El caso de Cataluña*, Ph.D thesis, Universitat Rovira i Virgili: Spain.

MUSLIMS IN PRISON AND PROCESSES OF RADICALISATION: THE UNITED KINGDOM

Muzammil Quraishi

The Statistical Background

The Muslim prison population has experienced significant expansion since records began. Between the years 1995 and 2005 the Muslim prison population grew by more than 150 per cent[1] and presently accounts for approximately 11 per cent of the prison population in England and Wales.[2] In September 2000, on average, the female and male Muslim prison population represented 3 per cent and 7 per cent respectively of the total prison population.[3] The prison population should be contrasted against the percentage of Muslims in the general British population. The census of 2001 revealed that 2.7 per cent (1.6 million out of a total population of 58,789,000) of the UK population declared Islam as their faith.[4] This therefore illustrates significant overrepresentation of Muslims in prison relative to their density in the general population.

The British Muslim population is ethnically diverse, however the majority of Muslims claim South Asian ethnicity with Pakistani (658,000) and Bangladeshi (260,000) populations accounting for approximately 918,000 of the 1.6 million Muslims in the UK. Furthermore, 8.5 per cent of the Indian population in the UK are also Muslim.[5] Therefore, one may expect the ethnic composition of British Muslim populations to be reflected in the incarcerated population. However, in 2001, the Home Office released statistical analysis of the prison population based on religious affiliation and ethnicity, which revealed that, in 2000, Black Muslims in prison constituted 34 per cent of the total Muslim inmate population while Asian Muslims constituted 42 per cent.[6] The percentage of Muslims who declared black ethnicity in the 2001 census is very small, with Black Caribbean Muslims recorded as 0.29 per cent and Black African Muslims as 0.09 per cent of the total Muslim population of the UK.[7] Although no statistics on conversion to Islam in prison have been published, the evaluation above suggests that many black prisoners are converts to Islam. The statistical picture is partly responsible for government and media engagement with this issue.

Media and Government Perspective

The British media has produced many articles raising concerns about potential radicalisation among Muslim prisoners and problems prompted by a rising Muslim prison population. The articles are, in part, reactions to the release of official reports and observations from prison-related organisations and watchdogs including the Prison Officers Association, the Independent Board of Monitors and HM Inspectorate of Prisons.

The concerns raised centre on the perceived vulnerability of prisoners to radical influences from extremist inmates (including those detained pursuant to terrorist offences) and in some rare cases from prison imams. It is worth emphasising that the reports tend to focus on maximum security prisons or those where the Muslim prison population is particularly large and are not representative of the prison estate as a whole. HMP Belmarsh has figured prominently in the media on account of some of its high-profile inmates while HMP Wandsworth has attracted attention over allegations of rival Muslim factions and disagreements between Muslim prisoners and an imam.

The government perceives the problem of radicalisation as a genuine and escalating issue, with the Ministry of Justice predicting a tenfold rise in the number of terrorist suspects held in prisons in England and Wales over the next ten years.[8] Policy has been recently extended by the Home Office to provide a nationwide 'de-radicalisation' programme and the deployment of £12.5 million for countering terrorism, including counter-radicalisation in prisons.[9] Furthermore, the Metropolitan Police Authority has acknowledged the operation of discreet 'de-radicalisation' teams headed by Islamic scholars to theologically de-programme extremist prisoners in some UK prisons.[10]

Experiences of Muslim prisoners

It must be stressed that what is understood by the term 'radicalisation' is highly contested. In the present context the term is used to describe the adoption and promotion of a type of Islam which advocates the rigorous application of Islamic law and morals upon non-Muslim populations to bring about spiritual and social change. The prison authorities are essentially concerned with incidents whereby violence and/or criminality are promoted as appropriate vehicles to bring about such change. How one monitors prison populations for outward signs of radicalisation remains a complex and vexing issue. The adoption of practices such as growing a beard or praying more regularly could be misunderstood as steps towards radicalisation. Distinctions have to be made when assessing behaviour among Muslim prisoners, between occasional spontaneous, frustrated outbursts such as praising well-publicised terrorist groups, and the steady absorption of a politicised Islam which produces sustained radicalisation within the adherent.

It follows, therefore, that individuals specifically detained for terrorist offences are more likely to have been exposed to the processes of radicalisation pre-incarceration rather than during their prison experience. In the maximum security prisons where such prisoners are held contact with fellow prisoners is infrequent. For example, prisoners do not share cells, and they have significant restrictions upon visits and recreation.

Furthermore, the opportunities which exist in British prisons for the process of radicalisation to be initiated must be questioned. The day-to-day existence of the majority of Muslim prisoners revolves around mundane domestic matters such as arranging for visits, receiving correspondence, applying for educational or rehabilitative courses, or disputes with fellow prisoners or staff. The opportunities for religious instruction or study depend upon many factors, such as the category of security of the institution, the category of security of the individual prisoner, the demographics of the prisoner population and the geographical location of the institution. Irrespective of these factors, the level of Islamic religious instruction across the prison estate tends to be elementary, concentrating upon teaching Qur'anic Arabic and how to perform obligatory prayers. Arguably, the immersion in intellectual theological debates and politicisation which sustained radicalisation requires is absent for the majority of Muslim prisoners. The experiences of Muslims who have converted to Islam in prison also tend to reflect the positive guidance their faith has provided for them rather than demonstrate radical indoctrination.

While the true extent of radicalisation among Muslim prisoners remains unknown, evidence of discrimination towards them within institutions can only serve to exacerbate tensions between staff and among inmates. Many Muslim prisoners, while belonging to a religious minority, are also ethnic minorities and so they are often unsure whether their maltreatment is due to their faith or ethnic identities. Discrimination from staff tends to be indirect and contextual, which means that it may occur in some institutions and not in others. The forms of discrimination may involve prisoners being prevented from joining congregational prayers or being supplied *halal* food which is not authenticated. Other forms of harassment include being subject to more-than-average cell searches, being closely 'policed' during Ramadan, or having religious articles such as texts, clothing and prayer mats defiled by staff and non-Muslim cellmates. There is the potential here for Muslim prisoners to feel that, in addition to their individual honour, it is Islam which is being dishonoured by such actions. The experiences of discrimination may be interpreted by some prisoners as concomitant with broader British domestic and foreign policies which target Muslim populations.

Imams

Prison imams were once termed Visiting Ministers which reflected the fact they occupied temporary positions. They were recruited mainly on a voluntary basis and their duties essentially involved leading congregational prayers and ad hoc advice to prison management on Muslim matters such as diet, prayers, religious holidays and funerals. Since the late 1990s, the situation for prison imams has altered quite significantly with the establishment of the Office of the Muslim Advisor to the Prison Service and the recruitment of Muslim chaplains on salaried contracts in prisons with sizeable Muslim prison populations. The shift to standardised recruitment procedures, job specifications and expanding the role of the imam to include statutory duties comes with benefits and disadvantages. The benefits include rewarding Islamic scholars, particularly those born and educated in the UK, with a clear career path. Furthermore, Muslim chaplains are able to sit on more internal management committees and make inroads in informing rehabilitation policies and programmes which have often excluded faith-based perspectives. Importantly, Muslim chaplains should not be viewed as the agents of radicalisation but more accurately as intermediaries in checking extremism.

Such benefits have to be balanced against the risk that the institutionalisation of Muslim chaplains may undermine the faith-based pastoral provision traditionally provided by imams in prison. Muslim prisoners may increasingly view the Muslim chaplain as part of the prison management and correspondingly are less likely to view him as a confidante. This may provide a vacuum for more radical prisoners to occupy, although precisely how much influence they can wield over fellow prisoners given the general constraints of prison is debatable.

Concluding comments

The historical relationship in the UK between Muslim (South Asian) populations and crime has been one of relative conformity and under-representation in official criminal statistics. Many factors have been offered to explain the rise in the recorded Muslim prisoner population since the 1990s, including demographic contexts and extra-legal factors in policing and sentencing. An exploration of the way in which particular populations are processed by the criminal justice system has the potential to reveal discriminatory practices which contribute to the overrepresentation of such populations in official criminal statistics. Youthful working-class urban populations have always been the subject of over-policing. The Muslim British population has a youthful demographic profile and the majority reside in urban areas. Therefore, if recent counter-terrorism strategies are also factored into the equation, a drift towards overrepresentation of Muslim male youth in criminal statistics is a likely consequence.

The picture is undoubtedly complex, but a moral panic over radicalisation only oversimplifies such complexity and acts as a distraction from engagement with the pressing issues of faith-based initiatives in rehabilitation and resettlement for a predominantly non-radical Muslim prison population.

Notes

1 Home Office (2006) Home Office Statistical Bulletin 18/06. Offender Management Caseload Statistics 2005, London: Home Office Research Development and Statistics.
2 Ministry of Justice (2007) Statistical Bulletin. Offender Management Caseload Statistics 2006, London.
3 Farid Guessous, Nick Hooper and Uma Moorthy (2001) *Religion in Prisons 1999 and 2000*, London: Home Office Research Development and Statistics.
4 Office for National Statistics (2003b). *Census April data set 2001: Religion by Ethnicity*, London.
5 Office for National Statistics (2003a). *Census April 2001*, London.
6 Guessous et al. *Religion in Prisons*.
7 Office for National Statistics. *Census April data set 2001*.
8 Alan Travis (2007) 'Tenfold rise in terrorism prisoners forecast', The *Guardian*, November.
9 Home Office (2006) Home Office Statistical Bulletin 18/06. Offender Management Caseload Statistics 2005, London.
10 Metropolitan Police Authority (2007) *Counter Terrorism: The London Debate*, London: MPA.

References

Beckford, James and Sophie Gilliat (1998) *Religion in Prison: Equal Rites in a Multi-faith Society*, Cambridge: Cambridge University Press.
Beckford, James, Daniele Joly and Farhad Khosrokhavar (2005) *Muslims in Prison: Challenge and Change in Britain and France*, Hampshire / New York: Palgrave Macmillan.
Guessous, Farid, Nick Hooper and Uma Moorthy (2001) *Religion in Prisons 1999 and 2000*, London: Home Office Research, Development and Statistics.
Home Office (2006) *Home Office Statistical Bulletin 18/06. Offender Management Caseload Statistics 2005*, London.
Marranci, Gabriele (2007) 'Living Islam in prison: faith, ideology and fear', *Media Releases*, University of Aberdeen, April. Available at http://www.abdn.ac.uk/mediareleases/release.php?id=889. Accessed 3 June 2008.

Metropolitan Police Authority (2007) *Counter Terrorism: The London Debate*, London: MPA.

Ministry of Justice (2007) *Statistical Bulletin. Offender Management Caseload Statistics 2006*, London.

Office for National Statistics (2003a) *Census April 2001*, London.

—— (2003b) *Census April data set 2001: Religion by Ethnicity*, London.

Quraishi, Muzammil (2005) *Muslims and Crime: A Comparative Study*, Aldershot: Ashgate.

Spalek, Basia and Salah El-Hassan (2007) 'Muslim Converts in Prison', *The Howard Journal of Criminal Justice,* 46 (2): pp. 99–114.

Travis, Alan (2007) 'Tenfold rise in terrorism prisoners forecast', The *Guardian*, November.

MUSLIMS IN PRISON AND PROCESSES
OF RADICALISATION: DENMARK

Jon Alix Olsen

According to Danish 'law concerning the execution of sentences', every inmate has the right to contact and have a conversation with a representative from his or her religious community. However, the right of inmates to contact representatives of their religion has been institutionalised in the context of the state church system and thereby limited – institutionally – to one religious community. In the rare cases where representatives from other religious societies have been needed, the minister of religion or the prison governor has made the required connections when possible. Today approximately 19 per cent of the inmates in Danish prisons are Muslim (according to a survey conducted by the Danish Prison and Probation Service in 2006),[1] and Danish prisons have begun employing imams. At the time of the survey, three of the seven maximum security prisons in Denmark had imams associated with them, two of the eight low security prisons had agreements with local mosques that prisoners could attend their Friday prayer, and of the 37 remand prisons only those placed at the above-mentioned prisons had any contact with an imam. Since the debate on Islam in prison began in late 2006 the Prison Service has gone from 'encouraging the prisons to employ imams', a policy which was followed by neither strategy nor funding, to having declared that 20 Muslim chaplains will be hired in 2009. The guidelines for this are still in the making.

One concern in the debate on Muslim chaplains in prison has been whether they might induce processes of radicalisation. So far only one study has examined this question on the basis of interviews with prison inmates of Muslim background who converted to Islam in prison as well as with Muslim chaplains.[2] In dealing with this subject, it is important to stress the special conditions inside penitentiary institutions which trigger processes of prisonisation. Inmates organise in strongly demarcated groups and often experience polarisation in the process of distancing themselves from some groups in order to cement their affiliation with others. The inmates are part of an environment in which social interaction is organised in small closed groups, based on visible signs and symbols, and where marked loyalty to one's own group is paired with a high degree of hostility towards others. Prisonisation and radicalisation are similar and mutually support each other in so far as both favour the polarisation of a given group's relationship to the outside and the adoption of an exclusionary attitude.

The Influence of the Imam

Many who were interviewed explain that their first meeting with the imam took place during solitary confinement, a practice frequently used in Danish prisons. The clerical employees of the prison hold a special status allowing them to visit prisoners in solitary confinement and they are often the inmates' only connection to the outside world other than police officers, prison officers or lawyers. The interviewed inmates explain that the five daily prayers and the reading of the Qur'an in particular have served as a way of structuring the day during the solitary confinement and motivating them to get up in the morning. It is not religion as an abstract metaphysical answer, but as an embodied enactment through practices, tasks and rituals that gives the inmates a sense of constructing an identity on their own premises and of being more than just prisoners that makes the construction of a religious identity attractive to them.

As a consequence, the inmates are very susceptible to the influence of the imam, who becomes a highly trusted and respected person among the Muslim inmates. He is capable of offering qualified religious guidance to religiously seeking inmates in the construction of a new identity, and he is able to provide religious literature and help the inmates to establish discussion-groups where they can meet for socialising, etc. Contrary to psychologists and other staff dedicated to helping the inmates, the imams are, according to the interviewees, viewed as having a 'special cause', 'a mission' or even to be 'sent from God'. Consequently, all of the interviewees were likely to adopt the theological standpoint as well as the worldviews of the imam. The positions defended by the imam, be they the possibility and the benefits of Muslims living in Denmark or the self-segregation of Muslims in Denmark, have a disproportionate influence on how converts position themselves in these matters.

The Radicalisation of Inmates

It is important to point out that none of the imams was found to deliver sermons or to disseminate ideas and practices which can be seen as radical. It is against this background that one has to note the high degree of convergence between the respective imam's understanding of the relationship between Muslims and the surrounding society on the one hand, and those of the inmates on the other. It is equally interesting that this relationship appears to determine whether the individual inmate has a polarised or exclusionary understanding of religion or not. A few examples should be mentioned here. One imam seemed intensely preoccupied with the discrimination of Muslims in Denmark and during the interview repeated phrases such as 'they always say you are immigrant not Danish' and 'My neighbour will never smile at me because I am Muslim. If I give him a box of chocolates, he will think I have poisoned it'. A similar position was apparent among members of his congregation. One said:

> I need to think about how this country is developing before it is too late and there will be [three] soldiers knocking at my door, giving me 30 minutes to pack a bag. (…) Because the way that the west develops, the wise knows how it develops and it is the children of Hitler trying to exterminate the Muslims.

This particular interviewee wanted to leave Denmark because, as he said, 'Maybe what I really want is to live like the Prophet, but I can't in a country like Denmark'. Here, the polarised understanding of the place of Muslims in Denmark held by the imam closely correlates and supports the way in which the inmate conceives of the relationship between Islam and the West, that is, in highly conflicting terms.

In the opposite case, when imams preached coexistence and tolerance despite inconveniences and experiences with discrimination, the members of the congregations did not consider their adherence to Islam to be in conflict with life in Denmark (despite still being very strong believers and even, in some cases, hoping for the implementation of the *shari'a*). For instance one interviewee said:

> Of course I would submit to Islamic law if it was realised anywhere in the world, but if I live in a country like Denmark, I have to practice as well as I can. I cannot take the consequences for the things that I can not do because of where I live. That would be against my religion.

Another said:

> It's no-one's business if my wife wears a headscarf or if I am wearing underpants. This is a democratic country and people can decide for themselves. I am religious, but I cannot tell others to be as well. That is none of my business.

In these cases, the imam's preaching of an inclusive view on Islam helped the inmates to break rather than reproduce the polarisation inherent in imprisonment.

Conclusion

Whether inmates converted to Islam adopt and extend the polarised worldview of the prisoner to their new religious identity is not simply a matter of Islamic theology. Rather, it depends on how individual Muslims come to understand their relationship to society and how they deal with experiences of discrimination. In the context of Danish prisons, imams and chaplains seem to play a crucial role in both respects.

Notes

1   Kriminalforsorgen (2006) *Rapport om gejstlig betjening af indsatte, der tilhører et andet trossamfund end den evangelisk-lutherske danske folkekirke*, Copenhagen: Kriminalforsorgen.
2   Jon A. Olsen (2006) *Religiøs identitetsdannelse i danske fængsler: en religionssociologisk undersøgelse af konvertering til islam under fængselsophold*, Ph.D thesis, Denmark: University of Copenhagen.

References

Clemmer, Donald (1958) *The Prison Community*, New York: Holt, Reinhart and Winston.
Kriminalforsorgen (2006) *Rapport om gejstlig betjening af indsatte, der tilhører et andet trossamfund end den evangelisk-lutherske danske folkekirke*, Copenhagen: Kriminalforsorgen.
Olsen, Jon A. (2006) *Religiøs identitetsdannelse i danske fængsler: en religionssociologisk undersøgelse af konvertering til islam under fængselsophold*, Ph.D thesis, Denmark: University of Copenhagen.

RASHID AL-GHANNUSHI

Lutz Rogler

Born into a peasant family in southern Tunisia in 1941, Rashid al-Ghannushi is one of the founders, leaders and ideologues of the mainstream current of the Tunisian Islamist movement which began to emerge at the beginning of the 1970s and proclaimed itself as the Islamic Tendency Movement in 1981. Since that year (with a short interruption between 1988 and 1991) al-Ghannushi has been the president of this movement, which changed its name to the Renaissance Movement (Harakat an-Nahda) in 1988. Due to his intellectual influence, he has also become one of the most prominent exponents of contemporary mainstream Islamism in the Arab world, in Europe and even beyond.

Although he attended a traditional religious school in his youth, al-Ghannushi later declared that 'intellectually' he grew up as a Nasserist. This attraction for Arab nationalist ideas directed him, in 1964, to the Arab East; at first to Cairo, then to Damascus where he studied philosophy until 1968. In Damascus too, he underwent a process which he described later as disenchantment with Arab nationalism and as conversion to 'original Islam'. His new religious engagement increased, both intellectually and socially, in Paris where he spent a year after graduating from the University of Damascus: it was in France that he became involved in activities with the Tablighi movement. After his return to Tunisia, while training to be a philosophy teacher at a secondary school, al-Ghannushi continued these religious activities which led – together with those of some other younger intellectuals – to the formation of the first nucleus of the Islamist movement in Tunis at the beginning of the 1970s. From that time on, al-Ghannushi's life course has been almost intrinsically tied to the trajectory of this movement, and at the end of the decade he became its leader.

Just as for the movement in its formative period, the main influences on al-Ghannushi's thinking in the 1970s came from inside the Middle Eastern Muslim Brotherhood current, but he was also inspired by the philosophical and political views of the Algerian thinker Malek Bennabi.

In 1981, when the Tunisian regime under President Bourguiba announced the end of the single-party system, Rashid al-Ghannushi was one of those among the Islamist movement's leadership who led the – at that time still clandestine – *Jama'a islamiyya* to publicly proclaim itself as the Islamic Tendency Movement and to express its intention to participate in a coming pluralistic political system and democratic elections. During the ensuing wave of state repression in July 1981, al-Ghannushi was arrested and sent to prison for ten years. Released in 1984, he played a determining role as the movement's leader when, during a short period of truce between the authorities and the Islamists, the latter extended their visible presence and became the main force of political opposition in the country. Once again sent to prison at the beginning of 1987, he was this time sentenced to life imprisonment but was released in May 1988 after the removal of Bourguiba by the coup of Ben Ali. Under the new regime, Rashid al-Ghannushi assumed the position as the official head and most prominent leader of the Islamist movement, renamed as Harakat an-Nahda (Renaissance Movement) in December 1988, its participation in the new 'political consensus' that was then supposed to emerge in the country, and its demands for legalisation as a political party. Although in person deprived of the right to be a candidate due to its former condemnation, he also took part in the first election campaign of Harakat an-Nahda during the pluralistic parliamentary election in April 1989.

Shortly after this event, when the political tension between the regime of President Ben Ali and an-Nahda movement began to rise once again, al-Ghannushi left Tunisia for a journey: he didn't return for more than two decades. Installed in exile in Great Britain since the early 1990s, he could thus escape the wave of repression against his movement in 1991–2; he was nevertheless sentenced to life imprisonment *in absentia* in 1991. In the same year, he re-took the position of president of an-Nahda movement which became, after its complete paralysis in Tunisia, a movement in exile too. As other exiled leaders of an-Nahda, al-Ghannushi then participated in some self-critical attempts to evaluate the experience of his movement which were published in his own name or in official declarations made in the name of *an-Nahda* and signed by him as its president. Since the mid-1990s, despite having also been overtly and frequently contested inside the movement for his tactical choices – in particular in view of an-Nahda's long-lasting political dilemma – he has been re-elected several times as 'president' on the occasion of 'congresses' held by the movement in Europe.

At the same time, Rashid al-Ghannushi has not only become – from his exile in London and mainly through his numerous writings and interviews in European, Arab or Arab-speaking media – the most largely known personality of an-Nahda, but he has also gained a reputation as one of the most outstanding and influential intellectuals in the contemporary Islamist mainstream, in the Arab world and beyond. First and foremost, this reputation is due to his theoretical contributions to the ongoing debate on the political project of contemporary Islamist movements. Taking up, to a certain degree, a critical stance against conservative viewpoints and inert attitudes in his own movement since the end of the 1970s, he subsequently contributed to laying down the ideological bases for the evolving readiness of the Arab Islamist mainstream currents to accept democratic principles and procedures as part of their political programme and conduct. His best known theoretical work in this respect is the book Public Liberties in the Islamic State, published in Arabic in Beirut in 1993,[1] where he elaborates on the contours of a contemporary Islamic public order which incorporates the principles of democracy such as civic and human rights, citizenship and pluralism. In the same line of thought, he later published several other books in Arabic dealing with solutions to controversial issues inside the Islamist ideology, in particular in respect of women's rights, the notion of civil society and the problems of secularism and authoritarianism. In so far as his contributions have been, to a large extent, expressing a critical revision of widespread views among the variety of Islamist movements more or less closely linked with the tradition of the Muslim Brotherhood, he is now considered as one of those thinkers whose positions are supporting and encouraging reformist trends and circles in the context of contemporary political Islam. In this regard too, he has established, since the 1990s, a close relationship with Yusuf al-Qaradawi and his transnational network of scholars and intellectuals inside the International Union of Muslim Scholars (IUMS, founded in 2004). While sharing with al-Qaradawi an uncompromising approach regarding the Arab–Israeli conflict, al-Ghannushi's political attitudes have also enabled him to establish good relations with secular nationalist and even leftist personalities and circles in Tunisia and the Arab world.

Undoubtedly, Rashid al-Ghannushi's thinking has been very much shaped by the specific Tunisian context where, under the influence of French cultural and ideological impact, the political and intellectual conflicts and discussions about religion and secularism, Islam and modernity, Islamism and democracy, etc. have been and still are more heated than elsewhere in the Arab region. Another factor which had a significant impact, especially on the development of his views on political modernity and the relation between state and religion, was the intellectual context of his long-lasting exile in Europe where, since the 1990s, he had become involved in the activities of academic institutions and forums of Muslim–Christian dialogue, mainly in Great Britain. However – and though also collaborating as a member in the European Council of Fatwa and Research (ECFR) – he is not primarily concerned with the issue of the presence of Muslims in European societies and the problems related to their integration. He remains, first and foremost, a Muslim intellectual whose main concerns are linked to the ideological and political developments in the contemporary Muslim and Arab worlds, where he strives towards an opening and modernisation of predominant Islamic (and Islamist) frameworks of thinking. It is primarily in this context that he is also engaged in the debate on the broader lines of the 'civilisational' relationship between the Muslim world and the West and on the universal relevance of concepts such as democracy, secularism, human rights and liberties.

After the overthrow of Ben Ali's regime by the revolutionary mass movement of January 2011, a completely new historical era began for Tunisian Harakat an-Nahda. For the first time since its foundation in the early 1970s, the movement could legally develop organisational structures and become socially active without any interference by state bureaucrats. On 1 March 2011 it received official permission to form a political party, almost 30 years after the unsuccessful attempt in June 1981 to gain formal recognition as the Islamic Tendency Movement. Subsequently, Rashid al-Ghannushi, who returned to Tunisia in February 2011, could play a crucial role in the rebuilding of his movement in the post-revolutionary context and its repositioning in the new political landscape. While excluding the taking up of any official position in the new political regime, his political involvement became of particularly great importance in order to mediate between the Islamist movement and secular/secularist forces in the context of the ongoing political transition, namely after the elections in October 2011 and the formation of a coalition government led by an-Nahda in December 2011. At the same time, his political influence and intellectual authority inside *an-Nahda* also enabled him to play a mediating role between different ideological sensibilities within his own movement, which had and still has to manage the reintegration of hundreds of members after years of exile on the one hand, and the influx of new, often young, members on the other. When, in July 2012, Harakat an-Nahda held its first party convention after the revolution in Tunis, Rashid al-Ghannushi was re-elected as the movement's president with 72.5 per cent of the votes.

While still being the best known leading figure of Harakat an-Nahda outside Tunisia, al-Ghannushi is, at this stage, more prominent and respected in large parts of the Muslim world – in particular in the Arabic-speaking countries from Morocco to the Gulf states

– as an intellectual in his own right who, through his books, articles, interviews and web columns, seeks to contribute critically to the ongoing debates about the political and intellectual issues of an accommodation between Islamic views and traditions and the globalising modern world.

Notes

1   Rashid al-Ghannushi (1993) *Public Liberties in the Islamic State*, Beirut: Centre for Arab Studies Unity.

References

Abdelsalam, El-Fatih A. (2005) 'Rashid al-Ghannoushi: portrait of a contemporary Islamic thinker and activist', in Zeenath Kausar (ed.), *Contemporary Islamic political thought: a study of 11 Islamic thinkers*, Kuala Lumpur: International Islamic University Malaysia, pp. 335–60.

Esposito, John L. and John O.Voll (2001) 'Rashid Ghannoushi: activist in exile' in John L. Esposito and John O. Voll, *Makers of contemporary Islam*, New York [u.a.]: Oxford University Press, pp. 91–117.

Ghannushi, Rashid (1993) *Public Liberties in the Islamic State*, Beirut: Centre for Arab Studies Unity.

Mahmoud, Muhammad (1996) 'Women and Islamism: the case of Rashid al-Ghannushi of Tunisia', in Abdel Salam Sidahmed and Anoushiravan Ehteshami (eds), *Islamic fundamentalism*, Boulder: Westview Press, pp. 249–65.

Tamimi, Azzam S. (2001) *Rachid Ghannouchi: a democrat within Islamism*, Oxford: Oxford University Press.

TARIQ RAMADAN

Frank Peter

Tariq Ramadan was born in 1962 in Geneva to Said Ramadan and Wafa' al-Banna, daughter of Hasan al-Banna, the founder of the Muslim Brotherhood (MB). Ramadan has studied in Geneva and completed a PhD in Islamic Studies in 1998. In his research he analysed the MB as part of the tradition of Islamic reformism. He also received private tutoring in Islamic sciences in Egypt. He is currently Professor of Contemporary Islamic Studies at the University of Oxford.

Ramadan is today the most prominent Muslim intellectual in Europe and North America. His career started in the early 1990s as a conference speaker in France. Ramadan's initial success was largely due to his ability to formulate a clear-cut discourse addressing European-born Muslims that articulated the possibility of Muslims living as Muslims and fully practising their religion without infringing upon the normative orders of European societies. While Ramadan was not the first Muslim to say so, because of his eloquence and the systematic and accessible nature of his discourse, he gave a singularly important impetus to the development of Muslim discourses in French and, subsequently, in other European languages. While his position in France initially benefited greatly from his close association with the Francophone Muslim network Présence musulmane (created in 1996), through which a new generation of Muslim activists received their education and contacts with human rights and leftist activists, his current status is due to his global activity as a prominent conference speaker and his numerous exchanges with intellectuals worldwide.

In his wide-ranging publications, a number of themes emerge repeatedly. Ramadan insists that the formation of a 'European Islam' (in earlier writings 'Islam of Europe') is possible and desirable. This practice of Islam would be European in the sense that Islam obliges all Muslims to be loyal to the legal orders of their European home countries. European Islam also refers to the idea that Muslims can and should produce a culture which is both European (in its mode of expression) and Islamic (in respect of normativity). The distinction between religion and culture is crucial to Ramadan's thought. It constitutes one element enabling him to argue for a reform of Muslim practices in Europe that necessarily includes a partial differentiation between European Muslims and Muslims elsewhere as far as their social and cultural practices are concerned. Another equally important element of his reform discourse is the reference to classical mechanisms of Islamic jurisprudence that determine the way in which the context of interpretation should be taken into account.

Ramadan's concern with the reform of Islam converges at some points with the expectations of European societies as they are articulated in the demands addressed to Muslims to 'integrate'. However, furthering this reform is not an aim in itself for Ramadan, but part of his broader objective to make Muslims an active and enriching component of European societies. Ramadan seeks to enable Muslims to put into practice the distinctive message with which they are entrusted and thus to fulfil their obligations as Muslims. Ramadan's thinking, indeed, never loses sight of the need, as he puts it, to relate the vertical relation between God and believers to issues concerning the horizontal relations between humans in society. This has led him, since the beginning of his career, to criticise Muslims for defensive and segregationist attitudes and for their lack of awareness of the possibilities to effect change and make a difference in Europe. While critical of the suspicions and attacks to which Muslims are systematically subjected today in Europe, Ramadan believes that, however necessary public criticism of this situation is, these criticisms should nevertheless not become the main concern of Muslims, who should instead be focused on cultivating dispositions and aims to proactively participate as Muslims in societal debates. This striving to have an impact on wider society and not to limit oneself to the defence of Muslim interests has led Ramadan early on to seek alliances with other non-Muslim groups, notably with leftist groups and actors associated with the anti-globalisation movement. These attempts have sometimes proved very problematic. Nevertheless, his pronounced openness to building alliances and his rejection of attempts to institutionalise Islam as a minority religion set him apart from many other Muslim activists.

While the years after 2001 have seen the rise of Ramadan as a world-renowned intellectual and interlocutor for various European governments, the suspicions and attacks against him have increased in proportion to his stature. Ramadan has been relatively successful in establishing himself as interlocutor for public authorities, notably in the United Kingdom and, for some time, in the Netherlands, and he has become a regular speaker in intellectual debates all over the world. However, many voices today strongly contest that Ramadan's views qualify his holding of such positions.

Ramadan has been associated with the support of terrorist organisations, more particularly Hamas, since he donated money to French charities that were classified as fundraising organisations for terrorist activities. Although this classification occurred only after Ramadan had donated money, his visa to the US was revoked for this reason in 2004, and he was thus unable to take up an academic position offered to him. In 2009 a US federal appeals court overturned a previous verdict upholding the government's decision to deny entry to Ramadan, and the case continues to the present day. Apart from the claim of Ramadan's support of terrorism, which is not central to the debate about Ramadan, Ramadan is regularly attacked for a variety of other reasons. His critics usually refer to a small number of specific statements he has made concerning the headscarf, mixed marriages, polygamy, homosexuality, anti-Semitism and the legitimacy of the Palestinian resistance. There can be no doubt that Ramadan's views on gender relations would be considered by an increasing number of people today to be very conservative. As to the issue of anti-Semitism, Ramadan had spoken out against Muslim anti-Semitism before the debate about the 'new' anti-Semitism started in France. However, he has also written a short article in which he identified a number of French intellectuals as Jewish and designated them as France's '(new) communalist intellectuals'. He criticised them for practising an 'identitarian closing-in' and abandoning 'universal principles' in favour of supporting Israel. While Ramadan's analysis of these intellectuals is in some passages crude, the thrust of his argument depends upon an uncritical adoption of the French republican opposition between universalism and communalism and not on anti-Semitic ideas. As to the Palestinian resistance, Ramadan defends its legitimacy while rejecting the use of violence. It is important to note that none of Ramadan's statements concerning these or other issues puts him outside the realm of the law. In fact, it is not Ramadan's statements (often incorrectly reported) which in themselves help explain the various criticisms to which Ramadan is subjected. Rather, these criticisms are based on the thesis that Ramadan is obscuring his real message and aims behind an innocuous-sounding discourse claiming to support the integration of Muslim citizens into Europe's multicultural societies. Ramadan's 'real' aims are usually identified as stemming from his family background. A common genealogical reading of Ramadan constructs him as a representative of the MB, imagined in these discourses simply as an extremist organisation striving to *Islamise* the world and implement *shari'a*. In this view, Ramadan is reduced to his position as grandson of the MB's founder, al-Banna. While Ramadan develops in his publications and talks a relatively specific reading of al-Banna, this is disregarded or interpreted as merely a new strategy serving the same ultimate aims. The constant reference to alleged ambivalences in Ramadan's discourse (which are thought to obscure his extremism) is crucial to this line of argument.

In spite of the wealth of books, articles and cassettes produced by Ramadan in the past 15 years articulating his stance, the accusations directed against him rely almost entirely upon the argument that his discourse signifies a meaning other than as it reads, and that his true intentions can be seen in occasional unwitting slip-ups in his talks or writings.[1] One simple yet relevant question this claim raises is what Ramadan would actually gain by constantly holding a discourse – not only in the broader public, but also among Muslims– that is in dissonance with his real aims. Another major problem with the thesis of Ramadan's double talk is that it is often merely a convenient means to avoid debate about the broader arguments put forward by Ramadan and to delegitimise him as an intellectual. The 'real' issue that Ramadan as Europe's most prominent Muslim intellectual raises is what kind of integration of Muslims European nations want – that is, what kind of 'reform' of Islam is deemed necessary – and whether they are willing to build diverse and inclusive societies. Ramadan is a Muslim who claims that Islam implies distinctively different notions from Europe's (post-) Christian societies – of how faith and reason relate to each other, how religion and politics are differentiated and how individual freedom can be exercised within a religious tradition. At the same time, Ramadan argues – and this argument cannot be easily dismissed – that Islam does not need to undergo a 'liberal' reform in order to be practised in Europe. For these reasons, Ramadan has become identified with the emergence of a Europe where religious differences may become more accentuated and it is this prospect – or, from the point of view of some, this threat – that nourishes many of the attacks directed against him.

The criticism of Ramadan is also based on his alleged associations with various institutions and people who are today considered extremist. At the centre of attention are his association with people identified as part of the MB movement and, more recently, his collaboration with a television channel funded by Iran. In 2009, this collaboration offered the pretext for terminating his professorship in Identity and Citizenship at Erasmus University in Rotterdam. Many believe that Ramadan is reluctant or ambivalent about marking his differences *vis-à-vis* other Muslims. In fact, while Ramadan stresses the legitimate plurality of opinions in many matters, he has regularly spoken out against a number of practices and discourses by Muslims. He notably supported a campaign against forced marriages and, more particularly, their justification on Islamic grounds, and he initiated a campaign for a moratorium on corporal punishments in Islamic countries. However, it is also true that Ramadan keeps in contact with various groups and institutions whose views he may not fully share. Ramadan has consistently made clear that his aim is to effect change in Muslim communities from the inside and through dialogue, rather than through wholesale denunciation of Muslims he disagrees with. In the current context, this position makes Ramadan an easy target for all those who seek to cast suspicion on his work.

Notes

1   See, for example, Caroline Fourest (2008) *Brother Tariq: The Doublespeak of Tariq Ramadan*, New York: Encounter Books.

References

Fourest, Caroline (2008) *Brother Tariq: The Doublespeak of Tariq Ramadan*, New York: Encounter Books.

(III) ISLAMIC KNOWLEDGE, EDUCATION AND MUSLIMS AT UNIVERSITIES

DENMARK: ISLAM CLASSES

Tina Gudrun Jensen

Introduction

The image of Islam as a threat to Western societies is frequently based on the imagined role of 'Islamic education' in processes of radicalisation. Radicalisation is generally conceptualised as a desire for wide-ranging societal change, a process of persuasion in which a person gradually acquires certain ideas that may lead to the legitimisation of political violence. Radicalisation is associated with the notion of conversion (in terms of identity change), which in public understanding implies the indoctrination and brainwashing of individuals with fundamentalist ideas. Muslim experts such as imams and others who teach Islam classes in mosques or other institutions are often pointed to as being largely responsible for this process, and are therefore at the centre of public attention. The imam is perceived as a figure of authority and power, and the mosque as a potential breeding ground for radicalism and even terrorism.

This perception of Islam classes assumes knowledge as fixed and unchangeable and posits a direct link between the discourses of various Muslim experts and their reception by those who attend the classes. The examination of the content and form of Islam classes in 21 educational settings in Denmark shows, in contrast, that the process of learning as it takes place here hardly involves a one-dimensional relationship between the religious expert, the religious messages and the followers.[1] Rather, this process is complicated by the religious pluralism and religious eclecticism of autonomous practitioners. This reflects the contemporary religious context – a market situation structured according to demand, supply and individual consumption – where multiple forms of relationships between the individual believer, the religious movement and society are possible.[2] Moreover, this religious market situation conditions the likelihood of Islam gaining ground and followers in competition with other new religious movements such as ISCKON (International Society for Krishna Consciousness), Scientology, etc.

Islam classes: content and form

Islam classes in Denmark comprise very different settings, varying from major institutionalised mosque milieus to smaller private study groups and internet-based courses on Islam, altering in orientation from Hizb ut-Tahrir and Wahhabi-Salafism to Sufism and modern holistic forms of 'New-Age Islam'. Most of these settings offer Islam classes on a weekly basis in Danish or in English. The major institutional settings include: the mainly Arabic Islamisk Trossamfund (The Islamic Belief Society) which is associated with the Muslim Brotherhood; the mainly Lebanese Islamisk Center for Europæiske Lande (Islamic Centre for European Countries) associated with al-Ahbash; the mixed Islamisk Kulturcenter (Islamic Cultural Centre); the Pakistani Muslimsk Kulturcenter (Muslim Cultural Centre); and new cross-ethnic ethically oriented institutions such as Muslimer i Dialog (Muslims in Dialoque), Islamisk–Kristent Studiecenter (Islamic–Christian Study Centre) and Forum for Kritiske Muslimer (Forum for Critical Muslims). Those who teach these courses are imams, preachers and Muslim intellectuals or other knowledgeable people who may have a more peripheral relationship to religious institutions.

Most of the classes are open to the public on a drop-in basis, implying loose client-like relations between the participants and the religious institutions. The participants who frequent Islam classes are generally young people between 17 and 29 years old and mainly so-called new Muslims, for example, young people with an immigrant background who are rediscovering Islam, or Danish converts to Islam. It is thus a new clientele, mirroring a new religious situation, with Islam being among the recent arrivals on the religious market. This novelty of Islam in Danish society is mirrored in the topics of lessons at Islam classes which, despite the institutional differences, share similarities in content. Some of the common topics are basic Islamic theological notions and practices, the history of Islam, the revelation of the Qur'an and the life of the Prophet Muhammad. Questions pertaining to how to live according to the Qur'an and *hadith*, often referring to the distinction between *halal* and *haram*, are also frequently discussed. A recurrent theme of discussion within the classes is how to be 'a good citizen' and Muslim exemplar to non-Muslims in society, and how to change the majority society's adversarial image of Islam and Muslims.

The form of Islam classes alternates between lectures and active participation through dialogue and discussion. The reflexive atitude of participants finds expression, for example, in their questioning of the reliability of religious sources. It is not uncommon for participants to criticise the religious expert's teaching after the classes, discussing his or her arguments and ways of interpretation. In this way, the participants challenge the authority of the teacher and continually reassert their individual autonomy.

Movements in Muslim Contexts: Pluralism and Eclecticism

The various voices of authority and representatives of 'true' Islam, within the field of Islam classes, mirror the pluralism of the religious market situation that characterises the Muslim field.[3] This situation is reflected among the participants who frequent the Islam classes, not only in the ways their participation in classes is characterised by reflexivity and autonomy, but also in the ways that they relate to the overall milieu of Islam classes. Participants often frequent different and contrasting forms of Islam classes, more or less simultaneously. They may therefore frequent Salafi, Sufi and other Muslim settings at the same time. These patterns of participation are both due to the participants' general ignorance about the differences between Muslim institutions and orientations, and to the eclectic nature of their individual religiosity which is comprised of various Muslim orientations. The participants therefore reflect a religious mobility and eclecticism that contradicts rigid categorisations of religious identity and memberships to groups. Instead, the participants' partaking of different Muslim institutional and private settings reflects a wavering between different forms of religiosity, representing a continuum between modern liberal and fundamentalist movements.

The forms of religiosity that participants in Islam classes tend to express do not differ from the kinds of modern religiosity expressed by other contemporary new religious movements. This overall picture questions the idea of adherence to fixed worldviews and memberships which imply a religious content that is purely transmitted and acquired by social actors. The milieu of Islam classes as characterised by autonomy, reflexivity, eclecticism and pluralism thus challenges the direct linking between sites, actors and forms of knowledge, which underlies the dominant understanding of the processes of 'radicalisation' today. Instead, it points to the differences between on the one hand, religious institutions and, on the other, the individual religiosity of the participants who frequent the institutions.

Concluding remarks

Islam classes should not be viewed as inherently related to radicalisation, and they cannot simply be understood as enrolment places for radical Islam. Such an understanding presupposes too simple a relationship between the religious expert, the religious messages and the followers. The general situation of religious pluralism that characterises the Muslim field consequently contradicts this image. This situation conditions a relationship between religious institutions and the audience frequenting the Islam classes based on loose client relations, which furthermore reflect the participants' religious eclecticism, privatised religiosity and autonomy. There is not necessarily any direct relationship, whether in form or in content, between the teachings of religious experts and the religious worldviews of the audience.

Notes

1 Tina Gudrun Jensen and Kate Østergaard (2007) *Nye muslimer i Danmark: møder og omvendelser*, Aarhus: Forlaget University.

2 See Peter Berger (1967) *The Sacred Canopy*, New York: Doubleday; Thomas Luckmann (1967) *The Invisible Religion: The Problem of Religion in Modern Society*, New York: Macmillan; and Thomas Luckmann (1999) 'The Religious Situation in Europe: the Background to Contemporary Conversions', *Social Compass*, 46 (3): pp. 251–8.

3 Patrick Haenni (2005) *L'Islam de marché: L'autre revolution conservatrice?*, Paris: Éditions du Seuil, Collection La république des idées.

References

Berger, Peter (1967) *The Sacred Canopy*, New York: Doubleday.

Haenni, Patrick (2005) *L'Islam de marché: L'autre revolution conservatrice?*, Paris: Éditions du Seuil, Collection La république des idées.

Jensen, Tina Gudrun and Kate Østergaard (2007) *Nye muslimer i Danmark: møder og omvendelser*, Aarhus: Forlaget University.

Luckmann, Thomas (1967) *The Invisible Religion: The Problem of Religion in Modern Society*, New York: Macmillan.

—— (1999) 'The Religious Situation in Europe: the Background to Contemporary Conversions', *Social Compass*, 46 (3) pp. 251–8.

ISLAMIC HIGHER EDUCATION IN THE NETHERLANDS: REPRESENTATION OF THE ISLAMIC UNIVERSITY OF ROTTERDAM IN THE DUTCH WRITTEN MEDIA

Firdaous Oueslati

Islamic institutions providing higher education have not been an important topic of public debate on Islam and Muslims in the Netherlands. It is only in relation to the training of imams at Dutch universities that this topic has been recently discussed. There are two Islamic universities in the Netherlands; the Islamic University of Rotterdam (IUR) and the Islamic University of Europe. Even though these institutions carry the designation 'university' in their name, they are not universities in the official sense, since their diplomas are not formally recognised. However, both institutions are making efforts to acquire accreditation for their BA and MA programmes.

The IUR was founded in 1997 and consists of three faculties: the faculty of Islamic Sciences, the faculty of Languages and Civilisations and the faculty of Islamic Art. The faculty of Islamic Sciences is the largest, with a few dozen students, and is considered to be the most vital for the university. Only a few students are enrolled in the programmes of the other two faculties.

In the following, I would like to outline the conditions – or, more particularly, some of the constraints – under which institutions of Islamic higher education develop, with a focus on media coverage. On several occasions the IUR received some coverage in the three major national newspapers; *NRC Handelsblad, de Volkskrant* and *Trouw*. The first time was when, shortly after his arrival as the new rector, Professor Akgündüz was interviewed by a *Trouw* journalist. In the very first paragraph of the article the new rector was introduced as follows:

> A Muslim woman can never marry a non-Muslim. A Muslim husband can hit his wife – provided that there is really no other option left. The fact that according to the Qur'an the portion of inheritance of a daughter is half that of a son, has a good reason. We cannot change these regulations that are embedded in authoritative Islamic sources. These are the convictions of Prof. Dr. Ahmed Akgündüz, the new rector of the Islamic University of Rotterdam (IUR).[1]

Naturally these statements provoked a lot of reactions – mostly condemnatory – and public figures, both Muslim and non-Muslim, began to wonder whether the IUR was an institution contributing positively to the position of Muslims in the Netherlands. The situation quickly became delicate, in response to which the IUR convened a press conference in order to make the necessary amends regarding the way the rector's statements were rendered. The rector stated that his words were distorted and that the Qur'an certainly does not allow for women to be beaten by their husbands.[2] The aim of the article seems to be the exposure of an orthodox or 'fundamentalist' institute by asking some yardstick questions against which the tendency of the university is measured. If the representative of the university gives the 'wrong' answers, then there is no doubt left and the institution is discredited as not fit for participation in Dutch society, which is imagined as a uniform space.

In public perception the only way Islamic education in general, and Islamic higher education in particular, can be approved of is when it teaches and disseminates a 'liberal' Islam – in other words, if the answers to litmus questions contain the 'right' opinions and concepts, such as, for instance, explicitly denouncing 'the implementation of "the" shari'a', and expressing support for gender equality in the secular liberal sense. It is not academic or scholarly quality that is at stake, but the value system which is assessed through addressing very specific issues.

Most attention in the written media has been centred around the IUR as an institution for the training of imams. The Islamic University clearly and actively pursues official recognition – since it is not validated by the Dutch government as a university – and applies several strategies to attain this end. One of these strategies is to constantly highlight its position as the only institution with sufficient expertise in the training of imams. Among the students of the IUR are several imams who want to improve their knowledge and acquire an academic degree. This was especially the case before September 2005, that is, prior to the start of various trajectories for the training of imams at Dutch universities and colleges at the incentive of the government. Some critics, however, expressed their scepticism as to whether the IUR would be able to provide Dutch society with imams with more 'liberal' convictions, in light of the highly orthodox opinions that are held there.

Anticipating the situation, the IUR started offering training trajectories to imams, the so-called *inburgeringscursussen*, or courses in Dutch citizenship. These courses comprise the study of Dutch language, history and culture and are intended to prepare imams educated in a non-Western (Muslim majority) context for offering his services in a Western (Muslim minority) environment. This initiative of the IUR might also be seen in light of its quest for recognition: one would then see it as the first step in gaining importance in the public sphere and in strengthening relations with the government by voluntarily implementing the latter's proposals.

Next to the IUR's training courses for imams, there have been three initiatives to train imams at Dutch institutions; two BA/MA courses at a university and one BA course at a college. It has been five years now since the first of these courses was initiated, but it is still hard to say whether all these initiatives are resulting in Dutch-trained imams taking the lead in mosques in the Netherlands. It is only now that students who have run through the full course are starting to graduate, and it will not be an easy task to accommodate these fresh graduates into their new professional environment in the mosque. For this to happen, the infrastructure around mosques needs to be further developed through an increase in resources and professionalisation. Only then will the office of the imam be an option worth considering for a Dutch graduate seeking to serve the community.

Notes

1   Rector IUR: je vrouw slaan mag, maar niet regelmatig, *Trouw*, 7 November 2000.
2   Slaan? Wat een vernieuwend idee, *Trouw*, 11 November 2000.

References

Boender, Welmoet (2006) 'From migrant to citizen: the role of the Islamic University of Rotterdam in the formulation of Dutch citizenship', in Gerdien Jonker and Valerie Amireaux (eds), *Politics of Visibility, Young Muslims in European Public Spaces*, Bielefeld: Transcript Verlag, pp. 103–22.

Oueslati, Firdaous (2008) 'Non-formal Islamic higher education in the Netherlands: with some comparative notes on France and the United Kingdom', in Willem B. Drees and Pieter Sjoerd Koningsveld (eds), *The Study of Religion and the Training of Muslim Clergy in Europe; Academic and Religious Freedom in the 21st Century*, Leiden: Leiden University Press, pp. 403–27.

ISLAMIC EDUCATION IN GERMANY: INSTITUT FÜR INTERRELIGIÖSE PÄDAGOGIK UND DIDAKTIK, COLOGNE AND ZENTRUM FÜR ISLAMISCHE FRAUENFÖRDERUNG UND FORSCHUNG

Jeanette Jouili and Melanie Kamp

Two Islamic centres in Germany – the Institut für Interreligiöse Pädagogik und Didaktik (IPD) and the Zentrum für Islamische Frauenförderung und Forschung (ZIF) – illustrate the development of new sites of Islamic knowledge dissemination designed specifically by and for women. In this case, both are set up by a group of like-minded intellectual women; those with a Turkish background and German converts. Although each group has its own distinguished profile and goals, both share the aim to transcend the fractures of the German-Islamic landscape wrought by ethnic strife. Further, they view themselves as independent from any of Germany's major Islamic organisations. Both institutes promote an Islamic understanding which takes a strong stance on gender equality and religious pluralism and refuses attachment to any particular school of law (*madhhab*), which means that they regard all four traditional Sunni schools of law as equally correct and valid interpretations of Islamic law. However, they are rarely recognised as such in the German public sphere given the close family ties of the involved women to the organisation Milli Görüş.[1] One founding member of both institutes, Amina Erbakan, is a German convert and lawyer and the sister-in-law of Necmettin Erbakan, a central figure of the Islamist party Saadet Partisi which today maintains links with Milli Görüş. Her daughter, Sabiha El-Zayat, is also a member of the ZIF. She is a medical doctor who holds an MA in Ethnology and Islamic studies. The conflation and accused affiliation of IPD/ZIF with Islamische Gemeinschaft Milli Görüş (IGMG) obscures the fact that the approaches – especially the feminist ones – adopted in both these institutes and transmitted to their members can hardly be reconciled with the main line of IGMG.

The IPD (Institute for Interreligious Pedagogy and Didactics) began work in 1993 under the name Internationales Institut für Pädagogik und Didaktik (Institute for International Pedagogy and Didactics). The name change reflected the international approach of the Institute, which collected Islamic curricula and teaching materials from all over the world in order to develop suitable curricula and teaching materials for Islamic instruction in Germany. In 1994, the founding members began training other Muslim women to support them in their pedagogical and didactical training courses. In 1998 they began offering regular correspondence courses for Muslim women. Approximately 300 people have studied with the IPD. This is remarkable because the training courses lack any formal recognition in Germany. Graduates may teach at local mosques on a voluntary basis and some teach privately, while others just pass on their knowledge to their own children. Recently the Institute has started to offer training courses in Switzerland that are no longer addressed exclusively to a female population, and since 2002/3 Swiss graduates have piloted teaching Islamic instruction at public schools in Luzern. With regard to the development of curricula, the IPD has been more successful than other Muslim organisations in Germany. The curriculum of the IPD is used by the Islamic Federation of Berlin in their Islamic instruction at public schools, whereas organisations such as the Central Council of Muslims in Germany did not get the chance to put their curricula into practice.

The curricula and the teaching material of the IPD aim at teaching Islam to children in close correspondence to their daily lives and showing them that there is no contradiction between Islam and life in a German society that is predominantly non-Muslim and secular. In order to achieve this, children are encouraged to think independently about religion in relation to their own world and experiences. The teaching materials as well as the training courses are designed to address students and pupils of different national and ethnic backgrounds and from various Muslim communities. Therefore they do not follow a set traditional Islamic school of law. For the same reason, the IPD almost exclusively refers to the Qur'an as a normative and pedagogical example and rarely to the prophetic tradition (Sunna). This approach is also a more or less direct criticism of the use of prophetic traditions whose reliability they question.

Although the Institute focuses in its training courses on religious pedagogy and didactics, it also disseminates knowledge about Islam. The students acquire a basic knowledge of Islamic jurisprudence (*fiqh*), Qur'an, pedagogical psychology based on the Qur'an, logic, philosophy and Arabic, as well as the practical aspects of organising lessons and seminars. Basic knowledge means, for example, that they learn to give ad hoc translations of Qur'anic verses that are suitable for children rather than doing intensive language training, or that they get an overview of the historical development of Islamic jurisprudence (*fiqh*) rather than a detailed introduction into the subject based on a specific school of law.

In 2003 the Institute changed its name to its current appellation. The new name is as programmatic as the old one and reflects the IPD's new emphasis on interreligious matters. The acceptance of a religiously plural society and guidelines for interreligious dialogue – an open philosophical conversation without a missionary framework, aggression or discrimination – are derived from the Qur'an. The closeness to the ZIF (discussed below) is apparent in the IPD's progressive stance towards gender issues as expressed in the curricula and in leaflets. The women from the IPD claim to question interpretations of Qur'an and Sunna that are invoked to argue for the subordinated status of women. According to them the Qur'an stresses the equality of men and women – they have been created from the same substance and therefore can never become unequal[2] – and it is the task of the religious instruction teachers to counteract attitudes of gender inequality. However, besides their feminist approach in their curricula and textbooks, the women from the IPD also revalue the traditional female role of mother and housewife – she is helpful, caring and kind – which children and teenagers often disregard in their explanation.[3]

Zentrum für Islamische Frauenförderung und Forschung (ZIF)

The ZIF's objective is twofold: undertaking a theological reflection corresponding to the needs of women, and carrying out social work aimed at helping Muslim women in their daily life. By combining these two objectives, the ZIF links grassroots activities with textual, exegetical work. This is also why the ZIF opts for a rather accessible language in its publications, until now consisting mainly of short brochures and articles and one small booklet. Unlike the IPD, the ZIF is not a regular teaching institute. It organises seminars on an irregular basis in its own small locations. Otherwise, it disseminates its ideas on interreligious conferences through the distribution of its writings and through its social work.

The ZIF's intellectual reflection situates itself critically towards the German majority society as much as towards the major Muslim organisations. On the one hand, it considers that the Muslim community, dominated by patriarchal structures, is not yet 'mature' enough to accept its own progressive readings of the Qur'an. This is also why the ZIF generally adopts a low profile and publishes its brochures only under the centre's name rather than signed by the individual authors. On the other hand, it questions the German conception of the integration of Muslims which seems to imply, according to the members, that abandoning one's Muslim identity and practice is the only way for Muslim women's emancipation. This is also why, according to the ZIF members, their work encounters so little response from the majority society where a feminist theology within Islam is considered inconceivable.

Like the IPD, the ZIF's approach focuses exclusively on the Qur'an, leaving out any discussion of the *ahadith*. The ZIF's publications express a profound criticism of mainstream orthodoxy, of the dominant religious scholars and of the classical Islamic sciences (*tafsir* and *fiqh*). They openly question the *'ulama's* legitimacy, accusing them of obscuring the 'authentic' message of the Qur'an as 'revolutionary in regard to women'. Starting with this assumption, the ZIF's publications propose a 'female centred hermeneutics' of the Qur'an resting on five principles:

1. The idea of the 'subjectivity' involved in the appreciation of the text stresses the personal relation of each individual with the text which cannot be replaced by any authority whatsoever. As a consequence, they argue for a 'declericalisation' of Islam.
2. An understanding of the inherent 'plural character' of the text leads to a recognition of the diversity of legitimate readings and substantiates the rejection of the monopoly of one specific reading.
3. The rejection of the idea of Islam's supremacy enables an acknowledgement of the legitimacy and value of other religious traditions.
4. The principle of a 'contextual application' expresses that the Qur'anic verses have to be understood in relation to the situation leading to their revelation (*asbab al-nuzul*). This contextual reading should not, however, as the ZIF insists, be confused with a secular approach that undertakes a 'historical' reading of the religious text.
5. Through the different above-outlined principles the aim is to determine the Qur'an's ahistorical, universal meaning.

Their hermeneutical method and their subsequent conclusions legitimise the ZIF's stance – which is more radical than the one disseminated by the IPD – on religious pluralism/religious freedom and gender equality. These positions situate the ZIF's thought clearly within the global trend of Islamic feminism that has emerged in Muslim majority societies (e.g. Iran, Malaysia) and in North America. In Europe, these voices are rather rare, and the ZIF's work can therefore be considered to be an exception. Indeed the ZIF's, but also the IPD's, perceived proximity with feminist tendencies also causes many Muslims in their environment to distance themselves from their approach – men and women alike – who consider feminism to be inherently non-Islamic.

Notes

1 'Die Probleme des Dialogs', *Taz*, 29 October 2001. Interview with Sabiha El-Zayat.
2 Irka-Christin Mohr (2006) *Islamischer Religionsunterricht in Europa. Lehrtexte als Instrumente muslimischer Selbstverortung im Vergleich*, Bielefeld: Transcript Verlag.
3 Ibid.

References

Mohr, Irka-Christin (2006) *Islamischer Religionsunterricht in Europa. Lehrtexte als Instrumente muslimischer Selbstverortung im Vergleich*, Bielefeld: Transcript Verlag.

ISLAMIC EDUCATION: SEMINARIES AND INSTITUTES: L'INSTITUT EUROPÉEN DES SCIENCES HUMAINES, FRANCE

Firdaous Oueslati

The foundations for l'Institut Européen des Sciences Humaines (the European Institute of Human Sciences) were laid when l'Union des organisations islamiques de France (UOIF, Union of French Islamic Organisations) and l'Union des organisations islamiques d'Europe (UOIE Union of European Islamic Organisations), based in Germany) created a non-profit association in 1990 known as L'institut européen des études islamiques, which served as a framework for the later Château-Chinon institute. From the outset, the aim of the Institute was to facilitate an 'intelligent' and 'positive integration' of the Muslim communities into European societies, through the formation of religious personnel, teachers and imams, who combine a mastery of Islamic sciences, both theological (*usul ad-din*) and legal (*usul al-fiqh*), with knowledge and understanding of European societies.[1]

The European Institute of Human Sciences (IESH) in Château-Chinon is the very first institution of Islamic Higher Education in France. The dire need for imams trained in the countries in which they exercise their profession made the UOIF consider establishing an imam training programme in France. After some years of preparation, the IESH in Château-Chinon was inaugurated in 1992. In the first year the institute counted 12 students, a number that increased in 2000 to 120, only to stabilise after a steady rise during subsequent years to around 130 students in 2006. The website of the institute states that the percentage of women students has never dropped below 40 per cent, a fact of which the institute is very proud, and that – according to the website – proves that 'authentic' Islam does not discriminate on the grounds of gender and never constitutes a barrier for women who want to acquire knowledge (http://www.iesh.org/). A fair share of the female student population aspires to assume an active role in their community following the completion of their training by transmitting their knowledge as teachers or counsellors. The institution does not provide a course for training female imams, and the existing imam training course is not pursued by women – which may be attributable to subtle social pressures rather than to explicit exclusion of women from this course. As yet, the debate in France on female imams has been eclipsed by debates on the training of home-grown imams and on improving both their training and working conditions.

It was apparently for economical reasons that the first branch of the IESH was set up in Château-Chinon – it is less costly to maintain outside an urban area. Being situated in the countryside is a good way for students to be immersed in the Arabic language and lets them focus on their studies, though it is hardly helpful in creating an institution that plays a key role for the Muslim communities that are mostly to be found in the larger cities. To cater to the needs of those communities in urban areas and offerthem training programmes in Islamic sciences, a branch of the institute was established in 2000 in Paris. By that time several institutions offering courses already existed, such as the Institut d'études islamiques de Paris (IEIP). The IESH is also represented in Britain, with a branch set up in Wales in 1998.

In France the educational programme consists of three main courses at the BA level:
an imam training course
an Islamic theology course
a course that aims at memorising and mastering the art of recitation of the Qur'an.

The content of the imam training track does not differ very much from that for Islamic theology: the programmes are the same, with the only difference being that one has to memorise a certain portion of the Qur'an – one-third – to receive a certificate of aptitude for the profession of imam. In fact, students that have accomplished the programme of Islamic theology can receive a certificate of aptitude for the profession of imam. There are no statistics available on the number of students and/or graduates who are currently employed as imams. People in charge of the programme estimate several dozens of graduates of both the Château-Chinon and the Paris branch work as full-time as well as part-time imams. Most students however, do not enrol in the programmes with the intention of becoming an imam; all they want is to increase their knowledge of their faith for personal development.

In addition to a programme of higher education taught in the Arabic language, the Parisian branch of the institute also provides introductory courses in Islamic sciences in French and an Arabic language training programme. Currently the latter two attract many students, considerably more than the programme of higher education. At the moment of writing, the institute counts around 1,000 students, 80 per cent of whom are enrolled in the introductory courses in Islamic sciences and Arabic language training. The majority of the students consist of French-born, second-generation North Africans, although there are also some first-generation immigrants among them. Generally the students are in their twenties, and many of them have already pursued a formal training, or are in the process of doing so while studying at the IESH.

The programme of Islamic theology requires a *baccalauréat* or comparable diploma granting admittance to university-level education. However, the degrees granted by the institute are not recognised by the French educational system. If students nonetheless wish to pursue their education at a formal French university after completing a degree at the IESH, they can submit their files for assessment upon which the university will decide on their admission.

Since the Château-Chinon institute engages in purely religious activities according to its own charter, it has the legal status of *établissement d'enseignement supérieur privé* (private institute of higher education). The Parisian branch has submitted a request for this status at l'Académie de Créteil.

The Parisian institute recently set about designing a graduate programme, comprising a two-year Master's programme and the possibility of doing a PhD. At the moment of writing not much is known about this programme, as it is still in its early stages. Another educational service the French branches of the IESH provides is *classes par correspondence* (distance learning). This entails studying the materials of the regular programmes on one's own and taking the exams at the institute. The students who enrol in this programme are not only from France, but also from other European countries such as Germany, the Netherlands and Belgium. Although the number of students is not very considerable – not more than a few tens – they still contribute to the development of the institute's international network.

The teaching staff mainly consists of people of North African origin, and most of them earned their university degrees both in their countries of origin and at French universities. The IESH is linked to other French or European Muslim associations through members of the teaching staff who are at the same time active members of, for instance, the UOIF or the European Council for Fatwa and Research (ECFR). There has also been one lecturer who was a member of an interfaith association, the Conférence mondiale des religions pour la paix. The institute in Château-Chinon is being directed by one of the founders of the UOIF, Zuhair Mahmoud, and the Parisian branch in Saint-Denis by Ahmed Jaballah, who regularly delivers the Friday sermon at the UOIF mosque in Paris. The latter is also a member of the ECFR, along with Abdelmajid an-Najjar and Ounis Guerguah, both lecturers at the French branches of the IESH.

From the start, the IESH faced political and public resistance to the fact that it had close relations with the Muslim Brotherhood (MB), adhered to its principles and that it received funding from the Gulf States. Despite these tensions, one can maintain that the IESH fits within the trend of *islamisme de minorité* (minority Islamism) (Amghar 2007). Living in a minority context as a Muslim is an important preoccupation tof the IESH. To carry 'Europe' in its name for instance, and to be closely linked to the ECFR – one of its aims being the development of an Islamic jurisprudence for Muslim minorities (*fiqh al-aqalliyat*) – already hints at a concern with developing a theoretical framework for Muslims living in Europe. In addition to the subjects of Islamic science –*fiqh* (jurisprudence), *hadith* and Qur'an – and the Arabic language, the programme of Islamic theology offers subjects such as the history of Islam in Europe, Western civilisation and schools of thought, French language (including translating from Arabic to French), French law and institutions. These latter classes often provide topics for heated debates in which both Western and Muslim societies are criticised.

Notes

1   Franck Frégosi (1998) 'Les filières nationales de formation des imams en France', in Franck Frégosi (ed.), *La formation des cadres religieux musulmans en France. Approches socio-juridiques*, Paris: l'Harmattan, pp. 101–40.

References

Amghar, Samir (2008) *Les mutations de l'islamisme en France ; Portrait de l'UOIF, porte-parole de l'islamisme de minorité*. Available at http://www.laviedesidees.fr/spip.php?page=print&id_article=accessed 28, February 12, 2008.

Frégosi, Franck (1998) 'Les filières nationales de formation des imams en France', in Franck Frégosi (ed.), *La formation des cadres religieux musulmans en France. Approches socio-juridiques*, Paris: l'Harmattan, pp. 101–40.

Godard, Bernard and Sylvie Taussig (2007) *Les musulmans en France: courants, institutions, communautés : un état des lieux*, Paris: Robert Laffont.

http://www.iesh.org/index.php?option=com_content&task=view&id=50&Itemid=102&lang=fr, accessed 27 March, 2008.

MUSLIM INTERNET SITES IN DENMARK

Birgitte Schepelern Johansen and Dorthe Høvids Possing

During the last decade the internet has gained considerable attention in Denmark as a potentially 'radicalising' media,[1] and politicians and security experts have pointed to internet-mediated communication as a space for the deployment of oppositional Muslim communication. What is ignored in these debates is the diversity of Muslim internet sites and the various functions they fulfil.

Organisations online

Some organisations with a Danish branch, such as the Hizb ut-Tahrir and the Minhaj ul-Qur'an, have sites where they present themselves in the Danish language with links to the main branch.[2] Such sites typically contain information about the historical background of the organisation, its purpose, guidelines for participation and contact information. Similar features can be identified when browsing through specific Danish organisations such as Islamisk Trossamfund (The Islamic Society), Muslimske Studerende og Akademikere (Muslim Students and Academics) and the recently founded Muslimernes Fællesråd (Muslim Council of Denmark). Even though these sites are a part of the virtual landscape of Muslim activism in Denmark, their actual use and dynamics obviously fluctuate over time. During 2007 and 2008, for example, the webpage of Hizb ut-Tahrir was rather inactive, with updates and comments that where up to a year old. However, at the moment the page appears rather active, with running updates, activities and comments. The point is that current updates and user active functions on these sites are not dominant, and it should be kept in mind that most of these organisations have existed for far longer than their websites. This means that their religious practice is not mainly structured as 'web activities' (as is the case with the Muslim message boards), but rather they can be seen as a means of internal contact and external visibility.

Message boards

The message boards have as their main audience young people debating Islam, Muslim identity and questions of belonging. Good examples of these are www.islam.dk, with their partly closed mailing list, and www.islamisk.dk and www.islamic.dk with their open and semi-open message boards, as well as approximately 450 users each. These are significant because they are among the most-used in Denmark and have been active for a relatively long period of time.[3] Furthermore, they are interesting because participants in the debates frequently conjoin identity positions which in public debates are often held to be contradictory; that is, Muslim and national identity. In most cases the sites are structured and designed in roughly the same way as the organisations' sites. The obvious differences are that their central feature is the user active part, and that the religious and political practices taking place there can be characterised as peer-debates. In other words they present intra-Muslim debates on various ways to live 'a good Muslim life'. This is in contrast to the question and answer sessions with a specific Muslim authority which can be seen at the various international online fatwa sections.[4] Rather, the debates unfold through relatively uncensored communication between young Muslims with various ethnic and sectarian backgrounds. Actual live fatwa sessions (that is, sessions where you can ask questions directly to a given Muslim authority) do not appear on Danish Muslim sites. However, some organisations such as Islamisk Trossamfund have a fatwa archive with frequently asked questions.[5]

A central feature of the peer-debates is the attempt to establish a globally unified Muslim identity position that *ideally* transcends national and ethnic loyalties. This is often done by referring to a transnational Muslim 'we' that stands apart from a Danish 'we'. The emphasis on a transnational identity could also be seen as a strategy used in response to events occurring within the Danish national context. This becomes obvious when observing the debates on, for instance, the Danish cartoon controversy, freedom of speech or other civil right issues.[6]

In such contexts the transnational identity is sometimes juxtaposed to the Danish national identity, the latter being defined as potentially backwards and not adapted to life in a new global world order. In other cases the national identity is subordinated to, rather than set apart from, being a Muslim, and the transnational orientation thus offers an opportunity to integrate the two. This is the case when Islam is articulated as a universal system of values common to all mankind, within which it is possible to belong to various national communities and be simultaneously a citizen and a Muslim. It should be mentioned that the actual content of this transnational Muslim community is highly contested. This is for instance seen particularly in the recurring debates about the truth claims of Hizb ut-Tahrir or Shi'a Islam.

Although structured as peer-debate, the inclusiveness of the message boards is restricted since the moderators can always close a topic or even remove specific communications should they compromise the official objective of the site. On some occasions it is an explicit requirement from the operators that users should avoid any discussions about the truth claims of specific branches within Islam.[7] Regardless of the transnational pretentions of the message boards, they are in Danish and thereby confined to a quite narrow national and linguistic context –interestingly enough this is not taken by the users as a sign of a specific national or cultural affiliation.

Though discourses on these sites may be termed Islamist – in the sense that they discuss 'the good life' and 'the good society' based on the Qur'an – they are equally focused on what, in a national political discourse, is mostly termed as 'integration', as for instance stated below:

> In a time where openness and tolerance are lacking in the debate about Islam, we try to supply interested parties with Danish translations of acknowledged Islamic texts and general authentic learning [...]. We firmly believe that dialogue based on tolerance is an important condition for peaceful coexistence in this society.[8]

The concept of 'authentic Islamic knowledge' is therefore not seen as an obstacle for a peaceful presence in Danish society, as is often assumed in public debates in Denmark.[9] However, the emphasis on values such as tolerance and dialogue does not always constrain the users from taking positions that would seem alarming to the public. These could be, for example, promoting the caliphate as a proper way to organise society, terming non-Muslims as *kuffar* or expressing support for suicide bombers in Palestine or Iraq.[10] Such issues aside, the political and religious practices on the sites mostly take the shape of debates on everyday life: what is *halal* and what is *haram* in specific situations? Is it *halal* to eat a McChicken sandwich? Or to work as an intern at a Danish bank that charges interest? Is a Danish university a proper place to learn Arabic? These questions are not answered authoritatively but are discussed with reference to individual experience as well as to scripture, and most often they do not involve explicit references to specific organisations, institutions or scholars; instead debaters on some occasions link to English-language sites.[11]

Perspectives

In a Danish context, internet-mediated communication often takes the shape of intra-Muslim communication and debates about how to relate to the non-Muslim majority. Some position themselves in direct opposition to the Danish state and society as a consequence of being Muslim, while others advocate the need to integrate religious and national identity. However, most debaters do not simply adopt a non-conflictual concept of living in a non-Muslim society, but neither do they explicitly oppose themselves to the Danish state or to Danish national identities. Rather, they use the conception of Islam as a universal religion 'that travels well' to dismiss their marginalised position within Danish society. Or, to put matters more bluntly, they position themselves as 'a citizen of the *umma* living in Denmark'. This also implies that the website cannot be evaluated as either 'radical' or 'moderate' depending on whether they merge or separate religious and national identities. Rather, it needs to be realised that the conjunction of these two identifications can relate to highly diverse practices and beliefs in the lives of Danish Muslims.

Notes

1   See, for example, Olivier Roy (2004) *Globalized Islam. The Search for a New Umma*, London: Hurst & Company; and Akil Awan (2007) 'Virtual jihadist media: function, legitimacy and radicalizing efficacy', *European Journal of Cultural Studies*, 10 (3) pp. 389–408.

2   Major organisations such as the Muslim World League, as well as various Tablighi-oriented organisations, also have Danish branches but are not online in Danish.

3   www.islamisk.dk has been active since 2002 and www.islamic.dk since 2003.

4   See, for example, www.islamonline.net (accessed 19 June 2014)

5   See http://www.wakf.com/wakfweb/faq.nsf/OnlineFatawaCat?OpenView. (link no longer functional)

6   See http://islamic.dk/forum/viewtopic.php?f=82&t=510288&p=163682&hilit=ytringsfrihed#p163682 or http://islamic.dk/forum/viewtopic.php?f=2&t=501727&p=156152&hilit=ummah#p156152 (link no longer functional)

7   See http://islamic.dk/v1/phpBB2/ftopic500966.html. (link no longer functional)

8   http://www.islamisk.dk/default.asp?side=information. (link accessed 19 June 2014)
9   Lene Kühle (2006) *Moskeer i Danmark: islam og muslimske bedesteder*, Aarhus: Aarhus Universitetsforlag, p. 15.
10 See, for example, http://www.islamic.dk/v1/phpBB2/ftopic509848.html. (link no longer functional)
11 See, for example, www.sunnipath.com. (link accessed 19 June 2014)

References

Awan, Akil N. (2007) 'Virtual jihadist media: Function, legitimacy and radicalizing efficacy', *European Journal of Cultural Studies*, 10 (3) pp. 389–408.
Kühle, Lene (2006) *Moskeer i Danmark: islam og muslimske bedesteder*, Aarhus: Aarhus Universitetsforlag.
Mandaville, Peter (2001) *Transnational Muslim politics. Reimagining the Umma*, Abingdon: Routledge.
Roy, Olivier (2004) *Globalized Islam. The Search for a New Umma*, London: Hurst & Company.

MUSLIM FREE SCHOOLS IN DENMARK

Tallat Shakoor

The Muslim population in Denmark was and still is dominated by Muslim immigrants and their direct descendants. Migration to Denmark from Muslim countries goes back to the mid-1960s, and has resulted in the establishment of free schools for children of these immigrants. In 2007, of a total of 500 free schools, there were 22 which were set up by Muslim immigrant parents. The number of pupils in these schools amounts to 3,600, which equals approximately 4 per cent of the entire population of children in free schools, and a little more than 0.5 per cent of Denmark's total population of children and young people of compulsory school attendance age. The schools are usually situated in major urban centres. While these schools are often designated in their entirety as Muslim schools in public debates, in 2007 only 14 of the 22 schools included Islamic religion in their curriculum and could therefore be considered Muslim schools. In addition, only one-third of these free schools actually makes reference to Islam in their statutes.

The free schools of Denmark are an institution which is approximately 150 years old, based partly on the constitutional right of Danish parents to teach their children according to their own beliefs and partly on the legal obligation that all children receive tuition.

The free schools differ in principle from the municipal primary and secondary schools in that they are granted specific privileges: the free schools enjoy freedom of teaching and freedom to employ or turn away job applicants or families on the basis of ideology. Also, the free schools differ from the municipal and private primary and secondary schools in terms of economic status. The Danish state covers 75 per cent of the expenses per pupil, as long as the school can muster a minimum of 28 pupils in total per school year. Danish law subsidises free schools under the condition that the founders of a new school can finance the acquisition of buildings as well as contribute to their maintenance.

The Muslim schools offer primary education to children of compulsory school attendance age. However, as free schools, they are legally bound to meet the standards of the Danish municipal schools in certain subject areas. This commitment requires the management and the staff to complete lesson plans, subsidiary goals and end goals regarding subject areas such as Danish, English, history, social studies, physical education or musical instruction. These requirements obviously do not apply to subject areas without a counterpart in public schools, such as the teachings in Islam and/or mother tongue education that is offered in the Muslim free schools.

The first free school offering basic tuition in Islamic religion was founded in 1978 in Copenhagen. During the following decade, the establishment of new free schools progressed relatively slowly and, by the end of the 1980s, fewer than ten free schools had been set up by immigrants from Muslim majority countries. The approach to Islam in the schools of the 1980s and early 1990s distinctly reflected the fact that founders, administration and the parents themselves were immigrants from Muslim countries. The teaching of Islam was strongly influenced by specific Middle Eastern, Turkish and Pakistani Islamic traditions, and the schools typically gravitated towards a particular religio-ethnic group. The ethnic origin of the founders, administration and parents would typically be reflected in the names of schools, for example Al-Aqsa or Al-Quds (servicing the Arabic-speaking community), Iqbal International School or Jinnah International School (servicing the Pakistani community) or the Danish–Moroccan School (servicing the Moroccan community).

New Muslim schools were founded in the 1990s and in the new millennium, carrying with them some new developments. The coexistence of formerly geographically divided Islamic traditions in Europe, back-to-back so to speak, created incentives among some Muslims to strengthen the common religious heritage in Islam and, rather than emphasising different ethnic identities, to 'root out' non-Islamic elements of the Islam transmitted to them by the first generation of Muslim immigrants. Therefore, the last decade has witnessed a surge in ethnically mixed schools, where ethnic identities play a less important role in the recruiting of staff and new pupils, as well as in the curriculum. Instead, these schools mark their difference from other private and public schools by an emphasis on a common Islamic ground. According to their own declarations, 19 of the 22 schools have mixed national populations, of which ten have pupils from the Arab-speaking world.

Depending on the individual school, there is a more or less pronounced Islamic slant to their ideological foundation. Formally, approximately one-third of the free schools in existence since 1978 have named Islam in their mission statements as a source of the ideological outlook of the school, although informally Islam may be viewed as part of other schools' ideological outlook as well.

Naturally, these accentuations have been changing over time, and it is interesting to note a shift in the purpose of the instillment of Islamic values in the children within the last 30 years. Whereas the schools of the 1980s focused on teaching children basic doctrinal beliefs and worship practices, the schools in the 1990s and beyond have increasingly incorporated a stronger focus on the transmission of Islamic values to their pupils regarding marriage and family life, public behaviour, food and eating habits and so on, as a way to strengthen their Muslim identity in a non-Muslim and secular society. Partly, this shift reflects an expectation on behalf of the parents that their children will have to live their lives in Denmark as Muslims, rather than return to the motherland of the parents or grandparents.

The Muslim school represents both a secure haven from external scepticism towards Muslims in general and an arena of internal dispute among Muslims themselves. The Muslim schools represent spaces of different and sometimes conflicting outlooks regarding the balance between the need for preservation and development of ethnic identities among the pupils on the one hand, and the need for strengthening Muslim identities that are seen as being more compatible with a life in Denmark on the other. For instance, the author witnessed how, in a Muslim free school recruiting primarily from the Pakistani community, ongoing discussions between parents and teachers on what it is to be Muslim were played out in the classroom, in the schoolyard and in homes. In this particular case, the teachers criticised the parents for nurturing a Muslim identity that was intertwined with a Pakistani ethnic identity, instead of cultivating a Muslim identity that was focused more on Islamic dogma and less on Pakistani culture. By insisting on this distinction, the teachers wanted to impress upon the children a sense of belonging to the Muslim community in Denmark at large, rather than strengthening an ethno-religious identity. The parents however, were not interested in these distinctions, but wanted to cultivate a basic Pakistani identity in their children in which Urdu, Pakistan and Islam were intertwined.

During the past 10 to 15 years, Muslim schools have received attention in the Danish integration debates on multiple occasions and given rise to much discussion by the Danish public.

Two sets of critiques have been raised against the schools. One strictly focuses on pedagogical issues: teaching proficiency among the teachers, teaching materials and pedagogic methods. The second critique of Muslim schools is part of a larger debate on the integration of Muslim migrants and their descendants into Danish society. This critique has shifted the focus from a direct scrutiny of the educational culture to the schools themselves. Within this view the Muslim schools are seen as proponents of a totalitarian worldview, which is seen as generally incompatible with democratic and secular values. This critique goes as far as comparing Muslim schools with Deobandi *madrasas* in Pakistan. To date, no-one has been able to pinpoint expressions of such fundamentalist views in the existing school regulations. What can be found are references to the desirability of preserving the children's religious and cultural background. In other words, the Muslim schools are seen as an obstacle to the assimilation process in which the children and their families are expected to take part.

FEDERATION OF STUDENT ISLAMIC SOCIETIES, UNITED KINGDOM

Shaida Nabi

The Federation of Student Islamic Societies (FOSIS) is a voluntary umbrella student organisation devoted to the pastoral, spiritual and political betterment of Muslims within British higher education. Over the years, the demographic and political profile of FOSIS members and activists has evolved considerably, although very little of this has been documented outside of or within accounts of the history of Islam in Britain.

Established in 1962 after a meeting held in Birmingham, FOSIS was initially led by international students from Dublin, Leeds, Liverpool and Birmingham. In 1967, with the support of UK Islamic Mission (UKIM) and funds from Arab states, FOSIS managed to found a hostel for Muslim students. By 1970 FOSIS had acquired a permanent office from which it organised annual conference events and camps for about 30 of its constituent member organisations.

Initially FOSIS's remit was largely pastoral and spiritual. Yet unlike their counterparts, their political attention in the 1960s and 1970s was not directed at Vietnam anti-war protests, but on issues that had been overlooked by the student body yet which resonated with Muslim communities: for instance, the execution of Sayyid Qutb by Nasser's regime in 1966 and the occupation of Palestine after the Arab–Israeli war in 1967. During this time, Jama'at-i Islami and the Muslim Brotherhood (MB) were both global Islamic movements said to be courting FOSIS.

This Islamist legacy has left a questionable impact on FOSIS since the 'Islamist' or 'Movement' commitments of members vary considerably, ranging from members identifying with a traditional Movement approach to those who express very little interest in its historical ties. However, what predominates in this range of identifications are political sensibilities marked by an ummatic discourse, signified in the FOSIS motto: 'hold fast to the rope of Allah, all of you together, and be not disunited'.[1]

FOSIS's historical relationship with the Muslim Association of Britain (MAB), an organisation thought to have links with the MB, has nonetheless been used by critics to discredit FOSIS success at national student conferences. This was the case in spite of the fact that MAB influence waned after the late 1990s with many non-MAB members assuming leadership positions.

In the early 1970s, members of FOSIS were mainly comprised of two types; international students hailing from Muslim countries and a 'string of indigenous and American hippies', who had converted to Islam. The third wave, 'not yet a dribble', was made up of Muslims born or raised in Britain.[2] What was once a 'dribble' of British-born Muslim students is now a characteristic feature of FOSIS membership.

Today FOSIS is an umbrella organisation made up of approximately 70 student Islamic societies from British universities across the UK and Ireland. Thirty are in London alone. Approximately ten Islamic societies across the country are considered FOSIS strongholds with the majority of these outside London. Organised into seven regions, FOSIS is run through a highly organised executive structure.

In the last decade, FOSIS has proved to be one vehicle through which Muslim students have been able to exercise their constitutional rights. While FOSIS's presence and influence across UK campuses is variable, its political prowess is demonstrated within the National Union of Students (NUS), a space in which Muslim students have, by and large, coordinated themselves politically as a *jama'a* (community). This is in contrast with other Muslim student collectives (for example, Hizb ut-Tahrir (HT), al-Muhajirun, the Muslim Public Affairs Committee) which have been subject to the NUS no-platform policy and thus excluded from the political process. FOSIS's political formalisation, however, precedes a much earlier grassroots politicisation developed through groups such as HT in the wake of the Rushdie affair, a period when FOSIS was largely considered ineffective.

While FOSIS remains committed to international causes, reflected in their campaigns for Palestine, Kashmir, Gujarat, and Iraq, the focus over this past decade has been centred on domestic issues that bear on the Muslim student experience on British campuses, with Islamophobia and Muslim student needs being pivotal. The Student Affairs Committee (SAC) is one example of this 'domestic' reorientation. This new wing of FOSIS was first introduced in 2003. Originally the brainchild of Manchester University student Al Khaffaf, it ran under the political leadership of Hasan Patel, a former NUS officer who was said to have been 'the man who really managed to garner and wake them up to their own power'.[3] As a working group of ten, it has supported a burgeoning political process that seeks to empower Muslim students within their respective unions and, quite importantly, make inroads into the NUS. This latter objective cannot be underestimated given the history of Islamophobia in the NUS and, in particular, the exclusion of Muslims from the political process through 'fundamentalist/ extremist' stigmatisation.

In 2003, for the first time in FOSIS history, the SAC actively encouraged a formalised political culture through the introduction of a Politics Guide and the delivery of 'politics seminars' across UK campuses. Both of these initiatives were aimed at increasing the competency and activism of Islamic societies (i.e. guidance on union motions and manifestos).

Within this recent political shift, this decade has also witnessed other notable trends: the significant presence and activism of Muslim women who, for the first time in April 2004, organised a national women's conference; increased liaison with the Home Office on a range of issues including prayer room provisions, top up fees and discussions centred on claims of Muslim campus extremism – which FOSIS has repeatedly held to be unsubstantiated; and finally the increasingly media-savvy role of FOSIS. This was a direct response to the London bombings and associated claims of Muslim campus extremism.

FOSIS's political energies have largely been directed at increasing a Muslim presence at the NUS conference, an annual conference decisive in determining the national student executive body and agenda for the coming year. Albeit still in its fledgling stages, the impressive constitutional literacy developed within FOSIS has paid off. This is evidenced in the exponential rise of Muslim students attending the NUS conference under the FOSIS *jama'at*. Over the course of five years the number more than quadrupled, from a mere seven students in 2001/02 to 120 in 2005/06. In 2006, Muslim students constituted the largest number of organised students to attend the NUS conference. Although this figure has since dwindled to some degree (70 in 2007 and 50–60 in 2008), FOSIS has retained a secure foothold within NUS politics. Not only has this bloc vote altered the traditional NUS balance of power, which previously rested in favour of Labour and Jewish society students, but it has also empowered Muslim students to steer student debates. This was most evident at the NUS 2006 conference when FOSIS confronted one of the most far-reaching issues in Muslim student history: the demonisation and no-platform policy of Hizb ut-Tahrir. As FOSIS activist Jamal el Shayyal put it at the time, 'it's about time, as Muslims, we decided what is extreme and what's not'.[4]

This successive shift in Muslim activism within FOSIS however is not coincidental. 2004, for example, marked a decisive turning point in FOSIS activist history in the NUS. Many students recall that in the preceding year the Union of Jewish Students (UJS) invited Shimon Peres to the NUS Conference, disrupting proceedings and subjecting Muslim students (and any one that appeared as such) to the intimidation of the Israeli security services. Many such junctures relate to an increased and unrelenting Islamophobia across British society, notwithstanding its institutionalisation in higher education. FOSIS's anti-religious discrimination campaigning across UK campuses reflects this 'new' and persistent concern.

Unfortunately, but not surprisingly, this increased activism has been explained away with clandestine undertones. However, as the president of FOSIS at the time put it, 'The simple fact is that all Muslim students have got a lot more organised'.[5] Indeed, Muslim student activism is clearly now a developing feature of the British student landscape.

Notes

1   Qur'an, 3: 103.
2   Ziauddin Sardar (2004) *Desperately Seeking Paradise: Journey of a Sceptical Muslim*, London: Granta Books, p. 24.
3   Shaida Nabi (n.d.). *Muslim Students and Institutionalised Islamaphobia in British Universities*. Ph.D Thesis, University of Manchester: United Kingdom (submitted).
4   Paul Lewis (2006) 'Adding Their Voice to The Debate', The *Guardian*, 4 April.
5   Ibid.

References

Gilliat-Ray, Sophie (2000) *Religion in Higher Education: The Politics of the Multi-Faith Campus*, Aldershot: Ashgate Publishing Company.
Lewis, Paul (2006) 'Adding Their Voice to The Debate', The *Guardian*, 4 April.
Nabi, Shaida (n.d.) *Muslim Students and Institutionalised Islamaphobia in British Universities*, Ph.D Thesis, University of Manchester: United Kingdom (submitted).
Sardar, Ziauddin (2004) *Desperately Seeking Paradise: Journey of a Sceptical Muslim*, London: Granta Books.

MUSLIMS AT BRITISH UNIVERSITIES

David Tyrer

Prior to the 1990s, Muslim students' activities reflected the large proportion of international students among them. Causes ranged from local and national concerns to international issues. Illustrative examples range from international students' key role in seeking funds for a student mosque in Sheffield during the 1970s to campaigns over Palestinian rights. Alliances were pursued with a broad range of anti-racist and anti-apartheid campaigners in mobilising support for Palestinian rights, and it was common for Muslim students to be primarily identified according to what were assumed to be their national or ethnic origins.

The political landscape was transformed by the Rushdie affair (1989) and protests against the Gulf War, which left a legacy of assertive mobilisation of Muslims as Muslims that manifested in the increasingly confident participation of Muslims in student politics. As more British-born Muslims entered universities, their political influence began to eclipse that of their international peers. The ideological backdrop to these developments was shaped by 'new right' conservative rule, which was closely associated with the emergence of 'new racism' coded in cultural terms, the decline of anti-racism, and a wider erosion of student political activism. Collectively, these saw increasingly visible activism by British Muslim students in the face of challenges to the 'no-platform' anti-racism politics they had previously prospered from, and growing Islamophobia.

Despite increasing Islamophobia, Muslim students mobilised with increasing confidence in often imaginative campaigns; for example, one 1994 campaign involved the production of a spoof erratum notice purporting to admit to students' union racism which was surreptitiously distributed in copies of a genuine students' union newspaper. Activities reflected a range of positions, including debates over the permissibility of engaging in union elections, and were mainly channelled through Islamic societies and the Federation of Student Islamic Societies (FOSIS). Activities ranged from campaigns against racism, requests for improved provision for Muslim students and charity fundraising, to support for causes affecting Muslims globally. Theological influences varied; Salafi influences were thought to be more prominent in the urban and metropolitan institutions while Tablighi Jama'at and Barelwi influences were noted in some provincial universities. Hizb ut-Tahrir (HT) became increasingly active during the early 1990s, with al-Muhajirun also visible during the mid-1990s following its split from HT. These groups emphasised transnational causes such as *Khilafa*. The influence of the two groups was often over-emphasised, both by the groups themselves (as a recruiting and publicity strategy) and by the NUS, which made campaigns against the groups a key priority in its treatment of Muslim students. These campaigns often focused on cases of harassment and intimidation carried out by members of al-Muhajirun in particular. However, this fairly specific focus often gave way to a wider Islamophobia in universities as Muslim students became increasingly identified and stereotyped in terms of extremism, irrespective of any actual involvement with groups such as al-Muhajirun or any evidence of wrongdoing. For instance, although these groups largely operated outside the hustings process, attempts to exclude Muslim students from constitutional forms of student politics were justified by individual union campaigns through claims of Islamic Society infiltration by these groups. The resulting exclusion in turn underlined the appeal of these groups, since they could offer political outlets outside the formal student politics in which Islamic Societies often faced hostility and barriers to participation.

Heightened scrutiny and frequently negative media reporting accompanied the increasing tensions. Reports in national newspapers alleged anti-Muslim hostility at the 1993 NUS Annual Conference and police harassment of Muslim delegates at the 1994 conference, while the socialist press later reported that Muslim and Asian students were harassed by other delegates at the 1995 conference. During 1994 and 1995, incidents involving HT were reported in the University of Central England, SOAS, King's College, London, and the universities of Birmingham, Leeds, Sheffield and Bristol. In 1995, London Guildhall University was closed for a day in response to an HT protest after a female Muslim student was allegedly showered with alcohol by rugby club members, while disturbances at King's College, London were reported a year earlier as student supporters of HT and their opponents clashed. Muslim students in Manchester mobilised in 1993 and 1994 over Palestine and union prayer facilities, amidst opposition and counterclaims of anti-Semitism.

Muslim students were increasingly stereotyped in terms of extremism and almost solely associated with HT and al-Muhajirun, despite the comparatively tiny size of these groups. As a result, even basic provision requests made by Muslim students could become politicised. The NUS exhorted the government to ban HT, and it was difficult for Muslim students to act politically without being accused of HT activity, irrespective of facts. In one incident during 1995, a Muslim elected as president of the University of North London Students' Union was reported by The *Guardian* newspaper as having found himself at the centre of a media storm over an alleged fundamentalist seizure of students' union power, despite having stood on a pro-sports platform and being disinterested in politics. Facing criticism over Islamophobia, the NUS reportedly began attempting to distinguish between 'good' and 'bad' Muslims. As the climate worsened, reports of Islamophobic harassment increased, often focusing on highly symbolic forms involving alcohol or targeting the *hijab*.

In response, challenging Islamophobia and improving provisions for Muslim students became increasingly central to Muslim student politics. Women played key roles in many campaigns by the late 1990s, (for example, a campaign for women-only sports sessions in Leicester). Despite the 'rights' focus of campaigns, the media often emphasised the alleged extremism of Muslim students and the threats they were assumed to pose to the rights of others. Claims of hardline targeting of Muslim students continued, and universities finally acted in concert, through the Committee of Vice Chancellors and Principals (CVCP), to issue guidance on *Extremism and Intolerance on Campus* in 1998, which was subsequently criticised for failing to clearly define key terms such as 'extremism', and reinforcing the wider stereotyping of Muslims.

After 9/11, increasing Islamophobia manifested in further reports of verbal abuse, harassment and threats against Muslim students and prayer rooms. Muslim students' activism continued, and a campaign on Palestine in the University of Manchester during 2002 (in alliance with socialist students) attracted widespread media coverage. Campaigns to raise awareness of racism and Islamophobia became more significant, and FOSIS intensified its capacity-building work with Islamic Societies and its dialogue with the Department for Education and Skills (DfES) and the NUS to challenge Islamophobia, for example by responding to DfES guidelines relating to the wearing of *niqab* and pressing the DfES to respond to Muslim concerns such as student loans. After the terrorist attacks in London on 7 July 2005, FOSIS produced a report highlighting students' experiences of Islamophobia and challenging racist stereotypes and assumptions about Muslim students' attitudes towards Britain. More negative coverage was attracted following the publication by the Social Affairs Unit of a report which claimed support and recruitment for terrorism among Muslim students. This report was criticised by Muslim students as inaccurate and methodologically unsound, described by Higher Education Minister Bill Rammell MP as an overstatement and rejected by most of the universities that it had named as sites of 'extremist' activities.

Growing awareness of Islamophobia and criticism of the CVCP's 1998 report led to its replacement in 2005 with a Universities' UK report: *Promoting good campus relations: dealing with hate crimes and intolerance.* This subtly changed emphasis, by recognising Muslims as victims of hate crimes rather than just perpetrators of 'extremism' and framing its focus with a recognition of universities' responsibilities under the race relations legislation. The following year saw a return to the earlier approach, with the publication of further guidance by the DfES targeted at Muslim students' alleged extremism. This was condemned by Muslim students, academic trade unions and universities, and was largely rejected by the higher education sector.

Throughout the 1990s, the lack of research on Muslim students cemented the centrality of often problematic media accounts in debates about Muslim students. Increasing research on Muslim students highlights tensions between their continued stereotyping in narrow terms (e.g. through the preoccupation with extremism), and the increasingly differentiated experiences of Muslim students in higher education. The diffuse (and gendered) nature of Islamophobia, and its persistence in universities, is increasingly recognised, while attention has slowly fallen away from the narrow fixation with Muslim students as extremists and emphasises a far more representative picture of the breadth of student experiences. Despite this, the government produced yet more updated guidance on dealing with Muslim student extremism in 2008, through the Department for Innovation, Universities and Skills. This followed controversy over attempts to ban *niqab* in a university, and has been criticised for implying that provisions for Muslim students, such as prayer rooms, segregate campuses and provide breeding grounds for extremism. Anecdotal reports suggest that some universities have put into place frameworks for implementing the report's advice and monitoring and reporting on the expression of political views by Muslim students in classrooms.

References

Committee for Vice Chancellors and Principals (1998) *Extremism and intolerance on Campus.* London: CVCP.

DfES (2006) *Promoting Good Campus Relations: Working with Staff and Students to Build Community Cohesion and Tackle Violent Extremism in the Name of Islam at Universities and Colleges,* London: DfES.

Federation of Student Islamic Societies (2005) *The Voice of Muslim Students*, London: FOSIS.

Lucas, Noah (1985) 'Jewish Students, the Jewish Community and the "Campus War" in Britain', *Patterns of Prejudice*, 19 (4), pp. 27–34.

Tyrer, David (2004) 'The Others: extremism and intolerance on campus and the spectre of Islamic fundamentalism', in Ian Law, Deborah Phillips, and Laura Turney (eds), *Institutional Racism in Higher Education*, Stoke-on-Trent: Trentham Books, pp. 35–48.

——— and Fauzia Ahmad (2006) *Muslim Women Students and Higher Education: Identities, Experiences and Prospects: A Summary Report*, Liverpool: Liverpool John Moores University.

PART 3

ISLAMIC MOVEMENTS IN EUROPE: ISLAMISM AND ISLAMOPHOBIA

INTRODUCTION

Frank Peter

Throughout Western Europe, the 'integration' of Muslims has become a salient issue which triggers broad public debate. The central question in these debates is whether Muslims can conform to a variously imagined consensus of norms and cultural values, or whether their practices and beliefs are so different that they transgress the limits of pluralism as defined by law. These debates are conducted with a remarkable sense of urgency. In part, the urgency is derived by participants from a link that is made between the integration issue and concerns over terrorist threats. This has given rise to various suspicions directed at Muslim institutions and actors. While not all Muslim groups are subjected to scrutiny many are, in particular those studied here. In the course of this scrutiny, the way in which they are perceived by outsiders has radically changed. Most notably, many so-called conservative Muslim groups have acquired the taint of illegality, or even criminality, since it is widely believed today that they constitute the milieus conducive to radicalisation. In the heat of the debate about whether and how 'conservative' Islam and radicalism are linked to each other, a central insight has been largely lost; that the fear of radical Islam has as much to do with the broader context of European societies and their transformations as with what Muslims – or to be precise, some Muslims – believe and do. It is this basic insight which we wish to further explore in greater detail by looking at eight European countries. Such a perspective does not deny the reality of security threats, even if their scope and gravity is difficult to assess. Rather, this perspective requires us to ask in what ways the identification of these threats and the political and public responses to them are partly contingent upon a variety of external factors: the ever incomplete homogenisation of the nation, the increasing usage of a civilisational discourse about 'Islam and Europe', and the memory work of European societies. Likewise, it is not in dispute that cultural and religious difference can raise specific problems with regard to citizenship and legal orders in plural societies. However, as the following chapters will show, the questions which are raised today in debates about Islam in Europe and the urgency with which these questions are asked do not simply derive from such concerns.

At the most basic level, the following chapters suggest that these debates should be situated in the context of the nation state. This not only means that it is problematic to frame debates about Islam, as so often today, by pitting it against Europe or the West. In this respect, the following chapters provide abundant examples to show that, inside Europe, the identification of contentious features in Muslim communities and the discourses about them vary greatly, and they do so largely along national lines. More importantly, as the study of Germany argues, antagonism towards Muslims is closely determined by a basic mechanism in national societies and is, to a great degree, not specific to Muslims. This mechanism pertains to the fact that nations, much as any other bounded community, need to maintain an opposition between inside(rs) and outside(rs). It is this master-opposition which permits the creation of clear-cut criteria for action, based on what is right versus wrong, proper versus improper, etc. At the same time, it permits a demarcation of the space within which individual responsibility is to be exercised. Muslims, as people identified as different yet living inside, challenge this master-opposition. The threat perceived in their presence is thus not solely constituted by them, and not only by any points of difference perceived in their lifestyle. The current anxiety about Muslims results from the much more fundamental threat of ambivalence – uncertainty about the nation's 'we' and blurred criteria for proper action – and, ultimately, from the fear that this 'we' may change as a result of fully including Muslims as equal citizens.

To say that antagonism towards Muslims is largely structured by specific national contexts does not mean, of course, that European nations are internally unified or sealed off from the outside. Indeed, as we shall see here, the homogenisation of the nation is an ongoing process which can intersect in different ways with policies aimed at Muslims and Muslim institutions. In the case of Belgium, counter-terrorism policies and the desire to homogenise the nation along the lines of a white, middle-class, liberal and secular imaginary are closely entwined. Anxiety about Muslims in Brussels is not rooted simply in a fear of terrorist violence or radicalisation, but in uncertainties about social marginalisation, phenomena of spatial disintegration, and religious practices which sit uncomfortably with secular norms. A similar picture emerges from the study of Denmark. Adopting a more historical approach, it argues that an unusually well-integrated nation state has been forged in the course of Denmark's protracted emergence as a centralised welfare state. At the same time, a pattern of government has been established built on regulation and intervention in many aspects of citizens' lives. In the context of the well-integrated welfare state, debates about whether Muslim ways of life conform to the Danish consensus can – as they currently do in Denmark – acquire a particular intensity and weight.

From a different perspective, the study of Italy shows how the emergence of an Islamic threat relates to regional divisions and conflicts inside the nation and to its changing political order. The political restructuring of Italy in the 1990s and the emergence of the Second Republic occurred in parallel to the rise of the regionalist Lega Nord, which aspires to greater autonomy for northern Italy. However, the defence of regional interests by this party aims not only at reshaping relations with central government and southern Italy. It has also launched a broad, strongly worded campaign against immigration and in particular against Muslim immigrants, making these issues a field where it seeks to distinguish its own profile from that of rival parties. The virulence of this campaign and the exceptional intensity of debates about Islam in Italy must be seen in the context of a generally more outspoken and aggressive political style introduced into Italian politics, in part by Lega Nord, during the 1990s. In Italy, then, the question of how to deal with Muslim immigration and Islam is bound up with major intra-regional conflicts and political competition and acquires its particular severity as part of broader changes in styles of political communication.

Much as it is important to consider the nation as internally fragmented, it is equally important to note the supranational and global dimensions of contemporary anxieties about Islam in Europe. Since the 1980s, European nations have been caught in the throes of globalisation and European unification processes which have fragmented national sovereignty and changed the way in which nations can see themselves as particular. At the same time, geopolitical changes in the wake of the communist collapse have partly rendered obsolete old understandings of Western identities and transformed the lines of political alliance forged during the Cold War. At the conjunction of these processes, and against the backdrop of a continued rise of Islamic movements internationally, heightened public visibility of European Muslims since the late 1980s has provided a crucial incentive for rethinking a European identity as defined culturally and with reference to the Judeo-Christian heritage, humanism or the Enlightenment. Europe's nations diverge in their usage of these terms, often employed as vaguely as they are boldly. Most importantly, it is widely recognised that the place of Christianity in the formation of Europe, and its relation to secularism, vary greatly both inside and between nations. However, what all the nations studied here share today is a framing of identity along the lines of more or less unified civilisational blocks – one Islamic, the other European – which are thought to be in tension with each other.

Through this civilisational framing, disparate issues have been interpreted in light of alleged propensities or essences of Islam. The headscarf – whatever the women wearing it might say about their motives – is thus widely tainted with the stigma of Islam's generally negative view of women. It has become patently difficult to offer accounts of this practice which do not conform to a civilisational hierarchy that credits Europe with the full implementation of gender equality and simultaneously casts fundamental doubt on the possibility that a 'proper' citizen might legitimately wear a headscarf.

The adoption of a civilisational discourse is not without its effects on European societies either. More often than not, the defence of 'Europe' against any Islam-related threats is one which both results from and furthers the transformation of European nations, their mode of political organisation, their interpretation of their legal order, and their identity. The case of the Netherlands shows that adhering to a discourse of civilisation is in fact not easily reconciled with the empirical realities of Dutch society, and it has triggered a re-reading of Dutch history and its secular character. The Netherlands is one of those European countries where the incompleteness of secularisation – if we understand it as a strict separation of state and religions – is particularly significant on an institutional level. Dutch modernisation was achieved through a 'pillarisation' of society, with the systematic creation of societal institutions along denominational and ideological lines. While this model has certainly lost some of its grip in recent decades, it is not simply a thing of the past. In the current context, however, where the creation of an Islamic pillar is, in principle, a serious option for engineering the incorporation of Muslims, the situation has changed. Now, influential voices have emerged to propose a radical break with an order which, they argue, blatantly contradicts the notion of a secularised and truly Occidental Dutch society.

The case of the Netherlands, like the other studies, demonstrates how much the shape and urgency of anxieties about Islam are related to the memory work of European societies. Today various features and practices of Muslims are taken and compared with elements from European national memories. Regularly, in this process of interpretation, Muslims are understood and measured with reference to criteria which are external to their own histories and tradition. In Germany, for example, the inclusion of Islam into society often raises fears about 'regression'. Whether with regard to gender relations, where Muslim women are seen as not fully emancipated, or to modes of religiosity, where the lack of a critical approach to scripture raises concerns, Muslims are considered to represent a cultural and intellectual formation which has been superseded in the course of German history, where societal conflicts have paid the price. This fear of regression is particularly virulent with regard to the question of Israel–Palestine and the 'new' anti-Semitism which some claim exists within Germany's Muslim community. In each instance, specifically German historical experiences are universalised, the equal status and legitimacy of alternative histories and conceptions of the good life denied, and the plurality of social norms in Germany simply dismissed.

Finally, the study on France draws attention to the colonial history which united France and North Africa until after World War II. The post-colonial dimension of current conflicts about Muslims is usually eclipsed in favour of a focus on secularism and integration. A major effect of this focus is to attribute the responsibility for current conflicts primarily to Muslims. The case of France strongly impresses upon the reader the need to broaden our perspective with regard to the determining factors in these conflicts. Not only is there a direct relationship between the traumatic evacuation of Algeria by France in 1962 and the success of the extreme-right party Front National in France which has greatly contributed to configuring Muslim immigrants and citizens as undesirable and problematic. More importantly, the French example also raises a general question about how the immense colonial investment required to place colonised North Africans in a position of political and cultural inferiority has affected the conditions under which Muslims are accepted or rejected as equal citizens. The fact that simple claims to equal rights by Muslims are regularly seen in public debate as impertinent justifies asking whether this colonial investment has been fully unravelled.

BRUSSELS AS A LANDSCAPE
OF FEAR: CONTAINING 'OTHERNESS'

Nadia Fadil

With its 1,031,215 inhabitants, Brussels Capital Region (Brussels) figures as one of the largest and most diverse cities of Belgium. Home to international organisations such as NATO and the European Union, the Belgian capital has recently grown into an important node in the international flow of individuals, capital and political decision-makers. This growing diversity is also reflected in the important multicultural composition of its population as 46 per cent is considered to be of non-Belgian origin.[1] Of these, individuals with a Muslim background represent an important segment and are estimated at between 16 and 25 per cent.[2] The distinctiveness and visibility of this group is manifested through the socio-geographic concentration in certain communes, as well as the prevalence of their associations, commercial activities and political weight in various local municipalities. The *Quartier Midi* in the city centre of Brussels, the *Chaussée de Gand* in Molenbeek or the famous *Rue de Brabant* in Schaarbeek – which harbour a large number of Islamic bookstores, Arabic music stores, *halal* restaurants and Islamic fashion shops – offer a good glimpse into the reality of this group. Yet while this diversity has often been celebrated, it has also emerged as the source of deep social anxieties.

In its weekly edition in April 2010, the largely read Francophone weekly *Le-Vif express* covered its front page with the title 'Brussels: A Muslim town in 2030?'. Citing a study that stated that one-third of the inhabitants of Brussels are Muslim and that this group shows larger fertility rates than non-Muslims, the magazine asked whether the capital was turning into a Muslim town. A few months later the organisation La Pensée et les Hommes (Thought and Men), headed by Chemsi Cheref Khan, organised a day-long seminar around this same question at the Free University of Brussels (ULB), framing the issue as follows:

> The demographic explosion awaited in Brussels in the next 10 to 20 years is a matter of concern, not to say anxiety [...]. While there is unanimity about the necessity to underline the urgency and rapid measures that need to be adopted to face the new needs in terms of schools, crèches, qualified teachers etc., there also seems to be a strange conspiracy of silence towards the question of knowing who the new inhabitants of the capital are'.[3]

And in April 2011, the largely read Francophone daily *Le Soir* devoted one of the episodes of its special series on the capital entitled 'The seven capital clichés on Brussels' to the

Islamic presence in Brussels. One of its central themes concerned the question of whether Brussels was turning into a Muslim town.[4] What is significant is that 77 per cent of its online readership agreed with the proposition that Brussels was turning into a Muslim town.

Dystopian imaginaries of the city are not new, nor are they limited to the case of Brussels and its Muslim population. Urban studies have extensively documented how such daunting representations have always accompanied celebratory accounts that view the city as modernity's apogee. Seen on the one hand as the primary harbour of modernity's successes (industrialisation, technological innovation), cities are also understood as a place that concentrate modernity's antithesis (poverty, criminality). Yet such dystopian imaginaries of the city are often also deeply racialised – as the moral anxiety illustrated above about the growing Muslim population in the Belgian capital shows. Commenting on the case of Brussels, the urban geographer Guy Baeten explains how such 'clichés of urban doom' fit in a broader policy of urban governance, which remains incapable of addressing the city's growing ethno-cultural diversity.[5] Such clichés – that he links with the urban exodus of the white middle class in the second half of the twentieth century and its gradual replacement by migrants – remain deeply informed by 'white, male, heterosexual and middle-class prejudice' which 'reinforce the supremacy of a homogeneous, mainstream urban society'.[6] David Theo Goldberg traces the genealogy of such racialised representations back to the colonial endeavour, which was organised around the necessity of spatially marking the differences between the self and the Other.[7] He understands such dystopian imaginaries, which he sees to emerge around the nineteenth century, to reflect a sense of destabilisation of these initial racial categories and hierarchies. Destabilisations that are especially pronounced in the modern city:

> Degeneracy, then, is the mark of a pathological Other, an other both marked by and standing as the central sign of disorder. Stratified by race and class, the modern city becomes the testing ground of survival, of racialised power and control. The paranoia of losing power assumes the image of becoming Other, to be avoided like the plague.[8]

This chapter seeks to examine the contours of such dystopian representations of Brussels and how these have found a new point of articulation around the Muslim presence in the capital. While much of this moral anxiety is generally linked with the post-9/11 context and the growing public awareness and fear of 'radical Muslim networks', in this particular chapter I try to show how such anxieties convey a broader concern about the loss of control of the national imaginary and the impossibility of containing 'Otherness'. In order to do so, I will offer a detailed analysis of two non-fictional books which have had a large impact on the debate around Brussels (and its Muslim population) in recent years: *Undercover in Klein-Marokko* by Hind Fraihi and *Brussel: Eurabia* by Arthur Van Amerongen. Both works recount the undercover journey of two journalists in their quest for hidden radical Muslim networks in the capital. My focus on these two books is motivated by the wide impact they have had, as well as the fact that they are written by two individuals who self-identify as defenders of multiculturalism. In analysing these works, I wish to understand how such cultural products contribute to the co-constitution of Brussels, and its Muslim community, as an 'other' that is in need of governmental control. The analysis will focus on two aspects of the authors' narrative. The first one is the auto-biographical genre adopted by both authors, which weaves personal anecdotes through their descriptions of the capital. The second is the undercover nature of their investigation, which reinforces the representation of Brussels as a zone of radical Otherness – or heterotopia (Foucault). More than viewing these works as studies on radical Muslim networks in the Belgian capital, I argue that the stories of Fraihi and Van Amerongen can be read as an allegory of the failed attempts by the nation to domesticate and governmentalise Otherness – failures which, as we will see, will be differentially evaluated.

Debating Brussels and its Muslim community

The idea of Brussels as a harbour of radical Muslim networks can already be traced back to the early 1980s. In their seminal book *Medias U Akbar* (1987), the Belgian sociologists Albert Bastenier and Felice Dassetto offer an account of the moral panic around the public demonstrations by hundreds of Muslims (and non-Muslims) against the American invasion of Benghazi and Tripoli in April 1986 in the streets of Brussels. They describe in a detailed manner how the Francophone national broadcasting service (RTBF) turned these demonstrations into a pro-Khomeini rally that was infiltrated by anti-Western and anti-Israeli 'fundamentalists'. This provoked several condemnations by journalists, opinion leaders and politicians – chief among them Charles Picqué, mayor of Saint-Gilles (one of the 19 communes of the Belgian capital), who prompted the Minister of the Interior to conduct an investigation on the 'subterranean networks of information dissemination in the radical milieus and on the influence of those radical milieus on the rest of the Muslim community').[9]

Since then, alarming discourses about the growing role of the Belgian capital in the organisation of international terrorism have regularly hit the news. The French anxieties about political Islam in the early 1980s have also had a strong impact on the Belgian capital, considering its relative cultural and geographical proximity to Paris. Terrorist expert Alain Grignard explains, for instance, that the turn of the Belgian security experts to the question of radical Islam was largely mediated by the events in France, citing the Fouad Saleh affair – a French Tunisian who committed 15 attacks in Paris between 1985 and 1986 as retaliation for the French support for Iraq during the Iran/Iraq war – as a first case in point.[10] The political successes of Islamist groups and the outbreak of the civil war in Algeria and the consequent attacks in Paris in 1996, furthermore, strongly impacted upon the Belgian scene as Brussels was considered a logistical platform in these operations.[11] By the late 1990s and the turn to the twenty-first century, this fear of Algerian-based political Islam would gradually extend to a broader concern with internationally organised networks such as Al-Qaeda. Nizar Trabelsi, a former professional football player, was arrested in September 2001 in Brussels for plotting an attack on the American military basis at Klein-Borgel. And, a few days before the 9/11 attacks in 2001, the Afghan leader Ahmed Shah Masoud was killed by Abdessatar Dahmane, a Belgian–Tunisian who lived in Brussels. Dahmane was also the husband of Malika El Aroud, a second-generation Belgian–Moroccan who lived in Brussels and who was arrested and condemned in May 2010 for her implication in international terrorism. Two other figures that are worth mentioning in this row are the 'radical imam' Bassam Ayachi, director of the Centre Islamique Belge located in Molenbeek. He was arrested in Italy in 2009 but released in July 2012. Also Muriel Degauque, a Belgian convert who was the first Western woman to conduct a suicide operation against the American military in Iraq, and who lived in Brussels for a short period before assuming this operation.[12]

Uncovering radical networks in Brussels

The arrests of several people accused of plotting attacks has been at the source of alarming discourses about the presence of radical networks in the capital. The well-known Flemish war reporter Rudi Vranckx asserted, for instance, in 2005 that Muslim extremist groups were actively recruiting for Iraq in Brussels, after making a documentary on the subject.[13] And in his popular and controversial nonfiction novel *While Europe Slept. How Radical Islam is Destroying the West from Within*, the American journalist Bruce Bawer warns the European liberals for their abdication to Islamist groups in the name of progressive values and multiculturalism, which paves the way for a take-over by Islamist groups. Discussing the case of different European cities, he describes Brussels as a city where 'Muslims living in the Brussels neighbourhood of Sint-Jans-Molenbeek already view it not as part of Belgium but as an area under Islamic jurisdiction in which Belgians are not welcome'.[14]

The books that are being discussed here fit and contribute to this dystopian representation of Brussels. While both works have been written in Dutch, their publication has had a large impact on both Flemish and Francophone audiences, provoking a large number of debates and controversies about the current state of affairs of the capital. *Undercover in Little-Morocco* (Undercover in Klein-Marokko) consists of a collection of newspaper articles that were written by the Belgian–Moroccan journalist Hind Fraihi for the popular daily *Het Nieuwsblad* in 2005. In these, she describes her undercover journey in the Belgian capital looking for radical Islamic networks. Fraihi lived for two months in Molenbeek-Saint-Jean, one of the poorest communes of Brussels with a high percentage of Muslims. The articles were broadly advertised by *Het Nieuwsblad* and received a large amount of public attention. They also provoked a debate about the integration of Muslims in Brussels and even lead to a parliamentary interpellation of the Minister of the Interior by a member of the right-wing political party *Vlaams Belang*.[15] The large attention given to her work stands in sharp contrast to the little factual information that is actually given about the presence of such radical groups. Fraihi's reports and book largely consist of an autobiographical account that is woven through the observations. She describes her visits to Islamic bookstores and Islamic organisations where conservative and women-unfriendly literature is sold, and holds a pessimistic diagnosis about the fate of Muslims in Belgium. While some conversations describe the support of some individuals for the *jihad* in Iraq and Afghanistan,[16] little information is provided about the seriousness of possible attacks in the capital.

Arthur Van Amerongen's *Brussel: Eurabia* shows large similarities with the work of Fraihi. His account is also the result of a lengthy undercover stay in the capital where he infiltrated a number of Islamic organisations passing as a Muslim convert. Autobiographical descriptions are woven through his descriptions: from his Calvinist youth, his life as a heroin addict, the psychological and emotional turmoil, and his professional career as a foreign correspondent in North Africa and the Middle East. As in the case of Fraihi, little evidence is given of the presence of militant networks in the Belgian capital, with the exception of one dubious encounter with a young man who hailed the *jihad*.[17] Despite the success of Van Amerongen's book (it was reprinted four times in 2008) and the media attention, a different fate would await him. In November 2007, the Francophone anti-racist movement MRAX filed a complaint against TV Brussels for broadcasting an interview with Arthur Van Amerongen that they considered racist. The movement challenged certain claims about Muslims made by Van Amerongen, who seemed to be drunk during his interview, and the journalist's incapacity to challenge those.[18] In addition, the board of the Nederlandse Fonds Bijzondere Journalistieke Projecten (Dutch Foundation for Particular Journalistic Projects), which funded part of the research stay of Van Amerongen, demanded a total reimbursement of the €16,500 grant after the publication of the book. They denounced the absence of actual undercover investigative journalism as well as the strong autobiographical components of the book.[19]

In analysing these works, the primary aim is not to offer an overview of their main findings about the presence of radical groups in the Belgian capital. The perspective that I adopt is rather one which tries to understand the performative role of such works, the kind of imaginaries they enable and co-constitute. For the successes of these works does not simply lie in the factual information they offer (which is quite limited), but more in the way their descriptions resonate with a wider cultural and historical context. In what follows, I will therefore try to show how these books can be read as a symptom of the growing anxiety over the multicultural composition of Belgium. An anxiety which, in the case of Fraihi and Van Amerongen, becomes articulated through the incapacity to contain the 'Other' through a number of (liberal) scripts which are taken as the common ground in the delineation of the nation.

Narrating the Self, establishing complicity

In her work *Autobiographics: A feminist theory of women's self-representation*, the cultural theorist Leigh Gilmore tries to unravel the particular work the genre of autobiography performs. A genre, she notes elsewhere, which has grown in popularity through the political mobilisation of historically disadvantaged minority groups such as women or people of colour.[20] The autobiographical genre firstly epitomises the primary mode through which individuals within Western modernity are instructed to talk about themselves; that is, by 'confessing' their interior truths. More than just describing inner truths, autobiographies also *produce* the 'truth' about oneself. They situate and inscribe the individual within a set of discourses or cultural formations by which he or she becomes readable at a particular moment of history.[21] The power of autobiographies, Gilmore notes, lies furthermore in their recognisability to the reader and their capacity to establish a sense of complicity, of identification, of *we-ness* with its audience. Drawing on an Althusserian perspective, which understands autobiographies as a moment of interpellation, Gilmore explains how this literary genre operates as an ideological vector in a double way. First, at the level of the autobiographical subject, who is produced through the story and who structures and frames her own story in relation to, or within, dominant cultural schemes.[22] Second, in relation to the reader who is hailed by the story and identifies with the 'representation of her position in relation to other familiar positions within cultural scripts'.[23]

Gilmore's account invites us to shed some light over the strong reflexive and autobiographical component of the works examined here. These autobiographical elements might, at first sight, seem striking, as they stand in sharp contrast to the detached, sober and objective tone that is generally assumed for investigative journalism. Both Fraihi and Van Amerongen disrupt this code by enacting as much about themselves as about the observed – something which, as has been noted earlier, will not remain without any consequences for Van Amerongen. Their accounts resonate with the journalistic genre known as 'new journalism' and describe a particular form of writing which challenges the very idea of the reporter as a detached, dislocated observer, an idea it considers as deeply 'deceiving'. Adopting a personal and autobiographical style becomes, thus, a means to achieve more authenticity and objectivity in one's relationship to the reader. Yet in these particular cases, the integration of personal elements seems to do something more than reflecting transparency. It turns the works of Van Amerongen and Fraihi into testimonies. Testimonies which address the reader and therefore establish a sense of intimate familiarity with the authors. A sense of complicity that, furthermore, is not abstract but clearly mediated by distinct cultural (i.e. liberal) scripts. The adoption of an autobiographical style can consequently be understood as a rhetorical style that individualises and naturalises the (liberal) interpretative categories that undergird the author's perception of the 'Other', and which enables the establishment of a liberal sense of commonality – a liberal we-ness – between the author and the reader.

Articulating self-critique

Hind Fraihi's self-presentation is an ambiguous one. One that could be characterised as that of an in-outsider or a hybrid position that sits midway between that of an external observer and of a witness.[24] Her position as a journalist, and the investigative role she adopts, implies holding a position as an extern towards the Muslim community. But Fraihi is not just any kind of journalist, but a journalist of *Muslim* background. This places her in a particular position, as it presupposes a certain degree of complicity and loyalty with the Muslim community. A large part of her account therefore consists of persistently marking her distance from the community, in order to remain an outsider. She firstly does so by highlighting her role as a journalist when she decides, for instance, not to try on a *burqa*: 'I take my job too seriously to dress as if it were Carnival'.[25] The idea of being an outsider is equally reflected when she decides to leave the city after a few weeks into her stay, to return to her native town in rural Flanders from where she will engage ino a daily commute to Brussels. In doing so, she defines herself through a dominant Flemish trope that represents the idea of 'home' (and Flanders) as rural, and the city – that is, Brussels – as a hostile environment. A final way in which she marks her position as an outsider is by presenting her Muslim background as an asset which grants her the necessary cultural and religious capital to easily infiltrate the Muslim community and to decode certain observations:

> I want, as an undercover journalist, to go to places where no cameras can go, where a Flemish journalist without a Muslim background will not have access, where people can speak openly in the Arabic language that I understand'.[26]

Her Muslim background becomes consequently primarily understood in its instrumental value.

Gradually we learn, however, that Fraihi's relationship with the Muslim community of Brussels is more complex than a mere professional engagement. This becomes especially apparent in one of the first sentences of the second chapter where she writes about the motives that inform her assignment:

> Salman Rushdie puts it beautifully: 'Muslims aren't the problem, Muslims have a problem'. Allah-damnit, we do not seem to want to advance, we are not even standing still. The only progress we are making seems to lie in our backwardness. It is as if our future lies behind us. Call it collective escapism from the social problems that we do not seem to want to resolve. It seems easier to dance to the rhythms of tyranny and fundamentalism. We behave like easy marionettes. Do I seem *pissed off*? Well, I am.[27]

A deep sense of anger about what she considers a situation of 'backwardness' among the Muslim community informs Fraihi's work. Two elements stand out in her diagnosis. The first one is the denouncement of the socio-economic precariousness in which the community lives, which is portrayed through images of poverty, degradation, filth and unemployment and is omnipresent in her descriptions. The second is what she describes as the absence of 'self-critique'. Self-critique emerges here as a narrative which articulates a distancing from the conservative and illiberal tendencies she observes in the community, ranging from the presence of strict segregationist views on gender[28] to hostile views on non-Muslims[29] or the apology of violence and *jihad*.[30] Self-critique consequently operates as an aesthetic of the self or a transformative practice that should allow the inscription of the Muslim community into the civil society, which is primarily encoded in liberal terms (cf. below). It is in this respect that the autobiographical components that she integrates in her narrative become relevant. As a reader, we learn about her family background that seems to emerge as a liberal horizon, which holds the promise of a 'different' Islam. The anecdotes she recounts about her family embody an Islam whose values are centred around the acquisition of knowledge and culture, a mother who reacts furiously to the condemnations to hell of unveiled Muslim women by Muslim theologians ('No God, no man, but the woman herself decides whether she will veil') and vivid and warm memories of her father playing, as a child, with his Jewish neighbours in Morocco.[31] Such memories counterbalance the Muslim practices she encounters in Brussels and which she experiences as dissonant to the Islam she was raised in. Fraihi's sense of anger can therefore be read as an expression of her own powerlessness at the sight of an Islam that emerges as 'Other', *even* to her own self-understanding.

By explicitly distancing herself from the Muslims she encounters in Molenbeek, *Undercover in Little-Morocco* articulates an ethical and ontological distance between herself and the 'other' Muslims of Brussels. The autobiographical or testimonial style she adopts is furthermore foregrounded upon a sense of complicity between herself and the reader. This observation resonates with the analysis offered by the cultural analyst John Beverley who, in his reading of testimonies by Latin-American revolutionaries, points at how this genre opens a 'discursive space' which allows for the possibility of political alliances 'without too much angst about otherness or othering'.[32] One could therefore understand Fraihi's work as an attempt to overturn the way in which processes of othering are predominantly articulated through a simple Muslim/non-Muslim, autochtonous/allochtonous dichotomy. A different 'we-ness' emerges here, one which is not articulated on ethnic or religious grounds, but rather according to the commitment one holds towards the promise of a liberal (national) imaginary.

The other as a failed promise

Brussel: Eurabia in many ways retraces the professional and personal journey of an author longing for a professional and personal tranquillity. The book recounts the various episodes of Arthur Van Amerongen's professional career as a journalist, which started through the stimulus of his mother who enrolled him for training as a journalist at one of the main Protestant Dutch newspapers to reinforce his piety.[33] We learn about his strict Calvinist education and how he gradually distanced himself from it and simultaneously started cultivating a fascination for Islam, to which he even considered converting. In difference to Fraihi, Van Amerongen's engagement with Islam seems to be primarily mediated by a fascination for something 'other' than that he grew up in. This fascination translated into a professional engagement as a foreign correspondent for a Dutch newspaper in the Middle East. The successive chapters describe his experiences in the region, his moments of deep complicity and solidarity with the Palestinians, his discovery of the Israeli oppression, and his collaborations with Islamist groups in Algeria or Lebanon.

Yet Van Amerongen's initial enthusiasm for the region gradually starts to dissipate. He describes how his fear of death leads him to abandon his work as a correspondent in the Middle East. This leaves him with a sense of bitterness about the value of his work and his own success: 'I had achieved nothing with my reporting. I never really had the illusion that I could change whatsoever with my reporting'.[34] These professional disappointments are, furthermore, tied with his numerous personal soul-searching episodes. We learn about his troubled life, the many experiences of loss, pain and solitude. The loss of his older brother, the existential break with the strong Calvinist ethos he was raised in, his turn to drugs and alcohol.[35] It is in this context that his assignment in Brussels emerges as a last attempt to save himself – personally, but also professionally:

> Only a miracle could still save me. The murder of Theo Van Gogh would change everything: I escaped from the Middle East, but it came now under the guise of Moroccan extremism towards me. The conflict had relocated in the heart of Europe. I considered Brussels as my last straw.[36]

The several months of undercover reporting he spends in the Belgian capital, however, fail to bring the professional and personal relief he yearns for. The picture he depicts of the capital is a dark one: streets full of dirt, social and economic despair, and a Muslim community that is ruled by conservative and intolerant mentalities. A conservatism which also reminds him of his Calivinist youth. These observations do not leave him unaffected, but provoke a deep political shift in his relationship:

> I had been completely wrong with my conclusion. At the end of my stay in Brussels I no longer heard my other sound. I was convinced that Islam was pernicious ('*Ik was ervan overtuigd dat de islam een splijtzwam was*'). Modern Muslims, if they already exist, always held mealy-mouthed talks about the possibility of a European Islam. But in Brussels, I only saw ghettos full of Muslims with Middle-Aged convictions that are in no way connected with Belgian society. Even more, they despise that society.[37]

What started as a promise of salvation through the interactions with the 'Other' turns out to be a grim disappointment. *Brussel:Eurabia* expresses a sense of disillusion by an author who had once been invested in the promises of the 'Other'. While a large part of his life had been governed by a deep sense of complicity with this other, the Muslim community of Brussels not only fails him, his experiences in Brussels even exacerbate new tensions and open the path for new fears; 'I felt chased and restless, Islam had not brought the peace that I needed so much. I was condemned to a life-long search for myself'.[38] In contrast to Fraihi, whose autobiographical components articulate the existence of a 'liberal Islam', *Brussel: Eurabia* is a testimony by an author who had once hoped to achieve personal stability through his journeys and interactions with 'the Other' (in the Middle East, in Brussels) only to return to himself grim, disappointed and full of bitterness. The 'Other', that had been temporarily imagined and experienced as an escape (from his Calvinist youth, from his addiction), only to turn into an obstacle to his own salvation. In what follows, we will see how this disappointment translates into a broader political position about multiculturalism and the (in)ability to domesticate and integrate this difference into society.

Domesticating heterotopia

In his short and suggestive essay *Des espaces autres. Heterotopies* (1967), Michel Foucault lays out the characteristics of a particular space that he sees emerging with modernity and which he describes as heterotopia or spaces of absolute otherness – *une sorte de contre-emplacement* – as he writes. A space which operates as a momentary escape (such as holiday villages) or which externalises those aspects of life that we no longer wish to confront (such as death and cemeteries). Heterotopia as a zone of absolute otherness that society creates and organises for its own self-preservation. A heterotopia, to Foucault, is therefore as much about the self as it is about the other. It is a way to become oneself, to organise oneself, to constitute a self by outsourcing certain elements which do not correspond with this dominant self-understanding.[39]

The accounts Fraihi and Van Amerongen offer of Brussels and its Muslim community places it into a trope of radical Otherness. This already emerges through the *undercover* nature of their operation. While both journalists do little more than visit Islamic bookstores, talk to representatives of the Islamic civil society, go to mosques and Islamic conferences or chat with youngsters in the streets, these become surrounded by an atmosphere of illegality and secrecy. The suggestion is even made that a deeper world exists – a heterotopia within a heterotopia – which conceals the secrets (about *jihad*, terrorism, etc.) of this world:

> The answers I get are very vague, unclear. This is typical for the conversations that I will carry out here in Molenbeek: giving some pieces of information and then pulling back. Why? Are Muslims in Molenbeek afraid to tell too much? Will their indiscretion be punished? Or is it about me? From the moment I know about something, I want to dig deeper. Suspiciously deeper. And that maybe turns the people of Molenbeek distrustful towards me.[40]

The author's relationship to this heterotopia is an ambiguous one. A sense of fascination characterises the position of both authors for the distinct temporalities that are seen to govern these different zones. Fraihi describes, for instance, her adventures in a fabric shop in Molenbeek as follows:

> I hide myself in metres of glittering fabric to silently dream away. I can already picture myself in a dream robe, with my black hair in waving arabesques. As a capricious romantic, I rival for the attention of men and the envy of women. I withdraw myself from the earthly and turn into an Arab princess.[41]

Molenbeek as a zone of fantasy, which allows her to enact a dream of beauty and seduction, and experience warmth that she (and her parents) too often seem to miss in Belgium: 'Shopping in Molenbeek is like spending one's summer in the Mediterranean without sun. Morocco is far from here, but Molokko lies at the centre of Belgium and attracts Moroccans from the whole country'.[42] Van Amerongen, on the other hand, underlines the *gemeinschaft* (Tönnies) or communal warmth he encounters there: 'As a potential convert, I had been welcomed with open arms by Muslims. They were happy about my presence at the Academy'.[43]

Yet this Orientalising fascination is equally traversed by fears of the unknown. Fraihi and Van Amerongen describe the security measures they adopt to keep their real identities undisclosed. Fraihi does so by being in touch at least once a day through SMS with her chief editor, by taking a new phone number and having a safe address in Molenbeek where she can escape to in case of necessity.[44] Their penetration into the mysterious, inaccessible zones uncovers the existence of ideas, visions, practices and worldviews which are the antipode of what they stand for: ideas about women, piety, religion, violence.

Brussels (and the Muslim community) as a heterotopia represents, therefore, more than a mere spectacle. The otherness that is uncovered by the journalists is one that disturbs, one that repulses one's liberal sentiments and also calls for an intervention. Throughout her study, Fraihi insists on the necessity of reconfiguring and transforming reigning viewpoints about Islam. We saw in the previous section how Fraihi's investigation in Molenbeek mirrored her own coming to terms with her Muslim background. It is through the other – through Molenbeek – that she understands that she longs for a different Islam:

> As expected I am accused by some of my co-believers of fouling my own nest. But it is because I love my nest that I do not want to see it spoiled by Muslim radicals. It is we, moderate Muslims, who should take the rotten elements away. With the right light you can make even the most rotten elements shine'.[45]

Challenging illiberal conceptions among the Muslim community, challenging the 'Otherness' she encounters in Brussels, becomes therefore a means of domesticating Muslims and of turning them into a part of the European body politics, of turning them into a part of 'history'. *Undercover in Little-Morocco* can therefore be read as an attempt to engage with the illiberal and orthodox facets of the Islamic tradition that she sees hindering Muslims from becoming full subjects. Dismantling the state of heterotopia by transforming the subject, by cultivating them, by domesticating them – these are words which resonate with what Foucault (1982) described as the pastoral power modernity conveys.

Van Amerongen's stand is, on the other hand, a more pessimistic one. His position is one of a radical disillusionment with the condition of Brussels and its Muslim community:

> I had lived as an ascetic and read hundreds of book about Islam, I had spent years in the Middle East, but all my knowledge about Islam seemed at the end to be nothing more than useless junk. I had been blinded by the beauty of Islam.[46]

His account represents a 'turn-away-from-multiculturalism' – a narrative that emerged in the early 1990s and has since grown in popularity among liberal and left-wing commentators (Fadil, 2010). He, furthermore, also considers this otherness untameable (contrary to Fraihi) and potentially dangerous. This idea is forcefully conveyed in the title of his book: Brussels figures not only as a heterotopia, but as a *Eurabia*. A haunting and dangerous zone because of its growing aspirations:

> Could the European Union, with almost 500 million inhabitants, be overrun by a small minority of 15 million Muslims? Could it be true that the Moroccan and Turkish migrants had been sent by their governments to Europe to start the Islamisation of Europe?.[47]

While he remains doubtful that this would be the case for the first generation of immigrants – who are represented as goodhearted, ignorant and naive – he becomes more suspicious towards their offspring. The space of heterotopia turns into a 'monster' that needs to be eradicated for one's own survival.

Brussel: Eurabia and *Undercover in Little-Morocco* can therefore be read as the authors' –and Belgian society's– attempts to domesticate otherness. An alterity it needs for the delineation of its own national identity, yet an alterity that needs to remain contained in a space of otherness, in a space of heterotopia. The moral pessimism that traverses their works reflects the struggle and failure in doing so, ranging from Fraihi's urgent calls for a liberal domestication of this other to Van Amerongen's sinister predictions of a Muslim takeover. These works can consequently be read as a comment upon the continuous destabilisations that are experienced in the various attempts to foreclose the national imaginary in liberal and secular terms.

Conclusion

In November 2009 the Belgian movie *Les Barons*, directed by the Belgian–Moroccan Nabil Ben Yadir, came out in the cinemas and was one of the most successful films of the year in Brussels. It tells the story of Hassan, Mounir, Aziz and Franck, young adults in their mid-twenties whose lives seem to be undecided between defeatism and the hope for a better tomorrow. They call themselves *les barons* because of the pleasure they take in hanging out and sleeping, rather than working. Yet this strong friendship will come to an abrupt end after Mounir's discovery of Hassan's amorous feelings for his sister. This causes a deep rift in the circle of friends, and Hassan decides to accept a job as a bus driver at the company where his father works and to settle for a marriage with a girl from his neighbourhood. He nevertheless keeps cultivating his secret passion – comedy – an art form which will have a decisive impact upon his journey and the outcome of the movie.

In *Les Barons*, Ben Yadir tries to offer a poignant critique of the defeatism he sees paralysing the youth. It is an attempt to re-empower the youth of Brussels by encouraging them to believe again in their own abilities. The movie, however, also offers a different image and aesthetic of the capital. The streets of Brussels are pictured in a colourful way and the whole movie is encapsulated with humour, which throws a certain degree of lightness over some of the tragic themes it raises. In one of the many interviews he gave, Ben Yadir explains his deep exhaustion about the stereotypical representations of Brussels and Molenbeek, the neighbourhood he grew up in.[48] With *Les Barons*, he wanted to offer a different image of Brussels and its Muslim community, by showing how 'mundane' many of their everyday problems are. An image of recognisability, of intelligibility, which brings us far away from the tropes of heterotopia observed in the work of Fraihi and Van Amerongen. Scenes where the local imam hysterically reacts to the discovery of a pack of cigarettes in the aspiring bride's handbag, or where a conservative Muslim restaurant owner passionately explains his boycott of Coca-Cola, only to serve Fanta a moment later, serve to underline the absurdity the director sees in certain Muslim orthodox tendencies. The movie has therefore also been praised as 'taboo-breaking', or as a movie that dared to raise a number of sensitive issues within the Muslim community and to articulate the much- needed 'self-critique'.[49] Yet, despite the different portrayal of Brussels (and its Muslim community) in *Les Barons*, what remains consistent with the accounts explored above is a consensus about who is to be considered as other. Whereas Fraihi and Van Amerongen's perspective is daunting and underscores the omnipresence of this other, Ben Yadir's lightness seems to downplay its importance by mocking it, and by mocking the audience's fears. Humour becomes, in *Les Barons*, a speech act or a discursive technique that serves to minimise, and therefore contain, the seriousness of a potential threat.

This chapter has tried to show the difficulty with which the question of difference seems to be understood in Belgium by taking two non-fictional books on Muslims in Brussels as a case study. Because of its symbolic role as a capital and the large presence of religious and cultural minorities – of which Muslims represent an important segment – Brussels has become the scene of several dystopian imaginaries about its gradual fragmentation and overtaking by radical and fundamentalist Muslims. Dystopian imaginaries which are a reflection, I have suggested, of the inability to address the question of pluralism in other terms than as a threat. More than being a work on the presence of radical Muslim networks in the Belgian capital, both works therefore illustrate the growing anxieties that surround the pluralistic composition of Belgium and Europe. Only time will and can tell whether alternative narratives will emerge which can grasp this reality in terms other than a threatening heterotopia. In the meantime, liberal and nationalistic homogenising fantasies remain pervasive, and the presence of Muslims persists as a haunting spectre.[50]

Notes

1   Didier Willaert and Patrick Deboosere (2005) *Buurtatlas van de bevolking van het Brussels Hoofdstedelijk Gewest bij de aanvang van de 21e eeuw*, Ministerie van het Brussels Hoofdstedelijk Gewest: Brussels Instituut voor Statistiek en Analyse.

2   See Ural Manço and Meryem Kanmaz (2005) 'From Conflict to Co-operation Between Muslims and Local Authorities in a Brussels Borough: Schaerbeek', *Journal of Ethnic and Migration Studies*, 31: p. 1106; and Felice Dassetto, Albert Bastenier and Abdelatif Elachy (1987) *Medias U Akbar*, Louvain-la-Neuve: CIACO.

3   'Une majorité musulmane à Bruxelles en 2030?' in *La Libre Belgique*, 14 January 2012, Available at www.lalibre.be/actu/bruxelles/article/713047/une-majorite-musulmane-en-2030.html. (link accessed 19 June 2014)

4   'Brussels, a Muslim town?' [Bruxelles, ville Musulmane?], *Le Soir*, 11 April 2011.

5   Guy Baeten (2001) 'Clichés of Urban Doom: The Dystopian Politics of Metaphors for the Unequal City – A View from Brussels', in *International Journal of Urban and Regional Research*, 25:1 pp. 55–69.

6   Ibid., p. 55.

7   David Theo Goldberg (1993) *Racist Culture. Philosophy and the Politics of Meaning*, Cambridge: Blackwell, p. 187.

8   Ibid., p. 200.

9   Dassetto, *Medias U Akbar*, p. 90.

10 Alain Grignard (2008) 'The Islamist networks in Belgium', in Rik Coolsaet (ed), *Jihadi terrorism and the radicalisation challenge in Europe*, London: Ashgate p. 86.

11 In 1994, the Belgian authorities arrested and condemned Ahmed Zaoui – a former FIS member who had fled the country to Europe after the failed elections of 1991 – for his complicity in organised crime and for using false passports.

12 Muriel Degauque's story has caught the attention of many commentators and has been the source of a bestseller by the investigative journalist Chris De Stoop (2010) *Vrede Zij met U Zuster* [Peace be upon you sister], Antwerpen/Amsterdam: De Bezige Bij.

13 In *Gazet Van Antwerpen*, 31 October 2005.

14 Bruce Bawer (2006) *While Europe Slept: How Radical Islam is Destroying the West from Within*, Anchor, p. 33.

15 This has also lead to a 'real' political interpellation of the Minister of the Interior by right-wing Vlaams Belang, MP: '*Interpellatie van de heer Francis Van den Eynde tot de vice-eerste minister en minister van Binnenlandse Zaken over "het bestaan van bendes van Brusselse boefjes die dermate ongemoeid gelaten worden dat zij hun wandaden op een weblog tentoonspreiden*"' (22 June 2005). Explicit references are made to Hind Fraihi's book to denounce the uninhabitable and ungovernable status of Molenbeek.

16 Hind Fraihi (2006) *Undercover in Klein-Marokko. Achter de gesloten deuren van de radicale Islam*, Leuven: Van Halewyck, pp. 18–9.

17 Arthur Van Amerongen (2008) *Brussel: Eurabia*, Amsterdam: Atlas, p. 166.

18 'Le Mrax se plaint à l'encontre de TV Brussel d'une interview de nature raciste et xenophobe', 13 December 2007.

19 Anne Brugmane 'Auteur "Brussel: Eurabia" moet subsidie wellicht terugstorten', 19 June 2008. Available at Brusselnieuws.be: http://www.brusselnieuws.be/cultuur/auteur-brussel-eurabia-moet-subsidie-wellicht-terugstorten. (link accessed 19 June 2014)

20 Leigh Gilmore (1994) *Autobiographics: a feminist theory of women's self-representation*, Ithaca: Cornell University Press, p. 2.

21 Ibid., p. 19.

22 Ibid., p. 25.

23 Ibid., p. 23.

24 For a similar analysis of the heterogeneous subject positions adopted by a Muslim spokesperson analysed through the case of the Dutch–Somalian Ayaan Hirsi Ali, see Marc De Leeuw and Sonja Van Wichelen (2005) '"Please, Go Wake Up!" Submission, Hirsi Ali and the "War on Terror" in the Netherlands', *Feminist Media Studies*, 5 (3) pp. 325–40.

25 Fraihi, *Undercover in Klein-Marokko*, p. 64.

26 Ibid., p. 34.

27 Ibid., p27–8. (Fraihi's emphasis).

28 Ibid., pp.90–1, 97.

29 Ibid., pp. 81, 98.

30 Ibid., pp. 99, 108–9.

31 Ibid., pp. 68–9, 91–2, 82.

32 John Beverley (1991) 'Through all things modern': second thoughts on testimonio', *Boundary*, 2 p. 4.

33 Van Amerongen, *Brussel: Eurabia*, p. 33.

34 Ibid., p. 90.

35 Ibid., p. 28.

36 Ibid., p. 95.

37 Ibid., p. 170–1.

38 Ibid., p. 175.

39 Foucault uses the metaphor of the mirror to elucidate the entangled – yet distinctive – relationship between utopia and heterotopia. While utopia emerges as a mirage, as an imaginary and perfect – yet non-physical – space (our image in the mirror), heterotopia is that 'other place' (i.e. the image in the mirror), which is real, and through which we can know ourselves.

40   Fraihi, *Undercover in Klein-Marokko*, p. 47.
41   Ibid., p. 37.
42   Ibid., p. 38.
43   Van Amerongen, *Brussel: Eurabia*, p. 29.
44   Fraihi, *Undercover in Klein-Marokko*, p. 48.
45   Ibid., p. 175.
46   Van Amerongen, *Brussel: Eurabia*, p. 175.
47   Ibid., p. 169.
48   Niels Ruëll (2009) '*Les Barons*. Comedie verbergt harde realiteit', 5 November. Available at http://www.brusselnieuws.be/cultuur/les-barons-komedie-verbergt-harde-realiteit. (link accessed 19 June 2014)
49   See for instance 'Nabil Ben Yadir. Les Barons' in *De Standaard*, 4 November 2009: 'Ben Yadir does not mince his words and describes with a lot of self-critique and panache the clumsy way in which the main character tries to deviate from the prescribed route.'
50   I am grateful to Sarah Bracke and Mathias Delori for their comments on earlier versions of this paper.

References

Baeten, Guy (2001) 'Clichés of Urban Doom: The Dystopian Politics of Metaphors for the Unequal City – A View from Brussels', *International Journal of Urban and Regional Research*, 25:1, pp. 55–69.

Bawer, Bruce (2006) *While Europe Slept: How Radical Islam is Destroying the West from Within*, Anchor.

Beeman, William O. (2000) 'Humor' in Allesandro Duranti (ed.), 'Linguistic Lexicon for the Millenium', *Journal of Linguistic Anthropology*, 9: 2.

Beverley, John (1991) 'Through all things modern': second thoughts on testimonio', *Boundary*, 2 pp. 1–21.

Dassetto, Felice, Albert Bastenier and Abdelatif Elachy (1987) *Medias U Akbar* Louvain-la-Neuve: CIACO.

De Leeuw Marc and Sonja Van Wichelen (2005) '"Please, Go Wake Up!" Submission, Hirsi Ali and the "War on Terror" in the Netherlands', *Feminist Media Studies*, 5 (3) pp. 325–40.

Fadil, Nadia (2010) 'Breaking the taboo of multiculturalism. The Belgian left and Islam', in Abdoolkarim Vakil and S. Sayyid (eds) *Thinking Through Islamophobia. Global Perspectives*, New York: Columbia University Press.

Foucault, Michel (1967) *Des espaces autres. Heterotopies.*

——(1982) Afterword. 'The Subject and Power', in Hubert L. Dreyfus and Paul Rabinow (eds), *Michel Foucault. Between Structuralism and Hermeneutics*, Brighton: Harvester Press.

Fraihi, Hind (2006) *Undercover in Klein-Marokko. Achter de gesloten deuren van de radicale Islam*, Leuven: Van Halewyck.

Gilmore, Leigh (1994) *Autobiographics: a feminist theory of women's self-representation*, Ithaca: Cornell University Press.

—— (2001) *The Limits of Autobiography. Trauma and testimony*, Ithaca / London: Cornell University Press.

Goldberg, David Theo (1993) *Racist Culture: Philosophy and the Politics of Meaning*, Cambridge: Blackwell.

Grignard, Alain (2008) 'The Islamist networks in Belgium', in Rik Coolsaet (ed), *Jihadi terrorism and the radicalisation challenge in Europe*, London: Ashgate, pp. 85–93.

Manço, Ural and Kanmaz, Meryem (2006) 'From Conflict to Co-operation Between Muslims and Local Authorities in a Brussels Borough: Schaerbeek', *Journal of Ethnic and Migration Studies*, 31 pp. 1105–23.

Van Amerongen, Arthur (2008) *Brussel: Eurabia*, Amsterdam: Atlas.

Willaert, D. and Deboosere, P. (2005) *Buurtatlas van de bevolking van het Brussels Hoofdstedelijk Gewest bij de aanvang van de 21e eeuw*, Ministerie van het Brussels Hoofdstedelijk Gewest: Brussels Instituut voor Statistiek en Analyse.

DENMARK

Heiko Henkel

The place of Islam and the Muslim minority in Denmark, and the debates and contro-versies surrounding them, shares many similarities with the situation in other Western European countries. The public debate concerning the legitimate place of Islam in Danish society was especially pronounced, however, with the Muhammad Cartoon Crisis of 2006 as its well-known high point. As elsewhere in Western Europe, the debate about Islam is closely connected with the debate over immigration and, at least since the 9/11 attacks, with the threat of 'fundamentalist' violence. To understand the enormous public interest in Islam and the central place 'Islam' has gained in Danish political debate, however, one also has to understand the important role the critique of Islam has acquired in the reshaping of Danish identity today. In the following, I discuss some of the important factors that have shaped Danish society and its contemporary engagement with its emerging Muslim society under the headings (1) 'Danishness' and the Welfare State (2) From Cultural Radicalism to Neo-nationalism (3) 'Danes' vs. 'Muslims', and (4) Uncertain hori-zons.

(1) 'Danishness' and the Welfare State

Perhaps the most important feature that distinguishes Denmark from many other European societies today is that, due to its particular historical trajectory, it has emerged as an unusually well-integrated nation state. The institutional backbone of this integration is Denmark's extensive welfare state, which strongly shapes the lives of virtually every resi-dent, whether wealthy or poor, citizen or refugee, through an array of interconnected institutions that supervise, facilitate and regulate most aspects of life. This tightly woven institutional matrix of the welfare state profoundly shapes the encounters of immigrants and their children with Danish society.

The welfare state was built during the twentieth century on the foundations of Denmark's increasingly centralised state as it had emerged since the seventeenth century. The 'abso-lutist' reforms of Frederik III in 1660 had greatly curtailed the power of the aristocracy in Denmark and concentrated power in the hands of a central bureaucracy. Parallel to the emergence of the bureaucratic state, the Lutheran reform movement of Nikolai Grundtvig (1783–1872) contributed greatly to the integration of Danish society in the nineteenth and twentieth centuries. Developing the Lutheran emphasis on civic virtues, Grundtvig succeeded in making the combined Christian and national education of all

Danes irrespective of their social background into a national credo. The Grundtvigian project was aided by the fact that Denmark lost a substantial part of its territory to neighbouring countries or separatist movements during the nineteenth century. The well-known phrase by the Danish writer Hans Peter Holst (1811–92), 'what is outwardly lost shall be inwardly gained', aptly captures the prevailing sentiment. A further influential factor was the cooperative movement of the nineteenth and twentieth centuries, which made cooperative ownership and management of a wide range of enterprises, from the processing and marketing of agricultural produce to urban housing, a common feature in Denmark.

During the twentieth century, the welfare state evolved into a broadly legitimate form of governance under the leadership of the Social Democratic party and the trade unions. The so-called 'Kanslergade agreement' of 1933 signals the onset of a consciously orchestrated mediation of interests between different social groups (classically: bourgeoisie, the farmers and the urban and rural working class) which has characterised Danish politics ever since. Even today, under the liberal-conservative government, the modernist legacy of the welfare state as an instrument of far-reaching intervention into the lives of the individual in the name of facilitating general welfare and shaping proper citizens remains strong.

(2) From Cultural Radicalism to Neo-nationalism

After World War II, Denmark experienced a period of particular social cohesion. In the wake of the Kanslergade agreement, a political framework had emerged that represented all major political constituencies, the experience of German occupation had further strengthened national cohesion, steady economic growth secured domestic peace and confidence, and the Cold War provided Denmark with a stable international environment. Perhaps paradoxically, this was not a time of widespread nationalist sentiment. Instead, modernisation theory, which in Denmark also reigned as the pre-eminent social philosophy of the time, seemed to suggest that the Danish way of life, as it was emerging in the postwar era, was not so much an expression of Danish particularity but somehow converged on the general trajectory of human history.

This conception of Danish culture as a progressive project oriented towards a shared international humanistic horizon was most explicitly formulated in the modernist movement of *kulturradikalisme* (cultural radicalism). In a narrow sense, *kulturradikalisme* was an avant-garde movement closely associated with the central figures of the Danish design movement (most notably Poul Henningsen (1894–1967), the public intellectual and designer of the PH lamp). In this narrow sense the movement was directly opposed both to romantic Danish nationalism and to conventionalised middle-class life, whether of a social democratic or conservative bent. In a wider sense, however, one can see *kulturradikalisme* as a liberal worldview broadly shared by the urban Danish elite. This worldview, on the one hand, legitimised the cultural hegemony of this elite (together with the progressive agendas of the welfare state) and, on the other hand, made it possible to perceive the way of life it championed not so much as a particular project tied to a particular tradition but as one converging with a much more universal historical trajectory.

Recent Danish history, notably the 2001 election victory of a coalition of (neo)liberal and conservative parties under Anders Fogh Rasmussen, and the era of dramatic political reforms that followed, can be seen as a sustained backlash against the long-lasting hegemony of liberal *kulturradikalisme*. This backlash brought with it a new emphasis on Danish particularity and, related to this, the often vehement critique of immigration, multiculturalism, and particularly of the presence of supposedly fundamentalist Muslims. Among the many reasons for this backlash, three historical developments stand out. While the postwar era was one of prosperity and stability, the increasing political and economic integration of Denmark into international trade regimes, financial markets and, above all, into the political structures of the European Union began to curtail the sovereignty of Danish national politics – and with it undermined the economical and political basis for pursuing a strong model of the welfare state upon which the *kultur-radikal* social model was premised. Moreover, the increasingly global circulation of discourses, images, commodities and desires has tied Danish lifeworlds more forcefully into transnational contexts, which also undermined the intellectual hegemony of *kultur-radikalisme*. Finally, the emerging ethnic and religious minorities have undermined the confident universalism of *kulturradikalisme*. With their very presence, these *nydanskere* (New Danes) made quite plain, if one recognised their presence, that mainstream Danish ways of life were rather less universal than *kulturradikal* universalism had suggested. The forms of life, aspirations and demands of the New Danes also challenged the carefully orchestrated political constellation that was premised on the mutual recognition of the major political constituencies in Denmark in the Kanslergade agreement.

(3) 'Danes' vs. 'Muslims'

The emergence of religious Muslim organisations in Denmark gathered pace in the 1980s and 1990s. Reflecting the heterogeneous constitution of the Muslim minority, these organisations were, from the beginning, diverse.[1] Many of these organisations cater quite narrowly to followers of particular subtraditions of Islam, often exclusively to those from a particular ethnic background. Others are branches of large international organisations or Sufi orders and some are sponsored by the governments of Muslim countries, as in the case of Turkey. Some increasingly draw practitioners with a variety of ethnic backgrounds, including ethnic Danes. While many of these organisations are organised as publicly registered associations, others are informal networks that, by their very nature, are difficult to track or describe. Very much like Muslim organisations elsewhere in Europe, Danish Muslim organisations fullfil a multitude of functions, from facilitating religious praxis to offering social services and acting as advocacy groups. Some of the activities, including religious instruction for children, are financed by municipal governments (this varies between municipalities). As elsewhere in Europe, many religious Muslims in Denmark engage with transnationally circulating news and debates (not least concerning the proper interpretations of Islam) through a multiplicity of media. These media may tie them into networks and discourses centred in their countries of origin or into transnational networks without clear geographic centres.

Almost all formal religious Muslim organisations in Denmark go out of their way to emphasise their commitment to working within the Danish legal framework and highlight their commitment to working towards the integration of religious Muslims into Danish society – while also stressing the need to maintain the integrity of their respective interpretations of the Islamic tradition and the identity of their members *as Muslims*. A high-profile exception has been the Danish branch of Hizb ut-Tahrir, whose noisy condemnations of the 'immoral' West (not least during the Cartoon Crisis of 2005–6 and its sequel in 2008), and its propagation of the advent of a new caliphate, have become a mainstay of scandal in the Danish media. Despite its marginal position among religious Muslim organisations in Denmark, Hizb ut-Tahrir's highly dramatised rhetoric seems to have gained the movement the status of representing the 'really Islamic' in the

Danish public imagination. The fact that the Muslim minority in Denmark is still very much in a dynamic phase of 'becoming' is indicated by the fluidity of its institutional framework. In a major new development, in March 2008 more than 30 religious Muslim organisations with a wide range of ethnic backgrounds and (Sunni) interpretations of Islam, founded the Danish Muslim Union (Dansk Muslimsk Union), an organisation that aims to represent 'all established organisations and associations recognised by Muslims in Denmark'.

Since the 1990s, the voices within the Danish public warning against an allegedly uncontrolled invasion of foreigners have become louder and increasingly influential. In concert with much of the Danish press, the political right and centre-right made the theme of immigration the focus of its political campaign to oust the Social Democratic government. At the centre of the critique of immigration is the claim that 'immigrants' – meaning, implicitly, 'non-Western' immigrants – are unable to integrate into Danish society, and thus undermine the cohesiveness and value base of Danish society. In 2001 the opposition succeeded after what was, by Danish standards, an extraordinarily aggressive campaign. A coalition government was formed by opposition leader Anders Fogh Rasmussen, which depended on the nationalist and openly xenophobic Dansk Folkeparti (Fogh Rasmussen remained prime minister until his appointment as NATO Secretary General in 2009). The Fogh Rasmussen government introduced highly restrictive immigration legislation and continued its high-profile critique of the supposed failure of Muslims to integrate properly into Danish society.

The critique of Muslims was by no means restricted to the new government and its supporters. Stories and commentaries about immigrants and particularly Muslims have gained a central place in the coverage of Danish print media. There is a strong tendency to portray the relationship of immigrants and Danish mainstream society as one of direct opposition, with the unsurprising correlate that the Danish side is generally portrayed positively in contrast to the immigrant others.[2] Significantly, in Denmark this critical assessment of the Muslim minority is widely shared by liberal and progressive sections of the public, the heirs to the *kulturradikal* tradition.

Analytically one can distinguish between a particular (nationalist) and a universal (liberal or progressive) aspect of the Danish critique of Islam. The first line of critique takes offence at the fact that foreigners, and particularly religious Muslims, appear to be incompatible with the particular values and ways of life (Danish culture) that are seen as characterising Danish society. This critique conforms to what Verena Stolcke (1995) has identified as the revival of 'cultural fundamentalism' in Europe since the 1980s. In its most aggressive form it is primarily associated with the nationalist Dansk Folkeparti (Danish People's Party), the populist tabloid *Ekstra Bladet* and, to a lesser degree, with the political centre-right. Much of the Danish critique of Islam, however, does not readily fit Stolcke's concept of 'cultural fundamentalism'. In fact, it is often formulated in the name of liberal or progressive values such as tolerance, democracy and gender equality. A wide range of practices (the headscarf, forced marriages, female circumcision, no hand-shakes with members of the opposite sex, 'honour' killings, general mistreatment of women, *shari'a* regulations concerning unequal inheritance, etc.), many of them wrongly perceived to be integral parts of mainstream Muslim ways of life, are the regular focus points of blistering public critique.

While some commentators express discomfort with or suspicion towards Islam and Muslims *in general*, most commentators have come to see 'Islamic fundamentalism' as the core of the problem. 'Fundamentalism' (or Islamism) is perceived as an ideology that justifies intolerance by religious decree and thus appears as the ultimate 'outside' to

Enlightenment reason – and therefore as incompatible with liberal Danish society. Most damagingly in the public discourse on Islam, religious Muslims (and Islamists or fundamentalists in particular) are regularly associated with violence. This association with violence, both in the form of terrorism and in the form of 'legal' violence through the *shari'a*, radically dramatises the urgency of the critique and tends to legitimise the intervention of state and its security services. Paradoxically, however, despite its central place in the Danish critique of Islam, it generally remains unclear what the terms Islamic fundamentalism or Islamism concretely describe – even though commentators seem to take their meaning for granted. Visiting a mosque or wearing a headscarf; visiting websites with 'fundamentalist content'; a particular theological standpoint (such as the assertion that the Qur'an is indeed God's revealed message to humankind); asserting the importance of the *shari'a* for guiding Muslim conduct; all of this can be equated with Islamic fundamentalism and, in turn, becomes part of one largely imaginary fundamentalist condition in the public perception of Islam in Denmark.

Importantly, the critique of Islam articulated as the critique of fundamentalism accommodates both nationalist and universalist forms of critique. Accusing a person or an organisation of fundamentalism does not require recourse to arguments concerning the 'foreignness' of Islam, or its 'reactionary' nature, but transcends the older opposition between the nationalist and the universalist camp. Instead, the equation of the Muslim minority with fundamentalism introduces a new divide: between proper Danes and fundamentalist Muslims.

To be sure, the demarcation line that is introduced here is by no means clear cut. In fact, it is profoundly ambivalent. For some it asserts a distinction between 'Danish Culture' and 'foreigners'; for others it subsumes under the category of 'Danish' also Muslim Danish residents with the exception of a tiny violent fringe of boneheaded jihadis. What the widely used opposition between Danishness and fundamentalism does, however, is to maintain a perpetual field of scrutiny of Muslim residents of Denmark. Danish Muslims have to prove over and again that *their* way of being Muslim falls within the limits of 'Danishness' because any association with 'fundamentalism', however spurious, puts their legitimate place in Danish society into question.

Accusations of political radicalism and proximity to terrorism have come to define the lives of Muslim minorities across European and North American societies. In the Danish context, however, the question of whether one lives a 'legitimate' way of life carries particular weight due to the ubiquitous presence of the welfare state. With its often implicit and sometimes explicit agenda for regulating social conduct and for facilitating certain forms of lives deemed desirable by the welfare bureaucracy, the welfare state introduces a particularly intensive field of conflict between Danish majority society and the Muslim minority.

(4) Uncertain horizons

An optimistic reading of the current tensions between the Danish majority public and its Muslim minority can claim that these tensions are part of the necessarily conflict-laden struggle for recognition that accompanies every instance of new social projects and ways of life being integrated into an established national society. In this reading, Danish mainstream society is likely to eventually recognise as legitimate certain demands made by its Muslim minority (just as Muslims recognise a re-negotiated Danish society) and to extend the notion of Danishness to include Danish Muslim identities. To support this optimistic view one could, for instance, point to the fact that the bitter conflict over the Muhammad cartoons has largely petered out, and that an (albeit grudging) recognition of mutual sensitivities has so far largely prevented similar crises. On the other hand, one could point out that many commentators continue to denounce mainstream Muslim aspirations as fundamentalist and that there is little evidence that the experiences and aspirations of Muslims in Denmark will be recognised as equally Danish anytime soon.

Moreover, there may be forceful systemic reasons that militate against the recognition of Muslims and their demands. The Danish critique of fundamentalist Islam has enabled Danes to imagine Danishness in new and productive ways, forging new alliances across formerly entrenched divides. For one, the critique of Islam has united nationalist, liberal and progressive political currents in their celebration of Danishness in contrast to Islamic fundamentalism, even if the virtues of Danishness are often defined somewhat differently. This current concept of Danishness integrates aspects of the *kulturradikal* tradition in so far as it claims Danish identity to be a version of a universal humanity. But it also integrates aspects of the nationalist tradition in so far as it prioritises the national horizon and sharply opposes Danish identity to those forms of life ascribed to Muslims and other 'foreigners'. In an era in which Danish society is under increasing pressure by global economic and political forces that challenge traditional Danish ways of life it seems questionable whether the mainstream Danish public will embrace the challenge of enlarging the notion of Danishness to include Muslim experiences in favour of re-emphasising Danish identity in opposition to the Muslim minority.

Defining Danish identity in this context seems particularly intuitive for many Danes because the definition of Danishness in opposition to Islam has already opened up new ways of imagining Danishness as part of a wider European identity. In this new constellation, Danishness is no longer constructed primarily in opposition to other national identities, such as Germanness or Swedishness, or in opposition to the EU. Rather, the juxtaposition of Danishness to fundamentalist Islam has enabled Danes to imagine Danishness as converging with other national identities on a shared European (or Western) identity. Danishness, like Germanness or Italianness, is defined in opposition to the Muslim minority. Given the enormous challenges that EU integration and other globalising processes pose for imagining collective horizons of solidarity, the construction of European identity in opposition to Europe's Muslim minorities may prove very tempting indeed in Denmark and elsewhere.

Notes

1   Jørgen Bæk Simonsen (1990) *Islam i Danmark: Muslimske Institutioner I Danmark 1970–1989*, Copenhagen: Statens Humanistiske Forskningsråd.
2   Peter Hervik (2002) *Mediernes Muslimer: En antropologisk undersøgelse af mediernes dækning af religioner I Danmark*, Copenhagen: Nævnet for ethnisk ligestilling.

References

Asad, Talal (2002) 'Muslims and European identity: Can Europe represent Islam?', in Anthony Pagden (ed.), *The Idea of Europe*, Cambridge: Cambridge University Press, pp. 209–27.
Brown, Wendy (2006) *Regulating Aversion: Tolerance in the Age of Identity and Empire*, Princeton: Princeton University Press.
Danmarks Statistik (2007) *Invandrere I Danmark 2007*, Copenhagen: Danmarks Statistik.

Danish Ministry for Integration website. http://www.nyidanmark.dk/en-us/. (website accessed 19 June 2014)

European Commission against Racism (2006) *Third Report on Denmark*, Strasbourg: ECRI-European Commission.

Fog Olvig, Karen and Karsten Pærregaard (eds) (2007) *Integraion: Antropologiske perspektiver*, Copenhagen: Tusculanums Forlag.

Hedetoft, Ulf (2003) *'Cultural transformation': how Denmark faces immigration*, OpenDemocracy Website www.opendemocracy.net. (website accessed 19 June 2014)

Henkel, Heiko (2006) '"The journalists of Jyllands-Posten are a bunch of reactionary provocateurs": The Danish cartoon controversy and the self-image of Europe', *Radical Philosophy*, 137, May/June.

Hervik, Peter (2002*) Mediernes Muslimer: En antropologisk undersøgelse af mediernes dækning af religioner I Danmark*, Copenhagen: Nævnet for ethnisk ligestilling.

—— (ed.) (1999) *Den generende forskellighed: Danske svar på den stigende multikulturalisme*, Copenhagen: Hans Reitzels Forlag.

Ihle, Annette Haaber (2007) *Magt, Medborgerskab, og Muslimske friskoler I Danmark: Traditioner, idealer, politikker*, Working paper, University of Copenhagen: Denmark.

Jensen, Erik and Arne Lund (eds) (2006) *Det antimuslimske univers: fra de høreekstremistiske grupper og partier til de nationale og liberale*, Copenhagen: Demos Press.

Jensen, Tina Gudrun (2006) 'Religious Authority and Autonomy Intertwined: The Case of Converts to Islam in Danmark', *The Muslim World*, 96 (4) pp. 641–58.

—— (2007) 'Danish Muslims: Catalysts of National Identity?', *ISIM review*, 19 pp. 28–9.

—— (2008) 'To be "Danish", becoming "Muslim": Contestations of National Identity?', *Journal of Ethnic and Migration Studies*, 34 (3) pp. 389–409.

Jöhnke, Steffen (2007) 'Velfærdsstaten som integrationsprojekt', in Karen Fog Olvig and Karsten Pærregaard, (eds), *Integraion: Antropologiske perspektiver*. Copenhagen: Tusculanums Forlag, pp.37–62.

Mahmood, Saba (2006) 'Secularism, Hermeneutics, Empire: The Politics of Islamic Reformation', *Public Culture*, 18 (2) pp. 323–47.

Rothstein, Klaus and Mikael Rothstein (2006) *Bomben i turbanen: Profeten, provokationen, protesten, pressen, perspektiver*, Copenhagen: Tiderne Skifter.

Simonsen, Jørgen Bæk (1990) *Islam i Danmark: Muslimske Institutioner I Danmark 1970– 1989*, Copenhagen: Statens Humanistiske Forskningsråd.

—— (2004) *Islam med danske øjne: Danskernes syn på Islam gennem 1000 år*, Copenhagen: Akademisk Forlag.

Stolcke, Verena (1995) 'Talking Culture: New Boundaries, new Rhetorics of Exclusion in Europe', *Current Anthropology*, 36 (1) pp. 1–24.

THE CONSTRUCTION OF RADICAL ISLAM IN FRANCE: THE HEADSCARF AFFAIR

Alexandre Caeiro and Frank Peter

Introduction

The presence and growing visibility of Muslims in France has given rise to important debates in the public sphere. While there have been various approaches and multiple topics have been dealt with, the issue of the Muslim headscarf often dominated discussions for the better part of the last two decades and structured mainstream perceptions of the 'Islamic threat' in France, leading to a legal ban on 'conspicuous religious signs' in public schools in early 2004. In order to understand the development from November 1989, when the headscarf was conditionally accepted in schools by the Conseil d'État, to the adoption of the law in February 2004, we have to analyse the process through which a specific perception of the headscarf has become hegemonic in France. In this process, a variety of counterclaims about the meaning and function of this practice, notably the claims made by covered women themselves, have become utterly unintelligible to the overwhelming majority of French.

If various spokespeople for the Republic felt that France was threatened by the presence of the headscarf in public spaces, particularly in public schools,[1] it is because the *hijab* has come to be understood as a phenomenon which embodies key political, social and cultural practices of Muslims. Here we attempt to provide a critical analysis of how such linkages have been established, what evidence has been mobilised to support such linkages, and what has been left out.

We begin by looking at Muslim understandings of the headscarf as a contested religious practice. We then proceed to evaluate how three specific arguments (namely, the defence of *laïcité*, the struggle against the Islamisation of France, and the protection of gender equality) have been mobilised in favour of the headscarf ban. In conclusion we point briefly to a series of historical factors that better explain France's particular anxiety about Islam and the headscarf.

Muslim Understandings of the *Hijab*

The veil is an Islamic practice that is usually related to two Qur'anic injunctions for modesty and recognition.[2] Most contemporary *'ulama'* argue that covering one's head is a religious obligation for Muslim women after puberty and before old age. In 2003, this view was reiterated unanimously in the wake of the proposal to ban the headscarf in public schools, by the recently established Muslim representative body in France, the Conseil Français du Culte Musulman (CFCM, French Council of the Muslim Cult), which reiterated this view in a unanimous statement issued in 2003. The most important grouping of imams in France, the Conseil des Imams led by Dhao Meskine, issued a similar statement.

There are, however, numerous dissenting opinions among Muslim public intellectuals in France. Soheib Bencheikh provided a reformulation of the meaning of the headscarf that appealed to many liberal Muslims. More recently, Leila Babès drew on the classical distinction between religious and social norms (*'ibadat* vs. *mu'amalat*) to argue that, since the headscarf belonged to the latter, it need not be considered universally valid. Various liberal Muslim intellectuals, often trained in the social sciences as Babès, have often converged in their analyses with dominant non-Muslim perceptions of the veil as a symbol of the inequality of women in Islam.

French Muslims of different sensibilities have remained divided over both the religious status of the headscarf and the need for its ban in public schools (as shown in various opinion polls). Many Islamic authorities in France have been critical of the importance the headscarf has acquired in French public debate and how it has polarised French society between 'Muslim fundamentalists' and everyone else. This is true for so-called 'moderate' figures such as Dalil Boubakeur of the Grande Mosquée de Paris (who famously coined the term *foulardisme* to designate the perceived Muslim politicisation of the headscarf), as well as leaders in the 'fundamentalist' Union des Organisations Islamiques de France (UOIF), including Tareq Oubrou, who publicly declared the headscarf to be 'a minor issue'.

There also exists a growing body of social scientific studies on covered Muslim women in France which serves to put into question the dominant view of the headscarf as having a clear and singular function – to affirm gender inequality. Such scholarship has often emphasised the various types of veils and multiple meanings attributed to the headscarf by covered Muslim women. If some don the headscarf because of family pressure, others do it against the family's wishes. The fact that the headscarf often enables women to move more freely in society – with their family's approval – may be an important stimulus for donning it.

While sociologists first pointed to a movement towards the spiritualisation of Islamic norms, such as that found in the statement '*je porte le voile à l'intérieur*,'[3] the growing prevalence of the veil among second, third and subsequent generations of French Muslims has come to be seen as symptomatic of the turn to Islam, an alternative identity that reconciles the complex attachments to one's more or less distant origins as well as to France, the country of residence or citizenship.

In recent years a number of publications have attempted to complement social scientific studies by providing unmediated explanations by covered women of the reasons that led them to veil in France. Two types of argumentation are typically mobilised, sometimes simultaneously: one emphasises veiling as the exercise of free choice by the individual, describing the advantages the headscarf confers in particular social contexts; the other invokes the religious command to veil as sufficient, and seeks to inscribe the act in a broader search for a pious self.

Laïcité and the Scarf – A Specifically French Problem?

Analyses of the French headscarf controversies usually insist on the specifically French nature of this conflict. It is said that it is the particularly categorical understanding of the separation of State and religion in France – referred to as *laïcité* – which underlies this conflict and goes a long way towards explaining why similar conflicts have not occurred in other European countries. Since the first covered girls were expelled from a high school in Creil in the Paris region in 1989, the argument that the *hijab* constitutes a transgression of the principle of *laïcité* and therefore needs to be prohibited has indeed been of central importance in French public debate. This type of argument is based on the perception that the *hijab* is an act of public identification with a particular group (here, the followers of one religion) inside the broader community of citizens and, as such, likely to threaten social cohesion. This line of argument is extremely powerful in French political life, attested to by the omnipresent use of the concept of *communitarisme*, which designates sub-national group identities seen in conflict with the national identity. The underlying assumption of this concept, namely that strong particular identities necessarily weaken social cohesion, is hardly ever questioned in public debates.

The public school has been a key site for the reproduction of the French abstract universalism that underlies *laïcité*. But participants in the headscarf debate over the years in France have argued that banning students' religious attire constitutes both a continuity and a rupture in the historical practice of *laïcité*. It would be wrong to consider the principle of *laïcité* simply the cause of certain conflicts pertaining to Muslims and Muslim practices. Rather, the more recent Muslim presence in France should be seen as an important factor which has crucially contributed to reshaping the understanding of *laïcité* over the last two decades or so. So far, this process of readaptation of *laïcité* has resulted primarily in severe constraints placed on the possibility for French Muslims to live as they deem fit. In fact, when the first headscarf affair erupted, the Conseil d'État took the position that the wearing of the *hijab* in public schools was not necessarily in contradiction to *laïcité* ('*Le port, par les élèves, de signes par lesquels ils entendent manifester leur appartenance à une religion n'est pas par lui-même incompatible avec la laïcité*' (27 November 1989)). Instead, the Council decreed that the legality of the *hijab* be decided on an individual basis by the school authorities concerned. The question to ask then is what changed between 1989 and 2004 – and who changed it – to make this conditional acceptance of the headscarf politically impossible to maintain?

The 'Islamic Threat'

The successful campaign for prohibiting headscarfs crucially depended on the widespread perception of a growing threat that is posed by 'radical Islamic movements' to France and to its secular institutions. Unlike the earlier debates, in 2003–4 even the staunchest arguments in favour of excluding covered girls from public school resorted primarily to a series of evaluative judgements over social problems in France, particularly in its *banlieues*. The need to rearrange the secular regime was defended by reference to the changed social context. Indeed, the historically changing nature of French *laïcité* was often recognised by proponents of the law. However, the conceptual distinction between politics and religion, understood as simply given, was never questioned in spite of the fact that the debate itself provided ample evidence for the contradictory entanglement of the two and the human labour necessary for separating them.

Disparate events – including rising delinquency, suburban violence against women, anti-Semitic attacks, student contestation of the Holocaust in history classes, demands for *halal* food in canteens or separate times in swimming-pools, the practices of polygamy, repudiation, female genital mutilation and forced marriages, more or less assertive demands for treatment by same-sex doctors in public hospitals, the recruitment of young French

Muslims for terrorism abroad – all these were mobilised to sustain the thesis of an Islamic threat requiring an urgent (and in part only symbolic) measure in the form of the headscarf ban. These events were represented as facets of a supposedly unified (and always ill-defined) phenomenon generating intense fear: the Islamisation of France.

The headscarf ban acquired its plausibility in French public discourse precisely through the *mise en relation* of these disparate events to the headscarf under a coherent politics. This highly problematic linkage has been established through references to the activities of obscure (and often unnamed) 'religious-political groups'. One of the few groups frequently named is the UOIF, one of France's most important Muslim federations, which rose to prominence during the first headscarf affair. This linkage is problematic in part because it ignores that the UOIF is far from monolithic and that its multiple relations and references to the movement of the Muslim Brotherhood are ambivalent. Significantly, the UOIF's leadership provides justification for only some of these acts (the headscarf, provision of *halal* food in canteens) while condemning most of the others (forced marriages, violence against women; polygamy in France; female genital mutilation; delinquency; terrorism; and anti-Semitism). It is indeed difficult to take seriously the anxieties which the UOIF continues to provoke when taking into account its relatively tight cooperation with French state authorities inside the CFCM and its regional bodies (not to mention the surveillance to which the UOIF is submitted). Juxtaposing these threat narratives about the UOIF with the strong criticism that the UOIF receives from some Muslims for its compromising attitude towards the French government, gives one a good measure of the monological nature of the French debate on the headscarf and, more generally, 'radical' Islam.

The linkage of the headscarf to various social phenomena was further consolidated by the almost unquestioned perception of veiling as containing a political statement (asserting something like the primacy of the *shari'a* over that of the French Republican order). To posit that such a normative clash, where it exists, poses a legal challenge to the Republic is nevertheless to mistake normative orders (plural in any multicultural society) for legal ones. Instead of attributing political programs to the headscarf one should instead acknowledge that the symbolism of religious practices is never fixed and listen carefully to what covered women themselves say.

Foulard, Islam, and Gender Equality

While the first debate on the headscarf started off as one about the 'right to difference' (*droit à la différence*) in relation to the principle of *laïcité*, the campaign against headscarves became, after the intervention of a number of French intellectuals, including some prominent feminists, tightly associated with the struggle against the supposed oppression of women in Islam (of which the headscarf was considered a part). This interpretive move would become a crucial factor structuring the debates preceding the adoption of the law when a group of Franco-Maghrebi women launched a movement in 2002 – Ni Putes Ni Soumises (Neither Whores Nor Submissives) – against the violence to which women in the *banlieues* were submitted. Highly sensationalised by the media, this movement, whose aims incidentally cannot be simply reduced to the fight against the headscarf,[4] was successfully instrumentalised by the anti-scarf campaign as further proof of the necessity to liberate women in the *banlieues*.

Based on the unquestioned assumption that the scarf stands as a symbol of female inferiority (and hence is discriminatory), Muslim women wearing the headscarf were perceived as falling into two categories: those forced to wear the headscarf were considered targets of the broader patriarchal system of Islam, which is slowly creating 'autonomous zones' in France's *banlieues*; and those who argued (implausibly in French public debates) that the headscarf was a personal choice and who were seen as manipulated because they contradicted the natural aspiration of women to lead a so-called self-determined life and to assume their femininity. The regular designations of covered women as *les folles d'Allah* encapsulates this idea in a concise way. Both of these arguments thus essentially construct Muslim women as victims – either of false consciousness or of various pressures by relatives or the social environment.

The assumption that the headscarf symbolises the inferiority of women needs to be challenged. While many, or perhaps even most, Muslims favourable to the headscarf would consider it an integral part of a societal order based on a gender-specific division of labour, this latter position does not imply necessarily – and indeed mostly does not in the case of France – the assignation of a status of inferiority to women. Muslim organisations in France – including the 'fundamentalist' UOIF – defend a vision of gender equality based on a natural complementarity of the sexes. What it suggests – and this brings us to the claim about the false consciousness of covered women – is that the idea of self-determination, which many French Muslim women espouse, does not necessitate excluding recognition of external authorities, in this case that of the Islamic tradition, over one's self. As many studies have shown, instead of attributing false consciousness to Muslim women, the simple recognition that supposedly natural aspirations and values are contingent and vary as a function of specific social environments is required. The invocation of a false consciousness type of argument merely demonstrates the unwillingness by many French intellectuals to question the universality of their own conceptions of femininity. Furthermore, if Muslim understandings of the nature of women – and more generally of humans, understood to be God's creatures – differ quite radically from those of the above-mentioned feminists, why divergent understandings of the self (as un/encumbered) should constitute a threat to the French Republic is, considering all available evidence, entirely unclear. The striking parallels between Muslim thinking on this subject and that which is found in other religions also leads one to think that the singular focus on the scarf is not justified.

Colonial Memories, Anti-Arab Racism and Islamophobia

Much of the preceding discussion has argued that the anxieties about the headscarf are not justified. Indeed, several observers have claimed that the debate on this topic is largely a false one. What is at stake then in this debate, and why have so many French been convinced in its course of the necessity to legislate against the headscarf?

A variety of answers can be given to this question. Some have argued that the most recent debate was a subterfuge intended to divert attention away from pressing social issues. Others have demonstrated how mechanisms of competition internal to French television have contributed to produce the various headscarf affairs. In a much broader perspective, the anti-headscarf campaigns have been interpreted as a reaction against the perceived threats to national sovereignty resulting from processes of globalisation and the unification of Europe. While these analyses are highly important, we want to address here more directly the question of why 'Islam' in particular can be manipulated to these ends.

In fact, what is striking in many discussions of Islam in France is the constant reference to France's unique secular constitution as an explanatory factor for its long-lasting and perhaps singular anxiety about Islam. While this is clearly one factor which defines and distinguishes France from other European countries in relation to Muslims, it is not the only one. Another at least equally important one is France's specific colonial history and its memories. What distinguishes France's colonial history from that of other European countries is its recentness and its 'traumatic' end. In 1962, one million French settlers had to abandon the(ir) country in which more than one million metropolitan French soldiers – the *Génération Algérie* from which stems a substantial part of the current political elite – had fought in the preceding decade to keep Algeria French. What the repatriation of the French settlers and the independence of Algeria in 1962 sets into motion is a 'transfer of memory'[5]– a transfer of attitudes, conducts and ways of thinking specific to colonial Algeria – and the instillment of a profound desire for revenge by those with a continued attachment to a French Algeria. It is the feelings of resentment generated by France's defeat which, to a large degree, underpin the success of France's right-wing movement Front National (founded in 1972) whose strength and long presence in the political field also set apart France from almost all other Western European countries. Considering the virulent Anti-Arab and Islamophobic campaigns of the Front National, and its remarkable success in transforming the terms of French political discourses on citizenship and Islam, the debate on the headscarf in France appears in a different light. From this specific perspective, the debate draws on and reactualises France's colonial past: by referring to a supposedly natural separation between religion and politics which needs to be reaffirmed against Islam, it has successfully built a political scenario in which the options for covered Muslim women are reduced to either assimilation or exclusion – not so dissimilar to the colonial context. Simultaneously, this debate has worked to obscure and erase this colonial past and present through the construction and naturalisation of an Islamic threat.

To say that the debate on the headscarf is a 'false' one is of course not meant to imply that it is without consequences. On the contrary, it is indicative of important social dynamics and its effects are equally significant. However, a serious contribution to the debate would demand that one first become cognisant of the ways in which its stakes exceed the mere issue of the legality of headscarves and their supposed effects in French society. It also demands that one recognises how a specific discourse of *laïcité* and various threat narratives about Islam have become the means to build up political authority over 'Muslims' and to define the conditions of their acceptance in France.

Notes

1   Hanifa Chérifi, the *médiatrice* of the Ministry of Education responsible for headscarf-related conflicts in schools, has estimated the number of covered girls at 2,000 (1994) and 400 (1999). The number of conflicts which necessitated her intervention was 300 in 1994 and 150 in 2002 (when the number of covered girls in schools was estimated at 1,250).

2   Qur'an, Surat al-Nur, verse 31 and Surat al-Ahzab, verse 59.

3   Jocelyne Cesari (1998) *Musulmans et républicains: Les jeunes. L'Islam et la France*, Bruxelles: Complexe. Indeed, the movement initially criticised in strong terms the idea of prohibiting the scarf. For considerations of political opportunism, the position was subsequently changed.

4   Benjamin Stora (1999) *Le transfert d'une mémoire. De l' 'Algérie française' au racisme anti-arabe*, Paris: La Découverte.

References

Bouzar, Dounia and Saida Kada (2003) *L'une voilée, l'autre pas. Le témoignage de deux musulmanes françaises*, Paris: Albin Michel.

Cesari, Jocelyne (1998) *Musulmans et républicains. Les jeunes. L'Islam et la France*, Brussels: Complexe.

Commission de réflexion sur l'application du principe de laïcité dans la République (2003) *Rapport au Président de la République*, December. Available at http://lesrapports.lado cumentationfrancaise.fr/BRP/034000725/0000.pdf. (link no longer accessible)

Deltombe, Thomas (2005) *L'islam imaginaire. La construction médiatique de l'islamophobie en France, 1975–2005*, Paris: La Découverte.

Geisser, Vincent (2003) *La nouvelle islamophobie*, Paris: La Découverte.

Lévy, Alma and Lila Lévy (2004) *Des filles comme les autres. Au-delà du foulard*, Paris: La Découverte.

Nordmann, Charlotte (ed.) (2004) *Le foulard islamique en questions*, Paris: Éditions Amsterdam.

Scott, Joan W. (2007) *The Politics of the Veil*, Princeton: Princeton University Press.

Stora, Benjamin (1999) *Le transfert d'une mémoire. De l' 'Algérie française' au racisme anti-arabe*, Paris: La Découverte.

Tévanian, Pierre (2005) *Le voile médiatique. Un faux débat: 'l'affaire du foulard islamique'*, Paris: Raisons d'agir.

Wieviorka, Michel (ed.) (2006) *La tentation antisémite. Haine des Juifs dans la France d'aujourd'hui*, Paris: Hachette.

THE IRRESPONSIBLE MUSLIM: ISLAM IN GERMAN PUBLIC CULTURE

Werner Schiffauer

During recent years a remarkable convergence of attitudes towards Islam has emerged all over Europe. The fundamental differences between a British, French, Dutch, German and Danish approach to religious difference in general, and to Islam in particular, which had been so clearly marked up to the turn of the millenium, have been replaced by approaches where the differences between nation states are reduced to nuances. This seems to be only partially related to the 9/11 attacks. It seems rather that these attacks have brought longstanding fears and anxieties related to the Muslim presence (and more general to migration) to the surface. A review of different European discourses shows that concerns about public culture play a crucial role in this process.

At the outset is the realisation of the fact that migration has become permanent and that the classical European nation states have de facto turned into countries of immigration. European societies today are confronted with the problem of the true stranger, with 'the man who comes today and stays tomorrow'.[1] Muslim immigrants pose the problem of ambivalence which Zygmunt Bauman has so brilliantly analysed.[2] They are neither friends – because, as confessing Muslims they represent a culture which has been and still is considered to be the quintessential other to the 'Christian occident' – nor enemies, because they live and work in Europe and are bound to stay. They are strangers who challenge the 'master-opposition between the *inside* and the *outside*' which is constitutive for all national societies.[3] They represent disorder, and this causes fear over the loss of agency: 'The main symptom of disorder is the acute discomfort we feel when we are unable to read the situation properly and to choose between alternative actions.'[4]

The fact that a sizeable group of 'strangers' (in the sense defined above) is actively entering the public debate leads to concerns that the rules of the game will be changed in this process. The growing weight of newcomers in the moral community creates fear with regard to values (will they adhere to the same standards?) as well as with regard to cohesion (will they speak the same language?). This fear is not restricted to Muslims but is related to migration in general (or, to be more precise, to the fact that migrants stay permanently). It seems, however, that Islam for several reasons currently concentrates these fears with regard to public culture. First, Islam, like all religions, provides a set of organised symbols which allow the formulation of difference. This creates the fear of a *systematic* difference, that is, a difference that is not restricted to bits and pieces but is a difference with regard to a structure which has its own logic that naturally makes it more difficult to be assimilated. Second, Islam and the West have a history of constructing alterity in Orientalist and Occidentalist discourses. Islam seems to be not just another religion (adding to the multi-religious landscape existing in Europe) but is seen as a religion which is the very opposite of the West's. Third, there exists a collective memory of the Muslim Wars (and correspondingly of the Crusades). On the basis of these historical narratives there is the suspicion that the other side is basically interested in conquest and taking over, but not in peaceful cohabitation. The attacks of 9/11 have finally proven to the worried public that Islam is not only different, but also dangerous.

While these fears are expressed all over Europe they take their concrete form in relation to the nation-specific civil cultures which have developed. The latter can be compared by analysing the different ways in which the republican key concepts are spelled out in different political cultures.[5]

Turning to Germany, liberty is mentioned noticeably often in the same breath as 'responsibility'. Only those who are capable of responsibility should enter into the free exchange of public culture in which the *volonté générale* emerges. This association of liberty with responsibility is remarkably different from the associations of liberty with equality (which is very often heard in France), liberty with inviolability of the private sphere (a British preoccupation) or liberty with tolerance (the Dutch version).

The German emphasis on a responsible use of freedom is related to a widespread conviction that a society can only function properly if every participant identifies with the common good or the political community as a whole. This identification is the basis for a responsible exercise of one's liberties. This type of identification with the common good differs from the identification with rules which is demanded in France and in Great Britain. I suspect that in both countries there is a feeling of trust that the common good will prevail if only the social preliminaries are correct: in France, if political and juridical equality is established and the individuals keep to the rules; in Great Britain, if the rules of liberty remain inviolate and the rules of fairness are observed. In both cases (1) affirmation of the rules is demanded, which then permits (2) ordered social competition, which finally (3) results in the formation of the common good. This trust in rules working is missing in Germany's political culture. There is a widespread notion that rules can easily be bent or manipulated in order to favour one's own strategic interest. In the collective memory this is related to the failure of the Weimar Republic which, by consequently sticking to the rules, lost power, enabling the National Socialists to take over. The emphasis on responsibility, or rather, identification with the whole, aims at avoiding these pitfalls of 'pure rule orientation': before and in addition to the affirmation of the rule, an inner identification with the general well-being is demanded. Nobody should participate in the free exchange until the *bien commun* has been internalised. One outcome of this process is the extreme hesitation with which citizenship is granted. It usually takes a generation longer in Germany to obtain citizenship than in other European countries. This is clearly related to the frequently heard statement that the 'acquisition of citizenship is the conclusion and not the beginning of the integration process'.

The growing number of Muslim citizens poses a particular challenge to this German construction. The question is posed explicitly as to whether orthodox Islam allows the identification with the common good at all (and thus a 'responsible use' of liberal rights). In an admittedly extreme form this was brought to the fore by the so-called Muslim Test. Baden Württemberg suggested that intensive interviewing be conducted in particular with Muslim applicants to citizenship that would focus less on knowledge but more on conscience. The idea was to filter out applicants who would *only* declare loyalty to the constitution but not *really* feel allegiance to it.

The problem of the relation of Qur'an and basic law are well known. The Qur'an is not only the 'holy script' of Islam corresponding to the Bible (in Christianity) but it is the Word of God which regulates all aspects of life. Whenever there is a conflict with secular law the latter is only of secondary importance according to the conviction of many Muslims. This is unacceptable for a Western understanding of the State. As nobody can see whether a Muslim applicant for citizenship adheres to the traditional understanding of the Qur'an or whether he ascribes to an 'enlightened' so-called Euro-Islam, general doubts exist. Doubts, well understood, no more. And these doubts should be answered by the conversation.[6]

This interrogative practice using trick questions in order to separate 'liberal Muslims' from 'orthodox Muslims' led to an outcry. The suggestion that a state agency engage in this kind of soul-searching practice was clearly in breach with liberal law. The outcry, however, concerned only the *consequences* that were drawn; the basic scepticism towards the inner loyalty of conservative Muslims that was reflected remained widespread.

The general distrust relates to the assumptions that Muslims have an incorrect understanding of freedom (*falschverstandene Freiheit*) and make a wrong, that is, irresponsible, use of the liberties granted by the constitution. The particular focus of these accusations are Muslim organisations. According to Dr Kandel from the Friedrich-Ebert-Stiftung, also a guiding intellectual force in the Sozialdemokratische Partei Deutschlands (SPD), they are nothing but ethnic entrepreneurs who try to push through 'their particular brand of Islam' in order to maintain their own position and dominance.[7]

The general fear that is reflected is that Muslims will use liberal freedoms in order to eventually undermine the very same liberties. This fear was brought to the fore when Fereshta Ludin won a (partial) victory in the constitutional court relating to the right of a teacher to wear a headscarf in school. This court decision triggered the fear that the Muslim organisations systematically make use of their legal rights and constitutional freedom in order to subvert it and eventually to abolish it. *Der Spiegel* commented on the case as follows:

> Ms. Ludin demands tolerance for intolerance. The severe headscarf-fetishists from the Islamic Council and the 'Central Council of Muslims in Germany' who supported her case, distinguish themselves from most Islamic associations active in Germany by their strange understanding of democratic rule of law. It is respected only until one is in the position to abolish it wherever it is possible in order install a theocracy without separation of the powers of the State and the Church [sic!].[8]

These fears are intensified by the interconnected processes of Islamisation of problems and Muslimisation of immigrants.[9] Problems such as violence at schools, which had been described in the 1990s as migration problems (and, one may add, in the 1980s as class problems), today are described as problems resulting from Muslim patriarchalism. According to this construction, it is the different set of values taught in Muslim families and communities which is at the heart of the matter. This can be generalised: in political debates in Germany today 'Islam' is named as the key factor leading to all kinds of problems from honour killings to unemployment. Corresponding to the Islamisation of problems is the Muslimisation of immigrants from the Muslim world. Migrants who had been treated as Turkish, Moroccan and Iranian nationals in the 1990s are treated as Muslims now. A key feature of Muslimisation is the construction of a homogenous

Muslim bloc. It goes hand in hand with the idea of a community which can be easily mobilised by cynical actors for their respective political causes.

These notions – the Islamisation of problems and Muslimisation of immigrants – magnify the problem (by relating the multitude of problems to a single key factor) and multiply the number of the problematic actors (by labelling all migrants from certain countries as Muslims). This leads to a discourse which does not bother to differentiate by space and time. A typical example of this discourse is again provided by the above-mentioned article on Fereshta Ludin. In order to prove its claim that Muslim activists are basically aiming at Islamising European societies, the article passed from Kaplan to Khomeini, to the murder of the liberal author Foda in Egypt in 1992, to the Rushdie affair, ending with suicide bombers. The reader is drawn into an argumentation which constantly shifts in space and time. The emotional message conveyed is fury about Muslim presumptuousness, and fear. The strong emotional drive evidently allows the reader and the author to pass over the logical flaws in the argument. The argument itself radicalises the existing fears as seemingly omnipresent and connected to everything.

The general fear with regard to the changing rules of civic culture by the inclusion of dedicated Muslims is spelled out differently by different actors in society.

Conservatives adhering to a communitarian vision of society fear the disintegration of society through Muslim identity politics. The argument goes that society needs a body of shared cultural convictions above and beyond the 'mere' acceptance of laws in order to be able to solve conflicts. If different cultural standards prevail, conflicts will escalate and violence will eventually become the dominant way of conflict resolution. Members of society will cease to speak the 'same' language. Parallel societies will emerge and society will fall apart into 'co-existing cultural ghettos which have no relation to each other' as the former governing mayor of Berlin, Eberhard Diepgen, emphasised during a debate in the Berlin House of Representatives.[10] These fears often focus on the situation in schools. Schools are the places where civil and political society reproduces itself. They are also the places which are shared by the majority population and immigrants. It is the opposition of many Muslims to co-educational swimming and school trips, as well as the insistence on headscarves, which seems to symbolise a resistance to national culture.

A second position, more characteristic of the political centre of society, shares these fears with regard to societal integration and emphasises the need for shared values. They criticise the former position, however, because it is unable to specify what they mean by a German *Leitkultur*. Rather than emphasising the need for shared national symbols and values, they refer to 'European values'; in particular the values of enlightenment such as freedom of opinion, equality, tolerance and secularism. Islam is seen as a problem from this perspective as it never underwent an enlightenment period. Representatives of this position often express strong doubts as to whether Islam can be democratic at all. After the murder of Theo van Gogh this position became more popular, particularly among people representing the political centre of society.

Many leftists would criticise this position as neglecting the role of power in this construction of seemingly universalist and rational values. Uncritically glorifying enlightenment and celebrating liberalism does not take into account the criticism voiced by Adorno, Foucault, Chantal Mouffe et al. Leftists worry about Muslim identity politics for different reasons. One concern is the establishment of strong communitarian counter-cultures which are dominated by old conservative men and exert strong social control over their members. This is seen as particularly problematic with regard to women's rights, the rights of homosexuals, and also the control of xenophobic (in particular anti-Semitic) tendencies.

In these circles the fears with regard to Islam relate to regression, that is, the fear of a civil society falling back behind the standards which have been achieved in historical struggles. Many feminists and gay and lesbian activists see their successes in the fight for women's emancipation threatened by the headscarf movement, which they interpret as a return of patriarchal culture. Another crucial concern relates to standards with regard to anti-Semitism. The fears concerning the latter are of special concern here because they are tied to the specific history of Germany. The constitutive vision and mission of the Federal Republic was the programme: Never again Auschwitz. This only became a generally accepted moral standard during the students' movement (which, much more than in other European countries, had the character of a conflict of generations in which the role of the fathers in the National Socialist era was made into a key moral issue). This is not to say that there is no anti-Semitism in Germany today – but that it is not acceptable to make anti-Semitic or anti-Zionist statements in public. The argument goes that immigration of Muslims leads to an import of anti-Semitic ideas and thus threatens the achievement with regard to political culture. The conflict in Palestine in particular leads to worries that solidarisation might lead to anti-Semitic agitation and anti-Semitic violence. This is also related to the observation that the classical European anti-Semitic rhetoric is taken up in the Islamic world. Both with regard to women's rights as well as with regard to anti-Semitism, one senses that the fears with regard to Muslims are as strong as they are because the establishment of these standards has occurred rather recently and are thus not anchored deeply. It is telling that an event at the Technical University in Berlin, where speakers of Hizb ut-Tahrir and representatives of the German right wing were joining ranks in critisising Israel, became the final reason for banning Hizb ut-Tahrir.

A third set of fears relates to the established balance between state and religion (or rather church) in Germany. It is defined as 'positive neutrality'. The State claims to be above and beyond the religious communities. At the same time it recognises religion as an essential part of political and civil culture. The outcome is the result of two eminent traumas in German history: the first was the religious wars of the seventeenth century (which are still very prominent in German collective memory) which led to the emergence of the State as guarantor of religious peace. The second experience was the totalitarianism of the Third Reich, the secular state per se in German history. Both experiences led to the concept of religion as basically ambivalent in nature: on the one hand 'too much' religion is dangerous because it can lead to civil war, intolerance and violence. On the other hand 'too little' religion is problematic because it leads to totalitarianism. A certain amount of religion is necessary for the project of creating responsible citizens able to stand up against tyranny. Religion thus has had to be tamed and promoted at the same time. This is expressed by the unique status of the Churches in Germany. They are *Körperschaften öffentlichen Rechts* – a status by which the Churches are at the same time given the character of state institutions and granted far-reaching independence (allowing them to stand up against the State). Thus the ideal is that of a religion in a democratic society which makes responsible use of its powers; that is, which limits itself to exert moral authority in everyday life but which would call for resistance in exceptional situations. This is also expressed in the vision of a dialogue between state and religion in which both sides respect each other.

Remarkably enough, these concerns about the return of fundamentalist religions are most prevalent in the higher ranks of the Protestant Church. With regard to Islam, this ambivalence is felt strongly: on the one hand it is argued that Islam has to be included in this particular German version of civil religion. On the other hand fears exist that

Islam is not able to engage in a responsible partnership with the State in the same way the Churches do: reference again is made to the fact that Islam has not developed a 'critical historical reading of the Qur'an'. Muslims do not interpret the Qur'an in the historical context but they take it literally. This presumably means that Muslims are bound slavishly to the letters of the text. They thus cannot make the compromises with the secular and democratic state which are necessary within this framework – and if they make compromises these are to be considered with scepticism. Again there is an outspoken fear of regression. The church establishment sees the reconciliation of religious tradition with a commitment to human rights, egalitarian values and democracy as an historical achievement. 'It took a long historical process to learn to deal critically with elements of the own tradition'.[11] This achievement again can be threatened by presumably intolerant religion and it seems that what is feared is not only the appearance of new conservative actors but also the re-appearance of conservative fundamentalists in their own ranks.

In Germany, the inclusion of Islam into society thus regularly raises fears about a 'regression'. Whether with regard to gender relations, where Muslim women are seen as not fully emancipated, or modes of religiosity, where the lack of a critical approach to scripture raises concerns, Muslims are seen to represent a cultural and intellectual formation which has been superseded in the course of German history. This fear of regression becomes particularly virulent with regard to the question of Israel–Palestine and the 'new' anti-Semitism which some claim is present inside Germany's Muslim community.

In all these cases, specifically German historical experiences are universalised; the equal status and legitimacy of alternative histories and conceptions of the good life denied; and the plurality of social norms and practices in Germany, whether among Muslims or non-Muslims, simply dismissed.

Notes

1   Georg Simmel (1908/1971) 'Exkurs über den Fremden', *Soziologie. Untersuchungen über die Formen der Vergesellschaftung*, Berlín: Duncker & Humblot, p. 685.
2   Zygmunt Bauman (1991) *Modernity and Ambivalence*, Cambridge: Polity Press.
3   Ibid., p. 53.
4   Ibid., p. 1.
5   See Werner Schiffauer (1997) 'Die civil society und der Fremde. Grenzmarkierungen in vier politischen Kulturen', in Werner Schiffauer (ed.), *Fremde in der Stadt*, Frankfurt am Main: Suhrkamp Verlag, pp. 35–49; and Werner Schiffauer, Gerd Baumann, Riva Kastoryano and Steven Vertovec (eds), (2004) *Civil enculturation: nation-state, schools and ethnic difference in the Netherlands, Britain, Germany and France*, New York / Oxford: Berghahn Books.
6   Protokoll der Dienstbesprechung anlässlich des vom Land Baden-Württemberg entwickelten 'Gesprächsleitfaden für Einbürgerungswillige' Innenministerium Baden-Württemberg AZ 5–1012 4/12.
7   Johannes Kandel (n.d) '"Lieber blauäugig als blind?" Anmerkungen zum "Dialog" mit dem Islam', *Islam und Gesellschaft Nr.2*. Berlin: Friedrich-Ebert-Stiftung, p. 7.
8   *Der Spiegel*, 29 September 2003, p. 84.
9   Werner Schiffauer (2007) 'Der unheimliche Muslim – Staatsbürgerschaft und zivilgesellschaftliche Ängste', *Soziale Welt*, Special issue (17) pp. 111–34.
10 Werner Schiffauer (2008) *Parallelgesellschaften. Wieviel Wertekonsens braucht unsere Gesellschaft? Ethnographische Überlegungen*, Bielefeld: Transcript, p. 119.

11   Evangelische Kirche Deutschlands (2006) *Klarheit und gute Nachbarschaft. Christen und Muslime in Deutschlaund. Eine Handreichung des Rates der EKD*, Hannover, p. 21.

References

Bauman, Zygmunt (1991) *Modernity and Ambivalence*, Cambridge: Polity Press.

Evangelische Kirche Deutschlands (2006) *Klarheit und gute Nachbarschaft. Christen und Muslime in Deutschlaund. Eine Handreichung des Rates der EKD*, Hannover.

Kandel, Johannes (n.d) '"Lieber blauäugig als blind?" Anmerkungen zum "Dialog" mit dem Islam', *Islam und Gesellschaft Nr.2*. Berlin: Friedrich-Ebert Stiftung.

——— (2004) *Organisierter Islam in Deutschland und gesellschaftliche Integration*, Berlin: Friedrich-Ebert-Stiftung.

Schiffauer, Werner (1997) 'Die civil society und der Fremde. Grenzmarkierungen in vier politischen Kulturen', in Werner Schiffauer (ed.), *Fremde in der Stadt*, Frankfurt am Main: Suhrkamp Verlag, pp. 35–49.

——— (2007) 'Der unheimliche Muslim – Staatsbürgerschaft und zivilgesellschaftliche Ängste', *Soziale Welt*, Special issue (17) pp. 111–34.

——— (2008) *Parallelgesellschaften. Wieviel Wertekonsens braucht unsere Gesellschaft? Ethnographische Überlegungen*, Bielefeld: Transcript.

———, Gerd Baumann, Riva Kastoryano and Steven Vertovec, (eds) (2004) *Civil enculturation: nation state, schools and ethnic difference in the Netherlands, Britain, Germany and France*, New York / Oxford: Berghahn Books.

Simmel, Georg (1908) 'Exkurs über den Fremden', *Soziologie. Untersuchungen über die Formen der Vergesellschaftung*, Leipzig: Duncker & Humblot pp. 685–91.

DOMES, MINARETS AND THE ISLAMIC THREAT IN ITALY. 'PIG DAY' AND MEDIA DEBATE

Ermete Mariani

Are Muslims living in Italy a serious threat to national security, and is their lifestyle in opposition to Italian identity and values? Is it really possible to live peacefully with Muslim populations and, eventually, integrate them into Italian society? These are, essentially, the most recurrent questions posed by Italian opinion makers and politicians with regard to Islam. As in other European countries, the Islamic veil and the building of monumental mosques are, today, the most effective catalysts of this kind of political debate and media attention. While these debates make apparent negative perceptions about Islam and Muslims, they also indicate a diversity of opinion towards Muslims. Indeed, these debates are as much about what 'Italy' stands for in terms of cultural and social practices and modes of political organisation as about Islam and Muslims. All the actors involved in this debate have to come to terms with a social and cultural landscape which is strongly characterised both by the predominance of the Catholic heritage and Church as well as by endemic localism. This localism, the most important political manifestation of which is the Lega Nord, together with the historical legacy of city states, makes it almost impossible to define unambiguously Italian national identity.[1] The understanding among the main actors of what is to be safeguarded in Italy 'against Islam', and how Italian identity conflicts with Islam and Muslims, thus differs greatly. Depending on ideology, beliefs, values and political aims, the 'Islamic threat' is constructed and deconstructed differently; at the same time the understanding of Italianness is also transformed.

The analysis of the media debate triggered by an attempt to construct a monumental mosque in Bologna in 2007 offers one opportunity to identify the complex set of actors involved in the process of construction and deconstruction of the Islamic threat. However, in order to understand their communication strategies and political aims it is first necessary to go back to the cultural and political 'revolution' which occurred in the 1990s, dubbed by Italian journalists as *Seconda Repubblica*, that is, the second Republic.

The return of Muslims in Italy: the growing Islamic threat and the Lega Nord party during the *Seconda Repubblica*

Historically the Islamic presence in Italy is a 'return', as Muslim Arabs had arrived in Italy, especially in the South and in Sicily, by the seventh century A.D. Those were the early days of Islam, and Muslims dominated the island from the ninth to the eleventh centuries. However, sociologically the presence of Muslims in Italy is a completely new phenomenon and a consequence of recent migration flows, as there is no living memory of their historical presence.[2]

Until long after World War II, Italy was a country of mass migration. Only in the 1980s and 1990s have immigrants started to arrive, coming from Muslim countries of the Maghreb, sub-Saharan Africa, the Middle East and Albania, plus predominantly Christian countries in Latin America and, more recently, Eastern Europe.[3] To date, Muslims number roughly one million and they are distributed all over the Italian territory but greater concentrations are in Lazio, Piemonte, Lombardia and Veneto.[4] Because of this rapid pace of immigration inflow and the novelty of the phenomenon, Muslims in Italy are still perceived as immigrants and foreigners, and essentially so different that they cannot be integrated. The characteristics that distinguish Muslims living in Italy from those in other European countries are: the diversity of countries of origin; the rapid pace of entry and settlement; the higher number of irregular immigrants; and the higher level of geographical dispersion. Consequently, the Muslim community in Italy is quite weak and not as structured as that in France, the United Kingdom or Germany.[5] Moreover, as Italy is a diverse nation with great regional differences in culture, politics and even spoken languages or dialects, migrants are not treated in the same way all over the Italian territory and are exposed to different cultural, as well as political and economical, contexts.[6]

The 1990s was a turning point for Italian political life in many respects. While the second wave of immigrants was arriving after the Berlin Wall had just fallen, Italian judges discovered a complex system of corruption, called *tangentopoli* by Italian media, involving the main political parties and leaders. This discovery eventually delegitimised almost the entire ruling political class. Out of the ashes of this system the *Seconda Repubblica* emerged, deeply marked by the personality and new communication styles of Silvio Berlusconi (media tycoon and four-times prime minister since 1994) and Lega Nord, a federation of northern independent parties led by Umberto Bossi.[7] The style of these political actors was disruptive of the *politichese*, the 'politically correct' language employed during the first Republic, as they used emphatic expressions and vulgar slogans. Thus, Lega Nord for ten years used a slogan claiming the virility of its leader as a political value. This new political language was adopted to discuss any topic, even the most complex subjects such as the integration of Muslim minorities or terrorism. Commenting upon a video showing Matteo Salvini, Lega Nord member of the European Parliament, singing a racist song against people from Naples, a famous Italian columnist wrote:

> Till 20 years ago, politicians were willing to show their difference from the most vulgar part of their voters. [...] Later on the would-be 'spontaneousness revolution' took place: politicians stopped talking with the people and they began, instead, speaking like the people.[8]

During this time period Italy was undergoing another major social transformation: the Islamic presence became much more relevant and consequently visible in the most industrialised regions of the North. Since then, the majority of Muslims has been made up of workers arriving from the Maghreb, and of poor origins, while prior to this a significant proportion were students coming from the Middle East, of Palestinian origins. The rapid acceleration of the immigration rate triggered harsh social and political reactions that partially sustained the growing role of the Lega Nord party.[9] Lega Nord – per l'Indipendenza della Padania (North League for the Independence of Padania) was formally founded in February 1991 as a federation of local independent parties in the North of

LORO HANNO SUBITO L'IMMIGRAZIONE

ORA VIVONO NELLE RISERVE!

LEGA NORD
PADANIA
BOSSI
Pensaci
www.leganord.org

They suffered immigration… now they live on reservations! Think about it!

Italy. The 8 per cent they obtained at the parliamentary elections in 1992 took Italian political analysts by surprise and gave the party the opportunity to join the first Berlusconi government in 1994.[10]

Initially, Lega Nord's main objective was to defend the rights of the industrialised north from the 'parasitical south of Italy' through secession from the central government of Rome, dubbed as 'the big thief', or at least through fiscal federalism and greater local autonomy. Later on, its main aim became to defend the people of the North from any kind of threat to their security and wellness, such as immigrants (either from the south of Italy or non-European countries), globalisation of markets, and a greater interference of European institutions into Italian domestic and economic affairs. During its 20-year history, the party led by Umberto Bossi developed a mythology about the Celtic origins of the hard-working people from the North versus the idle people from the South.

Lega Nord opposes any attempt to build mosques as they are 'meeting points for terrorists'. While this threat is in part nurtured by media reports of police operations against terrorist cells based in some mosques,[11] it is important to note that the reports of the intelligence service do not substantiate these fears. In fact, every six months, the central bureau of the Italian intelligence service reports to the Parliament's information and security policy, and assesses the various kinds of threats to Italian security and stability.[12] In the report presented on 29 February 2008 there is no reference to Islamic movements or ideology – either in the section 'Internal subversion and extremisms' or in 'Organised crime'. Only in the section 'International threats', is jihadism considered as a main threat with consequences inside the Italian territory and on Italian targets abroad: 'Extremists within our frontiers have kept on drawing the attention upon themselves mainly because of their logistic support to the organisations they belong to, as well as for routing *mujahidin* to Middle Eastern scenarios'.[13] While media and political leaders pay significant attention to mosques, the intelligence service has a wider scope and they collect information about Islamic associations, shops, meeting points such as internet cafés, *halal* butcheries and money transfer shops: 'From the constant monitoring of worship places (774 places to date, of which 78 were opened in 2007) and annexed education institutions, associations and foyers, we have noticed sporadic attempts by extremist individuals to prevail on moderates'.[14] Nevertheless, the global assessment they make about Islamic communities in Italy should not give rise to any worries: 'the majority of the Muslim community has demonstrated moderation and respect. [...] The community showed the same moderation during xenophobic episodes that happened in northern Italy and on the outskirts of the city of Milan from July till October 2007'.[15]

A 'Pig day' to contain the spreading of Islamic terrorism

Italian politicians and opinion makers seem more concerned about mosques than the intelligence service, even though mosques are not a new element in the Italian cultural landscape. During the Norman period, there were almost 300 mosques in Palermo alone and until recently new mosques were built notwithstanding some public critics. In some cases, public funds were even allocated to mosque projects. The first modern mosque in Sicily was built by an atheist Italian lawyer in Catania in 1980, with funds provided by Libya. The second modern mosque opened in Sicily was a deconsecrated church in Palermo which was heavily damaged during World War II and restored by the municipality for almost €750,000. The mosque was inaugurated on 7 November 1990 (the Tunisian national holiday) by the Tunisian Consul and Minister of Religious Affairs, and its imam continues to be nominated by the Tunisian government. However, the most important monumental mosque in Italy is surely the one in Rome, built in a field provided by the Rome municipality, funded by Saudi money, inaugurated in 1995 by the Italian President of the Republic, and managed by a cultural centre chaired by a previous Italian ambassador to Saudi Arabia converted to Islam.

Since the *Seconda Repubblica* was established and the new political language adopted, building monumental mosques, especially with domes and minarets, has always triggered harsh public debate. This subject is today perceived as a national political issue even if, according to Italian legislation, there is no need for government intervention since, like any other building, it falls under the jurisdiction of local authorities and the supervision of the Monuments and Fine Arts Office. In this new political climate, the strategies used to mobilise Italians against mosque construction may seem quite bizarre to external observers. The 'pig day' proposed in 2007 by Roberto Calderoli, Lega Nord exponent and deputy president of the Senate at that time, was not meant to celebrate this important animal but to desecrate a field in Bologna where Muslims were supposed to erect a mosque.[16]

In May 2007, the Bologna city council led by Sergio Cofferati, ex-leader of the leftist trade union CGIL, had given a 52,000m² field in San Donato to the local Muslim community to build a mosque of 6,000m² with a minaret and a dome, in exchange for a much smaller one already owned by the same cultural centre. In September 2007, just before

Wake up Padano!
With Lega Nord
against thieving Rome

the beginning of Ramadan, the debate became more intense because Calderoli announced his provocative initiative of the 'pig day'. Mayor Cofferati's concession to the Muslim community provoked strong response partly because it was perceived as an 'undue gift' to Unione delle Comunità Islamiche d'Italia (UCOII), which was accused of being the Italian branch of the Muslim Brotherhood and a Hamas supporter. The alleged link between mosques and terrorism was central to the project in Bologna. According to Lega Nord's Calderoli, 'Mosques are notably gathering centres for terrorists', or 'kamikaze's factories' as Magdi Allam, a prominent journalist of Egyptian origin who later converted to Catholicisim, defined them.[17] Criticisms spanned the range from the extreme right to the extreme left, passing through the Lega Nord, the Diocese and San Donato's citizens. These polemics immediately drew the attention of local and national mass media and the main political leaders as well as the Italian Minister of the Interior of that time, Giuliano Amato. This act of, formally, ordinary administration immediately became a source of contention also because Sergio Cofferati is a very well-known politician – for years he was the leader of the most important Italian trade union. However, his administration of Bologna, a prominent Italian town and historically administered by the communist party, is contested even by the leftist party Rifondazione Comunista, which criticises

0

Cofferati on many issues, such as his tough stance on security.

The Diocese, the Lega Anti-Diffamazione Cristiana (LADC, Christian anti-defamation league), the Lega Nord and San Donato's civic committee were the main opponents to the mosque's construction. For Calderoli, all mosques are a constant threat to security because imams preach hatred in Arabic and want to establish an Islamic Caliphate in Italy by exploiting 'the weakness of our legal system'. For Calderoli, the concession of opening a mosque or any kind of Islamic cultural centre should have only been taken by the *Viminale*, that is, the Italian Ministry of the Interior. The LADC is a non-profit association of Christians which declares itself to be under the patronage of the Blessed Virgin of San Luca (the most important sanctuary in Bologna). Its website functioned as a platform for publishing articles and arguments against the mosques and to mobilise public opinion against what it perceived as a threat to security. As an example, on 19 October 2007 they republished a poll commissioned by *Il Corriere della Sera* about how San Donato's citizens felt about the possibility of having a mosque in their neighbourhood; the result was that 35 per cent of the interviewees considered it a threat to security and between 51 and 55 per cent were decidedly against it. This association succeeded in stopping the mayor from proceeding with the construction by raising an international issue: apparently a gas pipeline which serves the NATO military base in Veneto passed just under the designated area for the mosque.

As to the official representatives from the Catholic Church, the Bologna Bishop Vicar, Monsignor Ernesto Vecchi, did not unambiguously oppose the construction of the mosque, however he underlined that the mosque was external to Italian identity, which he described as historically based on Christian values. The Catholic Church discourse about Islam and the mosque is indeed ambivalent:

> Although the Church representatives were in favour of the construction of the mosques and the cardinal of Lodi[18] condemned the priest that celebrated a mass in the Lega protest march of 14 October 2000, they at the same time defined popular 'fears [towards Muslim immigrants]' as 'normal' because hosting immigrants, rather than being emigrants themselves, is a new experience for Italians.[19]

The main local and national newspapers, from the right-wing *Il Giornale* and *Libero* to the more moderate and widely diffuse *Il Corriere della Sera* and *Repubblica*, covered the events extensively. *Il Giornale* and *Libero*, in the form of editorials signed by the directors and deputy directors, harshly criticised Cofferati's stand on this matter. *Repubblica's* coverage was quite moderate and its willingness not to contribute to the escalation of the polemic was apparent. On the other hand, *Il Corriere della Sera*, the most widely read daily newspaper in Italy, provided a forum for the harsh attacks of Magdi Allam as well as, in response to Allam, a letter by the UCOII's president Muhammad Nour Dacham on 9 November 2007. In this letter Dacham denied any relation to the planned mosque in Bologna and he dismissed Magdi Allam's allegations of supporting international terrorism.

After all these critiques, Cofferati and the city council decided to involve local citizens in the decision-making process and to postpone all further action until the end of negotiations with local inhabitants. The question is not yet a closed one as Muslims still want a mosque and the city council has, in the meantime, indicated a smaller area where the mosque could be erected. When Cofferati's administration publicly renounced the original project, Rifondazione Comunista harshly criticised the Mayor because he allegedly surrendered to the Lega Nord opposition. In June 2009 a new mayor was elected, still from the centre-left coalition, so presumably the dialogue will have to start again from the beginning.

As to the central government, the Italian Minister of the Interior stated clearly to the media that, according to his understanding, the real problem is not the concession of space but better monitoring of the messages spread inside mosques as well as of the centre's activities:

> It is not through repression that I can resolve problems. Of course, if it happens like in Perugia that the imam is preparing explosives I have to intervene, as we did. But we need to have open relations with Islam because it is religion as any other: so let's treat them all the same![20]

Conclusions

Previously built mosques, including the one situated in a former church in Palermo in 1990, did not come close to provoking the virulent debates that the attempt to erect domes and minarets in Bologna in 2007, or in other towns during the last ten years, did. This conservative and xenophobic attitude towards Muslims can be partially understood in the context of the high immigration pace of Muslims, who began arriving in Italy in the 1990s and now number almost one million. However, the 'pig day' proposed by Calderoli to contain the spreading of Islamic terrorism is also symptomatic of the new 'politically incorrect' communication style adopted by some Italian political leaders during the *Seconda Repubblica*.

Looking closely at the events in Bologna it becomes clear how a local debate about Islam can attract the immediate attention of national media and politicians trying to exploit it for their interests. The civic committee and Lega Nord's discourses are focused on safeguarding the national security threatened by the spreading of Islamism, allegedly represented in Italy by the UCOII and, to a lesser extent, on preserving Italy's cultural landscape. Actually, the Italian identity is a problematic concept for a federalist and some-times secessionist party like Lega Nord. The Church's stand on this subject is ambiva-lent as they condemn xenophobic attitudes but, at the same time, highlight, as Monsignor Vecchi did, that mosques are still an alien element to an Italian culture that is deeply marked by Catholic values. The town council, instead, wanted to implement a policy of integration but it did not succeed and postponed the problem, provoking the discontent of the extreme left party.

Unlike in other European countries, Islamic communities in Italy do not intervene directly in the media and political debate, probably because they are too new and frag-mented. However, the second generation of immigrants is growing and they have begun producing a new kind of Italian culture that will have, in the long run, an impact on the common perception of Muslim identity and the perceived Islamic threat.

Notes

1   See Gian Enrico Rusconi (1993) *Se cessiamo di essere una nazione*, Bologna: Il Mulino, and Ernesto Galli Della Loggia (1998) *L'identità italiana*, Bologna: Il Mulino.
2   Stefano Allievi (2003) *Islam italiano, viaggio nella Seconda religione del paese*, Turin: Einaudi.
3   The only institution that provides statistics about religions in Italy is the Foundation

Caritas/Migrantes which estimates that Muslims in Italy are just 26 per cent of all immigrants and are differentiated amongst themselves: 48 per cent come from North Africa, 26 per cent from Eastern Europe, 11 per cent from Western Africa and 10 per cent from the Indian subcontinent (Caritas/Migrantes, 2005). In this statistic Muslims with Italian nationality are not counted.

4   Istat (2007) *La popolazione straniera residente in Italia, al 1° gennaio 2007*. Available at www.istat.it/salastampa/comunicati/non_calendario/20071002_00/testointegrale 20071002.pdf. (link no longer accessible)

5   Stefano Allievi (2002) 'Islam in Italy', in Shireen Hunter (ed.), *Islam, Europe's second religion: the new social, cultural, and political landscape*, Washington DC: Praeger-CSIS.

6   Giovanna Zincone (ed.) (2000) *Secondo rapporto sull'integrazione degli immigrati in Italia*, Bologna: Il Mulino.

7   Norberto Bobbio (1997) *Verso la Seconda Repubblica*, Turin: La Stampa.

8   Massimo Gramellini (2009) 'Il Galateo secondo Matteo', *La Stampa*, July.

9   According to official figures, since the beginning of this century the foreign-born population in Italy has more than doubled and now numbers 2,938,922 (ISTAT 2007).

10   Lega Nord's voters are not homogeneously distributed throughout the Italian territory; in 2009 at the election for the European Parliament it obtained an average of 19 per cent of the vote in the northern part of Italy, as opposed to 2.97 per cent in the centre, 0.57 per cent in the South, and only 0.37 per cent in the islands.

11   Lorenzo Vidino (2006) *Al-Qaeda in Europe, the new battleground of international jihad*, New York: Prometheus Books.

12   Dipartimento delle informazioni per la sicurezza (2007) *Relazione sulla politica dell'informazione per la sicurezza*. Available at http://www.sicurezzanazionale.gov.it/ web.nsf/documenti/_relazione2007.pdf. (link accessed 19 June 2014)

13   Ibid., p. 66.

14   Ibid., p. 70.

15   Ibid., p. 69.

16   In 2006, Calderoli, at the time Minister of Reforms, had also displayed on TV a t-shirt with the Danish cartoons of the Prophet Muhammad, thus triggering riots in front of the Italian Consulate in Benghazi, during the course of which ten people died. Calderoli was asked to resign.

17   Magdi Allam, an Egyptian-born naturalised Italian, before becoming a member of the European Parliament in 2009 with the Unione Democratica di Centro, was one of the most influential journalists and columnists covering Islamic and Arab issues. Initially he wrote for *Il Manifesto* (a communist newspaper) and *La Repubblica* and, from 2003–8 he was deputy director *ad personam* of *Il Corriere della Sera*. He converted to Catholicism at Easter 2008, when he was baptised by Pope Benedict XVI himself.

18   Lodi is an important town near Milan where Calderoli had already organised a 'pig day' in 2000 against an attempt to build a mosque.

19   Anna Triandafyllidou (2002) 'Religious Diversity and Multiculturalism in Southern Europe: The Italian Mosque Debate', *Sociological Research Online*, 7 (1) p. 11.

20   Amato Islam (2007) 'Serve intesa con musulmani in particolare per quanto riguarda gli imam' *La Repubblica*, September.

References

Allievi, Stefano (2002) 'Islam in Italy', in Shireen Hunter (ed.), *Islam, Europe's second religion, the new social, cultural, and political landscape*, Washington DC: Praeger-CSIS.

—— (2003) *Islam italiano, viaggio nella Seconda religione del paese*, Turin: Einaudi.

Bobbio, Norberto (1997) *Verso la Seconda Repubblica*, Turin: La Stampa.

Caritas-Migrantes (2005) *Le religioni degli immigrati all'inizio del 2004: gli effetti della regolarizzazione*, Rome: Caritas-Migrantes.

Dipartimento delle informazioni per la sicurezza (2007) *Relazione sulla politica dell'informazione per la sicurezza*. Available at http://www.sicurezzanazionale.gov.it/web.nsf/documenti/_relazione2007.pdf (link last accessed 19 June 2014)

Galli Della Loggia, Ernesto (1998) *L'identità italiana*, Bologna: Il Mulino.

Gramellini, Massimo (2009) 'Il Galateo secondo Matteo', *La Stampa*, July.

Islam, Amato (2007) 'Serve intesa con musulmani in particolare per quanto riguarda gli imam', *La Repubblica*, September.

Istat (2007) *La popolazione straniera residente in Italia, al 1° gennaio 2007*. Available at www.istat.it/salastampa/comunicati/non_calendario/20071002_00/testointegrale20071002.pdf. (link no longer functional)

Rusconi, Gian Enrico (1993) *Se cessiamo di essere una nazione*, Bologna: Il Mulino.

Triandafyllidou, Anna (2002) 'Religious Diversity and Multiculturalism in Southern Europe: The Italian Mosque Debate', *Sociological Research Online*, 7 (1).

Vidino, Lorenzo (2006) *Al-Qaeda in Europe, the new battleground of international jihad*, New York: Prometheus Books.

Zincone, Giovanna (ed.) (2000) *Secondo rapporto sull'integrazione degli immigrati in Italia*, Bologna: Il Mulino.

THE END OF TOLERANCE. ISLAM AND THE TRANSFORMATIONS OF IDENTITY AND SECULARISM IN THE NETHERLANDS

Sarah Bracke

The Netherlands account for more than one million Muslims, which amounts to more than 6.5 per cent of the Dutch population, and ranks second in Western Europe (after France) in terms of the size of its Muslim population. Most Muslims in the Netherlands are of Turkish (about 380,000) and Moroccan (about 345,000) descent.[1] The presence of Islam in the material and imaginary space of the Netherlands is not confined to the present time or territory: the Netherlands colonised the largest Muslim country in the world, that is, Indonesia. Like a number of other national contexts in Europe, the 'Dutch case' has been much-discussed in relation to debates on multicultural issues and the place of Islam in Europe. Unlike some other cases, the Dutch colonial relationship to Muslim populations is rarely brought to bear on the contemporary debates about Islam in the Netherlands.

This chapter traces how Islam is framed in contemporary Dutch society. As such, it is very much a discussion of recent transformations of Dutch society, a discussion which proceeds on two terrains: first, the terrain of national security, where Islam gets framed as a security threat, and second, the terrain of national identity, where Islam gets framed as the civilisational 'Other' to Dutch identity. In the process of the transformation of Dutch identity, the role of sexual politics is central, which is addressed in a third section. By way of conclusion, the transformations of Dutch society are situated as a transformation of the Dutch secular regime.

Framing Islam part one: National Security

In a post-Cold War context in the Netherlands, like elsewhere, the national security apparatus is re-imagined and restructured. Part of this transformation can be traced through the reports of the Binnenlandse Veiligheidsdienst (BVD, the Interior Security Services), subsequently restructured and renamed as the General Information and Security Services (AIVD), which had been made public from the beginning of the 1990s onwards.[2] In 1992 the first available BVD annual report identifies 'political Islam' as a security problem for the Dutch state. Identifying and attending to new security threats in the course of the 1990s effectively enabled the expansion of the terrain of the Dutch security services and the enlargement of the terrain of surveillance in general. The end of the East–West Cold War antagonism not only entailed what the BVD describes as the growth and differentiation of the number of subjects and themes upon which security is brought to bear, but also a transformation of the nature of possible threats to national security. According to the BVD, the Netherlands now has to deal with *more* threats to democracy, and these have become more *intrinsic* to society, through the processes of migration and the informatisation of society (new digital media, the internet, etc.), both considered to be concerns to national sovereignty.

From the outset, the threat of political Islam was envisioned in a transnational way – first through an emphasis on connections between developments in 'the Muslim world' and migration from those parts of the world to the Netherlands, and subsequently through what is identified as 'a new development' of young, Dutch-born and integrated Muslims seeking to establish connections with radical political Islam organisations abroad. Political Islam, it is suggested, poses an inherent threat to national sovereignty, and this is reflected in the three categories, laid out by the 1992 report, of individuals in need of surveillance: first, those individuals who are considered to be 'serviceable' to foreign powers, and second, individuals who compromise Dutch security through their violent actions against other foreign powers. While these usual suspects of the national security services could and would subsequently be mobilised with respect to Muslims, it is the third category that comes to set the post-Cold War security agenda: those individuals who reject the established order and seek to replace it with an Islamic one – which amounts to the BVD's definition of political Islam.

Throughout the 1990s, these new threats, and the case for the expansion of surveillance in general, were articulated relatively independently from the securities services' concern with terrorism. A special report on terrorism at the dawn of the new millennium (published in April 2001) concludes that, although special attention needs to be given to political Islam and religiously inspired movements and organisations, the general threat of terrorism, nationally and internationally, has decreased. It is only in the wake of the events of 9/11, and in the subsequent annual reports, that the topics of terrorism and political Islam have been strongly interlaced, and closely linked to migration and the informatisation of society.

Moreover, the 2001 annual report explicitly identifies 'extreme religious ideas and conceptions' as the nature of the problem of contemporary terrorist threats. Religious radicalism, according to the security services, entails two sets of problems. First, it easily leads to terrorism, and second, it has a detrimental effect on the representation and acceptance of Islam by society at large – hence posing the question of integration. An analysis of the conceptual framework in which the security services construe the newly identified security threat reveals the centrality of the notion of 'integration'. While discursively connected to the issue of migration yet not confined to it, integration is taken as a crucial way to unnerve forces that could reject the established order. Hence, integration becomes conceptually embedded within the Dutch national security agenda as a 'security issue'. The more integrated Muslim populations are within Dutch society, the reasoning goes, the less chance they will turn to political Islam and thus seek to overthrow the established order and replace it with an Islamic one.

From the mid-1990s onwards, the security services discovered that the stigmatisation of Islam constitutes an important source of the non-integration of Muslim populations. As a result, the BVD envisioned yet another role for itself, that is, monitoring the representation of Islam and more specifically discouraging stereotypes about Muslims. The way forward, according to the security services, is a rigorous and ruthless investigation of the 'facts' of Islam and Islamic groups in the Netherlands. Thus the production of knowledge on Islam is acknowledged as part and parcel of the scope of operation of the security services.

This sustained attention to the need for more knowledge about Islam culminated in a first public publication, in 1998, entitled *Political Islam in the Netherlands*. The study asserts, among other things, that political Islam remains a rather small-sized problem in the Netherlands, but nevertheless one that is in constant need of monitoring. The focus of the security services' attention on political Islam is torn in two directions: on the one hand, Milli Görüş, an Islamic organisation within the Turkish diaspora, which is considered the largest political Islam organisation in the Netherlands (about 30,000 members) albeit by no means the most radical political Islam group; on the other hand, small, network-like organisations of young Dutch men of mostly Moroccan origin, such as the Hofstad network (to which Mohammed Bouyeri, the killer of Theo van Gogh, allegedly belonged), which are considered more of a real threat.

Framing Islam part two: Redefining Dutch National Identity

The framing of Islam as a security threat, whether through the direct threat of so-called political Islam or the indirect threat of a lack of integration of Islam in Dutch society, concurred with two decades of civilisation discourse in which Islam is framed as the other to Dutch identity. This framing of Islam is part and parcel of a redefinition of Dutch identity in the context of the crisis of the nation state. The 'cultural work' of redefining national identity takes place through the discussions about 'the multicultural society' and notably concerning the material and symbolic space of Islam within the Netherlands.

A landmark in this respect is the Lucerne speech by Frits Bolkestein at the Liberal International in Lucerne in 1991. The speech is a commentary on the geopolitical transformation inaugurated by the fall of the Soviet Union, wherein Bolkestein effectively established a link between the new geopolitical moment and the national debate on the multicultural society. He did so through his assertion of the incompatibility between Islam – the new geopolitical (f)actor – and Western liberal values. Bolkestein denounced 'the failure of integration' of the post-colonial labour migrants to the Netherlands, and pointed in two directions to take stock of this failure. First, he identified Islam as a fundamental problem. European civilisation, Bolkestein argued, and in particular the political tradition of liberalism, has generated a number of fundamental political principles (such as the separation of Church and State, freedom of expression, toleration and non-discrimination), which have universal validity and value, and Islam stands in tension with these principles. Secondly, Bolkestein denounced the 'cultural relativism' of the 1980s' minority policies grounded in the principle of 'integration with the conservation of one's own identity'. He concluded that it was time to draw limits on Dutch tolerance and multicultural society. His speech, which was subsequently elaborated and published as an op-ed in one of the leading newspapers *De Volkskrant*, effectively marked the beginning of the political use of the 'multicultural question' by voices other than the extreme right, which until then had been the home of this kind of civilisational discourse.

In many respects, Bolkestein's speech laid out the framework for debates on culture, religion and identity in the Netherlands in the decades to come. This framework was built upon a civilisational scheme which opposed Dutch society to Islam – as the great evil force threatening to take over and destroy Dutch society and culture, in Fortuyn's words – and became hegemonic. A large number of political and public figures, of which Pim Fortuyn, Ayaan Hirsi Ali, Theo van Gogh and Geert Wilders represent the most well known, took up the civilisational scheme and further elaborated on it. At the same time, some of these figures brought their own emphasis to the debate. Fortuyn embodied a new style in (party) politics previously unheard of in the Netherlands: transgressive, flamboyant, camp, and infused with his open and 'in your face' gayness. Hirsi Ali insisted more than anyone else on the values of the European Enlightenment and made women's emancipation and women's rights central in her fight against Islam.

The discourse that was elaborated in the process performed a break with previous understandings of Dutch identity and society – a transformation coded as 'the end of tolerance'. The substantive break is accompanied by one on the level of style, through the advent of what Baukje Prins qualifies as 'new realism' – that is, a mode of political rhetoric that derives its power from disavowing political and ideological processes and claiming direct access to reality. This was very much championed and consolidated by Fortuyn, and his repeated declarations that it was time to 'say things as they really are'. Moreover, in the case of Hirsi Ali, she claimed a position of 'native authority' for herself, and got it continuously ascribed to her, in yet another dimension of 'new realism': as 'a Muslim woman' she knows and speaks about Islam 'as it really is'.

Dutch Exceptionalism and Sexual Politics

The post-Cold War framing of geopolitics and global antagonism – whether it occurs through the 'Clash of Civilisations' as it emerged in the 1990s, or the War on Terror of the first decade of the new millennium – is profoundly infused with sexual politics (which is used here as shorthand for the politics of gender and sexuality). This entanglement is increasingly commented upon, drawing on post-colonial, feminist and queer theories and their intersections.

In the Dutch case, the emphasis on sexual politics is particularly strong, to the extent that it is a crucial element of Dutch exceptionalism. The Netherlands has a profound historical investment in an understanding of itself as a nation of emancipated women and sexual minorities, and this understanding is mobilised as a crucial terrain for civilisational politics. The subject of women's emancipation is omnipresent in discussions about Islam and multicultural society, and is indeed deployed as a distinctive cultural and civilisational marker. Hirsi Ali's discourse is prominent in this respect, including her film, *Submission*, in which Qur'anic verses about women are written on semi-nude female bodies.

Such appeal to women's emancipation is epitomised by a public statement by minister De Geus, responsible for emancipation at the time, on the occasion of International Women's Day in 2003. Women's emancipation was fully achieved for autochtonous women in the Netherlands, the minister declared, and subsequently emancipation policies needed only to focus on allochtonous women. Besides the very material consequences of such a reconceptualisation of women's emancipation, in which many autochtonous groups lost funding, this reflects the institutionalisation of cultural and racist demarcations on the grounds of women's emancipation.

The centrality of sexual politics in this civilisational redefinition of Dutch identity did not remain confined to women's emancipation, and included homosexuality as another crucial trope in the framing of Islam. Fortuyn's gayness, for instance, was not a marginal element but rather served to underscore a number of distinctions between open, sexually liberated Dutch culture on the one hand, and closed, sexually repressed Muslim culture on the other. A first public controversy revolving around homosexuality as a way of articulating Dutch identity occurred in the wake of the NOVA television programme in May 2001 in which an imam in Rotterdam, Khalil el Moumni, expressed a number of negative views on homosexuality (a contagious disease, etc.). NOVA's framing proved all but innocent: the focus was on el Moumni's condemnation of homosexuality, while his condemnations of violence against homosexuals was left out, as well any mention of the fact that the imam's views on homosexuality did not substantially differ from indigenous conservative Protestant and Catholic perspectives on the matter. Yet it is precisely this framing that is deployed for those cultural politics affirming the incompatibility of Islam and the liberal West.

This use of homosexuality in marking cultural identities also became institutionalised. The citizenship test (*nationale inburgeringstest*), which became compulsory in 2006 and functions as a way to establish whether immigrants can have residency in the Netherlands or not, contains a question about two men kissing in public. During the following year the Ministry for Education, Culture and Science released a document, entitled *Gewoon homo zijn* (Simply Being Gay) with a policy for the years 2008–11 'to make homosexuality the subject of societal discussion', including the 'Dialogue' project with 'other communities' where it was understood that the taboo of homosexuality needed to be broken. Both of these efforts by the Dutch government reflect institutionalised ways in which specific attitudes and outlooks to homosexuality are tied up with Dutch identity and deployed as a way to negotiate access to that identity and, indeed, citizenship.

A Transformation of the Dutch Secular Regime

A discussion of how Islam became framed through Dutch national security politics and Dutch identity politics reveals a tremendous transformation of Dutch society in the last two decades. There is yet another way to understand or situate that transformation, that is, from the perspective of Dutch secularism. Here it makes sense to reconsider Bolkestein's speech mentioned at the outset of this chapter. Bolkestein's critique focused on the Dutch policy of 'integration with conservation of one's own identity', which he argued must be brought to an end. This model of minority policy adopted by the Dutch state during the 1980s was problematic in many respects. It was explicitly inspired by the idea of facilitating the return of 'guest workers', as the labour migrants were called at the time, to their countries of origin when their labour was no longer needed. Moreover, it begs many questions about the construction of this 'own identity', which must conform to the spirit of the Dutch model of pillarisation, that is, a religious affiliation that should be at once recognisably religious and secular. Yet whatever the problems with the model, the point of the matter is that this mode of managing difference profoundly shapes Dutch society; it is part and parcel of its architecture, which was inspired by the notion of toleration that emerged as a philosophical and political answer to the religious wars of the seventeenth century.

Bolkestein explicitly highlighted the continuity between the 'integration with the conservation of one's own identity' policy and the Dutch model of pillarisation. This genealogical connection, however, is mobilised to dismiss the minority policies, as Bolkestein claims that Dutch society has moved *beyond* pillarisation. The point is the following: while at the time both Bolkestein's critique of the minority policies and his adoption of a civilisational discourse were heavily critiqued, his claim with respect to pillarisation remained largely unchallenged.

Pillarisation implies the organisation of the social body along confessional or sectarian lines in a segmented polity. A pillar is an integrated complex of societal organisations and/or institutions (such as schools, political parties, trade unions, newspapers, etc.) resting upon a confessional basis. Hence a certain cohesion internal to a pillar is mirrored in a separation from the rest of society, and a pillar can be recognised as a parallel network or social body. The theorist of Dutch pillarisation, Arend Lijphart, characterised pillarisation as a politics of accommodation and pacification, in which different faiths and ideologies are organised in a structurally similar way: Dutch nation formation began with a Protestant, a Catholic and a 'general' (humanist) pillar; a socialist pillar followed in the nineteenth century. Dutch pillarisation has been praised and ridiculed, defended and criticised, and analysed in terms of its functions: first, an emancipation strategy of structurally disadvantaged groups; second, the conservation and protection of identity; third, social control, or an instrument allowing elites to counter and channel claims for emancipation; and finally, the continuity of a tradition of pluralism and politics aimed at compromise.

Since the 1960s the 'de-pillarisation' (*ontzuiling*) of Dutch society has been announced over and over again, as a way to account for transformations of Dutch society and notably the decline of the binding force of confessions and ideologies in relation to societal institutions. If pillarisation provided a mode of modernisation in and of the Netherlands, in a more post-modern era the religious and ideological differences that comprise pillarisation have yielded to a more diffuse and playful understanding of pluralism and tolerance. Yet such declarations of the end of pillarisation need to be questioned in each instance that the resilience of the pillarised architecture of Dutch society reveals itself – after elections for instance, or in modalities of redistributing resources according to different religious and political lines. In other words, the Dutch pacification model has continued to be salient after the 1960s. As Lijphart put it in 1989: 'The politics of accommodation did not undergo a complete metamorphosis into its very opposite. No revolution ever happened.'

In relation to Islam, the pillarised structure of Dutch society would suggest an evident mode of incorporation of Islam in the Dutch nation state, that is, the development of a pillar of its own. The possibilities of the existing architecture of Dutch society have been noted before, for example by Yunas Samad in the following observation:

> 'Pillarisation' has incorporated religious minorities and retarded xenophobic and defensive developments among them. The Islam versus secularism debates, graphically represented by the vitriolic controversy around *The Satanic Verses* in Britain and the headscarf affair in France, are non-issues in the Netherlands, as Muslims there are already covered by blasphemy laws, allowed to have state-funded Muslim schools, and have access to the media in the form of an Islamic television channel. Clearly, then, the issues are not just about secularism and religion, but about forms of political activity that are deemed by national society to be legitimate in the light of existing structures.[3]

Perhaps it was precisely the great possibilities of the 'existing structures', when according to a civilisational logic Islam could *not* be integrated into Dutch society, that implied that there was a need for a fundamental break or discontinuity within Dutch society and its existing structures and identity. In this sense, Bolkestein's declaration that pillarisation is over and done with seems to be the most consistent one thus far: a declaration of death that does not so much occur in relation to a perceived general post-1960s decline of religious institutional affiliations, but rather in the light of a civilisational logic in which Islam and Dutch society are construed and imagined as incompatible opposites. The transformation of Dutch identity, in other words, is intrinsically linked with a transformation of the Dutch secular regime.

Conclusion

Islam is at the centre of heated and sometimes vitriolic public debates in the Netherlands nowadays, yet these debates reveal more about the significant transformations of Dutch identity and society in the last two decades than about the realities of Islam in the Netherlands. In discussions about identity, culture and civilisation, and in the public debate in general, notions of a Dutch self are established in relation to a cultural and civilisational 'Other', which is Islam. In a Dutch context, the terrain of sexual politics is crucial to these cultural definitions. This framing of Islam is not limited to public debate itself; rather the public debate reflects how hegemonic the framing of Islam as 'Other' has become. In relation to national security, we can trace how Islam came to occupy the centre stage in the post-Cold War redefinition of what constitutes a threat to the national body (and therefore also what and who constitutes the national body). In relation to the Dutch secular regime, we can trace how the potential for the integration of Islam in the existing Dutch pillarised structure comes to a halt through a civilisational logic. This implies a transformation of the Dutch secular regime as part of the transformations of Dutch identity and society. The actual integration or mooring of Islam in Dutch society, we could conclude, is accompanied by a relative lack of symbolic integration in which Islam and Muslims are recognised as part and parcel of Dutch identity and culture. For a viable future of the de facto multicultural and multi-religious Netherlands, this will have to change.

Notes

1   See Centraal Bureau voor de Statistiek Website. www.cbs.nl. (website last accessed 19 June 2014)
2   See www.minbzk.nl/aivd/. (website last accessed 19 June 2014)
3   Yunas Samad (1997) 'The plural guises of multiculturalism: conceptualising a fragmented paradigm', in Tariq Modood and Pnina Werbner (eds), *The Politics of Multiculturalism in the New Europe. Racism, Identity and Community*, London: Zed Books, pp. 240–60.

References

Asad, Talal (2003) *Formations of the Secular: Christianity, Islam, Modernity*, Stanford: Stanford University Press.

Binnenlandse Veiligheidsdienst (1998) *De politieke Islam in Nederland*, The Hague: Ministerie van Binnenlandse Zaken.

Bracke, Sarah (2007) 'Ex-corporation. The Dutch secular contract in transformation', in Rosi Braidotti, Charles Esche and Maria Hlavajova (eds), *Citizens and Subjects: The Netherlands, for example*, Zurich: JRP Ringier.

De Leeuw, Marc and Sonja Van Wichelen (2005) '"Please, Go Wake Up!" Submission, Hirsi Ali, and the "War on Terror" in the Netherlands', *Feminist Media Studies*, 5(3): pp. 325–40.

Ghorashi, Halleh (2003) 'Ayaan Hirsi Ali: daring or dogmatic? Debates on multiculturalism and emancipation in the Netherlands', *Focaal: European Journal of Anthropology*, 42: pp. 163–73.

Hoogenboom, Marcel (1996) *Een miskende democratie. Een andere visie op verzuiling en politieke samenwerking in Nederland*, Leiden: DSWO Press.

Lijphart, Arend (1989) 'From the Politics of Accommodation to Adversarial Politics in the Netherlands – A Reassessment', *West European Politics*, 12 (1): pp. 139–53.

Mahmood, Saba (2008) 'Feminism, democracy, and empire: Islam and the War of Terror', in Joan Scott (ed.), *Women Studies on the Edge*, Durham: Duke University Press.

Prins, Baukje (2000) *Voorbij de onschuld. Het debat over de multiculturele samenleving*, Amsterdam: Van Gennep.

Puar, Jasbir (2007) *Terrorist Assemblages. Homonationalism in Queer Times*, Durham: Duke University Press.

Samad, Yunas (1997) 'The plural guises of multiculturalism: conceptualising a fragmented paradigm', in Tariq Modood and Pnina Werbner, (eds), *The Politics of Multiculturalism in the New Europe. Racism, Identity and Community*, London: Zed Books, pp. 240–60.

Veer, Peter van der (2006) 'Pim Fortuyn, Theo van Gogh and the Politics of Tolerance in the Netherlands', *Public Culture*, 18 (1): pp. 111–24.

SPAIN: WHO'S AFRAID OF WHAT?

Elena Arigita

The political debate on Islam in Spain is very similar to that in other Western countries, and is also influenced by discourses and debates in those countries. Successive crises, in the form of attacks, violent events or media controversy, are echoed in Spain and, in turn, fuel the debate on Islam as a religion, on Muslims as a religious minority in Spain and on their loyalties (to Spain, to their country of origin, to their religion?). That is, the debate focuses on their ethno-religious identity, which is considered alien to Spain or to Spanish society and even, according to certain readings of Spanish history, capable of causing distrust, suspicion and, in the worst scenario, is something incompatible, hostile and dangerous. As a result, we are now witnessing a new tendency to observe and question Muslims about their feelings of belonging and loyalty to religion and to the country they live in, their commitment as citizens and their degree of acceptance of state institutions, democracy and the values of that system. Due to the effect of events that have fuelled global debates on Islam, individuals and communities have become the focus of interest, analysis, comparison and analogy, and sometimes also arouse suspicion.

In 2006 the Spanish Home Office began carrying out annual opinion surveys on 'the Spanish Muslim community'. These surveys were not fortuitous but rather the consequence of these debates on Islam. They are extremely important and are intended to be an ongoing initiative, since new studies have been carried out each year since the initiative was launched. The results of the first survey showed very clearly that 'the Muslim community resident in Spain has a positive opinion of both Spanish society and the Spanish political system'. The survey has developed into an annual study supported by the Spanish Home Office and also the Ministry of Justice and the Ministry of Labour and Immigration.

Year after year, the conclusions of these studies have highlighted the 'normality' of the responses given by the participants in the surveys. However, it is interesting to note that virtually no public voices have questioned the idea of questioning Muslims about their civil values and their vision of Spain, with certain exceptions such as the academician Gema Martín Muñoz, who referred in a Spanish newspaper to what she described as a worrying phenomenon, that is, the need to question Muslims simply because they are Muslims, and also condemned this as 'discriminatory' and even 'humiliating'.[1]

This is no trivial matter: the annual reports on the opinions of Muslims in Spain are part of a policy of prevention, control, security, resulting in the adoption – by different state departments responsible for security, immigration and relations with the different confessions – of specific policies for Muslims in the very particular scenario that has developed after the Madrid attacks on 11 March 2004. March 11 is a key moment in the development of a phenomenon that has become widely referred to as 'Islamic terrorism' (despite different attempts to disassociate that form of violence from Islamic religion as a source of motivation). As such, the attacks catalysed fear of Islam in Spain, a process precipitated by the events of 9/11, and related to the same logic. Moreover, the Madrid attacks became a point of inflection for a new visibility of Islam and Muslims in Spain. This visibility was seen as a challenge but also often as a problem. In this connection, the observation of and comparison with the situation in other countries with longer traditions of migration became a reference for addressing the visible Muslim presence in Spain which, in the decade marked by 9/11, is seen as a conflict and clash of cultural values.

However, although fear of Islam in Spain is encompassed within a broader context of Western public opinion on Islam and the Islamic threat, and is also fuelled by that situation, it must be understood specifically within Spanish dynamics resulting purely from national processes of political legitimation that have also developed as a result of the country's specific history. These dynamics are determined by three factors: first, Spain's history and the controversy surrounding the importance of Spain's Islamic heritage; second, the political, legal and institutional process that has regulated religious freedom and state aconfessionality during the period of democracy and recognises, institutionalises, regulates and gives visibility to Islam as a religion in Spain; and, third, migratory processes, influenced in particular by Spain's proximity to and historical links with Morocco.

The first of these factors relates to Spain as a nation and the function assigned to Islam within the nation, in the construction of Spanish identity and, in short, in the formation of a collective historical memory not without complexity and contradictions regarding the Islamic legacy of al-Andalus and its place in Spanish history. Therefore, although the new fear of Islam is not entirely the result of a process of continuity intrinsic to the Spanish national context, there are still elements that explain and fuel what is clearly a new fear.

The fear of Islam in Spain after 11 March has been fuelled by a certain historical revisionism that legitimises and justifies that fear, identifying reasons that may be traced to different periods of history; in short, and as revealed by the titles of certain essays and a new consumer literature on Islam, this historical revisionism presents and demonstrates that Islam is a religion essentially 'against Spain'.[2] The use of this historical legacy in the current context cannot be read from one perspective only, since it takes very different and sometimes opposing forms, ranging from the mythification of al-Andalus as the sole moment of perfect interreligious and inter-cultural coexistence, to completely opposite readings, that is, the demonstration that the aforementioned period was an exception in Spanish history before and after al-Andalus and that Spain had to fight against the Muslim invaders. The ideological debate on Spain's identity in relation to that historical past has been brilliantly dissected by contemporary historiography,[3] which has shown how, at certain moments and from very specific ideological positions, the narration of Spanish history has selected a series of events and data that 'demonstrate' that Islam and Muslims are not only foreign or alien but also 'against' Spain.

Within that logic, a relatively new discourse and literature have offered a new image of al-Andalus, defining it as an exceptional digression in the history of Spain that has been based on a hugely powerful stereotype arising from an accumulation of images on Muslim presence in the Iberian Peninsula during the invasion and as the enemy. The eight centuries of Muslim occupation which, in other cases and for other causes is recreated as an idyllic – and equally distorted – image of the coexistence of three cultures, are used, in the light of the attacks and wars in this decade, as part of the civilisational logic in which Islam is opposed to the West. That specific reading of history selects and explains events that continually present Spain as the frontier and 'shield of the West', where history is told as a succession of confrontations with the expansionism of Islam. Thus, all conflicts, from the 'Reconquest' to the Mediterranean wars with the Ottoman Empire, the Iraq wars or the 2002 crisis with Morocco over Perejil-Laila (a small islet in the Mediterranean whose sovereignty is disputed by both countries), are explained within the logic of Islam against Spain.[4] Within this logic, that 'coexistence' is described as not peaceful and the moral values of Islam are presented as a threat both to democratic values and to respect for human rights, in an amalgam of essentialist and distorting images that show that Islam is, by nature, violent. Thus, although the new fear of an Islamic threat has been elicited by specific international circumstances, it is fuelled and legitimised through a certain logic of continuity constructed by Spanish nationalist historiography, which has used certain historical facts to support the theory of an Islamic threat.

Apart from historiographical controversies and ideological debates on Spain as a nation, its collective identity and its (in)compatibility with Islam, the public visibility of Islam has been influenced by two events that have shaped it in very different ways: first, the signing of the Cooperation Agreements with the Islamic Commission of Spain in 1992, which underpinned the institutionalisation of Islam in Spain; and second, the March 11 terrorist attacks, which brought new attention to Muslims stimulated by fear, but also control, integration, dialogue between Muslim representatives and state administrations and institutions, specifically interreligious dialogue, etc.

The 1992 Cooperation Agreements were the result of a long process of recognition of religious freedom in Spain. The institutional treatment of religious identity in contemporary Spain prompted the separation of Church and State, and might indicate a break with the historical legacy of the confessional state. However, the history of the modern state, and the special relations with the Catholic Church have fostered a special relationship with Catholicism, which was the official religion until the 1978 Constitution.

That special relationship, which contradicts the aconfessionality of the Spanish State, has somehow served as an incentive for establishing relations with other minority confessions. The 1980 Organic Law on Religious Freedom defines that a privileged relationship between the State and certain confessions must comply with the condition of *notorio arraigo* (clear and deep-rooted influence), a concept that represents legal recognition of a specific confession taking into account its scope and number of believers. The concept of *notorio arraigo* is complex and difficult to define and prompted open interpretations, which at the time permitted the inclusion of history or 'historical scope' as an argument. Thus, although the incipient Muslim community in Spain was still small and limited in terms of its organisational capacity, in 1989 Islam was granted *notorio arraigo* status for the following specific historical reasons:

> Islam is one of the spiritual faiths that has shaped the historical personality of Spain. Our culture and tradition are inseparably linked to the religious foundations that have forged the deepest essences of the Spanish people and character...[5]

It was during this period, from 1989 to 1992, that the bases of dialogue between the State and the Muslim community were established, accompanied by parallel agreements signed with the Evangelist and Jewish confessions, culminating with the signing of the 1992 Cooperation Agreements. The date is also hugely symbolic because that year Spain celebrated a series of commemorative events: the 'discovery' of America, which was celebrated as a 'meeting' of two worlds; the World Expo in Seville; an exhibition at the Alhambra on the Andalusí Legacy; the Madrid Conference on Peace in the Middle East; the inauguration of the 'M30' mosque in Madrid by the King and Queen of Spain and the Prince of Saudi Arabia; and the Sefarad 1992 ceremony in Toledo, which attempted to demonstrate Spain's democratic normalisation in the international context through a re-reading of its history.

Given this backdrop, how is Islam seen in contemporary Spain? What elements are new and what images rooted in the collective conscience have remained? How are they reconstructed and what new content has been added?

With the consolidation of democracy in the 1980s, economic development, new immigration laws and the acquisition of religious freedoms enabled the installation, consolidation and also the enhanced visibility of an incipient Muslim associative network, although in that decade and even in the 1990s Muslims were still seen largely as emigrants. Thus, 'immigrant' Islam – sometimes also described as 'imported' Islam – referred to the religious practice of immigrant communities as something basically foreign, and also sometimes through opposition to the Islam of Spanish converts. The classification of different forms of Islam once again introduced a dichotomy between an imported tradition and another that demanded its place in Spain and Europe.

Institutional development since the late 1980s led to the creation of new associations, with and without links to existing federations, and officially represented before the State through the Islamic Commission of Spain, with the gradual development of different forms of local and regional representation, which have not been free of criticism in terms of their efficiency and representativeness. The new legal recognition afforded by the Agreements was followed by a certain period of institutional paralysis in which, due to the effect of immigration, Muslim communities continued to grow and became more heterogeneous.

In this context, March 11 added a new component to the visibility of Islam and Muslims, and had a decisive impact on the public debate, linking aspects such as the representation and management of Islam as a minority confession to security and immigration control issues. As a consequence of the Madrid terrorist attacks, Muslims attracted new attention (and concern) in the midst of a highly polarised debate on the reasons and responsibilities for the attacks. In the weeks following the attacks, some Muslim leaders contributed to the debates by issuing press releases condemning the attacks and expressing their concern that Muslim communities might suffer a backlash in their daily lives, while at the same time valuing the peaceful and positive response of Spanish society. That participation was also something new that timidly brought to an end the almost complete absence of Muslim voices in the media, and was accompanied by a growing awareness of the need to participate in political debates. Nevertheless, Muslim voices are still largely absent from Spanish public life.

As a result of the Madrid attacks, attention began to focus on the need to control imams and their authority and influence. In 2004–5, a series of controversial proposals were presented by the Spanish Home Office to control radical sermons at mosques, ranging from the possibility of finding a legal framework that would allow the State to control religious preaching (the ministry included all religions to avoid discrimination), to controlling the identity of imams by granting special permits for them to serve as imams or monitoring Friday sermons at mosques.[6]

In a climate of insinuations and mistrust, in March 2004 the new Spanish government reopened a new phase of dialogue with the Islamic Commission (as well as with the other confessions recognised in the 1992 process) that, paradoxically, received less attention than the above-mentioned control measures. This new dialogue was characterised by a new awareness of the need for Muslim leaders to participate in public debates. There was also new reorganisational drive to overcome the paralysis of the Islamic Commission, undoubtedly the result of the demographic growth of the Muslim community since the 1990s.

What consequences does this demographic growth have in terms of the public and organisational visibility of Islam? The new impetus given to associations and institutional visibility has been influenced by the demographic and sociological changes in the Muslim community.[7] Nevertheless, the current context in which public opinion is strongly influenced by a stereotyped and negative image of Islam also influences the new forms of mobilisation and leadership. So much so, that the demographic growth of the Muslim population influences political declarations and has prompted new collaboration between the government and Muslim representatives. Moreover, this new panorama has forced Muslim organisations to mobilise, creating new forms of organisation and representation. In spite of everything, these attempts at renewal have also prompted questions about whether these new initiatives are truly innovative or simply a continuation of the 1992 agreements and nothing more than another consequence of the new fear of Islam, placing Muslims at the core of the public debate on security.

Beyond the institutional sphere, 11 March has revealed an emerging dynamism in the forms of participation and growing public visibility of urban and youth groups that have mobilised to respond to what they see as very negative public opinion of Islam and their identity as Muslims.[8] This is still a fringe phenomenon when compared with traditional leadership in the Muslim community, but it is important because it seeks to explore new forms of public participation and social commitment, beyond religious practice, in order to interact with society in general. Thus, although its capacity to participate in public debates is very limited (or still even non-existent), the profile of this new associationism and its socio-cultural activity responds to new forms of Muslim visibility outside the institutional sphere, and to the idea of Islam as the religion of a confessional minority. A qualitative transformation in the mobilisation of Muslims and their public visibility is therefore likely in the near future.

In short, if 1992 established the base for Islam to achieve visibility as a religious minority and institutional normality acquired by religious freedom resulting from political developments, the situation after 11 March, despite in principle endorsing the 1992 model, also reveals a new awareness of the need for Muslims to participate as citizens in order to demand rights and do away with the stereotyped image of Islam.

Notes

1 Ciudadanos musulmanes, *El País*, 28 December 2007.
2 Different publications support the same thesis but to different extents, and in a more schematic or more complex and elaborate manner. See, for example, Cesar Vidal (2005) *España frente al Islam: de Mahoma a Ben Laden*, Barcelona: La Esfera de los Libros; Rosa María Rodríguez Magda (2006) *La España convertida al Islam*, Barcelona: Áltera; Rosa María Rodríguez Magda (2008) *Inexistente Al Ándalus: de cómo los intelectuales reinventan el islam*, Oviedo: Nobel; and Gustavo de Arístegui

(2006) *La Yihad en España: la obsesión por reconquistar al-Andalus*, Barcelona: La Esfera de los Libros.

3   Particularly important due to its reflection on the place of the Islamic legacy in the formation of Spanish nationalism, see Eduardo Manzano (2000) 'La construcción histórica del pasado nacional', in Juan Sisinio Pérez Garzón et al. (eds), *La gestión de la memoria. La historia de España al servicio del poder*, Barcelona: Crítica, pp. 33–62.

4   For example, the theory defended in Vidal (2005) *España frente al Islam*.

5   Iván Jiménez-Aybar (2004) *El islam en España: Aspectos institucionales de su estatuto jurídico*, Pamplona: Navarra Gráfica Ediciones, p. 68.

6   Luis R. Aizpeolea (2004) 'El Gobierno estudia una reforma legal para el control de mezquitas e imames', *El País*.

7   Jesus Garcia (2009) 'Sin mezquitas en mi barrio', *El País*, 14 September.

8   Virtudes Téllez (2008) 'La juventud musulmana de Madrid responde: lugar y participación social de las asociaciones socioculturales formadas o revitalizadas después de los atentados del 11-m', *Revista de Estudios Internacionales Mediterráneos* (6) September–December, pp. 133–43.

References

Aizpeolea, Luis R. (2004) 'El Gobierno estudia una reforma legal para el control de mezquitas e imames', *El País*, 8 May.

Arístegui, Gustavo de (2006) *La Yihad en España: la obsesión por reconquistar al-Andalus*, Barcelona: La Esfera de los Libros.

Garcia, Jesus (2009) 'Sin mezquitas en mi barrio', *El País*, 14 September.

Jiménez-Aybar, Iván (2004) *El islam en España: Aspectos institucionales de su estatuto jurídico*, Pamplona: Navarra Gráfica Ediciones, p. 68.

Manzano, Eduardo (2000) 'La construcción histórica del pasado nacional', in Juan Sisinio Pérez Garzón et al. (eds), *La gestión de la memoria. La historia de España al servicio del poder*, Barcelona: Crítica, pp. 33–62.

Rodríguez Magda, María Rosa (2006) *La España convertida al Islam*, Barcelona: Áltera.

——— (2008) *Inexistente Al Ándalus: de cómo los intelectuales reinventan el islam*, Oviedo: Nobel.

Téllez, Virtudes (2008) 'La juventud musulmana de Madrid responde: lugar y participación social de las asociaciones socioculturales formadas o revitalizadas después de los atentados del 11-m', *Revista de Estudios Internacionales Mediterráneos*, (6) September–December, pp. 133–43.

Vidal, Cesar (2005) *España frente al Islam: de Mahoma a Ben Laden*, Barcelona: La Esfera de los Libros.

THE RISE OF THE BRITISH NATIONAL PARTY: ANTI-MUSLIM POLITICS AND THE POLITICS OF FEAR

Chris Allen

In the preface to his revised edition of *Culture of Fear: risk-taking and the morality of low expectation*, Frank Furedi notes that, following the attacks on the World Trade Centre in 2001 (9/11), the *Los Angeles Times* wrote that the 'next big thing' was 'likely to be fear'.[1] As he went on, in today's Western societies, fear is a heavily influential and defining feature: 'the defining feature of this culture is the belief that humanity is confronted by powerful destructive forces that threaten our everyday existence'.[2] One of the most unfortunate consequences of fear is that any problem or new challenge that emerges is attributed with the capabilities of being able to be transformed into something that appears to be an issue of survival. Fear feeds itself, creating the disposition to speculate – and exaggerate – about ever more greater fears and threats that seem to be always lurking just around the corner. Yet, as Furedi also notes, when British newspapers were emblazoned with headlines asking 'Is this the end of the world?' or declaring 'Apocalypse' following the same attacks, few recognised these as being even potentially exaggerated. On the contrary, they were instead consumed as accepted realities. Only a few recognised that, in fact, 9/11 was little more than 'an old-fashioned act of terror, executed with low-tech facilities by a small number of zealots driven by unrestrained hatred'.[3]

It is possible that the widely documented events of 7 July 2005 (7/7), when four young men set off a series of bombs on the London public transport system, might also be understood in much the same way. With newspaper headlines that reflected those that followed 9/11 – including some that referred to 7/7 as being 'our 9/11' – much of the ensuing debate has focused not only on the fact that these four young men were of Muslim heritage, but that they were Muslims who were British born. Since 7/7, therefore, the phrase 'home-grown bomber' has entered into the social and political lexicon, joining other such negatively connotated words and phrases as 'radical', 'extremist', 'fundamental' and 'violent extremism' that are in many ways mere substitutions for either 'Muslim' or 'Islam'. Having occurred somewhat invisibly and without notice, however, and in line with Furedi's observation that events such as these create the disposition to speculate and exaggerate about other fears and potential threats, has been the wider impact of 7/7, implicated in debates and disagreements about such issues as cohesion, integration, identity and citizenship. And, for the majority of social and political commentators, the atrocities committed by four home-grown bombers have had even deeper ramifications. For them, the attacks exposed the inherent failure of British society and the multicultural model that Britain had structured itself around since the first waves of mass migration following World War II. For them, the 'death of multiculturalism' was the evidence needed to confirm the fear that contemporary British society was, to coin a popular political soundbite, a 'broken society'.

Little more than a year after 7/7, the Greater London Assembly (GLA) commissioned a piece of research to consider how Muslims and Islam were being represented in the media. The rationale for this research was that media representation was having an adverse impact on the way in which Londoners from different backgrounds were getting on with each other. Publishing the findings in 2007, the report – *The search for common ground: Muslims, non-Muslims and the UK media* – highlighted the intense newsworthiness of Muslims and Islam in British newspapers.[4] Making a very broad comparison between the report and research undertaken by Elizabeth Poole between 1994 and 1996,[5] it is possible that, in little more than a decade, the number of stories and reports that focused on Muslims or Islam in the British press had increased by around 270 per cent. In what was deemed a normal week, the GLA research found that around 70 per cent of all news stories focused on Muslims or Islam as presenting a threat. Reinforcing the findings from Poole's research a decade beforehand, not only was it that Muslims and Islam were increasingly being seen to be a threat to Britain and its values, but so too were Muslims being seen to be deviant, irrational and different.[6] As the report concluded, the findings of the research highlighted what 'normal' meant: 'normal in the sense that it showed what people in Britain think is normal – Islam is a threat'.[7]

The culmination of a climate of fear punctuated by the events of 7/7 would therefore appear to have further reified the more historical premise that Muslims and Islam present a very real threat. Add to that the disposition to speculate, and the threat of Muslims and Islam becomes such that it is perceived more readily and more 'normally': it becomes an inherent part of who and what Muslims and Islam are seen to be. Take for example the everyday activities of Muslims. As an article in *The Observer* newspaper, entitled 'The bomber will always get through' noted,[8] there are many others in Britain 'living very much the sort of lives as the four young men who perpetrated the [7/7] attacks'. In setting out the 'sort of lives' that home-grown bombers have, the article suggested they might be 'attending Friday prayers'. Given that Friday prayers are requisite and normal for many practising Muslims, its conflation with something so dangerous and different could be seen to be grossly misleading. In another article that also suggested that there remained a serious and significant threat from other young British Muslim men, the article exposed the 'missed clues' to spotting a terrorist. As it stated, 'after [one of the bombers] converted to Islam his behaviour changed'. It went on, the behaviour that changed and was a 'missed clue' was that 'religion increasingly became the main focus of his life'.[9]

Contextualised by the events of 7/7 and the botched attacks a fortnight later, a whole raft of other 'home-grown' activities have increased the fear – both perceived and real – about Muslims and Islam. As well as high-profile and widely reported events in Madrid, Bali and Mumbai, Britain has witnessed a failed attempt to set off explosives at Glasgow airport as well as various 'terror raids' that have exposed plots to set off explosives on trans-Atlantic flights and to behead a British Muslim serviceman among others. Irrespective of the outcome, whether judicial or otherwise, these plots have heightened suspicion and mistrust, deepened the sense of fear, increased anxiety and, essentially, reinforced all that is seen to be 'normal' about Muslims and Islam. Consequently, what can only be described as an 'us and them' dichotomy has not only emerged, but so too has it deepened. The argument therefore is that 'they' neither want to be nor can ever be all that 'we' are thought to be. And with this comes the perceived and oft-repeated premise that who 'we' are is clear and easily definable: definable through 'our' culture, 'our' values, 'our' institutions and 'our' way of life.

Muslims and Islam therefore are seen to present a real and direct threat to 'our' culture, 'our' values, 'our' institutions and 'our' way of life. And not only has this been put forward from more liberal political perspectives – in particular those espousing the 'death of multiculturalism'[10] – but so too has it been employed by those from the far-right whose ideologies are far more explicit and hating of Muslims and Islam. Indeed, at times, the voices emerging from both the left and right wings of the British political spectrum have been difficult to differentiate.[11] Most successful in exploiting this for political gain has been the far-right British National Party (BNP). Since 2001 – following the disturbances across a handful of northern towns in the summer of that year perpetrated largely by young Asian men – the BNP has become increasingly sophisticated and nuanced in the way in which it has spoken about and referred to Muslims and Islam. While much of this has been inciting, encouraging provocation and division, the BNP has routinely employed language and images that draw upon people's fear of the threat posed by Muslims and Islam.

In *Islam out of Britain,* one of the BNP's first campaigns after the disturbances, the party declared its clearest objectives: it sought to expose 'the threat Islam and Muslims pose to Britain and British society'. Shortly after, in a leaflet entitled *The truth about I.S.L.A.M.* – 'I.S.L.A.M.' being used as an acronym for 'Intolerance, Slaughter, Looting, Arson and Molestation of women' – a range of highly inflammatory justifications for hating Muslims was set out. As it put it, 'to find out what Islam really stands for, all you have to do is look at a copy of the Koran [sic], and see for yourself ... Islam really does stand for Intolerance, Slaughter, Looting, Arson and Molestation of Women'. By selectively quoting from the Qur'an, the BNP painted the most despicable picture of Muslims. Using the rhetoric of what Martin Barker described as 'new racism'[12] – racism that was based upon cultural or other markers of difference rather than any traditional racial or ethnic equivalent – the BNP declared that, 'no-one dares to tell the truth about Islam and the way that it threatens our democracy, traditional freedoms and identity'. Even at this early stage of the BNP's recent political and strategic development, the party was seeing the benefit of selectively employing the Qur'an to explain a whole raft of different events and activities at the same time as accentuating the threat posed by Muslims and Islam. By rooting this in the context of a pseudo-Islamic theology, the BNP set out an argument that stated that what demarcated 'them' from 'us' – 'Muslim' from *'kafir'* [sic] – was something required of Muslims by the religion of Islam: something that was entirely normal for Muslims to believe. What is interesting – and somewhat unprecedented – is how the BNP recruited a small number of fringe British Sikh and Hindu groups to support this viewpoint. In doing so, the BNP attributed further legitimacy to their message by offering what they termed an 'insiders' point of view.

Bolstered by the events of 7/7 and the emergence of home-grown terror, the BNP have continued to exacerbate the culture of fear and the perception of threat. Focusing on the alleged differences between the 'aboriginal' communities – a term sometimes employed by the BNP to describe what it recognises as the real British people – and Muslims, within days of the London tube train bombings the BNP had produced a leaflet showing the bombed out carcass of the bus in Tavistock Square. Emblazoned across it was a message that intoned 'we told you so': 'Maybe now it's time to start listening to the BNP'. Shortly afterwards, in early 2006, the BNP produced another leaflet that placed a picture of one the cartoons of the Prophet Muhammad from the Danish *Jyllands-Posten* newspaper alongside a photo of a cartoons-inspired protest in London where a number of aggressive young British Muslims held some of the most despicable placards that urged violence against those who insulted Islam. The BNP leaflet simply asked, 'Which do you find offensive'.

Despite public and political outcry at the inappropriateness of the leaflets, that year the BNP successfully fielded around 350 candidates in municipal elections across the country. Under a campaign entitled 'Islam Referendum Day', they asked, 'Are you concerned about the growth of Islam in Britain?'. In doing so, the BNP made unprecedented gains across the country: 33 candidates were initially declared to be winners with a further 70 being declared in second place. However, it was in Barking and Dagenham, a diverse and densely populated area of East London, where its success was most notable. Winning 11 of the 13 seats it contested, the BNP became the first far-right party in British history to be the official opposition in a British council chamber. At the first meeting of Barking and Dagenham Council in May 2006, the BNP attempted to try to force through an amendment to change the nature and emphasis of its commitment to anti-racism. Later that same evening, outside the tube station in Barking, a man of Afghan origin was repeatedly stabbed by four men who left a flag with the St George's Cross emblazoned on it draped across his body before running off and leaving the man to die.[13]

The exploitation of the perceived threat posed by Muslims to 'our' way of life has been one that has, to some degree, taken the mainstream of British politics by surprise. Potentially more worrying, however, is the extent to which this message has seemingly been accepted by a growing number of people across all of Britain's diverse communities. As research undertaken by the Democratic Audit at the University of Essex stated, in those parts of England where the BNP was targeting most of its resources around one in four voters were considering voting for them. In some parts of London, this figure was shown to be around one in five.[14] Emanating entirely from the successes gained on the back of their openly anti-Muslim campaigns, the BNP has found a much greater, near country-wide quasi-legitimacy that has seen their popularity mushroom into a party that many believe now offer a real political alternative. Targeting their seats directly and specifically, the BNP now has elected councillors across England, from Grays in the South, through Sandwell and Dudley in the Midlands, to its first stronghold in the North, in Burnley. Current estimates suggest it has around 56 local councillors. More significantly for the BNP, though, has been the recent successes in London and Europe. In 2008, it won one of 25 seats in the London Assembly having gained approximately 5.3 per cent of the capital's vote. Then, in 2009, the BNP further consolidated its position when it won two seats in the European Parliament with 9.8 per cent of the vote in Yorkshire and Humber and 8 per cent in the North West.

Without any doubt whatsoever, the growing success of the BNP has been achieved via its clear and acknowledged shift towards a more explicit anti-Muslim, anti-Islam agenda that both taps into and feeds the fear of threat. As the party's leader, Nick Griffin, told a group of activists in Burnley in March 2006:

We bang on about Islam. Why? Because to the ordinary public out there it's the thing they can understand. It's the thing the newspaper editors sell newspapers with. If we were to attack some other ethnic group – some people say we should attack the Jews ... But ... we've got to get to power. And if that was an issue we chose to bang on about when the press don't talk about it ... the public would just think we were barking mad...

It wouldn't get us anywhere other than stepping backwards. It would lock us in a little box; the public would think 'extremist crank lunatics, nothing to do with me.' And we wouldn't get power.[15]

What is interesting is the way that Griffin acknowledges how 'it's the thing the newspaper editors sell newspapers with': Muslims as threat, Muslims as Other, Muslims as against 'our' way of life. As Griffin put it on another occasion: 'We should be positioning ourselves to take advantage for our own political ends of the growing wave of public hostility to Islam currently being whipped up by the mass media.'[16]

Since 9/11, and more so 7/7, the BNP has used the climate in Britain to acquire social and political legitimacy, both of which have been undertaken on the back of an increasing receptivity to Islamophobia in the British, particularly English, domain. In today's public and political spaces, the threat that Muslims are most commonly seen to present is typically framed in debates associated with terrorism and securitisation. At one level this is the most obvious and apparent. However, this perceived threat is far more multi-layered, evident along the lines of new racist discourse where Islam and Muslims are seen to be incompatible with the dominant or perceived overriding culture and its heritage. That is, what it means to be 'us' rather than 'them'. And because of the growing acceptance of seeing Muslims and Islam as a threat, the increasing receptivity to anti-Muslim ideas and expressions, and the sense of justification that is recurrently evident across Britain, so being anti-Muslim and anti-Islamic for 'us' not only becomes increasingly seen to 'make sense' but so too does it appear to constantly justify itself. It does, to coin a popular phrase, constitute a vicious circle. Add to this the fact that when any plot – whether foiled or brought to fruition – involves Muslims claiming to be acting on behalf of 'the *umma*' or 'doing Allah's will', no matter how many times Muslims and their organisations distance themselves or claim that Islam is a religion of peace, the likelihood is that the plots will be seen as little more than proof that it makes sense to fear the threat posed by Muslims and Islam.

While the groundbreaking Runnymede Trust report, *Islamophobia: a challenge for us all*,[17] is now more than 17 years old, the need to understand and recognise the potential for Islamophobia is as necessary now – possibly even more so – than it was in 1997. A key part of this is being aware of the processes and discourses that remain in circulation in the wider public and political spaces, and how they feed into or even reinforce those messages that are anti-Muslim or anti-Islamic. In setting out the nature of Islamophobia and anti-Muslim prejudice, the Runnymede report noted how Muslims were seen as separate and Other, 'not having any aims or values in common' with Britain's non-Muslims.[18] In other words, the report suggested that Muslims were seen to be a 'them' that are inherently and irrevocably not a part of 'our way of life'. In addition, it went on to add that Islam and Muslims were seen to be 'violent, aggressive, threatening'.[19] From what has been noted here, little, if indeed anything, would appear to have changed in the decade and a half since that report was commissioned.

That all Muslims and Islam, without any differentiation whatsoever, are becoming increasingly understood in frames that identify them as a threat to all that British society holds dear, it may be worth remembering an observation that was first noted in 1997. Back then, the Runnymede report noted that anti-Muslim and anti-Islamic sentiment and feeling was not seen as problematic. Indeed, it was becoming more natural and accepted as normal. It could be that these sentiments and feelings have become ever more naturalised and normative in the ensuing years. As the report concluded:

The expression of anti-Muslim ideas and sentiments is becoming increasingly seen as respectable. It is a natural, taken-for-granted ingredient of the commonsense world of millions of people every day ... Islamophobic discourse, sometimes blatant but frequently subtle and coded, is part of the fabric of everyday life in modern Britain.[20]

It is interesting that this was written before the events of 7/7, before research that showed the number of stories and reports about Islam and Muslims in the British press had increased by approximately 270 per cent, and before the BNP made unprecedented political gains on the back of a concerted anti-Muslim, anti-Islam agenda. In this context, it is interesting to ask where the greatest threat exists, especially if something so damaging and dangerous is increasingly becoming a 'part of the fabric of everyday life in modern Britain'.

Notes

1   Frank Furedi (2002) *Culture of fear: risk-taking and the morality of low expectation*, London: Continuum, p. 7.
2   Ibid.
3   Ibid., p. 17.
4   INSTED (2007*) The search for common ground: Muslims, non-Muslims and the UK media*, London: GLA.
5   Elizabeth Poole (2000) 'Framing Islam: an analysis of newspaper coverage of Islam in the British press', in Kai Hafez (ed.), *Islam and the mass media: fragmented images in a globalizing world*, Cresskill: Hampton Press, pp. 157–79.
6   Ibid.
7   INSTED (2007) *The search for common ground*, p.30.
8   'The bomber will always get through', *The Observer*, 14 May 2006.
9   'Missed clues over the fanatical four', *Daily Mail*, 12 May 2006.
10   Chris Allen (2007) '"Down with multiculturalism, book-burning and fatwas": the death of multiculturalism and its implications for Muslims', *Journal for Culture and Religion*, 2 (8), Summer, pp. 125–38.
11   Chris Allen (2005) 'From race to religion: the new face of discrimination', in Tahir Abbas (ed.), *Muslim Britain: communities under pressure*. London: Zed Books, pp. 49–65.
12   Martin Barker (1981) *The new Racism: Conservatives and the ideology of the tribe*, London: Junction Books.
13   *The Observer*, 26 May 2006.
14   Peter John et al. (eds) (2006) *The BNP: the roots of its appeal*, Colchester: Democratic Audit, University of Essex.
15   BNPtv Films (2006) *Nick Griffin Speaking at Burnley Branch Meeting*. Available at http://video.google.co.uk/videoplay?docid=1269630805284168668#. Accessed 2 September 2009 (link no longer working).
16   Nick Griffin (2006) *By their fruits (or lack of them) shall you know them*. Available at http://web.archive.org/web/20071014195717/http://www.bnp.org.uk/columnists/chairman2.php?ngId=30.Accessed 30 October 2008.
17   Runnymede Trust (1997) 'Commission on British Muslims and Islamophobia, Islamophobia: a challenge for us all', *Report of the Runnymede Trust Commission on British Muslims and Islamophobia*, London: Runnymede Trust.
18   Ibid., p. 5.
19   Ibid.
20   Ibid., pp.10–1.

References

Abbas, Tahir (2005) *Muslim Britain: communities under pressure*, London: Zed Books.

Allen, Chris (2003) *Fair justice: the Bradford disturbances, the sentencing and the impact*, London: FAIR.

—— (2005) 'From race to religion: the new face of discrimination', in Tahir Abbas (ed.), *Muslim Britain: communities under pressure*, London: Zed Books, pp. 49–65.

—— (2007) '"Down with multiculturalism, book-burning and fatwas": the death of multiculturalism and its implications for Muslims', *Journal for Culture and Religion*, 2 (8), Summer, pp. 125–38.

Barker, Martin (1981) *The new racism: Conservatives and the ideology of the tribe*, London: Junction Books.

Furedi, Frank (2002) *Culture of fear: risk-taking and the morality of low expectation*, London: Continuum.

Hafez, Kai (2000) *Islam and the mass media: fragmented images in a globalizing world*, Cresskill: Hampton Press.

INSTED (2007) *The search for common ground: Muslims, non-Muslims and the UK media*, London: GLA.

John, Peter et al. (eds) (2006) *The BNP: the roots of its appeal*, Colchester: Democratic Audit, University of Essex.

Poole, Elizabeth (2000) 'Framing Islam: an analysis of newspaper coverage of Islam in the British press', in Kai Hafez (ed.), *Islam and the mass media: fragmented images in a globalizing world*, Cresskill: Hampton Press, pp. 157–79.

Runnymede Trust (1997) 'Commission on British Muslims and Islamophobia, Islamophobia: a challenge for us all', *Report of the Runnymede Trust Commission on British Muslims and Islamophobia*, London: Runnymede Trust.

NOTES ON CONTRIBUTORS

Samim Akgönül is a historian and political scientist, a professor at Strasbourg University and a researcher at the French National Centre of Scientific Research. He also teaches at Syracuse University and at several universities in Turkey. Executive editor of *Journal of Muslims in Europe*, he works mainly on religion-state relationships, contemporary Turkish history and minorities.

Chris Allen is a lecturer in Social Policy. He is based in the Institute of Applied Social Studies, School of Social Policy, at the University of Birmingham. He is the author of *Islamophobia* (Ashgate, 2010).

Samir Amghar is a political analyst for the Directorate for Strategic Affairs (Paris) and research fellow at the Université du Québec à Montréal. He has published *Salafism today: Sectarian Movements in the West* (Michalon Publishing, 2011) and *Islamic Activism in Europe: Reislamization, Preaching and Politics* (Infolio Publishing, 2013).

Schirin Amir-Moazami holds a PhD from the Department of Social and Political Sciences at the European University Institute in Florence and is currently Assistant Professor for Islam in Europe at Freie Universität Berlin. She has published a book on the headscarf controversies in France and Germany and articles relating to questions of secular orders and Muslims in Europe.

Elena Arigita holds a PhD in Arab and Islamic Studies and is affiliated to the University of Granada. She has worked on the relationship between traditional Islamic institutions and the State in contemporary Egypt. Her current research explores the interaction of transnational, national and local levels of Islamic activism in Spain, and debates about the memory of al-Andalus.

Akil N. Awan is a lecturer at the Department of History at Royal Holloway University of London. He has published widely on global jihadism and the use of virtual media and the internet by jihadist groups.

Jørgen Bæk Simonsen is a professor at the Department of Cultural and Regional Studies, University of Copenhagen. He has published widely on Islam and Muslims in Denmark and Europe.

Synnøve Bendixsen is a postdoctoral researcher at Uni Rokkan Centre. She holds a joint PhD in Social Anthropology from the Humboldt Universität and the École des Hautes Études en Sciences Sociales (2010). Bendixsen has conducted extensive fieldwork with Muslim youth in Germany. Currently she is working on the political mobilisation of irregular migrants in Norway.

Yahya Birt is Commissioning Editor at Kube Publishing. A visiting fellow at the Markfield Institute of Higher Education, he has published on various aspects of Muslim life in Britain and co-edited *British Secularism and Religion: Islam, Society and the State* (Markfield: Kube, 2011).

Sarah Bracke is Assistant Professor of Sociology of Religion and Culture at KU Leuven. She holds a PhD in Women's Studies from Utrecht University. Her work explores questions of modernity, religion and secularism in relation to subjectivity, agency and gender.

Alexandre Caeiro is an assistant professor at the Centre for the Study of Contemporary Muslim Societies, Qatar Faculty of Islamic Studies, Hamad Bin Khalifa University. His research deals primarily with European Islam, the development of an Islamic jurisprudence among minorities, and transformations of religious authority.

Mohammad Darif is a professor at the Faculty of Law of the University Muhammedia in Casablanca, and a leading figure in the study of Islamic movements in the Maghreb, with key works in the academic field and contributions in the international media.

Mohamed El Battiui holds a doctorate in Economic Sciences and Management from the Solvay Business School of the Université libre de Bruxelles. Currently, he is a visiting professor at the Haute École Francisco Ferrer, Brussels, and a research fellow at CECID, the Centre for Development Research at the Université libre de Bruxelles.

Nadia Fadil holds a PhD in Social Sciences from KU Leuven, where she also works as an assistant professor at the Interculturalism, Migration and Minorities Research Centre. Her research addresses the question of secularism and religion, subjectivity and governmentality, with an ethnographic focus on secular and pious Muslims in Belgium and Europe, questions on which she has published widely.

Annalisa Frisina, who holds a PhD in Sociology, is an adjunct professor at the University of Padova, where she teaches Qualitative Social Research. She sits on the Scientific Board for the Master in European Islam at the University of Padua. Her current research interests include religious diversity/religious pluralism from a generational and gender perspective, and visual research methods.

Bettina Gräf is a postdoctoral fellow at the Zentrum Moderner Orient in Berlin. Her fields of specialisation are Islamic political discourse and practice, and media developments in the Arab-speaking regions. She is currently working on an interdisciplinary research project called 'In Search of Europe: Considering the Possible in Africa and the Middle East'. In her present research she is examining ideological knowledge production in Egypt and the Levant in the 1940s and 1950s.

Sadek Hamid is a lecturer in Islamic Studies, most recently at Liverpool Hope University, and a visiting lecturer at the Cambridge Muslim College. He is a leading researcher in the areas of British Muslim youth, Islamic activism and religious radicalisation.

Jan-Peter Hartung is currently a senior lecturer in the study of Islam at the Department for the Study of Religions, SOAS, University of London. His research focuses on Muslim intellectual history from early modernity with a regional emphasis on South Asia and the wider Persianate world.

Heiko Henkel is an associate professor at the Department of Anthropology at the University of Copenhagen. His current work focuses on the often contentious encounters of Muslim minorities with established majority publics and the State in Denmark and across Europe.

Tina Gudrun Jensen is a senior researcher in the Department of Employment and Integration at the Danish National Centre for Social Research in Copenhagen. She is an anthropologist specialising in cultural complexity and interethnic relations. She has published on subjects such as multiculturalism, religion, ethnicity and integration.

Gerdien Jonker is a scholar in the history and ethnography of religion and has published widely on Muslim minorities in Europe. Currently affiliated to the University of Erlangen, she researches the history of the Muslim mission in Europe, in particular the Suleymanci and Ahmadiyya missions.

Jeanette S. Jouili is currently a postdoctoral fellow at the Women's Studies Programme at Duke University. In 2007 she obtained her PhD in Sociology and Anthropology jointly from the École des Hautes Études en Sciences Sociales in Paris and the European University Viadrina in Frankfurt an der Oder.

Melanie Kamp is a research associate at the Institute of Islamic Studies at Freie Universität Berlin. In her research she explores questions of religious authority and the transmission of religious knowledge among Muslims in Germany and Europe.

Martijn de Koning is a postdoctoral fellow at the Faculty of Religious Studies at Radboud University in Nijmegen. He has carried out research into identity formation and religious experience among Dutch–Morrocan youth and is the author of *Zoeken naar een 'zuivere' Islam* (Amsterdam: Bert Bakker, 2008).

Inge Liengaard holds a PhD in Religious Studies. She wrote her doctoral dissertation on Islamic authorities in Denmark and analysed the various grounds on which religious leaders base their authority. She also examined how they interacted with each other, both within and across ethnic boundaries. Today she works in public administration with issues related to integration and citizenship.

Philip Lewis has lived in Bradford for 25 years, following six years researching Christian–Muslim relations in Pakistan. He advises the Anglican Church on Islam and Christian–Muslim relations, and lectures in the Peace Studies Department at Bradford University on 'Islam in the West' and 'Religions, conflict and peacemaking'.

Ural Manço is a former guest professor at the Université Saint-Louis in Brussels and is associate professor and head of the Sociology Department at Aksaray University, Turkey. His research focuses on the social and cultural integration of the Muslim population in Europe; ethnicity and transnational identities; and the sociology of religion.

Ermete Mariani, an analyst of Middle East politics, security and new media, also has significant experience as a trainer working with non-formal education tools and methodology. He recently founded PlanetNext: information for change, www.planetnext.net, an association of journalists producing multimedia information packages on human security.

Seán McLoughlin is a senior lecturer in Islamic Studies at the School of Philosophy, Religion and the History of Science, University of Leeds. He works across the study of religion, ethnicity and migration from anthropological and sociological perspectives, with a special interest in the Pakistani-heritage Muslim diaspora in Britain.

Imran Mogra is a senior lecturer in Religious Education and Professional Studies in the School of Education (Faculty of Education, Law and Social Sciences) at Birmingham City University. He is involved in *maktab* teacher training. He also explores faith, pedagogy, identity and matters related to teaching and learning in the state sector.

Jordi Moreras is Professor of Social Anthropology at the Faculty of Humanities in the University Rovira i Virgili, Tarragona. His research topics are imams and religious authority, and the anthropology of Muslims in Europe.

Shaida Nabi completed her doctorate at the University of Manchester and is currently an independent researcher. Her doctoral research examines the way institutionalised racism against Muslim students in British universities functions through processes of racialised governmentality. Her current interests and forthcoming publications centre on the 'recognition' of Muslims in white institutions.

Jon A. Olsen holds an MA in Sociology of Religion and Minority Studies. He did his Master's thesis on conversion to Islam in Danish prisons and has studied religious and politically motivated violence, processes of radical identity formation, and the use of biological weapons in terrorism. Today he works with quality assurance in higher education.

Rafael Ortega is a historian with a PhD in Arab and Islamic Studies and is affiliated to the University of Granada, where he teaches at the Department of Semitic Studies. His research and publications deal with issues of Islamism in the Arab countries, in particular Sudan and Egypt, and its transnational links with Europe.

Firdaous Oueslati is currently a member of the Tunisian National Constituent Assembly. She holds a Master's degree in both Arabic Language and Islamic Studies from the University of Leiden. As a researcher in the field of Islamic Studies she specialises in Islam in Europe.

Frank Peter is Assistant Professor of Islamic and Middle Eastern Studies at the University of Bern. His research interests cover the history of the modern Middle East, secularism, political religion and Islamophobia. His current project examines how secular rationalities condition Islamism in contemporary France.

Dorthe Høvids Possing is an associate professor at Institute for Social Work, Department of International and Inter-cultural Social Work, Metropolitan University College, Copenhagen. Her scholarly interests include current global developments in international social work and social work with youth.

Muzammil Quraishi is a senior lecturer in Criminology and Criminal Justice at the University of Salford. He is a comparative criminologist using qualitative methodologies with a special focus on Muslim populations and crime. His wider interests involve research on racial discrimination, religious rights, colonialism and crime, and critical race theory.

Dietrich Reetz is a political scientist at the Zentrum Moderner Orient in Berlin, specialising in Non-Arabian Islam with a focus on South and South-East Asia, Central Asia and Europe. He is also an associate professor at Freie Universität Berlin and its Berlin Graduate School of Muslim Cultures and Societies.

Lutz Rogler is currently a visiting professor at the Institute of Islamic Studies, Freie Universität Berlin. His scholarly interests include the intellectual and social history of contemporary Islamic institutions and Islamist movements in the Arab world.

Dr Javier Rosón holds a PhD in Social Anthropology from the University of Granada and is currently researcher at Casa Árabe. His work as a researcher began in 1997 when he started working on diverse European research projects related, in various ways, to immigrant and/or Muslim populations in Spain.

Salman Sayyid is Reader in the School of Sociology and Social Policy, University of Leeds. He is the author of *A Fundamental Fear: Eurocentrism and the Emergence of Islamism* (Zed Press, 2nd edition: 2003) and co-edited *A postcolonial people: South Asians in Britian* (Hurst/Columbia University Press: London/New York, 2006).

Birgitte Schepelern Johansen is a postdoctoral fellow at the Institute for Cross-Cultural and Regional Studies, University of Copenhagen. Her research has mainly focused on the formation of secular space and secular identities, knowledge production on Muslim minorities in Europe, and the governance of normality and deviation in modern welfare states.

Werner Schiffauer is Professor for Comparative Social and Cultural Anthropology Europa-Universität Viadrina in Frankfurt an der Oder. He has worked on the transformation of rural and urban Turkey, labour migration, the organisation of diversity in European Societies, Islam in Europe, and recently on the anthropology of the State.

Tallat Shakoor was employed at the Department of Education at the University of Aarhus in Denmark. He holds a Master's degree in Sociology of Religion and Minority Studies from the University of Copenhagen. He has published on the origins, history and social dynamics of Muslim schools in Denmark and has conducted research and documentation on Muslims in Denmark and Europe for ten years.

Mohammad Siddique Seddon is a lecturer in Islamic and Religious Studies and Associate Director, Centre for Faiths and Public Policy at the Department of Theology and Religious Studies, University of Chester. In addition to teaching and supervising studies within the discipline, he has researched extensively on Islam and Muslim communities in Britain   and has published and co-authored a number of related works.

Guido Steinberg is a research fellow at the German Institute for International and Security Affairs. His more recent publications are concerned with Saudi Arabia, Islamism and terrorism.

Thijl Sunier is Professor of Anthropology and Head of the anthropological department at the VU University Amsterdam. He conducts research in the field of transnational Islamic movements, religious leadership, and nation-building and Islam in Europe and Turkey. He is chairman of the board of the Inter-academic School for Islam Studies in the Netherlands (NISIS).

Suha Taji-Farouki is a senior lecturer in Modern Islam at the Institute of Arab and Islamic Studies, University of Exeter. Her research addresses Islamic thought in the modern period in its diverse expressions, from Islamists to Islamic liberals and Sufis, in the Arab Sunni arena and beyond.

Hussam Tamam (d. 2011) was the founder of the first monitoring centre on Islamic movements in Egypt. He directed the section on Islamic movements for Islamonline.net and authored a large number of works on Islamic movements in the Arab world. He was a visiting professor at the University of Zurich. His last works address the question of 'salafisation' of the Muslim Brothers and were published by the Library of Alexandria.

Sol Tarrés holds a PhD in Social Anthropology and is a professor at the University of Huelva, Spain. She has published over 30 works, including articles in scientific journals and edited volumes. She is currently following two main threads of research: religiosity in transnational Islamic movements, and the religious expression of death among religious minorities in Spain.

Jörn Thielmann holds a PhD in Islamic Studies from Ruhr-University Bochum, and became managing director of the Erlangen Centre for Islam and Law in Europe (EZIRE) at the Friedrich Alexander University of Erlangen-Nuremberg in January 2009. From 2003 until 2008, he headed the Orient-Occident Center Mainz (KOOM) and lectured in Cultural Anthropology at the University of Mainz.

Dominique Thomas has published widely on global jihadism and jihadi groups in Britain. He is notably the author of *Londonistan. La voix du djihad* (Paris: Editions Michalon, 2003).

David Tyrer is a critical theorist based at Liverpool John Moores University, where he is employed as a senior lecturer in Sociology and Political Theory. He has interests in race, racism and Islamophobia, and in the politics and aesthetics of phobia.

Jenny White is Professor of Anthropology at Boston University and former president of the Turkish Studies Association and of the American Anthropological Association Middle East Section. She has authored numerous books and articles on Turkey regarding the economy and family life, political Islam and nationalism, ethnic identity, and gender issues.

INDEX